THE

HISTORY

OF THE

WORTHIES OF ENGLAND:

BY

THOMAS FULLER, D.D.

1608-1661

AUTHOR OF "ABEL REDIVIVUS," "THE CHURCH HISTORY OF BRITAIN," &c.

A NEW EDITION,

CONTAINING BRIEF NOTICES OF THE MOST CELEBRATED WORTHIES OF ENGLAND WHO
HAVE FLOURISHED SINCE THE TIME OF FULLER;

WITH EXPLANATORY NOTES AND COPIOUS INDEXES.

BY P. AUSTIN NUTTALL, LL.D.

AUTHOR OF THE "CLASSICAL AND ARCHÆOLOGICAL DICTIONARY;"
TRANSLATOR OF HORACE, JUVENAL, &c.

IN THREE VOLUMES.

VOL. II.

LONDON:

PRINTED FOR THOMAS TEGG, 73, CHEAPSIDE.

M.DCCC.XL.

1840

CONTENTS.

VOL. II.

LINCOLNSHIRE.

MIDDLESEX.

LONDON.

NOTTINGHAMSHIRE.

THE

WORTHIES OF ENGLAND.

HAMPSHIRE.

HAMPSHIRE hath Berkshire on the north, Surrey and Sussex on the east, the sea on the south, Dorset and Wiltshire on the west. From north unto south it extendeth unto fifty-four miles, not stretching above thirty miles from the east to the west thereof.

A happy country in the four elements, if culinary fire in courtesy may pass for one, with plenty of the best wood for the fuel thereof. Most pure and piercing the air of this shire; and none in England hath more plenty of clear and fresh rivulets of troutful water; not to speak of the friendly sea conveniently distanced from London. As for the earth, it is both fair and fruitful, and may pass for an expedient betwixt pleasure and profit; where, by mutual consent, they are moderately accommodated.

Yet much of the arable therein is stony ground, though not like that in the Gospel, where the grain grew up, and withered so soon, " having no deepness of earth;"* this bringing plenty of corn to perfection. Indeed, that in the parable may be presumed inwardly a rock, only faced over with superficial earth; whereas this hath solid earth enough; but abounding with little loose stones lying above it, which are conceived to keep the corn warmer; and therefore some skilful in husbandry have maintained, that the taking of them away doth more hurt than good to the ground.

The south-west part of this county is called The New Forest, not in the same sense as New College in Oxford, then at the founding the newest, which since hath gained many *puisnes* thereunto; but because the junior of all forests in England, many having been *dis-* none *in-forested* since the Conquest. True it is, king Henry the Eighth made a forest about his palace of Hampton in Middlesex, by the name of Hampton Forest;

* Matth. xiii. 5.

but it never obtained peaceable possession in *publique pronun-ciation* (blame not the people thereabout, if in point of profit their tongues would not cross their hearts) as this New Forest did. Whereof hereafter.

NATURAL COMMODITIES.

RED DEER.

Great store of these were lately in New Forest, so called be-cause newly made by king William the Conqueror. Otherwise, ten years hence, it will be six hundred years old. Indeed, as Augustus Cæsar is said to have said of Herod king of Judea, that it was better to be his hog than his child; so was it most true of that king William, that it was better to have been his stag than his subject; the one being by him spared and preserved, the other ruined and destroyed: such was the devas-tation he made of towns in this county, to make room for his game. And it is worth our observing the opposition betwixt the characters of

KING EDGAR.

" Templa Deo, templis monachos, monachis dedit agros." *

KING WILLIAM.

" Templa adimit Divis, fora civibus, arva colonis." †

And now was the south-west of this county made a forest indeed, if, as an antiquary‡ hath observed, a forest be so called, *quia foris est,* because it is set open and abroad. The stags therein were stately creatures, jealous, revengeful; insomuch that I have been credibly informed, that a stag, unable for the present to master another who had taken his hind from him, waited his opportunity, till his enemy had weakened himself with his wantonness, and then killed him. Their flesh may well be good, whose very horns are accounted cordial. Besides, there is a concave in the neck of a green-headed stag, when above his first crossing, wherein are many worms, some two inches in length, very useful in physic, and therefore carefully put up by Sir Theodore Mayerne and other skilful physicians. But, I believe, there be few stags now in New Forest, fewer harts, and not any harts-royal (as escaping the chase of a king); though in time there may be some again.

HONEY.

Although this county affordeth not such lakes of honey as some authors relate found in hollow trees in Muscovy;§ nor yieldeth combs equal to that which Pliny reporteth seen in Germany, eight feet long; || yet produceth it plenty of this necessary and profitable commodity.

* Camden's Britannia, in Somersetshire.   † Idem, in Hampshire.
‡ Sir Robert Cotton (under the name of Mr. Speed), in Huntingdonshire.
§ P. Jovius de Legatione Muscovitarum; et Munsterus de Muscoviâ.
|| Natural History, lib. xi. cap. 24.

Indeed Hampshire hath the worst and best honey in England; worst, on the heath, hardly worth five pounds the barrel; best, in the champaign, where the same quantity will well nigh be sold for twice as much. And it is generally observed, the finer the wheat and wool, both which are very good in this county, the purer the honey of that place.

Honey is useful for many purposes, especially that honey which is the lowest in any vessel. For it is an old and true rule, " the best oil is in the top; the best wine in the middle; and the best honey in the bottom."* It openeth obstructions, cleareth the breast and lights from those humours which fall from the head, looseneth the belly; with many other sovereign qualities, too many to be reckoned up in a winter's day.

However, we may observe three degrees, or kinds rather, of honey:—1. *Virgin honey*, which is the purest, of a late swarm which never bred bees.—2. *Chaste honey*, for so I may term all the rest which is not sophisticated with any addition.—3. *Harlot honey*, as which is adulterated with meal and other trash mingled therewith.

Of the first and second sort I understand the counsel of Solomon, " My son, eat honey, for it is good;"† good absolutely in the substance, though there may be excess in the quantity thereof.

WAX.

This is the cask, where honey is the liquor; and, being yellow by nature, is by art made white, red, and green, which I take to be the dearest colours, especially when appendant on parchment. Wax is good by day and by night, when it affordeth light, for sight the clearest; for smell the sweetest; for touch the cleanliest. Useful in law to seal instruments; and in physic, to mollify sinews, ripen and dissolve ulcers, &c. Yea, the ground and foundation of all cere-cloth (so called from *cera*) is made of wax.

HOGS.

Hampshire hogs are allowed by all for the best bacon, being our English Westphalian, and which, well ordered, hath deceived the most judicious palates. Here the swine feed in the forest on plenty of acorns (men's meat in the golden,‡ hogs' food in this iron age); which, going out lean, return home fat, without either care or cost of their owners. Nothing but fulness stinteth their feeding on the mast falling from the trees, where also they lodge at liberty (not pent up, as in other places, to stacks of peas), which some assign the reason of the fineness of their flesh; which, though not all glare (where no banks of lean can be seen for the deluge of fat), is no less delicious to the taste, and more wholesome for the stomach.

---

* " Naturæ liquor iste novæ cui summa natat fæx."—Ausonius.
† Prov. xxiv. 13.
‡ " Olim communis pecori cibus atque homini glans."—Ausonius.

Swines-flesh, by the way, is observed most nutritive of men's bodies, because of its assimilation thereunto. Yet was the eating thereof forbidden to the Jews, whereof this reason may be rendered (besides the absolute will of the law-giver), because in hot countries men's bodies are subject to the measles and leprosies, who have their greatest repast on swines-flesh. For the climate of Canaan was all the year long as hot as England betwixt May and Michaelmas; and it is penal for any butchers with us in that term to kill any pork in the public shambles.

As for the manufacture of clothing in this county (diffused throughout the same) such as deny the goodness of Hampshire cloth, and have occasion to wear it, will be convinced of its true worth by the price which they must pay for it.

THE BUILDINGS.

The cathedral in Winchester yieldeth to none in England for venerable magnificence. It could not be *opus unius sæculi*, perfected by the contributive endeavours of several successive bishops, whereof some lie most sumptuously interred in their chapel-like monuments.

On the walls of the choir on each side, the dust of the Saxon kings and ancient bishops of this church were decently entombed (many hundred years after) by Richard Fox bishop of this see, till, in the beginning of our civil wars, they were barbarously thrown down by the soldiers.

Josephus reports (what some hardly believe) how Herod took many talents of treasure out of the sepulchre of David. Sure I am they met with no such wealth here in this mine of mortality amongst the ashes, which did none any injury; and therefore why malice should scratch out that which did not bite it, is to me unknown.

As for the civil structures, Basing, built by the first marquis of Winchester, was the greatest of any subject's house in England, yea larger than most (eagles have not the biggest nests of all birds) of the king's palaces. The motto " Love Loyalty," was often written in every window thereof; and was well practised in it, when, for resistance on that account, it was lately levelled to the ground.

Next Basing, Bramsell, built by the last lord Zouch in a bleak and barren place, was a stately structure, especially before part thereof was defaced with a casual fire.

THE WONDERS.

There is an oak in this county, which by credible people is generally reported to put forth green leaves yearly on or about Christmas-day. It groweth nigh Lindhurst, in the New Forest; and perchance I could point more exactly at the position thereof, but am loath to direct some ignorant zealot, lest he cut it down under the notion of superstition, and make timber of this oak, as some lately have made fuel of the hawthorn at Glastonbury.

PROVERBS.

" Manners make a man, quoth William Wickham."]

This generally was his motto, inscribed frequently on the places of his founding; so that it hath since acquired a proverbial reputation. We commonly say, 1. In the *Church;* " God makes a man," as who truly created him. 2. In the *Court;* " Clothes make a man," as which habit and adorn him. 3. In the *Change;* " Money makes a man," which puts him in a solvable condition. 4. In the *Schools;* " Manners make a man," as which complete and accomplish him.

Grant the two middle expressions, the extravagancy of our pride and covetousness, the first and last must be allowed proportionable to piety and truth. Without manners, one is but a man-beast, or centaur.

Now seeing no man without manners, no manners without some learning, no learning without teaching, no teaching of youth to that in a grammar free-school, of men to that in a college in an university; how much thanks doth posterity owe to this Wickham's memory.

" Canterbury is the higher rack, but Winchester is the better manger."]

W. Edington, bishop of Winchester, was the author of this expression,* rendering this the reason of his refusal to be removed to Canterbury, though chosen thereunto. Indeed, though Canterbury be graced with a higher honour, the revenues of Winchester, lying entirely, are more advantageous to gather riches thereon. The proverb is appliable to such who prefer a wealthy privacy before a less profitable dignity.

Yet know that that manger did once partly maintain that rack; viz. when John White, bishop of Winchester, was enjoined by queen Mary to pay a thousand pounds a-year to cardinal Pole, archbishop of Canterbury, for the better support of his estate.

" The Isle of Wight hath no monks, lawyers, or foxes."†]

This speech hath more mirth than truth in it. That they had monks, I know; black ones at Carisbrook, white ones at Quarre, in this island.‡ That they have lawyers they know, when they pay them their fees; and that they have foxes their lambs know. However, because perchance they have fewer in proportion to places of the like extent (and few or none are often coupled in common discourse), let not that which was pleasantly spoken be frowardly taken, but pass as we found it to posterity.

PRINCES.

HENRY eldest son of king John and his wife ISABEL, born at Winchester, anno 1208, was one (besides the account of longevity) eminent in his generation. He was a most pious king,

* Bishop Godwin, in the Bishops of Winchester.
† Camden's Britannia, in the Isle of Wight.
‡ Speed's Catalogue of Religious Houses.

son to a profane father [king John] ; a very poor king, brother
to a most wealthy [Richard king of the Romans] ; a very weak
king, father to a most wise son, Edward the First. The tragi-
comedy of his life was eminent in many particulars. 1. He
had scarce half a kingdom in the beginning of his reign ; Lewis
of France being brought in to be king by the English in their
hot, and cast out in their cold blood. 2. He had no part of a
kingdom in the middle of his reign, embroiled with war with
his barons, beaten in battle, imprisoned, and no king in effect.
3. He had all the kingdom in the end of his reign ; for as soon
as prince Edward began to man it, this his son may be accounted his father, by whom he attained a comfortable old age.

He was not so weak but that he knew who were wiser than
himself, and would be governed by them, one main cause which
procured his death in peace, and burial in pomp in the abbey
of Westminster of his own foundation, anno Domini 1273.

ELEANOR, tenth daughter, sixteenth and youngest child of
king Edward the First, was born at Winchester, the 6th of
May 1306,* and died in her infancy ; so that the epitaph which
I find elsewhere of an infant of meaner birth, may be applied
unto her. (She lieth buried at Saint Peter's, Westminster,
having her picture upon her monument with three brothers.)

ARTHUR, eldest son to king Henry the Seventh and queen Elizabeth, was born (being *partus octomestris*,† yet vital and vigorous, contrary to the rules of physicians) at Winchester, the
20th day of September 1486.‡ Some will wonder at his name,
whereof no alliance, nor English prince, since the unhappy
Arthur duke of Britain, supposed to be made away by king
John, his cruel uncle. But because this prince, by his father's
side, was, with king Arthur, of British extraction, and because
born at Winchester where king Arthur kept his court, and his
(pretended) Round Table still to be seen, that name was bestowed upon him. He died at Ludlow, in the sixteenth year of
his age, anno 1502, and is buried in the cathedral of Worcester ;
more known to posterity by the widow he left, the lady Katherine Dowager (and the effects ensuing thereon), than by any of
his own personal performances.

SAINTS.

EDBURGH, eighth daughter of king Edward the elder, and his
first by queen Edgiva, gave, when but three years of age, a great
augury of her future piety ;§ her father presenting before her,
and leaving to her choice, on the one hand, the New Testament
and a chalice :|| on the other, jewels, rings, and bracelets.

---

* Speed's Chronicle, p. 565.   † Lord Verulam, in his Henry the Seventh.
‡ Speed's Chronicle, p. 763.
§ Henry Higgden, and Polychronicon, lib. vi. cap. 4.
|| Flowers of the English Saints, p. 570, June the 15th.

She took the New Testament and the chalice (conceive it not because of massy silver, but) acted with the principle of **infant** piety: hereupon her parents left her to her own disposal, who became a nun at Winchester after the order of Saint Benedict, undergoing the austerity of that order. It is reported of her (forgive me, reader, though I would not write these things they are so absurd, I cannot but write them they are so absurd) that she would by night play the part of a pious thief,* and steal the socks of all the other nuns, and, having carefully washed and anointed them, restore them to their bed sides.

This Saint Edburg died on the 15th of June 920. Some of her bones being kept at Winchester, others say at Wilton† (so facile the mistakes in Latin betwixt Wiltonia and Wintonia); and the rest were translated to Pershore, an abbey in the diocese of Worcester.

MARTYRS.

This county, being in the diocese of Winchester, escaped very well in the Marian days from any visible persecution. Under God, it might thank Stephen Gardiner, or rather Gardiner's policy. This bishop, like a cunning hunter, preserved the game fair at home, and killed it in the walks of other keepers. It was not he, but bloody Bonner, who procured the death of,

JOHN PHILPOT, son of Sir Peter Philpot, knight, born in this county;‡ whose family had an ancient habitation at . . . . . therein. He proceeded master of arts in New College in Oxford; and afterwards, being archdeacon of Lincoln, was a zealous promoter of the Protestant religion. In the first of queen Mary, being a member of the Convocation, "his heart was hot within; and while he was musing, the fire kindled, and he spake with his tongue," which afterwards occasioned his martyrdom.

If Papists account him a distracted man, none will wonder, who consider how the profane captains of Israel called the son of the prophet "a mad fellow."§ And if some vehement expressions fell from him during his imprisonment, his enemies' cruelty was the cause thereof; seeing ill usage, which once made a dumb beast to speak,‖ may make a sober man overspeak in his passion. But all his sufferings are reported by Mr. Fox so perfectly, "perfectum est cui nihil addi potest," that it is presumption for any to hope to make an essential addition thereunto. He was martyred anno Domini 1555, Dec. 18.

KATHARINE GOWCHES.

GUILLEMINE GILBERT.

* Idem, ibidem. † The English Martyrology, in the 15th of June.
‡ J. Bale, de Scriptoribus Britannicis, Cent. viii. num. 89. § 2 Kings ix 11.
‖ Numb. xxii. 28.

PEROTINE MASSEY; whose husband, a minister of God's word, was for fear fled out of the Island.

The first of these was the mother, a poor widow of St. Peter's Port, in the Isle of Guernsey; the other two her daughters (but married women). These, in the reign of queen Mary, were noted to be much absent from the church; for which they were presented before Jaques Amy, then dean of the Island; who, finding them to hold opinions against the real presence in the sacrament of the altar, condemned them to be burnt for heretics; which was done accordingly, July 18, 1556.

Add to these an infant without a christian name; and no wonder it is never named, seeing properly it was never born; but, by the force of the flame, burst out of his mother's belly, Perotine Massey aforesaid. This babe was taken up by W. House a by-stander, and by the command of Elier Gosselin the bailiff (supreme officer in the then absence of the governor of the Island) cast again into the fire, and therein consumed to ashes. It seems this bloody bailiff was minded, like the cruel tyrant, commanding, " Canis pessimi ne catulum esse relinquendum;" though this indeed was no dog, but a lamb, and that of the first minute, and therefore too young, by the Levitical law, to be sacrificed.

Here was a spectacle without precedent,—a cruelty built three generations high, that grandmother, mother, and grandchild, should all suffer in the same flame. And know, reader, these martyrs dying in the Isle of Guernsey, are here reckoned in Hampshire, because that Island with Jersey (formerly subordinate to the archbishop of Constance in Normandy) have, since the reign of queen Elizabeth, being annexed to the diocese of Winchester.

PRELATES.

WILLIAM WICKHAM was born at Wickham in this county, being the son of John Perot and Sibel his wife, over whose graves he hath erected a chapel at Titchfield in this county; and bred in the university of Oxford. He was otherwise called *Long*, from the height of his stature, as my author conceives,[*] though since it may be applied to the perpetuity of his memory, which will last as long as the world endureth, for his two fair foundations at

Oxford, begun 1379;[†] finished 1386. The charter of the foundation of St. Mary's-College in Oxford, was dated the 26th of November 1379, in his manor in Southwark, since called Winchester-house. The scholars entered thereunto about nine a clock on the 14th day of April, in the same year.

Winchester, begun 1387; finished 1393. The first stone was laid March 26, at nine o'clock in the morning, in the 69th year of the age of the founder.

---

[*] Godwin, in the Bishops of Winchester.
[†] These dates are exactly transcribed out of the records of New College.—F.

He died in the 37th year of his consecration, and 80th of his age, in the 5th year of the reign of king Henry the Fourth ; and his benefaction to learning is not to be paralleled by any English subject in all particulars.

JOHN RUSSEL was born in this county, in the parish of Saint Peter's in the suburbs of Winchester.* He was bred fellow of New College; and, when doctor of canon law, was chosen chancellor of Oxford. Yea, that office, annual before, was first fixed on him, as in Cambridge on Bishop Fisher, for term of life.†

By king Edward the Fourth he was advanced bishop of Lincoln, and by Richard the Third lord chancellor of England ;‡ having ability enough to serve any, and honesty too much to please so bad a king. And because he could not bring him to his bent, when the Lord Hastings was killed, this bishop, saith my author,§ was for a time imprisoned. He died January the 30th, anno 1490, leaving this character behind him: " Vir fuit summâ pietate, et ex rerum usu oppidò quàm prudens, doctrinâ etiam singulari."||

WILLIAM WARHAM was born at Ockley, of worshipful parentage in this county; bred fellow and doctor of the laws in New College ;¶ employed by king Henry the Seventh (who never sent sluggard or fool on his errand) to Margaret duchess of Burgundy, and by him advanced bishop of London, then archbishop of Canterbury, living therein in great lustre, till eclipsed in power and profit by Thomas Wolsey, archbishop of York.

It may be said, that England then had ten archbishops, if a figure and cipher amount to so many; or else, if it had but two, they were archbishop Thomas and archbishop Wolsey, drawing all causes to his court-legatine, whilst all other ecclesiastical jurisdictions in England kept a constant vacation. This, Warham bare with much moderation ; contenting himself, that, as he had less honour, so he had less envy, and kept himself cool, whilst Wolsey, his screen, was often scorched with just and general hatred.

In the case of king Henry's divorce, he was the prime advocate for queen Catherine ;** and carried it so cautiously, that he neither betrayed the cause of his client, nor incurred the king's displeasure. Nor will any wonder, that an archbishop of Canterbury did then plead before an archbishop of York, seeing the king at the same time was summoned before his subject.

He survived Wolsey's ruin ; but never recovered his former greatness, blasted with a *præmunire* with the rest of the clergy ;

* Register of New College, in anno 1449.
† Godwin, in Catalogue of Bishops of Lincoln.
‡ J. Philpot, in Catalogue of Chancellors, p. 65.
§ Harpsfield, Historia Ecclesiæ Anglicanæ, decimo quinto sæculo, c. 24.
|| Idem. ¶ New College Register, in the year 1475.
** Godwin, in the Archbishops of Canterbury.

and the heavier because the higher in dignity. He is said to have expended thirty thousand pounds in the repair of his palaces; the probable reason why he left no other public monuments, though archbishop twenty-eight years, dying anno Domini 1533.

ROBERT SHERBORN was born in this county;* and bred first in Winchester, and then in New College; was a great scholar, and prudent man; employed in several embassies by king Henry the Seventh; and by him preferred bishop, first of St. David's, then Chichester; which church he decorated with many ornaments and edifices, especially the south side thereof; where, on the one side is the history of the foundation of the church, with the images of the kings of England:† on the other, the statues of all the bishops of this see, both those of Selsey and of Chichester.‡

He often inscribed for his motto, " Dilexi decorem domûs tuæ, Domine," (I have loved the beauty of thy house, O Lord): and sometimes, " Credite operibus," (trust their works).§ Now although some may like his alms better than his trumpet, charity will make the most favourable construction thereof. Being ninety-six years of age, he resigned his bishopric, and died in the same year, anno Domini 1536.

JOHN WHITE was born in this county, of a worshipful house;‖ began on the floor, and mounted up to the roof of spiritual dignity in this diocese. First scholar in Winchester, then fellow of New College in Oxford, then master of Winchester school; then warden of that college, and at last (taking Lincoln bishopric in his passage) bishop of Winchester, all composed in this distich:¶

> " Me puero custos, ludi paulo ante magister,
> Vitus, et hac demum præsul in urbe fuit."

I may call the latter a golden verse; for it cost this White many an angel to make it true, entering into his bishopric on this condition, to pay cardinal Pole a yearly pension of a thousand pounds. Now though this was no better than simony, yet the prelate's pride was so far above his covetousness, and his covetousness so far above his conscience, that he swallowed it without any regret.

He was a tolerable poet; and wrote an elegy on the eucharist, to prove the corporal presence, and confute Peter Martyr,** the first and last, I believe, who brought controversial divinity

---

* New College Register, in the year 1474.
† Camden's Britannia, in Sussex.
‡ Godwin, in his Bishops of Chichester.   § Ibid.
‖ Sir J. Harrington, in the Bishops of Winchester.
¶ Made by Christopher Johnson, afterwards schoolmaster of Winchester.
** Pits, de Illustribus Angliæ Scriptoribus, p. 763.

into verses. He preached the funeral sermon of queen Mary (or, if you will, of public Popery in England), praising her so beyond all measure, and slighting queen Elizabeth without any cause, that he justly incurred her displeasure. This cost him deprivation and imprisonment, straiter than others of his order (though freer than any Protestant had under Popish persecutors) until his death, which happened at London about the year 1560.

SINCE THE REFORMATION.

THOMAS BILSON was born in the city of Winchester ;* bred first scholar in Winchester school, then (taking New College in his passage) schoolmaster thereof, afterwards warden of the college, and at last (taking Worcester in his way) bishop of Winchester. As reverend and learned a prelate as England ever afforded ; witness his worthy works, " Of the perpetual Government of Christ's Church," and of " Christ's Descent into Hell ;" not—1. *ad patiendum*, to *suffer*, which was concluded on the cross with " It is finished ;"† nor, 2. *ad prædicandum*, to *preach*, useless where his auditory was all the forlorn hope ; neither, 3. *ad liberandum*, to *free* any, pardon never coming after execution; but, 4. *ad possidendum*, to *take possession* of hell, which he had conquered ; and, 5. *ad triumphandum*, to *triumph*, which is honourable *in hostico*, in the enemies' own country.

The new translation of the Bible was by king James's command ultimately committed to his and Dr. Smith's‡ (bishop of Gloucester) perusal ; who put the completing hand thereunto. His pious departure out of this life happened 1618.

HENRY COTTON was born at Warblington in this county, being a younger son unto Sir Richard Cotton, knight, and privy councillor to king Edward the Sixth. Queen (whilst yet but a lady) Elizabeth, being then but twelve years of age, was his god-mother. He was bred in Magdalen College in Oxford, and was by the queen preferred bishop of Salisbury ; when she pleasantly said, " that formerly she had blessed many of her god-sons, but now her god-son should bless her;" reflecting on the solemnity of episcopal benediction. He was consecrated November the 12th, 1598 ; at which time William Cotton (of another family) was made bishop of Exeter ; the queen merrily saying (alluding to the plenty of clothing in those parts) " that she hoped that now she had well cottoned the west." By his wife, whose name was Patience, he had nineteen children, and died May the 7th, 1615.

ARTHUR LAKES was born in the parish of Saint Michael,§ in the town of Southampton ; bred first in Winchester school,

---

* New College Register, anno 1565.   † John xix. 30.
‡ See the Life of Dr. Smith, prefixed to his Sermon.
§ New College Register, anno 1589, wherein he was admitted.

then fellow of New College. In his own nature he preferred the fruitfulness of the vine, and fatness of the olive (painfulness in a private parish) before the government of the trees, had not immediate Providence, without his suit and seeking, preferred him successively warden of New College, prefect of Saint Crosses nigh Winchester, dean of Worcester, bishop of Bath and Wells.

He continued the same in his rochet, what he was in his scholar's gown; and lived a real comment upon Saint Paul's character of a bishop:

1. *Blameless.* Such as hated his order, could not cast any aspersion upon him.

2. *The husband of one wife.* He took not that lawful liberty; but led a single life, honouring matrimony in his brethren who embraced it.

3. *Vigilant.* Examining canonically in his own person all those whom he ordained.

4. *Sober, of good behaviour.* Such his austerity in diet (from university-commons to his dying day) that he generally fed but on one (and that no dainty) dish, and fasted four times a week from supper.

5. *Given to hospitality.* When master of Saint Crosses, he increased the allowance of the poor brethren in diet and otherwise. When bishop, he kept fifty servants in his family, not so much for state or attendance on his person, but pure charity, in regard of their private need.

6. *Apt to teach.* The living with his pious sermons, in his cathedral and neighbouring parishes; and posterity with those writings he hath left behind him.

7. *Not given to wine.* His abstemiousness herein was remarkable.

8. *No striker, not given to filthy lucre.* He never fouled his fingers with the least touch of Gehazi's reward, freely preferring desert.

9. *One that ruleth well his own house.* The rankness of house-keeping brake not out into any riot; and a chapter was constantly read every meal, by one kept for that purpose. Every night (besides cathedral and chapel prayers) he prayed in his own person with his family in his dining-room.

In a word, his intellectuals had such predominancy of his sensuals, or rather grace so ruled in both, that the man in him being subordinate to the Christian, he lived a pattern of piety.

I have read of one Arthur Faunt, a Jesuit, who, entering into orders, renounced his Christian name, because (forsooth) never legendary saint thereof, and assumed that of Lawrence.* This gracious Arthur was not so superstitiously scrupulous, and (if none before) may pass for the first saint of his name, dying in the fifty-ninth year of his age, anno Domini 1602.

* Burton's Description of Leicestershire, p. 105.

STATESMEN.

RICHARD RICH, Knight, was, in the words of my author, "a gentleman well descended and allied in this county ;"* bred in the Temple, in the study of our common law, and afterwards became solicitor to king Henry the Eighth. His deposition on oath, upon words spoken to him in the Tower, was the sharpest evidence to cut off the head of Sir Thomas More. He was under Cromwell a lesser hammer to knock down abbeys, most of the grants of which lands going through his hands, no wonder if some stuck upon his fingers.

Under king Edward the Sixth he was made lord chancellor of England, discharging his place with prudence and equity for the term of five years. Foreseeing he should be ousted of his office (being of the anti-faction to duke Dudley), to prevent stripping, he politically put off his robes of state (resigning his office) ; which done, no danger of catching cold, his own under-suit was so well lined, having gotten a fair estate about Lees Abbey in Essex, whereof he was created baron. He died in the beginning of the reign of queen Elizabeth, being direct ancestor unto the right honourable Charles Rich, now earl of Warwick.

[S. N.] WILLIAM POWLET (wherever born) had his largest estate and highest honour (baron of Basing, and marquis of Winchester) in this county. He was descended from a younger house of the Powlets of Hinton Saint George in Somersetshire, as by the crescent in his arms is acknowledged. One telleth us,† that he being a younger brother, and having wasted all that was left him, came to court on trust, where, upon the bare stock of his wit, he trafficked so wisely, and prospered so well, that he got, spent, and left, more than any subject since the Conquest.

Indeed he lived at the time of the dissolution of abbeys, which was the harvest of estates ; and it argued idleness, if any courtier had his barns empty. He was servant to king Henry the Seventh, and for thirty years together treasurer to king Henry the Eighth, Edward the Sixth, queen Mary, and queen Elizabeth. The latter, in some sort, owed their crowns to his counsel ; his policy being the principal defeater of duke Dudley's design to disinherit them.

I behold this lord Powlet like to aged Adoram, so often mentioned in Scripture, being over the tribute in the days of king David,‡ all the reign of king Solomon,§ until the first year of Rehoboam.|| And though our lord Powlet enjoyed his place not so many years, yet did he serve more sovereigns, in more

* J. Philpot, in his Catalogue of Chancellors, p. 73.
† Sir Robert Naunton, in his " Fragmenta Regalia."
‡ 2 Samuel xx. 24. § 1 Kings iv. 6. || 1 Kings xii. 18.

mutable times, being (as he said of himself) "no oak, but an osier."

Herein the parallel holds not. The hoary hairs of Adoram were sent to the grave by a violent death, slain by the people in a tumult.* This lord had the rare happiness of εὐθανασία, setting in his full splendour, having lived ninety-seven years, and seen 103 out of his body. He died anno Domini 1572.

Sir THOMAS LAKES was born in the parish of St. Michael, in the town of Southampton, and there bred in grammar-learning, under Doctor Seravia. By several under-offices he was at last deservedly preferred secretary of state to king James. Incredible his dexterity in dispatch, who at the same time would indite, write, discourse, more exactly than most men could severally perform them. Men resembled him to one of the ships-royal of queen Elizabeth, called the Swiftsure, such his celerity and solidity in all affairs. No less his secresy in concealing; and what was credited to his counsel was always found in the same posture it was left in. Add to all these, he was a good man, and a good man's brother, Dr. Arthur Lakes, bishop of Bath and Wells. King James (who always loved what was facile and fluent) was highly pleased with his Latin pen, who by practice had made Tully's phrase his own. He was one of the three noble hands, who at the court first led Mr. George Villers into the favour of king James.

At last he fell, for the faults of others, into the king's displeasure, being punished for the offences of one of his nearest relations; and of all them fined in the star-chamber, he was the only person generally pitied for his suffering; yet even then king James gave him this public eulogy in open court, "that he was a minister of state fit to serve the greatest prince in Europe." He was ousted his secretary's place, which needed him more than he it, having achieved a fair fortune, which he transmitted to posterity. How long he lived afterwards in a private life, is to me unknown.

SOLDIERS.

BEAVOIS, an Englishman, was earl of Southampton in the time of the Conqueror; and, being unable to comport with his oppression, banded against him, with the fragments of the Englishmen, the strength of Hastings the Dane, and all the assistance the Welch could afford; in whose country a battle was fought, near Carcliffe, against the Normans, anno Domini 1070, wherein three nations were conquered by one. Beavois being worsted (success depends not on valour) fled to Carlisle (a long step from Carcliffe); and afterwards no mention what became of him.

* 1 Kings xii. 18.

This is that Beavois whom the monks cried up to be such a man, that since it hath been questioned whether ever such a man, I mean, whether ever his person was in *rerum naturâ*: so injurious those are, who, in the reports of any man's performances, exceed the bounds of probability.

All I will add is this, that the sword preserved and showed to be this Beavoises in Arundel castle is lesser (perchance worn with age) than that of king Edward the Third, kept in Westminster church.

SEAMEN.

Sir JOHN WALLOP, born in this county, of a most ancient and respected family, was directed by his genius to sea-service, at what time our coasts were much infested with French piracies: for there was a knight of Malta, passing in our Chronicles by the name of Prior John (more proper, by his profession, to be employed against the Turks, lately so victorious in Hungary) who lived by *pickeering*, and undoing many English merchants.

But our Sir John made the French pay more than treble damages, who, with eight hundred men, landed in Normandy, burnt one-and-twenty towns,* with divers ships in the havens of Traport, Staples, &c.; and safely returned with wealth and victory.

Methinks the ancient arms of the Wallhops appear prophetical herein; viz. Argent, a bend undé Sable; interpreted by my author,† a wave, or surge of the sea, raised by some turbulent flaw of wind and tempest, prognosticating the activity of that family in marine performances.

ROBERT TOMSON, merchant, was born at Andover in this county; bred much at Bristol in sea employment.‡ Hence, anno 1553, he sailed into Spain, and thence two years after shipped himself for Nova Hispania, to make a discovery thereof; on the same token that in his passage thither, in a Spanish ship, a light like a candle (being nothing else but a meteor frequent by sea and land) fell on their mainmast, which the Spaniards on their knees worshipped for St. Elmo, the advocate of sailors.§ He afterwards wrote the Description of New Spain, with the city of Mexico, giving a good and the first account thereof of any Englishman.

During his abode many months in Mexico, at dinner he let fall some discourse against Saint-worship, for which he was imprisoned in the Holy-house, and enjoined solemn penance by the archbishop of Mexico; this Tomson, being the first (reputed) heretic, which was ever seen in America on a penitential

---

* Holinshed, Stow, ed. Herbert, in this year.
† Gwillim's Display of Heraldry, p. 50.
‡ Hackluit's Voyages, Vol. III. p. 437.   § Ibid. p. 450.

scaffold.   Hence he was sent into Spain ; and, after three years durance in the Inquisition, discharged.   Here a Spanish merchant's daughter, Mary de la Barrera by name, fell in love with him, and became his wife, worth to him in bars of gold and silver two thousand five hundred pounds, besides jewels of great price.*   Returning into England, he lived with great comfort and credit therein ; so that it may truly be said of him, " He had been undone, if (by the cruelty of his enemies) he had not been undone."

WRITERS.

LAMPRID of Winchester was bred a Benedictine therein, *Congregationis Giribenne,* saith my author,† wherein I am not ashamed to confess my ignorance.   Such his learning in those days, that he got the general name of *Doctor Eximius,* though his few works still extant answer not the proportion of so high a title.   He flourished anno 980.

WOLSTANUS of Winchester, bred a Benedictine, therein attained to the reputation of a great scholar.   I listen attentively to the words of W. Malmsbury‡ (who could *ken* a learned man) giving him this character: " Vir fuit eruditus, homo etiam bonæ vitæ et castigatæ eloquentiæ."   But, it seemeth, his eloquence was confined to poetry ; my author observing, that " Oratione solutâ nunquam politè scripsit."   He flourished anno 1000.

JOHN of Basingstoke, so called from a fair market town in this county, where he was born.   We have a double demonstration of his signal worth ; first, because Robert Grosthead that pious and learned bishop (who would not advance any thing which was under eminency) preferred him archdeacon of Leicester : secondly, the pens of Bale§ and Pits,‖ diametrically opposite one to the other, meet both in his commendation. Being bred first in Oxford, then in Paris, thence he travelled into Athens (Athens as yet was Athens, not routed by Turkish tyranny) ; where he heard the learned lectures of one Constantina, a noble woman¶ (not fully twenty years old),** of the abstruse mysteries of nature.   Coming home, he brought back many precious books, and had good skill in the Greek tongue (whereof he wrote a Grammar), and is justly reputed the first restorer thereof in England.   He was the author of many worthy works ; and died anno 1252, on whom Matthew Paris bestowed this eulogy, " Vir in trivio et quatrivio ad plenum eruditus."††

* Hackluit's Voyages, Vol. III. p. 451.   † Pits, ætate decima, num. 149.
‡ Libro secundo, de Gestis Reg. Angliæ.
§ Description of Britain, cent. quarta, p. 302.
‖ De Scriptoribus Britannicis.   ¶ Idem.   ** Idem.
†† In Chron, ad ann. 64.

JOHN of HIDE* was a monk in the abbey of Hide, in the suburbs of Winchester, and became a competent historian according to the rate of those times, writing certain Homilies, a book " Of the Patience of Job," and the " Story of his own Convent." He flourished anno 1284.

WILLIAM ALTON, a native of a known market-town in this county, was a Dominican, or preaching friar, famous even amongst foreigners for his sermons and sound judgment, avouching the Virgin Mary tainted with original corruption. He flourished anno 1330.

WILLIAM LILLIE was born at Odiam, a market-town in this county,† and travelled in his youth as far as Jerusalem. In his return, he staid at Rhodes, and studied Greek; which will seem strange to some, Rhodes not being Rhodes in that age (except casually some great critic was there); seeing otherwise to find elegant in modern Greek (soured with long continuance) is as impossible as to draw good wine out of a vessel of vinegar.

Hence he went to Rome, where he heard John Sulpitius and Pomponius Sabinus, great masters of Latin in those days. After his return, dean Colet made him the first master of St. Paul's school, which place he commendably discharged for fifteen years. Here he made his Latin grammar, which this great schoolmaster modestly submitted to the correction of Erasmus; and therefore such who will not take it on the single bond of Lillie may trust on the security of Erasmus.

Some charge it for surfeiting with variety of examples, who would have had him only to set down the bare rules, as best for children's remembrance. But they may know that such who learnt grammar in Lillie's time were not schoolboys, but schoolmen; I mean, arrived at men's estate. Many since have altered and bettered his grammar; and amongst them my worthy friend Dr. Charles Scarborough; calculating his short, clear, and true rules for the meridian of his own son; which in due time may serve for general use. Our Lillie died of the plague,‡ and was buried in the porch of Saint Paul's, anno Domini 1522.

SINCE THE REFORMATION.

MICHAEL RENEGER was born in this county,§ and bred fellow in Magdalen College in Oxford, where he gained great credit for his skill in learning and languages. He wrote a book in the Defence of Ministers' Marriage.

* Pits, de Illustribus Angliæ Scriptoribus.
† Bale, de Scriptoribus Britannicis, Cent. viii. num. 64.
‡ Stow's Survey of London, p. 370.
§ Bale, de Scriptoribus Britannicis, Cent. ix. num. 78.

THOMAS STERNHOLD was born in this county,[*] and was afterwards a servant to king Henry the Eighth. I find him a legatee in his will, thus mentioned : " Item, To Thomas Sternhold, groom of our robes, a hundred mark."

He was afterwards (saith my author)[†] *ab intimo cubiculo* to king Edward the Sixth; though I am not satisfied whether thereby he meant gentleman of his privy chamber, or groom of his bed chamber.

He was a principal instrument of translating the Psalms into English meter; the first twenty-six (and seven-and-thirty in all) being by him performed. Yet had he other assistance in that work. Many a bitter scoff hath since been past on their endeavours by some wits, which might have been better employed. Some have miscalled these their translations *Geneva gigs;* and, which is the worst, father, or mother rather, the expression on our virgin queen, as falsely as other things have been charged upon her. Some have not sticked to say, " that David hath been as much persecuted by bungling translators, as by Saul himself." Some have made libellous verses in abuse of them ; and no wonder if songs were made on the translators of the psalms, seeing drunkards[‡] made them on David the author thereof.

But let these translations be beheld by impartial eyes, and they will be allowed to go in equipage with the best poems in that age. However, it were to be wished that some bald rhymes therein were bettered ; till which time such as sing them must endeavour to amend them, by singing them with understanding heads, and gracious hearts, whereby that which is bad meter on earth will be made good music in heaven.

As for our Thomas Sternhold, it was happy for him that he died before his good master, anno 1549, in the month of August; so probably preventing much persecution, which had happened unto him if surviving in the reign of queen Mary.

DAVID WHITEHEAD (where born to me unknown) is here placed, because I find a worshipful and ancient family of his name in this county. He was bred a bachelor of divinity in Oxford ; and, flying into Germany in the reign of queen Mary, was in high esteem at Frankfort with the English congregation. After his return, queen Elizabeth proffered him great preferment. And it seems, in the first of her reign, the archbishop of Canterbury went a wooing to accept thereof; viz. to 1. John Feckenham, refusing it upon a popish account, because he would not subscribe to the queen's supremacy :[§] 2. Nicholas Wotton, doctor of law, and dean of Canterbury, refusing it on a politic account, suspecting the queen's short life, and fearing alterations

---

* Bale, de Scriptoribus Britannicis, Cent. ix. num. 79.   † Idem, ibidem.
‡ Psalm lxix. 12.   § Rinerius, in Historia Benedictinorum.

in the state :* 3. This Whitehead, who declined it out of his desire of privacy, though some causelessly suspected him for disaffection to church discipline.† For he was, by queen Elizabeth, offered the mastership of the hospital of the Savoy,‡ which he might have accepted without any subscription, but would not, affirming he could live plentifully on the preaching of the gospel ; a rare example of moderation. He was a deep divine, and was chosen one of the disputants, primo Elizabethæ, against the popish bishops. His many books, still extant, testify his learning and religion.

Queen Elizabeth highly valued his company, the rather because of his conscientious bluntness, wherein one repartee may be remembered. The queen, who ever was " iniquior in sacerdotes maritatos," said unto him, " Whitehead, I love thee the better, because thou art unmarried."§ " In truth, Madam," said he, " I love you the worse because you are unmarried." He died anno Domini 1571.

NICHOLAS FULLER was, as I have cause to conceive, born in this county; and, when a youth, was amanuensis or scribe to Dr. Horne, bishop of Winchester; afterwards he attended, as tutor servant, on Sir Henry Wallop to Oxford ; and returning thence, was made minister of Allington nigh Salisbury in Wiltshire, where he had a benefice rather than a living, so small the revenues thereof. But a contented mind extendeth the smallest parish into a diocese, and improveth the least benefice into a bishopric.

Here a great candle was put under a bushel, or peck rather, so private his place and employment. Here he applied his studies in the tongues, and was happy in pitching on (not difficult trifles, but) useful difficulties, tending to the understanding of Scripture. He became an excellent linguist; and his books found good regard beyond the seas, where they were reprinted.

Drusius, the Belgian critic, grown old, angry, and jealous that he should be outshined in his own sphere, foully cast some drops of ink upon him, which the other as fairly wiped off again. He charged Master Fuller for being his plagiary, taking his best notes from him without any acknowledgment thereof. Master Fuller confessed himself always desirous of Drusius's works, but never able, such his poverty, to purchase them, and therefore he could not steal out of those books which his eye never beheld ; and (not to be partial to my namesake) let the world judge whether Fuller's *miscellane* be not as good as Drusius's *wheat*.

Bishop Andrewes came to him, as the queen of Sheba to Solomon, to pose him with hard questions, bringing with him a heap of knots for the other to untie, and departed from him with good satisfaction. He afterwards bestowed on him a great

* Holinshed's Chronicle, p. 1403. † Heroologia Angliæ, p. 173.
‡ Idem, ibid. § Lord Verulam, in his Apophthegms,

living in this county, which Master Fuller did not long enjoy.
He was most eminent for that grace which is most worth, yet
costeth the least to keep it; I mean humility, who in his writings doth as fairly dissent from, as freely concur with, any man's
opinions.   He died about the year of our Lord 1626.

THOMAS JAMES was born in the Isle of Wight;* bred first
in Winchester, then at New College in Oxford, and afterwards
proceeded doctor in divinity.   He was chosen by Sir Thomas
Bodley the keeper of his inestimable library in Oxford.   And,
on serious consideration, one will conclude the library made for
him, and him for it; like tallies, they so fitted one another.
Some men live like moths in libraries, not being better for the
books, but the books the worse for them, which they only soil
with their fingers.   Not so Dr. James, who made use of books
for his own and the public good.   He knew the age of a manuscript by looking upon the face thereof, and by the form of the
character could conclude the time wherein it was written.

He was a member of the Convocation held with the Parliament of Oxford, primo Caroli, where he made a motion, that
some might be commissioned to peruse the manuscript Fathers
in all public and private English libraries, that thereby the forgery of foreign popish editions might be detected.

I believe his design had formerly been by him pursued for
many years, as appears by this passage in Mr. Camden :†

"Tho. James Oxoniensis, vir eruditus et verè φιλόβιβλος, qui
se totum literis et libris involvit, et jam publici boni studio in
Angliæ Bibliothecis excutiendis (Deus opus secundet!) id moli-
tur, quod Reipublicæ literariæ imprimis erit usui."

He never attained higher preferment than the subdeanery of
Wells ; and, dying 1628, was buried in the chapel of New College in Oxford.

[S. N.] CHARLES BUTLER was bred master of arts, in Magdalen College in Oxford, and afterwards beneficed in this
county.   An excellent musician, who wrote a book of "The
Principles of Music," in singing and setting, with the twofold
use thereof (ecclesiastical and civil) ; and a critical Englishman,
having composed a grammar of our language.   He also wrote a
"Book of Bees;" wherein, as if he had been their secretary, he
appears most knowing in the state mysteries of their commonwealth ; whence one, not unhandsomely, on his book :‡

> Aut à consiliis Apibus, Butlere, fuisti ;
> Aut à consiliis est Apis ipsa tuis.

> "Butler, he'll say (who these thy writings sees)
> Bees counsel thee, or else thou counsellest Bees."

I behold these his books as the receptacle of the leakage and
superfluities of his study ; and it is no trespass on grace for one

---

* New College Register, anno 1593.   † Britannia, in Monmouthshire.
‡ In the verses ad Authorem.

to walk and take a turn in the field of Nature. He was also a pious man, a painful preacher, and a solid divine: witness his excellent book of " The Marriage of Cousin Germans," approved and commended by Doctor Prideaux as the best ever written on that subject. I conjecture he died about the year 1640.

ROMISH EXILE WRITERS.

RICHARD WHITE was born at Basingstoke in this county ;* bred first in Winchester school, then in New College in Oxford. In the beginning of queen Elizabeth, leaving the land, he lived first at Louvain, then in Padua in Italy, where he proceeded doctor of the laws. Afterwards he became Regius Professor at Douay for the space of thirty years and more. He wrote many books, and, amongst the rest, a British and English History, which hitherto I have not been so happy as to see, save at the second hand, as often cited by Mr. Selden, which makes me believe much merit therein.

Surely he was better employed in the writing thereof, than in the large Comment he hath made on the enigmatical epitaph set up at Bononia: " Ælia Lælia Crispis, &c." Which many think merely made by a conceited brain, on design to puzzle intellects, to create sense by their ingenuity and industry, which was never intended therein; for I am clearly of his opinion, who said, " Qui ea scribit legi, quæ non vult intelligi, debet negligi."

I have nothing else to observe of this Richard White, save that, after he had successively married two wives,† he was made a priest by the special dispensation of Pope Clement the Eighth ; and that he was alive at Douay, 1611.

JOHN PITS was born in this county, nigh the market-town of Aulton ; witness his words, " in vicinio ‡ cujus oppidi natus sum ego." Son he was to Henry Pits and Elizabeth his wife, sister to Nicholas Sanders.§ It is hard to say whether his hands took more pains in writing, or feet in travelling, if the list of his laborious life be perused, whereby he will appear a very aged person. At eleven years of age he went to the school of Winchester, 11 ; seven years he staid there, until chosen unto New College, 18 ; two years he lived in Oxford, and then went beyond the seas, 20 ; one year he staid and studied in the college of Rheims, 21 ; thence going to Rome, he lived seven years there in the English college, and was ordained priest, 28 ; returning to Rheims, two years he there taught rhetoric and Greek, 30 ; then lived in Lorrain and in Triers two years, 32 ;

* He writeth himself, in his book, " of Basing-Stoak."
† Pits, de Illustribus Angliæ Scriptoribus, p. 806.
‡ Pits, in the Life of William Aulton, in anno 1330.
§ Idem, in his own Life, p. 817.

three years at Ingolstad in Bavaria, where he was made D.D. 35; made canon of Verdun in Lorrain, and lived there two years, 37; then for twelve years he was confessor to the duchess of Cleve, 49. Here he wrote many volumes of several subjects; one of the apostolical men, another of the kings and bishops in England; but, because he survived not to see them set forth, he was as good as his word, " mecum morientur, et sepelientur," (with him they died, and were buried.) Only that his book is brought to light, which is intituled, " De Illustribus Angliæ Scriptoribus;" a subject formerly handled by many; so that some stick not to say, *J. Leland* is the industrious *bee*, working all: *J. Bale* is the angry *wasp*, stinging all: *J. Pits* is the idle *drone*, stealing all.

For my part, I have made much use of his endeavours to help me with many writers, especially with such English Papists as have been since the Reformation. Nor will I pay him with railing, from whose pen I have borrowed much information. Some wonder at his invectiveness: I wonder more, that he inveigheth so little; and seeing he was sister's son to blackmouthed Sanders, it is much that he doth not more avunculize in his bitterness against Protestants.

After the death of Anthonia duchess of Cleve, he returned the third time into Lorrain, where the bishop of Toul (who formerly had been his scholar) gave him the deanery of Liverdune, a place of good credit and revenue, where quietly he reposed himself for the remainder of his life for many years; and, dying anno 1616, was there buried.

BENEFACTORS TO THE PUBLIC.

Besides bishop WICKHAM (of whom before), who alone may pass for ten, I meet with none of grand remark before the Reformation; since it, besides many of meaner note, I find two of signal charity.

Sir WILLIAM DODDINGTON, Knight, high sheriff of this county in the third of king James, kept a bountiful house at Bremer therein. Succeeding to an unexpected estate, he had the words of David frequently in his mouth; "What am I? or what is my Father's house, that thou hast brought me hitherto?" Having a godly jealousy that some former disasters in his family had been caused by God's displeasure on his ancestors for holding so many impropriations, he freely and fully restored them to the church, settling them as firmly as law could devise to a greater yearly value than many will believe, or any imitate. Yet was he a man of mourning, or son of affliction, all the days of his life. No sooner had he seen Herbert his eldest son, a most hopeful gentleman, married to a considerable co-heiress in Somersetshire, but he beheld him snatched away by an untimely death. What tragedies have since happened in his household,

is generally known.   All these he bare with saint-like patience ;
" hearing the rod," (that is, understanding and obeying it)
" and him who appointed it."* In a word, God, the skilful
lapidary, polished him with sharp instruments, that he then did
glister as a pearl here, who now shineth as a star in heaven.
He died about the year of our Lord 1638.

[S. N.] JOSEPH DIGGONS, Esquire, was of Dutch extraction
(whose father was a seaman of Trinity-house ;) but had his
longest habitation in this county, in a house of his own building at Wetham in the parish of Liss.   He was bred a fellow-
commoner of Clare Hall in Cambridge, and afterwards became
a barrister in the Temple.   By his will he gave to Clare Hall
(where none knew his face, nor remembered his name, save
the worthy master Dr. Pask) all his estate in land, of very
improvable rents, to the value of one hundred and thirty
pounds per annum, for the founding of fellowships and scholarships, at the discretion of the master and fellows.   He made
Mr. Pickering, an attorney of Clements-Inn (living at Oldham in
this county), an overseer of his will, who faithfully gave the college notice thereof, and was very useful and assistant to them in
the settling of the lands aforesaid.   Mr. Diggons died anno 1658.

MEMORABLE PERSONS.

We must not forget one (better known to me by his invention than his name) who, dwelling at Stockbridge in this county,
made so artificial a plough, that, by the help of engines and
some contrivances, it might be drawn by dogs, and managed by
one man, who would plough in one day well nigh an acre of the
light ground in this county.   This plough I saw (some thirty
years since) at Stockbridge aforesaid.

But the project was not taking, beheld rather as pretty than
profitable ; though in the judgment of wise men this ground-
work might have been built upon, and invention much improved by the skilful in mathematics ; for I have heard that
some politicians are back friends (how justly I know not) to
such projects, which (if accomplished) invite the land to a loss,
the fewer poor being thereby set a-work ; that being the best
way of tillage, which employeth most about it, to keep
them from stealing and starving ; so that it would not be
beneficial to the state, might a plough be drawn by butterflies,
as which would draw the greater burden on the commonwealth, to devise other ways for the maintenance of the poor.

 The mentioning of these plough-drawing dogs mindeth me
(one rarity attracteth another) of other dogs in this county,
more useful for the commonwealth, meeting with this passage in a modern author :†

---

* Micah vi. 9.   † Britannia Baconica, in Hampshire, p. 51.

" It is reported, that about Portsmouth is a race of small dogs, like beagles, that they use there to hunt moles, which they hunt as their proper natural game."

If this be true, I wish the continuance and increase of the breed of this kind of *canes venatici*. And though the pleasure be not so much as in hunting of hares, the profit is more in destroying those malignant pioneers, mischievous to grass, more to grain, most to gardens.

LORD MAYORS.

It is no less true than strange, that this county, so large in itself, so near to London, weekly changing cloth for money therewith, is Ἀσύμβολος ; I mean, hath not contributed one to this topic. Such as suspect the truth thereof will be satisfied, on their exact survey of Stow's "Survey of London."

THE NAMES OF THE GENTRY IN THIS SHIRE,

RETURNED INTO THE TOWER BY THE COMMISSIONERS IN THE TWELFTH YEAR OF KING HENRY THE SIXTH, ANNO 1433.

H. Ep'us Winton, cardinalis Angliæ; Reginaldus le Warre, miles;—Johannes Lysle, et Johannes Brewe de Stapule (knights for the shire);—Commissioners to take the oaths.

Walteri Sandes, chevalier.	Willielmi Clive.
Johannis Popham, chevalier.	Willelmi Chellys.
Johannis Uvedale.	Johannis Faukoner.
Willielmi Warbleton.	Johannis Mofunt.
Thomæ Tame.	Willielmi Tested.
Willielmi Fauconer.	Richardi Rumsey.
Roberti Dyngle.	Willielmi Burton.
Stephani Popham, chevalier.	Roberti Whittehede.
Willielmi Brokays.	Richardi Spicer.
Willielmi Ryngebourne.	Johannes atte Berwe, de Charleford.
Walteri Veere.	
Johannis Hampton.	Johannis Lawrence.
Johannis Gyffard.	Thomæ Rockley.
Johannis Brinkeley.	Thomæ Yardly.
Petri Condraye.	Thomæ Benebury.
Johannis Skilling.	Willielmi Wellis.
Thomæ Ringewood, senior.	Johannis Escote.
Willielmi Persh.	Johannis Rotherfield.
Jonannis Hacket.	Richardi Parkere.
Johannis Haymowe.	Johannis Kybbyll.
Roberti Fursey.	Johannis Barbour.
Roberti Tylbourgh.	Symonis Almayn.
Willielmi Astel.	Willielmi Farcy.
Johannis Balon.	Richardi Punchardon.
Johannis Bray.	Nicholai Bernard.
Johannis Purbyke.	Nicholai Banestre.
Johannis Catevan.	Thomæ Wayte.

It will be worth our inquiry, who this chief commissioner Henry bishop of Winchester was, with his insolent title of " Cardinal of England." I find many eminent epithets (but none of the quorum of Saint Paul's bishops) meeting in his person; viz. *noble, rich, valiant, politic, and long-lived :—Noble,* being son of John à Gaunt, by Katherine Swinford (born at Beaufort in France, whence he had his name), brother to king Henry the Fourth, uncle to king Henry the Fifth, great uncle to king Henry the Sixth :—*Rich,* commonly called the rich cardinal. In his time the king and courtiers cast a covetous eye on church-endowments, but were diverted from longer looking on them by the council of archbishop Chichly, and coin of this bishop Beaufort; the former putting the king upon the war with France, the latter lending him, on good security, twenty thousand pounds, a sum sounding high in those days. He was also called, κατ᾽ ἐξοχήν, the cardinal of England, though we had another (and his senior) at the same time of the same order; viz. Thomas Langley, bishop of Durham :—*Valiant,* being the pope's legate (in plain English, the pope's general), leading his army into Bohemia, in which service he behaved himself *fortius quam episcopum decebat :—Worldly politic,* venting words on his death-bed to this purpose, " that if all England " (some reporters take a longer circuit) " would preserve his life, he was able by his purse to purchase or by policy to procure it :"—*Long life,* having been bishop of Lincoln and Winchester fifty years; yet was he so far from being weaned from the world, he sucked the hardest (as if he would have bit off the nipples thereof) the nearer he was to his grave, dying anno 1447.

He was in his generation (by a charitable *antiperistasis*) fixed betwixt bishops Wickham and Wainfleet; but did not equal them in his benefactions to the public, though he founded a fair hospital in Winchester, a work (no doubt) more acceptable to God, than when he, anno 1417, undertook and performed a dangerous voyage to Jerusalem.

It is, in my apprehension, very remarkable, that the three aforesaid bishops of Winchester, Wickham, Beaufort, and Wainfleet, sat successively in that see six score years lacking two, not to be paralleled in any other bishopric.

To take our leave of this great cardinal, we read of king Josiah, " now the rest of the acts of king Josiah and his goodness,"* &c. But as for this prelate, the rest of his acts and his greatness, we leave to such as are desirous thereof to collect them out of our English historians.

SHERIFFS.

Anno	HENRY II.	Anno	
1		3	Turcinus vic.
2	Turcinus vic.	4	

* 2 Chronicles xxxv. 26.

Anno

5 Turcinus vic.

6

7 Rich. filius Turcini, for nine years.

16 Hugo de Gundevill, for four years.

20 Herudus de Stratton, et Hugo de Gundevill, for five years.

25 Hen. de Stratton, et Hugo de Gundevile.

26 Galf. filius Aze, for eight years.

RICHARD I.

1 Galf. filius Azon.

2 Ogerus filius Ogeri.

3 Joh. de Rebez.

4 Will. Briewere.

5 Ogerus filius Ogeri.

6 Hugo de Bosco, for five years.

REX JOHAN.

1 Hugo de Basco.

2 Idem.

3 Will. Briewere, et Rad. de Bray.

4 Galf. filius Petri. et Will. Stokes.

5 Idem.

6 Rog. filius Ade, for four years.

10 Walt. Briewere, et Alan de Bockland.

11 Idem.

12 Will. Briewere.

13 Hugo de Nevill, et Galf. de Salvaozins.

14 Idem.

15 Idem.

16 Will. de S'to Johanne.

17 Will. Briewere, et Will. de S'to Johanne.

HENR. III.

1

2 Pet. Winton. Epis. et

Anno

Will. de Schorewell, for seven years.

9 Rich. Epis. Saresb. et Bartholomew de Kemes.

10 Idem.

11 Rich. Epis. Saresb. et Gilb. de Staplebrigg.

12 Idem.

13 Nich. de Molis, et Walt. de Romsey.

14 Nich. de Molis, et Hen. de Bada.

15 Idem.

16 Idem.

17 Pet. Winton. Epis. et Rog. Wascelin.

18 Idem.

19 Hen. filius Nicholai.

20 Hen. filius Nich. et Rob. de Mara.

21 Galf. de Insula.

22 Idem.

23 Idem.

24 Emueus de Lacy.

25 Idem.

26 Idem.

27 R. Passelewe, for six years.

33 Rob. Passell.

34 Hen. Facull, for six years.

40 Hen. de Farneleg.

41 Ja. le Savage.

42 Joh. le Jac. Savage.

43 Idem.

44 Will. de Wintershull.

45 Regin. filius Petri, et Joh. de Flemer.

46 Idem.

47 Regin. filius Petri, et Hereward de Marisco.

48 Idem.

49 Joh. de Botele.

50 Idem.

51 Gerar. de Grue.

52 Joh. le Botele.

53 Idem.

54 Idem.

55 Will. de Wintershull.

56 Idem.

Anno

EDW. I.

1 Will. de Wintershull.
2 Hen. de Shotebroke.
3 Joh. de Havering, for four years.
7 Will. de Braybofe.
8 Idem.
9 Phil. de Foynil.
10 Idem.
11 Idem.
12 Simon. de Winton.
13 Idem.
14 Will. de Bremschete, for four years.
18 Ingeramus de Waleys.
19 Idem.
20 Rich. Aston.
21 Idem.
22 Hugo de Chickenhull, for four years.
26 Tho. de Warblington, for four years.
30 Joh. de Gerbg.
31 Tho. de Warblington.
32 Idem.
33 Idem.
34 Phil. de Foynil.
35 Idem.

EDW. II.

1 Tho. de Warblington, for five years.
6 Ja. de Norton, et Jo. de la Bech.
7 Idem.
8 Joh. de la Bech.
9 Idem.
10 Idem.
11 Rich. Byflett.
12 Rob. de Norton.
13 Ja. de Norton.

Anno

14 Joh. de Tichburne.
15 Nul. Tit. Com. in hoc Rotulo.
16
17 Joh. de Scures.
18 Idem.
19 Idem.

EDW. III.

1 Joh. de Scures, for twelve years.
13 Rob. Daundelin.
14 Rob. de Popeham, et Rob. de Daundelin.
15 Joh. de Palton, et Tho. de Chisenhall.
16 Joh. de Palton.
17 Th. de Apsall, for five years.
22 Hen. Sturmy.
23 Idem.
24 Idem.
26 Joh. de Winchester, for four years.
29 Will. de Overton.
30 Joh. de Palton.
31 Walt. de Haywood, for four years.
35 Tho. de Hampton, for five years.
40 Nich. Woodlocke.
41 Rad. Thurnbarne.
42 Idem.
43 Petr. Brugg.
44 Joh. Bottiller.
45 Idem.
46 Tho. Warner.
47 Phil. de Popham.
48 Laur. de S'to Martino.
49 Rich. Pauncefort.
50 Theob. de Gorges.
51 Tho. Boklands.

SHERIFFS OF HAMPSHIRE.

Anno	Name and Arms.	Place.
1	Rad. de Norton.	
	Arms: V. a lion rampant O.	
2	Joh. Butteshorne.	

3 Walt. Ramsey.
4 Will. Kingborne.
5 Hugo Crane.
6 Joh. Sandes.
    Arg. a cross ragulée trunked G.
7 Joh. Shownes.
8 Joh. de la Zouch.
9 Joh. Showne.
10 Rob. Cholmleigh.
    G. two helmets in chief and a garb in base proper.
11 Joh. Uvedale.
    Arg. a cross moline G.
12 Hen. Popham.
    Arg. on a chevron G. two bucks' heads cabossed O.
13 Nic. Dabrichcourt.
    Erm. three bars humetts G.
14 Phil. Baynard.
15 Rob. Cholmleigh   . . *ut prius.*
16 Rob. Dynlye.
17 Rob. Attemore.
18 Johan. Sands, et . . . *ut prius.*
    Tho. Warner.
19 Tho. Warner.
20 Joh. Waytes.
21 Will. Audley.
22 Idem.

HEN. IV.

1 Joh. Dovedale.
2 Joh. Waterton, et
    Joh. Chamfloure.
3 Joh. Barkley.
    G. a chevron betwixt ten crosses formée Arg.
4 Edw. Cawdrey.
    S. ten billets O. four, three, two, one.
5 Idem. . . . . *ut prius.*
6 Joh. Tichbourne.
    Vairy ; a chief O.
7 Joh. Berkeley, mil. . . *ut prius.*
8 Will. Marshull.
    S. three bars Arg. and a canton G.
9 Tho. Uvedall . . . . *ut prius.*
10 Will. Bremsheere.
11 Walt. Sands, mil.   . . *ut prius.*
12 Will. Warblington.

HEN. V.

Tho. Chaucer . . . . BERKSHIRE.
    Partie per pale Arg. and G. a bend counterchanged.

Anno   Name.   Place.

2 Joh. Uvedale . . . . *ut prius.*
3 Will. Brokes.
4 Tho. Wickham, mil.
5 Edw. Cowdrey . . . *ut prius.*
6 Will. Bremsbeth.
7 Joh. Uvedale . . . . *ut prius.*
8 Will. Kingborne.
9 Idem.

HENRY VI.

1 Joh. Uvedale . . . . *ut prius.*
2 Walt. Sands, mil. . . *ut prius.*
3 Joh. de Boys, mil.
    Arg. a chevron S. betwixt three acorns G.; on a canton
    Az. a pair of wings conjoined O.
4 Mauric. Brown . . . SURREY.
    S. three lions passant gardant betwixt two bends geme-
    ros Arg.
5 Joh. Uvedale . . . . *ut prius.*
6 Steph. Popham . . . *ut prius.*
7 Will. Brokes.
8 Tho. Thame.
9 Joh. Seymoure.
    G. two angels' wings paleways inverted O.
10 Walt. Veere.
    Quarterly G. and O. in the first a mullet Arg.
11 Joh. Giffard.
12 Joh. Uvedale . . . . *ut prius.*
13 Rob. Domley.
14 Will. Brokes.
15 Joh. Seymor, mil. . . *ut prius.*
16 Will. Fauconer.
    S. three falcons close Arg.
17 Tho. Uvedale . . . *ut prius.*
18 Joh. Lisle, mil.
    O. a fess betwixt two chevrons S.
19 Steph. Popham, mil. . *ut prius.*
20 Joh. Rogers.
21 Tho. Thame.
22 Hen. Trencard . . . DORSETSHIRE.
    Per pale Arg. and Az. three pallets S.
23 Tho. Montgomery.
    G. a chevron betwixt three flower-de-luces O.
24 Tho. Molegues.
25 Hen. Brum.
26 Tho Uvedale . . . . *ut prius.*
27 Rob. Fenns.

Anno	Name.	Place.

28 Rich. Dalingrug.
29 Tho. Warbleton.
30 Tho. Uvedale . . . *ut prius.*
31 Tho. Thame.
32 Joh. Seymor, mil. . . *ut prius.*
33 Joh. Wallop, arm.
      Arg. a bend wavy S.
34 Mau. Berkeley . . . *ut prius.*
35 Ber. Brokes.
36 Joh. Paulett.
      Arg. three swords in pile S. hilts O.
37 Hen. Brum.
38 Joh. Philpot.
      S. a bend Erm.

EDWARD IV.

1 Joh. Wallop, arm. . . *ut prius.*
2 Joh. Paulett, arm. . . *ut prius.*
3 Idem. . . . . . . *ut prius.*
4 Tho. Uvedale . . . . *ut prius.*
5 Edw. Berkeley, arm. . *ut prius.*
6 Galf. Gate, mil.
7 Mau. Berkeley, arm. . *ut prius.*
8 Joh. Roger, arm.
9 Joh. Whiteheed.
10 Rich. Darel, mil.
      Az. a lion rampant Arg. crowned O.
11 Mau. Berkeley, mil. . *ut prius.*
12 Edw. Berkeley . . . *ut prius.*
13 Joh. Rogers.
14 Carol. Bulkley.
      S. three bulls' heads cabossed Arg.
15 Tho. Troys, arm.
16 Edw. Berkeley . . . *ut prius.*
17 Will. Berkeley, arm. . *ut prius.*
18 Edw. Hardgill.
19 Joh. Cooke.
20 Will. Uvedal . . . . *ut prius.*
21 Edw. Berkeley . . . *ut prius.*
22 Joh. Brokes.

RICHARD III.

1 Rob. Pointz.
      Barry of six O. and V. a bend G.
2 Joh. Roger.
3 Rob. Carr, et
   Edw. Berkeley . . . *ut prius.*

HENTY VII.

Anno	Name.	Place.
1	Joh. Cooke.	
2	Will. Uvedale	*ut prius.*
3	Joh. Tichborne	*ut prius.*
4	Joh. Pound, arm.	
5	Tho. Troys, arm.	
6	Edw. Berkeley, mil.	*ut prius.*
7	Joh. Paulet, jun.	*ut prius.*
8	Will. Uvedale, mil.	*ut prius.*
9	Joh. Dudley, arm.	
10	Joh. Giffard, arm.	
11	Joh. Poundes, arm.	
12	Tho. Troys, arm.	
13	Will. Sands, mil.	*ut prius.*
14	Dau. Owen, mil.	
15	Joh. Paulett, arm.	*ut prius.*
16	Joh. Philpot, arm.	*ut prius.*
17	Rich. Wallop, arm.	*ut prius.*
18	Joh. Waller, arm.	Winch. Cast.

S. three walnut leaves O: betwixt two bendlets Arg.

| 19 | Joh. Pound, mil. | |
| 20 | Joh. Puterham, mil. | |

S. an helmet betwixt six crosslets in pale Arg.

| 21 | Rob. White, arm. | |

Az. a fess betwixt three flowers-de-luces O.

22	Joh. Lisle, mil.	*ut prius.*
23	Joh. Leigh, mil.	
24	Idem.	

HENRY VIII.

1	Rob. Wallop, arm.	*ut prius.*
2	Will. Sands, mil.	*ut prius.*
3	Will. Paulett	*ut prius.*
4	Will. Compton, mil.	Prierseen.

Erm. on a bend S. three helmets proper.

5	Ar. Plantagenet, mil.	
6	Rich. Norton, arm.	*ut prius.*
7	Rob. Wallop, arm.	*ut prius.*
8	Joh. Dawtree, mil.	

Az. four lozenges in fess Arg.

9	Joh. Lisley, mil.	*ut prius.*
10	Will. Paulett, arm.	*ut prius.*
11	Joh. Kaleway.	
12	Will. Frost.	
13	Will. Giffard, mil.	
14	Will. Paulett, arm.	*ut prius.*
15	Rob. Wallop, arm.	*ut prius.*

Anno	Name.	Place.
16	Pet. Philpot, arm. . .	*ut prius.*
17	Ant. Willoughby.	

S. a cross engrailed O.

18	Tho. Lisley, mil. . . .	*ut prius.*
19	Will. Berkeley, mil. . .	*ut prius.*
20	Rich. Andrews, arm.	
21	Lion. Morres.	
22	Tho. Lisley, mil. . .	*ut prius.*
23	Rich. Pexall, arm.	
24	Jo. Kaleway, mil.	
25	Jo. Paulett, arm. . .	*ut prius.*
26	Ant. Winsore, mil.	
27	Pet. Philpot, mil. . .	*ut prius.*
28	Will. Berkeley, mil. .	*ut prius.*
29	Tho. Lisley, mil. . .	*ut prius.*
30	Joh. Kingshall, arm.	
31	Ant. Winsore, mil.	
32	Rich. Andrews, arm.	
33	Joh. Kalevary, mil.	
34	Regi. Williams, arm. .	OXFORDSHIRE.

Az. an organ-pipe in bend sinister saltirewise, surmounted on another dexter betwixt four crosses patée Arg.

35 Joh. Kingsmil, arm.

Arg. crosslettée fitchée a chevron Erm. betwixt three mill-royndes S. and a chief of the second.

36	Will. Wacham, arm.	
37	Mich. Lister, mil.	

Erm. a fess S. three mullets O.

38	Geor. Paulett, arm. . .	*ut prius.*

EDWARD VI.

1	Nich. Tichborn . . .	*ut prius.*
2	Fran. Dawtrey, mil. . .	*ut prius.*
3	Mich. Lister, mil. . .	*ut prius.*
4	Nich. Pexall, mil.	
5	Joh. St. Lowe, mil.	
6	Joh. Norton, mil. . .	*ut prius.*

PHIL. et MAR.

1	Nich. Tichborn . . .	*ut prius.*
1, 2	Joh. Brain.	
2, 3	Joh. White, arm. . .	*ut prius.*
3, 4	Joh. Norton, arm. .	*ut prius.*
4, 5	Nich. Pexall, mil.	
5, 6	Oliu. Wallop, mil. .	*ut prius.*

ELIZ. REG.

1 Tho. Pace, arm.

Anno	Name.	Place.

2 Will. Pawlet, mil. . . *ut prius.*
3 Joh. Berkeley, mil. . . *ut prius.*
4 Geor. Mills, arm. . . SUSSEX.
  Per fess Arg. and S. a pale counterchanged, three bears of
  the last saliant, muzzled O.
5 Will. Kingsmil, arm. . *ut prius.*
6 Rich. Norton, arm. . . *ut prius.*
7 Rich. Pexall, mil.
8 Mil. Bulkley, arm. . . *ut prius.*
9 Rob. Oxenbridge.
  G. a lion rampant double queué O. within a border Az.
  charged with an entoir of escalops O.
10 Hen. Seymor, mil. . . *ut prius.*
11 Joh. Worsley, arm. . . Apledercomb.
  Arg. a chevron S. betwixt three Cornish choughs proper.
12 Gilb. Wells, arm.
13 Will. Waller, arm. . . *ut prius.*
14 Will. Jepham, arm.
15 Edw. White, arm. . . *ut prius.*
16 Edw. Aboroe, arm.
17 Rich. White, arm. . . *ut prius.*
18 Walt. Sands, arm. . . *ut prius.*
19 Jo. Thurnburgh, arm.
  Arg. fretty and a chief G.
20 Hen. Giffard, arm.
21 Ben. Tichburne, arm . *ut prius.*
22 Ja. Paget, arm.
23 Hen. Ughtread, arm.
24 Rob. White, arm. . . *ut prius.*
25 Tho. Dabridgcourt . . *ut prius.*
26 Will. Wright, arm.
27 Tho. West, arm.
28 Fra. Relway, arm.
29 Will. St. John, arm.
  Arg. on a chief G. two mullets pierced O.
30 Rich. Norton, arm. . . *ut prius.*
31 Edw. Goddard, arm.
32 Rich. Paulett, arm. . . *ut prius.*
33 Walt. Sands, mil. . . *ut prius.*
34 Joh. Seymor, mil. . . *ut prius.*
35 Nich. Mills, arm. . . *ut prius.*
36 Will. de Uvedale, arm. *ut prius.*
37 Rob. Oxenbridg . . . *ut prius.*
38 Rich. Norton, arm. . . *ut prius.*
39 Mar. Styward, arm.
40 Joh. White, arm. . . Southwick.
41 Will. Wallop, arm. . . *ut prius.*

Anno   Name.   Place.

42 Fran. Palmes, arm. . .   Oreton.
     G. three flower-de-luces Arg.; a chief parted bar-ways
        lozengée counter-lozengée Arg. and Az.; all within a
        border of the first.
43 Will. Kingsmil, mil.   . *ut prius.*
44 Ben. Tichbourn, mil.   . *ut prius.*
    He. Wallop, mil.   .   . *ut prius.*

JAC. REX.

 1 Hen. Wallop, mil.   . . *ut prius.*
 2 Will. Abarrow, mil.
 3 Will. Dodington.
 4 Will. Oglander, mil.
    Az. a stork betwixt three crosses patée fitchée O.
 5 Dan. Norton, mil.   . . *ut prius.*
 6 Joh. Knight, arm.
 7 Hen. Whitehead, mil.
 8 Tho. Stukeley, mil. . .   DEVONSHIRE.
    Az. three pears O.
 9 Will. Sandys, mil.   . . *ut prius.*
10 Will. Kingsmil, mil.   . *ut prius.*
11 Rich. Norton, mil.   . . *ut prius.*
12 Joh. Paulett, mil.   . . *ut prius.*
13 Edw. Richards, arm.
14 Ric. Worseley, mil. bar.   *ut prius.*
15 Hen. Clarke, mil.
16 Joh. Compton, arm.   . *ut prius.*
17 Tho. Neele, mil.
18 Tho. Lambert.
19 Geor. Philpot, mil.
20 Steph. Knight, arm.
21 Hen. Hook, arm.
22 Arth. Willmot, arm.

CAR. REG.

 1 Dan. Norton . . . . *ut prius.*
 2 Em. Gadder.
 3 Joh. Mills, bar. . . . *ut prius.*
 4 Fran. Douse, mil.
    O. a chevron lozengée Arg. and Az. betwixt three grey-
        hounds currant S.
 5 Hen. Wallop, mil.   . . *ut prius.*
 6 Tho. Cotcele.
 7 Rob. Pain, mil.
 8 Tho. Stewkly, mil.   . . *ut prius.*
 9 Edw. Hooper, arm.
10 Will. Beonsaw, mil.
11 Ric. Whitehead, arm.

12 Jo. Button, arm.
    Erm. a fess G.
13 Joh. Oglander, mil. . .   *ut prius.*
14 Jac. Hunt, arm.
15 Rich. Mayor, arm.
    G. an anchor Arg. ; on a chief O. three roses of the first.
16
17 Joh. Fielder, arm.
18
19
20
21
22 Rich. Bishop, arm.

THE FAREWELL.

When some five years since I visited Winchester, it grieved me at the heart to behold that stately structure so far run to ruin ; yea, my thoughts then interpreted those sad schisms and gaping chinks, the heralds of its downfall, deeming with myself that I discovered (as physicians in our bodies do *cadaverosam*) *faciem ruinosam* therein. But it rejoiced me, when coming there this last year, to find it so well amended, by the sovereign medicine of gold or silver charitably applied by its good bishop.* I wish all cathedrals in England, sick of the same distemper, as quick and happy a recovery.

WORTHIES OF HAMPSHIRE WHO HAVE FLOURISHED SINCE THE TIME OF FULLER.

Dr. BURGESS, Bishop of Salisbury, a voluminous writer; born at Odiham 1756 ; died 1837.

John CHAPMAM, divine and critic ; born at Strathfieldsay 1704; died 1784.

William COWARD, medical and metaphysical writer; born at Winchester 1656 ; died between 1722 and 1725.

William CROWE, divine, poet, and orator ; born at Winchester; died 1829.

William CURTIS, botanist, author of " Flora Londinensis ;" born at Alton 1746 ; died 1799.

Charles DIBDIN, writer and musical composer of numerous sea songs ; born at Southampton about 1748 ; died 1814.

Francis DOUCE, antiquary, virtuoso, and scholar; born 1761; died 1834.

Lady Emma HAMILTON, companion of Nelson ; born at Bere Forest; died 1816.

* Dr. Brian Duppa.—ED.

Jonas HANWAY, merchant, philanthropist, traveller, and author; born at Portsmouth 1712; died 1786.

Nathaniel HIGHMORE, physician, anatomist, and author; born at Fordingbridge 1613; died 1684.

Dr. Robert HOOKE, mathematician and natural philosopher, inventor of the pendulum-spring in watches; born at Freshwater, Isle of Wight, 1635; died 1702-3.

Philip HUNTON, nonconformist divine, and political writer, who on his declaring that the sovereignty of England was in the three estates, was ordered to be burnt; born at Andover; died 1682.

Giles JACOB, author of a Law Dictionary, some dramas and biographies; born at Romsey 1690; died 1744.

Admiral Sir R. G. KEATS; born at Chalton 1757: died 1834.

Robert LOWTH, Bishop of London, critic, antagonist of Warburton; born at Buriton 1710; died 1787.

Sir William PETTY, physician, writer on political economy, and practical philosopher; born at Romsey 1623; died 1687.

Richard POCOCKE, Bishop of Meath, oriental traveller; born at Southampton 1704; died 1765.

John POTTENGER, poet and translator; born at Winchester 1647; died 1733.

Dr. Joseph WARTON, divine, poet, critic, and translator; born at Basingstoke 1722; died 1800.

Thomas WHARTON, brother of the preceding, divine, antiquary, poet-laureat, author of " History of English Poetry;" born at Basingstoke 1728; died 1790.

Isaac WATTS, nonconformist divine, author of " Psalms " and " Hymns," &c.; born at Southampton 1674; died 1748.

Gilbert WHITE, writer on natural history, and author of the "History and Antiquities of Selborne;" born at Selborne 1720; died 1793.

Anne Countess of WINCHELSEA, ingenious poetess; born at Sidmonton; died 1720.

Dr. Edward YOUNG, divine and poet, author of " Night Thoughts," and " The Revenge;" born at Upham 1681; died 1765.

₊ Hampshire is destitute of a county historian. In 1793, however, the Rev. Richard Warner published Topographical Remarks relating to the south-western parts of Hampshire; and in 1795 the same author brought out Collections for the History of Hampshire, &c. In addition to these, a variety of works have been published relative to the history and topography of Winchester, Southampton, Selborne, Isle of Wight, &c.; the principal of which are the Histories of Winchester by Gale, Milner, Warton, and Britton.—ED.

HARTFORD or HERTFORD-SHIRE.

HERTFORDSHIRE is so called from Hertford, the chief town therein; as Hartford, so termed from the *Ford* of *Harts*,* a *hart* couchant in the waters being the arms thereof;† which convinceth me that HART not HERTfordshire, is the orthography of this county.‡   It hath Essex on the east, Middlesex on the south, Buckinghamshire on the west, Bedford and Cambridgeshire on the north thereof.   It might be allowed a square of twenty miles, save that the angular insinuations of other counties prejudice the entireness thereof.   I have been informed, from an ancient justice therein, that one cannot be so advantageously placed in any part of this shire, but that he may recover another county within the riding of five miles.   It is the garden of England for delight; and men commonly say, that such who buy a house in Hertfordshire pay two years' purchase for the air thereof.

It falls short in fruitfulness of Essex adjoining thereunto, to which it was also annexed under one sheriff (and one escheator, till after the reign of king Edward the Third) ; and painful Norden writes a bold truth :§

"For deep feedings, or sheep pastures, I take notice of few, and those especially about Knebworth.   To speak of the soil, as indeed it is most generally, for my part I take it but a barren country in respect of some other shires."

Indeed this foresty ground would willingly bear nothing so well as a crop of wood.   But, seeing custom is another nature, it hath for many years been contented to bring forth good grain, persuaded thereunto by the industrious husbandman.   Surely no county can show so fair a bunch of berries; for so they term the fair habitations of gentlemen of remark, which are called places, courts, halls, and manors, in other shires.

This county affording no peculiar commodity nor manufacture, we may safely proceed to other observations, when first we have given the due commendation to the horses of this shire.

---

* Camden's Britannia, in this county.   † Speed, in his Map of this county.
   ‡ The more modern and generally recognized orthography of HERTS is however adopted throughout this edition.—ED.
   § In his Description of Hertfordshire, p. 2.

Their teams of horses (oft-times deservedly advanced from the cart to the coach) are kept in excellent equipage, much alike in colour and stature, fat and fair; such is their care in dressing and well-feeding them. I could name the place and person (reader, be not offended with an innocent digression), who brought his servant with a warrant before a justice of peace for stealing his grain. The man brought his five horses tailed together along with him, alleging for himself, "that, if he were the thief, these were the receivers;" and so escaped.

THE BUILDINGS.

THEOBALDS did carry away the credit, built by Sir William, beautified by Sir Robert Cecil his son, both lord treasurers of England. The last exchanged it (too wise to do it to his loss) with king James for Hatfield-house; which king deceased therein, March 27, 1625. Yea, this house may be said to decease about its grand climacterical, some sixty-three years from the finishing thereof, taken down to the ground (for the better partage among the soldiery) anno 1651; and, from the seat of a monarch, is now become a little commonwealth; so many entire tenements, like splinters, have flown out of the materials thereof. Thus our fathers saw it built, we behold it unbuilt; and whether our children shall see it rebuilt, he only knows who hath written, "there is a time to cast away stones, and a time to gather stones together.*

HATFIELD-HOUSE was first the bishop's of Ely, then the king's, afterwards, by exchange, the earl's of Salisbury: for situation, building, contrivance, prospect, air, and all accommodations, inferior to none in England. Within a little mile thereof lieth a place called the Vineyard, where Nature, by the midwifery of art, is delivered of much pleasure; so that the reader must be a seer, before he can understand the perfection thereof. Had this place been in Græcia, or nigh Rome, where the luxuriant fancies of the poets, being subject-bound, improve a tree into a grove, a grove into a forest, a brook into a river, and a pond into a lake; I say, had this vineyard been there, it had disinherited Tempe of its honour; and hence the poets would have dated all their delights as from a little paradise, and staple-place of earthly pleasure.

MEDICINAL WATERS.

One hath lately been discovered near Barnet, in a common; as generally sanative springs are found in such places, as if Nature therein intimated her intention, designing them for public

* Eccles. iii. 5.

profit, not private employment. It is conceived to run through veins of alum, by the taste thereof. It coagulateth milk, and the curd thereof is an excellent plaister for any green wounds, besides several other operations.

But, as Alexander was wont to applaud Achilles, not as the most valiant, but the most fortunate of men, having Homer to trumpet forth his actions : so are these waters much advantaged with the vicinity of London, whose citizens proclaim the praise thereof. And indeed London in this kind is stately attended, having three medicinal waters within one day's journey thereof.* The catalogue of the cures done by this spring amounteth to a great number; insomuch that there is hope, in process of time, the water rising here will repair the blood shed hard by, and save as many lives as were lost in the fatal battle at Barnet betwixt the two houses of York and Lancaster.

PROVERBS.

" Hertfordshire clubs and clouted shoon."]

Some will wonder how this shire, lying so near to London, the staple of English civility, should be guilty of so much rusticalness. But the finest cloth must have a list, and the pure peasants are of as coarse a thread in this county as in any other place. Yet, though some may smile at their clownishness, let none laugh at their industry ; the rather because the high-shoon of the tenant pays for the Spanish-leather boots of the landlord.

" Hertfordshire hedgehogs."]

Plenty of hedgehogs are found in this high woodland county, where too often they suck the kine, though the dairy-maid conne them small thanks for sparing their pains in milking them. A creature always in his posture of defence, carrying a stand of pikes on his back, so that, if as well victualled as armed, he may hold out a siege against any equal opposition. If this proverb containeth any further reflection on the people in this county, as therein taxed for covetousness, and their constant nuddling on the earth, I will not so understand it, as hoping and believing this to be a false application.

" Ware and Wadesmill are worth all London."]

This, I assure you, is a master-piece of the vulgar wits in this county, wherewith they endeavour to amuse travellers, as if Ware, a thoroughfare market, and Wadesmill (part of a village lying two miles north thereof) were so prodigiously rich as to countervail the wealth of London. The fallacy lieth in the homonymy of Ware, here not taken for that town so named, but appellatively for all vendible commodities. We will not discompose the wit of this proverb, by cavilling that Weare is the proper name of that Town (so called anciently from the stop-

* Tunbridge, Epsom, Barnet.

pages which there obstruct the river), but leave it as we found
it, and proceed.

> " Hertfordshire kindness."]

This is generally taken in a good and grateful sense, for the
mutual return of favours received; it being [belike] observed
that the people in this county at entertainments drink back to
them who drank to them, parallel to the Latin proverbs, " Fri-
cantem refrica; Manus manum lavat; Par est de merente benè,
benè mereri." However, sometimes Hertfordshire kindness
may prove Hertfordshire cruelty, and amount to no less than a
monopoly, when this reciprocation of favours betwixt themselves
is the exclusion of all others from partaking thereof.

PRINCES.

WILLIAM, second son of king Edward the Third and Philippa his wife, took his christian name from his grandfather,
William earl of Henault, and his surname of Hatfield, from the
place of his nativity in this county, where he was born the ninth
of his father's reign, anno Domini 1335; and expired within few
days after. So that what I find written on the late monument
of a noble infant* may also serve for his epitaph:

> *Vivus nil poteram fari, quin mortuus infans*
> *Nunc loquor, ut mortis fis memor, atque vale.*

> " Living I could not speak, now dead I tell
> Thy duty; think of death; and so farewell."

It is uncertain where he was interred; but most believe him buried at Westminster.

EDMUND of LANGLEY, fifth son to king Edward the Third
and queen Philippa, was so surnamed from King's Langley in
this county, the place of his nativity. He was created earl of
Cambridge in the thirty-sixth year of the reign of his father, and
duke of York in the ninth year of his nephew king Richard the
Second. He married Isabel, daughter and co-heir of Peter king
of Castile; and they lie buried at Langley together. He had
(besides other children of both sexes) to his eldest son, Richard
duke of York; and he died anno Domini 1402.

EDMUND of HADDAM.— Reader, I presume thee to be so
much a gentleman, as in courtesy to allow him a prince, who
was son to queen Katherine by Owen Theodore her second husband, womb-brother to king Henry the Sixth, and father to king
Henry the Seventh. That he was born in this county, one may
well be confident, seeing there is no Haddam in any shire of
England save Hertfordshire alone.† I confess therein three
villages of that name; but sure no less than Great Haddam was

* On Charles Blunt, son to the earl of Newport, in St Martin's in the Fields.—F.
† As appeareth in " Villare Anglicanum."

the place of so eminent a native. He was solemnly created earl of Richmond at Reading, in the thirty-first of king Henry the Sixth.

Many good works no doubt he did when living, whose corpse when buried saved from destruction the fair cathedral of Saint David's. For his monument in the midst of the quire, saith my author* (as the prebendaries told him), spared their church from defacing in the days of king Henry the Eighth. I could wish all king Henry's nearest relations had after their decease been severally so disposed, preservatives from ruin and rapine, as the corpse of queen Catherine Dowager did, as some say, save the church of Peterburgh.† But this ill agreeth with that which Brooke reporteth,‡ viz. that this earl was buried in Carmarthen ; and because Vincent, his professed adversary (finding fault with him always when any, sometimes when no cause), taketh no exception thereat, I the more rely on his testimony. Only it is possible that this earl, first entered in Carmarthen, might be afterwards, for the more eminence of sepulture, removed to Saint David's. He died anno Domini 1456.

SAINTS.

Saint ALBAN, though (as Saint Paul§) a Roman by privilege, but Briton by parentage, was born in this county (though many hundreds of years before Hertfordshire had its modern name and dimensions) in the city of Verulam, and was martyred for Christianity under Dioclesian, anno 303. The cause and manner whereof (with the martyrdom of Saint Amphibalus hard by Rudborn) I have so largely related in my " Ecclesiastical History,"‖ that, as I will repeat nothing, I can add nothing of consequence thereto ; except any will conceive this to be remarkable ; that good liquorice groweth naturally out of the ruinous walls of Verulam, an old city (the mother of the new town of Saint Alban's), as a skilful eye-witness, antiquary, and zealous Protestant,¶ hath observed. Had some Papist taken first notice hereof, he might probably have made it a miracle, and assign the sanctity of this place for the root of this liquorice.

MARTYRS

It appeareth by the maps, that Africa lieth partly in the torrid and partly in the temperate zone. Nor is the wonder any at all, considering the vastness thereof, extending itself through many degrees. More strange it is that this small county should be partly in a temperate, viz. the western part thereof subjected to the bishop of Lincoln, and partly in the torrid climate, namely the eastern moiety belonging to the diocese of London,

---

* Speed, in the Description of Pembrokeshire.
† Lord Herbert, in the Life of king Henry the Eighth.
‡ In the Earl of Richmond.   § Acts xxii 25.   ‖ Cent. iv. p. 17, &c.
¶ Norden, in his Description of this county, p. 29.

which under Bonner was parched with persecution. Yet, not to make this monster worse than he was, though many in his jurisdiction were much molested, and though tradition points the very place in Bishop's Stortford where poor people were burnt at the stake; yet my book of martyrs, or eyes, or both, be defective, wherein I cannot recover the name of any particular person.

POPE.

NICHOLAS, son to Robert Breakspear (a lay-brother in the abbey of St. Alban's) fetched his name from Breakspeare, a place in Middlesex,* but was born at Abbot's Langley, a town in this county.† When a youth, he was put to such servile work in St. Alban's Abbey, that his ingenious soul could not comport therewith. Suing to be admitted into that house, he received the repulse, which in fine proved no *mishap*, but a *happy miss*, unto him; for, going over into France, he studied so hard and so happily at Paris, that for his worth he was preferred abbot of St. Rufus near Valentia, and afterward, by Pope Eugenius the Third, was made bishop of Alba nigh Rome. " Ad natalis soli memoriam," saith my author, that he who was refused to be *Monachus Albanensis* in England, should be *Episcopus Albanensis* in Italy. He was employed by the Pope for the conversion of the Norwegians; and though Bale saith (he were not Bale if he were not bitter) "Anti-christiano charactere Norwegios signavit;" yet his reducing them from Paganism to Christianity in the fundamentals was a worthy work, and deserves true commendation. He was afterwards chosen Pope of Rome, by the name of Adrian the Fourth. There is a mystery more than I can fathom in the changing of his name, seeing his own font-name was a papal one; yet he preferred rather to be Adrian the Fourth than Nicholas the Third. He held his place four years, eight months, and eight and twenty days: and, anno 1158, as he was drinking, was choked with a fly; which in the large territory of St. Peter's Patrimony had no place but his throat to get into. But, since a fly stopped his breath, fear shall stop my mouth, not to make uncharitable conclusions from such casualties.

CARDINALS.

[REM.] Boso (confessed by all an Englishman ‡) is not placed in this county out of any certainty, but of pure charity, not knowing where elsewhere with any probability to dispose him. But, seeing he was nephew to the late named Nicholas, or Pope Adrian, we have some shadow and pretence to make him of the same county. This is sure, his uncle made him car-

---

* Camden's Britannia, in Middlesex.
† Bale, de Scriptoribus Britannicis, Cent. ii. num. 90; and Pitseus, in anno 1159.
‡ Bale, de Scriptoribus Britannicis.

dinal in the month of December 1155;* and he was a great change-church in Rome, being successively— 1. Cardinal Deacon of Saints Cosma and Damian; 2. Cardinal Priest of St. Crosses of Jerusalem: 3. Cardinal Priest of St. Prudentiana: 4. Cardinal Priest of Pastor.

He was more than instrumental in making Alexander the Third Pope with the suffrages of nineteen cardinals, who at last clearly carried it against his Anti-Pope Victor the Fourth. This Boso died anno Domini 1180.

PRELATES.

RICHARD DE WARE: for this is his true name, as appears in his epitaph,† though some (pretending his honour, but prejudicing the truth thereby) surname him Warren. He was made abbot of Westminster 1260; and twenty years after treasurer of England, under king Edward the First. This Richard going to Rome, brought thence certain workmen, and rich porphyry. And for the rest, hear my author :‡

"By whom and whereof he made the rare pavement to be seen at Westminster, before the communion table, containing the discourse of the whole world, which is at this day most beautiful; a thing of that singularity, curiousness, and rareness, that England hath not the like again."

See, readers, what an enemy ignorance is to art. How often have I trampled on that pavement, so far from admiring, as not observing it; and since, upon serious survey, it will not, in my eyes, answer this character of curiosity. However, I will not add malice to my ignorance (qualities which too often are companions) to disparage what I do not understand: but I take it, on the trust of others more skilful, for a master-piece of art. This Richard died on the second of December 1283, the twelfth of king Edward the First; and lieth buried under the foresaid pavement.

RALPH BALDOCK, so called from the place of his nativity (a mungrel Market) in this county, was bred in Merton College in Oxford: § one not unlearned, and who wrote a "History of England," which Leland at London did once behold. King Edward the First much prized, and preferred him bishop of London. He gave two hundred pounds whilst living, and left more when dead, to repair the east part of St. Paul's, on the same token that, upon occasion of clearing the foundation, an incredible number of heads of oxen were found buried in the ground, alleged as an argument by some to prove that anciently

---

* Godwin, in Catalogue of Cardinals, p. 164.
† On his tomb, yet well to be seen in Westminster Abbey, on the north side of the tomb of Amer de Valens, earl of Pembroke.
‡ J. Philipot, in his Treasures of England, collected anno Domini 1636, p. 19.
§ Godwin, in his Bishops of London.

a temple of Diana.* Such who object that heads of stags had been more proper for her, the goddess of the game, may first satisfy us, whether any creatures *feræ naturæ* (as which they could not certainly compass at all seasons) were usually offered for sacrifices. This Ralph died July the 24th, 1313, being buried under a marble stone in St. Mary's Chapel in his cathedral.

JOHN BARNET had his name and nativity from a market town in this county, sufficiently known by the road passing through it. He was first by the Pope preferred, 1361, to be bishop of Worcester, and afterwards was translated to Bath and Wells. Say not this was a retrograde motion, and Barnet degraded in point of profit by such a removal; for though Worcester is the better bishopric in our age, in those days Bath and Wells (before the revenues thereof were reformed under king Edward the Sixth) was the richer preferment. Hence he was translated to Ely, and for six years was lord treasurer of England. He died at Bishop's Hatfield,† June 7, 1373; and was buried there on the south side of the high altar, under a monument, now miserably defaced by some sacrilegious executioner, who hath beheaded the statue lying thereon.

THOMAS RUDBURNE, no doubt, according to the fashion of those days, took his name from Rudburne, a village within four miles from St. Alban's. He was bred in Oxford, and proctor thereof anno 1402, and chancellor 1420.‡ An excellent scholar, and skilful mathematician; of a meek and mild temper (though at one time a little tart against the Wicliffites) which procured him much love with great persons. He was warden of Merton College in Oxford, and built the tower over the College Gate. He wrote a "Chronicle of England;"§ and was preferred bishop of St. David's. He flourished anno Domini 1419, though the date of his death be unknown.

Reader, I cannot satisfy myself, that any bishop since the Reformation was a native of this county, and therefore proceed to another subject.

STATESMEN.

Sir EDWARD WATERHOUSE, Knight, was born at Helmstedbury in this county, of an ancient and worshipful family, deriving their descent lineally from Sir Gilbert Waterhouse, of Kyrton in Low Lindsey, in the county of Lincoln, in the time of king Henry the Third. As for our Sir Edward, his parents were, *John Waterhouse*, Esquire, a man of much fidelity and sageness; auditor many years to king Henry the Eighth, of whom he obtained (after a great entertainment for him in his house) the grant of a weekly market for the town of Helmsted:

---

* Camden's Britannia, in Middlesex.
† Bishop Godwin, in Bishops of Ely.   ‡ Idem, in Catalogue of St. David's.
§ Bale, de Scriptoribus Britannicis, Cent. vii. num. 53; and Pitseus, anno 1419.

and *Margaret Turner*, of the ancient house of Blunt's Hall in Suffolk, and Cannons in Hertfordshire.

The king, at his departure, honoured the children of the said John Waterhouse, being brought before him, with his praise and encouragement ; gave a Benjamin's portion of dignation to this Edward, foretelling, by his royal augury, " That he would be the crown of them all, and a man of great honour and wisdom, fit for the service of princes."

It pleased God afterwards to second the word of the king, so that the sprouts of his hopeful youth only pointed at the growth and greatness of his honourable age ; for, being but twelve years old, he went to Oxford, where for some years he glistered in the oratoric and poetic sphere, until he addicted himself to conversation, and observance of state affairs, wherein his great proficiency commended him to the favour of three principal patrons.

One was Walter Devereux, earl of Essex, who made him his bosom friend ; and the said earl, lying on his death-bed, took his leave of him with many kisses, " O my Ned," said he, " farewell : thou art the faithfullest and friendliest gentleman that ever I knew." In testimony of his true affection to the dead father in his living son, this gentleman is thought to have penned that most judicious and elegant epistle (recorded in Holinshed's History, page 1266), and presented it to the young earl, conjuring him, by the cogent arguments of example and rule, to *patrizate*.

His other patron was Sir Henry Sidney (so often lord deputy of Ireland), whereby he became incorporated into the familiarity of his son Sir Philip Sidney ; between whom and Sir Edward there was so great friendliness, that they were never better pleased than when in one another's companies, or when they corresponded each with other. And we find, after the death of that worthy knight, that he was a close-concerned mourner at his obsequies, as appeareth at large in the printed representation of his funeral solemnity.

His third patron was Sir John Perot, deputy also of Ireland, who so valued his counsel, that in State affairs he would do nothing without him. So great his employment betwixt state and state, that he crossed the seas thirty-seven times, until deservedly at last he came into a port of honour, wherein he sundry years anchored, and found safe harbour ; for he received the honour of knighthood, was sworn of her majesty's privy council for Ireland, and chancellor of the Exchequer therein.

Now his graceful soul, coursing about how to answer the queen's favour, laid itself wholly out in her service, wherein two of his actions are most remarkable. First, he was highly instrumental in modelling the kingdom of Ireland into shires as now they are ; shewing himself so great a lover of the polity under which he was born, that he advanced the compliance therewith (as commendable and necessary) in the dominions annexed thereunto.

His second service was, when many in that kingdom shrouded themselves from the laws, under the target of power, making force their tutelary saint, he set himself vigorously to suppress them. And when many of the privy council, terrified with the greatness of the earl of Desmond, durst not subscribe the instrument wherein he was proclaimed traitor, Sir Edward, among some others, boldly signed the same (disavowing his and all treasons against his prince and country); and the council did the like, commanding the publication thereof.

As to his private sphere, God blessed him, being but a third brother, above his other brethren. Now though he had three wives, the first a Villiers, the second a Spilman, the third the widow of Herlakenden, of Woodchurch in Kent, esquire; and though he had so strong a brain and body, yet he lived and died childless, inter-commoning therein with many Worthies, who are, according to Ælius Spartianus, either improlific, or have children *in genitorum vituperium et famarum læsuram.* God thus denying him the pleasure of posterity, he craved leave of the queen to retire himself, and fixed the residue of his life at Woodchurch in Kent, living there in great honour and repute as one who had no design to be popular, and not prudent: rich, and not honest; great, and not good.

He died, in the fifty-sixth year of his age, the 13th of October 1591; and is buried at Woodchurch under a table marble monument, erected to his memory by his sorrowful lady surviving him.

Reader, I doubt not but thou art sensible of the alteration and improvement of my language in this character; owing both my intelligence and expressions unto Edward Waterhouse, now of Sion College, esquire, who, to revive the memory of his name-sake and great uncle, furnished me with these instructions.

HENRY CARY, viscount of Falkland in Scotland, and son to Sir Edward Cary, was born at Aldnam in this county. He was a most accomplished gentleman, and complete courtier. By king James he was appointed lord deputy of Ireland, and well discharged his trust therein. But an unruly colt will fume and chafe (though neither switched nor spurred) merely because backed. The rebellious Irish will complain, only because kept in subjection, though with never so much lenity; the occasion why some hard speeches were passed on his government. Some beginning to counterfeit his hand, he used to incorporate the year of his age in a knot flourished beneath his name, concealing the day of his birth to himself. Thus by comparing the date of the month with his own birth-day (unknown to such forgers) he not only discovered many false writings which were past, but also deterred dishonest cheaters from attempting the like for the future. Being re-called into England, he lived honourably in this county, until he by a sad casualty brake his leg on a stand in Theobald's Park, and soon after died thereof. He married the sole daughter and heir of Sir Lawrence Tanfield, chief baron of the Exchequer, by whom he had a fair estate in Oxfordshire. His death happened anno Domini 1620; being father to the most accomplished statesman, Lucius, grandfather to the present Henry Lord Falkland, whose pregnant parts (now clarified from juvenile extravagancies) perform much, and promise more useful service to this nation.

SOLDIERS.

[S. N.] Sir HENRY CARY, son to Sir William Cary and Mary Bollen his wife, was (wherever born) made by queen Elizabeth lord chamberlain, baron of Hunsdon in this county. A valiant man, and lover of men of their hands; very choleric, but not malicious. Once one Mr. Colt chanced to meet him coming from Hunsdon to London, in the equipage of a lord of those days. The lord, on some former grudge, gave him a box on the ear. Colt presently returned the principal with interest; and thereupon his servants, drawing their swords, swarmed about him. "You rogues," said the lord, "may not I and my neighbour change a blow but you must interpose?" Thus the quarrel was begun and ended in the same minute.

It was merrily said, "that his Latin and his dissimulation were both alike, and that his custom in swearing, and obscenity in speech, made him seem a worse Christian than he was, and a better knight of the carpet than he could be."* He might have been with the queen whatsoever he would himself; but would be no more than what he was, preferring enough above a feast in that nature.

He hung at court on no man's sleeve, but stood on his own bottom till the time of his death, having a competent estate of his own given him by the queen; who bestowed on him, in the first of her reign, Hunsdon-house in this county, with four thousand pounds a year (according to the valuation in that age) in fair desmesnes, parks, and lands lying about it. Yet this was rather restitution than liberality in her majesty; seeing he had spent as great an estate (left him by his father) in her service, or rather relief, during her persecution under queen Mary.

This lord suppressed the first northern commotion (the sole reason why we have ranked him under the title of soldier); for which this letter of thanks was solemnly returned unto him:

" By the QUEEN.

"Right trusty and well-beloved cousin, we greet you well: and right glad we are that it hath pleased God to assist you in

---

* Sir Robert Naunton, in his " Fragmenta Regalia."

this your late service, against that cankered, subtle traitor Leonard Dacres; whose force being far greater in number than yours, we perceive you have overthrown, and how he thereupon was the first that fled, having (as it seemeth) a heart readier to shew his unloyal falsehood and malice, than to abide the fight. And though the best we could have desired was to have him taken, yet we thank God that he is in this sort overthrown, and forced to fly our realm, to his like company of rebels, whom no doubt God of his favourable justice will confound with such ends as are meet for them. We will not now by words express how inwardly glad we are that you have such success, whereby both your courage in such an unequal match, your faithfulness towards us, and your wisdom is seen to the world; this your act being the very first that ever was executed by fight in field, in our time, against any rebel; but we mean also indeed, by just reward, to let the world see how much we esteem and can consider such a service as this is; and so we would have yourself also thank God heartily, as we doubt not but you do, from whom all victories do proceed, and comfort yourself with the assurance of our most favourable acceptation. We have also herewith sent our letter of thanks to Sir John Foster, and would have you namely thank our good faithful soldiers of Berwick, in whose worthy service we do repose no small trust. 26th of February 1569."

Thus far was written by the secretary of state; but the ensuing postscript was all the queen's own hand; the original being preserved by the right honourable Henry Earl of Monmouth (granchild to the Lord Hunsdon); by whose noble favour I carefully copied it forth as followeth:

"I doubt much, my Harry, whether that the victory given me more joyed me, or that you were by God appointed the instrument of my glory. And I assure you, for my country's good, the first might suffice; but for my heart's contentation, the second more pleaseth me. It likes me not a little, that with a good testimony of your faith, there is seen a stout courage of your mind, that more trusted to the goodness of your quarrel, than to the weakness of your number. Well, I can say no more; *beatus est ille servus quem, cum Dominus venerit, inveniet facientem sua mandata.* And that you may not think that you have done nothing for your profit (though you have done much for your honour) I intend to make this journey, somewhat to increase your livelihood, that you may not say to yourself, *Perditur quod factum est ingrato.*

"Your loving kinswoman,
"ELIZABETH REGINA."

Three times was this lord in election to be earl of Wiltshire, a title which in some sort belonged unto him in the right of Mary his mother; but still some intervening accident retarded it. When he lay on his death-bed, the queen gave him a gracious visit, causing his patent for the said earldom to be drawn, his robes to be made, and both to be laid down upon his bed; but this lord (who could dissemble neither well or sick) "Madam," said he, "seeing you counted me not worthy of this honour whilst I was living, I count myself unworthy of it now I am dying." He departed this life anno Domini 1596; and lieth buried in a most magnificent monument in Westminster Abbey, being the direct ancestor to the earls of Dover and Monmouth.

PHYSICIANS.

John Giles, or of St. Giles, was born at St. Alban's,* probably in the parish of St. Giles, long since (as some more in that town) demolished. He was bred beyond the seas, where he became so great a scholar, that he not only was physician in ordinary to Philip king of France, but also professor of that faculty in Paris and Montpelier. Then, waving the care of bodies, he took on him the cure of souls, and was made doctor of divinity. He afterwards became a Dominican, and was the first Englishman that ever entered into that order. In his old age he was famous for his divinity lectures read in Oxford.

But which most persuades me to a venerable reception of his memory, is what I read of him in Matthew Paris,† how "Robert Grosthead, the pious and learned bishop of Lincoln, being sick on his death-bed, sent for this Mr. John Giles, learned in physic and divinity, that from him he might receive comfort both for body and soul." How long this physician survived his patient (dying in October 1253) is to me unknown.

John de Gatesden was undoubtedly born in this county, wherein two villages the greater and less of that name. Such who except that they are written Gadesden will soon be satisfied in their sameness from those who know the sympathy betwixt T and D. He was bred in Merton College in Oxford, where he so profited in the study of physic, that a foreigner,‡ compiling a catalogue of men eminent in that faculty, acknowledgeth him a writer of high esteem therein. By one who hath made a list of learned men,§ he is styled Johannes Anglicus. I am informed that lately his books have been printed in Italy in a folio; no small honour (I assure you), seeing in physic the Italians account all Tramontane doctors but apothecaries in comparison of themselves. The first treatise in his book is

---

* Bale et Pitseus, de Scriptoribus Angliæ.   † In anno 1253.
‡ Symphorianus Champerius, in his fifth Tract de Medic. Art. Scriptoribus.
§ Mathæus Silvaticus, in Lexico.

termed "Rosa Anglica," the English Rose;* and I doubt not but, as it is sweet in the title, so it is sovereign in the matter therein contained. This John flourished in the year of our Lord 1320.

WRITERS.

ALEXANDER NEQUAM, or BAD in English, was born in St. Alban's. Many conceived themselves wondrous witty in making jests (which indeed made themselves) on his surname; whereof one eminent instance.

Nequam had a mind to become a monk in Saint Alban's, the town of his nativity; and thus laconically wrote for leave to the abbot thereof:

> "Si vis, veniam. Sin autem, tu autem."

To whom the abbot returned :

> "Si bonus sis, venias. Si *Nequam*, nequaquam."

Whereupon Nequam (to discompose such conceits for the future) altered the orthography of his name into Neckam.

Another pass of wit there was (saith my author†) betwixt him and Philip Repington bishop of Lincoln, the latter sending the challenge :

> "Et *niger* et *nequam*, cum sis cognomine *Nequam ;*
> *Nigrior* esse potes, *nequior* esse *nequis*."

> (Both *black* and *bad*, whilst *Bad* the name to thee ;
> *Blacker* thou may'st, but *worse* thou canst not be.)

To whom Nequam rejoined :

> "*Phi* nota fœtoris, *lippus* malus omnibus horis :
> *Phi* malus et *lippus*, totus malus ergo Philippus.

> (*Stinks* are branded with a *Phi*, *lippus* Latin for blear-eye :
> *Phi* and *lippus* bad as either ; then *Philippus* worse together.)

But, by the leave of my learned author, this Nequam must be much younger than our Alexander, or that Philip much older than bishop Repington; all agreeing that Alexander Nequam died 1227, under king Henry the Third, whereas Philip Repington was made bishop of Lincoln 1405, under king Henry the Fourth.‡

But, leaving Nequam's name, he is known to posterity by the title of Ingenii Miraculum, being an excellent philosopher, rhetorician, and poet; so true it is what Tully observeth, "Omnes artes, quæ ad humanitatem pertinent, habent quoddam commune vinculum, & quasi cognatione quadam inter se continentur." Besides, he was a deep divine, as his books do evidence. He was canon of Exeter, and (upon what occasion I know not) came to be buried at Worcester, with this epitaph :

---

* Bale, de Scriptoribus Britannicis, Cent. v. num. 7. et Pitseus, in anno 1320.
† Bishop Godwin, in Catalogue of the Bishops of Lincoln.
‡ Bale, and Pits, de Scriptoribus Angliæ.

Eclipsim patitur sapientia, sol sepelitur :
Cui si par unus, minus esset flebile funus.
Vir bene discretus, et in omni more facetus,
Dictus erat Nequam, vitam duxit tamen æquam.

" Wisdom's eclips'd, sky of the sun bereft,
  Yet less the loss if like alive were left.
  A man discreet, in manners debonair,
  Bad name, black face, but carriage good and fair."

Others say he was buried at St. Alban's,* where he found repulse when living, but repose when dead.

WILLIAM of WARE, born in that thoroughfare town, twenty miles from London, was a Franciscan, bred first in Oxford, then in Paris. Now because some may slight the praise of Bale or Pits (as *testes domesticos*, Englishmen commending Englishmen); know that John Picus Mirandula† highly extolleth this de Ware, though miscalling him John, as ambitious to have him his namesake. He was instructor to John Duns Scotus.‡

" And if the scholar to such height did reach,
  Then what was he who did that scholar teach."

He flourished under king Henry the Third, anno 1270; and is supposed to be buried in Paris.

JOHN MANDEVILE, Knight, born at Saint Alban's in this county,§ heir to a fair estate. He applied himself first to the reading of the Scriptures, then to the study of physic (wherein he attained to great perfection); afterwards to travel for thirty-four years together; and at last, like another Ulysses, returning home, was quite grown out of knowledge of all his friends. He wrote a book of his own Itinerary through Africa, the east and north part of Asia, containing a variety of wonders. Now though far travellers are suspected in their relations to wander from the truth, yet all things improbable are not impossible; and the reader's ignorance is sometimes all the writer's falsehood. He used to complain of the church corruptions in his age, being wont to say, " Virtus cessat, Ecclesia calcatur, Clerus errat, Dæmon regnat, Simonia dominatur." ||

He died anno Domini 1372; buried, say some, in the convent of the Williamites, at Liege in Germany; which St. Alban's will not allow, claiming his burial as well as his birth, where a rhyming epitaph is appendant on a pillar near the supposed place of his interment.

NICHOLAS GORHAM, a Dominican.—We cannot blame the Frenchmen, if desirous to gain so great a scholar to be their

---

* Weever's Funeral Monuments, in Hertfordshire.   † In suo Heptuplo.
‡ Bale, de Scriptoribus Britannicis, Cent. iv. p. 323, and Pits, p. 349.
§ Weever's Funeral Monuments, in this county.
|| Bale, de Scriptoribus Britannicis.

countryman; nor must the French blame us, if loath to lose what is duly and truly our own.

Three things are pretended to countenance his French nativity : 1. His long living (and dying at last) in that land : 2. The preferment he got there, being confessor to the king of France, which may seem a place of too much privacy to be conferred on a foreigner : 3. The great credit and esteem which his writings have gained in France, where his manuscript works are extant in many libraries.

These pleas are over-balanced with the like number to attest his English extraction. *Ham,* in Gorham, is notoriously known for no French, but a Saxon ordinary termination of a town. 2. Gorham was a village nigh St. Alban's in this county; where Gorhambury (the manor-house thereof) is extant at this day. The register of Merton College in Oxford mentioneth the admission of this Nicholas Gorham a student in their foundation. Add to all these, that learned Leland and other English antiquaries have always challenged him for their countryman.

Indeed he was an Englishman *Francised,* who, going over into France a young man, spent the rest of his life there. Many and learned are his books, having commented almost on all the Scriptures; and give me leave to say, no hands have fewer spots of pitch upon them who touched the superstition of that age he lived in. He died and was buried at Paris, about the year of our Lord 1400. I will only add, that since we have had another Nicholas of Gorham (though not by his birth, by his habitation) as famous for a statesman as the former for a divine. I mean Sir Nicholas Bacon, whose dwelling was at Gorhambury aforesaid.

HUGH LEGAT, born in this county;* bred in Oxford; at last became a Benedictine in the abbey of St. Alban's. Being much delighted in meditation, he wholly employed himself in commentary on, 1. John of Hanwell's† books of Lamentation. 2. Boetius of Consolation. Thus his soul may be presumed well poised betwixt *plumbum et plumam,* a weight and a wing, to suppress and support it. He flourished anno 1400.

JOHN WHETAMSTEAD was born at Wheathampstead in this county; not so famous for the production of the best wheat, whence the place hath its name, as for this John Whetamstead, who hath his name from that place. He was bred at the priory at Tynemouth in Northumberland (a long stride, I assure you, from the place of his birth); to which he bequeathed a chalice of gold.‡ He was afterwards abbot of St. Alban's, and the sixth of that christian name.

---

* Pits, de Illustribus Angliæ Scriptoribus, anno 1400.
† See WRITERS, in Middlesex.   ‡ Weever's Funeral Monuments, p. 569.

Vast were his expences in the adorning of that church, exceeding six thousand pounds.

Two criticisms in his buildings I cannot omit;* one, that on the north side of his church (which he enlightened with new windows) he set up the statues of those heathen philosophers who had testified of the Incarnation of Christ. 2. That in a little chapel he set up the similitudes of all the saints whose Christian names were John, with his own picture, and this prayer in a distich, that, though unworthy, he might have a place with his namesakes in heaven.

Besides, he procured from Humfrey the good duke of Gloucester, his great Mæcenas, who was buried at St. Alban's, a suit of vestments worth three thousand marks, and the manor of Pembroke in South Wales. Many are the books which he left to posterity, being counted no fewer than fourscore and odd several Treatises; and died about the year 1440.

[AMP.] JOHN BOURCHIER, baron Berners, was son of John Bourchier baron Berners, in the right of Margery his wife, daughter of Sir Richard Berners of West Horsley in Surrey.† Yet had that honourable family of the Berners an ancient habitation at Tharfield in this county;‡ which with some probability insinuateth the birth of this noble gentleman therein.

He was a martial man, well seen in all military discipline; and when Michael Joseph, the blacksmith, led the Cornish rebels against king Henry the Seventh, anno 1496, no man did better service than this lord in their suppression, for which he was made chief governor of Calais.

Having there gotten a repose, who formerly had been a far traveller and great linguist, he translated many books out of French, Spanish, and Italian, besides some of his own making.§ I behold his as the second (accounting the lord Tiptoft the first) noble hand, which, since the decay of learning, took a pen therein, to be author of a book. He died on the 16th of March 1532; and is buried in the great church in Calais. And I have read that the estate of the Berners is by an heir-general descended to the Knyvets of Ashwelthorp in Norfolk.||

SINCE THE REFORMATION.

ROGER HUTCHINSON was born in this county;¶ and bred fellow of St. John's College in Cambridge, where he was very familiar with Mr. Roger Ascham, who disdained intimacy with dunces. And as this is enough to speak him scholar; so it is a

---

* Manuscript in Sir Robert Cotton's library.
† Mills, in his Catalogue of Honour, p. 855.
‡ Camden's Britannia, in Hertfordshire.
§ Bale, de Scriptoribus Britannicis, Cent. vii. num. 1, and Pits, in anno 1532.
|| Mills's Catalogue, p. 256.
¶ Bale, de Scriptoribus Britannicis, Cent. ix. num. 95.

sufficient evidence to an intelligent jury, to prove him Protestant, that, being commended by Bale for writing a book in English of "The Image of God," he is wholly omitted by John Pits. He flourished anno Domini 1550; and probably died in the happy reign of Edward the Sixth, before the following persecution.

THOMAS CARTWRIGHT was born in this county,* and was admitted in Saint John's College in Cambridge, anno 1550. In the reign of queen Mary he left the university (being probably one of those scholars which, as Mr. Fox observeth, went (alias were driven) away from this college all at one time, and betook himself to the service of a counsellor. Here he got some skill in the common law, which enabled him afterwards to fence the better for himself by the advantage thereof.

In the reign of queen Elizabeth, he returned to Cambridge, was chosen fellow, first of St. John's, then of Trinity; how afterwards he was made Margaret Professor, ousted thereof for his non-conformity, travelled beyond seas, returned home, became the champion of the presbyterian party, is largely related in our " Ecclesiastical History."

Only I will add, that the Non-conformists, not agreeing which of them (where there is much choice, there is no choice) should answer Dr. Whitgift's " Reply," I read that Mr. Cartwright at last was chosen by lot to undertake it.† It seems the brethren concluded it of high and holy concernment; otherwise I know what Mr. Cartwright hath written of the appeal to lots : " Non nisi in rebus gravioribus, et alicujus magni momenti ad sortis judicium recurrendum, maximè, cum per sortem Deus ipse in judicio sedeat."‡

One saith " for riches he sought them not,"§ and another saith, " that he died rich;" ‖ and I believe both say true, God sometimes making wealth to find them who seek not for it, seeing many and great were his benefactors. He died and was buried in Warwick, where he was master of the hospital, anno 1603.

DANIEL DIKE was born at Hempstead in this county, where his father was a minister silenced for his non-conformity. He was bred in . . . . College in Cambridge, and became afterwards a profitable labourer in God's vineyard. Witness (besides his sermons) his worthy books, whereof that is the masterpiece which treateth of " The Deceitfulness of Man's Heart;" wherein he lays down directions for the discovery thereof; as also how, in other cases, one may be acquainted with his own condition, seeing many men lose themselves in the

---

* Samuel Clarke, in his Lives of English Divines, p. 367.   † Idem, p. 399.
‡ Idem, in his " Comment on Proverbs," 1633.   § Idem, p. 272.
‖ Sir George Paul, in his " Life of Whitgift," p. 54.

labyrinths of their own hearts : so much is the *terra incognita* therein. This book he designed for his pious patron John Lord Harrington. " But, alas ! when the child was come to the birth, there was no strength to bring forth ! " Before the book was fully finished, the author thereof followed his honourable patron into a better world ; so that his surviving brother (of whom immediately) set it forth. And to the Lady Lucy Countess of Bedford, the lord's sister, the same was dedicated. A book which will be owned for a truth, whilst men have any badness ; and will be honoured for a treasure, whilst men have any goodness in them. This worthy man died about the year 1614.

JEREMIAH DIKE, his younger brother, was bred in Sidney College in Cambridge ; beneficed at Epping in Essex ; one of a cheerful spirit. And know, reader, that an ounce of mirth, with the same degree of grace, will serve God farther than a pound of sadness. He had also a gracious heart, and was very profitable in his ministry. He was a father to some good books of his own ; and a guardian to those of his brother, whose *posthume* works he set forth. He was one " peaceable in Israel," and though no zealot in the practice of ceremonies, quietly submitted to use them. He lived and died piously ; being buried in his own parish church, anno Domini 1620.

ARTHUR CAPEL, Esquire, of Hadham in this county, was by king Charles the First created a baron, 1641. He served the king with more valour and fidelity than success, during the civil wars, in the Marches of Wales. After the surrender of Oxford, he retired to his own house in this shire, and was in some sort well cured of the (so then reputed) disease of loyalty, when he fell into a relapse by going to Colchester, which cost him his life, being beheaded in the Palace-yard in Westminster, 1648.

In his lifetime he wrote a book of meditation (published since his death) wherein much judicious piety may be discovered. His mortified mind was familiar with afflictions, which made him to appear with such Christian resolution on the scaffold, where he seemed rather to fright death, than to be frighted with it. Hence one not unhappily alluding to his arms (a lion rampant in a field Gules betwixt three crosses) thus expresseth himself :

> " Thus lion-like, Capel undaunted stood :
> Beset with crosses in a field of blood."

A learned doctor in physic (present at the opening and embalming of him and duke Hambleton) delivered it at a public lecture, that the Lord Capel's was the least heart (whilst the duke's was the greatest) he ever beheld. Which also is very proportionable to the observation in philosophy, that the spirits contracted in a lesser model are the cause of the greater courage.

God hath since been the husband to his widow (who, for her

goodness, may be a pattern to her sex) and father to his children, whom not so much their birth, beauty, and portions, as virtues, married to the best bloods and estates in the land, even when the Royalists were at the lowest condition.

EDWARD SYMONDS, born at Cottered in this county, was bred in Peter-house in Cambridge, where he commenced Master of Arts, afterwards minister of Little Rayne in Essex; a man strict in his life and profitable in his preaching, wherein he had a plain and piercing faculty. Being sequestered from his living for siding with the king; with David, 1 Sam. xxiii. 13. he went "wheresoever he could go," to Worcester, Exeter, Barnstaple, France, and lastly returned to London. He wrote a book "In Vindication of King Charles;" and was instrumental in setting forth his majesty's book called Εἰκὼν Βασιλική. Pens were brandished betwixt him and Mr. Stephen Marshal, though all was fair betwixt them before his death; for Mr. Symonds visited him, lying in his bed at Westminster; told him, "had I taken you for a wild beast, I would not have roused you in your den." He was very conscientious in discharging his calling. Being once requested by me to preach for me, he excused himself for want of competent warning; and when I pleaded, "that mine, being a country parish, would be well pleased with his performance;" "I can," saith he, "content them, but not mine own conscience, to preach with so little preparation." He died about anno Domini 1649; and was buried in St. Peter's, Paul's Wharf, in London.

BENEFACTORS TO THE PUBLIC.

NICHOLAS DIXON, parson for thirty years together of Cheshunt in this county. He was also clerk of the Pipe Office, belonging to the Exchequer. See we here why the officers of that place (as also those of the Chancery) were called Clerks, because priests in orders with cure of souls did formerly discharge those offices. He was also under-treasurer, and at last baron of the Exchequer, when, partly by his own bounty, and partly by collection of others, he built the parish church of Cheshunt (and that, I assure you, is a very fair one) with a chancel to the Virgin Mary. Now for an affidavit for the proof hereof, the reader is referred to this his epitaph inscribed in Cheshunt chancel, more to be respected for the truth than wit thereof:

> " O miserere, Jesu, famuli Dixon Nicolai,
> Cui brevis hospitium tumulus præstat satis amplum.
> Istud qui fanum ter denis rexerat annis,
> Ad cujus fabricam bursas proprias, alienas,
> Solvit et allexit: quo crevit in ardua templum.
> Pulchrum cancellum, tibi dat, pia Virgo, novellum :
> Dum laudaris eo, famulo suffragia præstes.
> Clericus hic Pipæ, Sub-thesaurarius, inde
> Baro Scaccarii, se justè gessit ubique

Pacem pauperibus dans,* cedat divitis iras.
Larga manus relevat quos pauperies fera pressit.
Anno Milleno C. quater, bis bis deca Christi
Octavo moriens, mutans terrestria cœlis,
Octobris luce ter denâ transit ad astra.
 Auxiliare prece qui perlegis hæc Nicholao,
 Ut sibi cum sanctis præstetur vita perennis.

The word *rexerat* doth intimate that Cheshunt was then a rectory, or parsonage, though since impropriated and made a vicarage. What a deal of do does this pitiful poet make with words at length, and figures, and Latin, and Greek, to describe the date of his death! which (if I understand his signs aright) was October the thirtieth, one thousand four hundred and forty eight.

Sir RALPH JOSCELINE, son to Jefferie Josceline, was born at Sabridgeworth in this county,[†] bred a draper in London, whereof he was twice mayor. Once, anno 1464 ; and ere the end of that year, was made knight of the Bath by king Edward the Fourth, in the field, saith my author.[‡] But seeing there is more of the carpet than of the camp in that order, it is more probable what another writes,[§] that he was invested knight of the Bath at the coronation of Elizabeth, queen to the king aforesaid. He was mayor again anno 1476, when he corrected the bakers and victuallers of the city, and by his diligence were the walls thereof repaired ;—walls, now a mere compliment, serving more for the dividing than the defending of the city ; so that as some foreign cities cannot be seen for the walls, here the walls cannot be seen for the city. Sad were the case of London, if not better secured with bones within, than stones about it. This Sir Ralph died October the 25th, anno 1478, and was buried in the church of Sabridgeworth.

JOHN INCENT, son of Robert Incent and Catherine his wife, was born at Berkhampstead in this county.[||] He was afterwards a doctor of law, and advanced, anno 1543 (when Richard Sampson was preferred bishop of Coventry and Lichfield) dean of St. Paul's. This John, probably invited by the example of another John (his mediate predecessor) Collet, dean of Paul's, founded a fair free-school in the town of his nativity, procuring it confirmed by act of Parliament, allowing the master twenty the usher ten pounds per annum. He died, as I collect, in the beginning of the reign of king Edward the Sixth.

Sir THOMAS WHITE, son to Thomas White, was born at

---

 * Were not that orthography, pseudography, which altereth the original copy, I had written *cedat* with an *st*, for so it ought to be written.—F.
 † Stow's Survey of London, p. 569. ‡ Idem, ibidem.
 § Weever's Funeral Monuments, p. 550.
 || Camden's Britannia, in Hertfordshire.

Rixmansworth in this county, and afterwards bred a merchant-tailor in London, of which city he was lord mayor anno Domini 1553. He first built Gloucester-hall, and afterwards built and endowed St. John's College in Oxford, the seminary of many flourishing wits. He bestowed also a vast sum of money on several corporations, to be employed circularly for the benefit of the poor freemen therein. I once intended to have presented the reader with an exact particular of his benefactions, till seasonably I reversed my resolution on this consideration : amongst the Jews it was an injury for one removed further off in blood to do the office of a kinsman to the childless widow, until the next of kin had first disclaimed his interest therein; as in the case of Ruth most plainly appeared.* A son, I am sure is nearer than a nephew; therefore it is a more proper performance for one bred in Oxford to collect the particulars of his bounty (who, whithersoever he went, left the finger-marks of his charity behind him,) than for me, distanced a *degree* farther off by my education in another university.

SINCE THE REFORMATION.

RICHARD HALE, Esquire, was born at Cudicot in this county, and bred a grocer in the city of London ; where his industrious endeavours were so blessed, that in a little time he got a great estate. Wherefore, in expression of his gratitude to God, the giver thereof, he founded a very fair school, allowing forty pounds a year to the master thereof, at Hertford in this county ; a place very prudently chosen for such a purpose. First, because the prime town in his native shire : secondly, great the want of a school in that populous place : and, lastly, because most pure the air thereof ; so that parents need not fear their children's loss of health for the gaining of learning. He died anno Domini 16.., whose wealthy family do still flourish with worth and worship at King's Walden in this county.

EDWARD BASH, Knight, was born at Aldnam in this county, in the manor-house then belonging to the noble family of the Careys; whereof Frances his mother, afterwards married to George earl of Rutland, was descended. He was a hearty gentleman, and a good English housekeeper, keeping a full table, with solid dishes on it, and welcome guests about it. And one may term him a valiant man, who durst be hospitable in these dangerous days. Whilst living, he was a benefactor to Peter-house in Cambridge, wherein he was bred a fellow-commoner; and at his death bequeathed more thereunto, the particulars whereof I have not yet attained. He gave also twenty pounds per annum for the maintenance of a schoolmaster at Stanstead in this county, where he had his constant habitation. He died anno Domini 1605.

* Ruth iv. 4.

Many other benefactors this shire hath of late afforded; and amongst them one born in Cheshunt parish, who founded a school and alms-house therein, whom we leave to be reckoned up by the topographists of this county.

MEMORABLE PERSONS.

THOMAS WATERHOUSE, Priest, was born at Helmstead in this county. His will acquainteth us with the wardrobe of men of his order towards the end of the reign of queen Mary:

" In the name of the Father, and of the Son, and of the Holy Ghost, Amen. I, Thomas Waterhouse, priest of the Catholic faith, whole of body, and of good and perfect remembrance, do make and ordain my last Will and Testament, the 25th day of May, in the year of our Lord 1557, in manner and form following: First, I bequeath my soul to God Almighty the Father of heaven, my Creator; and unto Jesus Christ, our Lord and God, my Redeemer. And I will my body to be buried in the chancel within the parish church of Hemelhempsted, near to the place where my mother lieth. I bequeath to the parish church of Quainton my vestment of crimson satin. I bequeath to the parish church of Great Barkemsted my vestment of crimson velvet. I bequeath to the parish church of Great Hemelsted my stole and fanon set with pearl. I bequeath to my cousin John Waterhouse, the queen's servant, my standing cup of silver and gilt, with the cover. I bequeath to my servant Thomas Ashton, ten pound in money, which I promised him. I bequeath to my priest, Sir Thomas Barker, my black gown faced with taffata, &c. And I ordain and make my brother John Waterhouse, and my cousin Richard Combe, gentlemen, mine executor. These being witnesses, &c."*

Such as jeer him for his gallantry (as one of the church triumphant) may remember that besides his worshipful extraction (which might the better countenance his clothes) these were not garments for his wearing, but vestments for his officiating; and, according to the opinion of that age, nothing could be too costly in that kind.

LORD MAYORS.

1. William Cromar, son of John Cromar, of Aldenham, Mercer, 1423.
2. Ralph Joceline, son of Geffrey Joceline, Draper, 1464.
3. William Martin, son of Walter Martin, of Sabridgworth, Skinner, 1492.
4. Ralph Ostrich, son of Geffrey Ostrich, of Hitchin, Fishmonger, 1493.

* Probatum fuit hoc Testamentum coram William Cooke, Leg. Doct. in Cur. Prerog. 17 Julii 1557.—F.

5. Thomas Bradbury, son of Will. Bradbury, of Braughin, Mercer, 1509.

6. Thomas White, son of Thomas White, of Rickmansworth, Merchant Taylor, 1553.

7. John Wats, son of Thomas Wats, of Buntingford, Clothworker, 1606.

Reader, this is one of the twelve shires whose Gentry were not returned by the Commissioners, the twelfth of Henry the Sixth, into the Tower.

SHERIFFS.

This county had the same with Essex until the ninth year of queen Elizabeth, when the distinction between the two Shires did begin, and these following peculiar to this county.

QUEEN ELIZ.

Anno	Name and Arms.	Place.

9 G. Penruddock, arm.
    G. a limb of a tree, raguled and trunked in bend Arg.

10 Row. Litton, arm. . Knebworth.
    Erm. on a chief indented Az. three crowns O.

11 Hen. Conisby, arm. . South Mims.
    G. three coneys seiant within a border engrailed Arg.

12 Will. Dods, arm.

13 Edw. Bash, arm. . Stansted.
    Per chevron Arg. and G.; in chief two martlets S.; in base a saltire, &c.

14 George Horsey, arm. . Digswel.
    Az. three horses' heads couped O. bridled Arg.

15 T. Leventhorp . . . Shingle-hall.
    Arg. a bend gobonée S. and G. cotised of the first.

16 Hen. Cocke, arm. . . Brocksborn.
    Quarterly, G. and Arg.

17 Johan. Gill, arm. . . Widjel.
    S. two chevrons Arg. each with three mullets of the first; on a canton O. a lion passant G.

18 Tho. Bowles, arm. . . Wallington.
    Arg. on a chevron betwixt three boars' heads couped S. as many scalops O. within a border V. bezantée.

19 Edw. Verney, arm.
    Az. on a cross Arg. five mullets G.

20 Phil. Butler, arm. . . Watton.
    (Vide the last of queen Elizabeth.)

21 Char. Morison, arm. . Cashiobery.
    O. on a chief G. three chaplets of the first.

22 Tho. Dockwray, arm. . Putridge.
    S. a chevron engrailed Arg. between three plates cha ed with as many pallets G.

Anno	Name.	Place.

23 Joh. Brocket, arm. . Broket Hall.
  O. a cross patoncée S.
24 Hen. Conisby, arm. . *ut prius.*
25 Fran. Haydon, arm. . Grove.
  Quarterly, Arg. and Az. a cross engrailed counterchanged.
26 Edw. Bash, arm. . . *ut prius.*
27 Hen. Capel, arm. . . Hadham.
  G. a lion rampant betwixt three crosses botonée-fitchée
  O.
28 Ed. Pawleter, arm. . . Wimondly.
  Arg. a bend voided S.
29 T. Leventhorp, arm. . *ut prius.*
  Tho. Sadler, arm. . Standon.
  O. a lion rampant partie per fess Az. and G.
30 Joh. Cutts, mil. . . . CAMBRIDGESHIRE.
  Arg. on a bend engrailed S. three plates.
31 Edw. Verney, arm. . . *ut prius.*
32 Wal. Mildmay, arm. . Pessobury.
  Arg. three lions rampant Az.
33 Th. Hanchet, arm. . . Hinkworth.
  S. three dexter hands Arg.
34 Arth. Capel, arm. . . *ut prius.*
35 J. Leventhorp, arm. . *ut prius.*
36 Row. Litton, arm. . . *ut prius.*
37 Th. Sadler, arm. . . . *ut prius.*
38 R. Coningsby, arm. . *ut prius.*
39 Rich. Spencer, arm. . . Offley.
  Quarterly Arg. and G. a fret O.; on a bend S. three
  escalops of the first.
40 T. Popeblunt, arm.
  Barry formy nebuly of six, O. and S.
41 Rob. Chester, arm. . . Cakenhatch.
  Per Pale Arg. and S. a chevron betwixt three rams' heads
  erased within a border engrailed roundelly, all counterchanged.
42 Tho. Hanchet, arm. . . *ut prius.*
43 Tho. Bowles, arm. . . *ut prius.*
44 Edw. Denny, mil. . . . ESSEX.
  G. a saltire Arg. betwixt twelve crosses O.
  H. Boteler, mil. . . Hatfield-woodhall.
  G. a fess checky Arg. and S. between six cross-croslets O.

KING JAMES.

1 Hen. Boteler . . . . *ut prius.*
2 Geo. Purient, arm. . . Digswel.
  G. three crescents Arg.

Anno	Name.	Place.

3 Tho. Dockwray, arm. . . *ut prius.*

4 Wa. Mildmay, arm. et . . *ut prius.*
Leon. Hide, mil. . . . Albury.
   O. a chevron between three lozenges Az.; on a chief G.
   an eagle displayed of the first.

5 J. Leventhorp, arm. . . *ut prius.*

6 Nich. Trot, arm. . . . Quickset.

7 Radu. Sadler, arm. . . *ut prius.*

8 Ric. Anderson, mil.
   Arg. a chevron betwixt three crosses formée S.

9 Rob. Boteler, mil. . . *ut prius.*

10 Johan. Wild, arm.

11 W. Franckland, arm.
   Arg. a chevron S. betwixt three torteaux, charged with
   as many scalops of the first.

12 Tho. Dacres, mil. et . . Cheshunt.
   Tho. Dacres, arm.

13 God. Pemberton, mil. Hartfordbury.
   Arg. a chevron between three buckets S.
   L. Pemberton, arm.

14 Tho. Newes, arm.
   S. two pallets Arg. a canton Erm.

15 Edw. Brisco . . . . Abbot's Langley.
   Arg. three greyhounds in pale S.

16 Tho. Read, arm. . . Broket-hall.
   G. a saltire betwixt four garbs O.

17 Nich. Hide, arm. . . *ut prius.*

18 R. Pemberton, arm. . . *ut prius.*

19 Will. Hale, arm. . . King's Wolden.
   Az. a chevron counterbattily O.

20 Edw. Newport, arm. . Pelham.

21 Cl. Skudamore, mil.
   G. three stirrups leathered and buckled O.

22 Rich. Sidley, arm. . . Digswell.
   Az. a fess wavy betwixt three goats' heads erased Arg.
   attired O.

KING CHARLES.

1 Will. Litton, mil. . . *ut prius.*

2 Joha. Jenning, mil. . . Hollywell.
   Az. on a fess G. three bezants.

3 Tho. Hide, bar. . . . *ut prius.*

4 Edw. Gardner, arm. . Thunderidge.
   Per pale O. and G. on a fess two mascles between three
   hinds passant counter changed.

5 Will. Hoe, arm. . . . Hoe.
   Quarterly S. and Arg.

Anno	Name.	Place.
6	Johan. Boteler, mil.	*ut prius.*
7	Rich. Hale, arm.	*ut prius.*
8	Hen. Cogshil, arm.	
9	Will Plomer, arm.	Radwell.

V. a chevron betwixt three lions' heads erased O. billeted G.

10 W. Prestly, arm.

S. a chevron Arg. charged with three anchors of the field, betwixt as many lions O. each issuant out of a tower of the second.

11 Will. Leaman, arm. . North-hall.

Az. a fess betwixt three dolphins Arg.

12 Rad. Freeman, arm. . Aspden.

Az. three lozenges Arg.

13 T. Coningsby, arm. . . *ut prius.*

14 Tho. Hewet, arm. . . Pesso-bury.

S. a chevron counter battellée betwixt three owls Arg.

15 Johan. Gore, arm. . . Gilsden.

G. a fess betwixt three croslets fitchy O.

16 Arth. Pulter . . . . *ut prius.*

17

18 Joh. Gerrard, bar.

19 Joh. Gerrard, bar.

20 Cha. Nodes, arm.

QUEEN ELIZABETH.

14. GEORGE HORSEY.—The Horseys had a free and competent estate at Digswell in this county, where they had lived long in good esteem. It happened that Sir John Horsey, of Clifton, in the county of Dorset (whose two daughters were married into the families of Mohune and Arnold) wanting an heir-male, settled the main of his estate, which was very great, on Ralph, the son of this George Horsey.

His father advised this Ralph his son (newly augmented with the addition of so great an estate), that in case he should have any occasion to sell lands, not to part with his Hertfordshire inheritance, which had continued so long in the family, but rather to make sale of some Dorsetshire land.

But the young gentleman, ill-advised, sold this his patrimony first of all; for which the rest of his means probably prospered no whit the better; not one foot thereof remaining at this day to his posterity. I write not this to grieve any of his surviving relations, but to instruct all in obedience to their parent's lawful commands.

16. HENRY COCK, Arm.—He was afterward knighted, and was cofferer to queen Elizabeth and king James, who lay at his

house May the second, at his first coming out of Scotland to London, where so abundant entertainment, "that no man, of what condition soever, but had what his appetite desired,"* which made the king, at his departure, heartily "thank the good knight for his great expences."† This Sir Henry's daughter was married to the Lord Delaware.

44. EDWARD DENNY, Knight, was high sheriff of this county when king James, coming from Scotland, passed through it. He was attended on by one hundred and forty men, suitably apparelled and well mounted, with whom he tendered his service to the king, presenting also his majesty with a gallant horse, rich saddle, and furniture. But, before the year of shrievalty was expired, king James created him baron Denny of Waltham, and another supplied the remainder thereof.

KING JAMES.

2. GEORGE PURIENT, Arm.—Let me do my best devoir and last office to preserve the memory of an ancient and now expired family. Digswell, I presume, was the place of their living, because of their interments therein, whereof this most remarkable:

"Hic jacent Johannes Purient, Armiger pro Corpore Regis Richardi Secundi, et Penerarius ejusdem Regis; et Armiger etiam Regis Henrici Quarti; et Armiger etiam Regis Henrici Quinti; et Magister Equitum Johanne filie Regis Navarre, et Regine Anglie, qui obiit ——————; et Johanna uxor ejus, quondam capitalis Domicilla —————— que obiit xxiv. . . . . anno Domini M.cccc.xv."

Surely he was a man of merit; being penon or ensign-bearer to *one*, esquire of the body to *three* successive kings; and master of the horse to one of their queens, to whom his wife was chief lady of honour.

THOMAS DACRES, Miles, et mort.—He was one of the three sheriffs in this county, who, within the compass of ten years, died in their shrievalties, as by this catalogue may appear. He was grandchild unto Robert Dacres, esquire, one of the privy council to king Henry the Eighth.

THOMAS HOE.—This most ancient name (which formerly had barons thereof) is now expiring in the male line; this gentleman's sole daughter being married unto —————— Kete, of London.

THOMAS CONISBY, Armiger.—When one told him, that his po-

---

tent adversary had prevailed to make him sheriff, "I will not," said he, "keep a man the more, or a dog the fewer, on that account."

THE FAREWELL.

I am sorry to hear that the fair font of solid brass, brought out of Scotland, and bestowed by Sir Richard Lea on the abbey church in St. Alban's, is lately taken away : I could almost wish that the plunderers' fingers had found it as hot as it was when first forged, that so these thieves, with their fault, might have received the deserved punishment thereof.

Had it been returned to the place whence it was taken, to serve for the same use, the matter had not been so much ; but, by an usual alchymy, this brass is since turned into silver. But let us not so much condole the late losing of the font, as congratulate our still keeping of baptism; which, if some men might have their minds, should utterly be denied to all infants. I wish all infants to be christened in this county and elsewhere, though not so fair a font, fair water, and, which is the best of all, the full concurrence of God's Spirit, effectually to complete the sacrament unto them.

WORTHIES OF HERTFORDSHIRE WHO HAVE FLOURISHED SINCE THE TIME OF FULLER.

Sir Henry CHAUNCEY, sergeant-at-law, historian of the county; born at Yardleybury; died 1700.

Isaac CHAUNCY, non-conformist divine and author; born at Ware; died 1712.

Robert CLUTTERBUCK, historian of the county; born at Watford 1772; died 1831.

William COWPER, poet; born at Berkhampstead 1731; died 1800.

John DUNCOMBE, poet and divine, author of "The Femineid," &c.; born at Stocks 1730; died 1786.

William DUNCOMBE, dramatic writer and translator of Horace; father of the preceding; born at Stocks 1690; died 1769.

John GUYSE, author of Paraphrase on the New Testament; born at Hertford 1680.

Robert HILL, a learned tailor, compared by Spence to Magliabechi; born at Miswell 1699; died 1777.

William KENRICK, miscellaneous writer; born near Watford; died 1779.

John SHUTE, first Viscount Barrington, statesman and author; born at Theobalds 1678; died 1754.

John WALKER, philologist, author of "Pronouncing Dictionary;" born at Barnet 1732; died 1807.
William WILLYMOT, divine and civilian; born at Royston;
died 1737.

‚ Hertfordshire can boast of three county historians, viz. Sir Henry Chauncey
(1700), N. Salmon (1728), and Robert Clutterbuck (1827). Accounts of St. Alban's Abbey have also appeared, dated 1795, and 1813; the former from the pen
of the Rev. P. Newcome.—ED.

HEREFORDSHIRE.

Herefordshire hath Worcestershire and Shropshire on the north, Gloucestershire on the east, Monmouthshire on the south, Brecknock and Radnor-shires on the west. In form it is almost circular, being from north to south (measured to the best improvement) thirty-five miles, though from east to west not altogether so much.

There cannot be given a more effectual evidence of the healthful air in this shire, than the vigorous vivacity of the inhabitants therein; many aged folk, which in other countries are properties of the chimneys, or confined to their beds, are here found in the field as able (if willing) to work. The ingenious sergeant Hoskin gave an entertainment to king James, and provided ten aged people to dance the Moorish before him; all of them making up more than a thousand years; so that what was wanting in one was supplied in another; a nest of nesters not to be found in another place.

This county doth share as deep as any in the alphabet of our English commodities, though exceeding in W. for Wood, Wheat, Wool, and Water. Besides, this shire better answereth (as to the sound thereof) the name of Pomerania than the dukedom of Germany so called, being a continued orchard of apple-trees, whereof much cider is made, of the use whereof we have treated before.*

There is a tract in this county called Gylden Vale; and if any demand how much gold is to be found therein, know that even as much as in *Chrusaroas,* or Golden-stream, the river of Damascus, so called from the yellowness of their water; as this vale is so named either because gilded with flowers in the spring, or because being the best of moulds, as gold is of metals.

Here I cannot but commend Master Camden's cautious commendation of this county: " Secunda fertilitatis laude inter Angliæ provincias acquiescere, haud facile est contenta;" (it is not willingly content to be accounted the second shire for matter of fruitfulness.)

But the aforesaid author in his whole book never expresseth

---

* In the Commodities of Gloucestershire.

which is the first, too politic to adjudge so invidious a pre-
eminence. And thus keeping the uppermost seat empty, such
competitor counties are allowed leave to put in their several
claims which pretend to the prime place of fertility.

Reader, I am sorry that having not hitherto seen the cathedral of Hereford, I must be silent about the buildings in this
county.

NATURAL COMMODITIES.
WOOL.

Such as are ignorant of the qualities thereof may inform
themselves therein from the common proverbs : 1. "White
as wool ; " a Scripture phrase,* though there be thereof black
by nature. 2. "Soft as wool ; " and therefore our judges anciently in the Parliament-house sat on wool-packs, as well for the
easier repose of their age, as to mind them to maintain this staple commodity in its legal privileges. 3. "As warm as wool."
And one said merrily, "Wooll must needs be warm, as consisting all of double letters."

Our English garments from head to foot were formerly made
thereof, till the beginning of the reign of king Henry the
Eighth, when velvet caps becoming fashionable for persons of
prime quality, discomposed the proverb, "If his cap be made of
wool," as formerly comprising all conditions of people how high
and haughty soever.

Great the plenty of wool in this county ; and greater God's
goodness, that generally our northern lands are well stored
therewith. The friar† rather descanted than commented, and
his interpretation not so much false, as improper for the place ;
"Dat nivem sicut lanam," (He giveth snow like wool ;)‡ that
where most snow falls, those places (if habitable) are best
provided with wool. It is well his wanton wit went no further,
"He scattered his hoar frost like ashes ; " freezing countries§
affording most fuel to burn ; so careful is Providence in dis-
pensing necessaries to mankind. As for the wool in this
county, it is best known, to the honour thereof, by the name of
Lempster Ore, being absolutely the finest in this county, and
indeed in all England, equalling, if not exceeding, the Apulian
or Tarentine in the south of Italy, though it cost not so much
charge and curiosity in the careful keeping thereof : for good
authors‖ inform us, that there the shepherds put in effect a
fleece over their fleece, using to clothe their sheep with skins,
to preserve their wool from the injury of earth, bushes, and
weather. How well this requiteth their cost, I know not, but
am sure no such trouble is used on our sheep here.

---

* Revelations i. 14.   † Cited by H. Stevens, in his Defence of Herodotus.
‡ Psalm cxlvii. 16.   § Muscovy, Poland, Norway.
‖ Var. de re rustic. 2 cap. 2.   Columell. 1. 7. c. 4.

SALMON.

A dainty and wholesome fish, and a double riddle in Nature: first, for its invisible feeding, no man alive having ever found any meat in the maw thereof. Secondly, for its strange leaping (or flying rather), so that some will have them termed salmons, *à saliendo*. Being both bow and arrow, it will shoot itself out of the water an incredible height and length. I might add the admirable growth thereof, if true what is confidently affirmed, that it increaseth from a spawn to a full-grown fish within the compass of a year. Plenty of these in this county, though not in such abundance as in Scotland, where servants (they say) indent with their masters, nor to be fed therewith above thrice a week.

Some will say, why salmons in Herefordshire, which are common in other counties? It is answered, in other counties, suitably with the buck, they are seasonable only in summer; whereas here, with buck and doe, they are in season all the year long. This county may say:

> *Salmo non æstate novus, nec frigore desit.*
> " Salmon in summer is not rare ;
>   In winter, I of them do share."

For the river of Wye affords brumal salmons, fat and sound, when they are sick and spent in other places.

THE WONDERS.

There is a little fountain called Bone-well nigh Richard's Castle in this county, the water whereof is always full of bones of little fishes,* or as others conceive, of little frogs; seeing, it seems, such their smallness they are hardly to be distinguished. It addeth to the wonder, because this spring can never be emptied of them, but as fast as some are drawn out, others instantly succeed them.

To this permanent, let us add two transient, Wonders, on the credit of excellent authors.† When a battle was fought in this county, anno Domini 1461, betwixt Jasper earl of Pembroke and James Butler earl of Ormond on the one side, and king Edward the Fourth of the other, three suns appeared together in the firmament.

Such a triple sun (one real, two representations) were seen in heaven a little before the Roman empire was rent betwixt three competitors, Galba, Otho, and Vitellius; as also since, when the kingdom of Hungary was cantoned betwixt John Vayvode, Ferdinand afterwards emperor, and the Great Turk; such meteors being sometimes prognostics of so many several pretenders at once to the same sovereignty.

Inquiring into the natural cause hereof, we find it to be no-

---

* Camden's Britannia, in Herefordshire.
† Quoted by Speed in his Maps of England, in Herefordshire.—F.

thing else but the image of the sun represented in an equal, smooth, thick, and watery cloud, not opposite thereunto (for then it would make the rainbow); nor under the sun (for then it would make those circles called crowns or garlands); but on one or either side thereof, in a competent or moderate distance: for, if it be too far off, then the beams will be too feeble to be reflected; if too near, the sun will disperse it; but in such a middle distance, wherein many suns may appear, as a man's face is expressed in all pieces of a broken glass.

To this wonder add a second, of Marcley Hill, which, anno Domini 1575, roused itself, as it were, out of its sleep.[*] Yea, in some sort it might seem to be in labour for three days together, shaking and roaring all that while,[†] to the great terror of all that heard or beheld it. It threw down all things that opposed it, and removed itself into a higher place. The best use we can make of such accidents is, to fear and not fear thereat, with a reverential awe to God, no servile dread of the thing itself: "Therefore we will not fear, though the earth be removed, and though the mountains be carried into the midst of the sea."[‡]

PROVERBS.

" Blessed is the eye,
  That is betwixt Severn and Wye."]

Some will justly question the truth hereof. True it is, the eyes of those inhabitants are entertained with a pleasant prospect; yet such as is equalled by other places. But it seems this is a prophetical promise of safety to such that live secured within those great rivers, as if privileged from martial impressions. But, alas! civil war is a vagrant, and will trace all corners, except they be surrounded with Gyges' ring. Surely some eyes in that place, besides the sweet rivers of Severn and Wye running by them, have had salt waters flowing from them, since the beginning of our late distractions.

" Lemster bread, and Weabley ale."[§]]

It seems both these are best in their kinds, though good in other places of the land. Thus, though Palestine was universally termed "a land of wheat,"[||] yet the Spirit of God takes signal notice of "the wheat of Minnith and Pannag,"[¶] as finer than the rest. Yet is there wheat in England, which jostleth for pureness with that of Weabley; viz. what groweth about Heston in Middlesex, yielding so fine flour, that for a long time the manchet for the kings of England was made thereof;[**] except any will say it is prized the more for the vicinity to London.

---

* Camden's Elizabeth, anno 1575.
† This kind of earthquake is called Brasmatias.—F.
‡ Psalm xlvi. 2.   § Camden's Britannia, in Herefordshire.
|| Deut. viii. 8.   ¶ Ezek. xxvii. 17.
** Camden's Britannia, in Middlesex.

SAINTS.

ETHELBERT was king of the East Angles, and went to Offa king of Mercia to treat of the marriage with his daughter; but queen Quendred, wife to Offa, more ambitious of her own unlawful than her daughter's lawful advancement, practised his death at a village now called Sutton Wallis, four miles from Hereford. His corpse was afterwards removed by Milfred (a petit prince of that country) to Hereford, where he obtained the reputation of a saint and martyr. His suffering happened anno Domini 793.

THOMAS CANTILUPE was of honourable extraction, whose father William lord Cantilupe had two fair habitations, Abergavenny castle in Monmouth, and Haringworth in Northamptonshire, which, by an heir-general of that family, afterwards descended to lord Zouch. He was bred in Oxford (whereof at last he became chancellor), and was preferred bishop of Hereford. A charitable man may believe him a person of holy life and great learning; but no wise man will credit what Walsingham writes of him, "That he was never guilty of any mortal sin." Going to (others say returning from) Rome, to assert his church from the encroachment of Peckham, archbishop of Canterbury, he died at a city in Tuscany, where his flesh was taken off his corpse and buried, whilst his bones were sent for reliques into England, and enshrined at Hereford. Now, though different dates be assigned of his death, I adhere to Bishop Godwin, noting his dissolution 1282.

He was afterwards canonized by Pope John the Twenty-second; and no fewer than four hundred twenty-five miracles are registered in that church, reported to be wrought at his tomb.* I say just four hundred and twenty-five, which falls out fewer by five-and-twenty than "the prophets of Baal," and more by five-and-twenty " than the prophets of the groves,"† in a middle number betwixt both, and all of them, I believe, honest and true alike. Yea, it is recorded in his legend, "that by his prayers were raised from death to life threescore several persons, one-and-twenty lepers healed, and three-and-twenty blind and dumb men to have received their sight and speech."‡

No wonder then what Mr. Camden observeth, that, in process of time, " parum abfuit quin pietatis opinione regio martyri Ethelberto præluxerit;" (he lacked but little to eclipse the lustre of Ethelbert, the royal saint and martyr§); formerly buried (as is aforesaid) in the same cathedral. Indeed it is given to superstition always to be fondest of the youngest saint. But long since king Henry the Eighth hath put a period to all emulations betwixt their memories.

---

* English Martyrology, October 2.   † 1 Kings xviii. 19.
‡ English Martyrology, ut prius.   § Britannia, in Herefordshire.

The bishops of Hereford so highly honoured this Thomas, that (waiving their ancient arms) they assumed the paternal coat of Cantilupe (viz. Gules, three leopards' heads inverted, each with a flower-de-luce in his mouth Or) to be successively the arms of their see. This Cantilupe lived the latest of any Englishman who was canonized; so that blind zeal may even close her stomach, and make up her mouth with the sweetmeats of his memory.

MARTYRS.

Sir John (son to Sir Thomas) Oldcastle was a native of this county, whereof he was sheriff in the seventh of Henry the Fourth; lord Cobham in the right of his wife; a right valiant man, but great follower of Wickliffe, so that he lost his life on that account.

As his body was hanged and burnt in an unusual posture at Tyburn, so his memory hath ever since been in a strange suspense betwixt malefactor and martyr; Papists charging him with treason against king Henry the Fifth, and heading an army of more than ten thousand men, though it wanted nine thousand nine hundred ninety and nine thereof, so far as it appears solidly proved.

But it hath ever been the practice of the devil and his instruments, angry with God's servants for their religion, to accuse them for sedition; perceiving princes generally more jealous of their own honour than God's glory, and most careful to cut off such as oppose their power or persons. Thus Christ was accused for disloyalty to Cæsar; and St. Paul, for raising of tumults; though they (as it is plain in the text*) either raised themselves, or were raised by the Pharisees and Sadducees, Paul's professed enemies. But I have so worn out the nib of my pen in my "Church History" about clearing the innocency of this worthy knight, that I have nothing to add new thereunto.

Marian martyrs this diocese affordeth none; such the moderation of Robert Parfew, the bishop thereof,

CARDINALS.

Adam de Easton.—We were at a great loss, had we but his bare surname to direct us to the place of his nativity, seeing scarcely one county in England, which hath not one or more Eastons or Eatons † (the same in effect) therein. But thanks be to our author,‡ who hath fixed his birth (though but with an *ut videtur*) in this shire.

Pretenders to skill in Palmistry would persuade us, that such, the table in whose hands is narrow beneath and broad above, are marked out for poverty in their youth, and plenty in their

---

* Acts xxiii. 6.
† Three Eatons there are in this county.
‡ Bishop Godwin, in his Catalogue of Cardinals, p. 173, out of whom this is collected.—F.

old age. I will not say, such the signature in the hands of our Adam; but sure I am, such his success. Mean his birth, homely his breeding, hard his fare, till by his industry he was advanced doctor of divinity in Oxford, wherein he became a great scholar, skilled in Greek and Hebrew (rare accomplishments in that age), and was very dexterous in all civil negotiations. He was afterwards made cardinal, with the title of St. Cicily, by Pope Urban, against whom Clement the Seventh was elected and erected by others.

Fierce the fight between bears and boars; but far fiercer betwixt two anti-Popes, giving no quarter to the opposite party, if brought into their power. Urban, suspecting treachery in some of his cardinals, imprisoned seven of them at once, and putting five of them into sacks, sank them into the sea. Oh, most barbarous *urbanity*! Our Adam, being the sixth, hardly escaped with life, and may be said in some sort put into a sack (though of a larger size); I mean, a strait dungeon, where he remained half-starved for five years together, till the death of Pope Urban. But Pope Boniface, his successor, restored him to all his honours and dignities, and sent him over into England to king Richard the Second with most ample commendation.

Returning to Rome, he lived there in all plenty and pomp; and died September the 17th, 1397. Pity it is so good a scholar should have so barbarous an epitaph, scarce worth our translation:

> *Artibus iste pater famosus in omnibus Adam,*
> *Theologus summus,* Cardi-*que*-nalis *erat.*
> *Anglia cui patriam, titulum dedit ista Beatæ*
> *Ceciliæque—morsque suprema polum.*

> " Adam a famous father in arts all,
> He was a deep divine, *Cardi*-and-*nall*,
> Whom England bred, St. Cicilie hath given
> His title—death at last gave heaven."

He was interred, when dead, in the church of St. Cicily, which intituled him when alive; though no happiness, an honour which no other Englishman (to my observation) of his order ever enjoyed.

PRELATES.

[S. N.] JOHN BRETON, alias BRITTON, Doctor of the Laws.—He meriteth a high place in this catalogue; and yet I am at a perfect loss where to fix his nativity, and therefore am forced to my last refuge, as the marginal character doth confess.

He was a famous lawyer, living in the reign of king Edward the First; at whose commandment, and by whose authority he wrote a learned book of "The Laws of England," the tenor whereof runneth in the king's name, as if it had been penned by himself. Take one instance thereof:

"Chapter XII. We will, that all those who are fourteen years old, shall make oath that they shall be sufficient and loyal unto us, and that they will be neither felons, nor assenting to felons: and We will that all be," &c.

This style will seem nothing strange to those who have read Justinian's " Institutions," which the Emperor assumed unto himself, though composed by others.

It is no small argument of the excellency of this book, that, notwithstanding the great variation of our laws since his time, his work still is in great and general repute. Thus a good face conquereth the disadvantage of old and unfashionable clothes. He was preferred bishop of Hereford in the reign of king Henry the Third. And although there be some difference betwixt authors about the time wherein he lived and died (some assign a later date), I confide in Bishop Godwin * (his successor in the same see) computing his death to happen May 12, in the third of king Edward the First, anno 1275.

ADAM de ORLTON was born in the city of Hereford. Proceeding doctor of law, he became afterwards bishop in the place of his nativity.† This is he so infamous in history for cutting off the life of king Edward the Second with his riddling unpointed answer: " Edwardum regem occidere nolite timere bonum est;" (to kill king Edward you need not to fear it is good.)

It is hard to say, which of these two were the original, and which the translation; it being equally probable that the English was Latined, as that the Latin was Englished, by such authors as relate this transaction.

This mindeth me of a meaner passage " Sic canibus catulos," which, to refresh both the reader and myself, I shall here insert.

A schoolmaster, being shut out of his school at Christmas, came to composition with his scholars, and thus subscribed the articles tendered unto him:

> Æqua est conditio non nego quod petitis.

But, being re-admitted into his house, he called all his scholars to account for their rebellion. They plead themselves secured by the act of oblivion he had signed. He calls for the original; and perusing it, thus pointed it:

> Æqua est conditio? non: nego quod petitis.

Thus power, in all ages, will take the privilege to construe its own acts to its own advantage.

But to return to De Orlton; he made much bustling in the land, passing through the bishoprics of Worcester and Winchester: and died at last, not much lamented, July 18, 1345.

JOHN GRANDESSON was born at Ashperton in this county;‡ a person remarkable on several accounts: 1. For his *High*

---

* In his Catalogue of the Bishops of Hereford.
† Godwin, in his Catalogue of Bishops.
‡ Idem, in his Catalogue of the Bishops of Exeter.

Birth; his father Gilbert being a baron, and his mother Sybill co-heir to the Lord Tregose. 2. *Great Learning;* being a good writer of that age, though Bale saith of him that he was " orator animosior quàm facundior." 3. *High Preferment;* attaining to be bishop of Exeter. 4. *Vivacity;* sitting bishop of his see two and forty years. 5. *Stout Stomach;* resisting Mepham archbishop of Canterbury, *vi et armis,* when he came to visit his diocese. 6. *Costly Buildings;* arching the beautiful roof of his cathedral; building and endowing a rich college of Saint Mary Ottery.

He was the better enabled to do these and other great bene-factions by persuading all the secular clergy in his diocese to make him sole heir to their estates. He died July 15, anno Domini 1369.

THOMAS BRADWARDINE, archbishop of Canterbury. (See him more properly in SUSSEX.)

RICHARD CLIFFORD bishop of London. (See him more conveniently in KENT.)

SINCE THE REFORMATION.

MILES SMITH, D.D. was born in the city of Hereford; * which I observe the rather, because omitted in his funeral sermon. His father was a fletcher, and a man of no mean estate, that vocation being more in use formerly than in our age. He was bred first in Brazennose College, then chaplain of Christ Church in Oxford. A deep divine, great linguist, who had more than a single share in the last translation of the Bible, as hereby will appear: 1. More than forty grave divines † were employed in several places on that work. 2. When it had passed their hands, it was revised by a dozen select ones. 3. This done, it was referred to the final examination of Bishop Bilston and Dr. Smith. 4. Doctor Smith at last was enjoined to make the preface to the translation, as a comely gate to a glorious city, which remains under his own hand in the University library in Oxford.

Yet was he never heard to speak of the work with any attribution to himself more than the rest.

He never sought any preferment he had; and was wont merrily to say of himself, that he was "nullius rei præterquam librorum avarus," (covetous of nothing but books.‡) King James preferred him bishop of Gloucester 1612, wherein he behaved himself with such meekness, that, in all matters of doubt, the bias of his inclination did still hang πρὸς τὸ φιλάνθρωπον. He wrote all his books with his own hand (in that faculty not being

---

* So Master Stephens, his secretary, informed me.—F.
† See their names in our " Church History."—F.
‡ See the preface of his works, written by Mr. Stephens.

short of the professors thereof); and, being seventy years of age, died and was buried in his own cathedral, 1624.

SOLDIERS.

ROBERT DEVEREUX, son of Walter Devereux earl of Essex, was born at Nethwood in this county, * November the 10th, 1567, whilst his father as yet was only Viscount of Hereford.

He was such a master-piece of court and camp, and so bright a light therein, that we will observe his morning, forenoon, high-noon, afternoon, and night.

His *morning* began at his first coming to court, the gates whereof he entered with four great advantages, of pity, kindred, favour, and merit : pity, on the account of his father lately dead (to say no more) and generally lamented ; kindred, on his mo-ther's side, Lettice Knowles, near allied to the queen ; favour, being son-in-law to Leicester, and so was a favourite's favourite at the first day, though he quickly stood on his own legs with-out holding ; merit, being of a beautiful personage, courteous nature, noble descent, fair (though much impaired) fortune.

Fore-noon : when the queen favourably reflected on him, as a grandmother on a grandchild, making him the wanton to her fond and indulgent affection, as by this letter, written with her own hand, doth appear :

     " ESSEX,

" Your sudden and undutiful departure from our presence, and your place of attendance, you may easily conceive how offen-sive it is, and ought to be, unto us. Our great favours bestowed upon you without deserts, hath drawn you thus to neglect and forget your duty ; for other construction we cannot make of these your strange actions. Not meaning therefore to tolerate this your disordered part, we gave directions to some of our privy councel to let you know our express pleasure for your im-mediate repair hither, which you have not performed as your duty doth bind you, increasing thereby greatly your former of-fence and undutiful behaviour, in departing in such sort with-out our privity, having so special office of attendance and charge near our person. We do therefore charge and command you, forthwith upon the receit of these our letters, all excuses and delayes set apart, to make your present and immediate repair unto us, to understand our further pleasure. Whereof see you fail not, as you will be loth to incur our indignation, and will answer for the contrary at your uttermost peril. The 15th of April, 1589."

This letter, angry in the first, and loving in the fourth degree, was written to him (sent by Sir Thomas Gorges) on this occa-sion. The earl, in pursuance of his own martial inclination, secretly left the court, to see some service in France. The

* Thomas Mills, in his Catalogue of Honours, p. 863.

queen, passionately loving his person, grievously complained of his absence, and often said, "We shall have this young fellow knockt on the head, as foolish Sidney was, by his own forwardness;" and was restless till his return.

I behold him in his *high-noon*, when he brought victory with him home from Cadiz, and was vertical in the esteem of the soldiery, and may be said to awaken the queen's jealousy by his popularity.

His *afternoon* followed; when he undertook the Irish action, too knotty service for his smooth disposition, being fitter for personal performance, than conduct and managing of martial affairs. And now his enemies' work was half done, having gotten such a gulf betwixt him and the queen; for, as Antæus is said to have recruited strength, when he touched his mother earth; so this earl, wrestling with his enemies, suppressed them, and supported himself, by his daily access to the queen, which distance now denied him.

His *night* approached; when, coming over without leave, he was confined by the queen to his house, to reclaim not ruin him. Hither a miscellaneous crew of swordsmen did crowd, tendering him their service, some of one persuasion, some of another, some of all, some of no religion. Their specious pretence was, to take evil counsellors from the queen, though it had been happy if they had been first taken away from the earl. What his company said they would do, the earl knew; but what would have been done by them, God knows. The earl rising, and missing of expected support from the city of London, quickly sunk in the queen's final displeasure, anno Domini 1600.

He was valiant, liberal to scholars and soldiers, nothing distrustful, if not too confident of fidelity in others. Revengefulness was not bred, but put into his disposition. 'Tis hard to say, whether such as were his enemies, or such as should be his friends, did him more mischief. When one flattered him to his face for his valour, "No," said he, "my sins ever made me a coward." In a word, his failings were neither so foul nor so many, but that the character of a right worthy man most justly belongs to his memory.

WRITERS.

ROGER of HEREFORD, born in that city, was bred in the university of Cambridge, being one of the prime promoters of learning therein after the re-foundation of the university by the abbot of Crowland.* He was an excellent astronomer; and, stars being made for signs, was a good interpreter what by these signs were intended. He wrote a book "Of Judicial Astrology;" whether to commend or condemn it, such only can sa-

---

* Bale, de Scriptoribus Britannicis, Cent. iii. num. 13. anno 1170.

tisfy themselves that have seen his book. He was also skilful
in all metals and minerals; and his pretty curiosities made him
acceptable to the nobility of England; flourishing under king
Henry the Second, anno Domini 1170.

WILLIAM LEMPSTER, a Franciscan, and a doctor of divinity
in Oxford, was born in that well-known town in this county.
He wrote "Collations on the Master of the Sentences, and
Questions in Divinity," as J. Pits informeth me,* adding withal,

> *Hæc scripsit, novi, sed non quo tempore novi.*

> "Well I know these works he wrot;
> But for the time I know it not."

And I am content (for company's sake) with him to be ignorant
of the exact date thereof.

SINCE THE REFORMATION.

RICHARD HACKLUIT was born of an ancient extract in this
county, whose family hath flourished at . . . . . . in good esteem.
He was bred a student in Christ Church in Oxford, and after
was prebendary of Westminster. His genius inclined him to
the study of history, and especially to the marine part thereof,
which made him keep constant intelligence with the most noted
seamen of Wapping, until the day of his death.

He set forth a large collection of the English sea voyages,
ancient, middle, modern; taken partly out of private letters
which never were, or without his had not been, printed; partly
out of small treatises, printed, and since irrecoverably lost,
had not his providence preserved them. For some pamphlets
are produced, which for their cheapness and smallness men
for the present neglect to buy, presuming they may procure
them at their pleasure; which small books, their first and last
edition being past (like some spirits that appear but once)
cannot afterwards with any price or pains be recovered. In
a word, many of such useful tracts of sea adventures, which
before were scattered as several ships, Mr. Hackluit hath
embodied into a fleet, divided into three squadrons, so many
several volumes: a work of great honour to England; it being
possible that many ports and islands in America, which, being base and barren, bear only a bare name for the present,
may prove rich places for the future. And then these voyages will be produced, and pleaded, as good evidence of
their belonging to England, as first discovered and denominated by Englishmen. Mr. Hackluit died in the beginning of
king James's reign, leaving a fair estate to an unthrift son,
who embezzled it on this token, that he vaunted, "that he
cheated the covetous usurer, who had given him spick and span
new money, for the old land of his great great grandfather.

JOHN GWILLIM was of Welch extraction, but born in this

* In Appendice Angliæ Scriptorum.

county;* and became a pursuivant of arms, by the name first of Portsmouth, then Rougecroix, but most eminent for his methodical "Display of Heraldry" (confusion being formerly the greatest difficulty therein); shewing himself a good logician in his exact divisions; and no bad philosopher, noting the natures of all creatures given in arms, joining fancy and reason therein. Besides his travelling all over the earth in beasts, his industry diggeth into the ground in pursuit of the properties of precious stones, diveth into the water in quest of the qualities of fishes, flieth into the air after the nature of birds, yea mounteth to the very skies about stars (but here we must call them estoiles) and planets, their use and influence. In a word, he hath unmysteried the mystery of heraldry, insomuch that one of his own faculty† thus descanteth (in the twilight of jest and earnest) on his performance:

"But let me tell you, this will be the harm—
 In arming others you yourself disarm;
 Our art is now anatomized so,
 As who knows not what we ourselves do know?
 Our corn in others' mill is ill apaid:
 'Sic vos non vobis,' may to us be said."

I suspect that his endeavours met not with proportionable reward. He died about the latter end of the reign of king James.

JOHN DAVIES of Hereford (for so he constantly styled himself) was the greatest master of the pen that England in his age beheld; for, 1. *Fast-writing;* so incredible his expedition. 2. *Fair-writing;* some minutes consultation being required to decide, whether his lines were written or printed. 3. *Close-writing;* a mystery indeed, and too dark for my dim eyes to discover. 4. *Various writing;* Secretary, Roman, Court, and Text.

The poetical fiction of Briareus the giant, who had a hundred hands, found a moral in him, who could so cunningly and copiously disguise his aforesaid elemental hands, that by mixing he could make them appear a hundred, and if not so many sorts, so many degrees of writing. Yet, had he lived longer, he would modestly have acknowledged Mr. Githings (who was his scholar, and also born in this county) to excel him in that faculty; whilst the other would own no such odious eminency, but rather gratefully return the credit to his master again.‡ Sure I am, when two such transcendant penmasters shall again come to be born in the same shire, they may even serve fairly to engross the will and testament of the expiring universe. Our Davies had also some pretty excursions into poetry, and could flourish matter as well as letters, with his fancy as well as with

---

* See J. Davis of Hereford challenging him for his countryman, in his verses on his Display of Heraldry.—F.
† Sir William Segar, in his verses before his book.
‡ So informed by Master Cox, Draper in London, his executor.—F.

his pen. He died at London, in the midst of the reign of king James; and lieth buried in St. Giles in the Fields.

ROMISH EXILE WRITERS.

HUMPHRY ELY, born in this county,* was bred in St. John's College in Oxford; whence flying beyond the seas, he lived successively at Douay, Rome, and Rheims, till at last he settled himself at Pont-muss in Lorraine, where, for twenty years together, he was professor of canon and civil law; and, dying 1604, was buried therein with a double epitaph.

That in verse my judgment commands me not to believe; which here I will take the boldness to translate:

> *Albion hæreseos velatur nocte, Viator,*
> *Desine mirari; Sol suus hic latitat.*

> "Wonder not, reader, that with heresies
> England is clouded; here her Sun he lies."

The prose-part my charity induces me to credit; "Inopiâ fermè laborabat, alios inopiâ sublevans;" (he eased others of poverty, being himself almost pinched therewith.)

BENEFACTORS TO THE PUBLIC.

JOHN WALTER was born in the city of Hereford. Know, reader, I could learn little from the minister† who preached his funeral, less from his acquaintance, least from his children. Such his hatred of vain-glory, that (as if charity were guiltiness) he cleared himself from all suspicion thereof. Yet is our intelligence of him, though brief, true, as followeth:

He was bred in London, and became clerk of Draper's-hall. Finding the world to flow fast in upon him, he made a solemn vow to God, that he would give the surplusage of his estate (whatever it was) to pious uses.‡ Nor was he like to those who at first maintained ten thousand pounds too much for any man; which when they have attained they then conceive ten times so much too little for themselves: but, after his cup was filled brim-full to the aforesaid proportion, he conscientiously gave every drop of that which overflowed, to quench the thirst of people parched with poverty.

I compare him to Elizabeth in the Gospel, who, as if "ashamed of her shame" (so then reputed) taken from her, "hid herself five months"§ (so great her modesty). Such his concealing of his charity, though pregnant with good works; and had not the lanthorn of his body been lately broken, it is believed the light of his bounty had not yet been discovered. He built and endowed a fair alms-house in Southwark, another at Newington (both in Surrey), on which, and other pious uses, he

---

* Pits, ætate xvii. numero 1053.
† Mr. Richard Henchman, of St. Mary Bothaw.
‡ Above ten thousand pounds.   § Luke i. 24.

expended well nigh ten thousand pounds, whereof twenty pounds per annum he gave to Hereford, the place of his nativity.

His wife and surviving daughters, so far from grudging at his gifts, and accounting that lost to them which was lent to God, that they much rejoiced thereat, and deserve to be esteemed joint-givers thereof, because consenting so freely to his charity. He died in the seventy-fourth year of his age, 29th December, anno Domini 1656; and was solemnly buried in London.

MEMORABLE PERSONS.

ROSAMUND, that is, saith my author,[*] Rosemouth (but by allusion termed Rose of the World) was remarkable on many accounts. First, for her father, Walter lord Clifford, who had large lands about Clifford's Castle in this county. Secondly, for herself, being the mistress-piece of beauty in that age. Thirdly, for her paramour, king Henry the Second, to whom she was concubine. Lastly, for her son, William Longspee, the worthy earl of Salisbury.

King Henry is said to have built a labyrinth at Woodstock (which labyrinth through length of time hath lost itself) to hide this his mistress from his jealous Juno, queen Eleanor. But *Zelotypiæ nihil impervium.* By some device she got access unto her, and caused her death.

Rosamund was buried in a little nunnery at Godstowe nigh Oxford, with this epitaph:

> *Hic jacet in tumbâ Rosa mundi, non Rosamunda;*
> *Non redolet, sed olet, quæ redolere solet.*

"This tomb doth inclose the world's fair rose, so sweet and full of favour; And smell she doth now, but you may guess how, none of the sweetest savour."

Her corpse may be said to have done penances after her death: for Hugh bishop of Lincoln, coming as a visitor to this nunnery, and seeing Rosamund's body lying in the choir, under a silken hearse, with tapers continually burning about it, thought the hearse of an harlot no proper object for eyes of virgins to contemplate on; therefore caused her bones to be scattered abroad. However, after his departure, those sisters gathered her bones together again, put them into a perfumed bag, and enclosed them in lead, where they continued until ousted again in the reign of king Henry the Eighth.

THE NAMES OF THE GENTRY OF THIS COUNTY,

RETURNED BY THE COMMISSIONERS IN THE TWELFTH YEAR OF KING HENRY THE SIXTH, ANNO 1433.

Thomas bishop of Hereford, and James de Audley;—John Skudamore, chevalier, and John Russell, (knights for the shire);— Commissioners for taking the oaths.

[*] Verstegan, Decayed Intelligence, p. 269.

Dom. Grey de Whilton, chev.
Walteri Lucy, chev.
Radulphi de la Bere, chev.
Roberti Whiteney, chev.
Johannis Baskervile, chev.
Johannis Merbury, arm.
Richardi de la Mare, arm.
Thomæ Bromwich, sen. arm.
Johannis Brugge, arm.
Thomæ Bromwich, jun. arm.
Johannis Melborn, arm.
Johannis Barre, arm.
Thomæ Donton, arm.
Hugonis Mortimer, arm.
Thomæ de Lastay, sen. arm.
Johannis Skudamore, arm.
Richardi Wigmore, arm.
Willielmi Croft, arm.
Walteri Hackluit, arm.
Willielmi Criketot, arm.
Ric. Walwain de Mayde, arm.
Maculmi Walwain, arm.
W. Walwain de Longford, arm.
Nicholai Wallwayn, arm.
Tho. Walwain de Stoke, arm.
R. Walweyn de Lugwardyn, arm.
Willielmi Byriton, arm.
Johannis Stapelton, arm.
Willielmi Hereford, arm.
Richardi Habberhale, arm.
Johannis Aberhale, arm.
Johannis Deverose, arm.
Richardi Deverose, arm.
Johannis de la Bere, arm.
Willielmi de la Bere, arm.
Rogeri Bodenham, arm.
Milonis Watier, arm.
Radulphi Baskervile, arm.
Thomæ de la Hay, jun. arm.
Rowlandi Lenthall, chev.
Henrici Oldcastle, arm.
Henrici Slake, arm.
Richardi ap Harry, arm.
Johannis Dansey, arm.
Henrici ap Griffith, arm.
Rogeri Wiggemore, arm.
Hugonis Moynington, arm.
Johannis Monyngton, arm.
Walteri Monington, arm.
Johannis Wise, arm.

Walt. ap Rosser Vaughan, arm.
Johannis Dumbleton, arm.
Thomæ Parker, arm.
Johannis Skellwick, arm.
Johannis Harper.
Willielmi Garnons.
Thomæ Brugge de Leye.
Thomæ Brugge de Brugge.
Thomæ Smith de Webley.
Edmundi Gomond.
Johannis Alton.
Johannis Wellynton.
Roberti Hunte, arm.
Roberti Bromwich.
Willielmi Bromwich.
R. Watteis de Bedingwey.
Richardi Leon.
Johannis Goure.
Willielmi Smethecote.
Willielmi Hackluit.
Hugonis Hackluit.
Jacobi Everard.
Thomæ Brugge de Yuenton.
Richardi Upton.
Johannis Upton.
Rogeri Erlyche.
Johannis de Ey.
Egidii Hackluit.
Thomæ Halle.
Hugonis Warton.
Johannis Bluwet.
Johannis Luntelye.
Philipi Lyngeyn.
Johannis Bevere.
Walteri Bradford.
Johannis Bradford.
Walteri Walker.
Thomæ Morton.
Johannis Salisbury.
Johannis Walker.
Willielmi Rafes.
Johannis Sherer.
Johannis Waldboet.
Richardi Windesley.
Joh. Mortimer de Bromyerd.
Thomæ Harlowe.
Johannis Ragon.
Johannis Broun.
Johannis Smith.
Thomæ Dovile.

Johannis Panton, jun.
Thomæ Petit.
Thomæ Horsenet.
Richardi Wynne.
Johannis Winter.
Thomæ Loveday.
Johannis Sheref.
Thomæ Everard.
Johannis Young.
Thomæ Tomkins.
Willielmi Shebrond.
Will. Waleyn de Bickerton.
Milonis Skulle.
Rogeri Admonsham.
Roberti Priour.
Johannis Watts.
Richardi Rovenhal.
Johannis Comyn.
Richardi Gambdon.
Henrici Comyn.
Willielmi Blanchard.
Willielmi Moynington.
Johannis Arundell.
Thomæ Arundell.
Thomæ Myntrick.
Willielmi Gray.
Johannis Brugge de Rosse.
Henrici White.
Richardi Coekes.
Johannis Wollrich.
Johannis de Wall.
Willielmi Lanke.
Will. ap Thomæ ap L.
Willielmi Gerrard.
Richardi Trevays.
Hugonis Cola.
Richardi de la Hay.
Hugonis Hergest.
Johannis Pu.
Walteri Puy.
Willielmi Huntington.
Willielmi Carwardine.

Johannis Chabenore.
Will. Smith de Tiberton.
Willielmi Chamberleyn.
Howel ap Howel ap Wil-
    miston.
Johannis Wiston.
Joh. Hunt de Snodhell.
Thomæ Lightfoot.
Joh. ap Thom. de Dorston.
Galfredi ap Thomas.
Johannis Pychard.
Thomæ Bruyn.
Georgii Braynton, Majoris Ci-
    vitatis Hereford.
Walteri Mibbe.
Henrici Chippenham.
Johannis Fulk, draper.
Johannis Mey.
Johannis Fuister.
Thomæ Hore.
Johannis Green.
Richardi Green.
Richardi Prat.
Thomæ Bradwardyn.
Richardi Russell.
Richardi Barbour.
Johannis Orchard.
Jacobi Orchard.
Johannis Dudley.
Richardi Houghton.
Rogeri Collyng.
Johannis Collier.
Thomæ Choppynham.
Henrici Cachepolle.
Thomæ Knobelle.
Hugonis Clerk.
Thomæ Combe.
Thomæ Verbum.
Johannis Elynner.
Joh. Heyward de Bodenham.
Rob. Wych de Ludwardyn.

SHERIFFS.

Anno.   HENRY II.
1
2 Walt. de Hereford, for
    five years.

Anno
7 Will. de Bello Campo,
    for nine years.
16 Idem, et Walt. Clicums.

Anno

17 Willielmus de la Lega.
18 Gilbertus Pypard.
19 Idem.
20 Willielmus de Braiose.
21 Idem.
22 Radulphus Pulcherus, for seven years.
29 Milo de Mucegros, et Willielmus Torelle.
30 Willielmus Torelle.
31 Radul. Arden.
32 Idem.
33 Idem.

RICH. I.

1 Radul. de Arden.
2 Hen. de longo Campo.
3 Willielmus de Braiosa.
4 Idem.
5 Hen. de longo Campo, et Willielmus de Braiosa.
6 Roger. Fitz-Mauricis.
7 Willielmus de Braiosa.
8 Idem.
9 Willielmus de Braiosa, et Willielmus de Burchhull.
10 Idem.

JOHAN.

1 Walter. de Clifford, et Gilbertus Clifford.
2 Willielmus de Braiosa, et Willielmus Burchull.
3 Hubert. de Burgo, et Rich. de Signes, for three years.
6 Willielmus de Cantulum, et Walter. de Puhier.
7 Idem.
8 Walt. de Clifford, et Osbert. fil. Willielmi.
9 Idem.
10 Gerer. de Atria, et Rich. de Burges.
11 Idem.
12 Endebard. de Cicomato, et Rich. de Burges.

Anno

13 Enozelcardus, de Cicomato, et Rich. Burgeis sive Burzeis, for four years.

HENR. III.

1 Walt. de Lascy, et
2 Tho. de Anesey.
3 Walt. de Lascy, et Warrinus de Grindon, for three years.
6 Walt. de Lascy, et Tho. de Anesey.
7 Walt. de Lascy.
8 Radulph. filius Nic. et Hen. filius Nic. frater ejus, for three years.
11 Radul. filius Nich. et Hen. frater ejus, et Jo. de East, for three years.
14 Joan. de Fleg.
15 Idem.
16 Johan. de Munemus.
17 Williel. filius Warrini.
18 Idem.
19 Amaricus de S'to Aman.
20 Amari. de S'to Amando, et Ricard. de Fardingston.
21 Idem.
22 Amari. de S'to Amando, et Matth. de Coddray, for three years.
25 Amaricus de Cancell, for seven years.
32 Waleranus.
33 Waleranus de Bradlegh.
34 Hugo de Kinardell.
35 Hen. de Bradlegh.
36 Idem.
37 Williel. de S'to Omero.
38 Idem.
39 Joan. de Brekon (sive Brecon) for three years.
42 Hen. de Penebrige.
43 Idem, et Ric. de Baggindin.
44 Robertus de Meysy.

Anno

45 Idem.
46 Robertus de Meysy, et
Adam. de Bideford, for
seven years.
53 Barthol. de Buly, et
Adam. de Botiler, for three
years.

EDW. I.

1 Barthol. de Stutely, et
Adam de Botiler.
2 Idem.
3 Joan. de Ware.
4 Egid. de Berkel, for three
years.
7 Roger. de Barghall.
8 Idem.
9 Rog. de Burghall, for ten
years.
19 Hen. de Solers, for three
years.
22 Johan. de Acton, for six
years.
28 Milo Picard, for six years.
34 Johan. de Acton.
35 Tho. Rossal.

EDW. II.

1 Walt. de Halits, for four
years.
5 Rog. de Chandos, for three
years.
8 Richard. de Baskervil.
9 Idem.
10 Hugo Hackluit.
11 Idem.
12 Roger. de Elmerugge.
13 Idem.
14 Roger. Chandos, for five
years.

Anno

EDW. III.

1 Roger. de Chandos, for
five years.
6 Johannes de Rous.
7 Idem.
8 Johan. Mauger,
Robert. Chandos, et
Jo. le Rous.
9 Idem.
10 Rich. Walwayn, for seven
years.
17 Johan. Walwayn.
18 Williel. de Radour, for
three years.
21 Tho. Pichard.
22 Joha. Scholle, et
Tho. Pichard.
23 Rich. Dansy, et
Johan. Sholle.
24 Rich. Dansy.
25 Tho. de Aston.
26 Rich. de Burges.
27 Idem.
28 Rich. Bregg.
29 Rich. de la Bere.
30 Tho. Atte Barre, et
Ric. de la Bere.
31 Ed. Hacklut, for three
years.
34 Thomas Chandois.
35 Ric. de la Bere, for ten
years.
45 Tho. Chandois.
46 Will. Devereux de Rod.
47 Tho. Chandois.
48 Idem.
49 Edw. de Burges.
50 Walter. Devereux, et
Tho. de la Bere.
51 Idem.

This county had sheriffs long before king Henry the Second,
as may appear by the direction of this writ, in the first of king
Henry the First.

"Henricus, Dei gratiâ Rex Angliæ, Hugoni de Boclande Vice-
comiti, et omnibus fidelibus suis, tam Francis quàm Anglicis,
in Herefordshire, salutem, &c."*

* Matthew Paris, anno Domini 1100

But such the uncertainty of their succession, it will be very well if we can continue our catalogue from the general era in other counties.

EDWARD II.

8. RICHARDUS de BASKERVIL.—This name is of great antiquity in these parts, whose ancestors immediately after the Conquest were benefactors to the abbey of Saint Peter's in Gloucester, as by the ensuing will appear :*

1. "Bernardus de Baskervile, cum semetipso, quando habitum monachi suscepit, dedit Ecclesiæ sancti Petri Glouc. unam hidam terræ in Cumbâ. Walterus et Robertus de Baskervile confirmant tempore Homelini Abbatis."

2. "Anno Domini 1109, Robertus de Baskervillâ, de Jerusalem† reversus, dedit Ecclesiæ Sancti Petri Glouc. unam hidam extra muros quidem Civitatis, ubi est nunc Hortus Monachorum, Rege Henrico confirmante, tempore Petri Abbatis."

As these came out of Normandy from a town so named, so are they extant at this day in this county; and have formerly been famous and fortunate for their military achievements.

SHERIFFS OF HEREFORDSHIRE.

RICH. II.

Anno	Name and Arms.	Place.
1	Rob. Whitney, arm.	Whitney.
	Az. a cross checky O. and G.	
2	Sim. de Brugge.	
	Arg. on a cross S. a leopard's head O.	
3	Joh. Walwayne.	
	G. a bend within a border Erm.	
4	Hugo Carew.	
	O. three lions passant gardant S.	
5	Sim. de Brugge . . . *ut prius.*	
6	Joh. Walwayne . . . *ut prius.*	
7	Rog. Pauncefort.	
	G. three lions rampant Arg.	
8	Tho. de la Barre . . . Kinnersley.	
	Az. a bend Arg. cotised O. betwixt six martlets of the same.	
9	Nic. Maurdin.	
10	Tho. Oldcastle.	
	Arg. a tower triple towered S.	
11	Rinardus, sive Kinardus, de la Bere.	
12	Tho. de la Barre . . . *ut prius.*	
13	Tho. Walwayn . . . *ut prius.*	
14	Hu. de Monington.	
	Arg. a chevron betwixt three unicorns S.	

* Monasticon Anglicanum, p. 113.   † Idem, p. 115.

Anno   Name.   Place.

15 Tho. Oldcastle . . . *ut prius.*
16 Mascre. de la Ma.
17 Tho. Walwayne . . . *ut prius.*
18 Joh. Walwayne . . . *ut prius.*
19 Tho. de la Barre . . . *ut prius.*
20 Idem . . . . . . *ut prius.*
21 Tho. Clanowe.
22 Idem.

HENRY IV.

1 Joh. ap Harry.
2 Will. Lucy, mil.
    G. crusulé O. three pikes hauriant Arg.
   Leon. Haklut, mil. . .   Yetton.
    G. three battle-axes O.
3 Joh. Bodenham.
    Az. a fess betwixt three chess-rooks O.
4 Idem . . . . . . *ut prius.*
5 Idem . . . . . . *ut prius.*
6 Joh. Merbury.
7 Joh. Oldcastle, mil. . . *ut prius.*
8
9 Joh. Skudamore, mil. . Holm Lacy.
10 Joh. Smert.
    G. three stirrups leathered and buckled O.
11 Joh. Bodenham . . . *ut prius.*
12 Will. Walwein . . . *ut prius.*

HENRY V.

1 Robert Whitney. . . *ut prius.*
2 Johan. Merbury.
3 Johan. Bodenham . . *ut prius.*
4 Johan. Brugge . . . *ut prius.*
5 Johan. Russel.
    Arg. a chevron betwixt three crosses crosslet fitchée S.
6 Thom. Holgot.
7 Johan. Merbury.
8 Rich. de la Bere.
9 Idem.

HENRY VI.

1 Rich. de la Mare.
2 Row. Lenthal.
    S. a bend lozengée Arg.
3 Guid. Whittington . . Hampton.
    G. a fess checky O. and Az.
4 Johan. Merbury.
5 T. de la Hay, jun.

Anno	Name.	Place.

6 Ro. Whitney, mil.

7 Ric. de la Mare . . . *ut prius.*

8 Joh. Merbury.

9 Joh. Skudemore, mil. . *ut prius.*

10

11 R. Whitney, mil.

12 T. de la Hay . . . . *ut prius.*

13 Tho. Merbury.

14 Tho. Mille.

15 Rob. Whitney . . . . *ut prius.*

16 J. Pauncefoote . . . *ut prius.*

17 Waltery Skull.

     Arg. a bend . . . . betwixt six lions' heads erased of the field.

18 Ric. Walwin . . . . *ut prius.*

19 Will. Lucy . . . . *ut prius.*

20 Idem . . . . . . *ut prius.*

21 Hen. Charleton . . . *ut prius.*

22 Tho. Parker.

23 Rad. Walwain . . . *ut prius.*

24 Tho. Mille.

25 Hum. Stafford.

     O. a chevron G. a quarter Erm.

26 Walter. Devereux . . Webley.

     Arg. a fess G. ; in chief three torteaux.

27 Walt. Skull, mil. . . *ut prius.*

28 Joh. Skudemore . . . *ut prius.*

29 Joh. Berry, mil.

30 Tho. Parker, arm.

31 Tho. Cornwayl.

     Erm. a lion rampant G. crowned O. within a border engrailed S. bezantée.

32 Will. Lucy, arm. . . *ut prius.*

33 Jo. Barry, mil.

34 Walt. Skul, mil. . . . *ut prius.*

35 Jo. Skudamore, mil. . *ut prius.*

36 Joh. Seymor, mil.

     G two angels' wings pale-ways inverted O.

37 W. Catesby, mil.

     Arg. two lions passant S. couronné O.

38 Jam. Baskervill . . . Erdssey.

     Arg. a chevron G. betwixt three heurts proper.

EDWARD IV.

1 Joh. Welford.

2 Tho. Monington . . . *ut prius.*

3 Idem . . . . . . *ut prius.*

4 Sim. Melburn, arm.

Anno   Name.   Place.

5 Joh. Baskervill, mil. . *ut prius.*
6 Joh. Lingein, arm.
    Barry of six, O. and Az. on a bend G. three cinquefoils Arg.
7 Tho. Cornwall, arm. . *ut prius.*
8 Wal. Wigmore.
    Arg. three greyhounds in pale currant S. collared G.
9 W. Baskervil, mil. . . *ut prius.*
10 Ric. Croft, sen., arm. . Croft Castle.
    Quarterly, per fess indented Az. and Arg.; in the first quarter a lion passant O.
11 Ric. Croft, sen., mil. . *ut prius.*
12 Joh. Lingein, mil. . . *ut prius.*
13 Tho. Monington . . . *ut prius.*
14 Jam. Baskervil, mil. . *ut prius.*
15 Rob. Whitney . . . *ut prius.*
16 Rich. Crofts, mil. . . *ut prius.*
17 Radulph. Hacluit . . *ut prius.*
18 J. Mortimer, mil.
    Barry of six O. and Az.; on a chief of the first three pallets inter two esquires dexter and sinister of the second, an inescutcheon Arg.
19 R. de la Bere, mil.
20 Simon Melborne.
21 Ja. Baskervil, mil. . . *ut prius.*
22 Johan. Mortimer . . *ut prius.*

RICHARD III.

1 Rich. de la Bere, mil.
2 Tho. Cornwal, mil. . . *ut prius.*
3 Rich. Crofts, mil. . . *ut prius.*

HENRY VII.

1 Johan. Mortimer . *ut prius.*
2 Johann. Lingeyn . . *ut prius.*
3 Roger. Bodenham . . *ut prius.*
4 Henr. Skudamore . . *ut prius.*
5 Joh. Devereux, mil. . *ut prius.*
6 Tho. Monington . . *ut prius.*
7 Rich. Greenway.
8 Ric. de la Bere, mil.
9 Jo. Mortimer, mil. . *ut prius.*
10 Edw. Blunt, arm.
    Barry nebulé of six O. and S.
11 Joh. Lingein, mil. . . *ut prius.*
12 Hen. Harper, arm.
    A. lion rampant within a border engrailed S.

Anno	Name.	Place.
13	Joh. Lingein, arm. . .	*ut prius.*
14	Rich. Greenway . . .	*ut prius.*
15	Hen. Mile, arm.	
16	Rich. Miners, arm.	
17	Joh. Mortimer, mil. . .	*ut prius.*
18	T. Cornwaile, mil. . .	*ut prius.*
19	Idem	*ut prius.*
20	Edw. Croft, arm. . .	*ut prius.*
21	J. Lingein, jun. mil. .	*ut prius.*
22	R. Cornwaile, arm. . .	*ut prius.*
23	Rad. Hackluit, arm. .	*ut prius.*
24	Hen. Mile, arm.	

HEN. VIII.

1	Edw. Croft, arm. . .	*ut prius.*
2	Rich. de la Bere, arm. .	*ut prius.*
3	Th. Monington, arm. .	*ut prius.*
4	Hen. Mile, arm.	
5	Edw. Croft, mil. . . .	*ut prius.*
6	Th. Cornwaile, mil. . .	*ut prius.*
7	Will. Herbert, mil.	

Partie per pale Az. and G. three lions rampant Arg.

8	Joh. Lingein, mil. . .	*ut prius.*
9	Edw. Croft, mil. . . .	*ut prius.*
10	Rad. Hackluit . . .	*ut prius.*
11	Rich. Cornwail . . .	*ut prius.*
12	Joh. Lingein, mil. . .	*ut prius.*
13	Edw. Croft, mil. . . .	*ut prius.*
14	Row. Morton.	

Quarterly G. and Erm.; in the first and fourth a goat's head erased Arg.

15	Jaco. Baskervile . . .	*ut prius.*
16	Jo. Skudemore, arm. .	*ut prius.*
17	Hen. Vain, arm. . .	KENT.

Az. three left-hand gauntlets O.

18	Rich. Cornwail . . .	*ut prius.*
19	Tho. Baskervil, arm. .	*ut prius.*
20	Tho. Lingein, mil. . .	*ut prius.*
21	Edw. Croft, mil. . . .	*ut prius.*
22	Ri. Vaughan, mil.	
23	Ric. Walwein, arm. . .	*ut prius.*
24	T. Monington, arm. .	*ut prius.*
25	Edw. Croft, mil. . .	*ut prius.*
26	Mic. Lister, arm.	
27	Will. Clinton, arm. et Tho. Clinton, arm.	
28	Joh. Skudamor, arm. .	*ut prius.*

Anno	Name.	Place.

29 Joh. Blount, arm. . . *ut prius.*
30 J. Packington, arm.
    Per chevron S. and Arg.; in chief three mullets O. in base as many garbs G.
31 Mich. Lister, arm.
32 Tho. Monington . . *ut prius.*
33 Rich. Vaughan.
34 Jac. Baskervil, mil. . *ut prius.*
35 Joh. Skudamore . . *ut prius.*
36 Joh. Leingein, arm. . *ut prius.*
37 Step. ap Harry, arm.
38 Rog. Bodenham . . . *ut prius.*

EDW. VI.

1 Joh. Cornwail, mil. . . *ut prius.*
2 Th. Baskervile, arm. . *ut prius.*
3 Johan. Harley, arm. . Brampton.
    O. a bend cotised S.
4 Jac. Baskervile . . . *ut prius.*
5 Jam. Baskervil . . . *ut prius.*
6 Joh. Skudamore, arm. . *ut prius.*

PHIL. et MAR.

1 Johan. Price, mil.
2 Tho. Howard, arm.
    G. a bend between six cross crosslets fitchée Arg.
3 Joh. Baskervil . . . *ut prius.*
4 Tho. Winston, arm. . *ut prius.*
5 Rich. Monington.
6 Rog. Bodenham, arm. . *ut prius.*

ELIZ. REG.

1 Geo. Cornwal, mil. . . *ut prius.*
2 Tho. Blount, arm. . . *ut prius.*
3 Joh. Harley, arm. . . *ut prius.*
4 Joh. Huband, arm.
5 Geo. ap Harry, arm.
6 Jam. Baskervil . . . *ut prius.*
7 Jo. Skudamore, arm. . Kein Church.
8 Georgius Price, arm.
9 Will. Shelley, arm. . . SUSSEX.
    S. a fess engrailed between three periwinkle shells O.
10 Tho. Clinton, arm.
11 Th. Baskervile, arm. . Nethwood.
12 Joh. Baskervil, arm. . *ut prius.*
13 Joh. Huband, mil.
14 Hugo ap Harry.

Anno   Name.   Place.

15 Joh. Abrahal, arm.
 Az. three porcupines O.
16 Jac. Whitney, mil. . . *ut prius.*
17 Georg. Price, arm.
18 Jac. Warcomb.
19 Tho. Morgan, arm.
20 Wa. Baskervil, arm. . *ut prius.*
21 Will. Cecil, arm. . . Altrinnis.
 Barry of ten Arg. and Az.; on six escutcheons three, two,
  and one, S. as many lions rampant of the first.
22 Fran. Blount, arm. . . *ut prius.*
23 Ja. Skudamore, arm. . *ut prius.*
24 Tho. Conisby, arm. . *ut prius.*
25 Ric. Walweyn, arm. . Langford.
 G. a bend with a border Erm.; in chief a hound
  passant O.
26 Hu. Baskervile, arm. . *ut prius.*
27 Ro. Bodenham, arm. . *ut prius.*
28 Ja. Whitney, mil. . . *ut prius.*
29 Jac. Boyle, arm.
 Partie per bend, embattled Arg. and G.
30 Joh. Berington, arm. . Courar.
31 Th. Baskervile, arm. . *ut prius.*
32 Cha. Brudges, arm. . . *ut prius.*
33 Will. Rudham, arm. . Rudham.
34 Rich. Tomkins, arm. . Moniton.
 Az. a chevron betwixt three pheasant-cocks O.
35 Ro. Bodenham, arm. . *ut prius.*
36 Tho. Harley, arm. . . *ut prius.*
37 Geo. Price, arm.
38 Eustac. Whitney . . *ut prius.*
39 Nich. Garnons, arm. . Garnons.
 G. two lions passant O. within a border Az.
40 Tho. Conisby . . . *ut prius.*
41 Will. Dauntsey, arm. . Brinsop.
 Barry wavy of six pieces Arg. and G.
42 Hen. Vaughan, arm.
43 Ja. Skudamore, mil. . *ut prius.*
44 Rich. Hyatt, arm. . . Sauntfield.
45 Tho. Harley . . . *ut prius.*

JAC. REX.

1 Tho. Harley, arm. . . *ut prius.*
2 Joh. Blount, arm. . . *ut prius.*
3 Joh. Berington, arm. . *ut prius.*
4 Jacob. Tomkins, arm. . *ut prius.*
5 Will. Rudhal, arm.

Anno	Name.	Place.

6 Joh. Kirle, arm. . . . Much Marcle.
 V. a chevron betwixt three flower-de-luces O.
7 Rich. Hopton, mil. . . Hopton.
 G. semé de cross crosslets a lion rampant O.
8 Hu. Baskervil, mil. . . *ut prius.*
9 Hum. Cornwall, arm. . *ut prius.*
10 Rob. Kirle, arm. . . . *ut prius.*
11 Joh. Colles, arm.
12 Fran. Smalman, arm. . Kinnesley.
13 Rich. Cox, arm.
14 Row. Skadmor, arm. . *ut prius.*
15 Ambro. Elton, arm. . . Lidbury.
 Paly of six O. and G. on a bend S. three mullets of the
  first.
16 Herb. Westfaling.
 Arg. a cross betwixt four cheval-traps O.
17 Will. Unet, arm. . . Cast. Frome.
 S. a chevron between three lions' heads couped Arg.
18 Edw. Leingein, arm. . *ut prius.*
19 Joh. Bridges, arm.
20 Sam. Aubrie, mil.
 G. a fess engrailed Arg.
21 Jac. Rodd, arm.
22 Fran. Pember, arm.
 Arg. three moor-cocks proper, combed and jealoped G.;
  a chief Az.

CAR. REG.

1 Egidius Bridges, arm. . Wilton.
 Arg. on a cross S. a leopard's head O.
2 Fitz Will. Conisby . . *ut prius.*
3 Will. Read, arm.
4 Johan. Kirle, bar. . . *ut prius.*
5 Jac. Kirle, arm. . . . *ut prius.*
6 Walop. Brabazon . . Eaton.
 G. on a bend Arg. three martlets of the first.
7 Rog. Dansey, arm. . . *ut prius.*
8 Ph. Holman, arm.
9 Joh. Abrahal, arm. . . *ut prius.*
10 Will. Skudamore . . *ut prius.*
11 Tho. Wigmore, arm.
 S. three greyhounds currant Arg.
12 Rog. Vaughan, arm.
13 Hen. Lingein, arm. . . *ut prius.*
14 Rob. Whitney, mil. . . *ut prius.*
15
16
17 Isaacus Seward.

Anno   Name.   Place.

18 ⎫
19 ⎪
20 ⎬ *Hæc fecit inania Mavors.*
21 ⎭

22 Amb. Elton, jun. arm. .   *ut prius.*

KING HENRY VI.

26. WALTER DEVEREUX.—I have vehement and (to use
the Lord Coke's epithet) necessary presumptions, to persuade
me that he was the same person who married Anne, daughter
and sole heir unto William Lord Ferrers of Chartley, and in her
right was afterwards by this king created Lord Ferrers. He
was father to, 1. John Lord Ferrers of Chartley, who married
Cecily sister to Henry Bourchier, Earl of Essex; and was father
to, 2. Walter Devereux Earl Ferrers, created Viscount Hereford by king Edward the Sixth; and was father to, 3. Sir
Richard Devereux, knight, dying before his father; and father
to, 4. Walter Devereux, first Earl of Essex of that family; of
whom largely hereafter, God willing, in Carmarthenshire, the
place of his nativity.

EDWARD IV.

14. JAMES BASKERVILE, Miles.
18. JOHN MORTIMER, Miles.
19. RICHARD de la BERE, Miles.
This leash of knights were persons of approved valour and
loyalty to king Henry the Seventh, by whom (being knights
bachelors before) they were made knights bannerets in the
beginning of his reign: I confess some difference in the date
and place; one assigning the Tower of London, when Jasper
was created duke of Bedford;* another with far more probability naming Newark, just after the fighting of the battle of Stoke
hard by.† Nor doth it sound a little to the honour of Herefordshire, that, amongst the thirteen then bannereted in the
king's army, three fall out to be her natives.

HENRY VIII.

11. RICHARDUS CORNWALL.—He was a knight, howsoever
it cometh to pass he is here unadditioned. I read how, anno
Domini 1523, in the 15th of king Henry the Eighth, he was
a prime person among those many knights which attended the
duke of Suffolk into France, at what time they summoned and
took the town of Roy; and Sir Richard was sent, with four hundred men, to take possession thereof, the only service of remark
performed in that expedition.‡

---

* Stow's Chronicles, p. 471.
† Selden, in his Titles of Honour, p. 700, *ex manuscripto*.
‡ Lord Herbert, in the Life of king Henry VIII., p. 151.

QUEEN ELIZABETH.

Reader, let me confess myself to thee. I expected to have found in this catalogue of sheriffs Sir JAMES CROFTS (knowing he was this countryman, whose family * flourished at Crofts Castle); but am defeated, seeing his constant attendance on court and camp privileged him from serving in this office. This worthy knight was accused for complying with Wiat; and notwithstanding his most solemn oath in his own defence, he was imprisoned by queen Mary, convicted of high treason; restored by queen Elizabeth, and made governor of the town and castle of Berwick.†

At the siege of Leith, he behaved him most valiantly in repelling the foe; and yet when, in a second assault, the English were worsted, the blame fell on him (as if he favoured the French, and maligned the lord Gray then general); so that he was ousted of his government in Berwick. Yet he fell not so into the queen's final disfavour, but that she continued him privy councillor, and made him comptroller of her househould. He was an able man to manage war, and yet an earnest desirer and advancer of peace, being one of the commissioners in 1588 to treat with the Spaniards in Flanders : I conceive he survived not long after. His ancient inheritance in this county is lately devolved to Herbert Croft,‡ D.D. and dean of Hereford.

40. THOMAS CONISBY, Mil.—I have heard from some of this county a precious report of his memory ; how he lived in a right worshipful equipage, and founded a place in Hereford for poor people; but to what proportion of revenue, they could not inform me.

43. JAMES SKUDAMORE, Knight.—He was father unto Sir John Skudamore, created by king Charles Viscount Sligo in Ireland. This lord was for some years employed Leiger ambassador in France; and, during the tyranny of the Protectorian times, kept his secret loyalty to his sovereign, hospitality to his family, and charity to the distressed clergy, whom he bountifully relieved.

THE FAREWELL.

I am credibly informed, that the office of the under-sheriff of this county is more beneficial than in any other county of the same proportion ; his fees, it seems, increasing from the decrease of the states of the gentry therein. May the obventions of his office hereafter be reduced to a lesser sum! And seeing God hath blessed (as we have formerly observed) this county with so many W's, we wish the inhabitants the continuance and

---

* Camden's Elizabeth, in apparatu. † Idem, anno 1560.
‡ Afterwards Bishop of Hereford, 1661-1691.—ED.

increase of one more, WISDOM, expressing itself both in the improving of their spiritual concernment, and warily managing their secular estates.

WORTHIES OF HEREFORDSHIRE WHO HAVE FLOURISHED
SINCE THE TIME OF FULLER,

Thomas BLOUNT, author on Manorial Tenures : born at Orleton about 1618 ; died 1679.

George Lord CARPENTER, general, victor at Preston ; born at Pitcher's Ocule 1667.

Catherine CLIVE, comic actress ; born at Hereford 1711 ; died 1785.

David GARRICK, the " English Roscius ;" born at Hereford 1716 ; died 1779.

Hon. Edward HARLEY, Auditor of the Imprest, benefactor ; born at Brampton Brian, 1664.

William HAVARD, song writer, author of " Banks of the Lugg ;" born at Hereford 1734.

Stringer LAWRENCE, East India Major-general ; born at Hereford 1697 ; died 1775.

Edward LONGMORE, " Hereford Colossus," 7 feet 6 inches high ; died 1777.

William POWELL, actor, pupil and protegé of Garrick ; born at Hereford ; died 1769.

John PRICE, historian of his native town ; born at Leominster ; died 1802.

John ROSS, Bishop of Exeter, classical scholar and author ; born at Ross 1719 ; died 1792.

‌‌* The county of Hereford is comparatively destitute of a general historian. In 1804, however, Collections towards the History of the County were published, in an imperfect state, by John Duncomb ; some Introductory Sketches having been previously given to the world, in 1791, by the Rev. John Lodge. Histories of the city have also appeared, from the pens of Dr. Rawlinson (1717), and of John Price (1796) ; the latter of whom published an Account of Leominister in 1795.

HUNTINGDONSHIRE.

HUNTINGDONSHIRE is surrounded with Northampton, Bedford, and Cambridge-shires; and, being small in extent, hardly stretcheth twenty miles outright, though measured to the most advantage. The general goodness of the ground may certainly be collected from the plenty of convents erected therein, at St. Neot's, Hinchingbrook, Huntingdon, Sautrie, St. Ives, Ramsey, &c; so that the fourth foot at least in this shire was abbey-land, belonging to monks and friars; and such weeds, we know, would not grow but in rich ground. If any say that monks might not choose their own habitations (being confined therein to the pleasures of their founders), know, there were few founders that did not first consult some religious person in the erection of convents; and such would be sure to choose the best for men of their own profession. Sure I am it would set all England hard to show in so short a distance so pleasant a park as Waybridge, so fair meadow as Portsholme, and so fruitful a town for tillage as Godmanchester; all three within so many miles in this county.

No peculiar commodity or manufacture (save with others equally intercommoning) appearing in this county, let us proceed.

THE BUILDINGS.

KIMBOLTON CASTLE.—This, being part of the jointure of queen Katherine dowager, was chosen by her to retire thereunto; as neither too near to London, to see what she would not; nor so far off, but that she might hear what she desired. Here she wept out the remnant of her widowhood (while her husband was yet alive) in her devotions. This castle came afterwards by gift to the Wingfields; from them by sale to the Montagues; Henry late earl of Manchester sparing no cost which might add to the beauty thereof.

HINCHINBROOK, once a nunnery, and which I am confident will ever be a religious house whilst it relateth to the truly noble Edward Montague, earl of Sandwich, the owner thereof. It sheweth one of the most magnificent rooms which is to be beheld in our nation.

We must not forget the house and chapel in Little Gedding (the inheritance of Master Ferrar) which lately made a great noise all over England.* Here three numerous female families (all from one grandmother)† lived together in a strict discipline of devotion. They rose at midnight to prayers; and other people most complained thereof, whose heads, I dare say, never ached for want of sleep. Sure I am, strangers by them were entertained, poor people were relieved, their children instructed to read, whilst their own needles were employed in learned and pious work, to bind Bibles; whereof one most exactly done was presented to king Charles. But their society was beheld by some as an embryo nunnery, suspecting that there was a Pope Joan therein; which causeless cavil afterwards confuted itself, when all the younger of those virgins practised the precept of St. Paul, to marry, bear children, and guide their houses.‡

MEDICINAL WATERS.

There is an obscure village in this county, near St. Neot's, called Haile-weston, whose very name soundeth something of sanativeness therein; so much may the adding of what is no letter, alter the meaning of a word; for, 1. *Aile* signifieth a sore or hurt, with complaining, the effect thereof. 2. *Haile* (having an affinity with Heile, the Saxon idol for Esculapius)§ importeth a cure, or medicine to a malady.

Now in the aforesaid village there be two fountain-lets, which are not far asunder: 1. One sweet, conceived good to help the dimness of the eyes: 2. The other in a manner salt, esteemed sovereign against the scabs and leprosy.

What saith St. James; "Doth a fountain send forth at the same place sweet water and bitter?"|| meaning in an ordinary way, without miracle. Now although these different waters flow from several fountains; yet, seeing they are so near together, it may justly be advanced to the reputation of a wonder.

PROVERBS.

"This is the way to Beggar's-bush."]

It is spoken of such who use dissolute and improvident courses, which tend to poverty; Beggar's-bush being a tree notoriously known, on the left hand of London road from Huntingdon to Caxton. I have heard how king James, being in progress in these parts with Sir Francis Bacon the lord chancellor, and having heard that morning how Sir Francis had prodigiously rewarded a mean man for a small present; "Sir Francis," said he, "you will quickly come to Beggar's-bush; and I may even go along with you, if both be so bountiful."

"Ramsey the Rich."¶]

This was the *Cresus*, or *Cræsus*, of all our English abbeys;

---

for, having but sixty monks to maintain therein, the revenues thereof, according to the standard of those times, amounted unto seven thousand pounds a year,* which, in proportion, was a hundred pounds for every monk, and a thousand for their abbot. Yet, at the dissolution of monasteries, the income of this abbey was reckoned but at one thousand nine hundred eighty-three pounds by the year,† whereby it plainly appears how much the revenues were under-rated in those valuations.

But how soon is *Crassus* made *Codrus,* and Ramsey the Rich become Ramsey the Poor! The wealth of the town, relative with the abbey, was dissolved therewith; and more the mendicants since in Ramsey than the monks were before. However, now there is great hope that Ramsey, after the two extremes of wealth and want, will at last be fixed in a comfortable mediocrity, the wish of Agur being granted unto him, " Give me neither poverty nor riches,"‡ especially since it is lately erected (or rather restored) to the dignity of a market-town. And surely the convenient situation thereof, since the draining of the fens, doth advantage it to be a staple place for the sale of fat and lean cattle.

SAINTS.

ELFLED, daughter of Ethelwold earl of East Angles (founder of the monastery of Ramsey in this county) was preferred abbess of Ramsey, and confirmed by king Edgar therein. She is reported to excel in austerity and holiness of life. When her steward complained unto her, that she had exhausted her coffers with the profuseness of her charity, she with her prayers presently recruited them to their former fulness.§ When her candle, as she read the lesson, casually went out, there came such a brightness from the fingers of her right hand, that it enlightened the whole choir; which is as true as the new lights to which our modern sectaries do pretend; the one having miracles, the other revelations, at their fingers' ends. She died anno Domini 992, being buried in the Lady Church at Ramsey with high veneration.

PRELATES.

WILLIAM de WHITLESEY.—No printed author mentioning the place of his birth and breeding, he was placed by us in this county, finding Whitlesey a town therein (so memorable for the Mere), and presuming that this William did follow suit with the best of his coat in that age, surnamed from the places of their nativity. Mr. Parker (I tell you my story

* Camden's Britannia, in Huntingdonshire.
† Speed's Catalogue of Religious Houses, folio 809.
‡ Proverbs xxx. 8.
§ R. Buckland, in Vitis Sanctarum Mulierum Angliæ, p. 242.

and my story's man), an industrious antiquary,* collecteth out of the records of the church of Ely, that (after the resignation of Ralph de Holbeach) William de Whitlesey, archdeacon of Hunt- ington 1340, was admitted third master of Peter House in Cam- bridge. Yet hath he left more signal testimony of his affection to Oxford, which he freed from the jurisdiction of the bishop of Lincoln, allowing the scholars leave to choose their own chancellor.†

He was kinsman to Simon Islip, archbishop of Canterbury, who made him vicar general, dean of the arches; and succes- sively he was preferred bishop of Rochester, Worcester, London; archbishop of Canterbury. An excellent scholar, an eloquent preacher; and his last sermon most remarkable, to the Convo- cation, on this text, "Veritas liberabit vos," (the truth shall make you free.‡) It seems by the story, that in his sermon he had a par- ticular reflection on the privileges of the clergy, as exempted by preaching the truth from payment of taxes, save with their own free consent. But all would not serve their turn; for, in the con- temporary parliament, the clergy, unwillingly-willing, granted a yearly tenth to supply the pressing occasions of king Edward the Third. This William died anno Domini 1375.

SINCE THE REFORMATION.

FRANCIS WHITE was born at St. Neot's in this county, and not in Lancashire, as I and others have been misinformed;§ witness the admission book of Caius College, and the testimony of his brother's son,‖ still alive (1661). The father to this Francis was a minister, and had five sons, who were divines, and two of them most eminent in their generation. Of these, this Francis was bred in Caius College, on the same token that when he was bi- shop of Ely (and came to consecrate the chapel of Peter-House) he received an entertainment at that college, where with a short speech he encouraged the young students to ply their books by his own example, who, from a poor scholar in that house, by God's blessing on his industry, was brought to that preferment.

By the Lord Grey of Grobie he was presented to Broughton Astley in Leicestershire, and thence (why should a candle be put under a bushel?) he was brought to be lecturer of St. Paul's in London, and parson of St. Peter's in Cornhill: whence he was successively preferred, first dean, then bishop of Carlisle, after bishop of Norwich, and at last of Ely.

He had several solemn disputations with popish priests and jesuits (Father Fisher and others); and came off with such good success, that he reduced many seduced Romanists to our

---

* MS. Scel. Cant. in the Masters of Peter House.
† Antiquit. Brit. p. 254.   ‡ John viii. 32.
§ By Master Holmes, his secretary, being himself deceived without intent to deceive.—F.   ‖ Mr. White, druggist, in Lombard Street.—F.

Church. He often chose Daniel Featley, **D.D.** his assistant in such disputes; so that I may call this prelate and his doctor, Jonathan and his armour-bearer (being confident that the doctor, if alive, would not be displeased with the comparison as any disparagement unto him) jointly victorious over the Romish Philistines. He died anno 1638, leaving some of his learned works to posterity.

WRITERS.

The candid reader is here requested to forgive and amend what in them is of casual transposition.

HENRY SALTRY was born in this county,* and became a Cistercian monk in the monastery of Saltry, then newly founded by Simon Saint Liz, earl of Huntington. He was also instructed by one Florentian, an Irish bishop. He wrote a profitable book for his own religion in the maintenance of purgatory, which made him esteemed in that superstitious age. He flourished anno Domini 1140.

GREGORY of HUNTINGTON, so called from the place of his nativity, was bred a Benedictine monk in Ramsey, where he became prior, or vice-abbot,† a place which he deserved, being one of the most learned men of that age for his great skill in languages.

For he was thorough-paced in three tongues, Latin, Greek (as appears by his many comments on those grammarians), and Hebrew, which last he learned by his constant conversing with the Jews in England.

But now the fatal time did approach, wherein the Jews (full loath I assure you) must leave the land, and many precious books behind them. Our Gregory, partly by love, partly by the king's power, (both together will go far in driving a bargain) purchased many of those rarities, to dispose them in his convent of Ramsey; which, as it exceeded other English monasteries for a library, so for Hebrew books that monastery exceeded itself.‡ After this Gregory had been prior of Ramsey no fewer than thirty-eight years,§ flourishing under king Henry the Third, he died in the reign of king Edward the First, about 1280.

HUGH of SAINT NEOT'S was born in that well-known market-town; bred a Carmelite in Hitching in Hertfordshire; hence he went to study in Cambridge, where, for his worth, the degree of doctorship was by the university gratis (quære whether

---

* J. Bale and J. Pits, de Scriptoribus Britannicis.

† Pits, de Scriptoribus Britannicis, Cent. iv. num. 22.

‡ Vide infra, p. 103, Jo. YONG, in the "Writers since the Reformation."

§ Pits, de Angliæ Scriptoribus, in anno 1255.

without paying of fees, or keeping of acts) conferred upon him.*
To him Bale (though that be the best Bale which hath the least
of Bale and most of Leland therein) giveth this testimony:
"that, living in the Egyptian darkness, he sought after the light
of truth," adding, that he was "Piscis in palude, nihil trahens
de sapore palustri," (a fish in the fens, drawing nothing of
the mud thereof); which is a rarity indeed.   Many his sermons:
and he wrote a Comment on Saint Luke.   He died 1340; and
was buried at Hitching.

WILLIAM RAMSEY was born in this county, famous for the
richest Benedictines' Abbey in England; but here he would not
stay, but went to Crowland, where he prospered so well that
he became abbot thereof.   He was a natural poet;† and therefore no wonder if faults be found in the feet of his verses; for
it is given to thorough-paced nags, that amble naturally, to trip
much; whilst artificial pacers go surest on foot.   He wrote the
life of St. Guthlake, St. Neot's, St. Edmund the king, &c.: all
in verse.

But that which may seem a wonder indeed is this, that, being
a poet, he paid the vast debts of others, even forty thousand
marks,‡ for the engagement of his convent, and all within the
compass of eighteen months, wherein he was abbot of Crowland.
But it rendereth it the more credible, because it was done by
the assistance of king Henry the Second, who, to expiate the
blood of Becket, was contented to be melted into coin, and
was prodigiously bountiful to some churches.   Our William
died 1180.

HENRY of HUNTINGTON, son to one Nicholas, where born
unknown, was first a canon of the church of Lincoln, where he
became acquainted with one Albine of Angiers, born in France,
but fellow canon with him of the same church.§   This Albine
he afterwards in his writings modestly owned for his master,
having gained much learning from him.

He was afterwards chaplain to Alexander, that great bishop of
Lincoln (magnificent unto madness), who made him archdeacon
of Huntingdon, whence he took his denomination.   A town
which hath received more honour from him than ever it can
return to him, seeing Huntingdon had never been mentioned in
the mouths, nor passed under the pens, of so many foreigners,
but for the worthy "History of the Saxon Kings," written by
this Henry.   Let me add, that, considering the sottishness of
superstition in the age he lived in, he is less smooted therewith than any of his contemporaries, and, being a secular priest,

---

* Bale, de Scriptoribus Britannicis, Cent. v. num. 29.
† Idem, Cent. iii. num. 9.   ‡ Pits, de Scriptoribus Britannicis, anno 1180.
§ Bale, Cent. ii. num. 92; and Pits, in anno 1148.

doth now and then abate the pride of monastical pretended perfection. He flourished under king Stephen, in the year of our Lord 1248; and is probably conjectured to die about the year 1260.

Roger of St. Ives was born at that noted town of this county, being omitted by Bale, but remembered by Pits* (though seldom sounding when the other is silent) for his activity against the Lollards and Sir John Oldcastle, against whom he wrote a book, flourishing in the year 1420.

SINCE THE REFORMATION.

[AMP.] John Yong was a monk in Ramsey Abbey at the dissolution thereof. Now, by the same proportion that a penny saved is a penny gained, the preserver of books is a mate for the compiler of them. Learned Leland looks on this Yong as a benefactor to posterity, in that he saved many Hebrew books of the noble library of Ramsey.

Say not such preserving was purloining, because those books belonged to the king, seeing no conscience need to scruple such a nicety: books (though so precious that nothing was worth them) being in that juncture of time counted worth nothing. Never such a massacre of good authors, some few only escaping to bring tidings of the destruction of the rest.

Seeing this Yong is inserted by Bale,† and omitted by Pits, I collect him to savour of the Reformation. As for such who confound him with John Yong, many years after master of Pembroke Hall, they are confuted by the different dates assigned unto them, this being his senior thirty years, as flourishing anno Domini 1520.

John White, brother to Francis White bishop of Ely, was born at St. Neot's in this county: bred in Caius college in Cambridge, wherein he commenced master of arts. He did not continue long in the university, but the university continued long in him; so that he may be said to have carried Cambridge with him into Lancashire (so hard and constant in his study) when he was presented vicar of Eccles therein. Afterwards Sir John Crofts, a Suffolk knight, being informed of his abilities, and pitying his remote living on no plentiful benefice, called him into the south, and was the occasion that king James took cognizance of his worth, making him his chaplain in ordinary. It was now but the third month of his attendance at court, when he sickened at London in Lombard street, died, and was buried in the church of Saint Mary Woolnoth ‡ 1615, without any other monument, save what his learned works have left to

* Anno 1420.   † De Scriptoribus Britannicis, Cent ix. num. 9.
‡ So I am informed by his son, Mr. White, a druggist, living in Lombard street.—F.

posterity, which all who have either learning, piety, or ingenuity do, yea must, most highly commend.

Sir ROBERT COTTON, Knight and Baronet, son to John Cotton, esquire, was born at Cunnington in this county; descended
by the Bruces from the blood royal of Scotland. He was bred
in Trinity College in Cambridge; where, when a youth, he discovered his inclination to the study of antiquity (they must
spring early who would sprout high in that knowledge); and
afterwards attained to such eminency, that sure I am he had no
superior, if any his equal, in the skill thereof.

But that which rendered him deservedly to the praise of present and future times, yea the wonder of our own and foreign
nations, was his collection of his library in Westminster;
equally famous for—1. *Rarity:* having so many manuscript
originals, or else copies so exactly transcribed, that, reader, I
must confess he must have more skill than I have to distinguish them. 2. *Variety:* he that beholdeth their number
would admire they should be rare; and he that considereth
their rarity, will more admire at their number. 3. *Method:* some
libraries are labyrinths, not for the multitude but confusion of
volumes, where a stranger seeking for a book may quickly lose
himself; whereas these are so exactly methodised (under the
heads of the twelve Roman emperors) that it is harder for one
to miss than to hit any author he desireth.

But what addeth a lustre to all the rest is, the favourable
access thereunto, for such as bring any competency of skill with
them, and leave thankfulness behind them. Some antiquaries
are so jealous of their books, as if every hand which toucheth
would ravish them; whereas here no such suspicion of ingenious
persons. And here give me leave to register myself amongst
the meanest of those who through the favour of Sir Thomas
Cotton (inheriting as well the courtesy as estate of his father
Sir Robert) have had admittance into that worthy treasury.

Yea, most true it is what one saith, that the grandest antiquaries have here fetched their materials:

> *Omnis ab illo*
> *Et Camdene tua, et Seldini gloria crevit.*
>
> " Camden to him, to him doth Selden, owe
> Their glory: what they got from him did grow."[*]

I have heard that there was a design driven on in the Pope's
conclave, after the death of Sir Robert, to compass this library
to be added to that in Rome; which, if so, what a Vatican had
there been within the Vatican, by the accession thereof! but,
blessed be God, the project did miscarry, to the honour of
our nation, and advantage of the Protestant religion. For
therein are contained many privities of princes and transactions

---

* Weever's Funeral Monuments, in the Preface.

of state ; insomuch that I have been informed, that the fountains have been fain to fetch water from the stream ; and the secretaries of state, and clerks of the council, glad from hence to borrow back again many originals, which, being lost by casualty or negligence of officers, have here been recovered and preserved. He was a man of a public spirit, it being his principal endeavour in all parliaments (wherein he served so often) [that the prerogative and privilege might run in their due channel; and in truth he did cleave the pin betwixt the sovereign and the subject. He was wont to say, "That he him-self had the least share in himself;" whilst his country and friends had the greatest interest in him. He died at his house in Westminster, May the 6th, anno Domini 1631, in the 61st year of his age ; though one may truly say, his age was adequate to the continuance of the creation; such was his exact skill in all antiquity. By Elizabeth, daughter and co-heir of William Brocas, esquire, he had only one son, Sir Thomas, now living, (1661), who, by Margaret, daughter to the Lord William Howard (grandchild to Thomas duke of Norfolk) hath one son, John Cotton, esquire, and two daughters, Lucie and Francis. The "Opera Posthuma" of this worthy knight are lately set forth in one volume, to the great profit of posterity.

STEPHEN MARSHALL was born at Godmanchester in this county, and bred a bachelor of arts in Emanuel College in Cambridge. Thence he went very early a reaper in God's har-vest, yet not before he had well sharpened his sickle for that service. He became minister at Finchfield in Essex ; and, after many years' discontinuance, came up to Cambridge to take the degree of bachelor of divinity, where he performed his exercise with general applause.

In the late long lasting parliament, no man was more gracious with the principal members thereof. He was their trumpet, by whom they sounded their solemn fasts, preaching more public sermons on that occasion, than any four of his function. In their sickness he was their confessor; in their assembly their counsellor ; in their treaties their chaplain ; in their disputations their champion.

He was of so supple a soul, that he brake not a joint, yea, sprained not a sinew, in all the alteration of times ; and his friends put all on the account, not of his inconstancy but pru-dence, who in his own practice, as they conceive, reconciled the various lections of St. Paul's precept, "serving the lord, and the times."*

And although some severely censure him for deserting his principles, yet he is said on his death-bed to have given full satisfaction to such who formerly suspected his sincerity to the

* Rom. xii. 11. τῷ Κυρίῳ τῷ καιρῷ δουλεύοντες.

presbyterian discipline, dying anno Domini 1655. He was solemnly buried in the abbey at Westminster.

ROMISH EXILE WRITERS.

RICHARD BROUGHTON was born at Great Stukeley in this
county ;* bred at Rheims in France, where he received the order
of priesthood ; and was sent over into England for the propo-
gation of his party. Here he gave so signal testimony and fidelity to the cause, that he was, before many others, preferred assistant to the English arch-priest.†

He wrote many books : and is most esteemed by those of his
own religion for his " English Ecclesiastical History, from the
first planting of the Gospel, to the coming in of the Saxons."
But, in plain truth, there is little milk, no cream, and almost all
whey therein, being farced with legendary stuff, taken from authors, some of condemned, most of suspected credit. If by the
Levitical law " a bastard should not enter into the congregation
of the Lord (understand it, to bear office therein) to the tenth
generation,"‡ it is pity that adulterated authors, being an ille-
gitimate off-spring, should be admitted to bear rule in church
history. This Broughton was living in the latter end of the
reign of king James.

BENEFACTORS TO THE PUBLIC.

AMBROSE (son to John) NICHOLAS was born at Needenworth
in this county, whence he went to London, and was bound apprentice to a salter, thriving so well in his trade, that, anno
1576, he became lord mayor of London. He founded twelve
alms-houses in Mungwel-street in that city, endowing them with
competent maintainance.

Sir WOLSTAN (son to Thomas) DIXIE was born at Catworth
in this county, bred a Skinner in London, whereof he became
lord mayor§ anno 1585. He was a man made up of deeds of
charity, the particulars whereof are too long to recite. He gave
600 pounds to Emanuel College in Cambridge, to the founding
of a fellowship ; erected a free-school at Bosworth in Leicestershire, and endowed it ; where his family flourish at this day
in a worshipful estate.

RICHARD FISHBOURN was born in the town of Huntingdon ;
cut out of no mean quarry, being a gentleman by his extraction.
Leaving a court-life (as more pleasant than profitable) he became servant to Sir Baptist Hickes, afterwards Viscount Camp-
den, and, by God's blessing on his industry, attained a great estate ; whereof he gave two thousand pounds for the buying out
of impropriations in the northern parts, and settling a preaching

---

* In the Preface of his Church History.   † Pits, de Scriptoribus Angliæ, p 815.
‡ Deut. xxiii. 2.   § Reckoned by Mr. Stow in his Survey of London.

ministry, where most want thereof; he bequeathed as much to the company of Mercers, whereof he was free; and the same sum to Huntingdon, the place of his nativity; with one thousand marks to Christ Church Hospital. The whole sum of his benefactions amounted to ten thousand seven hundred pounds and upwards, briefly summed up in his funeral sermon, commonly called "Corona Charitatis," preached by Master Nathaniel Shute, wherein, to use his expression, "he supped up many things with a very short breath," contracting his deeds of charity to avoid tediousness.

Nor must it be forgotten how this gentleman lying on his death-bed (when men are presumed to speak with unmasked consciences), did profess that, to his knowledge, "he had got no part of his goods unjustly." No man of his quality won more love in health, prayers in sickness, and lamentation at his funeral; dying a single man, and buried in Mercers' Chapel, May the 10th, 1625.

MEMORABLE PERSONS.

Sir OLIVER CROMWELL, Knight, son of Sir Henry Cromwell, Knight, of Hinchingbrooke, in this county, is remarkable to posterity on a four-fold account. First, for his hospitality and prodigious entertainment of king James and his court. Secondly, for his upright dealing in bargain and sale with all chapmen; so that no man whosoever purchased land of him was put to charge of three-pence to make good his title. Yet he sold excellent pennyworths; insomuch that Sir John Leamon (once lord mayor of London), who bought the fair manor of Warboise in this county of him, affirmed, "that it was the cheapest land that ever he bought; and yet the dearest that ever Sir Oliver Cromwell sold." Thirdly, for his loyalty; always beholding the usurpation and tyranny of his nephew, godson, and namesake, with hatred and contempt. Lastly, for his vivacity, who survived to be the oldest gentleman in England who was a knight; though not the oldest knight who was a gentleman; seeing Sir George Dalston, younger in years (yet still alive), was knighted some days before him. Sir Oliver died anno Domini 1654.

THE NAMES OF THE GENTRY IN THIS SHIRE,

RETURNED BY THE COMMISSIONERS IN THE TWELFTH YEAR OF KING HENRY THE SIXTH, 1433.

William Bishop of Lincoln, and John de Tiptofte, chevalier ;— Roger Hunt, and William Waton, (knights for the shire) ;— Commissioners.

Abbatis de Ramsey.
Abbatis de Sautrey.
Prioris de Huntington.
Prioris de S. Neoto.
Prioris de Stonle.
Archidiaconi Eliensis,

Rectoris de Somerham, prebendarii ecclesiæ Lincolniensis.
Domini de Leighton, rectoris ecclesiæ de Bluntesham.
Vicarii ecclesiæ de Gurmecest.

Vicarii ecclesiæ de S. Neoto.
Rect. ecclesiæ de Ript. Abbatis.
Nicholai Stivecle, militis.
Roberti Stonham, armigeri.
Everardi Digby, armigeri.
Radulphi Stivecle, armigeri.
Thomæ Devyll, armigeri.
Thomæ Nesenham, armigeri.
Henrici Hethe.
Johannis Bayons, armigeri.
Rogeri Lowthe.
Edwardi Parker.
Walteri Taillard.
Johannis Eyr.
Johannis Bekeswell.
Willielmi Castell.
Willielmi Waldesheefe.
Thomæ Freman.
Johannis Donold.
Walteri Mayll.
Roberti Boteler de Alyngton.
Roberti Boteler de Hilton.
Johannis Kirkeby.
Johannis Sankyn.
Roberti Langton.
Reginaldi Rokesden.
Johannis Pulter.
Roberti Wene.
Joh. Sampson de Somersh.
Thomæ Clerevax.
Radulphi Pakynton.
Willielmi Est.
Richardi Est.
Roberti Creweker.
Willielmi Maister.
Johannis Morys.
Willielmi Druell de Weresle.
Radulphi Joce.
Johan. Devyll de Chescerton.
Johannis Cokerham.
Richardi Basingham.
J. Cokeyn Parker de Kimbolton.
Richardi Burgham.
Richardi Parker de Bukden.
Thomæ Alcumbury.
Willielmi Boteler de Weresle.

Will. Judde de Sancto Ivone.
Willielmi Wassingle.
Willielmi Wardale.
Willielmi Colles.
Laurentii Merton.
Thomæ Judde.
Willielmi Boteler de Ramsey.
Thomæ Barboure de eadem.
Thomæ Rede.
Thomæ Irlle.
Willielmi Holland.
Will. Smith de Alcumbury.
Will. Hayward de Buckworth.
Richardi Boton.
Johannis Cross, senioris.
Edmundi Fairstede.
Willielmi Eryth.
Will. Skinner de Brampton.
Willielmi West.
Thomæ Daniel.
Willielmi Daniel.
Johannis Barbour.
Thomæ Parker de S. Neoto.
Edm. Faillour de Kymbolton.
Thomæ Bowelas.
Willielmi Peete.
Willielmi Talers,
Thomæ Aungevin.
Walteri Godegamen.
Johannis Cage.
Johannis Manypeny.
Johannis Copgray, clerici.
Willielmi Arneburgh.
Henrici Attehill.
Johannis Charwalton.
Edmundi Ulfe.
Willielmi Hare.
Johannis Dare.
Willielmi Sturdivale.
Richardi Brigge.
Mich. Carleton ballivi ejusdem ville Huntington.
Georgii Giddyng.
Johannis Chikson.
Johannis Pecke.
Thomæ Charwalton.
Johannis Abbotesle.

I meet with this uncomfortable passage in Mr. Speed's (or rather in Sir Robert Cotton's) description of this shire:

"Thus as this city, so the old families have been here with time out worn, few only (of the many former) now remaining, whose surnames before the reign of the last Henry were in this shire of any eminency."

Let others render a reason why the ancient families in this county (more in the proportion than elsewhere) are so decayed. This seemeth a probable cause why many new ones are seated herein; because Huntingdonshire being generally abbey-land (as is aforesaid), after the Dissolution many new purchasers planted themselves therein.

SHERIFFS OF THIS SHIRE ALONE.

KING CHARLES.

Anno	Name and Arms.	Place.
12	Tho. Cotton, bart. . .	Cunnington.
	Az. an eagle displayed Arg.	
13	Joh. Hewet, bart. . .	Waresly.
	S. a chevron counter-battelée between three owls Arg.	
14	Tho. Lake, knt. . . .	Stoughton.
	S. a bend betwixt six cross crosslets fitchée Arg.	
15	Will. Armyn, arm. . .	Orton.
	Erm. a saltire engrailed G. on a chief of the second a lion passant O.	
16	Will Leman	Warbois.
	Az. a fess between three dolphins Arg.	
17	Rich. Stone, mil. . . .	Stukeley.
	Arg. three cinquefoils S. a chief Az.	

Cambridgeshire and this county may pass for the emblem of man and wife, who have long lived lovingly together, till at last, upon some small disgust, they part bed and board, and live asunder. Even from the time of king Henry the Second these two shires were united under one sheriff,* (as originally they had one earl, of the royal blood of Scotland,) till in the twelfth of king Charles (on what mutual distaste I know not) they were divided.

But the best part of the emblem is still behind. As such separated persons do, on second thoughts, sometimes return together again, as most for their comfort, convenience, credit, and conscience; so these two counties (after six years' division) have been re-united under the same sheriff; and so continue to this day (1660).

THE FAREWELL.

Much of this county's profit depends on the northern road crossing the body thereof from Godmanchester to Wainsford

---

* Camden's Britannia, in Cambridgeshire.

Bridge ; a road which in the winter is the ready way, leading not only to trouble but danger ; insomuch that here it comes to pass (what war caused in the days of Shamgar), " The highways are unemployed, and travellers walk through byways," to the present prejudice and future undoing of all ancient stages.   And indeed though *Stif-clay* (commonly called Stukeley) be the name of one or two villages in the midst, yet their nature is extensive all over the county, consisting of a deep clay, giving much annoyance to passengers.   May a mean man's motion be heard ? Let the repairing or bad places in that highway (which is now the parish) be made the county charge, whereby the burden will become the less (borne by more backs), and the benefit the more, when the ways thereby shall effectually be mended and maintained.

WORTHIES OF HUNTINGDONSHIRE WHO HAVE FLOURISHED SINCE THE TIME OF FULLER.

Henry CROMWELL, son of Oliver, lord deputy of Ireland ; born at Huntingdon 1628; died 1674.

Richard CROMWELL, eldest son of Oliver, and successor to the Protectorate, which he resigned to facilitate the restoration of Charles II.; born at Huntingdon 1626; died 1712.

John MAPLETOFT, physician, scholar, and divine; born at Margaret Inge 1631; died 1721.

Samuel PEPYS, secretary to the Admiralty, president of the Royal Society, and author of an amusing " Diary ; " born at Bampton ; died 1703.

Samuel Jackson PRATT, novellist, poet, dramatist, and author of " Gleanings, or Travels Abroad and in England ;" born at St. Ives 1749; died 1814.

⁎ There has been nothing like a regular history of this little county, beyond what appears in the Magna Britannia and the Beauties of England.   In 1820, however, the Rev. G. C. Gorham published the History of Eynesbury and St. Neot's; and in 1831 Mr. Robert Fox produced the History of Godmanchester.   There is also extant a History of Somersham.—ED.

KENT.

KENT, in the Saxon Heptarchy, was an entire kingdom by itself, an honour which no other sole county attained unto. It hath the Thames on the north, the sea on the east and south, Sussex and Surrey on the west. From east to west it expatiateth itself into fifty-three miles: but from north to south expandeth not above twenty-six miles. It differeth not more from other shires than from itself; such the variety thereof. In some parts of it, health and wealth are at many miles' distance; which in other parts are reconciled to live under the same roof; I mean, abide in one place together. Nor is the wonder great, if places differ so much which lie in this shire far asunder, when I have read * that there is a farm within a mile of Gravesend, where the cattle, always drinking at one common pond in the yard, if they graze on one side of the house the butter is yellow, sweet, and good; but if on the other, white, sourish, and naught. Yet needeth there no Œdipus to unriddle the same, seeing one side lieth on the chalk, and hath much trefoil; the other on the gravel, abounding only with couch grass.

A considerable part of this county is called The Weald; that is, a woodland ground, the inhabitants whereof are called the Wealdish men. And here, reader, I humbly submit a small criticism of mine to thy censure. I read in Master Speed,† in Wyat's rebellion, how Sir Henry Isley and the two Knevets conducted five hundred Welchmen into Rochester. I much admire how so many Cambro-Britons should straggle into Kent; the rather because that rising was peculiar to that county alone; since I conceive these Welchmen should be Wealdishmen, viz. such who had their habitation in the woody side of this shire.‡

However, the goodness of the soil generally may be guessed from the greatness of the Kentish breed, where both the cattle

---

* Hartlib's Legacy, p. 170.
† In his Chronicle, page 845, paragraph 30.
‡ Hasted has given an interesting account of the Clothing Trade formerly carried on in the Weald, and also some notices of the families raised by that trade.—ED. *

---

* Many of the Editorial notes given in this County are the contributions of Sir Egerton Brydges, late of Lee Priory near Canterbury.

and the poultry are allowed the largest of the land. A giant ox, fed in Romney Marsh, was some six years since to be seen in London, so high, that one of ordinary stature could hardly reach to the top of his back.

Here let me observe a slip of the pen in industrious Master Speed. "The air," saith he, "of Kent, is both wholesome and temperate " (which is confessed most true, but mark what followeth,) " as seated nearest to the Equinoctial, and farthest from the northern pole." But let his own general map be appealed to as judge, being therein both true and impartial, and it will appear that some part of Devonshire lieth south of Kent well nigh a whole degree, or threescore miles. Thus we see other men's, other men see our mistakes; so necessary is mutual candour and charity, because he who forgiveth to-day may have need to be forgiven to-morrow. And yet I deny not but that Kent of all English counties is nearest to France; not because southernmost, but because the sea interposed is there the narrowest.

NATURAL COMMODITIES.

CHERRIES.

These were fetched out of Flanders, and first planted in this county by king Henry the Eighth, in whose time they spread into thirty-two parishes; and were sold at great rates. I have read that one of the orchards of this primitive plantation, consisting but of thirty acres, produced fruit of one year sold for one thousand pounds;* plenty, it seems, of cherries in that garden, meeting with a scarcity of them in all other places.

No English fruit is dearer than those at first, cheaper at last, pleasanter at all times; nor is it less wholesome than delicious. And it is much that of so many feeding so freely on them, so few are found to surfeit. Their several sorts do ripen so successively, that they continue in season well nigh a quarter of a year. It is incredible how many cherries one tree in this county did bear in a plentiful year; I mean not how many pound (being the fruit of other trees) have been weighed thereon (the common fallacy of the word *bear* amongst the countryfolk), but simply how many did naturally grow thereupon.

We leave the wholesomeness of this fruit, both for food and physic, to be praised by others, having hitherto not met with any discommending it. As for the outlandish proverb, " He that eateth cherries with noblemen, shall have his eyes spurted out with the stones," it fixeth no fault in the fruit; the expression being merely metaphorical, wherein the folly of such is taxed, who associate themselves equal in expence with others in higher dignity and estate, till they be losers at last, and well laughed at for their pains.

* Hartlib's Legacy, p. 15.

SAINT-FOIN.

Saint-foin, or *Holy-hay.* — Superstition may seem in the name; but I assure you there is nothing but good husbandry in the sowing thereof, as being found to be a great fertilizer of barren ground. It is otherwise called *polygala,* which I may English *much milk,* as causing the cattle to give abundance thereof. Some call it the small clover grass, and it prospereth best in the worst ground.

It was first fetched out of France from about Paris, and since is sown in divers places in England, but especially in Cobham park in this county, where it thriveth extraordinary well on dry chalky banks, where nothing else will grow. If it prospereth not equally in other dry places, it is justly to be imputed to some error in the managing thereof; as, that the ground was not well prepared, or made fine enough; that the seed was too sparing, or else old and decayed; that cattle cropt it in the first year, &c. It will last but seven years, by which time the native grass of England will prevail over this foreigner, if it be not sown again.

TROUTS.

We have treated of this fish before :* and confess this repetition had been a breach of the fundamental laws promised to this book, were it not also an addition; Kent affording trouts, at a town called Fordwich,† nigh Canterbury, differing from all others in many considerables :

1. *Greatness;* many of them being in bigness near to a salmon. 2. *Colour;* cutting white (as others do red) when best in season. 3. *Cunning;* only one of them being ever caught with an angle ;‡ whereas other trouts are easily tickled into taking, and flattered into their destruction. 4. *Abode;* remaining nine months in the sea, and three in the fresh water. They observe their coming up thereinto almost to a day; and the men of Forditch observe them as exactly, whom they catch with nets, and other devices.

WELD, or WOLD.

Know, reader, that I borrow my orthography hereof (if it be so) from the dyers themselves. This is a little seed, sown in this county some forty years since (when first it was brought into England) with barley, the growth whereof it doth not hinder in any degree; for when the barley is mowed down in harvest, then this Weld, or Wold, first peeps out of the earth, where it groweth till the May following, when it is gathered; and thus

---

* In Berkshire.
† Hasted speaks of the Littlebourne trout (a parish through which the Nail-bourne, or lesser Stour, runs in its course to the Stour) as distinct from the Fordwich trout.—ED.
‡ By Sir George Hastings.—Mr. Walton, in his Complete Angler, p. 94.

husbandmen with one sowing reap two crops; yet so as it taketh up their ground for two years.

The use hereof is for the dying of the best yellow. It hath sometimes been so low as at four pounds a load (which containeth fifteen hundred weight); and sometimes so dear that it was worth fifteen pounds; betwixt which prices it hath its constant motion; and now is in the equator betwixt both, worth seven pounds ten shillings. It was first sown in this county, and since in Norfolk and in other places.

MADDER.

This is very useful for dyers, for making of reds and violets. It is a weed whose root only is useful for dying (whilst the leaves only of woad are serviceable for that purpose); and there are three kinds thereof: 1. *Crop-Madder,* worth betwixt £4 and £5 the hundred: 2. *Umber-Owe,* worth betwixt £3 and £4: 3. *Pipe,* or *Fat Madder,* worth about £1. 10s.

Some two years since, this was sown by Sir Nicholas Crisp at Deptford, and I hope will have good success;—first, because it groweth in Zealand in the same (if not a more northern) latitude;—secondly, because wild madder grows here in abundance; and why may not tame madder, if cicurated by art?—lastly, because as good as any grew some thirty years since at Barn-Elms in Surrey, though it quit not cost, through some error in the first planter thereof, which now, we hope, will be rectified.

FLAX.

I am informed, by such who should know, that no county in England sends better or more to London; yet doth not our whole land afford the tenth part of what is spent therein; so that we are fain to fetch it from Flanders, France, yea, as far as Egypt itself. It may seem strange, that our soil, kindly for that seed, the use whereof and profit hereby so great, yet so little care is taken for the planting thereof, which, well husbanded, would find linen for the rich and living for the poor. Many would never be indicted *spinsters,* were they *spinsters* indeed; nor some to so public and shameful punishments, if painfully employed in that vocation.

When a spider is found upon our clothes, we use to say, "Some money is coming towards us." The moral is this, such who imitate the industry of that contemptible creature, "which taketh hold with her hands, and is in king's palaces,"* may, by God's blessing, weave themselves into wealth, and procure a plentiful estate.

MANUFACTURES.

Though CLOTHING (whereof we have spoken before) be diffused through many shires of England, yet is it as vigorously

* Prov. xxx. 28.

applied here as in any other place ; and Kentish cloth at the present keepeth up the credit thereof as high as ever before.

THREAD.

I place this the last, because the least of manufactures ; thread being counted a thing so inconsiderable : Abraham said to the king of Sodom, " that he would take nothing, from a thread to a shoe-latchet ;"* that is, nothing at all. It seems this Hebrew proverb surrounded the universe, beginning at a thread, a contemptible thing, and, after the encircling of all things more precious, ended where it begun, at a shoe-latchet, as mean as thread in valuation.

But, though one thread be little worth, many together prove useful and profitable ; and some thousands of pounds are sent yearly over out of England to buy that commodity. My author telleth me, that thread is only made (I understand him out of London) at Maidstone in this county, where well nigh a hundred hands are employed about it.† I believe a thousand might be occupied in the same work, and many idle women, who now only spin street thread (going tattling about with tales) might procure, if set at work, a comfortable livelihood thereby.

THE BUILDINGS.

The cathedral of Rochester is low, and little proportional to the revenues thereof. Yet hath it (though no magnificence) a venerable aspect of antiquity therein.

The king hath (besides other) three fair palaces in this shire : Greenwich, with a pleasant medley prospect of city, country, water, and land ; Eltham, not altogether so wholesome ; and Otford, which archbishop Warham did so enlarge and adorn with building, that Cranmer, his successor, was in some sort forced to exchange it with king Henry the Eighth on no gainful conditions,‡ to lesson the clergy to content themselves with decency without sumptuousness, lest it awaken envy, and in fine they prove losers thereby.

COBHAM, the house of the late duke of Richmond ; and . . . . the fair mansion of Sir Edward Hales, baronet (adequate to his large estate) when finished, will carry away the credit from all the buildings in this county.§

THE WONDERS.

A marvellous accident happened August 4, 1585, in the hamlet of Mottingham (pertaining to Eltham in this county) in a field which belongeth to Sir Percival Hart.‖ Betimes in the

* Gen. xiv. 23.   † Hartlib, in his Legacy, p. 32.   ‡ Cam. Brit. in Kent.
§ Cobham, the residence of Lord Darnley, is still in splendour ; but Sir Edward Hales's (Tunstal) is long gone.—Ed.   ‖ Villare Cantianum, p. 136.

morning the ground began to sink, so much that three great elm-trees were suddenly swallowed into the pit; the tops falling downward into the hole; and before ten of the clock they were so overwhelmed, that no part of them might be discerned, the concave being suddenly filled with water. The compass of the hole was about eighty yards, and so profound, that a sounding line of fifty fathoms could hardly find or feel any bottom. Ten yards' distance from that place there was another piece of ground sunk in like manner near the highway, and so nigh a dwelling house, that the inhabitants were greatly terrified therewith.

THE NAVY ROYAL.

It may be justly accounted a Wonder of Art. And know, the ships are properly here handled, because the most, best, and biggest of them have their birth (built at Woolwich) and winter abode nigh Chatham in the river of Medway in this county. Indeed, before the reign of queen Elizabeth, the ships royal were so few, they deserved not the name of a fleet; when our kings hired vessels from Hamborough, Lubeck, yea Genoa itself. But such who, instead of their own servants, use chair-folk in their houses, shall find their work worse done, and yet pay dearer for it.

Queen Elizabeth, sensible of this mischief, erected a navy royal (continued and increased by her successors) of the best ships Europe ever beheld. Indeed much is in the matter, the excellency of our English oak; more in the making, the cunning of our shipwrights; most in the manning, the courage of our seamen; and yet all to God's blessing, who so often hath crowned them with success.

If that man who hath *versatile ingenium* be thereby much advantaged for the working of his own fortune, our ships, so active to turn and wind at pleasure, must needs be more useful than the Spanish galleons, whose unwieldiness fixeth them almost in one posture, and maketh them the steadier marks for their enemies. As for Flemish bottoms, though they are finer built, yet as the slender barbe is not so fit to charge with, they are found not so useful in fight. The great sovereign, built at Woolwich, a lieger-ship for state, is the greatest ship our island ever saw. But great medals are made for some grand solemnity, whilst lesser coin are more current and passable in payment.

I am credibly informed, that that mystery of shipwrights, for some descents, hath been preserved successively in families, of whom the pets about Chatham are of singular regard. "Good success have they with their skill;" and carefully keep so precious a pearl, lest otherwise amongst many friends some foes attain unto it! It is no monopoly which concealeth that from common enemies, the concealing whereof is for the common good. May this mystery of ship-making in England never be lost, till this floating world be arrived at its own haven, the end and dissolution thereof !

I know what will be objected by foreigners, to take off the lustre of our navy royal; viz. that, though the model of our great ships primitively were our own, yet we fetched the first mould and pattern of our frigates from the Dunkirks, when in the days of the duke of Buckingham (then admiral) we took some frigates from them, two of which still survive in his majesty's navy, by the name of The Providence, and Expedition.

All this is confessed; and honest men may lawfully learn something from thieves for their own better defence. But it is added, we have improved our patterns, and the transcript doth at this day exceed the original. Witness some of the swiftest Dunkirks and Ostenders, whose wings in a fair flight have failed them, overtaken by our frigates, and they still remain the monuments thereof in our navy.

Not to disgrace our neighbouring nations, but vindicate ourselves, in these nine following particulars the navy royal exceeds all kingdoms and states in Europe:

1. *Swift Sailing; which will appear by a comparative induction of all other nations.*

First, for the Portugal, his *carvils* and *caracts*, whereof few now remain (the charges of maintaining them far exceeding the profit they bring in); they were the veriest drones on the sea, the rather because formerly their ceiling was dammed up with a certain kind of mortar to dead the shot, a fashion now by them disused.

The French (how dextrous soever in land battles) are left-handed in sea fights, whose best ships are of Dutch building.

The Dutch build their ships so floaty and buoyant, they have little hold in the water in comparison of ours, which keep the better wind, and so outsail them.

The Spanish pride hath infected their ships with loftiness, which makes them but the fairer marks to our shot.

Besides, the wind hath so much power of them in bad weather, so that it drives them two leagues for one of ours to the leeward, which is very dangerous upon a lee shore.

Indeed the Turkish frigates, especially some thirty-six of Algiers, formed and built much near the English mode, and manned by renegadoes, many of them English, being already too nimble-heeled for the Dutch, may hereafter prove mischievous to us, if not seasonably prevented.

2. *Strength.*

I confine this only to the timber whereof they are made, our English oak being the best in the world. True it is (to our shame and sorrow be it written and read) the Dutch of late have built them some ships of English oak, which (through the negligence or covetousness of some great ones) was bought here and transported hence. But the best is, that, as Bishop Latimer once said to one who had preached his sermon, that he had gotten his fiddlestick but not his rosin, so the Hollanders with our timber did not buy also our art of ship-building.

Now the ships of other countries are generally made of fir and other such slight wood; whereby it cometh to pass, that, as in the battle in the forest of Ephraim (wherein Absolom was slain), "the wood devoured more people that day than the sword,"* the splinters of so brittle timber kill more than the shot in a sea-fight.

3. *Comeliness.*

Our frigates are built so neat and snug, made long and low; so that (as the make of some women's bodies handsomely concealeth their pregnancy or great belly) their contrivance hideth their bigness without suspicion, the enemy not expecting thirty, when (to his cost) he hath found sixty pieces of ordnance in them. Our masts stand generally very upright; whereas those of the Spaniards hang over their poop, as if they were ready to drop by the board; their decks are unequal, having many risings and fallings, whereas ours are even. Their ports some higher in a tier than others, ours drawn upon an equal line. Their cables bad (besides subject to rot in these countries) because bought at the second hand; whereas we make our best markets, fetching our cordage from the fountain thereof.

4. *Force.*

Besides the strength inherent in the structure (whereof before), this is accessary, consisting in the weight and number of their guns; those of the

Sixth		10, 12, 14, 16, 18, 20,	
Fifth	Rates, carrying	22, 26, 28, 30,	Ordnance mounted.
Fourth		38, 40, 44, 48, 50,	
Third		50, 54, 56, 60,	
Second		60, 64, 70,	

The Royal Sovereign, being one of the first rates, when she is fitted for the seas, carrieth one hundred and four pieces of ordnance mounted.

5. *Seamen.*

Courageous and skilful.—For the first, we remember the proverb of Solomon : " Let another praise thee, not thy own mouth ; a stranger, not thy own lips."† The Spaniards with sad shrug, and Dutch with a sorrowful shaking of their heads, give a tacit assent hereunto.

---

* 2 Samuel xviii. 8.　　　　† Proverbs xxvii. 2.

Skilful.—Indeed navigation is much improved, especially since Saint Paul's time; insomuch that, when a man goes bunglingly about any work in a ship, I have heard our Englishmen say, "Such a man is one of St. Paul's mariners." For though, no doubt, they were as ingenious as any in that age to decline a tempest,* yet modern experience affords fairer fences against foul weather.

6. *Advantageous Weapons.*

Besides guns of all sorts and sizes, from the pistol to whole cannon, they have round-double-head-bur-spike-crow-bar-case-chain-shot. I join them together, because (though different instruments of death) they all concur in doing execution. If they be wind-ward of a ship, they have arrows made to shoot out of a bow with fire-works at the end, which, if striking unto the enemy's sails, will stick there, and fire them and the ship. If they lie board and board, they throw hand-grenades with stink-pots into the ship; which make so noisome a smell, that the enemy is forced to thrust their heads out of the ports for air.

7. *Provision.*

1. Wholesome our English beef and pork, keeping sweet and sound longer than any flesh of other countries; even twenty-six months, to the East and West Indies.

2. More plentiful than any prince or state in all Europe alloweth; the seamen having two beef, two pork, and three fish-days. Besides, every seaman is always well stored with hooks to catch fish, with which our seas do abound; insomuch that many times six will diet on four men's allowance, and so save the rest therewith to buy fresh meat, when landing where it may be procured. I speak not this that hereafter their allowance from the king should be less, but that their loyalty to him, and thankfulness to God, may be the more.

8. *Accommodation.*

Every one of his majesty's ships and frigate officers have a distinct cabin for themselves; for which the Dutch, French, and Portuguese do envy them, who for the most part lie *sub dio* under decks.

9. *Government.*

Few offences comparatively to other fleets are therein committed, and fewer escape punishment. The offender, if the fault be small, is tried by a court-martial, consisting of the officers of the ship; if great, by a council of war, wherein only commanders and the judge-advocate. If any sleep in their watches, it is pain of death. After eight o'clock none, save the captain, lieutenant, and master, may presume to burn a candle.

* Acts xxvi

No smoking of tobacco (save for the privilege aforesaid) at any time, but in one particular place of the ship, and that over a tub of water. Preaching they have lately had twice a week; praying twice a day; but my intelligencer could never hear that the Lord's Supper for some years was administered aboard of any ship; an omission which I hope hereafter will be amended.

But never did this navy appear more triumphant, than when in May last it brought over our gracious sovereign, being almost becalmed (such the fear of the winds to offend with over roughness); the prognostic of his majesty's peaceable reign.

The Farewell.

Being to take our leave of these our wooden walls; first, I wish that they may conquer with their mast and sails, without their guns; that their very appearance may fright their foes into submission.

But if, in point of honour or safety, they be necessitated to engage, may they always keep the wind of the enemy, that their shot may fly with the greater force, and that the smoke of their powder, pursuing the foe, may drive him to fire at hazard! May their gunner be in all places of the ship, to see where he can make a shot with the best advantage; their carpenter and his crew be always in the hold, presently to drive in a wooden plug (whereas a shot comes betwixt wind and water), and to clap a board with tar and camel's hair upon it till the dispute be over; their chirurgeon and his assistants be in the same place (out of danger of shot) to dress the wounded; their captain be in the uppermost, the lieutenant in every part of the ship, to encourage the seamen: the chaplain at his devotions, to importune heaven for success, and encouraging all by his good council, if time will permit!

MEDICINAL WATERS.

TUNBRIDGE-WATER.

It is usual for Providence, when intending a benefit to mankind, to send some signal chance on the errand, to bring the first tidings thereof; most visible in the news of medicinal waters.

The first discovery of this water (though variously reported) is believed from a footman to a Dutch lord, who passed this way, and drinking thereof found it in taste very like to that at the Spa in Germany.

Indeed, there is a great symbolizing betwixt them in many concurrences; and I believe it is as sovereign as the other, save that it is true of things as of persons, " Major è longinquo reverentia." Surely it runneth through some iron-mine, because so good for splenetic distempers. But I leave the full relation to such who, having experimentally found the virtue of it, can set their seal of *probatum est* unto the commendation thereof."

PROVERBS.

" A Kentish yeoman."]

It passeth for a plain man of a plentiful estate; yeomen in this county bearing away the bell for wealth from all of their rank in England.

Yeomen, contracted for *Yemen-mein*, are so called, saith a great antiquary,* from *gemein* (*g* in the beginning is usually turned into *y*, as *gate* into *yate*), which signifieth *common* in old Dutch; so that *Yeoman* is a *Commoner*, one undignified with any title of gentility!—a condition of people almost peculiar to England; seeing in France, Italy, and Spain (like a lame *dye*, which hath no points betwixt *duce* and *cinque*) no medium between gentlemen and peasants; whereas amongst us the yeomen, *Ingenui*, or *Legales Homines*, are in effect the basis of all the nation, formerly most mounting the subsidy-book in peace with their purses, and the muster-roll in war with their persons. Kent, as we have said, affordeth the richest in this kind; whence the rhyme,

> " A knight of Cales, and a gentleman of Wales,
>   And a laird of the north countree;
> A yeoman of Kent, with his yearly rent,
>   Will buy them out all three."

Cales Knights were made in that voyage, by Robert earl of Essex, anno Domini 1596, to the number of sixty, whereof (though many of great birth and estate) some were of low fortunes; and therefore queen Elizabeth was half offended with the earl for making knighthood so common. Of the numerousness of Welsh gentlemen we shall have cause to speak hereafter. Northern lairds are such who in Scotland hold lands in chief of the king, whereof some have no great revenue, so that a Kentish yeoman (by the help of an hyperbole) may countervail, &c.

Yet such yeomen refuse to have the title of Master put upon them, contenting themselves without any addition of gentility; and this mindeth me of a passage in my memory. One immoderately boasted, " that there was not one of his name in all England, but that he was a gentleman." To whom one in the company returned, " I am sorry, sir, you have never a good man of your name."

Sure am I in Kent there is many a hospital yeoman of great ability, who, though no gentleman by descent and title, is one by his means and state; let me also add by his courteous carriage, though constantly called but Good-man, to which name he desireth to answer in all respects.

* Verstegan, in his " Restoring of Decayed Intelligence."

" A Man of Kent."*]

This may relate either to the liberty or to the courage of this
county men; liberty, the tenure of villanage (so frequent else
where) being here utterly unknown, and the bodies of all Kentish
persons being of free condition. Insomuch that it is holden
sufficient for one to avoid the objection of bondage, to say " that
his father was born in Kent."† Now seeing " servi non sunt
viri, quia non sui juris," (a bond-man is no man, because not
his own man); the Kentish for their freedom have achieved to
themselves the name of men.

Others refer it to their courage; which from the time of king
Canutus hath purchased unto them the precedency of marching
in our English armies to lead the van.

" Ob egregiæ virtutis meritum, quod potenter et patenter
exercuit, Cantia nostra primæ cohortis honorem, et primos congressus hostium, usque in hodiernum diem in omnibus præliis
obtinet ;"‡ (For the desert of their worthy valour, which they
so powerfully and publicly expressed, our Kent obtaineth even
unto this day the honour of the first regiment, and first assault-
ing the enemy in all battles.)§

Our author lived in the reign of Henry the Second; and whether Kentish men retain this privilege unto this day (wherein
many things are turned upside down, and then no wonder if
also forward and backward) is to me unknown.

" Neither in Kent nor Christendom."]

This seems a very insolent expression, and as unequal a division. Surely the first author thereof had small skill in even
distribution, to measure an inch against an ell; yea, to weigh a
grain against a pound. But know, reader, that this home proverb is calculated only for the elevation of our own country, and
ought to be restrained to English Christendom, whereof Kent
was first converted to the faith. So then Kent and Christendom
(parallel to Rome and Italy) is as much as the first cut, and all the
loaf besides. I know there passes a report, that Henry the
Fourth, king of France, mustering his soldiers at the siege of a
city, found more Kentish men therein than foreigners of all
Christendom beside, which (being but seventy years since) is by
some made the original of this proverb, which was more ancient
in use: and therefore I adhere to the former interpretation;
always provided,

—————— *Si quid novisti rectius istis,*
Candidus imperti ; si non, his utere mecum.

" If thou know'st better, it to me impart ;
If not, use these of mine with all my heart."

* There is a dispute between East and West as to which part of the county at-
taches " Men of Kent," and to which only " Kentish Men."—ED.
† Fitzherbert 15, in title of Villanage.   ‡ Johannis Sarisburiensis,
§ De Nugis Curial. 6, cap. 16. Thus cited (for hitherto I have not read the
original) by Mr. Selden, in his Notes on Polyolbion, p. 303.—F.

For mine own part, I write nothing but *animo revocandi*, ready to retract it when better evidence shall be brought unto me. Nor will I oppose such who understand it for periphrasis of *nowhere;* Kent being the best place of England, Christendom of the world.

" Kentish long-tails."]

Let me premise, that those are much mistaken who first found this proverb on a miracle of Austin the monk, which is thus reported. It happened in an English village, where Saint Austin was preaching, that the Pagans therein did beat and abuse both him and his associates, opprobriously tying fish-tails to their backsides; in revenge whereof an impudent author re-lateth (Reader, you and I must blush for him who hath not the modesty to blush for himself) how such appendants grew to the hind parts of all that generation.* I say they are much mistaken; for the scene of this lying wonder was not laid in any part of Kent, but pretended many miles off, nigh Cerne in Dorsetshire.

To come closer to the sense of this proverb, I conceive it first of outlandish extraction, and cast by foreigners as a note of disgrace on all the English, though it chanceth to stick only on the Kentish at this day: for, when there happened in Palestine a difference betwixt Robert brother to Saint Lewis king of France and our William Longspee earl of Salisbury, hear how the Frenchman insulted over the nation:

" O timidorum *Caudatorum* formidolositas ! quàm beatus, quàm mundus præsens foret exercitus, si à *caudis* purgaretur et *caudatis !* "‡ (O the cowardliness of these fearful *Long-tails !* how happy, how clean would this our army be, were it but purged from *tails* and *long-tails !* "

That the English were nicked by this speech, appears by the reply of the earl of Salisbury, following still the metaphor: " The son of my father shall press thither to-day, whither you shall not dare to approach his *horse-tail.*"

Some will have the English so called from wearing a pouch or poke (a bag to carry their baggage in) behind their backs, whilst probably the proud Monsieurs had their lacqueys for that purpose; in proof whereof, they produce ancient pictures of the English drapery and armory, wherein such conveyances do appear. If so, it was neither sin nor shame for the common sort of people to carry their own necessaries; and it matters not much whether the pocket be made on either side, or wholly behind.

If any demand how this nick-name (cut off from the rest of England) continues still entailed on Kent? the best conjecture is, because that county lieth nearest to France, and the French are beheld as the first founders of this aspersion. But if any

* Hierome Porter, in the Flowers of the Lives of the Saints, p. 515.
† Matthew Paris, anno Domini 1250, p. 790.

will have the Kentish so called from drawing and dragging boughs of trees behind them, which afterwards they advanced above their heads, and so partly cozened, partly threatened, king William the Conqueror to continue their ancient customs; I say, if any will impute it to this original, I will not oppose.

" Kentish Gavel-kind."]

It is a custom in this county, whereby the lands are divided equally among all the sons; and in default of them amongst the daughters; that is, *give all kind,*—*kind* signifying a child in the low Dutch. This practice, as it appears in Tacitus, was derived to our Saxons from the ancient Germans:

Teutonibus priscis patrios succedit in agros
Mascula stirps omnis, ne foret ulla potens.

" 'Mongst the old Teuch, lest one o'ertop his breed,
To his sire's land doth every son succeed."

It appeareth that, in the eighteenth year of king Henry the Sixth, there were not above forty persons in Kent, but all their land was held in this tenure. But, on the petition of divers gentlemen, this custom was altered by act of Parliament in the 31st of king Henry the Eighth, and Kentish lands for the most part reduced to an uniformity with the rest in England.*

" Dover-court: all speakers, and no hearers."]

There is a village in Essex, not far from Harwich, called Dover-court, formerly famous for a rood burnt in the reign of king Henry the Eighth. But I take it here to be taken for some tumultuous court kept at Dover, the confluence of many blustering seamen, who are not easily ordered into awful attention. The proverb is applied to such irregular conferences, wherein the people are all tongue and no ears, parallel to the Latin proverb, " Cyclopum Respublica," being thus charactered that therein οὐδεὶς ἀκούει οὐδὲν οὐδενός.

" The father to the bough,
The son to the plough."]

That is, though the father be executed for his offence, the son shall nevertheless succeed to his inheritance.

In this county, if a tenant in fee-simple of lands in gavel-kind commit felony,† and suffer the judgment of death therefore, the prince shall have all his chattels for a forfeiture. But as touching the land, he shall neither have the escheat of it, though it be immediately holden of himself, nor the day, year, and waste, if it be holden of any other; for in that case the heir, notwithstanding the offence of his ancestor, shall enter immediately and enjoy the lands after the same customs and services by which they were holden before; in assurance whereof, the former proverb is become current in this county. But this rule

---

* No lands were allowed on tenure by the disgavelling acts, except those of the gentlemen named in those acts, who were mostly the principal noblemen and gentlemen in the county.—ED.

† W. Lambarde's " Perambulation of Kent," pp. 550 and 551.

holdeth in case of felony and of murder only, and not in case of treason, nor (peradventure) in piracy, and other felonies made by statutes of later times, because the custom cannot take hold of that which then was not in being. It holdeth moreover in case where the offender is justiced by order of law, and not where he withdraws himself after the fault committed, and will not abide his lawful trial.

" Tenterden's steeple is the cause of the breach in Goodwin Sands."]

It is used commonly in derision of such who, being demanded to render a reason of some important accident, assign " non causam pro causâ," or a ridiculous and improbable cause thereof. And hereon a story depends.

When the vicinage in Kent met to consult about the inundation of Goodwin Sands, and what might be the cause thereof, an old man imputed it to the building of Tenterden steeple in this county; " for those sands," said he, " were firm lands before that steeple was built, which ever since were overflown with sea-water." Hereupon all heartily laughed at his unlogical reason, making that the effect in Nature, which was only the consequent in time ; not flowing from, but following after, the building of that steeple.

But one story is good till another is heard. Though this be all whereon this proverb is generally grounded, I met since with a supplement thereunto. It is this. Time out of mind money was constantly collected out of this county to fence the east banks thereof against the eruption of the seas ; and such sums were deposited in the hands of the bishop of Rochester. But, because the sea had been very quiet for many years, without any encroachings, the bishop commuted that money to the building of a steeple, and endowing of a church, in Tenterden. By this diversion of the collection for the maintenance of the banks, the sea afterwards brake in upon Goodwin Sands.* And now the old man had told a rational tale, had he found but the due favour to finish it. And thus, sometimes, that is causelessly accounted ignorance in the speaker, which is nothing but impatience in the auditors, unwilling to attend the end of the discourse.

" A jack of Dover."]

I find the first mention of this proverb in our English Ennius, Chaucer, in his proem to the cook :

> " And many a jack of Dover he had sold,
> Which had been two times hot, and two times cold. "

This is no fallacy, but good policy, in an household, to lengthen out the provision thereof ; and, though less toothsome, may be wholesome enough. But what is no false logic in a family, is false ethics in an inn, or cook's-shop, to make the abused guest to pay after the rate of new and fresh for meat at he second and third hand.

* G. Sandys, in his notes on the 13th of Ovid's Metamorphoses, p. 282.

Parallel to this is the Latin proverb, " Crambe bis cocta;" *crambe* being a kind of colewort, which (with vinegar) being raw is good, boiled better, twice boiled noisome to the palate, and nauseous to the stomach.

Both proverbs are appliable to such who grate the ears of their auditors with ungrateful tautologies, of what is worthless in itself; tolerable as once uttered in the notion of novelty, but abominable, if repeated, for the tediousness thereof.

PRINCES.

John of Eltham, second son to king Edward the Second, by Isabel his queen, was born at Eltham in this county. He was afterwards created earl of Cornwall. A sprightly gentleman, and who would have given greater evidence of his abilities, if not prevented by death in the prime of his age. He died in Scotland, in the tenth year of the reign of king Edward the Third.

Be it observed that hitherto the younger sons to our English kings were never advanced higher than earls. Thus Richard, second son to king John, never had higher English honour than the Earl of Cornwall, though at the same time he were king of the Romans. But this John of Eltham was the last son of an English king who died a plain earl, the title of Duke coming afterwards into fashion. Hence it was that all the younger sons of kings were from this time forwards created dukes, except expiring in their infancy.

Bridget of Eltham, fourth daughter of king Edward the Fourth, and Elizabeth his queen, was born at Eltham in this county. Observing her three eldest sisters not over happy in their husbands, she resolved to wed a monastical life, and (no whit ambitious of the place of an abbess) became an ordinary votary in the nunnery at Dartford in this county, founded by king Edward the Third. The time of her death is uncertain; but this certain, that her dissolution happened some competent time before the dissolution of that nunnery.

Edmund, youngest son to king Henry the Seventh and Elizabeth his queen (bearing the name of his grand-father Edmund of Haddam) was born at Greenwich, in this county, 1495.[*] He was by his father created duke of Somerset; and he died, before he was full five years of age, at Bishop's Hatfield in Hertfordshire, which then was the nursery for the king's children. Little notice generally is taken of this prince; and no wonder, for

> " Who only act short paths in infant age
> Are soon forgot they e'er came on the stage."

He died anno Domini 1500, in the fifteenth year of his father's

---

[*] Vincent, in his Discovery of Brook's Errors, p. 481.

reign; and lieth buried (without any monument) in Westminster.

HENRY the EIGHTH, second son of king Henry the Seventh, was born at Greenwich. A prince whom some praise to the skies, others depress to the pit, whilst the third (and truer) sort embrace a middle way betwixt both.

Extreme.—Some carry him up as the paragon of princes; the great advancer of God's glory and true religion; and the most magnificent that ever sate on the throne. Master Fox, in his "Acts and Monuments," is sometimes very superlative in his commendation; and so are most Protestant authors who wrote under his reign.

Mean.—Polydore Vergil hath an expression of him to this effect: "Princeps in quo æquali quasi temperamento magnæ inerant virtutes, ac non minora vitia;" (a prince in whom great virtues, and no less vices, were in a manner equally contemperated.)

Extreme.—Sir Walter Raleigh, in his preface to his great "History," whose words may better be read there than transcribed thence, makes him the truest map of tyranny. Insomuch, that king James (who could not abide that any under a king should speak against a king) was much offended thereat. And those words worst became the writer so much advanced by the daughter of the said king Henry.

For mine own part, I humbly conceive, God effected more by his work as the instrument, than he was directed by God's word as the principal. Indeed he was a man of uncontrollable spirit, carrying a mandamus in his mouth, sufficiently sealed when he put his hand to his hilt. He awed all into obedience, which some impute to his skilfulness to rule, others ascribe to his subjects' ignorance to resist.

Let one pleasant passage (for recreation) have its pass amongst much serious matter. A company of little boys were by their schoolmaster not many years since appointed to act the play of "King Henry the Eighth," and one who had no presence, but (an absence rather) as of a whining voice, puling spirit, consumptionish body, was appointed to personate king Henry himself, only because he had the richest clothes, and his parents the best people of the parish: but, when he had spoken his speech rather like a mouse than a man, one of his fellow actors told him, "If you speak not *Hoh* with a better spirit, your Parliament will not grant you a penny of money."

But it is vain to glean in the stubble; seeing the Lord Herbert hath so largely wrote the life of this king, that nothing of moment can be added thereunto. He died January 28, 1546.

MARY, eldest daughter to king Henry the Eighth and queen Katherine of Spain, was born at Greenwich, the 18th of February 1518. She did partake of both her parents in her person and properties; having from her father a broad face, big voice, and undaunted spirit; from her mother a swarthy complexion, and a mind wholly devoted to the Romish religion. She attained the crown by complying with the gentry of Norfolk and Suffolk, promising them to continue religion as established by king Edward the Sixth; after the breach of which promise she never prospered. For, first, she lost the hearts of her subjects, then her hopes of a child, then the company, not to say affection, of her husband, then the city of Calais, then her mirth, then her health, then her life, which ended on the 17th of November, 1558.

Queen ELIZABETH, second daughter to king Henry the Eighth, was born at Greenwich, September 7, 1533. She was heir only to the eminences of her father, his learning, bounty, courage, and success; besides grace and true goodness, wherein she was daughter to her mother.

Her learning appears in her two Latin speeches to the university; and a third, little better than extempore, to the Poland ambassador. Her bounty was better than her father's, less flowing from humour, and more founded on merit, and ordered with moderation; seeing that is the best liberality that so enricheth the receiver that it doth not impoverish the giver.

Her courage was undaunted, never making herself so cheap to her favourites but that she still valued her own authority, whereof this an eminent instance:

A prime officer with a white staff, whose name I purposely forbear, coming into her presence, the queen willed him to confer such a place now void on one of her servants whom she commended unto him. "Pleaseth your highness, madam," saith the lord, "the disposal thereof pertaineth to me by virtue of this white staff conferred upon me." "True," said the queen; "yet I never gave you your office so absolutely, but I still reserved myself of the *quorum*." "But of the *quarum*, madam!" returned the lord, presuming on the favour of her highness. Hereat the queen, in some passion, snatching the staff out of his hand, "You shall acknowledge me," said she, "of the *quorum, quarum, quorum*, before you have it again." The lord waited staff-less almost a day (which seemed so long unto him as if the sun stood still) before the same was reconferred upon him.

Her success was admirable, keeping the king of Spain at arms-end all her reign. She was well skilled in the queen-craft; and, by her policy and prosperity, she was much beloved by her people; insomuch that since it hath been said, "that queen Elizabeth might lawfully do that which king James might not." For, although the laws were equally the rule to them both, yet her popularity sugared many bitter things; her subjects thanking her for taking those taxes which they refused to pay to her successor. She died at Richmond, March 24, anno Domini 1602.

MARY, daughter to king James and Anne of Denmark his queen, was born at Greenwich, April 8, about eleven o'clock at night, and soon after baptized with greater state than the memory of any then alive in England could recover.* King James was wont pleasantly to say, " that he would not pray to the Virgin Mary, but he would pray for the Virgin Mary ;" meaning his own daughter. But, it seems, his prayers prevailed not (Divine Providence having otherwise determined it) for her long life, who expired in her infancy, and lies buried at Westminster.

SOPHIA, youngest daughter to king James and queen Anne, was born at Greenwich the 22nd day of June 1606 ; and departed this life three days after.† This royal babe lieth buried nigh queen Elizabeth, in the north part of the chapel of king Henry the Seventh, represented sleeping in her cradle, wherewith vulgar eyes, especially of the weaker sex, are more affected (as level to their cognizance, more capable of what is pretty than what is pompous) than with all the magnificent monuments in Westminster.

CHARLES, eldest son of king Charles and queen Mary, was born at Greenwich, anno 1629. A fright of his mother is generally reported to have accelerated, or rather antedated, his nativity. The popish priests belonging to the queen stood ready, watching to snatch the royal babe to their superstitious baptism ; but the tender care of king Charles did out-vigil their watchfulness, commanding Doctor Webb (his next chaplain in attendance) to christen it according to the church of England. This done, within few hours he expired ; and lies buried at Westminster.

SAINTS.

EALPHAGE, born of good parentage, had his education during his youth in Gloucestershire ; then he became a monk at Glastonbury. But, that place not sufficiently suiting the severity of his solitary soul, removing thence he built himself a hut at Bath, which small cell in process of time (the longest line proceedeth from a little point at first) proved the beautiful priory in that place. Hence by Dunstan he was preferred bishop of Winchester, continuing therein twenty-two years ; and at last became bishop of Canterbury.‡

* Stow's Chronicle, p. 862.
† Stow, in his Survey of London, continued by How, p. 512.
‡ Godwin, in his Catalogue of Archbishops of Canterbury.

It happeneth that the cruel Danes seizing on that city put it under decimation. Start not, loyal reader, at the word, if in the late tyranny of the times thou thyself hast been against all right and reason decimated in thy purse, as now the poor citizens of Canterbury were in their persons. For the Danes (under pretence of tribute detained), saved the tenth part of the citizens alive amounting unto eight hundred and four : destroyed the other nine parts, no fewer than seven thousand two hundred and thirty-six.

As for archbishop Alphage they demanded of him a greater sum than he could pay or procure, whose wealth consisted chiefly in his piety, no current coin with the pagan Danes ; so that, after seven months' imprisonment, they barbarously murdered him, near Greenwich, about the year 1013.

His corpse was first buried in St. Paul's ; and then removed, by the command of king Canutus, to Canterbury. Impudent monks have almost as much wronged his memory, as the Danes did his person ; farcing his life with such abominable lies, that thereby the very truth therein is rendered suspected.

AGELNOTH, son to count Agelmar, was a calendared saint in this county, being elected archbishop of Canterbury, from being dean over the canons in that convent.*

This is the first time I find the dignity of Decanus, or Dean, in England ; so called from Δέκα, ten,† having (it seemeth), at the first, inspection just over that number, though since an Heteroclite in England ; as, either over fewer, but six in Norwich, Bristol, &c. ; or many more in other cathedrals.

He was so pious in his life, that he was commonly called the Good. And here one may justly wonder ; God having two grand epithets, Optimus and Maximus, most give the former the go-by, and strive only for the latter, to be the greatest ; though greatness without goodness is both destructive to him that hath it, and dangerous to all others about him.

Going to Rome to get his pall from the Pope, by him he was courteously entertained, and deserved his welcome, who gave him (saith my author‡) for the arm of Saint Augustine bishop of Hippo, one hundred talents of silver, and one talent of gold, citing bishop Godwin for his author : but indeed that bishop, though reporting the hundred talents of silver, mentioneth not at all that of gold.

Perchance Mr. Weever had lately read (still obversing his fancy) how Pharaoh king of Egypt, having taken away king Jehoahash, " condemned the land in an hundred talents of silver, and a talent of gold."§ And to me it is a double wonder ; first, that this archbishop *would* give ; secondly, that he *could*

* Weever, Funeral Sermon, p. 301.
† Cowel's Interpreter, on the word Dean.   ‡ Weever, ut prius.
§ 2 Chronicles xxxvi. 3.

give, living in a harraged land (wherein so much misery and little money) so vast a sum.

However, this mindeth me of a passage in Saint Augustine, speaking of the relics of the deceased, "Si tamen martyrum," (if so they be of martyrs); and let me choose the words of this Father on this Father, "Si tamen Augustini:" If this were the arm of Saint Augustine, and not of some other ordinary (not to say infamous) person.

Well, were one as good a mathematician as he who collected the stature of Hercules from the length of his foot, it were easy to proportion the price of Saint Augustine's whole body, from this valuation of his arm. And now, having so dearly bought it, let him dispose thereof as he pleaseth; and let no man grudge if he gave it to Coventry rather than Canterbury.

He expended much in repairing (or rather renewing) of his cathedral of Canterbury, lately destroyed by the Danes; assisted therein by the bounty of king Canutus, who, at the instance and by the advice of this prelate, did many worthy works. Our Agelnoth, after he had sat seventeen years in his see, died October 29, in the year 1038.

MARTYRS.

WILLIAM WHITE was born in this county; and entering into orders, became a great maintainer of the opinions of Wicliffe.* He was the first married priest in England since the Pope's solemn probibition thereof. I find Johan his wife commended for her modesty and patience, and that she was "conjux tali digna marito."† Indeed she shared very deep in her husband's sufferings, hardly coming off with her life at the last; for he, though leaving his living (as unsafe to hold), still kept his calling, and preached about all the eastern parts of the land.

The same mouth which commanded the disciples in time of peace, "Go not from house to house,"‡ so to avoid the censure of levity, advised them also, "When ye are persecuted in one city, fly to another,"§ so to provide for their own security. Such the constant practice of this William White, who was as a partridge daily on the wing, removing from place to place. At last he was seized on at Norwich by William Alnwick, the cruel bishop thereof, and charged with thirty articles, for which he was condemned, and burnt at Norwich in September 1428.|| He was the Proto-martyr of all born in this county; and had not five before him in all England who suffered merely for religion, without any mixture of matter of state charged upon them.

As for Marian martyrs, we meet with many in this county, though not to be charged on cardinal Pole archbishop of Canterbury, further than his bare permission thereof.

It is observed of bears, that they love to kill their own

---

* Bale, de Scriptoribus Britannicis, p. 564.　† Idem, ibidem.
‡ Luke x. 7.　　§ Matthew x. 23.　　|| Fox, Acts and Monuments.

prey, and (except forced by famine) will not feed on what was dead before. Such a bear was bloody Bonner, who was all for the quick, and not for the dead; whilst, clean contrary, cardinal Pole let the living alone, and vented his spleen only on the dead (whom he could wrong, but not hurt); burning the bones of Martin Bucer and Paulus Phagius at Cambridge. Such martyrs, therefore, as suffered in this shire, were either by the cruelty of Griffin bishop of Rochester, or of Thornton suffragan of Dover.

CONFESSORS.

Simon Fish, Esquire, was born in this county, bred a lawyer in Gray's Inn, London.* Here he acted that part in a tragedy, wherein the pride of Cardinal Wolsey was personated, and wherewith that prelate was so offended, that Fish was fain to fly, and live two years beyond the seas. There he made, and thence sent over into England, a small but sharp treatise, called "The Supplication of Beggars," termed by Master Fox a libel, understand him a little book;† otherwise prizing and praising it for a master-piece of wit, learning, and religion, discovering the superstition of that age. This by queen Anna Bolen, was presented by king Henry the Eighth, who therewith was so highly affected, that he sent for the author home, and favoured him in great proportion.

However, many nets were laid by the Popish party against him, especially by Sir Thomas More, his implacable enemy; yet Fish had the happiness to escape the hands of men, and to fall into the hand of God more immediately; dying of the plague, 1531, and lieth buried at St. Dunstan's in London.

Sir James Hales was born, did live, and was richly landed, in this county,‡ one of the justices of the Common Pleas, a man of most signal integrity. When the rest of the judges (frighted at the frowns of the duke of Northumberland) subscribed the disinheriting of the Lady Mary and Lady Elizabeth, he only refused, as against both law and conscience.

Yet afterwards, in the first of queen Mary, he fell into the displeasure of bishop Gardiner (which, like juniper coals, once kindled hardly quenched) for urging the observation of some laws of king Edward the Sixth. For this he was imprisoned, hardly used, and so threatened by his keeper, that he endeavoured to have killed himself; which, being after let at liberty, he afterwards effected, drowning himself in a small water near his house; fear and melancholy so much prevailing upon him. Mr. Fox concludeth the sad poem of his final estate with this distich:

---

* J. Bale, in his book titled "Scriptores nostri Temporis," p. 102.
† Acts and Monuments, page 1014.
‡ His house was at the Dane-john, or Dungeon, Canterbury.—Ed.

Cum nihil ipse vides, propria quin labe laboret,
  Tu tua fac cures, cætera mitte Deo.

" Seeing nought thou seest, but failing in the best,
  Mind thy own matters, and leave God the rest."

We must look on his foul deed with anger, and yet with pity on the doer thereof; frown on the one, and weep for the other: for, seeing he had led a right godly life, and had suffered so much on the account of his conscience, I hope that his station in this place will not be cavilled at by any charitable persons. He died anno Domini 1555.

CARDINALS.

JOHN KEMP, son to Thomas, grand-child to Sir John Kemp, nephew to Sir Roger Kemp, both knights, was born at Wye in this county (where he built a fair college for seculars); bred also in Merton College in Oxford; successively bishop of Rochester, Chichester, and London; afterwards archbishop of York and Canterbury; cardinal, first by the title of Saint Balbine, then of Saint Rufine in Rome: all his preferments are comprehended in the old following verse: *

  " Bis primas, ter præsul erat, bis cardine functus."

He had another honour, to make up the distich, being twice lord chancellor of England; so that I may add:

  " Et dixit legem bis cancellarius Anglis."

Such are mistaken who report him the first raiser of his family to a knightly degree, which he found in that equipage, as is aforesaid, though he left it much improved in estate by his bounty; and some of his name and blood flourish in Kent at this day. He died a very old man, March the 22d, anno 1453.

RICHARD CLIFFORD.—His nativity may bear some debate, Herefordshire pretending unto him: but because Robert Clifford was his brother † (in the first of king Henry the Fourth high-sheriff of this county, and richly landed therein), I adjudge him a Cantian, and assign Bobbing as the most probable place of his birth. His worth preferred him bishop of London 1407; and he was sent by king Henry the Fourth as his ambassador of the council of Constance. I could [not] hold my hand from ranking him under the topic of Cardinals, confident that no ingenious person would take exception thereat. For, first, he was one in merit and desert. Secondly, in general desire and designation. Thirdly, (though no actual cardinal) he acted as a cardinal when joined to their conclave to see fair play amongst them at the choosing of a new Pope. Yea, some mentioned him for the place, who (counting it more credit to make, than be, a pope) first nominated cardinal Columna, and he clearly

---

  * Made by Thomas Kemp, his kinsman, Bishop of London.
  † Villare Cantianum, p. 24.

carried it by the name of Martin.* During his abode at Constance, he preached a Latin sermon before the emperor and Pope. He answered his name *de clivo forti*, or of the strong rock indeed, viz. David's.† Being a most pious person, returning home he lived in good esteem with prince and people, until his death, which happened 1421, being buried nigh the present monument of Sir Christopher Hatton.

PRELATES.

RALPH of MAYDENSTAN.—I presume this the ancient orthography of Maidstone (a noted town in this county); the rather because I met with no other place in England offering in sound or syllables thereunto.

An author giveth him this short but thick commendation: " Vir magnæ literaturæ et in theologiâ nominatissimus."‡ Insomuch that, in the reign of king Henry the Third, 1234, he was preferred bishop of Hereford.

This prelate bought of one Mount-hault, a nobleman, a fair house in, and the patronage of, St. Mary Mount-hault (commonly, but corruptly, called Mount-haw) in London, leaving both to his successors in the see of Hereford. Know, reader, that all English bishops in that age had palaces in London for their conveniency, wherein they resided, and kept great hospitality, during their attendance in Parliament.

Now, although the schoolmen generally hold that episcopacy is *Apex consummatæ religionis,* than which *nihil amplius,* nothing higher or holier in this life; and though many friars have been preferred bishops as a progressive motion both in dignity and sanctity; yet our Ralph was of a different judgment herein. This made him, in the year 1239, turn his mitre into a cowl, and become a Franciscan,§ first at Oxford, then at Gloucester, where he died about the year 1244.

HENRY de WINGHAM (a well-known town in this county) was, by king Henry the Third, preferred chancellor both of England and Gascony, dean both of Totten-hall (query, where this place is?) and St Martin's, and twice ambassador into France.‖

It happened that one Ethelmar, womb-brother to king Henry the Third, was then bishop of Winchester: a person who properly comes not under my pen; first, for his foreign nativity; secondly (so much as he was English), he was an UN-WORTHY, wanting age, ability, and orders to qualify him in that place.¶

Hereupon the monks of Winchester, endeavouring to eject him, chose Wingham, a man of merit (and might in the court),

---

* All collected out of Godwin's Bishops of London.
† " Lord, be thou my strong rock," Psalm xxxi. 3.
‡ Thomas Wike, in his Chronicle of Osney.
§ Godwin, in the Bishops of Hereford.
‖ Idem, in the Bishops of London.
¶ Idem, in the Bishops of Winchester.

to be their bishop; which honour he wisely refused, fearing to incur the king's displeasure. It was not long before his modesty and discretion was rewarded with a peaceable (instead of that litigious) bishopric, when chosen to London 1259. But he enjoyed his see not full two years, dying July 13, 1261; and was buried in his own cathedral.

HENRY of SANDWICH, archdeacon of Oxford, was consecrated bishop of London 1263. He took part with the seditious barons against king Henry the Third, for which he was deservedly excommunicated by Othobon, the Pope's legate.* Going to Rome, it cost him well nigh an apprenticeship of patience, dancing attendance almost seven years before he could gain absolution; which obtained, he returned home, and dying September 16, 1273, was buried in his own church of St. Paul's.†

RICHARD of GRAVESEND, archdeacon of Northampton, was (after Fulk Lovel had freely refused it) consecrated [at Coventry] bishop of London, anno 1282. He was the first founder of a convent of Carmelites at Maldon in Essex, and, dying at Fulham 1303, was buried in his own cathedral.

SIMON MEPHAM was born at Mepham in this county.‡ He was bred in Merton College in Oxford. He was a good scholar, as those days went, chosen by the monks of Canterbury, approved by king Edward the Third, and consecrated, by the command of the Pope, archbishop of Canterbury. He is only famous for two things; his expensive suit with the monks of Canterbury, wherein at last he got the better, though it cost seven hundred pounds, in the court of Rome. Secondly, his magnificent visitation in person of the dioceses south of Thames, till he was resisted by Grandison bishop of Exeter. This affront did half break Mepham's heart; and the Pope siding with the bishop against him, brake the other half thereof, hastening his death, which happened anno Domini 1333.

HAYMO of HITHE was born therein, a small town on the seaside; *hithe* in old English signifying a landing-place, as Queenhithe, Garlic-hithe, &c. in London. He was made bishop of Rochester in the twelfth of king Edward the Second, to whom he was confessor. I believe him owner of good temporal means. First, because he made so much building on a mean bishopric, erecting the great hall and fair frontispiece at his palace in Halling, and repairing all the rooms thereof; not forgetting the town of his nativity, where he erected and endowed the hospi-

* So was also his countryman Benedict of Gravesend, bishop of Lincoln, otherwise not to be remembered.—F.
† Godwin, in his Catalogue of the Bishops of London.
‡ W. Lambarde in his Perambulation of Kent.

tal of St. Bartholomew for ten poor people.* Secondly, because in his old age he lived on his own estate, resigning his bishopric, which the charitable conceive done not out of discontent but desire of retirement, to compose himself the better for his dissolution, which happened about the year 1355.

JOHN of SHEPPY, prior of Rochester, succeeded Haymo aforesaid in the same see; and for some time was treasurer of England. His death happened anno Domini 1360.

WILLIAM REDE.—I place him in this county with confidence, having clearly conquered all suspicions to the contrary: first, because of his name then flourishing at Read in Marden in this county.† Secondly, because the Provost-place of Wingham College therein was his first public preferment. To which I may add, that he was bred fellow of Merton College (abounding with Cantians, since a bishop in Kent was founder thereof); and he merited much of that foundation,‡ not only building a fair library§ therein, but furnishing it with books, and astronomical tables of his own making, which (they say) are still to be seen therein, with this lively picture inserted.||

In his reduced age he applied himself to divinity, and by king Edward the Third was preferred bishop of Chichester. Retaining his mathematical impressions, he commendably expressed them in architecture, erecting a castle *egregii operis*, saith my author,¶ at Amberley in Sussex. His death happened anno Domini 1385.

THOMAS KEMP, brother's son to John Kemp archbishop of Canterbury, was born of a knightly family in this county; bred in Oxford, whereof he became proctor anno 1437. By papal provision he was made bishop of London, consecrated by his uncle at York-house, (now White Hall), and sate in his see** forty years, from the twenty-eighth of Henry the Sixth till the fifth of Henry the Seventh; so that he saw the wars between Lancaster and York begun, continued, concluded; and the two Roses tied together in one royal posy. I know not whether his benefactions were adequate to his long possessing of so wealthy a place, finding him to have curiously arched and leaded the Divinity schools in Oxford, and built the cross nigh the church of St. Paul's, as it stood in our memories; but lately demolished,

---

* Godwin, in his Bishops of Rochester.
† Villare Cantianum, p. 321.
‡ He left also a fund, as did Sir Thomas Bodley, to be occasionally borrowed by the fellows on proper security. Chalmers's Oxford, p. 7.—ED.
§ He was an architect of great skill. The library was built from a plan furnished by him.—Ed.
|| Godwin, in his Bishops of Chichester.   ¶ Baleus.
** Godwin, in his Bishops of London.

though guilty of no other superstition, save accommodating the preacher and some about him with convenient places. Methinks, though idle crosses, standing only for shew, were published for offenders, this useful one, which did such service, might have been spared; but all is fish which comes to the net of sacrilege. This bishop died anno Domini 1489.

JAMES GOLDWELL was born at Great Chart in this county; bred in All Souls College, in Oxford; promoted first to be dean of Salisbury, and secretary to king Edward the Fourth, and at last made bishop of Norwich. He not only repaired the church at Great Chart, where he was born; but also founded a chapel on the south-side thereof, where his picture is in the east window, with his rebus [viz. a *golden well*] in every quarry of the same.* He died anno Domini 1498.

THOMAS GOLDWELL was born at Goldwell in the parish of Great Chart in this county, where his family had long flourished, till lately alienated.† He was by queen Mary preferred bishop of St. David's; and, as a volunteer, quitted the land in the first of queen Elizabeth. Going to Rome, he made a deal of *do* to *do* just nothing; prevailing by much importunity with the Pope to procure large indulgences for such who superstitiously were in pilgrimage to, and offered at, the Well of Saint Winifred in his diocese. The obscurity of his death denieth us the exact date thereof.

Reader, I am sensible how imperfect my list is of the bishops in this county; the rather because I have heard from my worthy friend and excellent historian Mr. Fisher, fellow of Merton College, that this his native shire of Kent had twelve bishops at one time, whilst I can hardly make up twelve bishops at all times before the Reformation: but my defects will be perfectly supplied by such who shall topographically treat of this subject in relation to this county alone.

SINCE THE REFORMATION.

JOHN POYNET was born in this county;‡ bred (say some) in King's College in Cambridge. Sure I am, he was none of the foundation therein, because not appearing in Master Hatcher's exact manuscript catalogue. Bale is rather to be believed herein, making him to be brought up in Queen's College in the same university.§

But, wherever he had his education, he arrived at admirable learning, being an exact Grecian, and most expert mathematician. He presented king Henry the Eighth with a *horologium* (which I might English *dial, clock,* or *watch,* save that it is

---

* Weever's Funeral Monuments, p. 296.   † Villare Cantianum, p. 145.
‡ Bishop Godwin, in his Bishops of Winchester.
§ Bale, de Scriptoribus Britannicis, Cent. 8. numb. 62.

epitheted *sciotericum**) observing the shadow of the sun, and therein shewing not only the hours, but days of the month, change of the moon, ebbing and flowing of the sea, &c. I confess the modern mystery of watchmaking is much completed (men never being more curious to divide, more careless to employ, their time); but surely this was accounted a master-piece in that age.

His sermons so endeared him to king Edward the Sixth. that he preferred him (whilst as yet scarce thirty-six years of age) to the bishopric of Rochester, then of Winchester. But, alas! these honours soon got were as soon lost, being forced to fly into High Germany in the first of queen Mary, where, before he was fully forty, and before he had finished his book begun against Thomas Martin in defence of ministers' marriage, he died at Strasburg, the 2d of August 1556, and was buried there with great lamentation.

RICHARD FLETCHER was born in this county, brother to doctor Giles Fletcher the civilian and ambassador in Russia, and bred in Bennet College in Cambridge.† He was afterwards dean of Peterborough at what time Mary queen of Scots was beheaded at Fotheringhay, to whom he made, saith my author,‡ " verbosam orationem," (a wordy speech), of her past, present, and future condition, wherein he took more pains than he received thanks from her who therein was most concerned.

Hence he was preferred bishop of Peterborough, and at last of London; my author saith he was *Præsul splendidus*,§ and indeed he was of a comely presence, and queen Elizabeth knew full well,

> *Gratior est pulchro veniens è corpore virtus :*
> " The jewel virtue is more grac'd
> When in a proper person cas'd."

Which made her always, on an equality of desert, to reflect favourably on such who were of graceful countenance and stature.

In one respect this bishop may well be resembled to John Peckham archbishop of Canterbury, of whom I find this character : " Quanquam gestu et incessu, sæpe etiam in sermone gloriosus videretur et elatus; animo tamen fuit benignissimo et perquam comi."|| (Athough he seemed a boaster, and puffed up both in gesture and gait, and sometimes in his speech also ; yet was he of a loving disposition and exceeding courteous).

Such a one was bishop Fletcher, whose pride was rather on him than in him, as only gait and gesture-deep, not sinking to his heart, though causelessly condemned for a proud man, as

* Bishop Godwin, ut prius. † So his near relation informed me.—F.
‡ Camden's Elizabeth, anno 1589. § Idem, in anno 1596.
|| Bishop Godwin, in his Catalogue of the Archbishops of Canterbury, and the Life of J. Peckham.

who was a good hypocrite, and far more humble than he appeared.

He married a lady of this county,* who one commendeth for very virtuous; which if so, the more happy she in herself, though unhappy that the world did not believe it. Sure I am, that queen Elizabeth (who hardly held the second matches of bishops excusable) accounted his marriage a trespass on his gravity, whereupon he fell into her deep displeasure. Hereof this bishop was sadly sensible, and, seeking to lose his sorrow in a mist of smoke, died of the moderate taking thereof, June the 15th, 1596.†

BRIAN DUPPA, D.D. the worthy bishop of Winchester, was born at Lewisham in this county. Staying for farther instructions, I am forced to defer his life to our Additions.‡

STATESMEN.

Sir EDWARD POYNINGS, Knight, was in martial performances inferior to none of his age, and a native of this county, as from the catalogue of the sheriffs therein may be collected. We will insist only on his Irish action, being employed by king Henry the Seventh to conjure down the last walking spirit of the house of York which haunted that king; I mean Perkin Warbeck.

Having ferreted him out of Ireland, he seriously set himself to reclaim that barbarous nation to civility; and, in order thereunto, passed an act in Parliament, whereby "all the statutes made in England before that time were enacted, established, and made of force, in Ireland." He caused also another law to be made, that no act should be propounded to any parliament in Ireland, till first it had been transmitted into England, approved there by the king, and returned thence under his broad seal.

Now though this act seemeth, *primâ facie*, prejudicial to the liberty of the Irish subjects; yet was it made at the request of the Commons upon just and important cause, being so sensible of the oppression and laws imposed by private lords, for their particular ends, that they rather referred themselves to the king's justice than to the merciless mercy of so many masters.

Also, to conform Ireland to England, he procured the passing of an act, that the Irish barons should appear in parliament in their robes, which put a face of grandeur and state on their convention. And indeed formalities are more than formalities in matters of this nature, essential to beget a veneration in barbarous people, who carry much of their brain in their eyes.

He thriftily improved the king's revenues, and obtained a sub-

---

* Sir Richard Baker, in his Chronicle.
† Camden's Elizabeth, in anno 1596.
‡ This addition Dr. Fuller did not live to make.—The bishop of Winchester died in 1662.—ED.

sidy, of twenty-six shillings eight pence, payable yearly for five years, out of every six score acres manured. The worst was, the burden fell on their backs whose islands were most industrious, whereby the sovereign became not more wealthy, but the subjects more lazy, the mischief being as apparent as the remedy impossible. Many more large laws of his making found but narrow performance, viz. only within the pale. Nor was Henry the Seventh (though in title) in truth lord of all Ireland, but, by the favour of a figure and large synecdoche, of a part for the whole. These things thus ordered, Sir Edward was recalled into England, created a baron, and, dying in the beginning of king Henry the Eighth, left a numerous natural but no legitimate issue.

Sir ANTHONY ST. LEGER is rationally reputed a Kentish man (though he had also a Devonshire relation), as will appear to such who peruse the sheriffs of this county. He was properly the first viceroy of Ireland, seeing shadows cannot be before their substance: and in his deputyship Henry the Eighth (in the thirty-third year of his reign) assumed the title of King and Supreme Head of the Church of Ireland.

To him all the Irish nobility made their solemn submission, falling down at his feet upon their knees, laying aside their girdles, skeines, and caps. This was the fourth solemn submission of the Irish to the kings of England; and most true it is, such seeming submissions have been the bane of their serious subjection: for, out of the pale, our kings had not power either to punish or protect, where those Irish lords (notwithstanding their complimental loyalty) made their list the law to such whom they could overpower. He caused also certain ordinances of state to be made not altogether agreeable with the rules of the law of England, a satisfactory reason hereof being given in the preamble to them : *

"Quia nondum sic sapiunt leges et jura, ut secundùm ea jam immediatè vivere et regi possint;" (because the [Irish] as yet do not so savour the laws [of England] as immediately to live after and be ruled by them.)

Thus the greatest statesman must sometimes say "by your leave" to such as are under them, not acting always according to their own ability, but others' capacity.

He seized all the abbey lands in Ireland for the king's use; a flower of the crown which alone had made a posy, if continued thereunto. But, alas! the revenues of abbey lands are as ruinous as their buildings, nothing more than the rubbish thereof remaining in the king's Exchequer. He made a law, " that no children should be admitted to church livings : " which importeth the frequency of that abuse in former times. He persuaded

* In the Council-book of Ireland, in the 33rd of king Henry VIII.

O'Neile, O'Brian, &c. to go over to England, to surrender their lands into the king's hands; promising they should receive them again from him by letters patent, with the addition of Earls, which was done accordingly. At his desire the king conferred on them houses nigh Dublin, that, residing there, they might suck in civility with the court air. These things thus settled, he returned into England; and died (as I take it) in the reign of king Edward the Sixth.

Sir HENRY SIDNEY was son to Sir William Sidney, of Penshurst in this county, who, by his own worth was advanced into the favour of queen Elizabeth (never a wit the less for marrying Mary Dudley, sister to Robert earl of Leicester); he was by her made knight of the Garter, lord president of Wales, and for eleven years (off and on) deputy of Ireland.

Now, though generally the Irish are querulous of their deputies (what patient for the present will praise his chirurgeon, who soundly searcheth his sore?) yet Sir Henry left a good memory and the monuments of a good governor behind him. 1. He made Annaly, a territory in Loynsteresse by the Sept of Offerralles, one entire shire by itself, called the county of Longford: he likewise divided the province of Connaught into six counties.* 2. In a parliament held the eleventh of Elizabeth, he abolished the pretended and usurped captain-ships, and all extortions incident thereunto. 3. He caused an act to pass, whereby the lord deputy was authorized to accept the surrenders of the Irish seignories, and to regrant estates unto them, to hold of the crown by English tenures and services. 4. Because the inferior sort of the Irish were poor, and not amenable by law, he provided, that five of the best persons of every Sept should bring in all the persons of their surname, to be justified by the law. 5. A law was made, that, for the civil education of the youth, there should be one free school at least in every diocese. 6. To acquaint the people of Munster and Connaught with the English government again (disused amongst them for two hundred years), he instituted two presidency courts in those two provinces. 7. To augment the revenues of the crown, he resumed and vested therein (by the power of the same parliament) more than half the province of Ulster, upon the attainder of Shane O'Neale. 8. He raised customs upon the principal commodities of the kingdom, and reformed the abuses of the Exchequer by many good instructions from England. 9. He established the composition of the pale, in lieu of purveyance and sess of soldiers.

It must not be forgotten, that he caused the statutes of Ireland unto his own time to be printed; and so (saith my author†) " ex umbrâ in solem eduxit," (he brought them out of the

---

* Sir John Davis, in his Discovery of Ireland, p. 251.

† J. Wareus, de Scriptoribus Hiberniæ, p. 136.

shadow into the sunshine); whereas formerly they were only in manuscript: a sad case, that men should be obliged to the observation of those laws, scarce ever seen by one in a hundred subjected thereunto.

Being to leave Ireland, anno 1578, and now ready to go up into his ship, he took his leave thereof with the words of the Psalmist, " When Israel came out of Egypt, and Jacob from a strange people ;"* rejoicing in heart, that he came with a clear conscience from that dangerous employment.† He died at Worcester, May 5, 1586 ; and his corpse being brought to Penshurst, was there solemnly interred amongst his ancestors. I will close his life with this encomium, which I find in a worthy author :‡ " His disposition was rather to seek after the antiquities and the weal-public of those countries which he governed, than to obtain lands and revenues within the same; for I know not one foot of land that he had, either in Wales or Ireland."

Sir PHILIP SIDNEY.—Reader, I am resolved not to part him from his father ; such the sympathy betwixt them, living and dying both within the compass of the same year. Otherwise this knight, in relation to my book, may be termed an ubiquitary, and appear amongst Statesmen, Soldiers, Lawyers, Writers, yea Princes themselves, being (though not elected) in election to be king of Poland, which place he declined, preferring rather to be a subject to queen Elizabeth, than a sovereign beyond the seas."§

He was born at Penshurst in this county, son to Sir Henry Sidney (of whom before), and sister's son to Robert earl of Leicester; bred in Christ-church in Oxford. Such his appetite to learning, that he could never be fed fast enough therewith; and so quick and strong his digestion, that he soon turned it into wholesome nourishment, and thrived healthfully thereon.

His home-bred abilities travel perfected with foreign accomplishments, and a sweet nature set a gloss upon both. He was so essential to the English court, that it seemed maimed without his company, being a complete master of matter and language, as his " Arcadia" doth evidence.

I confess I have heard some of modern pretended wits cavil thereat, merely because they made it not themselves : such who say, that his book is the occasion that many precious hours are otherwise spent no better, must acknowledge it also the cause that many idle hours are otherwise spent no worse, than in reading thereof.

At last, leaving the court, he followed the camp, being made governor of Flushing, under his uncle earl of Leicester. But

* Psalm cxiv. 1.   † Camden's Elizabeth, anno 1578.
‡ Doctor Powel, in his History of Wales : Epistle to the Reader.
§ Fragmenta Regalia, in his Character.

the walls of that city (though high and strong) could not confine the activity of his mind, which must into the field, and before Zutphen was unfortunately slain with a shot, in a small skirmish, which we may sadly term a great battle, considering our heavy loss therein. His corpse, being brought over into England, was buried in the choir of St. Paul's, with general lamentation.

Sir FRANCIS WALSINGHAM, Knight, was born in this county, wherein his family long flourished at Chiselhurst; though I read,* that originally they fetched their name from Walsingham in Norfolk. He was bred in King's College in Cambridge, and gave the king of Spain's bible to the library thereof. As a traveller many years beyond the seas, he learnt experience; as an agent, he practised it there; and after his return, as secretary of state, he taught it to many emissaries employed under him.

None alive did better ken the secretary craft, to get counsels out of others, and keep them in himself. Marvellous his sagacity in examining suspected persons, either to make them confess the truth, or confound themselves by denying it to their detection. Cunning his hands, who could unpick the cabinets in the Pope's conclave; quick his ears, who could hear at London what was whispered at Rome; and numerous the spies and eyes of this Argus dispersed in all places.

The Jesuits, being outshot in their own bow, complained that he out-equivocated their equivocation, having a mental reservation deeper and farther than theirs. They tax him for making heaven bow too much to earth, oft-times borrowing a point of conscience, with full intent never to pay it again, whom others excused by reasons of state and dangers of the times. Indeed his *simulation* (which all allow lawful) was as like to *dissimulation* (condemned by all good men) as two things could be which were not the same.

He thought that gold might, but intelligence could not, be bought too dear; the cause that so great a statesmen left so small an estate, and so public a person was so privately buried in Saint Paul's, anno Domini 1590. His only daughter Frances was successively matched to three matchless men, Sir Philip Sidney, Robert earl of Essex, and Richard earl of Clanricarde.

CAPITAL JUDGES, AND WRITERS ON THE LAW.

Sir JOHN FINEUX was by all probability born at Swinkfield in this county (as I am informed from my good friend Mr. Thomas Fineux, a descendant from him); " a place," saith Mr. Camden,† " bestowed on his ancestor by T. Criol, a great lord in Kent, about the reign of king Edward the Second." I learned from the same gentleman, that he was eight and twenty

---

* Camden's Britannia, in Norfolk.   † In his Remains, p. 118.

years of age before he betook him to the study of the law; that
he followed that profession twenty-eight years before he was
made a judge; and that he continued a judge for twenty-eight
years, whereby it appears that he lived fourscore and four years.
This last exactly agrees with Sir Henry Spelman,* making him
continue lord chief justice of the King's Bench from the
eleventh of king Henry the Seventh until the seventeenth of
king Henry the Eighth.

He was a great benefactor unto Saint Augustine's in Canterbury; whose prior, William Mallaham,† thus highly commendeth him in a manuscript instrument: " Vir prudentissimus,
genere insignis, justitiâ præclarus, pietate refertus, humanitatis
splendidus, et charitate fœcundus," &c.

Now though some will say, his convent may well afford him
good words who gave them good deeds; yet I believe this character of him can in no part be disproved. He died about the
year 1526, and lies buried in Christchurch in Canterbury; who
had a fair habitation in this city, and another at Herne in this
county, where his motto still remains in each window, " Mise-
ricordias Domini cantabo in æternum."

Sir ROGER MANWOOD, born at Sandwich in this county,‡
applying himself from his youth to the study of the common
law; wherein he attained to such eminency, that by queen
Elizabeth he was preferred second justice of the Common Pleas,
in which place he gave such proof of his ability and integrity,
that not long after, in Hilary Term in the twenty-first of queen
Elizabeth, he was made chief baron of the Exchequer, discharging that office, to his great commendation, full fourteen years,
till the day of his death.§ He was much employed in matters
of state, and was one of the commissioners who sat on the trial
of the queen of Scots. His book on " The Forest Laws" is a
piece highly prized by men of his profession. In vacation time,
his most constant habitation was at Saint Stephen's in Canterbury, where, saith my author, the poor inhabitants were much
beholden to his bounteous liberality.‖ He erected and endowed a fair free-school at Sandwich, the place of his nativity;
and died in the thirty-fifth of queen Elizabeth, anno Domini
1593.

Sir HENRY FINCH, Knight, was born in this county, of right
worshipful extraction (their ancient surname being Herbert), a
family which had, and hath, an hereditary happiness of eminency
in the study of the laws. He was sergeant at law to king James;
and wrote a book of the law, in great esteem with men of his own

---

* In his Glossary, *verbo* Justiciarius.
† William Somner, in his Antiquities of Canterbury.
‡ Lambarde, in his Perambulation of Kent, p. 131.
§ Sir Henry Spelman, in his Glossary, *verbo* Justiciarius.
‖ Camden's Britannia, in Kent.

profession : yet were not his studies confined thereunto. Witness his book of "The Calling of the Jews." And all ingenious persons which dissent from his judgment will allow him learnedly to have maintained an error, though he was brought into some trouble by king James, conceiving that on his principles he advanced and extended the Jewish commonwealth, to the depressing and contracting of Christian princes' free monarchies. He was father unto Sir John Finch,* lord chief justice, and for a time lord keeper, and baron of Foredwiche, who is still alive.

SOLDIERS.

Kent hath so carried away the credit, in all ages, for manhood, that the leading of the front, or van-guard (so called from *avant-guard,* or *go on guard,* because first in marching) in former times hath simply and absolutely belonged unto them ; I say absolutely, for I find two other shires contending for that place. The best is, it is but a book combat betwixt learned writers ; otherwise, if real, such a division were enough to rout an army, without other enemy. But let us see how all may be peaceably composed.

It is probable that the Cornish men led the van in the days of king Arthur, who, being a native of Cornwall, had most cause to trust his own countrymen.† But I behold this as a temporary honour which outlasted not his life who bestowed it.

The men of Archenfeld, in Herefordshire, claimed by custom to lead the van-guard ;‡ but surely this privilege was topical, and confined to the Welch wars, with which the aforesaid men, as borderers, were best acquainted.

As for Kent, "Cantia nostra primæ cohortis honorem, et primos congressus hostium usque in hodiernum diem in omnibus præliis obtinet," saith my author.§

[Reader, it may rationally be concluded that the ensuing topic had been as large in this as in any county in England, seeing it is bounded on the sea on the east and south sides thereof, had not the author departed this life before the finishing of the same.]

SEAMEN.

WILLIAM ADAMS was (as his own pen reporteth) born at Gillingham in this county ;‖ and take the brief account of his life, being the first Englishman who effectually discovered Japan.

---

* Sir John Finch was appointed Lord Keeper 23 Jan. 15 Car. I. ; and 7th April 16 Car. I. was created Baron Finch of Fordwiche. He was twice married ; but died Nov. 20, 1660, without issue ; and was buried at St. Martin's, Canterbury.— ED.

† Michael Cornubiensis ; see Cornwall, title SOLDIERS.
‡ Camden's Britannia, in Herefordshire.
§ Joannes Sarisburiensis, de Nugis Curial. 6, cap. 18.
‖ Purchas's Pilgrims.

Twelve years he lived at home with his parents: twelve years he was apprentice and servant to Nicholas Diggins, a brave seaman; for some time he was master of one of the queen's ships: ten years he served the English Company of Barbary merchants: fourteen years (as I collect it) he was employed by the Dutch in India; for he began his voyage 1598, pilot to their fleet of five sail, to conduct them to Japan; and, in order to the settlement of trade, endured many miseries. He who reads them will concur with Cato, and repent that ever he went thither by sea whither one might go by land. But Japan being an island, and inaccessible save by sea, our Adams's discretion was not to be blamed, but industry to be commended in his adventures. He died at Firando in Japan about 1612.

CIVILIANS.

NICHOLAS WOTTON, son to Sir Robert, was born at Bockton Malherb in this county, a place so named, as it seems, from some noxious and malignant herbs growing therein. What the natural plants there may be, I know not. Sure the moral ones are excellent, which hath produced so many of the honourable family of the Wottons; of whom this Nicholas, doctor of civil laws, bred in Oxford, may be termed a centre of remarkables, so many met in his person. 1. He was dean of the two metropolitan churches of Canterbury and York. 2. He was the first dean of those cathedrals. 3. He was privy councillor to four successive sovereigns, king Henry the Eighth, king Edward the Sixth, queen Mary, queen Elizabeth. 4. He was employed thirteen several times in embassies to foreign princes.

Now because there are some of so diffident natures, that they will believe no total sum, except they peruse the particulars, let them satisfy themselves with what followeth:

Five times to Charles the fifth emperor: once to Philip his son, king of Spain: once to Francis the First, king of France: once to Mary queen of Hungary, governess of the Netherlands: twice to William duke of Clive: once to renew the peace between England, France, and Scotland, anno Domini 1540: again to the same purpose, at Cambray, 1549: once sent commissioner with others to Edinburgh in Scotland 1560.

We must not forget how, in the first of queen Elizabeth, the archbishopric of Canterbury was proffered unto, and refused by him.* He died January the twenty-sixth, anno Domini 1566, being about seventy years of age, and was buried in Canterbury.

GILES FLETCHER (brother of Richard Fletcher, bishop of London) was born in this county, as I am credibly informed.† He was bred first in Eton, then in King's College in Cambridge,

---

* Holinshed's Chronicle, page 1403.

† From the mouth of Mr. Ramsey, minister of Rougham in Norfolk, who married the widow of Mr. Giles Fletcher, son to this doctor.—F.

where he became doctor of law. A most excellent poet (a quality hereditary to his two sons, Giles and Phineas); commissioner into Scotland, Germany, and the Low Countries, for queen Elizabeth, and her embassador into Russia, secretary to the city of London, and master of the Court of Requests.

His Russian embassy to settle the English merchandize was his master-piece, to Theodore Juanowich, duke of Muscovy. He came thither in a dangerous juncture of time, viz. in the end of the year 1588. First, some foreigners (I will not say they were the Hollanders) envying the free trade of the English, had done them bad offices. Secondly, a false report was generally believed, that the Spanish Armada had worsted the English Fleet; and the duke of Muscovy (who measured his favour to the English by the possibility he apprehended of their returning it) grew very sparing of his smiles, not to say free of his frowns, on our merchants residing there.

However, our doctor demeaned himself in his embassy with such cautiousness, that he not only escaped the duke's fury, but also procured many privileges for our English merchants, exemplified in Mr. Hackluit.* Returning home, and being safely arrived at London, he sent for his intimate friend Mr. Wayland, prebendary of St. Paul's, and senior fellow of Trinity College in Cambridge (tutor to my father, from whose mouth I received this report,) with whom he heartily expressed his thankfulness to God for his safe return from so great a danger; for the poets cannot fancy Ulysses more glad to be come out of the den of Polyphemus, than he was to be rid out of the power of such a barbarous prince; who, counting himself, by a proud and voluntary mistake, emperor of all nations, cared not for the law of all nations; and who was so habited in blood, that, had he cut off this ambassador's head, he and his friends might have sought their own amends; but the question is, where he would have found it?

He afterwards set forth a book, called, "The Russian Commonwealth," expressing the government, or tyranny rather, thereof; wherein, saith my author,† are many things most observable. But queen Elizabeth, indulging the reputation of the duke of Muscovy as a confederate prince, permitted not the public printing of that which such who have private copies know to set the valuation thereon. I cannot attain the certain date of his death.

PHYSICIANS.

ROBERT FLOID, who by himself is Latined *Robertus de Fluctibus*, was born in this county, and that of a knightly family, as I am informed; bred (as I take it) in Oxford, and beyond the seas:

---

* In his volume of English Navigation, p. 473.

† Camden, in his Elizabeth, anno 1583, when he was agent in Muscovy, as afterward ambassador.—F.

a deep philosopher, and great physician, who at last fixed his habitation in Fenchurch-street, London. He was of the order of the Rosa-Crucians, and I must confess myself ignorant of the first founder and sanctions thereof. Perchance none know it but those that are of it. Sure I am, that a rose is the sweetest of flowers, and a cross accounted the sacredest of forms or figures, so that much of eminency must be imported in their composition.

His books written in Latin are great, many, and mystical. The last some impute to his charity, clouding his high matter with dark language, lest otherwise the lustre thereof should dazzle the understanding of the reader. The same phrases he used to his patients; and, seeing conceit is very contributive to the well working of physic, their fancy, or faith natural, was much advanced by his elevated expressions.

His works are for the English to slight or admire, for French and foreigners to understand and use: not that I account them more judicious than our own countrymen, but more inquiring into such difficulties. The truth is, here at home his books are beheld not so good as crystal, which (some say) are prized as precious pearls beyond the seas. But I conclude all with the character which my worthy (though concealed) friend thus wrote upon him: "Lucubrationibus quas solebat edere profusissimas semper visus est plus sumere laboris, quam populares nostri volebant fructum, quia hunc ferè negligebant, præ tædio legendi, et prejudicio quodam oleam perdendi operamque, ob CABALAM, quam scripta ejus dicebantur olere magis quam PERIPATUM, et ob ferventius hominis ingenium, in quo plerique requirebant judicium." He died on the eighth of September anno Domini 1637.

WILLIAM HARVEY, son of Thomas Harvey, was born at Folkstone in this county. His father had a week of sons; whereof this William, bred to learning, was the eldest; his other brethren being bound apprentices in London, and all at last ended in effect in merchants. They got great estates, and made their father the treasurer thereof; who, being as skilful to purchase land, as they to gain money, kept, employed, and improved their gainings, to their great advantage; so that he survived to see the meanest of them of far greater estate than himself.

Our William was bred in Caius College in Cambridge, where he proceeded doctor of physic. Five years also he studied at Padua, making a good composition of foreign and domestic learning; so that afterwards he was (for many years) physician to king Charles the First; and not only *doctor medicinæ*, but *doctor medicorum*.

For this was he that first found out the circulation of the blood; an opinion which entered into the world with great disadvantages. For, first, none will be acquainted with strangers at the first sight, as persons generally suspected; as if to be unknown were part of being guilty. Secondly, the grandees of this profession were of the opposite judgment, heavy enough without any argument to overlay (and so to stifle) any infant opinion by their authority.

But truth, though it may be questioned for a vagrant, carrieth a passport along with it for its own vindication. Such have since shaken friendly hands with Doctor Harvey, which at first tilted pens against him. And amongst the rest Riolanus, that learned physician, if not *ambabus ulnis,* with one arm at the least, doth embrace his opinion, and partly consent thereunto.

This doctor, though living a bachelor, may be said to have left three hopeful sons to posterity: his books, 1. "*De Circulatione Sanguinis,*" which I may call his son and heir; the doctor living to see it at full age, and generally received. 2. "*De Generatione;*" as yet in its minority; but, I assure you, growing up apace into public credit. 3. "*De Ovo;*" as yet in the nonage thereof; but infants may be men in due time.

It must not be forgotten, that this doctor had made a good progress, to lay down a practice of physic, conformable to his thesis of the Circulation of Blood; but was plundered of his papers in our civil war. Unhappy dissensions, which not only murdered many then alive; but may be said by this (call it mischief or mischance) to have destroyed more not yet born, whose diseases might have been either prevented or removed, if his worthy pains had come forth into the public; and I charitably presume that grateful posterity will acknowledge the improvements of this opinion, as superstructures on his foundation; and thankfully pay the fruit to his memory, who watered, planted (not to say made) the root of this discovery.

He hath since been a second Linacre and great benefactor to the college of physicians in London, where his statue stands with this inscription:

"GULIELMO HARVEO,
Viro monumentis suis immortali,
Hoc insuper Coll. Med. London. posuit,
Qui enim Sanguin. motum (ut et animal. ortum) dedit
Meruit esse Stator perpetuus."

He died in the eightieth year of his age, June 3, anno Domini 1657.

WRITERS.

JOHN of KENT, so called because born in this county;* after he had studied at home with good proficiency, went over into France, where he became canon in the church of Saint Mary's

---

* J. Pits, in Angliæ Scriptoribus, 1248.

in Angiers. But afterwards, being weary of worldly wealth, he quitted that place, and turned a Franciscan friar; and by Pope Innocent the Fourth he was sent a joint legate into England. He flourished in the year of our Lord 1248.

HAIMO of FEVERSHAM both had his first breath at, and fetched his name from, Feversham in this county. When a man, he left the land, and, repairing to Paris, applied his studies so effectually, that Leland saith he was "inter Aristotelicos Aristotelissimus."

He became a Franciscan in the church of St. Denis itself; and, returning into England, was elected Provincial of his order. Afterwards he was called to reside in Rome for his advice; where, quitting his provincialship to his successor, he was chosen general of the Franciscans. Surely he had much real or reputed merit, being so highly prized by the Italians, who generally do as much undervalue us English as they over admire themselves. "Speculum honestatis," (the glass of honesty), saith one,* was the title given unto him; though dark and false this glass, if Bale may be believed, who taxeth him for being an inquisitor after, and persecutor of good people, especially when employed by the Pope into Grecia.† Lying on his death-bed at Anagnia in Italy, the Pope in person came to visit him, which was no small honour unto him: but all would not prolong his life, which he ended anno 1260; having first, at the command of Pope Alexander the Fourth, corrected and amended the Roman Breviary.

SIMON STOCK was born in this county; and, when but twelve years of age, went into the woods (whereof this shire then afforded plenty), and became a hermit.‡ This Christian Diogenes had for his tub the stock of a hollow tree, whence he fetched his name, and (abating his sex) was like the nymphs called Hamadruids, which were the properties of oak trees. "Here he had," saith Leland, "water for his nectar, and wild fruits for his ambrosia." One may admire how this man here met with learning, except by inspiration, and except books (as at the original) were written on barks of trees, wherewith he conversed: yet the university of Oxford would force a bachelor of divinityship upon him: and many are the superstitious writings he left to posterity.

Reader, behold here how the roaring lion hath translated himself into a mimical ape, endeavouring a mock parallel betwixt this Simon and Simeon in the Gospel.

Old Simeon had a revelation that he should not die till he had seen our Saviour come in the flesh.§ This Simon, aged

---

* Pits, anno 1260.   † Bale, de Scriptoribus Britannicis, Cent. iv. num. 27.
‡ Bale, ibidem, Cent. iv. num. 7; et Pits, in anno 1265.
§ Luke ii. 26.

eighty years, had a revelation, that before his death he should behold a holy order of Carmelites come out of Syria, which fell out accordingly.*

At their arrival in England, our Simon quitted his oak, and advanced forward to meet them, as of whom, though he had no sight, he had a vision before, which is probably as true as that he was fed seven years with manna in Mount Carmel. He was chosen the general governor of their order all over Europe ; and died in the hundredth year of his age, anno Domini 1265, and was buried at Bordeaux in France.

[AMP.] THOMAS HASELWOOD. I find the name very ancient in a worshipful family in Northamptonshire ; and profess not only my inclination, but propensity, to gain him for the credit of my native country. But that needs not to be (and I ought not to make it) rich with the wrong of others. Indeed I find a Haselwood (transposition makes no mutation) in Suffolk, and another in Northumberland : but their vast distance from the monastery of Leeds in this county, wherein our Haselwood was bred an Augustinian Friar (with some other insinuations, too long to report) prevail with me to fix him in this place. He was an excellent scholar himself, and a fortunate schoolmaster to teach others, and became a faithful and painful historian. Bale (out of William Botiner, an industrious collector of antiquities) assigneth him to flourish under king Edward the Second, 1321 ;† but Mr. Weever lighted on a manuscript of his making, in Sir Robert Cotton's library, wherein he particularly speaks of the achievements of Edward the Black Prince,‡ which I here thought fit to exemplify :

" Edwardus filius Edwardi Tertii primogenitus, Princeps Walliæ fortunatissimus, et miles in bello audacissimus, inter validissima bella gesta militaria, magnificè ab eodem peracta, Johannem regem Franciæ apud Poyteizes debellavit; et pluribus, tam nobilibus quam aliis, de dicto regno captis et interfectis, eundem regem captivavit, et ipsum potenter in Angliam ductum patri suo præsentavit. Henricum etiam intrusorem Hispaniæ potentissimè in bello devicit, et Petrum Hispaniæ regem dudum à regno suo expulsum, potenti virtute in regnum suum restituit. Unde propter ingentem sibi probitatem, et actus ipsius triumphales, memoratum principem, inter regales regum memorias, dignum duximus commendandum."

Thus have I (not killed two birds with one bolt, but) revived two men's memories with one record, presenting the reader (according to my promise§) with the character of this prince, and style of this writer, speaking him, in my conjecture, to have lived about the reign of king Richard the Second.

* Bale, ibidem.   † De Scriptoribus Britannicis, Cent. v. num. 20.
‡ Funeral Monuments, p. 206.
§ In our Description of Oxfordshire, in this Prince's Life.—F.

SINCE THE REFORMATION.

Sir THOMAS WIAT, Knight, commonly called the Elder, to distinguish him from Sir Thomas Wiat, raiser of the rebellion (so all call it, for it did not succeed) in the reign of Queen Mary, was born at Allington castle in this county, which afterwards he repaired with most beautiful buildings. He was servant to king Henry the Eighth, and fell, as I have heard, into his disfavour, about the business of queen Anna Boleyn, till, by his innocence, industry, and discretion, he extricated himself.

He was one of admirable ingenuity, and truly answered his anagram, WIAT, "a wit." Camden saith he was "Eques auratus, splendidè doctus."*

It is evidence enough of his Protestant inclination, because he translated David's Psalms into English metre; and though he be lost both to Bale and Pits in the catalogue of writers, yet he is plentifully found by Leland,† giving him this large commendation:

> *Bella suum meritò jactet Florentia Dantem;*
> *Regia Petrarchæ carmina Roma probat:*
> *His non inferior patrio sermone Viattus,*
> *Eloquii secum qui decus omne tulit.*

> "Let Florence fair her Dante's justly boast,
>   And royal Rome her Petrarch's numbered feet:
> In English Wiat both of them doth coast,
>   In whom all graceful eloquence doth meet."

This knight being sent ambassador by king Henry the Eighth to Charles the Fifth emperor, then residing in Spain, before he took shipping, died of the pestilence in the West Country, anno 1541.‡

LEONARD DIGGS,§ Esquire, was born in this county; one of excellent learning and deep judgment. His mind most inclined him to mathematics; and he was the best architect in that age for all manner of buildings, for conveniency, pleasure, state, strength, being excellent at fortifications. Lest his learning should die with him, for the public profit he printed his "Tectonicon," "Prognostic General," "Stratiotic," about "the Ordering of an Army," and other works. He flourished anno Domini 1556; and died, I believe, about the beginning of the reign of queen Elizabeth.

Nothing else have I to observe of his name, save that hereditary learning may seem to run in the veins of his family; witness, Sir Dudley Diggs of Chilham castle in this county, made Master of the Rolls 1636, whose abilities will not be for-

---

* In Britannia, in Kent.   † In suis Næniis.
† Weever's Funeral Monuments, p. 853.
§ Leonard Digges resided at Wootton Court in this county, which was sold by his son Thomas, father of Sir Dudley.—F.

gotten whilst our age hath any remembrance. This knight had a younger son, fellow of All Souls in Oxford, who, in the beginning of our civil wars, wrote so subtile and solid a treatise, of the difference betwixt King and Parliament, that such royalists who have since handled that controversy have written *plura, non plus;* yea, *aliter* rather than *alia* of that subject.

THOMAS CHARNOCK was born in the Isle of Thanet, in this county, as by his own words doth appear.* He discovereth in himself a modest pride; modest, styling himself (and truly enough) the UNLETTERED SCHOLAR; pride, thus immoderately boasting of his book discovering the mysteries of the philosopher's stone:

> " For satisfying the minds of the students in this art,
> Then thou art worthy as many books as will lie in a cart."

However, herein he is to be commended, that he ingeniously confesseth the persons (viz. William Byrd, prior of Bath, and Sir James, a priest of Sarisbury) who imparted their skill unto him.

This Charnock, in the pursuance of the said stone (which so many do touch, few catch, and none keep), met with two very sad disasters. One on New-year's day (the omen worse than the accident) anno 1555, when his work unhappily fell on fire. The other three years after, when a gentleman, long owing him a grudge, paid him to purpose, and pressed him a soldier for the relieving of Calais. Whence we observe two things; first, that this Charnock was no man of estate, seeing seldom, if ever, a subsidy-man is pressed for a soldier; secondly, that though he practised surgery,† yet he was not free of that society, who, by the statute 32d Hen. VIII. are exempted from bearing armour. But the spite of the spite was, that this was done within a month‡ (according to his own computation, which none can confute) of the time wherein certainly he had been made master of so great a treasure. Such miscarriages, frequent in this kind, the friends of this art impute to the envy of evil spirits maligning mankind so much happiness; the foes thereof conceive that chemists pretend (yea, sometimes cause) such casualties to save their credits thereby. He was fifty years old anno 1574; and the time of his death is unknown.

FRANCIS THINNE was born in this county, and from his infancy had an ingenuous inclination to the study of antiquity, and especially of pedigrees. Herein he made such proficiency, that he was preferred, towards the end of the reign of queen Elizabeth, to be an herald, by the title of Lancaster. A gentleman painful, and well deserving, not only of his own office, but all the English nation. Whosoever shall peruse the voluminous

* In his Breviary, p. 298.   † Theatrum Chymicum Britanniæ, p. 176.
‡ In his Breviary of Philosophy, cap. 4.

works of Raphael Holinshed, will find how much he was assisted therein by the help of Mr. Thinne, seeing the shoulders of Atlas himself may be weary, if sometime not beholden to Hercules to relieve him. He died 15 . .

ROBERT GLOVER, son to Thomas Glover and Mildred his wife, was born at Ashford in this county.* He addicted himself to the study of heraldry, and in the reward of his pains was first made a Pursuivant Porcullis, and then Somerset herald. When the earl of Derby was sent into France, to carry the Garter to king Henry the Third, Mr. Glover attended the embassage, and was, as he deserved, well rewarded for his pains.† He by himself in Latin began a book, called "The Catalogue of Honour of our English Nobility," with their arms and matches. Being the first work in that kind, he therein traced untrodden paths ; and therefore no wonder if such who since succeeded him in that subject have found a nearer way, and exceed him in accurateness therein.‡ Being old rather in experience than years, he died not forty-six years old, anno 1583 ; and lieth buried under a comely monument in Saint Giles without Cripplegate, London, on the south wall of the choir. Let Mr. Camden's commendation pass for his epitaph: "Artis Heraldicæ studiosissimus, peritissimusque, qui in Fæcialium Collegio Somerseti titulum gessit, Robertus Gloverus."§

THOMAS MILLS, sister's son to Robert Glover aforesaid, was born at Ashford in this county, and, following his uncle's direction, applied himself to be eminent in the genealogies of our English nobility. If the expression were as properly predicated of a nephew as of the next brother, one might say, he raised up seed unto his uncle Glover, in setting forth his "Catalogue of Honour" in English, as more useful therein, because chiefly of our national concernment. He was employed on a message of importance from queen Elizabeth unto Henry the Fourth king of France, being then in Normandy; which trust he discharged with great fidelity, and incredible celerity, being returned home with a satisfactory answer to her highness before she could believe him arrived there. In memory of which service he had given him, for the crest of his arms, a chapeau with wings, to denote the *Mercuriousness* of this messenger. He died anno 16 . .

JOHN PHILPOT was born at Faulkston, in this county, and from his childhood had a genius inclining him to the love of antiquity. He first was made a Pursuivant extraordinary, by

---

* Out of his epitaph on his monument.
† Weever's Funeral Monuments.
‡ Ralph Brooke, York ; Augustine Vincent, Windsor Herald.
§ Britannia, in his Description of Berkshire.

the title of Blanch Lion, then in ordinary, by name of Rouge-Dragon, and afterwards Somerset herald. He made very pertinent additions to the second edition of Mr. Camden's Remains; and deserved highly well of the city of London, proving, in a learned and ingenious book, that gentry doth not abate with apprenticeship, but only sleepeth during the time of their indentures, and awaketh again when they are expired. Nor did he contribute a little to the setting forth of his uncle's "Catalogue of Honour." He died anno 1645, and was buried in Bennet, Paul's-wharf.

THOMAS PLAYFERD was born in this county, as some of his nearest relations have informed me. He was bred fellow of Saint John's College in Cambridge, and chosen 1597 to succeed Peter Barrow in the place of Margaret Professor. His fluency in the Latin tongue seemed a wonder to many, though since such who have seen the sun admire no more at the moon; doctor Collins not succeeding him so much in age, as exceeding him in eloquence.

The counsel of the apostle is good, Φρονεῖν εἰς τὸ σωφρονεῖν. His foe-friends commending of him, and his own conceiting of himself, made too deep an impression on his intellectuals. It added to his distemper, that when his re-election to his place (after his last two years' end) was put into the Regent-house, a great doctor said, "Detur Digniori." However, he held his professorship until the day of his death, 1609; and lieth buried, with an hyperbolical epitaph, in St. Botolph's in Cambridge.

JOHN BOIS, D.D., was descended of a right ancient and numerous family in this county,* deriving themselves from J. de Bosco, entering England with William the Conqueror, and since dispersed into eight branches extant at this day in their several seats.† Our John was bred fellow of Clare-hall in Cambridge, and afterwards preferred dean of Canterbury, famous to posterity for his Postils in defence of our Liturgy. So pious his life, that his adversaries were offended that they could not be offended therewith. A great prelate in the church did bear him no great good-will for mutual animosities betwixt them, whilst gremials in the university; the reason, perchance, that he got no higher preferment, and died (as I conjecture) about the year 1625.

BENEFACTORS TO THE PUBLIC.‡

Sir JOHN PHILPOT was born in this county, where his family

---

* Now all extinct, except the issue of the late antiquary of Sandwich, who are derived from a remote younger branch, Vincent Boys, in the time of queen Elizabeth.—ED.

† Villare Cantianum, p. 251.

‡ To the Benefactors to the Public in this county should be added the name of William Caxton, who is placed by Dr. Fuller in Cambridgeshire.—ED.

hath long resided at Upton-court, in the parish of Sibbertswood. He was bred a citizen and grocer in London, whereof he became mayor, 1378.

In the second of king Richard the Second our English seas wanted scouring, overrun with the rust of piracies, but chiefly with a canker fretting into them, one John Mercer, a Scot, with his fifteen Spanish ships; to repress whose insolence, our Philpot on his own cost set forth a fleet, a project more proportionable to the treasury of a prince, than the purse of a private subject. His success was as happy as his undertaking honourable; and Mercer brought his wares to a bad market, being taken with all his ships and rich plunder therein.*

Two years after he conveyed an English army into Britain, in ships of his own hiring; and with his own money released more than 1000 arms there, which the soldiers formerly engaged for their victuals. But this industry of Philpot interpretatively taxed the laziness of others, the nobility accusing him (drones account all bees pragmatical) to the king, for acting without a commission. Yea, in that ungrateful age, under a child-king, " pro tantorum sumptuum præmio, veniam vix obtinuit." However, he, who whilst living was the scourge of the Scots, the fright of the French, the delight of the Commons, the darling of the merchants, and the hatred of some envious lords, was at his death lamented, and afterwards beloved of all, when his memory was restored to its due esteem.

WILLIAM SEVENOCK was born at Sevenoaks in this county; in allusion whereunto he gave seven acorns for his arms,† which if they grow as fast in the field of heraldry as in the common field, may be presumed to be oaks at this day. For it is more than 200 years since this William (bred a grocer at London) became, anno 1419, lord mayor thereof. He founded at Sevenoaks a fair free-school for poor people's children, and an almshouse for twenty men and women, which at this day is well maintained.‡

SINCE THE REFORMATION.

Sir ANDREW JUD, son of John Jud, was born at Tunbridge in this county, bred a skinner in London, whereof he became lord mayor anno 1551. He built alms-houses nigh Saint Ellen's in London, and a stately free-school at Tunbridge in Kent, submitting it to the care of the company of Skinners. This fair school hath been twice founded in effect, seeing the defence and maintenance whereof hath cost the company of Skinners, in suits of law and otherwise, four thousand pounds.§ So care-

* Stow's Chronicle, p. 281.
† Stow's Survey of London.
‡ Idem, p. 88.
§ Dr. Willett, in his "Catalogue of good Works since the Reformation."

ful have they been (though to their own great charge) to see the will of the dead performed.

WILLIAM LAMBE, Esquire, sometime a gentleman of the chapel to king Henry the Eighth, and in great favour with him, was born at Sutton-Valens in this county, where he erected an alms-house, and a well-endowed school.* He was a person wholly composed of goodness and bounty, and was as general and discreet a benefactor as any that age produced. Anno 1557, he began, and within five months finished, the fair conduit at Holborn-bridge, and carried the water in pipes of lead more than two thousand yards at his own cost, amounting to fifteen hundred pounds. The total sum of his several gifts, moderately estimated, exceeded six thousand pounds. He lies buried with his good works in Saint Faith's church under Saint Paul's; where this inscription (set up, it seems, by himself in his life-time) is fixed on a brass plate to a pillar:

> " O *Lamb* of God, which sin didst take away,
>   And (as a *Lamb*) wast offered up for sin;
>   Where I (poor *Lamb*) went from thy flock astray,
>   Yet thou, good Lord, vouchsafe thy Lamb to win
>   Home to thy fold, and hold thy Lamb therein,
>   That, at the day when *Goats* and *Lambs* shall sever,
>   Of thy choice lambs, *Lamb* may be one for ever."

The exact time of his death I cannot meet with; but, by proportion, I conjecture it to be about 1580.

FRANCES SIDNEY, daughter of Sir William, sister to Sir Henry (lord deputy of Ireland, and president of Wales), aunt to the renowned Sir Philip Sidney, was born (and probably at Penshurst, the ancient seat of the Sidneys) in this county;—a lady endowed with many virtues, signally charitable, expending much in large benefactions to the public. She bestowed on the abbey church of Westminster a salary of twenty pounds per annum for a divinity lecture; and founded Sidney Sussex college in Cambridge, of which largely in my "Church History." She was relict of Thomas Ratcliff, the third earl of Sussex. This worthy lady died childless (unless such learned persons who received their breeding in her foundation may be termed her issue) on the ninth day of May, anno 1588, as appeareth by her epitaph.†

Sir FRANCIS NETHERSOLE, Knight, born at Nethersole‡ in this county, was bred fellow of Trinity College in Cambridge, and afterwards became orator of the university. Hence he was preferred to be ambassador to the princess of the Union, and secretary to the lady Elizabeth, queen of Bohemia; it is hard

* Stow's Survey of London, p. 93.
† On her monument in Westminster Abbey.—F.
‡ Nethersole House was pulled down about 50 years ago.—ED.

to say whether he was more remarkable for his doings or sufferings in her behalf. He married Lucy, eldest daughter of Sir Henry Goodyear of Polesworth in Warwickshire, by whose encouragement (being free of himself to any good design) he hath founded and endowed a very fair school at Polesworth aforesaid, and is still living.[*]

MEMORABLE PERSONS.

SIMON, son of William LYNCH,[†] Gent. was born at Groves, in the parish of Staple, in this county, December 9, 1562. But see more of his character under this title in Essex, where his life and death were better known.

MARY WATERS was born at Lenham in this county; and how abundantly entitled to memorability, the ensuing epitaph in Markeshall church in Essex will sufficiently discover:

" Here lieth the body of Mary Waters, the daughter and co-heir of Robert Waters of Lenham in Kent, esquire, wife of Robert Honywood [‡] of Charing in Kent, esquire, her only husband, who had at her decease, lawfully descended from her, three hundred sixty-seven children; sixteen of her own body, one hundred and fourteen grandchildren, two hundred twenty-eight in the third generation, and nine in the fourth. She lived a most pious life; and in a Christian manner died here at Markeshall, in the ninety-third year of her age, and in the forty-fourth year of her widowhood, the eleventh of May, 1620."

Thus she had a child for every day in the (though Leap) year, and one over. Here we may observe, that (generally) the highest in honour do not spread the broadest in posterity. For time was, when all the earls in England (and those then seventeen in number) had not, put together, so many sons and daughters, as one of them had, viz. Edward Somerset, earl of Worcester.[§] And yet of both sexes he never had but thirteen.[||] But to return to Mistress Waters; she since hath been much out-stript in point of fruitfulness by one still surviving; [¶] and therefore this worthy matron (in my mind) is more memorable on another account, viz. for patient weathering out the tempest of a troubled conscience, whereon a remarkable story dependeth. Being much afflicted in mind, many ministers repaired to her, and amongst the rest the Reverend Mr. John

---

* He died in 1652.—ED.

† The last of the Lynches of Grove were, Sir William Lynch, K. B. and his younger brother Dr. John Lynch, dean of Canterbury. Sir William's widow died at Grove in 1808.—ED.

‡ The last of the Markshall branch of Honywood was General Honywood, who devised it to his remote collateral relation the late Filmer Honywood, esq. M.P. for Kent, on whose death it came to his nephew William Honywood, esq. M.P. younger brother to the late Sir John Honywood, bart.—ED.

§ Camden, in his Elizabeth, anno 1589.

|| Mills, in his Catalogue of Honour, p. 106.

¶ Dame Hester Temple. See Memorable Persons in Buckinghamshire.—ED.

Fox, than whom no more happy an instrument to set the joints of a broken spirit. All his counsels proved ineffectual, insomuch that, in the agony of her soul, having a Venice-glass in her hand, she brake forth into this expression, " I am as surely damned as this glass is broken;" which she immediately threw with violence to the ground.

Here happened a wonder: the glass rebounded again, and was taken up whole and entire. I confess it is possible (though difficult) so casually to throw as brittle a substance, that, lighting on the edges, it may be preserved; but happening immediately in that juncture of time, it seemed little less than miraculous.

However the gentlewoman took no comfort thereat (as some have reported, and more have believed); but continued a great time after (short is long to people in pain) in her former disconsolate condition without any amendment; until at last, God, the great clock-keeper of time, who findeth out the fittest minutes for his own mercies, suddenly shot comfort like lightning into her soul; which once entered, ever remained therein (God doth not palliate cures, what he heals it holds); so that she led the remainder of her life in spiritual gladness. This she herself told to the Reverend Father Thomas Morton, bishop of Duresme, from whose mouth I have received this relation.

In the days of queen Mary she used to visit the prisons, and to comfort and relieve the confessors therein. She was present at the burning of Mr. Bradford in Smithfield; and resolved to see the end of his suffering, though so great the press of people, that her shoes were trodden off, and she forced thereby to go barefoot from Smithfield to Saint Martin's before she could furnish herself with a new pair for her money. Her dissolution happened, as is aforesaid, anno 1620.

NICHOLAS WOOD was born at Halingborne in this county, being a landed man, and a true labourer. He was afflicted with a disease called *Boulimia,* or *Caninus Apetitus;* insomuch that he would devour at one meal what was provided for twenty men, eat a whole hog at a sitting, and at another time thirty dozen of pigeons, whilst others make mirth at his malady.* Let us raise our gratitude to the goodness of God, especially when he giveth us appetite enough for our meat, and yet meat too much for our appetite; whereas this painful man spent all his estate to provide provant for his belly, and died very poor about the year 1630.

We will conclude this topic of Memorable Persons with a blank mention of him whose name hitherto I cannot exactly attain, being an ingenuous yeoman in this county, who hath two

---

* Sandys, in his notes on the Eighth Book of Ovid's Metamorphoses, p. 162.

ploughs fastened together so finely, that he plougheth two fur-rows at once, one under another, and so stirreth up the land twelve or fourteen inches deep, which in so deep ground is very good.* Scholars know that *Hen-dia-duo* is a very thrifty figure in rhetoric ; and how advantageous the improvement of this de-vice of a twin plough may be to posterity, I leave to the skilful in husbandry to consider.

LORD ·MAYORS.

1. William Sevenock, son of William Rumshed, of Sevenoaks, Grocer, 1418.
2. Thomas Hill, son of William Hill of Hilstone, Grocer, 1484.
3. Richard Chawry, son of William Chawry of Westram, Salter, 1494.
4. Andrew Jud, son of John Jud, of Tonbridge, Skinner, 1550.
5. John Rivers, son of Richard Rivers, of Penshurst, Grocer, 1573.
6. Edward Osburne, son of Richard Osburne, of Ashford, Cloth-worker, 1583.
7. Thomas Polloccil, son of William Polloccil, of Footscray, Draper, 1584.
8. William Rowe, son of Thomas Rowe, of Penshurst, Ironmon-ger, 1592.
9. Cuthbert Aket, son of Thomas Aket, of Dartford, Draper, 1626.

THE NAMES OF THE GENTRY OF THIS COUNTY,†

RETURNED BY THE COMMISSIONERS IN THE TWELFTH YEAR OF KING HENRY THE SIXTH, ANNO 1433.

Henry archbishop of Canterbury, and Robert de Poynings, knight ;—Richard Widvile, and John Perye, (knights for the shire) ;—Commissioners to take the oaths.

Willielmi prioris ecclesiæ Christi Canter.
Prioris de Rouchester.
Abbatis Sancte Radgundis.
Abbatis de Langedon.
Abbatis de Boxle.
Abbatis de Lesnes.
Prioris Sancti Georgii Cartur.
Prioris de Ledes.
Prioris de Tunbregge.
Prioris de Bilsington.
Prioris de Horton.
Rogeri Heron, magistri Coll. de Maydston.
Thomæ Ward, rectoris ec-clesiæ de Wroham.
Thomæ Mome, rectoris ec-clesiæ de Dele.

* Hartlib's Legacy, p. 6.
† There are still remaining out of this list, Oxenden, Finch, Monins (a younger branch), Twisden, Toke, Carter of Crundal, probably ancestor of William Carter of Canterbury, M. D.—The long-standing names of Haute, Cheyney, Clifford, Isaac, Septuans, Norton, Malmain, Apulderfield, Goldwell, Hadde, Wotton, Ro-berts of Goudhurst, Barham, Cobham, Brent, Fineaux, have been long extinct. The following old families became extinct in the last century; Guilford, St. Leger, Walsingham, Digges, Aucher, Watton, Colepepper, Hardres, Engham, Lovelace, Monins, Godfrey.—ED.

Henrici Benwortham, rectoris
ecclesiæ de Bourne.

Mathei Ashton, prepositi Coll.
de Wingham.

Will. Palmer, rectoris eccl.
de Smerden.

Rich. Corden, archidiaconi
Roffensis.

Johannis Gladwyn, magistri
Collegii de Cobham.

Will. Lyef, rectoris ecclesiæ
de Heriettesham.

Johan. Corwel, magistri de
Stode.

Roberti rectoris ecclesiæ de
Redelegh.

Fratris Andree Birchford, mil.
de Swynfeld, magistri Hosp.
de Osprenge.

Simonis Chepynden, rectoris
ecclesiæ de Wornesel.

Johannis Petthe, mil.

Rogeri Chamberleyn, mil.

Galfridi Louther.

Johannis Darsel.

Willielmi Haute.

Willielmi Cheyney.

Willielmi Clifford.

Edwardi Gilfford.

Rogeri Cliderowe.

Thomæ Browne.

Reignaldi Peckham.

Johannis Seyntleger.

Johannis Bamburgh.

Lodewici Clifford.

Willielmi Garnel.

Johannis Cheyney.

Thomæ Walsingham.

Willielmi Warner.

Johannis Dennis de Welle.

Valentini Baret.

Willielmi Manston.

Johannis Berton.

Johannis Isaac.

Thomæ Ballard.

Willielmi Septuans.

Willielmi Pikhill.

Thomæ Septuans.

Johannis Greneford.

Edmundi Hardes.

Johannis Digges.

Edwardi Lymsey,

Johannis Shyngleton.

Richardi Bamme.

Richardi Chiche.

Roberti Shandeford.

Willielmi Frogenale.

Richardi Combe.

Thomæ Betenham.

Johannis Kelsham.

Edmundi Passhele.

Henrici Horne de Apledre.

Thomæ Achier.

Johannis Cokeham de Hoo,

Roberti Watten.

Stephani Cossington.

Willielmi Channz.

Rogeri Honyngton.

Johannis Horne de Lenham,

Walteri Colepepar.

Nicholai Colepepar.

Willielmi Burys.

Willielmi Gullby.

Johannis Norton.

Johannis Feerby de Paulstrey.

Johannis Erhithe.

Stephani Norton.

Willielmi Kereby.

Rogeri Appulton.

Roberti Mollyngton.

Willielmi Isle de Sondrish.

Willielmi Hodestle.

Thomæ Hardes.

Johannis Oxenden.

Thomæ Brokhill de Saltwode.

Nichol. Brokhill de Saltwode.

Adomari Digge.

Willielmi Bertyn.

Edwardi Seint John.

Richardi Malman.

Roberti Cappes.

Johannis Vinche.

Richardi Horn de Westwell.

Will. Lane de Cantuaria.

Will. Chilton de eadem.

Will. Benet de eadem.

Will. Bellington de eadem.

Joh. Rose de eadem.

Will. Osborn de eadem.

Rob. Stopingdon de eadem.

Gilberti Germayn.

Thomæ Normayne de Cant.

Johannis Foochunt de eadem.

Willielmi Bryan de eadem.

Richardi Curteler de eadem.

Richardi Prat de eadem.

Edmundi Wykes de eadem.

Willielmi Baker de eadem.

Rogeri Manston.

Johannis Hetesle.

Thomæ Salisbury.

Johannis Carleton.

Johannis Gotysle.

Johannis Dandylion.

Willielmi Isaak.

Thomæ Apuldrefeld.

Willielmi Steveday.

Johannis Moyne.

Johannis Gerwinton.

Johannis Feneaux.

Will. Sutton de Northburne.

Stephani Monyn.

Johannis Broke de Snaxton.

Johannis Petit de Chartham.

Willielmi Valence.

Tho. Hollys de Godmarsham.

Johannis Rolling.

Nicholai Hame.

Roberti Yerde.

Richardi Bruyn.

Willielmi Brokman.

Guidoni Elys.

Thomæ Simond de Hertley.

Johannis May.

Thomæ Horden.

Thomæ Burgeys.

Johannis Golde.

Johannis Hoigges.

Thomæ Springet.

Rogeri Twisden.

Johannis Hore.

Johannis Derby.

Will. Collings de Thameto.

Walteri Gore.

Thomæ Champion.

Johan. Chamberlain.

Henr. Hicks de Rouchestre.

Willielmi Sidenore.

Radulfi Towke.

Johannis Wareve de Wy.

Will. Goldwell de Godyinton.

Will. Goldwell de Chart.

Richardi Sprot.

Thomæ Chiterynden.

Will. Enfynge.

Will. Spert.

Rob. Tropham de Wingham.

Roberti Goodebarne.

Thomæ Bevesle.

Will. Iuenet.

Johannis Iuenet.

Johannis Brenchesle, sen.

Johannis Brenchesle, jun.

Laur. Betleston de Bydyn-
den.

Joh. Pitlesden de Tynderdi.

Thomæ Hames de eadem.

Thomæ Berkynden.

Thomæ Gosebourne.

Will. Gosebourne.

Johannis Edyngham.

Richardi Edyngham.

Hugonis Godwyn.

Peteri Colepeper.

Walt. Baker de Maidston.

Steph. Colney de eadem.

Laur. Stonstreet de eadem.

Will. Enton.

Thomæ Mellere de Lenham.

Caur. Mellere de eadem.

Hen. Boycote.

Will. Hadde.

Roberti Purse.

Johannis Laurence.

Roberti Norton.

Richardi Dawdemere.

Willielmi Roger.

Thomæ Grymston.

Johannis Tuttesham.

Galfrid Yong.

Simonis Goldsmith.

Johannis Croweche de Water-
ingbery.

Joh. Reve.

Joh. Westbery.

Thomæ Stydolf.

Tho. Hilles de Brenchesle.
Laur. Hilles.
Joh. Slyhand.
Wil. Woadlond de Westgate.
Joh. Philpot de eadem.
Thomæ Tenham de Thaneto.
Thome Pawlyn de Thaneto.
Joh. Roger de Whitstaple.
Johannis Salmon de Whit-
staple.
Will. Hall de Eastrey.
Tho. Hunt de Cruddeswode.
Will. Licheffeld de Norbourn.
Henrici Bynton.
Adde Chanceler.
Thome Newman de Chistlet.
Richardi Bomoure de eadem.
Thome Causant de eadem.
Will. Philip de Hierne.
Thomæ Loucher.
Roberti Lovelass.
Thomæ Cadbery.
Thomæ Rokesle.
Roberti Virle.
Joh. Rose de Shorham.
Will. Holden de Hunten.
Joh. Rolff de Wrotham.
Johannis Swan de Southfleet.
Johannis Mellere de Wimel-
ingwelde.
Johannis Eythorst de Tenham.
Will. Blosme de Tenderden.
Jacobi Budde de Whittresham.
Richardi Combre.
Willielmi Wotton de Denton.
Johannis Biunham.
Roberti Hothe de Ryvere.
Thomæ Willok de Wy.
Will. Willok de Wy.
Johannis Atte Cambre de
Bokton Aluph.
Johannis Sandre de Bokton
Aluph.
Johannis Colman de Eastwell.
Jo. Walter de Eastwell.
Tho. Richard de Wy.
Thomæ Cartere de Crundale.
Will. Lucas de Essheford.
Rich. Atte Sole Kenington.

Johahnis Roberd de eadem.
Johannis Sandre de Cony-
broke.
Thomæ Chapman.
Johannis Ely
Will. Ixning.
Nicholai Roger de Mersham.
Nicholai Kenet.
Johannis Weston.
Henrici Tepynden.
Barthol. Atte Boure.
Will. Bregges de Ore.
Reginaldi Drylonde.
Nicholai Dane.
Richardi Langedon.
Stephani Hoigge.
Simonis Harry.
Willielmi Iden.
Johannis Hewet de Chertham.
Willielmi Egerden.
Johan. Bertlot de Cantuaria.
Johannis Lynde de eadem.
Rob. Becket de eadem.
Johan. Edle de eadem.
Joh. Edmond de eadem.
Johan. Osburn de eadem.
Johan. Pikerel de eadem.
Laur. Winter de eadem.
Will. Atte Wode de eadem.
Thomæ Cherch de eadem.
Johan. Bronns de eadem.
Rob. Pycot de eadem.
Rich. Galding de eadem.
Thomæ Pollard de eadem.
Johan. Pende de eadem.
Thomæ Mott de eadem.
Thomæ Lamsyn de eadem.
Joh. Mallyng de eadem.
Joh. Cosyn de eadem.
Joh. Bertholt de eadem.
David Marryes de eadem.
Ade Body de eadem.
Henrici Piers de eadem.
Joh. Robart de Cranebroke.
Will. Hert de Wodecherche.
Richardi Fawconer.
Johannis Bakke.
Johannis Bereham.
Johannis Bettenham.

Johan. Watte de Hankherst.
Will. Bernes de eadem.
Richardi Hodingfold.
Nicholai Piers.
Willielmi Piers de Molash.
Richardi Monyn.
Willielmi Cobham.
Johannis Baily de Hoo.
Roberti Reynold.
Henrici Rowe.
Richardi Groucherst de Hors-
     monden.
Johannis Jud.
Walteri Fletcher de Tun-
     bridge.
Johannis Picot de eadem.
Willielmi Randolf de eadem.
Rich. Johnson de eadem.
Simonis Fitzraufe.
Tho. Barbour de Wrotham.
Willielmi Menyware.
Johannis Rowe.
Richardi Ruxton.
Stephani Atte Bourn de Gon-
     therst.
Will. Robert de eadem.
Joh. Thorp de Gillingham.
Jo. Spencer de Melton.
Joh. Spencer de eadem, jun.
Jo. Petyge de Gravesend.
Joh. Pete de eadem.
Will. Doget de eadem.
Robert Baker de eadem.
Joh. Igelynden de Bydinden.
Richardi Smith de Shorne.
Michaelis atte Dean.
Richardi Lewte.
Johannis Bottiler de Clyne.
Thomæ Gardon de eadem.
Thomæ Peverel de Cukston.
Joh. Chambre de eadem.
Will. Holton de Heo.
Simonis Walsh de Creye.
Johannis Mayor de Rokesle.
Tho. Shelley de Farnburgh.
Joh. Mellere de Orpington.
Joh. Shelley de Bixle.
Willielmi Bery.
Johannis Bery.

Thomæ Cressel.
Johannis Manning de Code-
     ham.
Roberti Merfyn.
Roberti Chesman de Green-
     wich.
Philippi Dene de Woolwich.
Radulphi Langle de Becon-
     ham.
Will. Wolty de eadem.
Joh. Smith de Sevenock.
Joh. Cartere of Nemesing.
Tho. Palmer de Otford.
Nich. atte Bore de Bradest.
Rog. Wodeward de eadem.
Willielmi Rothel.
Roberti Allyn.
Johannis Knolls.
Richardi Rokesle.
Johannis Steynour.
Radolphi Stanhall de Wester-
     ham.
Rich. Yong de eadem.
Rich. Paris de eadem.
Tho. Martin de Edenbregge.
Thomæ Peny.
Joh. Dennet de Edonbregge.
Will. Kirketon de Fankham.
Johannis Crepehegge.
Johannis Hellis de Dernthe.
Johan. Chympeham.
Rob. Coats de Stone.
Roberti Stonestrete de Ive-
     chesch.
Johan. Hogelyn de eadem.
Johannis Lewys.
Petri Thurban.
Thomæ Beausrere.
Steph. Ive de Hope, sen.
Will. Newland de Brokland.
Hen. Aleyne de eadem.
Willielmi Wolbale.
Johannis Creking.
Stephani Wyndy.
Henrici Dobil.
Simonis Odierne.
Rob. Hollynden de Stelling.
Will. Bray de eadem.
Petri Neal de Elmestede.

Steph. Gibbe de Stonting.
Rich. Shotwater de eadem.
Rogeri Hincle de Elham.
Andree Wodehil de eadem.
Nicolai Campion.
Will. Atte Berne de Lymyne.
Johan. Cartere de Abyndon.
Rich. Knight de Stelling.
Will. Kenet de Bonyngton.
Jacobi Skappe.
Jacobi Godefray.
Joh. Baker de Caldham.
Roberti Dolyte.
Roberti Woughelite.
Joh. Chilton de Newington.
Tho. Chylton de eadem.
Tho. Turnour de Rochester.

Joh. Cust de eadem.
Joh. Houchon de eadem.
Stephani Riviel.
Warini Wade.
Thomæ Groveherst.
Will. Berford de Newington.
Joh. Grendon de Upcherche.
Johannis Hethe de Bakchild.
Rich. Groveherst de Synding-
    bourn.
Joh. Sonkyn de eadem.
P. Haidon de Borden.
Thomæ Waryn de Lenham.
Rich. Dene de Hedecrone.
Walteri Terold.
Hugonis Brent.

SHERIFFS.*

HENRY II.
Anno
1 Rualons.
2 Radul. Picot, for six years.
8 Hugo de Dovera, for seven years.
15 Gerv. de Cornhilla, for six years.
21 Gervat. et Rob. filius Bernardi.
22 Rob. filius Bernardi, for eight years.
30 Will. filius Nigelli.
31 Alanus de Valoigns, for four years.

RICH. I.
1 Regnal. de Cornhill, for six years.
7 Will. de Sancta Mardalia. Walt. filius Dermand.
8 Reginald. de Cornhill.
9 Idem.
10 Idem.

REX. JOHAN.
Anno
1 Reginald de Cornhill, for eleven years.
12 Johan. Fitz Vinon et Reginald. de Cornhill, for six years.

HENR. III.
1 Hubert de Burgo, Hugo de Windlesore, for seven years.
8 Hub. et Roger de Grimston for three years.
11 Huber. de Burozo, et Will. de Brito, for six years.
17 Bartholomeus de Criol, for six years.
24 Humf. de Bohun, Comes Essex.
25 Idem.
26 Petrus de Sabaudia et Bertram de Criol.

* The Cobhams, Colepeppers, Norwoods, and St. Legers, appear very early in the list of Sheriffs. Afterwards, among the principal, Septuans, Guilford, Digges, Darrell, Clifford, Haute, Cheyney, Waller, Fogge, Scott, Isaac, Roberts, Kemp, Walsingham, Wotton, Vane, Sonds, Poynings, Wyat, Hart, Sidley, Crisp, Tufton, Cromer, Hales, Boys, Baker, Fineux, Hardres, Leonard, Palmer, Twisden, Knatchbull, Aucher, Filmer, Dixwell, Lewknor, Polhill, Brockman, and Honywood.—Ed.

Anno

27 Bertram de Criol et Joh. de Cobham.

28 John de Cobham, for five years.

33 Reginald de Cobham, for eight years.
Walterus de Bersted.

41 Reginaldus de Cobham.

42 Fritho. Poysorer.

43 Idem.

44 Johannes de Cobham.

45 Idem.

46 Idem.

47 Rob. Walerand.
Tho. de la Wey.

48 Rogerus de Layburne.

49 Idem.

50 Rog. et Hen. de Burne, for three years.

53 Steph. de Penecester, et Henricus de Ledes, for three years.

56 Henricus Malemeins.

EDW. I.

1 Hen. Malemenis Mort.

2 Will. de Hents.

3 Will. de Valoigns, for four years.

7 Robertus de Schochon.

8 Idem.

9 Idem.

10 Idem.

11 Petrus de Huntinfend.

12 Idem.

13 Idem.

14 Hamo de Gatton.

15 Will. de Chelesend.

16 Idem.

17 Idem.

18 Will. de Brimshete.

19 Idem.

20 Johan. de Northwod.

21 Johannes de Burne.

22 Johan. de Burne.

23 Idem.

24 Idem.

25 Will. Trussel.

Anno

26 Will. Trussel.

27 Hen. de Apuldrefeld.

28 Johan. de Northwod.

29 Hen. de Cobham.

30 Idem.

31 Warresius de Valoynes.

32 Idem.

33 Johan. de Northwod.

34 Idem.

35 Will. de Cosington.

36 Galfridus Colepepar, for four years.

EDW. II.

1 Henricus de Cobham.

2 Johan. de Blound, for five years.

7 Will. de Basings et Johannes de Haulo, jun.

8 Idem.

9 Hen. de Cobham.

10 Johannes de Malemeyns de Hoo.

11 Idem.
Johannes de Fremingham.

12 Joh. et Hen. de Sardenne.

13 Hen. et Will. Septuans.

14 (*Nul. tit. Com. in hoc rotulo.*)

15 Williel. Stevens et Radulphus Savage.

16 (*Nul. tit. Com. in rotulo.*)

17 Johannes de Shelvinge.

18 Johannes de Fremingham.

19 Idem.

EDW. III.

1 Radulph. de Sancto Laur.

2 Will. de Orlaston.

3 Joh. de Shelvingges,
Will. de Orlaston.

4 Johannes de Bourne,
Johannes de Shelvingges.

5 Johannes de Bourne.

6 Tho. de Brockhull.
Laur. de Sancto Laur.

7 Tho. de Brockhull.

8 Steph. de Cobham.

Anno

 9 Steph. de Cobham.
10 Idem.
11 Tho. de Brockhull.
12 Will. Morants.
13 Idem.
14 Henricus de Valoyns.
15 Johannes de Mereworth.
15 Johannes de Widleston,
     Johannes de Mereworth.
17 Johannes de Widleston, for
     four years.
21 Williel. de Langele.
22 Johan. de Fremingham.
23 Willielmi de Langele.
     Arnaldus Sauvage.
24 (*Nul. tit. Com. in hoc ro-
     tulo.*)
25 Will. de Langele.
26 Jacobus Lapin.
27 Will. de Apelderfeld.
28 Jacobus Lapin.
29 Reginal. de Duk, sive Dyk.

Anno

30 Gilb. de Helles.
31 Will. de Apelderfeld.
32 Radulphus Fremingham.
33 Williel. Wakenade.
34 Will. de Apelderfeld.
35 Idem.
36 Idem.
37 Willielmi Pimpe.
38 Will. de Apelderfeld.
39 Johannes Colepepar.
40 Idem.
41 Ric'us Atte Les.
42 Johannes de Brockhull.
43 Johannes Colepepar.
44 Will. de Apelderfeld.
45 Williel. Pimp.
46 Johannes Barry.
47 Galfr. Colepepar.
48 Rob. Notingham.
49 Williel. Pimpe.
50 Nic. Atte Crouch.
51 Henrici Apulderfeld.

HENRY III.

1. HUBERT de BURGO et HUGO de WINDLESORE.—This is that Hubert so famous in our chronicles, late lord chamberlain unto king John, and lord chief justice of England. In this year of his shrievalty, he not only valiantly defended the castle of Dover against Lewis the French king's son, but also in a naval conflict overthrew a new supply of soldiers sent to him for his assistance. I behold this Hugo joined with him (as the shadow to the substance) as his under-sheriff, acting the affairs of the county in his absence.

11. HUBERT de BUROZO* et WILL. de BRITO.—This year, anno 1227, Hugo de Burgo (of whom immediately before) was, in the month of February, by the king made earl of Kent; and, for a farther reward, had granted unto him the third penny of all the king's profits arising in the said county; and Hubert de Burozo succeeded him in his office. But I humbly conceive him the same person, who was both Comes and Vice-comes of Kent at the same time, a conjunction often precedented in other counties; the rather, because this Hubert lived many years after, till at last he got the king's ill will for doing him so many good offices, not dying till the twenty-seventh year of his reign, anno 1243.

* *Burozo* is but our English borough, barbarously Latinized, and the same with *Burgo*.—F.

EDWARD I.

20. JOHAN. de NORTHWOD.—This was a right ancient family in this county; for I find, in the church of Minster in Sheppey, this inscription :

" Hic jacent Rogerus Norwod et Boan uxor ejus, sepulti ante Conquestum."

Possibly they might be buried here before the Conquest; but the late character of the letter doth prove it a more modern inscription. The chief residence of the Norwods was a house of their own name in the parish of Milton-church, where they have many fair monuments, but with defaced epitaphs. One of their heirs was married into the family of the Nortons, of whom hereafter.*

SHERIFFS.

RICH. II.

Anno	Name and Arms.	Place.
1	Tho. de Cobham	Roundall.
	G. on a chevron O. three crescents S.	
2	Jo. de Fremingham	Freming.
3	Jac. de Peckham	Yaldham.
	S. a chevron O. between three cross-croslets fitchée Arg.	
4	Will. Septuans	Milton.
5	Arnald. Savage	Bobbing.
	Arg. six lioncels, three, two, and one, S.	
6	Tho. Brockhul	Cale-Hill.
	G. a cross engrailed, between twelve cross-croslets fitchée Arg.	
7		
8	Rob. Corby	Boughton.
9	Arnald. Savage	*ut prius.*
10	Rad'us Seintleger	Ulcomb.
	Az. frettée Arg.; a chief G.	
11	Will. de Guldeford	Hempsted.
	O. a saltire betwixt four martlets S.	
12	Jacobus Peckham	*ut prius.*
13	Will. Burcestre	HAMPSHIRE.
14	Rich. de Berham	Berham.
	Arg. three bears S. two and one, muzzled O.	
15	Tho. Chich	Dungeon.
	Az. three lions rampant, within a border Arg.	
16	Will. Barry	Sevington.
17	Joh. Fremingham.	
18	Tho. Colepeper	Pepenbury.
	Arg. a bend engrailed G.	

* In the fifth of king Henry the Eighth.

Anno	Name.	Place.
19	Will. Haut	Waddenhal.

O. a cross engrailed G.

20	Tho. Seintleger	*ut prius.*
21	Nich. Potyne	Queen-Co.
22	Joh. Botiller	Gravenev.

Arg. on a chief S. three cups covered O.

HENRY IV.

| 1 | Rob. Clifford | Bobbing. |

Checky O. and Az. a fess within a border G.

| 2 | Tho. Lodelow | WILTSHIRE. |
| | Joh. Diggs | Digs Court. |

G. on a cross Arg. five eaglets displayed S.

| 3 | Tho. Hyach. | |
| 4 | Rich. Cliderow | Goldstanton. |

Arg. on a chevron G. betwixt three spread-eagles S. five
annulets O.

5		
6	Valent. Baret	Lenham.
7	Hen. Horn.	
8	Edw. Haut	*ut prius.*
9	Will. Snayth.	
10	Reginald. Pimpe	Pimps Court.

Arg. four barrulets G.; on a chief S. a bar nubilée of
the first.

| 11 | Joh. Darel | Cale-Hill. |

Az. a lion rampant O. crowned Arg.

| 12 | Will. Notebeame. | |

HENRY V.

1	Will. Clifford	*ut prius.*
2	Rob. Clifford	*ut prius.*
3	Will. Langley.	
4	Will. Darel	*ut prius.*
5	Joh. Darel	*ut prius.*
6	Rich. Cliderow	*ut prius.*
7	Joh. Burgh.	
8	Will. Haut	Hautsburn.

Arms, *ut prius.*

| 9 | | |
| 10 | Joh. Darel | *ut prius.* |

HENRY VI.

| 1 | Joh. Darel | *ut prius.* |
| 2 | Will. Cheney | Shutland. |

Az. six lions rampant Arg. a canton Erm.

| 3 | Joh. Rykeld | Eastlingham. |

Anno	Name.	Place.
4	Will. Clifford	*ut prius.*
5	Will. Culpeper . . .	Preston.
	Arms, *ut prius.*	
6	Tho. Ellis	Burton.
	O. on a cross S. five crescents A.	
7	[AMP] Will. Scot . .	Braborne.
8	Joh. Peach	Lullingston.
9	Joh. Seintleger . . .	*ut prius.*
10	Edward Gulfort . . .	Halden.
	Arms, *ut prius.*	
11	Will. Burys	Bromley.
12	Rich. Wodveile . . .	NORTHAMPTON.
	Arg. a fess and canton G.	
13	Will. Clifford	*ut prius.*
14	Will. Manston . . .	Manston.
15	Jacobus Fienis . . .	Kemsing.
	Az. three lions rampant O.	
16	Rich. Waller	Grome-Bride.
	S. three walnut-leaves O. between two bendlets Arg.	
17	Edw. Guldeford . . .	*ut prius.*
18	Gervasius Clifton . .	Brabourn.
	S. semée de cinquefoils, a lion rampant Arg.	
19	Joh. Yeard	Denton.
20	Joh. Warner . . .	Foot's Cray.
21	Will. Mareys . . .	Ufton.
22	Tho. Brown	SURREY.
	S. three lions passant in bend, double cotised Arg.	
23	Will. Crowmer . . .	Tunstal.
	Arg. a chevron betwixt three ravens S.	
24	Joh. Thornbury . .	Feversham.
25	Will. Isley	Sundridge.
	Erm. a fesse G.	
26	Will. Kene	Well-Hall.
27	Steph. Seintleger . .	*ut prius.*
28	Hen. Crowmer . . .	*ut prius.*
29	Gervasius Clifton . .	*ut prius.*
30	Rob. Horn	Horn's Place.
31	Tho. Ballard	Horton.
32	Joh. Fogge	Repton.
33	Joh. Cheyney, mil. .	*ut prius.*
34	Phil. Belknap, arm. .	The Moat.
35	Alex. Eden, arm. . .	Westwell.
36	Joh. Guldeford, arm. .	*ut prius.*
37	Gervas. Clifton, mil. .	*ut prius.*
38	Tho. Brown, mil. et .	*ut prius.*
	Joh. Scot, arm. vicis. Vic.	Scots-Hall.
	Arms, *ut prius.*	

EDW. IV.

Anno	Name.	Place.
1	Joh. Isaac, arm. . . .	Howlets.
2	Will. Peach, mil.	
3	Idem.	
4	Job. Diggs, arm. . .	*ut prius.*
5	Alex. Clifford, arm. . .	*ut prius.*
6	Will. Haut, mil. . .	*ut prius.*
7	Joh. Colepeper, mil. .	*ut prius.*
8	Rad. Seintleger, arm. .	*ut prius.*
9	Hen. Ferrers, arm. . .	WARWICKSHIRE.
10	Joh. Bromston, arm. .	Preston.
11	Rich. Colepeper, arm.	Oxenhoath.
	Arms, *ut prius.*	
12	Ja. Peckham, arm. .	*ut prius.*
13	Joh. Fogge, mil.	
14	Joh. Isley, arm. . . .	*ut prius.*
15	Will. Haut, mil. . . .	*ut prius.*
16	Joh. Green, arm. . .	Scadbury.

G. a cross croslet Erm. within a border gobony Arg. and S.

17	Will. Cheyney, arm. .	*ut prius.*
18	Rich. Haut, arm. . .	*ut prius.*
19	Rich. Lee, arm. . . .	Delce.
20	Joh. Fogge, mil.	
21	Geo. Brown, mil. . .	*ut prius.*
22	Rich. Haut, arm. . .	*ut prius.*

RICHARD III.

1	Will. Haut, mil. . . .	*ut prius.*
2	Joh. Banne	Grench.
3	Ri. Brakenbury, mil. et .	The Moat.
	Will. Cheyney . .	*ut prius.*

HENR. VII.

1	Will. Cheyney . . .	*ut prius.*
2	Joh. Pymp, arm. . .	*ut prius.*
3	Hen. Ferrers, mil. . .	*ut prius.*
4	Walt. Roberts . . .	Glastenbury.
5	Will. Boleyn, mil. . .	NORFOLK.

Arg. a chevron G. inter three bulls' heads couped S. armed O.

6	Will. Scot, mil. . . .	*ut prius.*
7	Joh. Darel, arm. . .	*ut prius.*
8	Tho. Kemp, arm. . .	Ollantie.
9	Rich. Gulford, mil. . .	Halden.
	Arms, *ut prius.*	
10	Joh. Peach, arm.	

Anno	Name.	Place.
11	Joh. Diggs, arm. . .	*ut prius.*
12	Ja. Walsingham, arm. .	Scadbury.

Paly of six Arg. and S. a fesse G.

13	Lodow. Clifford, arm. .	*ut prius.*
14	Rob. Wotton, arm. .	Bocton.

Arg. a saltire engrailed S.

15	Alex. Colepeper, arm. .	*ut prius.*
16	Tho. Eden, arm.	
17	Will. Scot, mil. . . .	*ut prius.*
18	Rad. Seintleger . . .	*ut prius.*
19	Will. Crowmer, arm. .	*ut prius.*
20	Joh. Langley, arm. . .	Knowlton.
21	Tho. Kemp, mil.	
22	Alex. Colepeper, arm. .	*ut prius.*
23	Henry Vaine	Tunbridge.

Az. three gauntlets sinister O.

24	Reginald Peckham . .	*ut prius.*

HEN. VIII.

1	Will. Crowmer, mil. .	*ut prius.*
2	Jacobus Diggs, arm. .	*ut prius.*
3	Tho. Boleyn, mil. . .	*ut prius.*
4	Tho. Kemp, mil.	
5	Jo. Norton, mil. . . .	Northwood.
6	Alex. Colepeper, arm. .	*ut prius.*
7	Tho. Cheyney, arm. .	*ut prius.*
8	Will. Scot, mil. . . .	*ut prius.*
9	Tho. Boleyn, mil. . .	*ut prius.*
10	Joh. Crisps, arm. . .	Quekes.
11	Joh. Wiltshire, mil. .	Stone.
12	Joh. Roper, arm. . .	Eltham.

Party per fess Az. and O. a pale counterchanged, three roe-bucks' heads erased of the second.

13	Rob. Sonds, arm. . .	Town-place.

Arg. three blackmoors' heads couped proper between two chevronels S.

14	Joh. Fogge, mil.	
15	Geo. Guldeford, mil. .	*ut prius.*
16	Will. Haut, mil. . . .	*ut prius.*
17	Hen. Vane, arm. . .	*ut prius.*
18	Will. Whetnal, arm. .	Hextal.

V. a bend Erm.

19	Joh. Scot, mil. . . .	*ut prius.*
20	Will. Kemp, arm.	
21	Edw. Wotton, mil. . .	*ut prius.*
22	Will. Waller, mil. . .	*ut prius.*
23	Rich. Clement, mil. . .	Ightham.
24	Will. Finch, mil. . .	Eastwell.

Arg. a chevron between three griffins passant S.

Anno	Name.	Place.

25 Tho. Roberth, arm. . . Glastenbury.
26 Tho. Ponings, mil. . . Ostenhanger.
    Barry of six O. and V. a bend G.
27 Edw. Wotton, mil. . . *ut prius.*
28 Tho. Wyat, mil. . . . Allington.
29 Will. Haut, mil. . . . *ut prius.*
30 Will. Sidney, mil. . . Penshurst.
    O. a pheon Az.
31 Ant. Seintleger, mil. . *ut prius.*
32 Anth. Sonds, arm. . . *ut prius.*
33 Reginald. Scot, mil. . . *ut prius.*
34 Henry Iseley, mil. . . *ut prius.*
35 Humph. Style, mil. . . Langley-pa.
    S. a fess engrailed frettée between three flowers-de-luce O.
36 Joh. Fogge, mil.
37 Percival Hart, mil. . . Lullingstone.
38 Hen. Crisps, arm.

EDWARD VI.

1 Will. Sidley, arm. . . Scadbury.
    Az. a fess vairy between three goats' heads erased Arg.
    attired O.
2 Geo. Harper, mil. . . Sutton.
    S. a lion rampant within a border engrailed G.
3 Tho. Culpeper, arm. . *ut prius.*
4 Tho. Wyat, mil.
5 Hen. Isley, mil. . . . *ut prius.*
6 Joh. Guldeford, mil. . *ut prius.*

PHIL. et MAR.

m. 1 Rob. Southwel, mil. . Merworth.
m. 1 & 2 Will. Roper, arm. *ut prius.*
2 & 3 Tho. Kemp, mil.
3 &4
4 & 5 Geo. Vane, arm. . . *ut prius.*
5 & 6 Tho. Wotton, arm. . *ut prius.*

ELIZ. REG.

1 Nich. Crisps, arm.
2 Warh. Seintleger, arm. . *ut prius.*
3 Joh. Tufton, arm. . . Hothfield.
    S. an eagle displayed Erm. a border Arg.
4 Rich. Baker, arm. . . Sisingherst.
    Az. a fess O. between three swans' heads erased, beaked G.
5 Tho. Walsingham, arm. *ut prius.*
6 Tho. Kemp, mil.
7 Joh. Mayney, arm.
    Will. Isley, arm. . . . *ut prius.*

Anno	Name.	Place.

8 Joh. Sidley, arm.   .   Southfleet.
9 Will. Crowmer, arm.   .   *ut prius.*
10 Joh. Brown, arm.   .   . Brown's-place.
    Az. a chevron between three escalops O. within a border engrailed G.
11 Edw. Isaac, arm.   .   . Patrick's-b.
12 Joh. Leonard, arm. .   . Chevening.
    O. on a fess G. three flowers-de-luce of the first.
13 Wal. Mayne, sen. arm. .   Spilsil.
14 Tho. Vane, sen. mil.   . Badsel.
    Arms, *ut prius.*
15 Tho. Willoughby, arm. .   Bore-place.
    O. frettée Az.
16 Jacobus Hales, mil. .   . Woodchurch.
    G. three arrows O. headed and feathered Arg.
17 Joh. Tufton, arm.   .   . *ut prius.*
18 Tho. Scot, mil.   .   .   *ut prius.*
19 Edw. Boys, arm.   .   . Fredville.
    O. a griffin segreant S. within two borders G.
20 Tho. Wotton, arm. .   .   *ut prius.*
21 Tho. Copinger, arm.
    Bendy of six, O. and G. on a fess Az. three plates.
   Tho. Vane, arm. .   .   *ut prius.*
22 Tho. Sonds, arm.   .   . *ut prius.*
23 Geo. Hart, mil. .   .   . *ut prius.*
24 Rich. Baker, mil.   .   . *ut prius.*
25 Just. Champneys, arm. .   Hall-place.
    Per pale Arg. and S. a lion rampant within a border engrailed counterchanged.
26 Nich. Sonds, arm.   .   . *ut prius.*
27 Will. Cromer, arm. .   . *ut prius.*
28 Jacobus Hales, mil. .   . *ut prius.*
29 Joh. Fineux, arm.   .   . Haw-court.
    V. a chevron between three eaglets displayed O.
30 Rich. Hardres, arm.
31 Will. Sidley, arm.   .   . *ut prius.*
32 Tho. Willoughby, arm. .   *ut prius.*
33 Sampson Leonard, arm.   *ut prius.*
34 Rob. Bing, arm. .   .   . Wrotham.
    Quarterly S. and Arg. a lion rampant in the first quarter of the second.
35 Mich. Sond, arm.   .   . Throughley.
    Arms, *ut prius.*
36 Edw. Wotton, mil. .   . *ut prius.*
37 Tho. Palmer, arm.
38 Moile Finch, mil. .   . Eastwell.
    Arg. a chevron betwixt three griffins passant S.
39 Tho. Kemp, arm.

Anno	Name.	Place.

40 Martin Barnham, arm.
    S. a cross engrailed between four crescents Arg.
41 Rog. Twisden, arm. . . East Peckham.
    Gyronny of four Arg. and G. a saltire between as many
       croslets, all counterchanged.
42 Joh. Smith, arm. . . . Ostenhanger.
43 Tho. Scot, arm. . . . *ut prius.*
44 Petr. Manwood, arm. . St. Stephen's.
45 Ja. Cromer, mil. . . . *ut prius.*

JAC. REX.

1 Jacob. Cromer, mil, . . *ut prius.*
2 Tho. Baker, mil. . . . *ut prius.*
3 Moilus Finch, mil. . . *ut prius.*
4 Nort. Knatchbul, mil. . Mersham.
    Az. three croslets fitchée between two bendlets O.
5 Rob. Edolph, mil. . . Hinx-hill.
6 Edw. Hales, mil. . . . *ut prius.*
7 Will. Withens, mil. . . South-end.
8 Nich. Gilborn, mil. . . Charing.
9 Max. Dallison, mil. . . Halling.
    G. three crescents O. a canton Erm.
10 Will. Steed, mil. . . Steed-hill.
11 Anth. Awcher, mil. . . Hautsbourn.
12 Edw. Filmer, mil. . . East Sutton.
    S. three bars, and as many cinquefoils in chief O.
13 Edwin Sandis, mil. . . Northborn.
    O. a fess dancetté between three croslets G.
14 Will. Beswick, arm. . . Spelmonden.
    G. six besants ; a chief O.
15 Gabr. Livesey, arm. . . Hollingborne.
    Arg. a lion rampant G. between three trefoils V.
16 Tho. Norton, mil. . . Bobbing.
17 Edw. Scot, arm. . . . *ut prius.*
18 John Sidley, bar. . . *ut prius.*
19 Tho. Roberts, mil. et bar. Glastenbury.
20 George Fane, mil. . . *ut prius.*
21 Joh. Hayward, mil. . . Hollingborne.
22 Tho. Hamond, mil. . . Brasted.
    Arg. on a chevron engrailed betwixt three martlets S.
    as many cinquefoils O.

CAR. I.

1 Isa. Sidley, mil. et bar. . Great Chart.
    Arms, *ut prius.*
2 Basilius Dixwel, arm. . Folkstone.
    Arg. a chevron G. between three flowers-de-luce S.

Anno	Name.	Place.
3	Edw. Engham, mil. . .	Goodnestone.

Arg. a chevron S. between three ogresses; a chief G.

| 4 | Will. Campion, mil. . | Combwel. |
| 5 | Rich. Brown, arm. . . | Singleton. |

Arms, *ut prius.*

| 6 | Rob. Lewkner, mil. . . | Acris. |

Az. three chevrons Arg.

| 7 | Nich. Miller, arm. . . | Crouch. |
| 8 | Tho. Style, bar. . . . | Watringbury. |

Arms, *ut prius.*

9	Joh. Baker, bar. . . .	*ut prius.*
10	Edw. Chute, arm. . .	Surrenden.
11	Will. Culpeper, bar. .	*ut prius.*
12	Geo. Sands, mil. . . .	*ut prius.*
13	Tho. Hendley, mil. . .	Courshorn.
14	Edw. Maisters, mil. . .	East Langdon.
15	David Polhill, arm. . .	Otford.
16	Jacob. Hugeson, arm. .	Lingsted.
17	Will. Brokman, mil. .	Bithborow.
	Joh. Honywood, mil. .	Evington.
18		
19		
20	Joh. Rayney, bar.	
21	Edw. Monins, bar. . .	Waldershare Court.

Az. a lion passant betwixt three escalops O.

| 22 | Joh. Hendon, mil. | |

RICHARD II.

5. ARNOLD SAVAGE.—He was a knight, and the third constable of Queenborough Castle. He lieth buried in Bobbing church, with this inscription :

" Orate specialiter pro animabus Arnoldi Savage, qui obiit in vigil. Sanc. Andreæ Apost. anno 1410, et Domine Joanne uxoris ejus, quæ fuit fil. &c."

The rest is defaced.

16. GULIELMUS BARRY.—In the parish church of Sevington in this county, I meet with these two sepulchral inscriptions :

" Orate pro anima Isabelle quondam uxoris Willielmi Barry, Militis."
" Hic jacet Joanna Barry, quondam uxor Willielmi Barry, Militis."

There is in the same church a monument, whereupon a man armed is portrayed, the inscription thereon being altogether perished, which in all probability, by the report of the parishioners, was made to the memory of Sir William Barry aforesaid.

HENRY IV.

6. VALENTINE BARRET.—He lieth buried in the parish

church of Lenham in this county, under a grave-stone, thus inscribed :

" Hic jacet Valentine Barret, Arm. qui obiit Novemb 10, 1440, et Cecilia uxor ejus, quæ obiit Martii 2, 1440, quorum animabus ——"

HENRY VI.

7. WILLIAM SCOT.—He lieth buried in Braburne church, with this epitaph :

" Hic jacet Willielmus Scot de Braburne, Arm. qui obiit 5 Feb. 1433, cujus anim—
    Sis testis, Christe, quod non jacet hic lapis iste,
    Corpus ut ornetur, sed spiritus ut memoretur.
    Quisquis eris qui transieris, sic perlege, plora,
    Sum quod eris, fueramque quod es, pro me precor ora."

His family afterwards fixed at Scot's-hall in this county, where they flourish at this day in great reputation.

9. JOHN SEINTLEGER.—I find him entombed in Ulcombe church, where this is written on his grave, " Here lieth John Seintleger, Esq. and Margery his wife, sole daughter and heir of James Donnet, 1442." Wonder not that there is no mention in this catalogue of Sir Thomas Seintleger, a native and potent person in this county, who married Anne the relic of Henry Holland duke of Exeter, the sister of king Edward the Fourth, by whom he had Anne, mother to Thomas Manners, first earl of Rutland ; for the said Sir Thomas Seintleger was not to be confided in under king Henry the Sixth ; and afterwards, when brother-in-law to king Edward the Fourth, was above the office of the shrievalty.

16. RICHARDUS WALLER.—This is that renowned soldier, who, in the time of Henry the Fifth, took Charles duke of Orleans, general of the French army, prisoner at the battle of Agincourt, brought him over into England, and held him in honourable restraint or custody at Gromebridge, which a manuscript in the Herald's office notes to be twenty-four years.* In the time of which his recess, he newly erected the house at Gromebridge upon the old foundation, and was a benefactor to the repair of Spelhurst church, where his arms remain in stonework over the church-porch : but, lest such a signal piece of service might be entombed in the sepulchre of unthankful forgetfulness, the prince assigned to this Richard Waller and his heirs for ever an additional crest, viz. the arms or escutcheon of France, hanging by a label on an oak, with this motto affixed, " Hæc Fructus Virtutis." From this Richard, Sir William Waller is lineally descended.

23. WILLIELMUS CROWMER.—This year happened the barbarous rebellion of Jack Cade in Kent. This sheriff, unable

* Villare Cantianum, p. 320.

with the *posse comitatús* to resist their numerousness, was taken
by them, and by those wild justicers committed to the Fleet in
London; because, as they said (and it must be so if they said
it), he was guilty of extortion in his office. Not long after,
these reformers sent for him out of the Fleet, made him to be
brought to Mile-end, where, without any legal proceedings, they
caused his head to be smitten off, and set upon a long pole on
London-bridge, next to the lord Say aforesaid, whose daughter
he had married.*

38. JOHN SCOT, *Arm. et vicissim Vic.*—I understand it thus;
that his under-sheriff supplied his place whilst he was busied in
higher affairs. He was knighted, much trusted, and employed
by king Edward the Fourth. I read in a record,

"Johannes Scot, Miles, cum CC. Soldariis, ex mandato Domini Regis, apud
Sandwicum, pro salvâ custodiâ ejusdem."†

The aforesaid king, in the twelfth year of his reign, sent this
Sir John (being one of his privy council, and knight marshal
of Calais) with others, on an embassy, to the dukes of Burgundy
and Britain, to bring back the earls of Pembroke and Richmond,
whose escape much perplexed this king's suspicious thoughts.
But see his honourable epitaph in the church of Braburne:

"Hic jacet magnificus ac insignis Miles Johannes Scot, (quondam Regis domûs,
invictissimi Principis Edwardi Quarti, Controll.), et nobilissima integerrima-
que Agnes uxor ejus. Qui quidem Johannes obiit anno 1485, die mens.
Octob. 17."

RICHARD III.

3. RICHARDUS BRAKENBURY, Mil. et WILLIELMUS CHE-
NEY.—The former was of an ancient extraction in the north. I
behold him as nearly allied (if not brother) to Sir Robert Brakenbury, constable of the Tower, who dipped his fingers so deep
in the blood of king Edward the Fifth and his brother. It
concerned king Richard, in those suspicious times, to appoint
his confident sheriff of this important county; but he was soon
un-sheriffed by the king's death, and another of more true integrity substituted in his room.

HENRY THE SEVENTH.

5. WILL. BOLEYN, Mil.—He was son to Sir Jeffery Boleyne,
lord mayor of London, by his wife, who was daughter and co-
heir to Thomas Lord Hoo and Hastings. This Sir William
was made knight of the Bath at the coronation of king Richard
the Third. He married one of the daughters and co-heirs of
Thomas Butler earl of Ormond; by whom, besides four daughters married into the worshipful and wealthy families of Shelton,
Calthrop, Clere, and Sackvil, he had Sir Thomas Boleyn, earl of
Wiltshire, of whom hereafter.

* Stow's Chronicle, p. 391.
† Inter. Bundell. Indent. de Guerrâ, apud Pelles Westm.

10. Joh. Peach, Arm.—This year Perkin Warbeck landed at Sandwich in this county, with a power of all nations, contemptible, not in their number or courage, but nature and fortune, to be feared, as well of friends as enemies, as fitter to spoil a coast, than recover a country. Sheriff Peach, knighted this year for his good service, with the Kentish gentry, acquitted themselves so valiantly and vigilantly, that Perkin shrunk his horns back again into the shell of his ships. About 150 of his men being taken, and brought up by this sheriff to London, some were executed there, the rest on the sea coasts of Kent and the neighbouring counties; for sea-marks to teach Perkin's people to avoid such dangerous shores.*

HENRY THE EIGHTH.

5. Joh. Norton, Mil.—He was one of the captains, who in the beginning of the reign of king Henry the Eighth went over with the 1500 archers, under the conduct of Sir Edward Poynings, to assist Margaret, duchess of Savoy (daughter to Maximilian the emperor, and governess of the Low Countries) against the incursions of the duke of Guelders; where this Sir John was knighted by Charles, young prince of Castile, and afterwards emperor. He lieth buried in Milton church, having this written on his monument;

" Pray for the souls of Sir John Norton, knight, and Dame Joane his wife, one of the daughters and heirs of John Norwood, Esq. who died Feb. 8, 1534."

7. Thomas Cheyney, Arm.—He was afterwards knighted by king Henry the Eighth, and was a spriteful gentleman, living and dying in great honour and estimation; a favorite and privy counsellor to four successive kings and queens, in the greatest turn of times England ever beheld; as by this his epitaph in Minster Church, in the Isle of Sheppey, will appear.

" Hic jacet Dominus Thomas Cheyney, inclitissimi ordinis Garterii Miles, Guarduanus Quinque Portuum, ac Thesaurarius Hospitii Henrici Octavi ac Edwardi Sexti, regum, reginæque Mariæ ac Elizabethæ, ac eorum in secretis consiliarius, qui obiit—mensis Decembris, anno Dom. M.D.LIX. ac reg. reginæ Eliz. primo."

11. John Wiltshire, Mil.—He was controller of the town and marches of Calais, anno 21 of king Henry the Seventh. He founded a fair chapel in the parish of Stone, wherein he lieth entombed with this inscription:

" Here lieth the bodies of Sir John Wiltshire, knight, and of Dame Margaret his wife; which Sir John died 28 Dec. 1526; and Margaret died ———— of ————"

Bridget, his sole daughter and heir, was married to Sir Richard

* Stow's Annals, p. 480.

N 2

Wingfield, knight of the Garter, of whom formerly in Cambridgeshire.

12. JOHN ROPER, Arm.—All the memorial I find of him, is this inscription in the church of Eltham :

> " Pray for the soul of Dame Margery Roper, late wife of John Roper, esquire, daughter and one of the heirs of John Tattersall, esquire, who died Feb. 2, 1518."

Probably she got the addition of Dame (being wife but to an esquire) by some immediate court attendance on Katharine first wife to king Henry the Eighth.

KING JAMES.

3. MOILE FINCH, Mil.—This worthy knight married Elizabeth, sole daughter and heir to Sir Thomas Heneage, vice-chamberlain to queen Elizabeth, and chancellor of the duchy of Lancaster. She, in her widowhood, by the special favour of king James, was honoured Viscountess Maidstone (unprecedented, save by one,* for this hundred years) ; and afterwards, by the great grace of king Charles the First, created countess of Winchelsea, both honours being entailed on the issue-male of her body ; to which her grandchild, the Right Honourable Heneage (lately gone ambassador to Constantinople) doth succeed.

THE FAREWELL.

Having already insisted on the courage of the Kentish men, and shown how in former ages the leading of the van-guard was entrusted unto their magnanimity, we shall conclude our description of this shire, praying that they may have an accession of loyalty unto their courage, not that the natives of Kent have acquitted themselves less loyal than those of other shires ; but, seeing the one will not suffer them to be idle, the other may guide them to expend their ability for God's glory, the defence of his majesty, and maintenance of true religion.

CANTERBURY.

CANTERBURY is a right ancient city; and, whilst the Saxon Heptarchy flourished, was the chief seat of the kings of Kent. Here Thomas Becket had his death; Edward, surnamed the Black Prince, and king Henry the Fourth, their interment. The Metropolitan dignity, first conferred by Gregory the Great on

* Mary Beaumont, or Villers, extraordinarily created countess of Buckingham.—F.

London, was, for the honour of Augustine, afterwards bestowed on this city.* It is much commended by William of Malmesbury for its pleasant situation, being surrounded with a fertile soil, well wooded, and commodiously watered by the river Stour, from whence it is said to have had its name *Durwhern;* in British, a *swift river*.† It is happy in the vicinity of the sea, which affordeth plenty of good fish.

THE BUILDINGS.

CHRIST CHURCH, first dedicated, and (after 300 years' intermission to Saint Thomas Becket) restored to the honour of our Saviour, is a stately structure, being the performance of several successive archbishops. It is much adorned with glass windows. Here they will tell you of a foreign ambassador, who proffered a vast price to transport the east window of the choir beyond the seas. Yet artists, who commend the colours, condemn the figures therein, as wherein proportion is not exactly observed.

According to the maxim, " pictures are the books," painted windows were in the time of popery the library of lay-men; and after the Conquest grew in general use in England. It is much suspected annealing of glass (which answereth to dying in grain in drapery), especially of yellow, is lost in our age, as to the perfection thereof. Anciently colours were so incorporated in windows, that both of them lasted and faded together: whereas our modern painting (being rather on than in the glass) is fixed so faintly, that it often changeth, and sometimes falleth away. Now, though some, being only for the innocent white, are equal enemies to the painting of windows as faces, conceiving the one as great a pander to superstition as the other to wantonness; yet others, of as much zeal and more knowledge, allow the historical uses of them in churches.

PROVERBS.

" Canterbury Tales."]

So Chaucer calleth his book, being a collection of several tales, pretended to be told by pilgrims in their passage to the shrine of Saint Thomas in Canterbury. But since that time, Canterbury Tales are parallel to *Fabulæ Milesiæ*, which are charactered, *Nec veræ, nec verisimiles;* merely made to mar precious time, and please fanciful people. Such are the many miracles of Thomas Becket. Some *helpful* (though but narrow, as only for private conveniency); as, when perceiving his old palace at Otford to want water, he struck his staff into the dry ground (still called Saint Thomas's well), whence water runneth plentifully to serve that house (lately rebuilt) unto this day. Others *spiteful;* as when (because a smith dwelling in that town had clogged his horse) he ordered, that no smith after-

* Camden's Britannia, de Cant.
† By Mr. Somner, in his Description of Canterbury, p. 37.

wards should thrive within that parish.*   But he who shall go
about seriously to confute these tales, is as very a fool, as he
was somewhat else who first impudently invented and vented
them.

PRELATES.

[S. N.]   STEPHEN LANGTON.—Here we are at a perfect
loss for the place of his birth, his surname affording us so much
direction; in effect it is none at all. *Inopes nos copia fecit*,—
finding no fewer than twelve Langtons (though none very near to
this place), which makes us fly to our marginal refuge herein.
Stephen, born in England, was bred in Paris, where he became
one of the greatest scholars of the Christian world in his age.
He was afterwards consecrated cardinal of Saint Chrysogone;
and then, by Papal power, intruded archbishop of Canterbury,
in defiance of all opposition which king John could make
against him.

Many are his learned works, writing comments on all the
Old, and on some of the New, Testament.   He was the first
that divided the whole Bible into chapters,† as Robert Stephens, a Frenchman, that curious critic and painful printer,
some six score years since, first subdivided into verses.

A worthy work, making Scripture more manageable in men's
memories, and the passages therein the sooner to be turned to;
as any person is sooner found out in the most populous city, if
methodized into streets and houses with signs, to which the
figures affixed do fitly allude.

Say not this was a presumption, incurring the curse de-
nounced to such who add to Scripture; it being no addition,
but an illustration thereof.   Besides, God set the first pattern to
men's industry herein, seeing the distinction of some verses may
be said to be *Jure Divino*, as those in the Lamentations and elsewhere, which are alphabetically modelled.

As causeless their complaint, who cavil at the inequality of
chapters, the eighth of the first of Kings being sixty-six, the last
of Malachi but six verses, seeing the entireness of the sense is
the standard of their length or shortness.   It is confessed, some
few chapters end, and others begin, abruptly: and yet, it is
questionable whether the alteration thereof would prove advantageous, seeing the reforming of a small fault, with a great
change, doth often hurt more than amend: and such alterations
would discompose millions of quotations, in excellent authors,
conformed to the aforesaid received divisions.

Here it must not be concealed, that notwithstanding this
general tradition of Langton's chaptering the Bible, some
learned men make that design of far ancienter date, and par-

---

* Lambarde, in his Perambulation of Kent, p. 37.

† Bale, de Scriptoribus Britannicis, Cent. iii. numb. 87.; and Matthew Parker
in the Life of Langton.

ticularly that able antiquary Sir Henry Spelman.* This I am confident of, that Stephen Langton did something much material in order thereunto; and the improver is usually called the inventor, by a complimental mistake.

However, though I believe Langton well employed in dividing the Bible, he was ill busied in rending asunder the church and kingdom of England, reducing king John to sad extremities. He died, and was buried at Canterbury, anno Domini 1228.

SOLDIERS.

WILLIAM PRUDE, Esquire, (vulgarly called Proud) was born in this city, where his stock have continued for some hundreds of years; bred a soldier in the Low Countries, where he attained to be lieutenant colonel. He was slain July 12, 1632, at the siege of Maestrich. His body (which I assure you was no usual honour) was brought over into England, and buried in the cathedral of Canterbury, in Saint Michael's chapel, on the south side of the choir, with this inscription on his monument:

> " Stand, soldiers; ere you march (by way of charge)
> Take an example here, that may enlarge
> Your minds to noble action : here in peace
> Rests one whose life was war, whose rich increase
> Of fame and honour from his valour grew
> Unbegg'd, unbought, for what he won he drew
> By just desert : having in service been
> A soldier, till nearly sixty from sixteen
> Years of his active life, continually
> Fearless of death ; yet still prepar'd to die
> In his religious thoughts ; for, 'midst all harms,
> He bare as much of piety as arms.
>   Now, soldiers, on ; and fear not to intrude
>   The gates of death by th' example of this Prude.

" He married Mary daughter of Sir Adam Sprackling, knight; and had issue by her four sons and three daughters; to whose memory his surviving son Searles Prude hath erected this monument."

WRITERS.

OSBERN of CANTERBURY, so called because there he had his first birth, or best being, as chanter of the cathedral church therein. An admirable musician, which quality endeared him (though an Englishman) to Lanfranc, the lordly Lombard, and archbishop of Canterbury. He was the English Jubal,† as to the curiosity thereof in our churches : an art which never any spake against who understood it; otherwise Apollo is in a sad case, if Midas's ears must be his judges. However, in divine service, all music ought to be tuned to edification (that all who hear may understand it); otherwise it may tend to delight not devotion; and true zeal cannot be raised where knowledge is depressed. This Osbern wrote the life of Saint Dunstan in

---

* In Glossario, verbo *Heptateuchus.*   † Genesis iv. 21.

pure Latin, according to that age, flourishing under William the Conqueror, anno 1070.

[S. N.] SIMON LANGTON was, by his brother Stephen Langton the archbishop, preferred archdeacon of Canterbury; who, " Carne et sanguine revelante " (saith the Record)* made the place much better, both to him and his successors, in revenue and jurisdiction. A troublesome man he was, and, on his brother's score, a great adversary to king John, even after that king had altered his copy, and became, of a fierce foe, a son-servant to the Pope, by resigning his crown unto him. But our Simon could not knock off when he should, having contracted such a habit of hatred to king John, that he could not depose it, though commanded under the pain of excommunication. This caused him to trudge to the court of Rome, where he found little favour. For such who will be the Pope's white boys must watchfully observe his signals, and not only charge when he chargeth, but retreat when he retreateth. This Simon (besides others) wrote a book of " The Penitence of Magdalene," in relation (it seems) to himself, though she found more favour in the court of heaven than he at Rome. He died anno Domini 12 . .

BENEFACTORS TO THE PUBLIC.

JOHN EASDAY was alderman and mayor of this city, anno 1585. He found the walls thereof much ruined; and, being a man but of an indifferent estate, began the reparation thereof at Ridingate, and therein proceeded so far as his name is inscribed on the wall;† whose exemplary endeavours have since met with some to commend, none to imitate them.‡

THOMAS NEVILE,§ born in this city of most honourable extraction, as his name is enough to notify and avouch. He was bred in Cambridge, and master first of Magdalen then of Trinity College, and dean of Canterbury. He was the first clergyman (sent by Archbishop Whitgift,) who carried to king James tidings of the English crown; and it is questionable whether he brought thither or thence more welcome news (especially to the clergy), acquainting them with the king's full intentions to maintain church discipline, as he found it established.||

But the main matter commending his memory is his magnificency to Trinity College, whose court he reduced to a spacious and beautiful quadrangle. Indeed he plucked down as good building as any erected; but such as was irregular, intercepting

---

* Somner, in his Catalogue of the Archdeacons of Canterbury.
† Idem, in his Survey of Canterbury, p. 15.
‡ Alderman Simmons, who died M.P. for Canterbury in 1806, by his munificent expences on the Dane-John, &c. proved that this remark is no longer applicable.—ED.
§ He had a brother Alexander, a poet and scholar.—ED.
|| Sir George Paul, in the Life of Archbishop Whitgift.

the sight, disturbing the intended uniformity of the court, whereby the beauty at this day is much advanced; for, as the intuitive knowledge is more perfect than that which insinuates itself into the soul gradually by discourse; so more beautiful the prospect of that building, which is all visible at one view, than what discovers itself to the sight by parcels and degrees. Nor was this doctor like those poets, good only at translation, and bad at invention; all for altering, nothing for adding of his own; who contributed to this college, (I will not say a widow's mite, but) a bachelor's bounty; a stately new court of his own expence, which cost him three thousand pounds and upwards.* Much enfeebled with the palsy, he died, an aged man, May 7, 1615.†

THE FAREWELL.

I am heartily sorry that the many laudable endeavours for the scouring and enlargement of the river Stour (advantageous for this city) have been so often defeated, and the contributions given by well-disposed benefactors (amongst whom Mr. Rose, once an alderman of Canterbury, gave three hundred pounds) have missed their ends; praying that their future enterprises in this kind may be crowned with success.

For the rest, I refer the reader to the pains of my worthy friend Mr. William Somner, who hath written *justum volumen* of the antiquities of this city. I am sorry to see him subject-bound (betrayed thereto by his own modesty); seeing otherwise not the city but diocese of Canterbury had been more adequate to his abilities. I hope others, by his example, will under-take their respective counties; it being now, with our age, the third and last time of asking the banns, whether or no we may be wedded to skill in this kind, seeing now, " use, or for ever hold your pens; " all church monuments, leading to know-ledge in that nature, being daily irrecoverably embezzled.

WORTHIES OF KENT WHO HAVE FLOURISHED SINCE THE TIME OF FULLER.

Jeffery Lord AMHERST, general; born at Riverhead in Seven-oaks 1717; died 1797.

Nicolas AMHURST, author of " Terræ Filius," and " The Crafts-man;" born at Marden 1706; died 1742.

Sir Richard BAKER, author of " Chronicle;" born at Sissing-hurst 1568; died 1645.

William BOYS, surgeon, historian of Sandwich; born at Deal 1735; died 1703.

* Dean Neville's beautiful little chapel was removed about fifty years-ago.—ED.
† See Todd's Lives of the Deans of Canterbury.—ED.

Sir Egerton BRYDGES, miscellaneous writer and critic; born at Wootton Court 1762; died 1837.

George BYNG, first Viscount Torrington, admiral; born 1663; died 1733.

Elizabeth CARTER, translator of Epictetus; born at Deal 1717; died 1806.

Thomas CURTEIS, divine and poet; born 1690.

John DENNE, divine and antiquary; born at Littlebourne 1693.

Andrew Coltee DUCAREL, English topographer, and Anglo-Norman antiquary; born at Greenwich 1714; died 1785.

Sir Robert FILMER, political writer; born 1688; died 1747.

William GOSTLING, antiquary; born at Canterbury 1696.

Stephen HALES, Christian philosopher; born at Beckesbourn 1677; died 1761.

John HARRIS, historian of Kent, encyclopædist, &c.; died 1719.

Edward HASTED, historian of Kent; born at Hawley 1732; died 1812.

John HAWKESWORTH, author of "The Adventurer;" born at Bromley, 1715.

Benjamin HOADLY, bishop of Winchester, originator of the Bangorian controversy; born at Westerham 1676; died 1761.

George HORNE, bishop of Norwich, commentator on the Psalms; born at Otham 1730; died 1792.

William HUNTINGDON, "Sinner Saved," a religious enthusiast; born at Cranbrook 1744; died 1813.

Edward JACOB, historian of Faversham; died 1788.

Basil KENNET, author of "Roman Antiquities;" born at Postling 1674; died 1714.

Richard KILBURNE, author of "Topographie of Kent;" died 1678.

Nath. LARDNER, defender of Christianity; born at Hawkhurst 1684; died 1768.

Cath. MACAULAY (Graham), party historian; born at Ollantigh 1730; died 1791.

John MONRO, physician, eminent in cases of insanity; born at Greenwich 1715; died 1791.

Elizabeth MONTAGU, author of "Observations on Shakespeare;" born at Horton 1720; died 1800.

William NEWTON, historian of his native town; born at Maidstone; died 1744.

William PITT, eminent statesman; born at Hayes-place 1759; died 1806.

Admiral Peter RAINIER, public benefactor; born at Sandwich; died 1808.

Sam. Foart SIMMONS, physician and author; born at Sandwich 1750; died 1813.

Christopher SMART, poet; born at Shipbourne 1722; died 1771.

Sir Thomas STAINES, gallant naval officer; born at Dent-de-Leon, Margate; died 1813.

Algernon SYDNEY, patriot; born at Penshurst 1617; executed in 1683.

Lord TENTERDEN, chief juctice of the King's Bench; born at Canterbury 1762; died 1832.

Lewis THEOBALD, dramatic writer, commentator on Shakspeare; born at Sittingbourne : died 1741.

Admiral Sir Thomas Boulden THOMPSON, captain of the Leander in engagement with Le Genereux; born at Barham 1766.

John THORPE, physician, and antiquary; born at Newhouse, in Penshurst 1682; died 1750.

John THORPE, editor of " Custumale Roffensi ;" born at Penshurst 1714; died 1792.

James WOLFE, major-general, conqueror of Quebec; born at Westerham 1726; died 1759.

William WOOLLETT, engraver; born at Maidstone 1735.

Philip YORKE, first earl of Hardwicke, Lord Chancellor; born at Dover 1690.

*** The county of Kent has perhaps been more extensively illustrated by the pen of the historian, and the pencil of the artist, than any other in the kingdom. So early as 1576, appeared the " Perambulation of Kent," by William Lambarde ; and in 1659, Mr. Rich. Kilburne produced a work, entitled, " A Topographie or Survey of the County of Kent." In 1719 appeared the History of Kent, by the Rev. Dr. Harris ; and in 1776, two works, The Villare Cantianum, by Tho. Philipott, and a Topographical Survey of Kent, by Cha. Seymour, made their appearance. In 1778, Mr. E. Hasted published a regular history of the county, which has been held in much esteem ; and Mr. Hanshall produced another in 1798. Numerous local histories have also been produced at different times ; amongst which may be enumerated the following, in chronological order :—Monasticon Favershamiense in agro Cantiano, by T. Southouse, 1671. Treatise on the Roman Ports and Forts in Kent, by W. Somner, 1693. Somner's Antiquities of Canterbury, by N. Battely, 1703. History of Rochester Cathedral, by Dr. R. Rawlinson, 1717. History of Thanet, by J. Lewis, 1726 ; also by R. E. Hunter, 1815. History of the Abbey of Faversham, &c., by J. Lewis, 1727. Rev. W. Newton's History of Maidstone in 1741. Denne's History of Rochester, 1772. Duncombe's Antiquities of Richborough and Reculver, from the Latin of Archd. Batteley, 1774. More's History of Tunstall, 1780. Thorpe's Antiquities of Kent, 1783. Duncombe's Description of Christ Church, Canterbury, &c. 1783. History of the Three Archiepiscopal Hospitals at Canterbury, by J. Duncombe, and N. Batteley, 1785. Boys's History of Sandwich, 1786-92. Account of Cranbrook, 1789. Cozens's Tour through the Isle of Thanet, 1793. Pocock's History of Gravesend, Milton, &c., 1797. Wilson's Description of Bromley, 1797. Excursions in the Counties of Kent, &c., 1802 ; and by J. P. Malcolm, 1814. History of Maidstone, by W. Rowles, 1809. History of Tunbridge Wells, by T. B. Burr, 1766 ; also by P. Amsinck, 1810. History of Dover, by the Rev. J. Lyon, 1813. Journey round the Coast of Kent, by L. Fussell, 1818. Account of the Weald of Kent, by T. D. W. Dean, 1814. Graphical Illustration of Canterbury Cathedral, by W. Woolnoth, 1816. Picturesque Views of Ramsgate, by H. Moses, 1817. Sketch of Knowle, by J. Bridgeman, 1817. Horn's Description of Dover, 1819. Clifford's Guide to Tunbridge Wells, 1823. Gostling s Walk through Canterbury, 1825. Sketch of Dover, 1828. Account of Eltham Palace, by J. Buckler, 1828. Berry's Kentish Genealogies, &c.

LANCASHIRE.

LANCASHIRE hath the Irish Sea on the west, Yorkshire on the east, Cheshire (parted with the river Mersey) on the south, Cumberland and Westmoreland on the north. It rangeth in length, from Mersey to Wenander-Mere, full fifty-five miles, though the broadest part thereof exceedeth not one and thirty. The air thereof is subtil and piercing, being free from fogs saving in the mosses; the effects whereof are found in the fair complexions and firm constitutions of the natives therein, whose bodies are as able as their minds willing for any laborious employment. Their soil is tolerably fruitful of all things necessary for human sustenance: and, as that youth cannot be counted a dunce, though he be ignorant, if he be docible, because his lack of learning is to be scored on the want of a teacher; so sterility cannot properly be imputed to some places in this county, where little grain doth grow, because capable thereof, as daily experience doth avouch, if it were husbanded accordingly.

This shire, though sufficiently thick of people, is exceedingly thin of parishes, as by perusing this parallel will plainly appear:

Rutland hath in it forty-eight parishes.[*]

Lancashire hath in it thirty-six parishes.[†]

See here how Rutland, being scarce a fifth part of Lancashire in greatness, hath a fourth part of parishes more therein.

But, as it was a fine sight to behold Sir Thomas More, when lord chancellor of England, every morning in term time, humbly ask blessing in Westminster-hall of Sir John More, his father, then a puisne judge;[‡] so may one see in this shire some chapels, exceeding their mother-churches in fairness of structure and numerousness of people; yet owning their filial relation, and still continuing their dutiful dependance, on their parents. But for the numerosity of chapels, surely the church of Manchester exceedeth all the rest, which, though anciently called but Villa de Manchester, is for wealth and greatness co-rival with some cities in England, having no less than nine chapels, which, before these our civil wars, were reputed to have five hundred communicants a-piece. Insomuch that some clergymen, who have consulted God's honour with their own credit and profit, could not better desire for themselves, than to have

---

* Camden's Britannia, in Rutland.
† Idem, in Lancashire. Speed (I think mistaken) says but 28.
‡ Stapleton, in his Life.

a Lincolnshire church, as best built; a Lancashire parish, as largest bounded; and a London audience, as consisting of most intelligent people.

The people, generally devout, are (as I am informed), northward and by the west, popishly affected; which in the other parts (intended by *antiperistasis*) are zealous Protestants. Hence is it that many subtile papists and jesuits have been born and bred in this county, which have met with their matches, to say no more, in the natives of the same county; so that thereby it hath come to pass, that, "the house of Saul hath waxed weaker and weaker, and the house of David stronger and stronger."*

NATURAL COMMODITIES.

OATS.

If any ask why this grain, growing commonly all over England, is here entered as an eminent commodity of Lancashire? let him know, that here is the most and best of that kind; yea wheat and barley may seem but the adopted, whilst oats are the natural issue of this county; so inclined is its genius to the production thereof. Say not oats are horse-grain, and fitter for a *stable* than a *table*; for, besides that the meal thereof is the distinguishing form of gruel or broth from water, most hearty and wholesome bread is made thereof. Yea, anciently, north of Humber, no other was eaten by people of the primest quality; for we read, how William the Conqueror bestowed the manor of Castle Bitham in Lincolnshire upon Stephen earl of Albemarle and Holderness, chiefly for this consideration, that thence he might have wheaten bread to feed his infant son, oaten bread being then the diet of Holderness and the counties lying beyond it.†

ALUM.

I am informed that alum is found at Houghton in this county, within the inheritance of Sir Richard Houghton, and that enough for the use of this and the neighbouring shires, though not for transportation. But, because far greater plenty is afforded in Yorkshire, the larger mention of this mineral is referred to that place.

OXEN.

The fairest in England are bred (or, if you will, made) in this county, with goodly heads, the tips of whose horns are sometimes distanced five feet asunder. Horns are a commodity not to be slighted, seeing I cannot call to mind any other substance so hard, that it will not break; so solid, that it will hold liquor

* 2 Sam. iii. 1.   † Camden's Britannia, in Lancashire.

within it ; and yet so clear, that light will pass through it.   No
mechanic trade, but hath some utensils made thereof : and even
now I recruit my pen with ink from a vessel of the same.   Yea,
it is useful cap-a-pie, from combs to shoeing horns.   What shall
I speak of the many gardens made of horns, to garnish houses ?
I mean, artificial flowers of all colours.   And, besides what is
spent in England, many thousand weight are shaven down into
leaves for lanthorns, and sent over daily into France.   In a
word, the very shavings of horn are profitable, sold by the sack,
and sent many miles from London for the manuring of ground.
No wonder then that the Horners are an ancient corporation,
though why they and the Bottle-makers* were formerly united
into one Company passeth my skill to conjecture.   The best
horns in all England, and freest to work without flaws, are what
are brought out of this county to London, the shop-general of
English industry.

THE MANUFACTURES.

FUSTIANS.

There anciently were creditable wearing in England for persons of the primest quality, finding the knight in Chaucer thus
habited :

> " Of fustian he weared a gippon
> All besmottered with his haubergeon."†

But it seems they were all foreign commodities, as may appear by their modern names : 1. *Jen Fustians*, which I conceive
so called from Jena, a city in Saxony: 2. *Ausgburg Fustians*,
made in that famous city in Suabia; 3. *Milan Fustians*,
brought over hither out of Lombardy.

These retain their old names at this day, though these several
sorts are made in this county, whose inhabitants, buying the
cotton, wool, or yarn, coming from beyond the sea, make it here
into fustians, to the good employment of the poor, and great
improvement of the rich therein, serving mean people for their
outsides, and their betters for the linings of their garments.
Bolton is the staple-place for this commodity, being brought
thither from all parts of the county.

As for Manchester, the cottons thereof carry away the credit
in our nation, and so they did a hundred and fifty years ago.
For when learned Leland,‡ on the cost of king Henry the
Eighth, with his guide, travelled Lancashire, he called Manchester the fairest and quickest town in this county; and sure I
am, it hath lost neither spruceness nor spirits since that time.

Other commodities made in Manchester are so small in themselves, and various in their kinds, they will fill the shop of an
haberdasher of small wares.   Being, therefore, too many for me

* Stow's Survey of London, p. 638.   † Chaucer, in his Prologue.
‡ In his Itinerary.

to reckon up or remember, it will be the safest way to wrap
them altogether in some Manchester-ticking, and to fasten
them with the pins (to prevent their falling out and scattering),
or tie them with the tape, and also, because sure bind sure find,
to bind them about with points and laces, all made in the same
place.

THE BUILDINGS.

Manchester, a collegiate as well as a parochial church, is a
great ornament to this county. The choir thereof, though but
small, is exceeding beautiful, and, for wood-work, an excellent
piece of artifice.

THE WONDERS.

About Wigan, and elsewhere in this county, men go a-fishing
with spades and mattocks ;* more likely, one would think, to
catch moles than fishes with such instruments. First, they
pierce the turfy ground, and under it meet with a black and
deadish water, and in it small fishes do swim. Surely these
pisces fossiles, or subterranean fishes, must needs be unwholesome, the rather because an unctuous matter is found about
them. Let them be thankful to God, in the first place, who need
not such meat to feed upon. And next them, let those be
thankful which have such meat to feed upon when they need it.

PROVERBS.
" Lancashire fair women."]

I believe that the God of Nature having given fair complexions to the women in this county, art may save her pains (not
to say her sins) in endeavouring to better them. But let the
females of this county know, that though in the Old Testament
express notice be taken of the beauty of many women, Sarah,†
Rebekah,‡ Rachel,§ Abigail,|| Thamar,¶ Abishag,** Esther ;††
yet in the New Testament no mention is made at all of the fairness of any woman ; not because they wanted, but because grace
is chief gospel-beauty. Elizabeth's unblameableness ;‡‡ the
Virgin Mary's pondering God's word ;§§ the Canaanitish wo-
man's faith ;|||| Mary Magdalen's charity ;¶¶ Lydia's attention
to Paul's preaching ;*† these soul-piercing perfections are far
better than skin-deep fairness.

" It is written upon a wall in Rome,
Ribchester was as rich as any town in Christendom."*‡]

And why on a wall? Indeed the Italians have a proverb, " A
wall is the fool's paper," whereon they scribble their fancies.
But, not to be over curious in examining hereof, we suppose

---

* Camden's Britannia, in Lancashire.   † Gen. xii. 11.   ‡ Gen. xxiv. 16.
§ Gen. xxix. 17. || 1 Sam. xxv. 3.   ¶ 2 Sam. xiii. 1.   ** 1 Kings i. 4.
†† Esther ii. 7.   ‡‡ Luke i. 6.   §§ Luke ii. 19. |||| Matth. xv. 28.
¶¶ John xii. 3.   *† Acts xvi. 14.   *‡ Camden's Britannia, in Lancashire.

some monumental wall in Rome, as a register, whereon the names of principal places were inscribed, then subjected to the Roman empire: and probably this Ribchester anciently was some eminent colony, as by pieces of coins and columns there daily digged out doth appear. However, at this day, it is not so much as a market town; but whether decayed by age, or destroyed by accident, is uncertain.

Here, reader, give me leave. The historian must not devour the divine in me, so as to debar me from spiritual reflections. What saith St. Paul? "We have here no continuing city; and no wonder, seeing mortal men are the efficient, mouldering buildings the material, and mutable laws the formal cause thereof. And yet St. Paul was well stocked with cities as any man alive; having three, which in some sort he might call his own; Tarsus, where he was born;* Jerusalem, where he was bred at the feet of Gamaliel; and Rome, whereby he received the privilege of freedom.† All which he waived as nothing worth, because of no abiding and continuance.

MARTYRS.

JOHN ROGERS was born in this county, and bred in the university of Cambridge;‡ a very able linguist and general scholar. He was first a zealous Papist, till, his eyes being opened, he detested all superstition, and went beyond the seas to Wittenburg, where (some years after Tindal) he translated the Bible, from Genesis till the Revelation, comparing it with the original. Coming to England, he presented it in a fair volume to king Henry the Eighth, prefixing a dedicatory epistle, and subscribing himself (those dangerous days required a disguise) under the name of Thomas Matthew.§

And now, reader, that is unriddled unto me which hath puzzled me for some years; for I find that king James, in the instructions which he gave to the translators of the Bible, enjoined them to peruse the former translations of—1. Tindal; 2. Matthews; 3. Coverdale; 4. Whitchurch; 5. Geneva.|| Now at last I understand who this Matthews was (though unsatisfied still in Whitchurch); believing his book never publicly printed, but remaining a manuscript in the king's library.

Yet this present could not procure Mr. Rogers his security, who, it seems, for fear of the Six Articles, was fain to fly again beyond seas; and, returning in the reign of king Edward the Sixth, became a preacher of London. He and Mr. Hooper were the two greatest sticklers against ceremonies, though otherwise allowing of Episcopal government. He was the first

---

* Acts xxii. 3. † Acts xxii. 27.
 ‡ J. Bale, de Scriptoribus Britannicis, Cent. viii. num. 83; and Fox, Acts and Monuments.
 § Bale, ut prius.
 || See my Church History, 10th Book, 17th Century.

martyr who suffered in Smithfield in queen Mary's days, and led all the rest; of whom we may truly say, that, "if they had not been flesh and blood, they could not have been burnt: and if they had been no more than flesh and blood, they would not have been burnt."

The Non-conformists account it no small credit unto them, that one of their opinion (as who would not flinch from the faith) was chosen by Divine Providence the first to encounter the fire. Such may remember, that no army is all front; and that as constant did come behind as went before. Had those of an opposite judgment been called first, they had come first to the stake; and in due time the defenders of ceremonies were as substantial in their sufferings. This John Rogers was martyred Feb. 4, 1555.

JOHN BRADFORD was born at Manchester in this county;[*] and bred first a lawyer in the inns of court, and for a time did solicit suits for Sir John Harrington: afterwards (saith my author,[†]) *ex rixoso causidico mitissimus Christi apostolus:* going to Cambridge a man n maturity and ability, the university by special grace bestowed on him the degree of Master of Arts: and so may he be said to commence, not only *per saltum,* but *per volatum.* The Jesuit doth causelessly urge this his *short standing* for an argument of his little *understanding;* whereas he had always been a hard student from his youth; and his writings and his disputings give a sufficient testimony of his learning.

It is a demonstration to me that he was of a sweet temper, because persons,[‡] who will hardly afford a good word to a Protestant, saith, "that he seemed to be of a more soft and mild nature than many of his fellows." Indeed he was a most holy and mortified man, who secretly in his closet would so weep for his sins, one would have thought he would never have smiled again; and then, appearing in public, he would be so harmlessly pleasant, one would think he had never wept before. But Mr. Fox's pains have given the pens of all posterity a writ of ease, to meddle no more with this martyr, who suffered anno Domini 1555.

GEORGE MARSH was born at Dean in this county;[§] bred a good scholar in a grammar-school, and then lived in the honest condition of a farmer: after the death of his wife, he went to Cambridge,[||] where he followed his studies very closely; and afterwards solemnly entering into orders, became a profitable

---

* Fox, Acts and Monuments.
† J. Bale, de Scriptoribus Britannicis, Cent. viii. num. 87.
‡ In his Examination of J. Fox's "Martyrs."
§ Fox, Acts and Monuments, p. 1561. || Idem, ibidem.

preacher and curate to Mr. Lawrence Sanders, the worthy martyr. Causelessly therefore doth persons* asperse him, that he of a farmer turned a preacher, as if he had done it immediately (with many of our age leaping from the plough to the pulpit), concealing his academical breeding; such is the charity of his jesuitical reservation.

As little is his charity for condemning him for answering dubiously and fearfully at first to such who examined him about the Sacrament of the Altar, seeing the said Marsh condemned himself for doing it, as therein too much consulting carnal respects to save his life, as appears in Master Fox, whence the jesuit fetcheth all his information. But Marsh made amends for all these failings with his final constancy, being both burnt and scalded to death (having a barrel of pitch placed over his head, an accent of cruelty peculiar to him alone) when he was martyred at Westchester, April 24, 1555.

CARDINALS.

WILLIAM ALAN was born in this county (saith my author)† *nobilibus parentibus,* of gentle parentage. He was bred in Oriel College, in the university of Oxford, and became head of St. Mary's-hall therein. Then, going beyond the seas, he became king's professor at Douay, canon of Cambray and Rheims; and at last, by Pope Sixtus Quintus, made cardinal priest of St. Martin's in Rome, 1587; and deserved his *red hat* by his good service the year after against his native country. But hear what different characters two authors of several persuasions bestow upon him. "He was somewhat above an ordinary man in stature, comely of countenance, composed in his gait, affable in all meetings; and for the gifts of his mind, pious, learned, prudent, grave, and, though of great authority, humble, modest, meek, patient, peaceable; in a word, beautified and adorned with all kinds of virtues."‡ "He was the last of our English cardinals in time, and first in wickedness; deserving not to be counted among Englishmen, who, as another Herostratus, to achieve himself a name amongst the grandees of earth, endeavoured to fire the church of England, the noblest (without envy be it spoken) in the Christian world; so that his memory deserveth to be buried in oblivion."§

He collected the English exiles into a body, and united them in a college, first at Douay, then at Rheims; so great an advancer, that we may behold him as founder of that seminary. He died at Rome, anno 1594; and preferred rather to be buried in the English school, than in the church of St. Martin's, which gave him the title of cardinal.

* In his Examination of Fox's "Martyrs."   † Pits, p. 792.
‡ Pits, de Angliæ Scriptoribus, p. 792.
§ Godwin, in his Catalogue of Cardinals, p. 479.

PRELATES.

HUGH OLDHAM, born in this county, at Oldham, a village some six miles from Manchester, bred in Queen's College in Cambridge, was no ill scholar, and a good man, most pious according to and above the devotion of the age he lived in. He was afterwards bishop of Exeter; a foe to monkish superstition, and a friend to university learning. Brazen-nose College in Oxford, and Corpus Christi College therein, will for ever bear witness of his bounty, to advance religion and learning. Besides, the town of Manchester have good cause to remember him who founded and endowed a school therein, with large revenue, appointing the warden of the college therein *Caput Scholæ*.

This bishop having a tough contest with the abbot of Tavistock, was excommunicated for refusing to stand to the decision of the court of Rome. He had formerly built a chapel in the south side of his cathedral; and, dying excommunicate (on the aforesaid account), was buried, not in the very church, but brink thereof, and body of the wall. He died anno Domini 1520.

JAMES STANLEY, D.D. brother of Thomas earl of Derby, was born in this county; and was by king Henry the Seventh (his kinsman by marriage) preferred bishop of Ely 1506; a man more memorable than commendable, who never resided at his own cathedral. I can partly excuse his living all the summer with the earl his brother in this county; but must condemn his living all the winter at his manor at Somersham in Huntingdonshire,* with one who was not his sister, and wanted nothing to make her his wife save marriage. However, if Jehu allowed a burial to his most professed enemy, on this account, that she was a king's daughter,† none, I hope, will grudge his memory a room in this book, were it only because he was an earl's brother. He died anno 1515.

HENRY STANDISH was, as I have just cause to conclude, extracted from the Standishes of Standish in this county; bred a Franciscan, and doctor of divinity in Cambridge, and afterwards made bishop of St. Asaph. I neither believe him so good as Pits doth character him, *pietate et doctrinâ clarum;* nor so bad as Bale doth decry him, making him a doating fool. Sure I am, there was *impar congressus* betwixt him and Erasmus; as unequal a contest as betwixt a child and man, not to say dwarf and giant. This Standish is said to have fallen down on his knees before king Henry the Eighth, petitioning him to continue the religion established by his ancestors; and, entering

---

* Godwin, in his Bishops of Ely, and Camden's Britannia, in the Description of Huntingdon.
† 2 Kings ix. 34.

into matters of divinity, he cited the Colossians* for the Corinthians; which being but a memory-mistake in an aged person, need not to have exposed him so much as it did to the laughter of the standers-by. After he had sat sixteen years bishop of St. Asaph, he died, very aged, 1535.

JOHN CHRISTOPHERSON was born in this county;† bred first in Pembroke Hall, then fellow of St. John's, and afterwards master of Trinity College, in Cambridge: an excellent scholar, and linguist especially. I have seen a Greek tragedy, made and written by his own hand (so curiously that it seemed printed), and presented to king Henry the Eighth. He no less elegantly (if faithfully) translated Philo and Eusebius into Latin. Besides his own benefaction to the Master's lodgings and library, he was highly instrumental in moving queen Mary to her magnificent bounty to Trinity College. In the visitation of Cambridge he was very active in burning the bones of Bucer, being then elect bishop of Chichester, scarcely continuing a year in that place.

All expected that, at his first coming into his diocese, he should demean himself very favourably. For why should not the poet's observation of princes be true also of prelates?

——————— *Mitissima sors est*
Regnorum sub rege novo ——

" Subjects commonly do find
New-made sovereigns most kind."

But he had not so much mercy as Nero, to begin courteously, having no sooner put on his episcopal ring, but presently he washed his hands in the blood of poor martyrs; whereof in due place.‡ In the first of queen Elizabeth he was deprived, and kept in some restraint; wherein he died, about the year 1560.

SINCE THE REFORMATION.

JAMES PILKINTON, D.D. was the third son of James Pilkinton of Rivington in this county,§ esquire, a right ancient family; being informed by my good friend Master William Ryley, Norroy, and this countryman, that the Pilkintons were gentlemen of repute in this shire before the Conquest,‖ when the chief of them, then sought for, was fain to disguise himself, a thresher in a barn. Hereupon, partly alluding to the head of the flail (falling sometime on the one, sometime on the other side), partly to himself embracing the safest condition for the present, he gave for the motto of his arms, " Now thus, now thus."

* Bale, de Scriptoribus Britannicis, Cent. ix. num. 3.
† Bale, Pits, and Bishop Godwin, in the Bishops of Chichester.
‡ See Martyrs in Sussex.
§ Parker's Scel. Cant. MS. in the Masters of St. John's.
‖ Others make this of far later date.—F.

This James, bred fellow of St. John's in Cambridge, was in the first of queen Mary forced to fly into Germany, where he wrote a Comment on Ecclesiastes and both the Epistles of St. Peter.* After his return, in the first of queen Elizabeth, he was chosen Master of St. John's; and, March 2d, 1560, was consecrated bishop of Durham.

Nine years after, the northern rebels came to Durham, and first tore the Bible, then the English Liturgy, in pieces.† Unhappy (though most innocent) book, equally odious to opposite parties; such who account the Papists heretics esteeming it Popish, whilst the Papists themselves account it heretical. The bishop had fared no better than the book, could he have been come by. But, when the rebellion was suppressed, the bishop commenced a suit against queen Elizabeth for the lands and goods of the rebels attainted in the bishopric, as forfeited to him by his charter; and had prevailed, if the Parliament had not interposed, and, on special consideration, *pro hoc tempore*, adjudged them to the queen. He died anno Domini 1576.‡

EDWIN SANDYS was born at Conisby in this county; whose good actings, great sufferings, pious life, and peaceable death, 1588, are plentifully related in our "Church History."

RICHARD BARNES was born at Bold near Warrington in this county;§ bred in Brazen-nose College in Oxford, and afterwards advanced suffragan bishop of Nottingham; thence he was preferred to Carlisle, 1570, and seven years after to Durham. He was himself one of a good nature (as by the sequel will appear), but abused by his credulity, and affection to his brother John Barnes, chancellor of his diocese.

"A man, of whom it is hard to say, whether he was more lustful, or more covetous: who, whereas he should have been the man who ought to have reformed many enormities in the diocese, was indeed the author of them, permitting base and dishonest persons to escape scot-free for a piece of money, so that the bishop had a very ill report every where." ‖

By the suggestion of this ill instrument, the patriarchal man Mr. Gilpin fell into this bishop's displeasure, and by him was suspended from his benefice.

But the good bishop afterwards restored him; and, visiting him at his house, took him aside into the parlour, and thus accosted him:

"Father Gilpin, I acknowledge you are fitter to be bishop of Durham, than myself to be parson of this church of yours: I

* Bale, de Scriptoribus Britannicis, pagina penult.
† Camden's Elizabeth, in anno 1569.
‡ Camden's Britannia, in Bishops of Durham.
§ Out of a Manuscript of the great Antiquary, Mr. Dodsworth.
‖ Bishop Carleton, in the Life of Mr. Gilpin.

ask forgiveness for errors passed; forgive me, father; I know you have hatched up some chickens that now seek to pick out your eyes; but, so long as I shall live bishop of Durham, be secure, no man shall injure you."*

This bishop sate about eleven years in his see, and died a very aged man, a little before the Spanish invasion, anno Domini 1588.

JOHN WOOLTON was born at Wigan in this county, of honest parents, and worshipful by his mother's side.† He was bred a short time in Oxford; and in the reign of queen Mary, attended his uncle Alexander Nowell in his flight beyond the seas. Returning into England, he was made first canon residentiary; and after, anno 1579, bishop of Exeter, being an earnest assertor of conformity against opposers thereof. He met, whilst living, with many hard speeches; but after his death (when men's memories are beheld generally in their true colours) he was restored to his deserved esteem, even by those who formerly had been his adversaries. He indited letters, full of wisdom and piety, becoming the strength of one in health, not two hours before his death, which happened March the 13th, 1593. It is a part, though not of his praise, of his happiness, that his daughter was married to Francis Godwin bishop of Hereford, whose learned pen hath deserved so well of the Church of England.

MATTHEW HUTTON.—I have given a large account of him formerly, in my "Ecclesiastical History." However, having since received an exact Annary, as I may so say, from his nearest relation, of his life, I will here insert an abridgment thereof.

1. Being son to Matthew Hutton of Priest Hutton in this county, he was born anno Domini 1529. 2. He came to Cambridge in the 17th year of his age, anno 1546, the 38th of king Henry the Eighth. 3. Commenced bachelor of Arts 1551; master of Arts 1555. 4. Chosen Margaret professor of divinity, December 15, anno 1561, in the 4th of queen Elizabeth. 5. In the same year commenced bachelor of divinity. 6. Elected master of Pembroke-hall May the 12th; and the same year, September the fifth, admitted regius professor, anno 1562. 7. Answered a public act before queen Elizabeth and her court at Cambridge, anno 1564. 8. Married in the same year Katharine Fulmetby (niece to Thomas Goodrick, late bishop of Ely) who died soon after. 9. Made dean of York anno 1567. 10. Married for his second wife Beatrix Fincham, daughter to Sir Thomas Fincham of the Isle of Ely. 11. Resigned his mastership of Pembroke-hall, and his professor's place to Dr. Whitgift, April 12, anno 1567. 12. Married

* Bishop Carleton, in the Life of Mr. Gilpin.
† Godwin, in his Catalogue of the Bishops of Exeter.

Frances, widow of Martin Bowes, son of Sir Martin Bowes, alderman of London, Nov. 20, 1583. 13. Chosen bishop of Durham, June 9, anno Domini 1589. 14. Confirmed by the dean and chapter July 26. 15. Consecrated by John arch-bishop of York, July 27. 16. Translated to York, and conse-crated at Lambeth, anno 1594, the thirty-seventh of queen Eli-zabeth, by John archbishop of Canterbury and others, March 24. 17. He died in Jan. 1605, in the 76th year of his age.

He gave a hundred marks to Trinity College in Cambridge; and founded an hospital at Wareton in this county. In a word, he was a learned prelate, lived a pious man, and left a precious memory.

MARTIN HETON was born in this county, as by his epitaph on his monument, lately set up by his daughters in the church of Ely, may appear; and bred first a student, then a canon of Christ Church, on whom queen Elizabeth bestowed the bishop-ric of Ely, after twenty-nine years' vacancy thereof. Now, al-though his memory groweth under the suspicion of simoniacal compliance, yet this due the inhabitants of Ely do unto him, that they acknowledge him the best housekeeper in that see within man's remembrance. He died July 14, 1609, leaving two daughters, married in those knightly families of Fish and Filmer.

RICHARD BANCROFT was born at .... in this county;* bred in Jesus College in Cambridge; and was after-wards, by queen Elizabeth, made bishop of London; by king James, archbishop of Canterbury. Indeed he was in effect archbishop whilst bishop, to whom Doctor Whitgift, in his de-crepit age, remitted the managing of matters; so that he was the soul of the high commission.

A great statesman he was, and grand champion of church dis-cipline, having well hardened the hands of his soul, which was no more than needed for him who was to meddle with nettles and briars, and met with much opposition. No wonder if those who were silenced by him in the church were loud against him in other places.

David speaketh of "poison under men's lips."† This bishop tasted plentifully thereof from the mouths of his enemies, till at last (as Mithridates) he was so habited to poisons, they became food unto him. Once a gentleman, coming to visit him, pre-sented him a libel, which he found pasted on his door, who, nothing moved thereat, "Cast it," said he "to an hundred more which lie here on a heap in my chamber."

Many a libel (*lie*, because false; *bell*, because loud) was made upon him. The aspersion of covetousness, though cast,

* So I find in the manuscript of Mr. Dodsworth; and so Mr. Richard Line (this Archbishop's servant lately deceased) did inform me.—F.   † Psal. cxl. 3.

doth not stick on his memory; being confuted by the estate which he left, small in proportion to his great preferment.

He cancelled his first will, wherein he had bequeathed much to the church; which gave the occasion for scurrilous pens to pass on him:

> " He who never repented of doing ill,
>   Repented that once he made a good will."

Whereas indeed, suspecting an impression of popular violence on cathedrals, and fearing an alienation of what was bequeathed unto them, he thought fit to cancel his own, to prevent others cancelling his testament.

This partly appears by his second will, wherein he gave the library at Lambeth, the result of his own and three predecessors' collections, to the university of Cambridge, which now they possess, in case the archiepiscopal see should be extinct.

How came such a jealousy into his mind? What fear of a storm, when the sun shined, the sky clear, no appearance of clouds? Surely his skill was more than ordinary in the complexion of the commonwealth, who did foresee what afterward, for a time, came to pass. This clause, providentially inserted, secured this library in Cambridge during the vacancy of the archiepiscopal see; and so prevented the embezzling, at the least the dismembering thereof, in our late civil distempers. He died anno Domini 1610; and lieth buried at the church in Lambeth.

THOMAS JONES was born in this county; bred master of arts in Cambridge, but commenced doctor of divinity in the university in Dublin.* He was first chancellor, then dean of St. Patrick's in that city; and thence was made bishop of Meath, anno 1584, and the next month appointed by queen Elizabeth one of her privy council in Ireland. Hence he was translated to be archbishop of Dublin, anno 1605; and at the same time was by king James made chancellor of Ireland, which office he discharged thirteen years, dying April 10, 1619.

As he was a good officer for the king, he was no bad one for himself, laying the foundation of so fair an estate, that Sir Roger Jones, his son, was by king Charles created Viscount Ranelagh. Thus, whilst the sons of the clergymen in England never mounted above the degree of knighthood, two† of the clergymen in Ireland attained to the dignity of peerage. I say no more, but " Good success have they with their honour," in their persons and posterity!

RICHARD PARR was born in this county;‡ bred fellow of Brazen-nose College in Oxford. Whilst he continued in the university, he was very painful in reading the arts to young

---

* Sir James Ware, de Præsulibus Lageniæ, p. 40.
† The other, Viscount Ely, son to Archbishop Loftus.—F.
‡ M. James Chaloner, in his Description of the Isle of Man, p. 7.

scholars; and afterwards, having cure of souls, no less industrious in the ministry.

He was afterwards preferred to be bishop of Man, by the earl of Derby, lord thereof: for the lords of that island have been so absolute patrons of that bishopric, that no lease made by the bishop is valid in law without their confirmation. This prelate excellently discharged his place, and died anno Domini 1643.

SOLDIERS.

Sir WILLIAM MOLINEUX, Knight, of Sefton in this county. He was, at the battle of Navarre in Spain, made knight banneret by Edward the Black Prince, anno 1367; under whose command he served in those wars, as also for a long time in the wars of France. From whence returning homewards, he died at Canterbury, anno 1372; on whom was written this epitaph :

> " Miles honorificus Molineux subjacet intus;
> Tertius Edwardus dilexit hunc ut amicus:
> Fortia qui gessit, Gallos Navarosque repressit,
> Sic cum recessit, morte feriente decessit,
> Anno Milleno trecento septuageno,
>   Atque his junge duo : sic perit omnis homo."[*]

His monument is not extant at this day; and it is pity that so good a sword did not light on a better pen; and that Pallas (so much honoured by him in her military relation) did not more assist in his epitaph in her poetical capacity.

Sir WILLIAM MOLINEUX, junior, Knight, descendant from the former, flourished under king Henry the Eighth, being a man of great command in this county, bringing the considerable strength thereof to the seasonable succour of the duke of Norfolk, with whom he performed signal service in Flodden Field.

It is confessed, on all sides, that the Scots lost the day by not keeping their ranks; but not agreed on the cause thereof.[†] Buchanan (who commonly makes the too much courage of his countrymen the cause of their being conquered) imputes to their indiscreet pursuing of the English, routed at the first. Others say, they did not break their ranks; but they were broken, unable to endure the Lancashire archers, and so forced to sunder themselves. In this battle the Scotch king and chiefest gentry were slain; the English losing scarce any *of*, the Scots scarce any *but of*, prime note. The king afterwards wrote his gratulatory letter to Sir William Molineux, in form following :

" Trusty and well-beloved, We greet you well; and understand, as well by the report of our right trusty cousin and counsellor the duke of Norfolk, as otherwise, what acceptable service you amongst others lately did unto us, by your valiant towardness in the assisting of our said cousin, against our great enemy the

---

[*] Weever's Funeral Monuments, p. 234.   [†] Paulus Jovius.

late king of Scots ; and how courageously you, as a very hearty
loving servant, acquitted yourself for the overthrow of the said
late king, and distressing of his malice and power, to our great
honour, and the advancing of your no little fame and praise :
for which we have good cause to favour and thank you, and so
we full heartily do ; and assured may you be, that we shall in
such effectual wise remember your said service in any your
reasonable pursuits, as you shall have cause to think the same
right well employed to your comfort and weal hereafter.   Given
under our signet, at our castle at Windsor, the 27th of November."*

It appears by our author, that the like letters, *mutatis mutan-
dis*, were sent unto Sir Edward Stanley and some other men of
principal note in Lancashire and Cheshire.   I have nothing
more to observe, save that these two worthy Sir Williams were
ancestors unto the truly honourable the lord Molineux, viscount
Maryborough in Ireland, lately deceased.

WRITERS.

Hugh of Manchester was, saith my author,† when *Ado-
lescens* [a youth] a Dominican ; but when *Juvenis* (a young
man) he changed his copy, and turned a Franciscan.   Say not
he degraded himself, choosing a later order than he left ; for it
seems that amongst them the last is counted the best, as of a
more refined perfection.   He was a great scholar, and highly
esteemed in that age for his severity and discretion.

An impostor happened at this time, pretending himself first
blind, then cured at the tomb of king Henry the Third,‡ so
to get coin to himself, and credit to the dead king.   But our
Hugh discovered the cheat ; and, writing a book " De Fanaticorum Diliriis," dedicated it to king Edward the First, who kindly
accepted thereof, preferring that his father's memory should
appear to posterity with his true face, than painted with such
false miracles.   This Hugh, with another Franciscan, was employed by the same king to Philip king of France, to demand
such lands as he detained from him in Aquitaine.   Such who
object, that fitter men than friars might have been found for
that service, consider not how in that age such mortified men
were presumed the most proper persons, peaceably to compro-
mise differences between the greatest princes.   This embassy
was undertaken anno Domini 1294.

Richard Ulverston was born in this county, at Ulver-
stone, a well known market-town in Lonsdale hundred.§   A
great antiquary‖ (ambitious of all learned men's acquaintance)

* Stow's Chronicle, p. 495.
† Pits, de Angliæ Scriptoribus, in anno 1294.
‡ Bale, de Scriptoribus Britannicis, Cent. iv. num. 62.
§ Idem, ibidem, 1430.   ‖ Leland.

complained, that he knew him not so well as he desired. He was bred in Oxford, and wrote a book, entituled, " The Articles of Faith, or the Creed of the Church." This lay latent a good while, till John Stanberry bishop of Hereford rescued it from the moths some thirty years after the author's death, and bestowed a double light upon it; one in producing it into the public, the other illustrating it with a commentary he wrote thereon. Say not this was false heraldry, but true humility, to see a bishop commenting (which is not usual) on the book of a priest. Bale concludeth all thus :

—————————————————— *longum*
Non doctrina potest obscuro carcere claudi.
" ——————————— —— nor will worth
Long be confin'd, but make its own way forth."

The time and place of his death are equally uncertain; but, by probability, about 1434, under the reign of king Henry the Sixth.

Thomas Penketh,* so was his true name (though wrested by some Latinists into Penchettus, and miswritten Penthy and Penker, by some English), taken from a village in this county. He was bred an Augustinian in Warrington, and a doctor of divinity in Oxford; a deep Scotist, and of so great a memory, that foreigners† (amongst whom he lived) report of him, that, had all the books of Scotus been lost, he could easily have restored every word of them. He was called to be professor at Padua, and, returning into England, became Provincial of his order.

But his last act stained his former life, who promoted the bastardizing of the issue of king Edward the Fourth; and, as Dr. Shaw ushered, his flattery held up the train of the usurper's praises, in a sermon at St. Paul's; in preaching whereof, he who had formerly forfeited his honesty, lost his voice;‡ a proper punishment for a parasite. His disgrace had some influence on his order, which, then vertical and numerous, daily decayed in England to their dissolution. This Thomas died, and was buried in London, 1487.

John Standish.—Short mention shall serve him, who might have been left out without loss. He was nephew to Henry Standish, bishop of St. Asaph, of no mean family in this county. One would suspect him not the same man called by Bale a scurrilous fool, and admired by Pits for piety and learning, jealous lest another man should be more wise to salvation than himself. He wrote a book against the translation of Scripture into English, and presented it to the parliament. His

* Bale, de Scriptoribus Britannicis, Cent. viii. num. 47.
† Ambrosius Coriolanus et Jacobus Bergomensis. ‡ Speed's Chronicle, p. 717.

death happened seasonably for his own safety, 1556, a little before the death of queen Mary.

SINCE THE REFORMATION.

THOMAS LEAVER was born in this county,* where his family and name still remain, at two villages called Leaver at this day. He was bred a fellow and bachelor of divinity of St. John's College in Cambridge, whereof he was chosen master 1552. He was also preferred master of Sherburne House, or Hospital, in the bishopric; a place, it seems, of good profit and credit, as founded by Hugh Pudsey, bishop of Durham, and earl of Northumberland.

In the beginning of queen Mary he was forced to fly beyond the seas, and became the principal pastor; for they had three other, of the English exiles at Arrow in Switzerland; which congregation I behold, as the least, so the freest, from factions of any in that age of our nation. He was, saith my author,† "Virtutum in omni mansuetudine seminator;" and, besides some sermons and a "comment on the Lord's Prayer," he wrote a book, intituled, "The right Pathway to Christ."

After the death of queen Elizabeth, coming over into England, he took a journey to Durham, to visit his old hospital at Sherburne; and, falling sick by the way, died at Ware, anno 1558, in that very juncture of time when what church preferment he pleased courted his acceptance thereof.‡ I find two more of his name, Ralph Leaver and John Leaver (probably his kinsmen) exiles for their conscience in Germany in the reign of queen Mary.

WILLIAM WHITACRE was born at Holme in this county, whose life hath been formerly twice written by me.§ He died anno 1596.

ALEXANDER NOWELL was born 1510, of a knightly family at Read in this county;‖ and at thirteen years of age being admitted into Brazen-nose College in Oxford, studied thirteen years therein.¶ Then he became schoolmaster of Westminster.

It happened in the first of queen Mary he was fishing upon the Thames, an exercise wherein he much delighted, insomuch that his picture kept in Brasen-nose College is drawn with his lines, hooks, and other tackling, lying in a round on one hand, and his angles of several sorts on the other. But, whilst Nowel was catching of fishes, Bonner was catching of Nowel; and, understanding who he was, designed him to the shambles, whither he had certainly been sent, had not Mr. Francis Bowyer,

---

* Bale, de Scriptoribus Britannicis, Cent. ix. num. 86.   † Idem, ut prius.
‡ Parker, in his Scelet. Cantab. MS. in the Masters of St. John.
§ In my "Holy State," and "Church History."
‖ See the Latin Life of his nephew Dr. Whitaker, near the beginning.
¶ In his epitaph on his monument in St. Paul's.—F.

then merchant, afterwards sheriff of London, safely conveyed him beyond the seas.

Without offence it may be remembered, that leaving a bottle of ale, when fishing, in the grass, he found it some days after, no bottle, but a gun, such the sound at the opening thereof: and this is believed (casualty is mother of more inventions than industry) the original of bottled ale in England.

Returning the first of queen Elizabeth, he was made dean of St. Paul's; and, for his meek spirit, deep learning, prudence, and piety, the then parliament and convocation both chose, enjoined, and trusted him, to be the man to make a catechism for public use, such a one as should stand as a rule for faith and manners to their posterity.

Catechising (by the way) is an ancient church ordinance, as appears by Theophilus* and Apollos,† both exercised therein. It remained in *state* during the primitive church, and did not decline till popery began to increase; for, had catechising continued, it had made the laity more wise in religion than would well have stood with the interest of the church of Rome. It was therefore ousted by school divinity; and then a fruitful olive was cut down, to have a bramble set in the room thereof. In the first Reformation, Protestants revived this ordinance; and by the use thereof, religion got the speed, and great ground of superstition; till the Jesuits, sensible thereof, have since outshot us in our own bow, most careful to catechise their novices; whilst English Protestants (for I will not condemn foreign churches) grew negligent therein. What is the reason that so much cloth so soon changeth colour? even because it was never well woaded. And why do men so often change their opinions? even because they were never well catechised.

He was confessor to queen Elizabeth, constantly preaching the first and last lent sermons before her. He gave two hundred pounds per annum to maintain thirteen scholars in Brasennose College. He died, being ninety years of age, not decayed in sight, February 13, 1601.

[S. N.] JOHN DEE, where born I cannot recover, was a man of much motion, and is mentioned in this place, where he had his (though last) best fixation. He was bred, as I believe, in Oxford, and there *doctorated*, but in what faculty I cannot determine.

He was a most excellent mathematician and astrologer, well skilled in magic, as the ancients did, the Lord Bacon doth,‡ and all may accept the sense thereof, viz. in the lawful knowledge of natural philosophy.

This exposed him, anno 1583, amongst his ignorant neigh-

* Luke i. 4. περι ὦν κατηχθης. † Acts xviii. 25. οὗτος ἦν κατηχημενος.
‡ In his "Advancement of Learning."

bours, where he then lived, at Mortlake in Surrey, to the suspicion of a conjurer; the cause, I conceive, that his library was then seized on, wherein were four thousand books, and seven hundred of them manuscripts.*   This indignity, joined with the former scandal, moved him to leave the land, and go over with Sir Edward Kelly into Bohemia, as hereafter shall be more fully related.†

Returning to Mortlake, 1592, the same scandal of being a conjurer haunted him again.   Two years after, viz. 1594, he was under a kind of restraint, which caused him to write to the Lady Scydemore, to move queen Elizabeth, either that he might declare his case to the council, or have liberty under the broad seal to depart the land.   Next year he wrote an apological letter to archbishop Whitgift, which, it seems, found good reception: yea, at last he gave such satisfaction of the lawfulness and usefulness of his studies, that the queen (besides many considerable new year's gifts sent unto him) presented him warden of Manchester in this county, 1596, where he had many contests and suits with the fellows of that college.

The last mention I find of him is in Mr. Camden, to whom he presented an ancient Roman inscription found about Manchester; and Mr. Camden, in his requital, presented him with this commendation :‡

" Hanc mihi descripsit, qui vidit, Cl. Mathematicus, J. Dee, Collegii Manchestrensis custos."

And indeed all the books he hath left behind him speak him a *learned*, as those " De usu Globi Terrestris," " De Nubium, Solis, Lunæ, ac Planetarum distantiis," &c. an *aged* man; being dedicated to king Edward the Sixth, and he dying about the beginning of king James.

ROGER FENTON, D.D. fellow of Pembroke Hall in Cambridge, was born in this county, as appeareth by his epitaph in St. Stephen's, Walbrook, London, being the painful, pious, learned, and beloved minister thereof.   Little is left of him in print, save a solid treatise against usury.   Great was his intimacy with Dr. Nicholas Felton, being contemporaries, collegiates, and city ministers together, with some similitude in their surnames, but more sympathy in their natures.

Once my own father gave Dr. Fenton a visit, who excused himself from entertaining him any longer.   " Mr. Fuller," said he, " hear how the passing-bell tolls at this very instant, for my dear friend Dr. Felton, now a-dying; I must to my study, it being mutually agreed upon betwixt us in our healths, that the surviver of us should preach the other's funeral sermon."   But

* Theatrum Chymicum, p. 480.
† See Sir Edward Kelly's Life, in Worcestershire.
‡ In his Britannia, in Lancashire.

see a strange change.   God, " to whom belongs the issues from death,"* was pleased (with the patriarch Jacob blessing his grand-children) " wittingly to guide his hands across, reaching out death to the living and life to the dying."† So that Dr. Felton recovered, and not only performed that last office to his friend Dr. Fenton, but also survived him more than ten years, and died bishop of Ely.   Roger Fenton died in the fiftieth year of his age, anno Domini 1615, buried in his own church, under a monument at the expence of the parish.

ROBERT BOLTON was born at Blackburne in this county, on Whitsunday 1572; a year as infamous for the massacre of many Protestants in France, so for the birth of some eminent in England.   His parents, having a narrow estate, struggled with their necessities, to give him liberal education ; and he was bred first in Lincoln, then in Brazen-nose College in Oxford. He had Isocrates' six marks, or properties of a good scholar : Ἐυφυὴς, Μνήμων, Ζητειτικὸς, Φιλομαθὴς, Φιλόπονος, Φιλήκοος.‡   His want of means proved an advancement unto him : for, not having whence to buy books, he borrowed the best authors of his tutor, read over, abridged into note-books, and returned them. He was as able to express himself in Latin or Greek, as English; and that *stylo imperatorio.*   He was chosen one of the disputants before king James, at his first coming to the university ; and performed it with great applause.

Thus far I have followed my author mentioned in the margin ; but now must depart from him a little in one particular.   Though Mr. Bolton's parents were not overflowing with wealth, they had a competent estate (as I am informed by credible intelligence) wherein their family had comfortably continued long time in good repute.

Sir Augustine Nicolls presented him to the rectory of Broughton in Northamptonshire; sending him his presentation unexpectedly, from his chamber in Sergeant's Inn, where Dr. King, bishop of London, being accidentally present, thanked the judge for his good choice; but told him withal, that he had deprived the university of a singular ornament.   Besides his constant preaching, he hath left behind him many useful books, the witnesses of his piety and learning ; and died, in the 59th year of his age, December 17, 1631.

JOHN WEEVER was born at ...... in this county ; bred in Queen's College, in Cambridge, under Dr. John Person, his worthy tutor.   He was very industrious in the study of antiquity; and composed a useful book of " Funeral Monuments " in the diocese of Canterbury, Rochester, London, and Norwich.

* Psal. lxviii. 20.   † Gen. xlviii. 14.
‡ See the particulars justified in his Life at large, written by my worthy friend Edward Bagshaw, Esq.—F.

He died in London in the fifty-sixth year of his age; and was buried in St. James's, Clerkenwell, where he appointed this epitaph for himself:

> " Lancashire gave me breath,
>   And Cambridge education.
> Middlesex gave me death,
>   And this church my humation.
> And Christ to me hath given
> A place with him in heaven."

The certain date of his death I cannot attain; but, by proportion, I collect it to be about the year of our Lord 1634.

RALPH CUDWORTH, D.D. the second son of Ralph Cudworth, of Wernith-hall near Manchester, esquire, chief lord of Oldham, was bred fellow of Emanuel College, in Cambridge. A most excellent preacher, who continued and finished some imperfect works of Mr. Perkins, and, after his decease, supplied his place in St. Andrew's in Cambridge. He was at last presented by the college to the parish of Aller in Somersetshire anno 16 . .*

LAWRENCE CHADERTON was born at Chadderton in this county, of ancient and wealthy parentage; but much nuzzled up in Popish superstition. He was intended for a lawyer; and in order thereunto, brought up some time in the Inns of Court, till he changed his profession, and admitted himself in Christ's College in Cambridge. His father, hearing that he had altered his place, studies, and religion, sent him a *poke* with a groat therein, for him to go a begging therewith; disinheriting him of that fair estate which otherwise had descended upon him. But God, who taketh men up "when their fathers and mothers forsake them," provided him a comfortable subsistence, when chosen fellow of the college. He was for many years lecturer at St. Clements, in Cambridge, with great profit to his auditors; afterwards made, by the founder, first master of Emanuel. He was chosen by the Non-conformists to be one of their four representatives in Hampton Court conference, and was afterwards employed one of the translators of the Bible. He had a plain but effectual way of preaching. It happened that he, visiting his friends, preached in this his native country, where the word of God (as in the days of Samuel) was very precious; and concluded his sermon, which was of two hours' continuance at least, with words to this effect, "that he would no longer trespass upon their patience." Whereupon all the auditory cried out (wonder not if hungry people craved more meat), "for God's sake, sir, go on, go on." Hereat Mr. Chaderton was surprised into a longer discourse, beyond his expectation, in satisfaction

---

* His son, the celebrated Dr. Ralph Cudworth, was born at Aller in 1617. The father died in 1624.—ED.

of their importunity, and (though on a sudden) performed it to their contentment and his commendation. Thus constant preachers, like good housekeepers, can never be taken so unprovided, but that (though they make not a plentiful feast) they can give wholesome food at a short warning.

He commenced doctor in divinity, when Frederick Prince Palatine (who married the lady Elizabeth) came to Cambridge. What is said of Mount Caucasus, "that it was never seen without snow on the top," was true of this reverend father, whom none of our father's generation knew in the university before he was grey-headed, yet he never used spectacles till the day of his death, being ninety-four years of age.

He was not disheartened with that common saying, "he that resigneth his place before his death, burieth himself alive;" but put off his clothes long before he went to bed; divested himself of the mastership of Emanuel College, that so he might see a worthy successor in his life-time. The blessing which befell Job, was in some sort appliable unto him : he saw his successors to "the fourth generation."* I mean Doctor Preston, and after his death Doctor Sancroft, and after his death Doctor Holesworth, who preached his funeral sermon anno 1640, about the ninety-fourth year of his age.

GEORGE WALKER was born at Hawkshead in Furnifells, of religious parents. Being visited, when a child, with the small-pox, and the standers-by expecting his dissolution, he started up out of a trance with this ejaculation, "Lord, take me not away till I have shewed forth thy praises!" which made his parents devote him to the ministry after his recovery.

He was bred B.D. in St. John's College in Cambridge, where he attained to be well skilled in the Oriental tongues, an excellent logician and divine. Mr. Foster (formerly his tutor) resigned unto him his living of St. John the Evangelist, London; wherein Mr. Walker continued the painful preacher well nigh forty years, refusing higher preferment often proffered him. Dr. Felton (the same morning he was elected bishop of Ely) made him his chaplain; and Dr. Featly chose him his second in one of his disputations against Father Fisher; yea, Mr. Walker alone had many encounters with the subtilest of the Jesuitical party.

He was a man of a holy life, humble heart, and bountiful hand, who deserved well of Sion College library; and, by his example and persuasion, advanced about a thousand pounds towards the maintenance of preaching ministers in this his native county. He ever wrote all his sermons, though making no other use of his notes in the pulpit, than keeping them in his pocket, being wont to say, "that he thought he should be out if he had them

* Job xlii. 15.

not about him." His sermons, since printed, against the profanation of the sabbath, and other practices and opinions, procured him much trouble, and two years' imprisonment, till he was released by the parliament. He died, in the seventieth year of his age, anno Domini 1651.

ROMISH EXILE WRITERS.

EDWARD RISHTON was born in this county,* and bred some short time in Oxford, till he fled over to Douay, where he was made master of arts. Hence he removed to Rome; and, having studied divinity four years in the English college there, was ordained priest, 1580. Then was he sent over into England to gain proselytes; in prosecution whereof he was taken and kept prisoner three years. Yet was the severity of the state so merciful unto him, as to spare his life, and only condemn him to banishment.

He was carried over into France, whence he went to the university of Pontmuss in Lorraine, to ply his studies. During his abode there, the place was infected with the plague. Here Rishton forgat the physicians' rule, "Citò, procul, longè, tardè," (fly away soon, live away far, stay away long, come again slowly:) for he remained so long in the town, till he carried away the infection with him, and, going thence, died at St. Manhow, 1585. I presume no ingenious papist will be censorious on our painful Munster, learned Junius, godly Greenham, all dying of the pestilence, seeing the most conscientious of their own persuasion subject to the same; and indeed neither love nor hatred can be collected from such casualties.

THOMAS WORTHINGTON was born in this county,† of a gentle family; was bred in the English College at Douay, where he proceeded bachelor in divinity, and a little before the eighty-eight was sent over into England as an harbinger for the Spanish invasion, to prepare his party thereunto. Here he was caught, and cast into the Tower of London; yet found such favour, that he escaped with his life, being banished beyond the seas.

At Triers he commenced doctor in divinity; and, in process of time, was made president of the English College at Rheims. When, after long expectation, the Old Testament came out in English at Rheims (permitted with some cautions for our lay-catholics to read) this Worthington wrote his notes thereupon, which few Protestants have seen, and fewer have regarded. He was alive in 1611; but how long after is to me unknown.

If not the same (which, for his vivaciousness,‡ is improbable) there was a Father Worthington, certainly his kinsman and countryman, very busy to promote the Catholic cause in England, about the beginning of king Charles. He dining, some

* Pits, de Angliæ Scriptoribus, p. 787.   † Idem.
‡ See "His One Foot out of the Snare."

thirty years since, with a person of honour in this land (at whose table I have often eaten) was very obstreperous in arguing the case for transubstantiation and the ubiquitariness of Christ's body: "Suppose," said he, "Christ were here." To whom the noble master of the house (who till then was silent) returned, "If you were away, I believe he would be here." Worthington perceiving his room more welcome than his company, embraced the next opportunity of departure.

—————— ANDERTON, whose christian name I cannot recover, was born in this county, and brought up at Blackburne school therein; and (as I have been informed*) he was bred in Christ's College in Cambridge, where for his eloquence he was commonly called Golden-mouth Anderton; afterwards he went beyond the seas, and became a popish priest, and one of the learnedest amongst them.

This is he, who, improving himself on the poverty of Mr. Robert Bolton, sometime his schoolfellow (but then not fixed in his religion, and fellow of Brazen-nose College), persuaded him to be reconciled to the church of Rome, and go over with him to the English seminary, promising him gold enough, a good argument to allure an unstable mind to popery; and they both appointed a meeting. But it pleased the God of heaven, who holdeth both an hour-glass and reed in his hand to measure both time and place, so to order the matter, that, though Mr. Bolton came, Mr. Anderton came not accordingly; so that Rome lost, and England gained, an able instrument. But now I have lost J. Pits to guide me; and therefore it is time to knock off, having no direction for the date of his death.

BENEFACTORS TO THE PUBLIC.

WILLIAM SMITH was born at Farnworth in this county;† bred fellow in Pembroke-hall in Cambridge; and at last, by king Henry the Eighth, preferred bishop of Lichfield and Coventry. That politic prince, to ease and honour his native country of Wales, erected a Court of Presidency, conformable to the parliaments of France, in the Marshes thereof; and made this bishop first president, those parts lying partly in his diocese. He discharged the place with singular integrity, and general contentment, retaining that office till the day of his death, when he was removed to be bishop of Lincoln.

"A good name is an ointment poured out," saith Solomon; and this man, wheresoever he went, may be followed by the perfume of charity he left behind him.

1. At Lichfield, he founded an hospital, for a master, two priests, and ten poor people. 2. In the same place, he founded a school, procuring from king Henry the Seventh, that the hospital of Downhall in Cheshire, with the lands thereunto be-

* In the Life of Mr. Bolton.　　† Bishop Godwin, in the Bishops of Lincoln.

longing, should be bestowed upon it. Say not this was robbing the spittle, or at the best robbing Peter to pay Paul; seeing we may presume so charitable a prelate would do nothing unjust, though at this distance of time we cannot clear the particulars of his proceedings.

At Farnworth, where he was born, he founded a school, allowing ten pounds annually (in that age no mean salary) for the master thereof.

The University of Oxford discreetly chose him (Oxford being in his diocese of Lincoln) their chancellor, and lost nothing thereby; for he proved a more loving nephew than son; so bountiful to his aunt Oxford, that therein he founded Brazen-nose College; but died 1513, before his foundation was finished.

———— MOLINEUX, a famous preacher about Henry the Eighth's time, descended of the house of Sefton in the county of Lancaster, builded the church at Sefton anew, and houses for schools about the church-yard; and made the great wall about Magdalen College in Oxford.*

EDWARD HALSALL, in the county of Lancaster, Esquire, sometime chamberlain of the Exchequer at Chester, founded a free-school in Halsall, and endowed it with competent revenue, for the maintenance of a schoolmaster there for ever. When this party lived, I cannot as yet recover.

THOMAS WEST was younger brother to the Lord de la Ware, and parson of Manchester; on whom the barony was devolved, his brother dying issueless. The Pope allowed him to marry for the continuance of so honourable a family, upon condition that he would build a college for such a number of priests (fellows under a warden) as the bishops of Durham and Lichfield should think fit; which he did accordingly, in Manchester. The endowment of this collegiate and parochial church were the glebe and tithes of the parsonage of that parish; and besides them, scarce any other considerable revenue.

I say the glebe, esteemed about 800 acres of that county (half as much more as the statute) measure; besides a considerable part of the town, commonly called the Dean's Gate, corruptly for St. Dionise Gate (to whom, with the Virgin Mary and St. George, Manchester church was dedicated), built upon the glebe-land belonging to the church. As for the tithes of the parish, they lie in two-and-thirty hamlets, wherewith the collegiates were to be maintained, which were, one warden and four fellows, and the integrated and incorporate rector, unto whom the parsonage was appropriated. There were also two chaplains, singing-men, choristers, and organists.

* Both these notes were taken out of a manuscript of Mr. Roger Dodsworth.—F.

This college hath passed many dissolutions and re-foundations; but was lately dissolved, and the lands thereof sold by the late act for sale of dean and chapters' lands : some, skilful in the Gospel, much bemoaning it; and some learned in the law, conceiving, that, being but the glebe of that rectory, it came not within the compass of that act. But, blessed be God, it since hath reverted to its former condition.

SINCE THE REFORMATION.

JOHN SMITH was born at . . . . in this county ; bred in Magdalen College, in Cambridge ; whereof he became fellow, and proctor of the university, when past sixty years of age ; when the prevaricators gave him this *homonymous* salute, " Ave, Pater."

This man could not fiddle, could not tune himself to be pleasant and plausible to all companies : but he could, and did, make that little college great, wherein he had his education.

The poets feign how Bacchus, by reason of his mother Semele's untimely death, was taken out of his mother's womb, and sewed into the thigh of Jupiter his father, where he was bred until the full time of his nativity : a fiction which finds a moral in this Magdalen College, whose mother may be said to decease before the infant was fit to be born ; and that Mr. Smith performed the rest of the parent's part thereunto.

Indeed Edmund Stafford duke of Buckingham, the first founder thereof, gave it little more than a name. The lord Audley bestowed on it a new name, with little buildings and less endowment. Magnificent Dr. Nevil for a time was master thereof ; but (according to the fashion of the world, the rich shall still have more) his affections were all for Trinity College, to which he was afterwards removed.

Only Mr. Smith, by his long life and thrifty living, by what he gave to, and what he saved for, the college, so improved the condition thereof, that, though he left it *lateritium* as he found it, yet what he found poor and empty, he left rich and full of scholars.

Nor must we forget his painfulness, when, with Dr. Gouge he solicited the suit called Magdalen College Case : nor yet his patience, when he lay so long in the Fleet, for refusing to submit to an order of Chancery (fearing their cause would be prejudiced thereby) ; so that he may be called the confessor of the college. From inconsiderable income, he raised by his carefulness considerable profit to the fellows of that house ; and, by observing the statutes, brought the college into such reputation for learning, that yearly it afforded one or more eminent scholars. In a word, he was a true servant to the college all his life, and at his death, to which he bequeathed all he had, six hundred pounds at least, and died anno Domini 163 .

GEORGE CLARKE, haberdasher, a plain honest man, just, temperate, and frugal; and, according to his understanding, (which, in the world's esteem, was not great), devout, a daily frequenter of the prayers in the college church, and the hearer of sermons there. Not long before the breaking forth of our civil dissensions, dying without issue, he made the poor his heir; and did give them one hundred pounds per annum in good lands, lying in a place called Crompsall, within a mile of Manchester. I have not yet attained the certain date of his death.

HUMPHREY CHETHAM, third son of Henry Chetham of Crompsall, gentleman, is thought (on just ground) to descend from Sir Jeffrey Chetham of Chetham (a man of much remark in former days); and some old writings, in the hands of worshipful persons not far remote from the place, do evidence as much : but the said Sir Jeffrey falling in troublesome times into the king's displeasure, his family (in effect) was long since ruinated.

But it seems his posterity was unwilling to fly far from their old (though destroyed) nest; and got themselves a handsome habitation at Crompsall hard by, where James, elder brother to this Humphrey Chetham, did reside. The younger brethren, George, Humphrey, and Ralph, betook to the trading of this county, dealing in Manchester commodities sent up to London; and Humphrey signally improved himself in piety and outward prosperity. He was a diligent reader of the Scriptures and of the works of sound divines; a respecter of such ministers which he accounted truly godly, upright, sober, discreet, and sincere. He was high-sheriff of this county, 1635, discharging the place with great honour; insomuch that very good gentlemen of birth and estate did wear his cloth at the assize, to testify their unfeigned affection to him; and two of them, of the same profession with himself, have since been sheriffs of the county.[*]

Grudge not, reader, to go through so long a porch; for, I assure thee, it leads unto a fair palace; to as great a masterpiece of bounty as our age hath afforded. This Mr. Chetham, by his will, bearing date the 16th of January, 1651, gave £7000, to buy a fee-simple estate of £420 for ever, for the education of forty poor children in Manchester at school, from about six till fourteen years of age, when they are to be bound out apprentices. They must be the children of poor but honest parents; no bastards, nor diseased at the time wherein they are chosen; not lame or blind; in regard the town of Manchester hath ample means already (if so employed) for the maintenance of such impotents. Indeed, he intended it for a seminary of religion and ingenuity, where the aforesaid boys were to have

[*] John Huntley and H. Wrigley, Esquires.—F.

diet, lodging, apparel, and instruction. He gave £1000 for books to a library, and £100 to prepare a place for them. He bequeathed £200 to buy books (such as he himself delighted in) for the churches of Manchester, Bolton, and other chapels thereabouts. He gave the remainder of his estate (debts and legacies first paid) to the increase of the books in the library.

Now as the loaves in the Gospel multiplied in the breaking; so Mr. Chetham's estate did not shrink, but swell, in the calling of it in; insomuch that the aforesaid surplusage is known to be the better part of two thousand pounds. Dying a bachelor, he appointed George Chetham, esquire, citizen and grocer of London (wherefore he was chosen alderman 1656, and fined for the same), and Edward Chetham, gentleman, executors of his will and testament. God send us more such men, that we may dazzle the eyes of the Papists with the light of Protestant good works! And know, reader, I am beholding, for my exact information herein, to my worthy friend Mr. Johnson, late preacher of the Temple, and one of the feoffees appointed by Mr. Chetham for the uses aforesaid.

MEMORABLE PERSONS.

Sir EDMUND de TRAFFORD, et Sir THOMAS de ASHTON, Knights, were persons of high esteem, as anciently descended, and richly revenued in this county. How great their skill was in chemistry will appear by the following patent (faithfully transcribed with mine own hand out of the original in the Tower) granted unto them by king Henry the Sixth, in the four and twentieth year of his reign:

"REX omnibus ad quos, &c. salutem. Sciatis, quòd cùm dilecti et fideles nostri, Edmundus de Trafford, miles, et Thomas Ashton, miles, nobis per quandam supplicationem monstraverint, quod quamvis ipsi super certis metallis, per artem sive scientiam philosophiæ, operari vellent, metalla imperfecta de suo proprio genere transferre, et tunc ea, per dictam artem sive scientiam, in aurum sive argentum perfectum transubstantiare, ad omnimodas probationes et examinationes, sicut aliquod aurum sive argentum in aliqua minerâ crescens, expectandum et indurandum, ut dicunt; nihilominus certæ personæ, illis malevolentes et malignantes, supponant ipsos per artem illicitam operari, et sic ipsos in probatione dictæ artis sive scientiæ impedire et perturbare possunt: Nos præmissa considerantes, ac conclusionem dictæ operationis sive scientiæ scire volentes, de gratiâ nostrâ speciali concessimus et licentiam dedimus iisdem Edmundo et Thomæ, et ipsorum servientibus, quod ipsi artem sive scientiam prædictam operari et probare possint licitè et impune, absque impetitione nostrâ vel officiariorum nostrorum quorumcunque; aliquo statuto, actu, ordinatione, sive provisione in contrarium facto, ordinato, sive proviso,

non obstante. In cujus, &c. T. R. apud Westmonast. septimo
die Aprilis.*"

("The king to all unto whom, &c. greeting. Know ye, that
whereas our beloved and loyal Edmund de Trafford, knight, and
Thomas Ashton, knight, have by a certain petition shown unto
us, that although they were willing, by the art or science of
philosophy, to work upon certain metals to translate imperfect
metals from their own kind, and then to transubstantiate them
by the said art or science, as they say, into perfect gold or
silver, unto all manner of proofs and trials, to be expected and
endured, as any gold or silver growing in any mine; notwithstanding, certain persons, ill-willing and maligning them, conceive them to work by unlawful art, and so may hinder and
disturb them in the trial of the said art and science: We, considering the premises, and willing to know the conclusion of the
said working or science, of our special grace have granted and
given leave to the same Edmund and Thomas, and to their servants, that they may work and try the aforesaid art and science,
lawfully and freely, without any hindrance of ours, or of our
officers whatsoever; any statute, act, ordinance, or provision,
made, ordained, or provided to the contrary notwithstanding.
In witness whereof, the king at Westminster, the 7th day of
April.")

Mr. . . . . . Kidson.—Reader, I presume not now to direct
thee, who myself am at a loss, and grope for a guide. Leland,
in his Itinerary, speaking of Warton, a village in this county,
observeth, that Mr. Kidson was born there; a passage which
never had fallen from his pen, had he not been one of signal
remark. Who this Mr. Kidson was, where he lived, what he
did, where he died, I shall be thankful so such as give me satisfaction.

Richard Rothwell was born at or near Bolton in the
Moors, in this county.† Taking the ministry (after his education in Cambridge) upon him, he disposed his temporal estate to
his friend to live of the Gospel. I remit the reader to his Life,
extant at large in print, wherein this most remarkable, viz. his
dispossessing of John Fox near Nottingham of a devil, there
passing betwixt them a large discourse, by way of question and
answer. I know that such confabulations are common in the
church of Rome; to whose exorcists, Satan's language is as
familiar as Erasmus's Dialogues are well known to men, or those
of Corderius to schoolboys. But such accidents amongst Protestants are very rare, and therefore the more to be observed.
There are, I confess, more Thomases than myself, much given
to mistrust (whose faith will be at a stand herein). However,

* Pat. 24 of Hen. VI. memb. 14.
† Mr. Clark, in his Lives of Modern Divines, p. 450.

finding it attested by an honest and able person,* I dare not deny the truth thereof. All I will say is this, that is the best belief, which is neither over-forward, nor over-froward; which, as it will not run itself out of breath with too much speed, will not be like a restive horse, which no force can make to go farther. He died at Mansfield in Nottinghamshire, 1627, in the sixty-fourth year of his age. Nor could I write less of him, whom one termeth "Orbis Terrarum Anglicarum Oculum," (The eye of our English world;)† and my book would seem dark and blind, if passing him over in silence.

LORD MAYORS.

1. Nicholas Mossey, son of Edward Mossey, of Hough, Clothworker, 1599.
2. James Pemberton, son of James Pemberton, of Ecclestone, Goldsmith, 1611.

Reader, Lancashire is one of the twelve pretermitted counties, the names of whose gentry were not returned into the Tower in the twelfth year of king Henry the Sixth.

SHERIFFS.

ELIZ. REG.

Anno   Name and Arms.   Place.

1 Johan. Talbot, arm.
     Arg. three lions rampant Purpure.
2 Rob. Worseley, mil.
3 Joh. Atherton, mil. . . Atherton.
     G. three falcons O.
4 Joh. Southworth.
5 Tho. Hesketh, mil.
     Arg. on a bend S. three garbs O.
6 Tho. Houghton, arm. . Houghton.
     S. three bars Arg.
7 Edw. Trafford, arm. . . Trafford.
     Arg. a griffin rampant G.
8 Ric Mollineux, mil. . . Sheffton.
     Az. a cross moline O.
9 Tho. Laughton, mil.
     Arg. three chevrons G.
10 Edw. Holland, arm.
     Az. a lion rampant, semée de fleurs-de-lis Arg.
11 Joh. Preston, arm.
     Arg. two bars on a canton G. a cinquefoil O.
12 Tho Butler, arm.
13 Edw. Trafford, arm. . . *ut prius.*

---

* Mr. Stanley Gower, minister of Dorchester, who penned his Life full of many Observables.—F.

† Idem, ibidem.

Anno   Name.   Place.

14 Fran. Holt, arm.

    Arg. on a bend engrailed S. three flowers-de-luce of the first.

15 Rich. Holland, arm. . . *ut prius.*

16 Will. Boothe, arm.

    Arg. three boars' heads erased and erected S.

17 Fran. Holt, arm. . . . . *ut prius.*

18 Rich. Bold, arm.

    Arg. a griffin rampant S. lozengée of the field and Sables.

19 Rob. Dalton, arm.

20 Johan. Fleetwood   . .   Rossehall.

    Party per pale nebulé Az. and O. six martlets counter-changed.

21 Rad. Ashton, arm.

    Arg. a mullet S.

22 Edw. Trafford, mil. . . *ut prius.*

23 Joh. Byron, mil.

    Arg. three bendlets G.

24 Rich. Holland . . . . *ut prius.*

25 Joh. Atherton, arm. . . *ut prius.*

26 Edwar. Trafford . . . *ut prius.*

27 Tho. Preston, arm. . . *ut prius.*

28 Richard. Asheton   . . *ut prius.*

29 Johan. Fleetwood   . . *ut prius.*

30 Tho. Talbot, arm.   . . *ut prius.*

31 Rich. Mollineux .   . . *ut prius.*

32 Rich. Bold, arm. .   . . *ut prius.*

33 Jac. Asheton, arm. .   . *ut prius.*

34 Edw. Fitton, arm.

    Az. on a bend Arg. three garbs O.

35 Richard. Asheton   . . *ut prius.*

36 Radulph. Asheton   . . *ut prius.*

37 Tho. Talbot, arm.   . . *ut prius.*

38 Richard. Holland   . . *ut prius.*

39 Rich. Molleneux .   . . *ut prius.*

40 Richard. Asheton   . . *ut prius.*

41 Rich. Houghton .   . . *ut prius.*

42 Robert. Hesketh .   . . *ut prius.*

43 Cut. Halsall, mil.

    Arg. three griffins' heads erased Az.

44 Edward. Trafford   . . *ut prius.*

JAC. REX.

1 Nic. Moseley, mil.

    S. a chevron betwixt three pick-axes Arg.

2 Thom. Baker, mil.

3 Edw. Fleetwood, arm. . *ut prius.*

4 Rich. Ashton, mil. . . *ut prius.*

5 Rob. Hesketh, arm. . . *ut prius.*

Anno	Name.	Place.
6	Edw. Trafford, mil. . . *ut prius.*	
7	Roger. Nowell, arm.	
	Arg. three cups covered S.	
8	Johan. Fleming, arm.	
9	Cut. Halsall, mil. . . *ut prius.*	
10	Rob. Bindlose, arm.	. Borwick.
	Quarterly per fess indented G. and on a bend O.	
11	Rich. Shirborn, arm.	
12	Edw. Stanley, arm.	
	Arg. on a bend Az. three stags' heads caboshed O.	
13	Rolan. Moseley, arm. . *ut prius.*	
14	Edw. Trafford, mil. . . *ut prius.*	
15	Ric. Shutleworth.	
	S. three weavers' shuttles Arg.	
16	Leonar. Ashawe, arm.	
17	Ed. Moore, arm.	
	V. ten trefoils, four, three, two, and one, Arg.	
18 to 24		

CAR. REX.

1 to 22

Courteous reader, do not behold these vacuities as the effect of my laziness. Nor will I excuse myself by accusing others. The rather, because " in gratuitis nulla est injusticia;" it was no wrong in any to deny, what was bounty in them to bestow on me. But know, all my industry and importunity could not procure the seasonable sight of the records of this county (not kept, as the rest, in the Exchequer, but in a proper place by themselves), thereby to supply the beginning and finishing of this our catalogue.

THE BATTLES.

At Preston in Anderness, August 17th, 1648, Duke Hambleton, resolving to play an after-game of loyalty, entered England with an army more numerous than well disciplined. Most beheld him as one rather cunning than wise; yet rather wise than valiant. However, he had officers who did ken the warcraft as well as any of our age. He would accept of no English assistance, so to engross all the work and wages to himself. Some suspect his officers' trust was undermined (or over-moneyed rather); whilst others are confident they were betrayed by none save their own security. Indeed, the common soldiers were persuaded that the conquest would be easy; rather to be possessed than purchased. Their van and rear were many miles asunder, and they met the resistance of major-general Lambert before they expected it. He at Preston gave the Scotch army such a blow, as settled or stunned it, though it reeled on some miles more southward into Staffordshire, where, at Ulceter, the duke was taken prisoner, and utterly defeated.*

As for the defeat of James earl of Derby in this county, at the end of August anno 1651, it amounted not to a battle; which properly is the engagement of two formed armies. Whereas the forces of the earl were scattered before fully gathered to a firm consistency. Yet this had been a battle if, not prevented by the vigilancy of colonel Lilburn and others, whose seasonable service to the parliament was not so great in itself, as in the most considerable consequences thereof.

THE FAREWELL.

I am informed that Pillyn-moss is the fountain of fuel [turf] in this county, and is conceived inexhaustible by the vicinage. May it prove so! But, if it should chance to fail, may God's grace (which the vulgar, in their profane proverb, equally yoke therewith)—I say, may God's grace never be drained to those that stand in need thereof!

And because this county may be called the cock-pit of conscience, wherein constant combats betwixt religion and superstition, (may the contest betwixt them prove like the morning twilight), wherein (after some equal conflict betwixt them) the light gaineth the final conquest of the darkness.

One word more to this shire, and I have done. Let me be the remembrancer, that Hugh of Manchester† in this county wrote a book in the reign of king Edward the First, intituled, " De Fanaticorum Deliriis," (Of the Dotages of Fanatics.) At which time an impostor had almost made Eleanor the queen-mother mad, by reporting the posthume miracles done by her husband, king Henry the Third, till this our Hugh settled her judgment aright.‡ I could wish some worthy divine (with such Lancashire doth abound) would resume this subject, and shew how ancient and modern fanatics, though differing much in their wild fancies and opinions, meet together in a mutual madness and distraction.

WORTHIES OF LANCASHIRE WHO HAVE FLOURISHED SINCE THE TIME OF FULLER.

Robert AINSWORTH, grammarian, and author of Latin Dictionary, born at Woodvale or Eccles, 1660; died 1743.

* By Colonel Waite.　　† Vide supra, p. 202, titulo WRITERS.
‡ Bale, de Scriptoribus Britannicis, Cent. iv. numb. 62 ; and Pits, de Angliæ Scriptoribus, anno 1294.

Sir Richard ARKWRIGHT, inventor of cotton machinery, born at Preston 1732; died 1792.

Dr. William ASSHETON, divine, voluminous author, and philanthropist; born at Middleton 1641; died 1711.

Dr. Thomas BARNES, learned dissenting divine, and author, born at Warrington 1747; died 1810.

Barton BOOTH, eminent tragedian; born 1681; died 1733.

John Byrom, poet and stenographic writer, born at Kersal 1691; died 1763.

John COLLIER, writer, musician, caricaturist, author of "A View of the Lancashire Dialect," by "Tim Bobbin," born at Urmston near Warrington 1708; died 1786.

Thomas FALKNER, jesuit, author of Description of Patagonia; born at Manchester; died 1780.

Matthew GREGSON, topographer and antiquary; born at Liverpool 1749; died 1824.

James HARGRAVE, inventor in 1767 of improved Spinning-jenny; born at Blackburn.

Mrs. Felicia Dorothea HEMANS, poetess; born at Liverpool; died 1835.

Edward HARWOOD, author of "Editions of the Classics," born 1729.

Francis HAYWARD, physician and scholar; born at Warrington 1738-9.

Nathaniel HEYWOOD, nonconformist divine and author; born at Little Leaver, 1633; died 1677.

Samuel HEYWOOD, serjeant-at-law, learned author, born at Liverpool 1753; died 1828.

Edmund LAW, Bishop of Carlisle, editor of Stephens's Thesaurus, and Locke; born at Cartmel, 1703; died 1787.

John Leland, author of "View of Deistical Writers;" born at Wigan 1691; died 1766.

Jeremiah MARKLAND, critic and collector, born at Childwall 1693; died 1776.

Sir Jonas MOORE, mathematician, surveyor-general of the ordnance, and author; born at Whittle-le-Woods 1617; died 1679.

Sir Robert PEEL, improver of the cotton machinery, M.P. author, and father of the present baronet; born at Peel's Cross, Lancaster 1750: died 1830.

Thomas PERCIVAL, physician, philosopher, and moralist; born at Warrington 1740; died at Manchester in 1804.

Christopher RAWLINSON, antiquary and Saxonist; born at Carkhall 1677; died 1733.

Legh RICHMOND, amiable divine, author of the "Dairyman's Daughter," &c. born at Liverpool 1772; died 1827.

George ROMNEY, painter, royal academician; born at Beckside, near Dalton 1734; died 1802.

William Roscoe, poet and politician, born at Liverpool 1752; died 1831.

George Stubbs, R.A. painter of animals; born at Liverpool 1724; died 1806.

Dr. John Taylor, Unitarian divine, teacher, and author of an Hebrew-English Concordance, born at Lancaster 1694; died 1761.

Charles Townley, antiquary and skilful collector; born at Townley Hall 1737; died 1805.

John Townley, military hero, translator of Hudibras into French; born at Towneley 1697; died 1782.

Thomas West, catholic priest, historian of Furness and the Lakes; born at Ulverston; died 1779.

John Whitaker, divine, antiquary, and historian of Manchester, where he was born 1735; died 1808.

Dr. John Worthington, divine and author, born at Manchester 1618; died 1671.

** It is to be regretted that the important and populous county of Lancaster is without a regular historian. Many local histories of great merit, however, have made their appearance; as the Histories of Manchester by Dr. Aikin (1795), by J. Aston (1816), and by the Rev. J. Whitaker (1818); the History of Liverpool, by Mr. Wallace (1795); the Histories of Whalley and Clitheroe, and of the Parish of Cartmel, by Dr. T. D. Whitaker (1818); Antiquities of Furness, by the Rev. T. West (1774); Description of Blackpool, by W. Hutton (1804); and Fragments relative to the History of Lancashire, by Mr. Gregson (1817.) There have also appeared two Gazetteers of Lancashire; one by J. Aston (1822), and another by S. R. Clarke (1830); besides two anonymous works, entitled, The Stranger in Liverpool 1807; and the History of Liverpool (1819.)

LEICESTERSHIRE.

THIS county is (though not exquisitely) circular in the form; whilst Leicester, the shire town, is almost the exact centre thereof; and the river Soare, diameter-like, divides it into two equal halves; having Lincoln and Rutlandshire on the east, Derby and Nottinghamshire on the north, Warwickshire on the west, and Northamptonshire on the south. It extendeth from north to south thirty and three miles (measured from the utmost angle): but exceedeth not twenty-seven in the breadth thereof.

Here, to avoid all offence, we will collect the quality of this soil from a native thereof: * who may be presumed exact in this quadri-partition.

South-West. Rich ground, plentiful in corn and pasture, but wanting wood; forcing the inhabitants to make use of straw, cowshern, &c.

North-West. For the most part hard and barren, yielding fruit not without labour and expence, but well-stored with wood and pit-coal.

North-East. Good soil, apt to bear corn and grass, and sufficiently provided with fuel.

South-East. Much like the last for fruitfulness, and, of the two, better furnished with fuel.

However, these four quarters, being put together into the body of one shire, competently supply their mutual defects.

NATURAL COMMODITIES.

BEANS.

Plenty of these in this county, especially about Barton in the Beans, in the hundred of Sparkenhoe, where they appear like a forest toward the time of harvest. Wherefore the scouts of Charles duke of Burgundy, who mistook a field full of high thistles near unto Paris, for the army of the king of France with their lances held upright,† might here commit the like mistake with more probability. Though beans be generally beheld but as horse and hog-grain, yet were they man's meat even in

* Burton, in his Description of Leicestershire, p. 2.
† Phil. Comineus, lib. i. cap. 11.

the plentiful country of Canaan,* called קלי (*Pholl*) in the Hebrew; whence some deduce the word *pulse*, though none dare affirm that Daniel's pulse was made thereof. But more of this grain hereafter.†

COAL.

These are digged up plentifully at Cole-Orton, in the hundred of West Goscote. I say Cole-Orton, for there is another village called Cold-Orton in this shire: an addition which no less truly than sadly would be prefixed to most towns in this county, if not warmed in winter with this under-ground fuel, that above ground is so much decayed.

I confess, Θησαυρὸς ἀνθρακῶν (a *treasure of coals*), passeth both in the Greek and Latin proverb for a frustrated expectation; and his hopes fall very low, who, looking for gold, either in specie or in ore, lighteth only on a heap of coals, which anciently used to be buried in the earth, for boundaries or limits of lands.‡ However, such mines of coals as these, without any help of alchemy, are quickly turned into gold and silver, sold at good rates to the counties round about.

MANUFACTURES

In this county are not to be expected; for where the husbandman's acre-staff and the shepherd's hook are, as in this county, in *state*, there they engross all to themselves, and command manufactures to observe their distance from them.§

THE BUILDINGS.

This county affordeth no cathedrals; and as for parish churches therein, they may take the eye, not ravish the admiration of the beholder. Bottesford is one of the primest, very fair and large, with a high spire steeple. At the suppression of abbeys, many ancient monuments of the Albanies and Rosses were removed hither out of the priory of Belvoir, by the command of Thomas earl of Rutland;‖ and pity it was that his commendable care was not imitated in other places.

As for civil structures, there is a seeming parity betwixt many fair houses in this shire; only something monarchical (above the ordinary aristocracy of fabrics) appears in the height, strength, and workmanship of the Stone Tower built by William lord

---

* 2 Sam. xvii. 28, and Ezek. iv. 9.

† In the proverb of Beanbelly Leicestershire, see p. 225.

‡ Austin, de Civitate, lib. xxi. c. 4.

§ The manufacture of stockings was successfully established in this county soon after the death of Dr. Fuller; and the navigable canals, which cross this county in every direction, have infused a spirit of commercial industry.—ED.

‖ A beautiful series of the Monuments of eight successive Earls of Rutland may still be seen in Bottesford Church.—ED.

Hastings at Ashby de la Zouch. Also the fair, large, and beautiful palace built at Broadgate * by Thomas Grey marquis of Dorset challengeth the pre-eminence above the rest.†

THE WONDERS.

There is a village in this county named Carleton, surnamed Curley, and all that are born therein have a harsh and rattling kind of speech, uttering their words with much difficulty and wharling in the throat, and cannot well pronounce the letter R. Surely this proceedeth not from any natural imperfection in the parents (whence probably the tribual lisping of the Ephraimites ‡ did arise); because their children, born in other places, are not haunted with that infirmity. Rather it is to be imputed to some occult quality in the elements of that place. Thus a learned author informeth us, that some families at Lablonne in Guienne in France do naturally stut and stammer, which he taketh to proceed from the nature of the waters.§

As for the inability distinctly to pronounce R, it is a catching disease in other counties. I knew an Essex man,‖ as great a scholar as any in our age, who could not for his life utter *Carolus Rex Britanniæ* without stammering. The best was, the king had from him in his hearty prayers what he wanted in his plain pronunciation.

My father hath told me, that in his time a Fellow of Trinity College, probably a native of Carleton in this county, sensible of his own imperfection herein, made a speech of competent length, with select words both to his mouth and for his matter, without any R therein, to shew that men may speak without being beholden to the dog's letter.

PROVERBS.

" Bean-belly Leicestershire."]

So called from the great plenty of that grain growing therein. Yea, those in the neighbouring counties use to say merrily, " Shake a Leicestershire yeoman by the collar, and you shall hear the beans rattle in his belly;" but those yeomen smile at what is said to rattle in their bellies, whilst they know good silver ringeth in their pockets.

Indeed I read a Latin proverb, " A fabis abstineto," (forbear beans) ; whereof some make a civil interpretation, " Meddle not with matters of state;" because anciently men cast in a bean when they gave their suffrages in public elections. Others ex-

---

* This noble edifice, the residence of Lady Jane Grey, was burnt down at the close of the seventeenth century.—ED.

† Of the houses built since Fuller's time, Staunton Harold, the seat of the Earl Ferrers; Castle Donington, Earl Moira's; and Kirkby Malory, Lord Viscount Wentworths, claim pre-eminence.—ED.

‡ Judges xii. 6. § Jo. Bodin, Method. Hist. cap. 5.

‖ Mr. Joseph Mede.

pound it physically, because beans are windy, and discompose the tranquillity of men's minds by their flatuous evaporation; the reason assigned for the general report that Pythagoras prohibited the eating of them to his scholars. Yet an excellent author informs me, that Pythagoras had his repast on beans more than on any other kind of pulse.*

However, nothing will put Leicestershire men out of conceit of their beloved beans: the rather because their plenty argueth the goodness of their ground; for, whereas lean land will serve for puling peas and faint fetches, it must be a strong and fruitful soil indeed, where the masculine beans are produced.

" If Bevoir have a cap,
      You churls of the vale look to that." †]

That is, when the clouds (as he expoundeth it) hang over the towers of the castle, it is a prognostic of much rain and moisture, to the much indamaging of that fruitful vale, lying in the three counties of Leicester, Lincoln, and Nottingham. But, alas! though the cap may be there still, the head (or the crown therefore) I am sure is not there [I mean Belvoir Castle itself], being lately demolished in our civil wars, though I hear some part thereof is rebuilding. I wish the workmen good success, though I suspect the second edition (to use a scholar's metaphor) of this castle will not be so full and fair as the former.

PRINCES.

JANE GREY,‡ eldest daughter of Henry Grey, duke of Suffolk, by Frances Brandon, eldest daughter to Mary, second sister to king Henry the Eighth, was born at Broadgates, near unto Leicester.

No lady, which led so many pious, lived so few pleasant days; whose soul was never out of the non-age of afflictions, till death made her of full years to inherit happiness; so severe her education.

Whilst a child, her father's was to her a house of correction; nor did she write *woman* sooner than she did subscribe *wife;* and, in obedience to her parents, was unfortunately matched to the Lord Guildford Dudley; yet he was a goodly, and (for aught I find to the contrary) a godly gentleman, whose worst fault was, that he was son to an ambitious father.

She was proclaimed, but never crowned queen; living in the Tower, which place, though it hath a double capacity of a palace and a prison, yet appeared to her chiefly in the latter relation.

For she was longer a captive than a queen therein, taking no contentment all the time, save what she found in God and a clear conscience.

Her family, by snatching at a crown which was not, lost a

* Aristoxenus apud Aulum Gellium, lib. iv. cap. 11.
† Burton's Description of Leicestershire, page 2.
‡ Her Life is written at large in my " Holy State."—F.

coronet which was their own, much degraded in degree, and more in estate. I would give in an inventory of the vast wealth they then possessed, but am loath to grieve her surviving relations with a list of the lands lost by her father's attainture. She suffered on Tower-hill, 1554-5, on the twelfth of February.

KATHARINE GREY was second daughter to Henry duke of Suffolk. 'Tis pity to part the sisters, that their memories may mutually condole and comfort one another. She was born in the same place, and (when her father was in heighth) married to Henry Lord Herbert, son and heir to the earl of Pembroke; but the politic old earl, perceiving the case altered, and what was the highway to honour, turned into the ready road to ruin, got pardon from queen Mary, and brake the marriage quite off.

This Heraclita, Lady of Lamentation, thus repudiated, was seldom seen with dry eyes for some years together, sighing out her sorrowful condition; so that though the roses in her cheeks looked very wan and pale, it was not for want of watering. Afterward Edward Seymour earl of Hertford married her privately without the queen's licence; and concealed, till her pregnancy discovered it.

Indeed our English proverb, "It is good to be near a-kin to land," holdeth in private patrimonies, not titles to crowns, where such alliances have created to many much molestation. Queen Elizabeth beheld her with a jealous eye, unwilling she should match either foreign prince or English peer, but follow the pattern she set her of constant virginity.

For their presumption, this earl was fined fifteen thousand pounds, imprisoned with his lady in the Tower, and severely forbidden her company. But love and money will find or force a passage. By bribing the keeper, he bought (what was his own) his wife's embraces; and had by her a surviving son, Edward, ancestor to the right honourable the duke of Somerset. She died January 26th, a prisoner in the Tower, 1567, after nine years' durance therein.

MARY GREY, the youngest daughter, frighted with the infelicity of her two elder sisters, Jane and this Katharine, forgot her honour, to remember her safety; and married one whom she could love, and none need fear, Martin Kayes, of Kent, Esq. who was a judge at court (but only of doubtful casts at dice, being serjeant-porter); and died without issue, the 20th of April 1578.

MARTYRS.

HUGH LATIMER was born at Thurcaston in this county.* What his father was, and how qualified for his state, take from

---

* Fox, Acts and Monuments, p. 32.

his own mouth, in his first sermon before king Edward, being confident the reader will not repent his pains in perusing it.

" My father was a yeoman, and had no lands of his own; only he had a farm of three or four pounds a-year at the uttermost; and hereupon he tilled so much as kept half a dozen men. He had walk for an hundred sheep; and my mother milked thirty kine. He was able, and did find the king an harness, with himself and his horse, whilst he came unto the place that he should receive the king's wages. I can remember I buckled his harness when he went to Blackheath-field. He kept me to school; or else I had not been able to have preached before the king's majesty now. He married my sisters with five pounds, or twenty nobles, a-piece; so that he brought them up in godliness and fear of God. He kept hospitality for his poor neighbours, and some alms he gave to the poor. And all this did he of the same farm where he that now hath it payeth sixteen pounds by the year and more, and is not able to do anything for his prince, for himself, nor for his children; or give a cup of drink to the poor."

He was bred in Christ's College in Cambridge; and converted, under God, by Mr. Bilney, from a violent Papist to a zealous Protestant. He was afterwards made bishop of Worcester; and four years after ousted, for refusing to subscribe the Six Articles. How he was martyred at Oxford, 1555, is notoriously known.

Let me add this appendix to his memory. When the contest was in the House of Lords, in the reign of king Henry the Eighth, about the giving all abbey lands to the king, there was a division betwixt the bishops of the Old and New learning, for by those names they were distinguishing. Those of the Old learning, unwillingly willing, were contented that the king should make a resumption of all those abbeys which his ancestors had founded, leaving the rest to continue according to the intention of their founders. The bishops of the New learning were more pliable to the king's desires. Only Latimer was dissenting; earnestly urging, that two abbeys at the least in every diocese, of considerable revenues, might be preserved for the maintenance of learned men therein. Thus swimming a good while against the stream, he was at last carried away with the current.

EMINENT PRELATES BEFORE THE REFORMATION.

Gilbert Segrave, born at Segrave in this county, was bred in Oxford, where he attained to great learning, as the books written by him do declare. The first preferment I find conferred on him was, the provost's place of St. Sepulchre's in York; and the occasion how he obtained it is remarkable.

The Pope had formerly bestowed it on his near kinsman, which argueth the good value thereof; seeing neither eagles nor eagles'-birds do feed on flies. This kinsman of the Pope's, lying on his death-bed, was troubled in conscience (which speaketh loudest when men begin to be speechless, and all sores pain most when near night) that he had undertaken such a cure of souls upon him, who never was in England nor understood English; and therefore requested the Pope his kinsman, that after his death the place might be bestowed on some learned Englishman, that so his own absence and negligence might in some sort be repaired by the residence and diligence of his successor:* and this Segrave, to his great credit, was found the fittest person for that performance. He was afterwards preferred bishop of London, sitting in that see not full four years, dying anno Domini 1317.

WALTER de LANGTON was born at West Langton in this county. He was highly in favour with king Edward the First, under whom he was bishop of Coventry and Lichfield, and treasurer of England. He granted him also liberty of free-warren in West and Thorpe Langton in this county, the patrimonial inheritance of this prelate.†

With his own innocence and friends' assistance, at long sailing he weathered out the tempest of the Pope's displeasure.

Longer did he groan under the undeserved anger of king Edward the Second: chiefly because this bishop sharply reproved him, when as yet but prince, for his debauchery.‡

See here the great difference betwixt youth: some hopefully, some desperately riotous. Of the former was Henry the Fifth, who, when king, is said to have rewarded and advanced such who had reproved and punished him when prince. Of the latter was king Edward, not only wild, but mad in his viciousness. But our Langton at length was brought, saith my author,§ "in regis semi-gratiam," (into the king's half favour); let me add, " et in populi sesque-gratiam," (and into the people's favour and half) who highly loved and honoured him.

His tragi-comical life had a peaceable end in plenty and prosperity. He found his cathedral of Lichfield mean, and left it magnificent; and it will appear by the instance of our Langton, Josceline of Wells, and others, that bishops continuing unremoved in their see have achieved greater matters than those who have been often translated, though to richer bishoprics. Indeed prodigious was his bounty in building and endowing his cathedral, wherein he continued almost twenty-five years; and, dying 1321, was buried in the chapel of St. Mary, of his own erection.

ROGER de MARTIVAL,‖ son and heir to Sir Aukitell de Martivall, Knight (who gave for his arms Argent a cinquefoil Sable),

---

* Bishop Godwin, in vità T. Corbridge,
† Burton's Description of this County, p. 257.
‡ Godwin, in the Bishops of Bath and Wells.   § T. Walsingham.
‖ Bishop Godwin writeth him " Mortivall."

was born at Nowsley in this county. He was first archdeacon of Leicester, then dean of Lincoln, and at last consecrated bishop Salisbury, in the reign of king Edward the Second, 1315. Now seeing Bishop Godwin hath nothing more of him save his name and date, it is charity further to inform posterity that he was the last heir male of his house, and founded a college at Nowsley, temp. Edw. I. for a warden and certain brethren, which in the 24th of Henry VI. was valued to dispend yearly (besides all charges) 6l. 13s. 4d. His estate descended to Joyce de Martivall, his sister, married unto Sir Ralph Hastings, lineal ancestor to the now Earl of Huntingdon. As for the manor of Nowsley, as it came with the mother, so it went away with her daughter, into the family of the Herons; and by her daughter into the family of the Hazelriggs, who at this day are possessors thereof.* This bishop died in the midst of Lent, 1329.

ROBERT WIVILL was born of worthy and wealthy parentage at Stanton Wivill in this county.† At the instance of Philippa, queen to king Edward the Third, the Pope, anno 1329, preferred him bishop of Salisbury. It is hard to say whether he were more dunce or dwarf, more unlearned or unhandsome, insomuch that T. Walsingham tells us, that had the Pope ever seen him (as no doubt he felt him in his large fees) he would never have conferred the place upon him.

He sate bishop more than forty-five years, and impleaded William Mountague earl of Salisbury in a writ of right for the castle of Salisbury. The earl chose the trial by battle; which the bishop accepted of, and both produced their champions into the place. The combatant for the bishop coming forth all clad in white, with the bishop's own arms, viz. Gules fretty Vaire, a chief Or,‡ impaled no doubt with them of his see, on his surcoat.

Some highly commended the zeal of the bishop, asserting the rights of his church; whilst others condemn this in him, as an unprelatical act, God allowing duels no competent deciders of such differences. And moderate men, to find out an expedient, said, he did this, not as a bishop, but baron. The best was, the matter was taken up by the king's interposing; and the bishop, with 2500 marks, bought of the earl the quiet possession of the castle; and died anno Domini 1375, being buried under a marble stone about the middle of the choir.

SINCE THE REFORMATION.

JOSEPH HALL was born at Ashby de la Zouch in this county, where his father, under the earl of Huntingdon, was governor or bailiff of the town. So soon almost as Emanuel College was

---

* Burton, in his Description of Leicestershire, page 211.
† Idem, page 269.
‡ Godwin, in the Bishops of Salisbury. Burton, ut prius.

admitted into Cambridge, he was admitted into that college, within few years after the first foundation thereof. He passed all his degrees with great applause. First, noted in the university for his ingenuous maintaining (be it truth or paradox) that " Mundus senescit," (the world groweth old). Yet, in some sort, his position confuteth his position, the wit and quickness whereof did argue an increase rather than a decay of parts in this latter age.

He was first beneficed by Sir Robert Drury at Halstead in Suffolk ; and thence removed by Edward Lord Denny (afterward Earl of Norwich) to Waltham Abbey in Essex. Here I must pay the tribute of my gratitude to his memory, as building upon his foundation, beholding myself as his great-grandchild in that place, three degrees from him in succession : but oh ! how many from him in ability. His little catechism hath done great good in that populous parish ; and I could wish that ordinance more generally used all over England.

Being doctor of divinity, he was sent over by king James to the Synod of Dort, whence only indisposition of body forced him to return before the rest of his colleagues. He was preferred first dean of Worcester, then bishop of Exeter, then bishop of Norwich, then bishop of no place : surviving to see his sacred function buried before his eyes. He may be said to have died with his pen in his hand, whose writing and living expired together. He was commonly called our English Seneca,* for the pureness, plainness, and fulness of his style. Not unhappy at controversies, more happy at comments, very good in his characters, better in his sermons, best of all in his meditations. Nor will it be amiss to transcribe the following passage out of his will :

" In the name of God, Amen. I Joseph Hall, D.D., not worthy to be called bishop of Norwich, &c. First, I bequeath my soul, &c. My body I leave to be interred, without any funeral pomp, at the discretion of my executors ; with this only monition, that I do not hold God's house a meet repository for the dead bodies of the greatest saints."†

He died September the 8th, anno Domini 1656; and was buried at Higham near Norwich.

STATESMEN.

GEORGE VILLIERS was born at Brokesby in this county, fourth son to his father Sir George Villiers, and second son to his mother Mary Beaumont. Being debarred (by his late nativity) from his father's lands, he was happy in his mother's love, maintaining him in France, till he returned one of the completest courtiers in Christendom, his body and behaviour mutually gracing one another.

* Sir H. Wotton, in his Letter to Dr. Collins.—F.
† Examinat. R. Richard.

Sir Thomas Luke may be said to have ushered him into the English court; whilst the Lady Lucy, Countess of Bedford, led him by the one hand, and William Earl of Pembroke by the other, supplying him with a support far above his patrimonial income. The truth is, Somerset's growing daily more wearisome, made Villiers hourly more welcome to king James.

Soon after, he was knighted, created successively Baron, Viscount Villiers, Earl, Marquis, Duke of Buckingham; and, to bind all his honours the better together, the noble Garter was bestowed upon him. And now offices at court (not being already void) were voided for him. The earl of Worcester was persuaded to part with his place of Master of the Horse, as the earl of Nottingham with his office of Admiral; and both conferred on the duke.

He had a numerous and beautiful female kindred, so that there was hardly a noble stock in England into which one of these his scions was not grafted. Most of his nieces were matched with little more portion than their uncle's smiles, the forerunner of some good office or honour to follow on their husbands. Thus with the same act did he both gratify his kindred, and fortify himself with noble alliance.

It is seldom seen that two kings (father and son) tread successively in the same tract as to a favourite; but here king Charles had as high a kindness for the duke as king James. Thenceforward he became the plenipotentiary in the English court, some of the Scottish nobility making room for him by their seasonable departure out of this life. The earl of Bristol was jostled out, the bishop of Lincoln cast flat on the floor, the earls of Pembroke and Carlisle content to shine beneath him, Holland behind him, none even with, much less before him.

But it is generally given to him who is the little god at the court, to be the great devil in the country. The commonalty hated him with a perfect hatred; and all miscarriages in church and state, at home, abroad, at sea and land, were charged on his want of wisdom, valour, or loyalty.

John Felton, a melancholy mal-contented gentleman, and a sullen soldier, apprehending himself injured, could find no other way to revenge his conceived wrongs, than by writing them with a point of a knife in the heart of the duke, whom he stabbed at Portsmouth, anno Domini 1620. It is hard to say how many of this nation were guilty of this murder, either by public praising, or private approving thereof.

His person from head to foot could not be charged with any blemish, save that some hypercritics conceived his brows somewhat over-pendulous, a cloud which in the judgment of others was by the beams of his eyes sufficiently dispelled. The reader is remitted for the rest of his character to the exquisite epitaph on his magnificent monument in the chapel of Henry the Seventh.

CAPITAL JUDGES.

[AMP.] Sir ROBERT BELKNAP.—Being bred in the study of the laws, he became chief justice of the Common Pleas, October the 8th, in the 48th of king Edward the Third; and so continued till the general rout of the judges, in the wonder-working parliament, the eleventh of Richard the Second, when he was displaced on this occasion.

The king had a mind to make away certain lords; viz. his uncle the duke of Gloucester, the earls of Arundel, Warwick, Derby, Nottingham, &c. who in the former parliament had been appointed governors of the kingdom. For this purpose, he called all the judges before him to Nottingham, where the king's many questions in fine were resolved into this, "Whether he might by his regal power revoke what was acted in parliament?" To this all the judges, Sir William Skipwith alone excepted, answered affirmatively, and subscribed it.

This Belknap underwrote unwillingly, as foreseeing the danger, and, putting to his seal, said these words:

" There wants nothing but a hurdle, a horse, and a halter, to carry me where I may suffer the death I deserve; for, if I had not done this, I should have died for it; and because I have done it, I deserve death for betraying the lords."

Yet it had been more for his credit and conscience, to have adventured a martyrdom in the defence of the laws, than to hazard the death of a malefactor in the breach thereof. But judges are but men; and most desire to decline that danger which they apprehend nearest unto them.

In the next parliament, all the judges were arrested in Westminster-hall of high treason; when there was a vacation in term time, till their places were re-supplied. Sir R. Tresilian, chief justice of the King's Bench, was executed: the rest thus named and reckoned up in the printed statutes;* Robert Belknap, John Holt, John Cray, William Burgh, Roger Fulthorp, all judges and knights, with J. Locktan, serjeant at law, had their lands (save what were entailed) with their goods and chattels, forfeited to the king, their persons being banished; and they, by the importunate intercession of the queen, hardly escaping with their lives.

Belknap is placed in this county, only because I find a worshipful family of his name fixed therein, whereof one was high sheriff in the 17th of king Henry the Seventh; provided this be no prejudice to Sussex, the same name† being very ancient therein.

Sir ROBERT CATELIN, descended from the ancient family

* Anno 11 Rich. II. cap. 4.   † Camden's Britannia, in Sussex.

of the Catelins of Raunds in Northamptonshire (as doth appear
by the heralds' visitation) was born at Beby in this county.*
He was bred in the study of the municipal laws; profiting so
well therein, that, in the first of queen Elizabeth, he was made
lord chief justice of the King's Bench.   His name hath some
allusion to the Roman senator† who was the incendiary of that
state, though in nature far different, as who by his wisdom and
gravity was a great support to his nation.

One point of law I have learned from him, at the trial of
Thomas duke of Norfolk, who pleaded out of Bracton, " that
the testimonies of foreigners" (the most pungent that were
brought against him) " were of no validity."   Here Sir Robert
delivered it for law, " that, in case of treason, they might be
given in for evidence ; and that it rested in the breast of the
peers, whether or no to afford credit unto them." ‡

He had one (as what man hath not many) fancy, that he had
a prejudice against all those who write their names with an
alias ; and took exceptions at one in this respect, saying, " that
no honest man had a double name, or came in with an *alias.*" §
The party asked him what exceptions his lordship could take at
Jesus Christ, *alias* Jesus of Nazareth.

He died in the sixteenth year of queen Elizabeth ; and his
coat of arms [viz. Partie per chevron Azure and Or, three
lions passant gardant counterchanged, a chief pearl] is quartered by the right honourable the Lord Spencer, earl of
Sunderland ; this judge's daughter and sole heir being married
to his ancestor.

Some forty years since, a gentleman of his name and kindred
had a cause in the Upper Bench ; to whom the chief justice
therein said, " Your kinsman was my predecessor in the court,
and a great lawyer."   " My lord (replied the gentleman) he
was a very honest man, for he left a small estate."   But indeed,
though his estate was not considerable, compared to his successors then present, it was in itself of a good valuation.

WRITERS.

WILLIAM DE LEICESTER, otherwise called William de
Montibus (which I would willingly English William of the
Wolds), was born in Leicester in this county ; bred in Oxford, where he was doctor and professor of divinity, so eminent
for his learning that he was known to and much beloved by the
nobility of the land.|| He was also known by the name of
Mr. William,¶ an evidence, I assure you, sufficient to avouch
his magisterialty in all learning.

He was removed to Lincoln ; and became first canon, then

---

* So I have learned by his relations.—F.   † L. Catilina.
‡ Camden's Elizabeth, anno 1572.   § Idem, in his Remains, p. 147.
|| Pits, de Angliæ Scriptoribus, p. 285.   ¶ Idem, ibidem.

chancellor of the church. Boston of Bury reckoneth up many and learned books of his making. He flourished under king John, 1210; and lieth buried at Lincoln.

RICHARD BELGRAVE was born, saith J. Pits,* at Chichester in Sussex; but at Belgrave in Leicestershire, saith Mr. William Burton,† whom I rather believe, because he wrote a particular description of this county. Now surely the more is the exactness of the author, the less the extent of his subject, especially making it his set-work (what was Pits's by-work) to observe the natives of this shire. But both agree him to be a Carmelite, bred in Cambridge, an excellent divine and good schoolman, more learned than eloquent. He wrote one book of "Theological Determinations," and another of "Ordinary Questions," flourishing in the year 1220, under king Edward the Second.

ROBERT de LEICESTER was born therein, but bred in Oxford a Franciscan friar. He was one of those who brought preaching into fashion in that age, and was much esteemed for his faculty therein, by most of the nobility. But Robert Mascall bishop of Hereford (as pious and learned as any in that age) had an extraordinary affection for him.‡ Our Leicestrian Robert appeareth also a good chronologer, having written judiciously of the Hebrew and Roman computation. In his reduced age, he retired to Lichfield, where he died, and was buried in the monastery of the Franciscans, 1348.§

THOMAS RATCLIF, born at Ratcliffe in this county, was bred an Augustinian in Leicester, where he was *Ordinis sui Episcopus*,‖—strain the word no higher than to *overseer* of his order. He had *ingenium fecundum et amplum;* and pity it was, that he had *vitæ institutum sterile et angustum.* However, to enlarge his soul, he wrote divers books, and flourished anno 1360.

BARTHOLOMEW CULIE was born at Radcliffe-Culie in this county, as the exact describer thereof avoucheth.¶ And therefore Pits committeth a double mistake about this one writer, first calling him Conway, and then making him a Welchman by his nativity.** How hard is it to commit one, and but one, error! This Bartholomew was an excellent philosopher, and wrote a book of "Generation and Corruption;" and although J. Pits confesseth himself ignorant of the time he lived in, my author assureth me that he flourished under king Edward the Third.

* De Scriptoribus Britannicis, in anno 1320.
† In his Description of Leicestershire, p. 40.
‡ Understand it after the death of Robert of Leicester.
§ Pits, de Angliæ Scriptoribus, hoc anno.   ‖ Bale, Cent. vi. num. 14.
¶ Burton, in his Description of Leicestershire, p. 229.   ** In Appendice.

WILLIAM de LUBBENHAM was born at Lubbenham in this county; brought up in Oxford; a good philosopher and a divine;* was after a White friar, or Carmelite, in Coventry; and after became provincial of the order, which place he kept till he died. He wrote upon "Aristotle's Posteriors;" and one book of "Ordinary Questions." He died in the White Friars, in Coventry, 1361, in the 36th year of king Edward the Third.

JEFFERY de HARBY was born at Harby in this county; and bred in Oxford, where he became provincial of the Augustines, and confessor to king Edward the Third. Wonder not when meeting with so many confessors to that king, presuming he had but one at one time, conscience not standing on state and variety in that kind. For know king Edward reigned fifty years; and confessors being aged before admitted to their place, his vivaciousness did wear out many of them. Besides, living much beyond the seas, it is probable that he had his foreign and his home confessors. Our Jeffery was also of his privy council, being as prudent to advise in matters politic, as pious in spiritual concernments. Such as admired he was not preferred to some wealthy bishopric, must consider that he was ambitious and covetous to be poor, and wrote a violent book in the praise and perfection thereof against Armachanus. Dying in London, he was buried in the church of the Augustines, about the year 1361.

WILLIAM de FOLVIL was born at Ashby-Folvil in this county; and therefore, when Bale calleth him *Lincolniensem*,† understand him not by county, but by diocese. He was bred a Franciscan in the university of Cambridge; and engaged himself a great master of defence in that doughty quarrel *pro pueris induendis*, that children under the age of eighteen might be admitted into monastical orders: for whereas this was then complained of as a great and general grievance; that by such preposterous cowling of boys, and veiling of girls, parents were cozened out of their children, and children cozened out of themselves, doing in their minority they knew not what, and repenting in their maturity, not knowing what to do; our Folvil, with more passion than reason, maintained the legality thereof. He died and was buried in Stamford,‡ anno 1384.

HENRY de KNIGHTON was born at Knighton in this county; sometime abbot of Leicester; who wrote his "History from William the Conqueror to the time of king Richard the Second," in whose reign he died.

It seemeth *Lelandus non vidit omnia*, nor his shadow Bale,

---

* Leland, de Scriptoribus Britannicis, 265.
† Bale, de Scriptoribus Britannicis, Cent. vi. num. 72.   ‡ Idem, p. 491.

nor his shadow Pits; all three confessing that the history of this Knighton never came to their hands; whereas of late it hath been fairly printed, with other historians, on the commendable cost of Cornelius Bee. Thus it is some comfort and contentment to such whom nature hath denied to be mothers that they may be dry nurses, and dandle babes in their laps, whom they cannot bear in their wombs. And thus this industrious stationer (though no father) hath been foster-father to many worthy books, to the great profit of posterity.

WILLIAM WOODFORD.—I cannot fix his nativity with any certainty, because so many Woods and Fords; (and would the former did continue as well as the latter!) and consequently so many towns called Woodfords in England. He is placed here, because his surname in this age flourished in great eminency in this county.* He was bred a Franciscan; and though bilious Bale giveth him the character of *Indoctè Doctus*,† we learn from Leland, that he was one of profound learning, and Thomas Waldensis‡ owneth and calleth him *magistrum suum*, his master.

Indeed Woodford set him the first copy of railing against Wickliffe, being deputed by Thomas Arundel archbishop of Canterbury to confute, publicly in writing, his opinions. He died and was buried at Colchester 1397.

THOMAS LANGTON was born at West-Langton in this county; bred a Carmelite in London, but first brought up in Oxford. He wrote a book of their own "Ordinary Acts;" another called "The Trial of Henry Crump, Doctor in Divinity;" another book against the errors of the said Doctor Crump. Reader, we are beholden to my author§ for retrieving this writer's memory, which otherwise appears not in Leland, Bale, or Pits. He flourished under king Henry the Fourth, anno Domini 1400.

ROBERT de HARBY was born at Harby in this county; bred a Carmelite in their convent at Lincoln. He seems to be a doctor in divinity,‖ and surely was a great adorer of the Virgin Mary, writing many sermons of her festivities. He flourished 1450.

RICHARD TURPIN was born at Knaptoft¶ in this county,

* Burton, in his Description of Leicestershire, p. 23.
† De Scriptoribus Britannicis, Cent. vii. num. 33.
‡ Libro de Sacrament. c. 50.
§ Burton, in his Description of this Shire, p. 157.
‖ Pits, de Angliæ Scriptoribus, anno 1450.
¶ Burton, in his Description of Leicestershire, p. 153.

very lately (if not still) in the possession of that ancient family,* and was one of the gentlemen of the English garrison of Calais in France in the reign of king Henry VIII.   Such soldiers generally in time of war had too much, in time of peace too little work, to employ themselves therein.   Commendable therefore the industry of this Richard, who spent his spare hours in writing of a " Chronicle of his Time."   He died anno Domini 1541, in the thirty-fifth year of the aforesaid king's reign.†   This I observe the rather, that the reader may not run with me on the rock of the same mistake, who in my apprehension confounded him with Richard Turpin the herald, first Blue-mantle, and then created Windsor, in the beginning of queen Elizabeth.

WRITERS SINCE THE REFORMATION.

HENRY SMITH, commonly called silver-tongued Smith, preacher at St. Clement Danes.   But I refer the reader to his life writ by me at large, and preposed to his printed sermons.

JOHN DUPORT, D. D. son to Thomas Duport, esquire, was born at Shepeshead in this county ; bred fellow, then master, of Jesus College in Cambridge ; once proctor, and thrice vice-chancellor, of that university.   He was one of the translators of the Bible, and a reverend man in his generation, who bestowed the perpetual advowsance of the rectory of Harston on the college.   Men generally in Scripture are notified by their fathers, seldom by their sons ; as, Simon of Cyrene, father of Alexander and Rufus,‡ persons (no doubt) of signal worth in that age. Thus this doctor is remarkable for his son (by Rachel daughter to Richard Cox bishop of Ely) James Duport, D. D. fellow of Trinity College, and lately Greek professor ; happy in the education of many hopeful pupils of worship and honour, as they more happy in so able a tutor.   His father, Dr. John Duport, deceased 1617.

WILLIAM BURTON, Esquire, son of Ralph Burton of Lindley in this county (who had a more ancient inheritance belonging to his name at Falde in Staffordshire) a place remarkable, because no adder, snake, or lizard (common in the confines) were ever seen therein ;§ as if it were a land-island, and an Ireland in England. This William was born at Lindley, August 24, 1575 ;‖ bred in Brazen-nose College ; and wrote an alphabetical description of the towns and villages in this county, with the arms and pedigrees of the most ancient gentry therein.   The sparks of his ingenuity herein have since set fire on Mr. Dugdale, my worthy friend, to do the like to Warwickshire (lately under one

---

* Not only the ancient family of Turpin, but their mansion, and even the parish church, are blended in one common ruin ; and Knaptoft is now a deserted village.—ED.   † Weever's Funeral Monuments, p. 682.   ‡ Mark xv. 21.
  § Description of Leicestershire, p. 174.   ‖ Idem, p. 68.

sheriff with Leicestershire;) and I hope in process of time they may inflame many others into imitation, that so (give me leave to match an English and Greek word together) the county-graphy of our land may be completed.

ROBERT BURTON, his younger brother, born Feb. 8, 1575, afterwards student of Christ's Church Oxon, and bachelor of divinity. He wrote an excellent book (commonly called "Democritus Junior,") of "The Anatomy of Melancholy" (none to the native, to describe a country), wherein he hath piled up variety of much excellent learning. On whose tomb is this epitaph:

> " Paucis notus, paucioribus ignotus ;
> Hic jacet Democritus junior,
> Cui vitam pariter et mortem
> Dedit Melancholia.

Scarce any book of philology in our land hath in so short a time passed so many impressions. He died rector of Segrave (presented by his patron George Lord Berkeley) in this county, about 1636.*

RICHARD VINES was born at Blaston in this county; and bred in Magdalen College in Cambridge, where he commenced master of arts. Now although many healthful souls in their age break out in their youth, he was never given to any extravagancy. Hence he was chosen school-master of Hinckley in this county, a profession wherein many a good minister hath been (and it is pity that any but a good man should be) employed. Entering the ministry, after other intermediate places (such as are his censurers would be his compurgators, if privy to the weighty causes of his just removal), he was fixed at last at St. Lawrence Jewry in London.

An excellent preacher, skilful to cut out doctrines in their true shape, naturally raised, to sew them up with strong stitches, substantially proved, and set them on with advantage on such backs who should wear them, effectually applied.

He was one (yea, I may say one of sevenscore) in the assembly; the champion of their party, therefore called their Luther, much employed in their treaties at Uxbridge and Isle of Wight. His majesty, though of a different judgment, valued him for his ingenuity, seldom speaking unto him without touching (if not moving) his hat; which by Master Vines was returned (though otherwise blunt and unobservant) with most respectful language and gestures; which I will not say was done by all his fellow divines there present.

He was most charitably moderate to such as dissented from him, though most constant to his own principles; witness his

---

* He died Jan. 25, 1639. See the "History of Leicestershire," Vol. III. p. 418, where a portrait of him is given.

forsaking of his mastership of Pembroke-hall for refusing of the engagement. Such who charged him with covetousness, are confuted with the small estate he left to his wife and children.

It seemeth that the sand in his hour-glass (though sticking high on each side) was but hollow in the middle, for it sunk down on sudden. Visible decays appeared in him a year before his death, though rather in his limbs than parts, spirits than spirit. But, alas, the best mind cannot make good music where the instrument of the body is out of tune; his speech grew very low. Not a week before his death, preaching in St. Gregory's, a rude fellow cried out unto him, "Lift up your voice, for I cannot hear you;" to whom Mr. Vines returned, "Lift you up your ears, for I can speak no louder."

Indeed his strength was much spent by his former pains, so that some suppose, had he wrought less, he had lived longer. He was buried Feb. the 7th, 1655, in his own parish church, where Mr. Jacomb modestly and learnedly performed his funeral sermon. Much lamented, as by many others, so by his own parish, where he piously endeavoured to make them all of one piece who were of different colours, and to unite their judgments who dissented in affections.

JOHN CLEVELAND was born in this county at Hinckley (where his father was vicar), and bred therein under Mr. Richard Vines his schoolmaster. He was afterwards scholar of Christ's, then fellow of St. John's, in Cambridge; and during the late civil wars was much conversant in the garrison of Newark, where, as I am informed, he had the place of advocate general.

A general artist, pure Latinist, exquisite orator, and (which was his master-piece) eminent poet. His epithets were pregnant with metaphors, carrying in them a difficult plainness, difficult at the hearing, plain at the considering thereof. His lofty fancy may seem to stride from the top of one mountain to the top of another, so making to itself a constant level and champaign of continued elevations.

Such who have *Clevelandized*, endeavouring to imitate his masculine style, could never go beyond the hermophrodite, still betraying the weaker sex in their deficient conceits. Some distinguish between the vein and strain of poetry, making the former to flow with facility, the latter pressed with pains, and forced with industry. Master Cleveland's poems do partake of both, and are not to be the less valued by the reader, because most studied by the writer thereof. As for his anagram "JOHN CLEVELAND," (Heliconean Dew), the difficult trifle, I confess, is rather well endeavoured than exactly performed. He died on Thursday morning the 29th of April 1658, at his chamber in Grey's Inn, from whence his body was brought to Hunsdon House, and on Saturday, being May-day, was buried at College

Hill Church, Mr. John Pearson, his good friend, preaching his funeral sermon. He rendered this reason why he cautiously declined all commending of the party deceased, because such praising of him would not be adequate to any expectation in that auditory, seeing such who knew him not, would suspect it far above, whilst such who were acquainted with him did know it much beneath, his due desert. The self-same consideration shall put a period to my pen in his present character; only this I will add, that never so eminent a poet was interred with fewer (if any remarkable) elegies upon him.

I read in an excellent author,[*] how one Johannes Passerativus, professor of the Latin tongue in the university of Paris, being no bad poet (but morose and conceited of himself) forbade by his dying words, under an imprecation, "that his hearse should be burthened with bad funeral verses;" whereupon out of fear to offend his ghost, very few verses were made upon him. Too much the modesty and charity of Mr. Cleveland, by any such injunction to obstruct his friends expressing their affection to his memory. Be it rather imputed to the royal party, at that juncture of time generally in restraint, so that their fancies may seem in some sort to sympathise with the confining of their persons, and both in due season may be enlarged.

Of such verses as came to my hand these were not the worst, made by my good friend[†] since deceased.

"Ye Muses, do not me deny,
   I ever was your votary;
And tell me, seeing you do deign
   T' inspire and feed the hungry brain,
With what choice cates, with what choice fare
Ye Cleveland's fancy still repair?
Fond man, say they, who dost thou question thus?
Ask rather with what nectar he feeds us."

But I am informed, that there is a book intended by the poets of our age, in the honour of his memory, who was so eminent a member of their society.

BENEFACTORS TO THE PUBLIC.

Sir JOHN POULTNEY, Knight, was born in this county, at Poultney in the parish of Misterton; bred in the city of London, and became four times lord mayor thereof.[‡] He built a college, to the honour of Jesus and Corpus Christi, for a master and seven chaplains in St. Laurence church in Candleweek Street in London, in the 20th of Edward the Third, which church was after denominated of him St. Laurence Poultney.

He built the parish church of Allhallows the Less in Thames-street, and the monastery of White Friars in Coventry,

---

[*] Thuanus, de Obit. Virorum Illustrium, anno 1602.
[†] Mr. Edward Martin, of London.
[‡] Burton's Description of Leicestershire, p. 191.

and a fair chapel on the north side of St. Paul's in London, where he lieth buried, who died 1349, the 24th year of Edward the Third. He was a great benefactor to the hospital of St. Giles by Holborn, and gave many great legacies to the relief of prisoners and the poor.*

SINCE THE REFORMATION.

Reader, if any demand of me the names of the natives of this county, benefactors to the public since the Reformation, all my answer is, "Non sum informatus;" and let the court judge whether this be the fault of the council of or the client; and I doubt not but the next age will supply the defects hereof. Only, *postliminio*, I have, by the help of my good friend,† at last recovered one who may keep possession of the place till others be added unto him.

ROBERT SMITH, citizen and merchant tailor of London, was born at Market Harborough in this county, and became controller of the chamber of London, and one of the four attorneys in the mayor's court. A painful person in his place, witness the many remaining monuments of his industry, whilst he acted in his office, betwixt the years 1609 and 1617. Nor was his piety any whit beneath his painfulness, who delivered to the chamberlain of London seven hundred and fifty pounds to purchase lands for the maintenance of a lecturer in the town of his nativity, as also for several other pious uses, as in the settlement of those lands are particularly expressed.‡ He died, as I collect, about 1618.

MEMORABLE PERSONS.

Know, reader, that by an unavoidable mischance the two first following persons, who should have been entered under the topic of Soldiers, are (with no disgrace, I conceive) remembered in this place.

EDMOND APPLEBIE, Knight, was son to John Applebie, esquire, and born at Great Appleby, whence their family fetched their name, and where at this day (I hope) they have their habitation. He was a mighty man of arms, who served at the battle of Cressy, the 20th of king Edward the Third, where he took Monsieur Robert du Mailarte, a nobleman of France, prisoner.§ Now know, though the pens of our home-bred historians may be suspected of partiality, yet English achievements acknowledged by French authors, such as Froissart is, who

---

* Stow's Survey of London, p. 81.
† Mr. Rawlins, one of the Lord Mayor's Court.
‡ For an account of these benefactions, still honourably supported, see Nichols's History of Leicestershire, vol. II. p. 498.—ED.
§ Burton's Leicestershire, p. 14.

taketh signal notice thereof, commandeth belief. Afterwards, in the eighth year of Richard the Second, he went into France, with John of Gaunt duke of Lancaster, to treat of a peace betwixt both kingdoms. Lastly, in the ninth of Richard the Second, he accompanied the said duke and the lady Constance his wife, daughter and co-heir of Peter king of Castile, in his voyage into Castile, who then went over with a great power to invest himself in the said kingdom, which by descent belonged to his wife, and was then usurped by Henry, base brother unto king Peter.

JOHN HERDWICKE, Esq. born at Lindley in this county, was a very low man (stature is no standard of stoutness) but of great valour, courage, and strength. This is he, though the tradition goeth by an unknown name, by whose good conduct, Henry earl of Richmond, afterwards king Henry the Seventh, in the battle of Bosworth, got the advantage of ground, wind, and sun, each singly considerable, but little less than an army in themselves when all put together.[*] Besides, he assisted him with the service of many men and horses. He died 1511, leaving six daughters and co-heirs; and was buried at Nuneaton in Warwickshire.

JOHN POULTNEY, born in Little Sheppey, was herein remarkable, that in his sleep he did usually rise out of his bed, dress himself, open the doors, walk round about the fields, and return to his bed not wakened. Sometimes he would rise in his sleep, take a staff, fork, or any other kind of weapon that was next his hand, and therewith lay about him, now striking, now defending himself, as if he were then encountered or charged with an adversary, not knowing (being awaked) what had passed. He afterwards went to sea with that famous but unfortunate Sir Hugh Willoughby, knight, and was (together with all the fleet) frozen to death in the north-east passage, about Nova Zembla.[†]

HENRY NOEL, Esquire.—I will incur the reader's deserved displeasure, if he appear not most memorable in his generation. He was younger son to Sir Andrew Noel, of Dalby in this county, who for person, parentage, grace, gesture, valour, and many other excellent parts (amongst which, skill in music), was of the first rank in the Court. And though his lands and livelihood were small, having nothing known certain but his annuity and pension as gentleman to queen Elizabeth, yet in state, pomp, magnificence, and expences, did ever equalize the barons of great worth. If any demand whence this proceeded, the Spanish proverb answers him,

"That which cometh from above, let no man question."

Being challenged by an Italian gentleman to play at *baloun,* he so heated his blood, that, falling into a fever, he died thereof, and, by her majesty's appointment, was buried in the Abbey of Westminster, and chapel of St. Andrew, anno 1596.

LORD MAYORS.

1. Geffrey Fielding,* son of William Fielding, of Lutterworth, Mercer, 1452.
2. William Heriot, son of John Heriot, of Segrave, Draper, 1481.
3. Robert Billesdon, son of Alex. Billesdon, of Queeningsborough, Haberdasher, 1483.
4. Christoph. Draper, son of John Draper, of Melton-Mowbray, Ironmonger, 1566.
5. George Bolles, son of Thomas Bolles, of Newbold, Grocer, 1617.

SHERIFFS

OF LEICESTER AND WARWICK-SHIRE.

HEN. II.

Anno
1 Geffrey Clinton.
2 Robert Fitz Hugh.
3 Idem.
4 William de Bello Campo, et Robert Fitz Hardulph.
5 Bertram de Bulmer, et Raph Basset.
6 Raph Basset.
7 W. Basset, for Raph his brother.
8 Robert Fitz Geffrey, et William Basset.
9 William Basset.
10 Rap. Glanvil, et W. Basset.
11 William Basset, for five years.
16 Bert. de Verdun, for ten years.
26 Raph de Glanvil, et Bertram de Berder.
27 Raph de Glanvil, et Bert. de Verdun, Arn. de Burton, Arn. de Barton, et Adam de Aldedelega.
28 Raph de Glanvil, Adam de Aldedelega, Bertram de Verdun, A. de Barton.
29 Idem.

Anno
30 Raph de Glanvil, et Bertram de Verdun.
31 Raph de Glanvil, et Michael Belet.
32 Idem.
33 Idem.

RICH. I.

1 Michael Belet.
2 Hugh Bishop of Coventry.
3 Hugh Bardolph et Hugh Clarke.
4 Hugh Bp. of Coventry, Gilbert de Segrave, et Reginald Basset.
5 Reginald Basset.
6 Regin. Basset, et Gilbert Segrave.
7 Regin. Basset, Will. Aubein, et Gilb. Segrave.
8 Regin. Basset.
9 Regin. Basset, Will. Aubein, et Gilb. Segrave.
10 Robert Harecourt.

REX JOHAN.

1 Regin. Basset.
2 Robert Harecourt.
3 Rob. Harecourt, et Godfry de Liege.

* He was privy councillor to king Henry VI. and king Edward IV.—F.

Anno

4 William de Cantelupe.
   Robert de Poyer.
5 Robert Poyer.
6 Hugh Chaucomber, for
   four years.
10 Robert Roppest.
11 Idem.
12 William de Cantelupe.
   Rob. Poyer.
13 Rob. Poyer, for five years.

HEN. III.

2 Will. de Cantelupe, et
   Phil. Kniton.
3 Philip de Kniton.
4 Idem.
5 Will. de Cantelupe, et
   Will. de Luditon.
6 Will. de Luditon.
7 Idem.
8 John Russell, et
   John Winterborne.
9 Rob. Lupus.
10 Idem.
11 Idem.
12 Will. Stutewill, et
   Will. Ascellis.
13 Will. Ascellis.
14 Stephen. de Segrave, et
   Will. Edmonds.
15 Will. Edmonds.
16 Idem.
17 Steph. de Segrave.
   Joh. de Ripariis.
18 Raph Bray.
19 Raph Fitz Nichol.
   Raph Brewedon.
20 Raph et Will. Erleg.
21 Will. de Lucy.
22 Idem.
23 Hugh Pollier, et
   Philip Ascett.
24 Hugh Pollier, for eight
   years.
32 Baldwin Paunton.
33 Idem.
34 Philip Murmuny.

Anno

35 Idem.
36 Idem.
37 Will. Maunsel, for four
   years.
41 Alan Swinford.
42 Anketill Martivaus.
43 Idem.
44 Will. Bagot, for twelve
   years.
56 Will. Morteyn, et
   Will. Bagot.

EDW. I.

1 William Mortimer.
2 Idem.
3 Idem.
4 William Hamelin.
5 Idem.
6 Idem.
7 Tho. de Hasele, et
   Robert Verdon.
8 Robert Verdon, et Osb.
   Bereford, for five years.
13 Rob. Verdon, Osbert Bereford, et Tho. Farendon.
14 Idem.
15 Tho. Farendon, et
   Foulk Lucy.
16 Foulk Lucy.
17 William Bonvill.
18 Idem.
19 Stephen Baber.
20 Idem.
21 Steph. Baber, et
   Will. de Castello.
22 Will. de Castello, for five
   years.
27 John Broughton.
28 Idem.
29 Philip Gayton.
30 Idem.
31 John Deane, et
   Richard Herehus.
32 Idem.
33 Idem.
34 Richard Whitnere.
35 Idem.

Anno   EDW. II.

1 John Deane, et
     Geffrey Segrave.
2 Richard Herthull.
3 Idem.
4 John Deane.
5 Idem.
6 John Olney.
7 Idem.
8 William Trussell.
9 Idem.
10 Walter Beauchamp.
11 Walter Beauchamp, et
     Will. Nevill.
12 Raph Beler.
13 William Nevill.
14 Thomas le Rous.
15 Idem.
16
17 Hen. Nottingham, Rob.
     Morin, et Oliver Walleis.
18 Idem.
19 Idem.

EDW. III.

1 Roger Aylesbury.

Anno

2 Thomas Blancfront.
3 Robert Burdet.
4 Rob. Burdet, et
     Roger la Zouch.
5 Roger Aylesbury.
6 Idem.
7 Hen. Hockley, et
     Roger de la Zouch.
8 Roger de la Zouch, for
     seven years.
15 William Peito.
16 Robert Bereford.
17 John Wallis.
18 Idem.
19 Tho. Beauchamp, Earl of
     Warwick, for twenty-
     five years.
44 John Peach.
45 William Catesby.
46 Richard Harthull.
47 Roger Hillary.
48 John Boyvill.
49 John Burdet.
50 William Breton.
51 Richard Harthull.

SHERIFFS OF LEICESTER AND WARWICK.

RICHARD II.

Anno	Name and Arms.	Place.
1	Roger Perewich.	
2	J. de Bermingham.	
	Per pale indented Arg. and S.	
3	Williel. Flamvil . . .	Aston, Leic.
	Arg. a manche Az.	
4	Thomas Ralegh . . .	Farnborough.
	Arg. semé of croslets G. a cross moline S.	
5	T. de Bermingham . .	*ut prius.*
6	Willielm. Baggot.	
7	Idem.	
8	Joh. Bermingham . .	*ut prius.*
9	Jo. Calveleigh, mil.	
	Arg. a fess G. between three calves S.	
10	Johannes Parker . . .	Olney, Warw.
11	Richardus Ashby.	
	Az. a chevron Erm. between three leopards' heads O.	

Anno	Name.	Place.

12 Williel. Flamvil . . . *ut prius.*
13 Ado. de Lichfeld.
14 Rob. de Harington.
   S. a fret Arg.
15 Johann. Mallory . . . Swinford, Leic.
   O. three lions passant gardant S.
16 Th. de Woodford . . Sproxton, Leic.
   S. three leopards' heads feasant G. three flower-de-luces
   Arg.
17 Thomas Ondeby.
18 Robertus Veer.
   Quarterly G. and O. a mullet Arg.
19 [AMP.] Henricus Nevill.
20 Robert Goushul.
21 Johan. Eynesford.
22 Adomar de Lichfeld.

HEN IV.

1 Johan. Berkely, mil. . Wymondham.
   G. a chevron betwixt ten cinquefoils Arg.
2 Hen. Nevill, mil. . . . *ut prius.*
3 Alex. Trussel, mil.
   Arg. fretty G. ; on every point a bezant.
4 Johannes Blaket . . . Nowesly, Leic.
   Az. a bend cotised between six cross croslets fitchée O.
5 Idem. . . . . . . *ut prius.*
6 Jon. Berkley, mil. . . *ut prius.*
7 Thomas Lucy . . . Charlcot, Warw.
   G. semé de croslets, three lucies hauriant Arg.
8 Johannes Parr.
   Arg. two bars Az. a border engrailed S.
9 Hen. Nevill, mil. . . *ut prius.*
10 Will. Brokesby.
   Undée Arg. and S. ; a canton G.
11 Robertus Castell . . . Withibroke.
   G. two bars and a castle in a canton Arg.
12 Barth. Brokesby. . . *ut prius.*

HEN. V.

1 Tho. Crewe, arm.
2 Rich. Hastings, mil.
   Arg. a manche S.
3 Tho. Burdet, mil. . . Newton Burdet.
   Az. on two bars O. six martlets G.
4 Johannes Mallory . . *ut prius.*
5 Will. Bishopston.
   O. three bends S. ; a canton Erm.
6 Johann. Salveyn.
7 Barth. Brookesby . . *ut prius.*

Anno   Name.   Place.

 8 Tho. Ardington, et
   Tho. Maureward   .   .   Cole-Orton, Leic.
      Az. a fess Arg. between three cinquefoils O.

      HEN. VI.

 1 Rich. Hastings, mil.   .   *ut prius.*
 2 Humph. Stafford   .   .   Huncote, Leic.
      O. a chevron G. and a quarter Erm.
 3 Johann. Mallory   .   .   *ut prius.*
 4 Richar. Cloddale.
 5 Rich. Hastings, mil.   .   *ut prius.*
 6 Thomas Stanley.
      Arg. on a bend Az. three bucks' heads O.
 7 Willielmus Payto   .   .   Chesterton.
      Barry of six pieces Arg. and G. per pale indented and
      counterchanged.
 8 Nichol. Ruggeley.
 9 Humphr. Stafford   .   .   *ut prius.*
10 W. Mountford, mil.
      Bendy of ten pieces, O. and Az.
11 Rich. Hastings, mil.   .   *ut prius.*
12 Thom. Foulshurst.
13 Thom. Ardington.
14 Willielmus Lucy   .   .   *ut prius.*
15 Wil. Payto, mil.   .   .   *ut prius.*
16 Robertus Ardern.
      Erm. a fess checky O. and Az.
17 Hum. Stafford, mil.   .   Grafton.
18 Laurenc. Berkley   .   .   *ut prius.*
19 Thomas Ashby   .   .   Lowesby.
      Arms, *ut prius.*
20 Will. Mountford   .   .   *ut prius.*
21 W. Bermingham .   .   .   *ut prius.*
   Lawr. Sherrard   .   .   Stapleford, Leic.
      Arg. a chevron G. betwixt three torteaux.
22 Idem.   .   .   .   .   .   *ut prius.*
23 Rob. Harecourt   .   .   Bosworth, L.
      O. two bars G.
24 Tho. Erdington   .   .   Barrow, L.
      Arg. two lions passant O.
25 Th. Everingham.
      G. a lion rampant vairy, couronné O.
26 Tho. Porter, arm. et
   Will. Purefoy, arm.   .   Drayton, L.
      S. three pair of gauntlets clipping (or joined together)
      Arg.
27 Will. Purefoy.   .   .   *ut prius.*

Anno	Name.	Place.
28	Willielm. Lucy . . .	*ut prius.*
29	W. Mountford, mil. .	*ut prius.*
30	Rob. Motun, mil. . .	Pekleton, L.
	Arg. a cinquefoil Az.	
31	W. Bermingham . .	*ut prius.*
32	Leonard Hastings . .	Kerby, L.
	Arms, *ut prius.*	
33	Thomas Berkley . .	*ut prius.*
34	Williel. Hastings . .	*ut prius.*
35	Tho. Walsh, arm. . .	Wanlip, L.
	G. two bars gemews, a bend Arg.	
36	Tho. Maston, arm.	
37	H. Filongley, arm. . .	Filongley, Warw.
38	Edm. Mountford . .	*ut prius.*

EDW. IV.

1	[AMP.] Tho. Ferrers, arm.	
2	Joh. Grevil, arm.	
	S. a bordure and cross engrailed O. ; thereon five pellets.	
3	Idem.	*ut prius.*
4	Will. Harecourt . . .	*ut prius.*
5	Joh. Huggford, arm.	
6	Th. Throgmorton . .	Coughton, W.
7	Rad. Woodford, arm. .	Knipton, L.
	G. on a chevron Arg. three bars gemellée S.	
8	Edw. Rawleigh, mil. .	*ut prius.*
9	Tho. Ferrers, mil. . .	*ut prius.*
10	Joh. Grevil, mil. . .	*ut prius.*
11	Sim. Mountford . . .	*ut prius.*
12	Will. Motun, arm. . .	*ut prius.*
13	Joh. Higgford, arm. . .	*ut prius.*
14	Joh. Grevil, mil. . . .	*ut prius.*
15	Will. Lucy, arm. . . .	*ut prius.*
16	W. Trussell, mil. . .	Elmesthorp, L.
17	Johan. Bransitz.	
18	Joh. Grevill, mil. . .	*ut prius.*
19	Thom. Poultney . . .	Misterton, L.
	Arg. a fess indented G. ; in chief three leopards' heads S.	
20	Rich. Boughton . . .	Lauford, W.
	S. three crescents O.	
21	Thomas Cokesey.	
22	Edward Felding . . .	Newnham, W.
	Arg. on a fess Az. three lozenges O.	

RICH. III.

1	Thom. Entwysel.	
	Arg. on a bend S. three martlets of the field.	

Anno   Name.   Place.

2 Humph. Beaufort . . Guiesclif, W.
  Erm. on a bend Az. three cinquefoils O.
3 R. Broughton, arm. et . *ut prius.*
  R. Throgmorton . . . *ut prius.*

HENRY VII.

1 Johannes Digby.
  Az. a flower-de-luce Arg.
2 Henricus Lisle.
  O. a fess betwixt two chevrons S.
3 R. Throgmorton . . . *ut prius.*
4 Will. Lucy, mil. . . . *ut prius.*
5 Tho. Brereton, arm.
  Arg. two bars S.
6 Johan. Villars, arm. . . Brokesby, L.
  Arg. a cross G. five escalops O.
7 R. Throgmorton . . . *ut prius.*
8 Tho. Pulteney, mil. . . *ut prius.*
9 Rad. Shirley, mil. . . Staunton, L.
  Paly of six O. and Az. a canton Erm.
10 Johan. Villars, arm. . *ut prius.*
11 Ed. Rawleigh, mil. . . *ut prius.*
12 W. Brokesby.
13 Tho. Nevill, arm. . . *ut prius.*
14 Rich. Pudsey, mil.
15 Joh. Villars, arm. . . *ut prius.*
16 Tho. Hasilrig, arm. . . Nouseley, L.
  Arg. a chevron betwixt three hazel-leaves V.
17 Edw. Belknap, arm.
18 Nich. Mallory, arm. . *ut prius.*
19 Henricus Lysle, arm. . *ut prius.*
20 Nich. Brome, arm.
21 H. Willoughby.
  O. on two bars G. three water bougets Arg.
22 Edw. Raleigh, mil. . . *ut prius.*
23 Tho. Trussel, arm. . . *ut prius.*
24 Will. Skevington . . Skevington.
  Arg. three bulls' heads erased S.

HENRY VIII.

1 Simon Digby, arm. . . *ut prius.*
2 Johan. Aston, mil.
3 Maur. Berkley, arm. . . *ut prius.*
4 Will. Turpin, arm. . . Knaptoft, L.
  G. on a bend Arg. three lions' heads erased S.
5 [AMP.] Edw. Ferers, mil.
6 Johan. Digby, mil. . . *ut prius.*
7 Will. Skevington . . *ut prius.*

Anno	Name.	Place.
8	Maur. Berkley, mil. . .	*ut prius.*
9	Simon Digby, arm. . .	*ut prius.*
10	Edw. Ferrers, mil. . .	*ut prius.*
11	Hen. Willoughby . .	*ut prius.*
12	Edw. Digby, arm. . .	*ut prius.*
13	Will. Skevington . .	*ut prius.*
14	Will. Browne, arm.	
15	Edw. Conway, arm. . .	Ragley, W.

S. on a bend between two cotises Arg. a rose G. between two annulets of the first.

16	Tho. Lucy, mil. . . .	*ut prius.*
17	H. Willoughby, mil. .	*ut prius.*
18	G. Throgmorton, mil. .	*ut prius.*
19	Tho. Pultney, mil. . .	*ut prius.*
20	Rog. Ratcliffe, mil.	

Arg. a bend engrailed S.

21	Rich. Verney, arm.	

Az. on a cross Arg. five mullets G.

22	Christ. Villars, arm. .	*ut prius.*
23	Johan. Villars, mil. . .	*ut prius.*
24	Joh. Harrington . . .	*ut prius.*
25	Johan. Audley, arm.	
26	Regin. Digby, arm. . .	*ut prius.*
27	W. Broughton, arm.	
28	Walt. Smith, arm.	
29	Johan. Villars, mil. . .	*ut prius.*
30	Tho. Nevill, arm.	

G. a saltire Erm.

31	Johan. Digby, arm. . .	*ut prius.*
32	Rich. Catesby, arm.	

Arg. two lions passant S. couronné O.

33	Rog. Wigston, arm. . .	Wolston, W.
34	Fulco Grevil, mil. . .	Beachamp, W.

S. a border and cross engrailed O. thereon five pellets.

35	G. Throgmorton . . .	*ut prius.*
36	Regin. Digby, arm. . .	*ut prius.*
37	Rich. Catesby, mil. . .	*ut prius.*
38	Fran. Poultney, et . .	*ut prius.*
	Will. Leigh, arm. . .	*ut prius.*

G. a cross engrailed Arg.; in the first quarter a lozenge O.

EDWARD VI.

1	Fulco Grevill, mil. . .	*ut prius.*
2	Ambros. Cave, mil.	

Az. frettée Arg.

3	Rich. Munnar, mil.	
4	Edw. Hastings, mil. .	*ut prius.*

Anno	Name.	Place.
5	W. Wigesten, arm.	*ut prius.*
6	Tho. Nevill, mil.	*ut prius.*

PHIL. et MAR.

1	R. Throgmorton	*ut prius.*
2	Tho. Hastings, mil.	*ut prius.*
3	Edw. Grevill, mil.	*ut prius.*
4	Fran. Shirley, arm.	*ut prius.*
5	W. Wigeston, mil.	*ut prius.*
6	Bran. Cave, arm.	*ut prius.*

ELIZ. REG.

1	Tho. Lucy, arm.	*ut prius.*
2	Will. Skeffington	*ut prius.*
3	Tho. Nevill, mil.	*ut prius.*
4	Rich. Verney, mil.	*ut prius.*
5	Johan. Fisher, arm.	Pakington.

Per bend G. and O. a griffin rampant counterchanged within a border vairy.

6 Williel. Devereux.

Arg. a fess G.; in chief three torteaux.

7 Geor. Turpin, mil. . . *ut prius.*

8 Fran. Smith, arm. . . Ashby, L.

Arg. a cross G. betwixt four peacocks proper.

The reader may perceive some (not considerable) difference betwixt this our catalogue and the printed one set forth by Mr. Burton in his description of this shire. I will neither condemn his, nor commend my own; but leave both to the examination of others.

RICHARD II.

16. THOMAS de WOODFORD.—He was the eldest son of Sir Robert de Woodford, a wealthy knight, who, dying before his father, left five sons, viz. John, Walter, Humphrey, Ralph, and John. Sir Robert their grandfather, out of design to perpetuate his posterity (adventured in five bottoms) made all his grand-children in effect elder brothers, dividing his vast estate amongst them; an equal unequal partition, to be injurious to the heir (without his demerit), that he might be bountiful to his other brethren: but it thrived accordingly. For that great family (which had long continued in great account and estate), by reason of this division, in short space utterly decayed; not any part of their lands (thus disposed) now in the tenure of the name, and some of the male heirs descended from the five bre-thren now living in a low condition;* and no wonder they soon made a hand of all, where the thumb was weakened to strengthen the four fingers.

* Burton, in his Description of Leicestershire, p. 264.

HENRY V.

3. THOMAS BURDET, Mil.—The sameness of name and nearness of kindred giveth me here a just occasion to insist on a memorable passage concerning Thomas Burdet, esquire, grandchild and heir to Sir Thomas here named. When as king Edward the Fourth (in his absence) had killed a fat white buck in his park at Arrow in Warwickshire, which he greatly esteemed; upon the first hearing of it, wished the buck's head and horns in his belly that moved the king to kill it. Upon the misconstruing of which words, he was accused of treason; attainted, and beheaded, 18 Edward IV. 1477; and was buried in the Grey Friers in London.

Thus far our English Chronicles with joint consent agree in the same tune; but I meet with one author, reaching one note higher than all the rest, adding as followeth: "These words spoken and so wrested were the colour of his death; but the true cause was the hard conceit and opinion which the king had of him, for that he had ever been a faithful friend and true councillor to George duke of Clarence his brother, between whom there had been bitter enmity.*

Whatsoever was the cause of such severity against him, Burdet patiently and cheerfully took his death, affirming he had a bird in his breast (his own innocency) that sung comfort unto him.

HENRY VI.

2. HUMPHREY STAFFORD.—Being afterwards knighted, he was by king Henry the Sixth made governor of Calais; and coming over into England, was slain by Jack Cade: but God hath a blessing for those whom rebels curse. Sir Humphrey Stafford, his grandchild, fixed himself at Blatherwick in Northamptonshire, where his posterity doth flourish to this day.

34. WILLIAM HASTINGS. — The reader needeth not my dim candle to direct him to this illustrious person. He was son to Sir Leonard Hastings (sheriff two years before); and was he whom king Edward the Fourth, or rather Edward Plantagenet (because more in his humane than royal capacity) so delighted in, that he made him his lord chamberlain, Baron Hastings of Ashby de la Zouch, &c. As he loved the king very well, so after this king's death he is charged to have loved Jane Shore too well; and Richard Duke of Gloucester, perceiving him to obstruct the way to his ambitions designs, ordered his removal, causing him to be beheaded, 1 Edward V. As when living he was dear, so being dead his corpse lies near to Edward IV.; buried under a very fair monument in Windsor Chapel. He was grandfather to George Hastings, first earl of Huntingdon.

* Burton, in the Description of Leicestershire, p. 201.

EDWARD VI.

4. EDWARD HASTINGS, Mil.—Queen Mary, much delighting in his devotion, created him baron of Loughborough. He founded and endowed a handsome hospital at Stoke Pogeis in Buckinghamshire, whither (after the queen's death), weary of the world, he retired himself, and therein died without issue.

The foresaid (and that a very fair) town of Loughborough hath since again afforded the title of a baron to a younger branch of the same honourable family, Henry Hastings, second son to Henry (second of that christian name) earl of Huntingdon, who by his virtues doth add to the dignity of his extraction.*

QUEEN ELIZABETH.

5. JOHN FISHER, Arm.—His father Thomas Fisher, alias Hawkins, being a colonel under the duke of Somerset in Musselborough Field, behaved himself right valiantly, and took a Scotchman prisoner, who gave a griffin for his arms. Whereupon the said duke conferred on him the arms of his captive, to be borne within a border vairy, in relation to a prime coat which the said duke (the granter thereof) quartered as descended from the Lord Beauchamps of Hatch.†

SHERIFFS OF LEICESTERSHIRE ALONE.

ELIZ. REG.

Anno	Name and Arms.	Place.
9	Geo. Sherard, arm.	Stapleford.
	Arg. a chevron G. betwixt three torteaux.	
10	Hen. Poole, arm.	
11	Brian. Cave, arm.	
	Az. frettée Arg.	
12	Jac. Harington, mil.	Pekleton.
	S. a fret Arg.	
13	Geo. Hastings, mil.	
	Arg. a maunche S.	
14	Fr. Hastings, arm.	
	The same, with due difference.	
15	Edw. Leigh, arm.	
	G. a cross engrailed Arg. ; in the first quarter a lozenge O.	
16	Geor. Turpin, mil.	Knaptoft.
	G. on a bend Arg. three lions' heads erased S.	
17	Rog. Villers, arm.	
	Arg. on a cross G. five escalops O.	

* The Title having again become extinct, was revived in 1780, in the person of Alexander Wedderburne, Esq. an eminent Lawyer, afterwards Lord High Chancellor of Great Britain, and in 1801 elevated to the earldom of Rosslyn.—ED.

† Mr. Dugdale, in the Description of Warwickshire, p. 365.

Anno   Name.   Place.

18 Tho. Skevington . . . Skevington.
    Arg. three bulls' heads erased S.
19 Nic. Beaumont, arm. . Cole-Orton.
    Az. semé de flower-de-luces, a lion rampant O.
20 Tho. Ashby, arm.
    A chevron Erm. betwixt three leopards' heads.
21 Tho. Cave, arm. . . . *ut prius.*
22 Fran. Hastings, arm. . *ut prius.*
23 Geor. Purefey, arm. . . Drayton.
24 Brian Cave, arm. . . . Ingersby.
    Arms, *ut prius*, with due difference.
25 Andr. Noell, arm. . . Dalby.
    O. fretty G. ; a canton Erm.
26 Hen. Turvile, arm. . . Aston.
    G. three chevrons vairy.
27 Will. Turpin, arm. . . *ut prius.*
28 Anth. Faunt, arm. . . Foston.
    Arg. crusulé fitché, a lion rampant G. with due difference.
29 Will. Cave, arm. . . . Pickwell.
30 Tho. Skeffington . . . *ut prius.*
    —Belgrave . . . . Belgrave.
    G. a chevron Erm. betwixt three mascles A.
31 Edw. Turvile, arm. . . Thurlston.
    Arms, *ut prius*, with due difference.
32 Geor. Purefey, arm. . . *ut prius.*
33 Geor. Villers, arm. . . Brokesby.
    Arms, *ut prius.*
34 Thom. Cave, arm. . . *ut prius.*
35 Will. Turpin, arm. . . *ut prius.*
36 Hen. Beaumont . . . *ut prius.*
37 Williel. Cave, arm. . . *ut prius.*
38 Henri. Cave, arm. . . *ut prius.*
39 Will. Skipwith, arm. . Cores.
    Arg. three bars G. ; in chief a greyhound cursant S.
40 Will. Digby, arm. . . Welby.
    Az. a fleur-de-lis Arg.
41 T. Skeffington, arm. . *ut prius.*
42 Rog. Smith, arm. . . Withcock.
    G. on a chevron O. between three bezants three croslets
      formée fitchée.
43 Georg. Ashby, arm. . . Queenby.
44 Tho. Humfreys . . . Swepston.

       JAC. REX.

1 Will. Faunt, mil. . . Fauston.
    Arms, *ut prius.*
2 Will. Noell, arm. . . Wellsborough.
    Arms, *ut prius.*

Anno	Name.	Place.

3 Basil. Brook, mil. . . Lubbenham.
4 Tho. Nevill, mil. . . . Holt.
  G. a saltire Erm.
5 Hen. Hastings, mil. . . LEICESTER.
  Arms, *ut prius.*
6 Will. Villers, arm. . . Brokesby.
7 Joh. Plummer, arm. . . Marston.
  Erm. a bend vairy, cotised S.
8 T. Beaumont, mil. . . Cole-Orton.
9 Brian Cave, mil. . . . Ingersby.
10 Tho. Hasilrig, mil. . . Nowsley.
  Arg. a chevron betwixt three hazel-leaves V.
11 Tho. Staveley, arm.
  Barry of eight Arg. and G. ; over all a flower-de-luce S.
12 Wolstan. Dixy, mil. . Bosworth.
  Az. a lion rampant and chief O.
13 Will. Faunt, mil. . . *ut prius.*
14 W. Halford, mil. . . Welham.
15 Edw. Hartopp, arm. . Buckminster.
  S. a chevron betwixt three otters Arg.
16 W. Jerveis, arm. . . . Peatling.
  Wil. Roberts, mil. . . Sutton.
  Per pale Arg. and G. a lion rampant S.
17 Johan. Cave, arm. . . Pickwell.
18 Alex. Cave, mil. . . . Bagrave.
19 Richard. Halford . . Wistowe.
20 Geo. Bennet, arm.
21 Johan. Bale, mil. . . Carleton-Curley.
  Per pale V. and G. an eagle displayed Arg. beaked and
  armed O.
22 Hen. Shirley, mil. . . Stanton.
  Paly of six O. and Az.; a canton Erm.

CAR. REX.

1 Hartopp, mil. . . . . . *ut prius.*
2 Nathan. Lacy, arm.
3 Georg. Ashby, arm.
4 Er. de la Fontaine, mil.
  G. a bend O. ; in the sinister chief a cinquefoil Erm.
5 W. Wollaston, arm.
  S. three mullets pierced Arg.
6 Joh. Bainbrigge, arm. . Lockinton.
  Arg. a chevron embattled betwixt three battle-axes S.
7 Johann. Brokesby . . *ut prius.*
8 Joh. St. John, mil.
  Arg. on a chief G. two mullets O.
9 Tho. Burton, bart. . . Stockerston.
  S. a chevron between three owls Arg. crowned O.

10 Fran. Sanders, arm.
    Partie per chevron Arg. and S. three elephants' heads
      counterchanged.
11 Joh. Poultney, arm. . . Misterton.
    Arg. a fess indented G. ; three leopards' heads in chief S.
12 Hen. Skipwith, mil. . *ut prius.*
13 Rich. Roberts, mil.
14 Joh. Whatton, arm.
15 Will. Halford, arm.
16 Johan. Pate, arm.
17 Archdale Palmer, arm.
18 Henry Hastings.
19 Peter Temple.
20 Arthur Staveley.
21 Johan. Stafford, arm.
22 Will. Hewett, arm.
    S. a chevron counterbattellée betwixt three owls Arg.

QUEEN ELIZABETH.

14. FRANCIS HASTINGS. — I believe him the same person
with Sir Francis Hastings, fourth son of Francis, second earl of
Huntingdon of that surname, to whose many children Mr. Camden giveth this commendation, " that they agreed together in
brotherly love, though not in religion ; "* some Protestants, others
Papists, all zealous in their persuasion. Our Sir Francis wrote
a learned book in the defence of our religion (rather carped at
than confuted by Parsons in his " Three Conversions") ; and
was an eminent benefactor to Emanuel College. But, if I
be mistaken in the man, and these prove two different persons, the reader will excuse me for taking occasion, by this
his namesake and near kinsman, of entering here the memorial
of so worthy a gentleman.

28. ANTHONY FAUNT, Esquire.—He was a gentleman of
a comely person and great valour (son unto William Faunt,
apprentice of the law of the Inner Temple, one of great
learning and wisdom) ; and had in the Low Countries served
under William prince of Orange, where he gained much martial experience. Returning into his country, he underwent
some offices therein with good esteem, being this year chosen
sheriff of the shire. In the next year (which was 1588)
he was chosen lieutenant-general of all the forces of this shire,
to resist the Spanish invasion. But his election being crossed
by Henry earl of Huntingdon (lord lieutenant of the county)
he fell into so deep a fit of melancholy, that he died soon
after.†

* In his Elizabeth, anno 1560.   † Burton, in Leicestershire, p. 105.

39. WILLIAM SKIPWITH, Esq.—He was afterwards deservedly knighted, being a person of much valour, judgment, learning, and wisdom, dexterous at the making fit and acute epigrams, poesies, mottoes, and devices, but chiefly at impresses, neither so apparent that every rustic might understand them, nor so obscure that they needed an *Œdipus* to interpret them.*

THE FAREWELL.

Being now to take my leave of this county, it is needless to wish it a Friday market (the Leap-day therein, and it is strange there should be none in so spacious a shire), presuming that defect supplied in the vicinage. Rather I wish that the leprosy may never return into this county; but if it should return (we carry the seeds of all sins in our souls, sicknesses in our bodies,) I desire that the lands may also (without prejudice to any) return to the hospital of Burton Lazars in this shire, if not entire, yet in such a proportion as may comfortably maintain the lepers therein.

WORTHIES OF LEICESTERSHIRE WHO HAVE FLOURISHED SINCE THE TIME OF FULLER.

Dr. John AIKIN, surgeon and miscellaneous author; born at Kibworth 1747; died 1822.

William BEVERIDGE, bishop of St. Asaph, orientalist, and voluminous writer on theological and philological subjects; born at Barrow-upon-Soar 1638; died 1708.

F. BROKESBY, nonjuring divine, biographer of Dodwell; born at Stoke; died 1718.

William CAVE, son of John Cave, writer and preacher, author of " Historia Literaria;" born at Pickwell 1637; died 1713.

William CHESELDEN, anatomist and lithotomist, and professional author; born at Burrow-on-the-Hill 1688; died 1752.

Roger COTES, mathematician and astronomer, a friend of Sir Isaac Newton; born at Burbach 1682; died 1716.

Joseph CRADOCK, miscellaneous writer, and author of " Memoirs;" born at Leicester 1741-2; died 1826.

Luke CRANWELL, nonconformist divine and author; born at Loughborough; died 1683.

Richard DAWES, author of " Miscellanea Critica;" born at Stapleton 1708; died 1766.

Dr. Richard FARMER, divine, elegant scholar, author on the Learning of Shakspeare; born at Leicester 1735; died 1797.

* Burton, in Leicestershire, p. 77.

George Fox, founder of Quakerism; born at Fenny Drayton 1624; died 1690.

Robert HALL, A.M. orator and dissenting divine; born at Arnsby; died 1831.

Ralph HEATHCOTE, divine, projector of the General Biographical Dictionary; born at Barrow-upon-Soar 1721; died 1795.

John HENLEY, "Orator Henley," eccentric divine; born at Melton Mowbray 1692; died 1756.

John HOWE, nonconformist divine and author; born at Loughborough 1630; died 1705.

Elizabeth JERVIS, wife of Dr. Samuel Johnson; born at Peatling; died 1753.

Dr. David JENNINGS, learned dissenting divine and author; born at Kibworth 1691; died 1762.

Daniel LAMBERT, weighed, at his death in 1809, 739lbs.; born at Leicester 1770.

William LILLY, astrologer, the "Sydrophel" of Butler's Hudibras; born at Diseworth 1602; died 1681.

Sir John MOORE, founder of Appleby School, lord mayor of London in 1681; born at Appleby.

Christopher PACKE, lord mayor of London, republican; born at Prestwould; died 1682.

David PAPILLON, author on Fortification; born at Papillon Hall in Lubbenham.

Ambrose PHILLIPS, pastoral poet and dramatist; born 1671; died 1749.

Dr. Richard PULTENEY, eminent physician, conchologist, and botanist; born at Loughborough 1730; died 1801.

William SHERARD, founder of botanical lecture at Oxford; born at Bushby 1659; died 1728.

John SIMPSON, dissenter, biblical critic; born at Leicester 1746.

Thomas STAVELEY, lawyer, author of "History of Churches;" born at East Langton 1626; died 1683.

Styan THIRLBY, critic, editor of Justin Martyr; born at Leicester 1692; died 1753.

John THROSBY, parish clerk, tourist of Leicestershire, and historian of his native town; born at Leicester 1746; died 1803.

William WHISTON, learned and ingenious but variable divine, and clever mathematician; born at Norton-juxta-Twycross 1667; died 1752.

Hugh WORTHINGTON, eloquent dissenting divine; born at Leicester 1752.

Sir Nathan WRIGHTE, lord keeper; born at Barwell; died 1721.

*** This county has been fertile in historians. So early as 1622 Mr. Wm. Burton published a Description of Leicestershire; in 1777 Mr. J. Throsby brought out the Memoirs of the Town and County; and so late as 1831, a Topographical History of the County was published in one vol. 8vo. by the Rev. J. Curtis. There have also appeared various publications of a local nature; as Throsby's Views (1790); Macaulay's History of Claybrook (1791); Harrod's History of Market Harborough (1808); Hanbury's Account of Church Langton; Rouse's Account of the Charities at Market Harborough; Histories of Aston Flamvill, Burbach, Hinckley, &c. But the most extended history of this or of any other county, was produced by Mr. John Nichols, in four thick imperial volumes. It is a concentration (as he himself observes) of all that had been previously published; with the addition of private documents, communications, memoirs, monumental inscriptions, family anecdotes, pedigrees, &c.; in short of every thing (important or non-important) which was calculated to feed the vanity of subscribers, or gratify the family pride of personal friends. While the motto, assumed for his family arms, " Labor ipse voluptas," was here truly realized, he entirely lost sight of the valuable adage of the Roman poet, " Brevis esse laboro,"—so admirably displayed in the works of that great exemplar of topography, Dr. Whittaker.

LINCOLNSHIRE.

THIS county, in fashion, is like a bended bow, the sea making the back, the rivers Welland and Humber the two horns thereof, whilst Trent hangeth down from the latter like a broken string, as being somewhat of the shortest. Such persecute the metaphor too much, who compare the river Witham (whose current is crooked) unto the arrow crossing the middle thereof.

It extendeth 60 miles from south to north, not above 40 in the middle and broadest part thereof. Being too voluminous to be managed entire, it is divided into three parts, each of them co-rival in quantity with some smaller shires; Holland on the south-east, Kesteven on the south-west, and Lindsey on the north to them both.

Holland (that is *Hoyland*, or *Hayland*, from the plenty of hay growing therein), may seem the reflection of the opposite Holland in the Netherlands, with which it sympathized in the fruitfulness, and low and wet situation. Here the brackishness of the water, and the grossness of the air, is recompensed by the goodness of the earth, abounding with dairies and pasture. And as " God hath " (to use the Apostle's phrase) " tempered the body together,"* not making it all eye or all ear (nonsense that the whole should be but one sense), but assigning each member the proper office thereof; so the same Providence hath so wisely blended the benefits of this county, that take collectively Lincolnshire, and it is defective in nothing.

NATURAL COMMODITIES.

PIKES.

They are found plentifully in this shire, being the fresh-water wolves; and therefore an old pond pike is a dish of more state than profit to the owners, seeing a pike's belly is a little fish-pond, where lesser of all sorts have been contained. Sir Francis Bacon † alloweth it (though tyrants generally be short-lived) the survivor of all fresh-water fish, attaining to forty years, and some beyond the seas have trebled that term. The flesh thereof must needs be fine and wholesome, if it be true what is affirmed,

---

* 1 Cor. xii. 24.   † In his History of Life and Death.

that in some sort it cheweth the cud; and yet the less and middle size pikes * are preferred for sweetness before those that are greater. It breedeth but once † (whilst other fishes do often) in a year; such the providence of nature, preventing their more multiplying, lest the waters should not afford subjects enough for their tyranny. For want of other fish, they will feed one on another; yea, what is four-footed shall be fish with them, if it once come to their jaws (biting sometimes for cruelty and revenge, as well as for hunger); and because we have publicly professed, that to delight as well as to inform is our aim in this book, let the ensuing story (though unwarranted with a cited author) find the reader's acceptance.

A cub fox, drinking out of the river Arnus in Italy, had his head seized on by a mighty pike, so that neither could free themselves, but were engrappled together. In this contest a young man runs into the water, takes them out both alive, and carrieth them to the duke of Florence, whose palace was hard by. The porter would not admit him, without promising to share his full half in what the duke should give him; to which he (hopeless otherwise of entrance) condescended. The duke, highly affected with the rarity, was about giving him a good reward; which the other refused, desiring his Highness would appoint one of his guard to give him a hundred lashes, that so his porter might have fifty, according to his composition. And here my intelligence leaveth me how much farther the jest was followed.

But to return to our English pikes, wherein this county is eminent, especially in that river which runneth by Lincoln, whence grew this proverb,

> " Witham pike
> England hath none like."

And hence it is that Mr. Drayton ‡ maketh this river, poetising in her praises, always concluding them,

> "Thus to her proper song the burden still she bare:
> Yet for my dainty pikes I am without compare."

I have done with these pikes, when I have observed (if I mistake not) a great mistake in Mr. Stowe, affirming that pickrels were brought over (as no natives of our land) into England at the same time with carps, and both about the beginning of the reign of king Henry the Eighth.§ Now if pickrels be the diminutives of pikes (as jacks of pickrels), which none, I conceive, will deny, they were here many hundred years since, and probably of the same seniority with the rivers of England; for I find, in the bill of fare made at the prodigious feast at the installing of George Nevil archbishop of York, anno 1466, that there were spent three hundred *lupi fluviatiles*, that is, river pikes, at that entertainment.‖ Now, seeing all are children before

---

* Mr. Walton, in his Complete Angler, p. 197.   † Idem, p. 199.
‡ Polyolbion, 25th Part, 111.   § In his Chronicle, p. 948.
‖ Bishop Godwin in his Catalogue of the Bishops of York.

they are men, and pikes pickrels at the first, pickrels were more anciently in England than that author affirmeth them.

WILD FOWL.

Lincolnshire may be termed the aviary of England, for the wild fowl therein; remarkable for their, 1. *Plenty;* so that sometimes, in the month of August, three thousand mallards, with birds of that kind, have been caught at one draught, so large and strong their nets; and the like must be the reader's belief. 2. *Variety;* no man (no not Gesmar himself) being able to give them their proper names, except one had gotten Adam's nomenclature of creatures. 3. *Deliciousness* ; wild fowl being more dainty and digestible than tame of the same kind, as spending their gross humour with their activity and constant motion in flying.

Now as the eagle is called *Jovis ales,* so here they have a bird which is called the king's bird, namely, *Knut's,* sent for hither out of Denmark, at the charge, and for the use, of Knut, or Canutus, king of England. If the plenty of birds have since been drained with the fens in this county, what Lincolnshire lacks in her former fowl, is supplied in flesh (more mutton and beef); and a large *first* makes amends for a less *second* course. But amongst all birds we must not forget

DOTTERELS.

This is *avis* γελοτοποῖος, a mirth-making bird, so ridiculously mimical, that he is easily caught (or rather catcheth himself) by his over-active imitation. There is a sort of apes in India, caught by the natives thereof after this manner : they dress a little boy in his sight, undress him again, leave all the child's apparel behind them in the place, and then depart a competent distance. The ape presently attireth himself in the same garments, till the child's clothes become his chains, putting off his feet by putting on his shoes, not able to run to any purpose, and so is soon taken.

The same humour, otherwise pursued, betrayeth the dotterels. As the fowler stretcheth forth his arms and legs going towards the bird, the bird extendeth his legs and wings approaching the fowler, till surprised in the net. But it is observed, that the foolisher the fowl or fish (woodcocks, dotterels, codsheads, &c.) the finer the flesh thereof.

FEATHERS.

It is pity to part Lancashire ticking (lately spoken of) and Lincolnshire feathers, making so good beds together. I cannot find the first beginning of feather-beds. The Latin word *pulvinar* for a cushion, pillow, or bolster, sheweth, that the entrails of such utensils amongst the Romans were made but of dust; and our English plain proverb, " de puerperis," (they are in the straw), shows feather-beds to be of no ancient use amongst the common sort of our nation; and beds of down (the cream of feathers) are more modern than they. The feathers of this county are very good (though not so soft as such as are imported from Bordeaux in France); and although a feather passeth for the emblem of lightness itself, they are heavy enough in their prices to such as buy any quantity; and daily grow dearer.

PIPPINS.

With these we will close the stomach of the reader, being concluded most cordial by physicians. Some conceive them to be of not above a hundred years seniority in England: however, they thrive best, and prove biggest (not Kentish excepted) in this county, particularly in Holland, and about Kirton therein, whence they have acquired addition of Kirton pippins, a wholesome and delicious apple; and I am informed that pippins graffed on a pippin stock are called *renates*, bettered in their generous nature by such double extraction.

FLEET HOUNDS.

In Latin called *petronii*, or *petrunculi*, from *petra* a rock, either because their feet are sound and solid (and therefore named Εὔποδες by Xenophon), or from the hard and rocky ground whereon they were accustomed to hunt. These, with much certainty of scent and quickness of feet, will run down a hare in a short time.

Janus Ulitius, a Dutchman, some fifteen years since came into England; and, though a man of the gown (employed in public affairs), for diversion he went down into this county, to spend one winter; where, conversing with some young gentlemen, he hunted twice a week with so great content, that the season (otherwise unpleasant) was past before he perceived how it went. Hear him expressing himself: " Sed et petrunculi illi, qui vestigiis eorum non minus celeriter quam sagaciter instant, haud facile trihorio minus leporem aliquem defatigant, ut in Lincolniensi montium æquijugi tractu aliquoties ipse vidi." And yet I assure you, the hares in this county on Ancaster Heath do (though lesser) far exceed in swiftness and subtilty of doubling those of the valleys and plains.

Such a *petronius*, or fleet hound, is two hounds in effect.

> *Sed premit inventas, non inventura latentes.*
> *Illa feras, quæ* petroniis *bene gloria constat.*

> " To the *petronian*, both the praise is due,
> Quickly to find, and nimbly to pursue."

GREYHOUNDS.

In Latin termed *veltraga*, or *vertragus*, or *vertagus*, derived, it seems, from the Dutch word *velt* a field, and *rach*, or *brach*, a dog. And of how high esteem the former, and these, were amongst the ancients, the reader may infer from the old Bur-

gundian law : " Siquis canem veltraum, aut segutium, vel pe-
trunculum præsumpserit involare, jubemus ut convictus coram
omni populo posteriora ipsius osculetur."

Martial, speaking of these greyhounds, thus expresseth himself :

> *Non sibi sed domino venatur vertragus acer ;*
> *Illæsum leporem qui tibi dente feret.*

> " For's master, not himself, doth greyhound toil,
> Whose teeth to thee return the unhurt spoil."

I have no more to observe of these greyhounds, save that
they are so called (being otherwise of all colours) because
originally employed in the hunting of *grays* ; that is, *brocks*
and *badgers*.

MASTIFFS.

Known to the Romans by the name of *molossi*, from Molos-
sia a county in Epirus, whence the fiercest in that kind were
fetched at first, before better were brought out of Britain.

Gratius, an ancient poet, contemporary with Virgil, writing
his Cynegeticon, or poem of hunting, giveth great praise to
our English mastiffs, highly commending their valour; only
taxing them that they are not handsomely made :

> *Hæc una est catulis jactura Britannis.*

> " The British whelps no blemish know,
> But that they are not shap'd for show."

Which thing is nothing in my mind, seeing beauty is no whit
material to a soldier.

This county breedeth choice mastiffs for the bull and bear;
and the sport is much affected therein, especially about Stamford, whereof hereafter. What remaineth concerning mastiffs
is referred to the same topic in Somersetshire.

Thus the three kinds of ancient hunting, which distinctly
require fleetness, scent, and strength, are completely performed
in this county, by a breed therein, which are answerably qualified. This I have inserted, because as to my native country in
general, so to this in particular, I would not willingly do less
right than what a stranger hath done thereunto.

Before we come to catalogue the WORTHIES of this county,*
it is observable, that as it equalled other shires in all ages, so it
went beyond itself in one generation, viz. in the reign of queen
Elizabeth, when it had natives thereof, 1. *Edward Clinton*, lord
admiral; 2. *William Cecil*, lord treasurer; 3. *Sir Edmund Anderson*, lord chief justice; 4. *John Whitgift*, archbishop of
Canterbury; 5. *Peregrine Bartu*, lord general in France; 6.
Thomas Wilson, doctor of law, and secretary of state: — all
countrymen and contemporaries.† Thus sea and land, church

---

* Reader, pardon this true but (abortive) notation casually come in before the
due time thereof.—F.

† Here I mention not Sir Thomas Heneage, at the same time a grand favourite,
and privy counciilor to queen Elizabeth.—F.

and camp, sword and mace, gospel and law, were stored with prime officers out of this county. Nor must it be forgotten, though born in the same shire, they were utterly unrelated in kindred, and raised themselves independently (as to any mutual assistance) by God's blessing, the queen's favour, and their own deserts.

THE BUILDINGS.

Here the complaint of the prophet taketh no place, taxing men to live " in ceiled palaces, whilst the temple of God lay waste,"* no county affording worse houses, or better churches. It addeth to the wonder, that seeing in this soft county a diamond is as soon found as a flint, their churches are built of polished stones; no natives, but naturalized by importation from foreign parts.

I hope the inhabitants of this shire will endeavour to disprove the old proverb, "the nearer to the church the further from God;" because they have substituted a better in the room thereof; viz. "the further from stone, the better the churches."

As for the cathedral of Lincoln, whose floor is higher than the roof of many churches, it is a magnificent structure, proportionable to the amplitude of the diocese. This I dare boldly say, that no diocese in Christendom affordeth two such rivers — Thames and Trent; for the southern and northern bounds; and two such universities, Cambridge and Oxford, both in the content thereof, before three small bishoprics,† were carved out of it.

Amongst the houses of the nobility, I take signal notice of two. One I may call a premeditate building, viz. Tattershall (belonging to the Right Honourable the earl of Lincoln), advanced by degrees at several times to the modern magnificence thereof. But Grimsthorp I may term an extempore structure, set up on a sudden by Charles Brandon duke of Suffolk, to entertain king Henry the Eighth, in his progress into these parts. The hall therein was fitted to a fair suit of hanging, which the duke had by his wife Mary the French queen, and is now in the possession of the Right Honourable Montague Earl of Lindsey.

THE WONDERS.

At Fishtoft in this county, no mice or rats are found, insomuch that barns, built *party per pale* in this and the next parish, on one side are annoyed; on the other side (being Fishtoft moiety) are secured from this vermin. Surely no piper (what is notoriously known of Hamel in Westphalia) did ever give them this mice-delivery by his music.

It is easier to conjure up many than allay one difficulty; other places in England affording the like. At one of the Rodings in Essex no hogs will root: in another common no mol

---

* Haggai i. 4.   † Ely, Peterborough, and Oxford.

will cast. In Lindley in Leicestershire, no snakes are found.* I believe they overshoot the mark, who make it a miracle ; they undershoot it, who make it magic : they come the nearest to truth, who impute it to occult qualities. If some men will swoon at some meat, yea but smelling it unseen, by their disaffection thereunto, why may not whole species and kinds of creatures have some antipathetical places, though the reason thereof cannot be rendered ? Surely, as Samson at his marriage propounded a riddle to his companions to try their wits thereon ; so God offereth such enigmas in nature, partly that men may make use of their admiring as well as of their understanding ; partly that philosophers may be taught their distance betwixt themselves, who are but the lovers, and God, who is the giver wisdom.

Let it also pass (for this once) for a wonder, that some seven-score years since, nigh Harlaxton in this shire, there was found (turned up by one ploughing the ground) a golden helmet of antique fashion ;† I say, " cassis non aurata, sed aurea," (a helmet not gilt, but of massive gold), studded with precious stones, probably of some prime Roman commander. Whence I observe, first, that though no edge tool to offend may be made of gold and silver, yet defensive weapons may thereof be compounded. Secondly, that the poetical fiction of Glaucus's golden arms is founded on history ; for (not to speak of Solomon's golden shields) great commanders made use of arms of that metal, if not for strength, for state and ornament. Lastly, it was presented to queen Katharine, first wife to king Henry the Eighth, who, though not knowing to use it as a helmet, knew how to employ it as made of gold and rich jewels.

PROVERBS.

" Lincolnshire bagpipes."]

I behold these as most ancient, because a very simple sort of music, being little more than the oaten pipe improved with a bag, wherein the imprisoned wind pleadeth melodiously for the enlargement thereof. It is incredible with what agility it inspireth the heavy heels of the country clowns, overgrown with hair and rudeness, probably the ground-work of the poetical fiction of dancing satyrs. This bagpipe, in the judgment of the rural Midas's, carrieth away the credit from the harp of Apollo himself; and most persons approve the blunt bagpipe above the edge-tool instruments of drums and trumpets in our civil dissensions.

" As loud as Tom of Lincoln."]

This shire carries away the *bell* for *round-ringing* from all in England; though other places may surpass it for *changes*, more pleasant for the variety thereof; seeing it may be demonstrated

---

* Burton, in his Description of Leicestershire.
† Camden's Britannia, in this county.

that twelve bells will afford more changes than there have been hours since the creation. Tom of Lincoln may be called the Stentor (fifty lesser bells may be made out of him) of all in this county. Expect not of me to enter into the discourse of Popish baptising and naming of bells, many charging it on them for a profane, and they confessing enough to make it a superstitious, action.

"All the carts that come to Cowland are shod with silver."]

Venice and Crowland, "sic canibus catulos," may count their carts alike; that being sited in the sea (this in a morass and fenny ground), so that a horse can hardly come to it. But whether this place, since the draining of the fens, hath acquired more firmness than formerly is to me unknown.

"Tis height makes Grantham steeple stand awry."*]

This steeple seems crooked unto the beholders (and I believe will ever do so, until our age erect the like by it for height and workmanship), though some conceive the slenderness at such a distance is all the obliquity thereof. Eminency exposeth the uprightest persons to exception; and such who cannot find faults in them, will find faults at them, envying their advancement.

"As mad as the baiting bull of Stamford."]

Take the original hereof. William earl Warren, lord of this town in the time of king John, standing upon the castle walls of Stamford, saw two bulls fighting for a cow in the meadow, till all the butchers' dogs, great and small, pursued one of the bulls (being madded with noise and multitude) clean through the town. This sight so pleased the said earl, that he gave all those meadows † (called the Castle Meadows) where first the bull duel began, for a common to the butchers of the town (after the first grass was eaten), on condition that they find a mad bull, the day six weeks before Christmas day, for the continuance of that sport every year. Some think that the men must be mad as well as the bull, who can take delight in so dangerous a waste-time: whereby that no more mischief is done, not man's care but God's providence is to be praised.

"He looks as the devil over Lincoln."‡]

Lincoln Minster is one of the stateliest structures in Christendom. The south side of it meets the travellers thereunto twenty miles off, so that their eyes are there many hours before their feet.

The devil is the map of malice, and his envy, as God's mercy, is over all his works. It grieves him whatever is given to God, crying out with that flesh devil, "Ut quid hæc perditio," (what needs this waste?§) On which account he is supposed to have overlooked this church, when first finished with a torve and tetric countenance, as maligning men's costly devotion, and that they should be so expensive in God's service. But it is suspicious that

---

* Mr. John Cleiveland.   † R. Butcher, in his Survey of Stamford, p. 40.
‡ See the Proverbs in Oxfordshire.   § Matt. xxvi. 8.

some who account themselves saints behold such fabrics with little better looks.

"He was born at Little Wittham."*]

This village in this county by orthography is Witham, near which a river of the same name doth rise. But such nominal proverbs take the advantage of all manner of spelling as due unto them. It is applied to such people as are not overstocked with acuteness. The best is, all men are bound to be honest, but not to be witty.

"Grantham gruel, nine grits and a gallon of water."]

Gruel (though homely) is wholesome spoon-meat physic for the sick, and food for persons in health. Water is the matter, grits the form thereof, giving the being thereunto. Now gruel thus imperfectly mixed is wash rather, which one will have little heart to eat, and get as little heart thereby. The proverb is applicable to those who in their speeches or actions multiply what is superfluous, or (at best) less necessary; either wholly omitting, or less regarding, the essentials thereof.

"They held together as the men of Marham† when they lost their common."]

Some understand it ironically; that is, they were divided with several factions, which proverb, "mutato nomine," is used in other counties. Yea, long since, Virgil said the same in effect of the men of Mantua, when they lost their lands to the soldiers of Augustus:

> —————— En quò discordia, cives,
> Perduxit miseros ! En queis consevimus agros !‡

> "See, townmen, what we by our jars are grown ;
> And see for whom we have our tillage sown !"

Indeed, when a common danger calls for a union against a general enemy, for any then to prosecute their personal quarrels and private grudges, is a folly always observed, often reproved, sometimes confessed, but seldom reformed.

Others use this proverb only as an expression of ill success, when men strive to no purpose, though plotting and practising together to the utmost of their power, being finally foiled in their undertakings.

PRINCES.

HENRY eldest [surviving] son of John of Gaunt duke of Lancaster, was born at the castle of Bollingbroke in this county, and bred (according to the discipline of those days) in camp and court, in both which he proved a good proficient. By nature he was made more to command than obey, being ambitious, choleric, and withal courageous, cunning to catch, careful to keep, and industrious to improve all advantages.

Being nettled with some injuries received from king Richard

---

* Heywood, in his Epigrams, cent. v. num. 19.
† Though this Proverb be frequent in this shire, Marham is in Norfolk.—F.
‡ Eclogue the first.

the Second, he complotted with a good party of the nobility to depose him. Miscarriages in his government (many by mismanaging, more by the mis-succeeding of matters) exposed him to just exception, besides his own debauchery; and how easily is a dissolute government dissolved!

Having, by the murder of king Richard, achieved the government to himself, he reigned with much difficulty and opposition. Though his father was a great patron, *he* was a great persecutor of the Wickliffites; though not so much out of hatred to them, as love to himself, thereby to be ingratiated with the clergy, then potent in the land.

When duke, he wore on his head an antique hood, which he cast not off when king, so that his picture is generally known by the crown superadded thereon. Lying on his death-bed, he was rather querulous than penitent, much complaining of his sufferings in keeping, nothing bewailing his sin in getting, the crown. Fire and faggot was first kindled in his reign in England, to burn (pardon the prolepsis) poor Protestants; and happy had it been, had they been quenched at his death, which happened anno Dom. 1413.

This Henry was the only prince born in this county since the Conquest, though a good author by mistake entituleth this county to another, an ancienter Henry; yet so that he giveth him with one hand to it in his Book of Maps, and takes him away with the other in his Chronicle.

J. Speed (in his description of Lincolnshire, parag. 7.)— "This shire triumpheth in the birth of Beauclerk king Henry the First, whom Selby brought forth."

J. Speed (in his chronicle in the life of W. I. pag. 436.)— "Henry fourth, and youngest son of king William, was born at Selby in Yorkshire."

I believe Mr. Speed the *chronicler* before Mr. Speed the *chorographer*, because therein concurring with other authors. Besides, consult the alphabetical index of his Map, and there is no Selby in this shire. We have therefore placed king Henry the First in Yorkshire; and thought fit to enter this observation, not to reprove others, but lest I be reproved myself.

SAINTS.

Here I make no mention of St. Botolph, because there is no *constat* (though very much probability) of his English Nativity, who lived at, and gave the name to, Botolph's town (corruptly Boston) in this county.

GILBERT de SEMPRINGHAM, there born in this county, was of noble extraction, Joceline his father being a knight, to whom he was eldest son, and heir to a great estate.* In body he was

---

* Bale, de Scriptoribus Britannicis, cent. iii. n. 25. and Camden's Britannia, in Lincolnshire.

very deformed, but of subtile wit and great courage. Travelling over into France, there he got good learning, and obtained leave from the Pope to be founder of those Epicæne and Hermaphrodine convents, wherein monks and nuns lived together, as under one roof, but with partitions betwixt them.

Sure it was to him a comfort and credit (which is confidently related by credible authors) to see 13 convents, 700 monks, 1100 nuns (women out-superstition men) of his order, being aged one hundred and six years. He appointed the fair convent at Sempringham (his own rich inheritance) to be mother and prime residence of his new-erected order. He died anno 1189.

HUGH was a child, born and living in Lincoln,* who by the impious Jews was stolen from his parents, and in derision of Christ and Christianity, to keep their cruel hands in use, by them crucified, being about nine years old. Thus he lost his life, but got a Saintship thereby; and some afterwards persuaded themselves that they got their cures at his shrine in Lincoln.

However, this made up the measure of the sins of the Jews in England, for which not long after they were ejected the land, or, which is the truer, unwillingly willing they departed themselves. And whilst they retain their old manners, may they never return, especially in this giddy and unsettled age, for fear more Christians fall sick of Judaism, than Jews recover in Christianity. This Hugh was martyred anno Dom. 1255, on the 27th of July.

MARTYRS.

ANNE ASKEWE, daughter of Sir William Askewe, knight, was born at Kelsey in this county. Of her piety and patience, when first wracked in the Tower, then burnt in Smithfield, I have largely treated in my "Church History." She went to Heaven in a chariot of fire, July 16, 1546.

CARDINALS.

[AMP.] ROBERT SOMMERCOT.—There are two villages, North and South Sommercot, in this county (and to my notice, nowhere else in England); from one of which, I presume, he took his nativity in name. Yet because Bale affirmeth Lawrence Sommercot, his brother or kinsman, born in the South of England,† we have affixed our note of dubitation. But out of doubt it is, he was a right learned man, to whom Matthew Paris gives this short but thick commendation; "Vir fuit discretus, et circumspectus, omnibus amabilis meritò et gratiosus."‡ By Pope Gregory the Ninth he was made Cardinal of St. Stephen's, anno 1231.

* Jo. Capg. in SS. Ang. Matth. Westm. et Paris. ann. 1255.
† De Scriptoribus Britannicis, Cent. iv. num. 2. ‡ In anno 1241, pag. 576.

He was a true lover of his countrymen, and could not abide to hear them abused; the cause that his choler was twice raised, when the Pope said, in his presence, " that there was not a faithful man in England;"* though wisely he repressed his passion.

After this Pope Gregory's death, he was the foremost of the three Elects for the Papacy; and, on fair play, the most probable person to carry the place; but he was double barred : first, because an honest man as any in that age : secondly, because an Englishman: the Italians desiring to monopolize the choice to themselves. Hereupon, in the holy conclave (the better place the better deed) he was made away by poison, to make room for Celestine to succeed him, who sate that skittish place but a short time, dying seventeen days after our Sommercot's death, which happened anno Domini 1241.

PRELATES.

WILLIAM of GAINSBOROUGH was born in that fair market town, which performeth more to the eye, than fame hath reported to the ear thereof. He was bred a Franciscan in Oxford, and became the twenty-fifth lecturer of his order. He was afterwards sent over by king Edward the First, with Hugh of Manchester, to Philip king of France, to demand reparation for some damages in Aquitaine.

He was a mighty champion of the Pope's infallibility : avowing that what David indulged to his son Adonijah, never saying unto him, " why didst thou so ? "† ought to be rendered by all to his Holiness; being not to be called to an account, though causing the damnation of thousands.

I remember, when I was in Cambridge some thirty years since, there was a flying though false report, that Pope Urban the Eighth was cooped up by his cardinals in the castle of St. Angelo. Hereupon a waggish scholar said, " Jam verissimum est Papa non potest errare," "it was then true (according to their received intelligence) that the Pope could not straggle or wander."

But our Gainsborough stoutly defended it in the literal sense against all opposers, for which his good service Pope Boniface the Eighth preferred him bishop of Worcester, where he sate 6 years, and died 1308.

WILLIAM AYRMIN was descended of an ancient family in this county, still extant in great eminency of estate at Osgodby therein. He was for some time keeper of the Seal and vice-chancellor to king Edward the Second; at what time, anno 1319, the following misfortune befell him; and take the original thereof out of an anonymal croniclering manuscript.

"Episcopus Eborum, Episcopus Elie, thesaurarius, Abbas

---

* Bale, ut prius, in anno 1240, pp. 524 and 542.   † 1 Kings i. 6.

Beate Marie Eborum, Abbas de Selbie, Decanus Eborum, Dominus Willielmus Arymanée vice-cancellarius Anglie, ac Dominus Johannes Dabeham, cum 8000 fermè hominum, tam equitum quàm peditum, et civibus, properanter civitatem egredientes, quoddam flumen Swale nuncupatum sparsis cuneis * transeuntes, et indispositis seu potiùs confusis ordinibus, cum adversariis congressi sunt. Scoti siquidem in Marte gnari amplitudinem eorum exercitûs cautè regentes, in nostris agminibus strictis audacter irruerunt; nostrorum denique in brevi laceratis cuneis atque dissipatis, corruerunt ex nostris, tam in ore gladii quàm aquarum scopulis suffocati, plusquam 4000 ; et capti sunt Domini Johannes de Papeham, et Dominus Willielmus de Arymanée, ut prefertur, de cancellaria," &c.

("The Archbishop of York, the Bishop of Ely, lord treasurer, the Abbot of St. Mary's in York, the Abbot of Selby, the Dean of York, Mr. William Ayrmane, vice chancellor, and Mr. John Dabehame, with almost 8000 men, as well horse as foot, and citizens, hastily going out of the city, passing over a certain river called Swale, with scattered parties,* and with disordered or rather confused ranks, encountered the enemy. The Scotch, cunning in war, warily ruling the greatness of their army, boldly rushed on our men with well-ordered troops ; and afterwards in short time having broken, and scattered our parties, there fell of our men, with the mouth of the sword, and choked with the water, more than 4000 : and Mr. John de Papeham and Mr. William Arymane of the chancery, as aforesaid, were taken prisoners.")

Afterwards recovering his liberty, he was made chancellor of England, and bishop of Norwich, in the 18th year of king Edward the Second. He gave two hundred pounds, to buy land, to maintain priests to say mass for his soul. He died anno Domini 1337, at Charing Cross nigh London, when he had been eleven years bishop. I am credibly informed, that he bestowed the manor of Silk Willoughby in this county on his family, which, with other fair lands, is possessed by them at this day.

WILLIAM WAYNFLET was born at Waynflet in this county, whence he took his denomination, according to the custom of clergyman in that age : for otherwise he was eldest son to Richard Pattin, an ancient esquire in this county; and I understand that at this day they remain at Barsloe in Derbyshire, descended from the said knight. But of this worthy prelate, founder of Magdalen College in Oxford, abundantly in my "Church History."

WILLIAM LYNWOOD was born at Lynwood in this county,† and proceeded Doctor of the Laws (probably rather by incorpo-

---

* Fashioned in form of a wedge.—F.   † Harpsfield, in his History.

ration than constant education) in Oxford, long living a commoner in Gunvil Hall in Cambridge. He was chancellor to the archbishop of Canterbury, keeper of the Privy Seal to king Henry the Sixth, and was employed in several embassies into Spain and Portugal. He wrote a learned comment on the English provincial constitutions, from Stephen Langton to archbishop Chichley : and his pains at last were rewarded with the bishopric of St. David's, where he died 1446.

WILLIAM ASCOUGH was descended of a worshipful and very ancient family now living at Kelsey in this county, the variation of a letter importing nothing to the contrary. I have seen at Sarisbury his arms, with allusion to the arms of that house, and some episcopal addition. Such likeness is with me a better evidence than the sameness, knowing that the clergy in that age delighted to disguise their coats from their paternal bearing. He was bred Doctor of the Laws, a very able man in his profession ; became bishop of Sarum, confessor to king Henry the Sixth, and was the first (as T. Gascoigne relateth) of bishops who discharged that office, as then conceived, beneath the place. Some will say, if king Henry answered the character commonly received of his sanctity, his confessor had a very easy performance. Not so: for always the most conscientious are the most scrupulous in the confession of their sins, and the particular enumeration of the circumstances thereof.

It happened that Jack Cade with his cursed crew (many of them being the tenants of this bishop) fell foul on this prelate at Edington in this shire. Bishop Godwin saith, " Illi quam ob causam infensi non habeo compertum ; " he could not tell " why they should be so incensed against him." But, I conceive, it was because he was learned, pious, and rich — three capital crimes in a clergyman. They plundered his carriages, taking ten thousand marks (a mine of money in that age) from him ; and then, to secure their riot and felony, by murder and high-treason, dragged him as he was officiating from the high altar. And although they regarded difference of place no more than a wolf is concerned whether he killeth a lamb in the fold or field, yet they brought him out of the church to a hill hard by, and there barbarously murdered him, and tore his bloody shirt in pieces, and left his stripped body stark naked in the place :

> Sic concussa cadit populari mitra tumultu,
> Protegat optamus nunc diadema Deus.

> " By people's fury mitre thus cast down,
> We pray henceforward God preserve the crown."

This his massacre happened June 29, 1450, when he had sate almost twelve years in the see of Salisbury.

RICHARD FOX was born at Grantham in this county, as the fellows of his foundation in Oxford have informed me. Such who make it their only argument to prove his birth at Grantham, because he therein erected a fair free-school, may on the same reason conclude him born at Taunton in Somersetshire, where he also founded a goodly Grammar school. But what shall I say ? "Ubique nascitur qui orbi nascitur;" he may be said to be born every where, who with Fox was born for the public and general good.

He was very instrumental in bringing king Henry the Seventh to the crown, who afterwards well rewarded him for the same. That politic prince (though he could go alone as well as any king in Europe, yet) for the more state, in matters of moment he leaned principally on the shoulders of two prime prelates, having archbishop Morton for his right, and this Fox for his left supporter, whom at last he made bishop of Winchester. He was bred first in Cambridge, where he was president of Pembroke-hall (and gave hangings thereunto with a fox woven therein) ; and afterwards in Oxford, where he founded the fair college of Corpus Christi (allowing per annum to it 401*l.* 8*s.* 11*d.*) ; which since hath been the nursery of so many eminent sholars. He expended much money in beautifying his cathedral in Winchester, and methodically disposed the bodies of the Saxon kings and bishops (dispersedly buried in this church) in decent tombs erected by him on the walls on each side of the choir, which some soldiers, to show their spleen at once against crowns and mitres, valiantly fighting against the dust of the dead, have since barbarously demolished. Twenty-seven years he sat bishop of this see, till he was stark blind with age. All thought him to die too soon, one only excepted, who conceived him to live too long, viz. Thomas Wolsey, who gaped for his bishopric, and endeavoured to render him to the displeasure of king Henry the Eighth, whose malice this bishop, though blind discovered, and in some measure defeated. He died anno Domini 1528, and lies buried in his own cathedral.

SINCE THE REFORMATION.

THOMAS GOODRICH was son of Edward Goodrich and Jane his wife, of Kirkby in this county, as appeareth by the Yorkshire visitation of heralds : in which county the allies of this bishop seated themselves, and flourish at this day. He was bred in the university of Cambridge, D.D. say some ; of Law, say others, in my opinion more probable, because frequently employed in so many embassies to foreign princes, and at last made by king Henry the Eighth bishop of Ely (wherein he continued above twenty years), and by king Edward the Sixth lord chancellor of England.   Nor will it be amiss to insert and translate this distich made upon him.

> *Et bonus et dives, benè junctus et optimus ordo* ;
> *Præcedit bonitas, ponè sequuntur opes.*

> " Both good and rich, well joined, best rank'd indeed :
> For grace goes first, and next doth wealth succeed."

I find one pen spirting ink upon him * (which is usual in his writings) ; speaking to this effect, " that if he had ability enough he had not too much to discharge his office." I behold him as one well inclined to the Protestant religion ; and after his resignation of the chancellor's † place to Stephen Gardiner, his death was very seasonable for his own safety, May 10, 1554, in the first of queen Mary, whilst as yet no great violence was used to Protestants.

JOHN WHITGIFT was born at Grimsby in this county ; successively bred in Queen's, Pembroke-hall, Peter-house, and Trinity College, in Cambridge, Master of the latter ; bishop of Worcester, and archbishop of Canterbury. But I have largely written his life in my "Ecclesiastical History ;" and may truly say, with him who constantly returned to all inquirers, " Nil novi novi," (I can make no new addition thereunto) ; only since I met with this anagram :‡ " JOANNES WHITEGIFTEUS," (*non vi egit, favet Jesus*).

Indeed he was far from violence ; and his politic patience was blessed in a high proportion. He died anno 1603, Feb. 29.

JOHN STILL, D. D. was born at Grantham in this county, and bred, first, fellow of Christ's, then master of St. John's, and afterwards of Trinity College in Cambridge, where I have read in the register this commendation of him, " that he was ἀγαθὸς κουρότροφος, nec collegio gravis aut onerosus." He was one of a venerable presence, not less famous for a preacher than a disputant. Finding his own strength, he did not stick to warn such as he disputed with in their own arguments, to take heed to their answers, like a perfect fencer, that will tell aforehand in what button he will give his venue. When, towards the end of the reign of queen Elizabeth, there was an (unsucceeding) motion of a diet, or meeting, which should have been in Germany, for composing matters of religion ; Doctor Still was chosen for Cambridge, and Doctor Humfred for Oxford, to oppose all comers for the defence of the English church.§

Anno 1592, being then the second time vice-chancellor of Cambridge, he was consecrated bishop of Bath and Wells, and defeated all causeless suspicion of symoniacal compliance ; coming clearly thereunto, without the least scandal to his person, or loss to the place. In his days God opened the bosom of the earth, Mendip Hills affording great store of lead, wherewith and with his own providence (which is a constant mine of wealth) he raised a great estate, and laid the foundation of three families,

---

* Sir John Hayward, in the Life of king Edward the Sixth.
† Peruse Sir Henry Spelman's Glossary, in verbo *Chancellariorum*.
‡ Camden's Remains, page 184.
§ Sir John Harrington, in his Continuation of Bishop Godwin's Catalogue of Bishops.

leaving to each of them a considerable revenue in a worshipful condition. He gave five hundred pounds for the building of an alms-house in the city of Wells ; and, dying February 26, 1607, lies buried in his own cathedral, under a neat tomb of alabaster.

MARTIN FOTHERBY, D.D. was born at Great Grimsby in this county, of a good family, as appeareth by his epitaph on his monument in the church of All-hallows, Lombard street, London. He was bred fellow of Trinity College in Cambridge, and became afterwards one and twenty years prebendary of Canterbury ; then he was preferred by king James bishop of Salisbury ; he died in his calling, having begun to put in print an excellent book against Atheists, most useful for our age, wherein their sin so aboundeth. His death happened March 11, 1619, not two full years after his consecration.

STATESMEN.

EDWARD FINES, lord Clinton, knight of the Garter, was lord admiral of England for more than thirty years : a wise, valiant, and fortunate gentleman. The master-piece of his service was in Musselborough field, in the reign of king Edward the Sixth, and the battle against the Scots.* Some will wonder, what a fish should do on dry land, what use of an admiral in a land fight. But know, the English kept themselves close to the shore, under the shelter of their ships ; and whilst their arrows could do little, their spears less, their swords nothing, against the Scots (who appeared like a hedge of steel, so well armed and closed together) : the great ordnance from their ships at first did all, making such destruction in the Scottish army, that though some may call it a land fight, it was first a victory from the sea, and then but an execution on the land.†

By queen Elizabeth (who honoured her honours by bestowing them sparingly) he was created earl of Lincoln, May 4th, 1574 ; and indeed he had breadth to his height, a proportionable estate, chiefly in this county, to support his dignity, being one of those who, besides his paternal inheritance, had much increased his estate. He died January the sixteenth, 1585 ; and lieth buried at Windsor, in a private chapel, under a stately monument, which Elizabeth his third wife, daughter to the earl of Kildare, erected in his remembrance.

THOMAS WILSON, doctor of laws, was born in this county ;‡ bred fellow of King's College in Cambridge ; and afterwards was tutor in the same university to Henry and Charles Brandons, successively dukes of Suffolk. Hard shift he made to

* Sir John Hayward, in the reign of king Edward the Sixth, page 15.
† Sir John Hayward, ubi supra, page 31.
‡ Bale, de Scriptoribus Britannicis, Cent. ix.

conceal himself in the reign of queen Mary. Under queen Elizabeth he was made Master of the hospital of St. Katherine's nigh the Tower of London, upon the same token that he took down the choir, which, my author saith, (allow him a little hyperbole) was as great as the choir at St. Paul's.* I am loath to believe it done out of covetousness, to gain by the materials thereof, but would rather conceive it so run to ruin, that it was past repairing. He at last became secretary of state to queen Elizabeth for four years together. It argues his ability for the place, because he was put into it; seeing in those active times, under so judicious a queen, weakness might despair to be employed in such an office. He died anno Domini 15 . .†

THOMAS Lord BURGE, or BOROUGH, son to William Lord Burge, grandson to Thomas Lord Burge (created baron by king Henry the Eighth) was born in his father's fair house at Gainsborough in this county.‡

His first public appearing was, when he was sent ambassador into Scotland, anno 1593, to excuse Bothwell's lurking in England, to advise the speedy suppressing of the Spanish faction, and to advance an effectual association of the Protestants in that kingdom for their king's defence; which was done accordingly.

Now when Sir William Russel, lord deputy of Ireland, was recalled, this lord Thomas Burge was substituted in his room, anno 1597. Mr. Camden doth thus character him, "vir acer, et animi plenus, sed nullis ferè castrorum rudimentis."§ But where there is the stock of valour with an able brain, experience will soon be graffed upon it. It was first thought fit to make a month's truce with Tyrone; which cessation, like a damn, made their mutual animosities for the present swell higher, and, when removed for the future, run the fiercer. The lord deputy (the truce expired) straitly besieged the fort of Blackwater, the only receptacle of the rebels in those parts (I mean, besides their woods and bogs), and the key of the county of Tyrone. This fort he took by force; and presently followed a bloody battle, wherein the English paid dear for their victory, losing many worthy men, and amongst them two that were foster-brothers (*fratres collactanei*) to the earl of Kildare, who so laid this loss to his heart (amongst the Irish, foster-brethren are loved above the sons of their fathers), that he died soon after. Tyrone's credit now lay a bleeding; when, to staunch it, he rebesieged Blackwater; and the lord deputy, whilst endeavouring to relieve it, was struck with untimely death, before he had continued a whole year in his place. All I will add is this, that it brake the heart of valiant Sir John Norris (who had promised the deputy's place unto himself, as due to his deserts) when this

---

* Stow's Survey of London, in Tower-street Ward.
† Dr. Wilson died in 1581.   See Wood's Fasti, vol. I. p. 98.—ED.
‡ Camden's Britannia, in this County.   § In his Elizabeth, anno 1597.

lord Burge was superinduced into that office. His relict lady (famous for her charity, and skill in chirurgery) lived long in Westminster, and died very aged some twenty years since.

WILLIAM CECIL.—Know, reader, before I go farther, something must be premised concerning his position in this topic. Virgil was profane in his flattery to Augustus Cæsar; proffering him his free choice after his death, to be ranked amongst what heathen gods he pleased; so that he might take his place either amongst those of the land, which had the oversight of men and cities; or the sea-gods, commanding in the ocean; or the sky-gods, and become a new constellation therein.* But, without the least adulation, we are bound to proffer this worthy peer his own election; whether he will be pleased to repose himself under BENEFACTORS TO THE PUBLIC, all England in that age being beholden to his bounty (as well as the poor in Stamford, for whom he erected a fair bead-house) acknowledging, under God and the queen, their prosperity the fruit of his prudence. Or else he may rest himself under the title of LAWYERS, being long bred in the Inns of Court, and more learned in our municipal law than many who made it their sole profession. However, for the present, we lodge this English Nestor (for wisdom and vivacity) under the notion of STATESMEN, being secretary and lord treasurer for above thirty years together. Having formerly written his life at large,† it will be enough here to observe, that he was born at Bourne in this county, being son to Richard Cecil (esquire of the robes to king Henry the Eighth, and a legatee in his will) and Jane his wife, of whom hereafter. He was in his age *moderator aulæ*, steering the court at his pleasure; and whilst the earl of Leicester would endure no equal, and Sussex no superior therein, he, by siding with neither, served himself with both.

Incredible was the kindness which queen Elizabeth had for him, or rather for herself in him, being sensible that he was so able a minister of state. Coming once to visit him, being sick of the gout at Burleigh-house in the Strand, and being much heightened with her head attire (then in fashion); the lord's servant who conducted her through the door, "May your highness," said he, "be pleased to stoop." The queen returned, "For your master's sake I will stoop, but not for the king of Spain's." This worthy patriot departed this life, in the seventy-seventh year of his age, August the 4th, 1598.

CAPITAL JUDGES.

[REM.] Sir WILLIAM de SKIPWITH was bred in the study of the laws, profiting so well therein, that he was made, in

* Georgic. l. i.   † In my "Holy State."—F.

Trinity term, lord chief baron of the Exchequer, in the thirty-fifth, continuing therein until the fortieth, of the reign of king Edward the Third.* I meet not with any thing memorable of him in our English histories; except this may pass for a thing remarkable, that, at the importunity of John of Gaunt duke of Lancaster, this Sir William condemned William Wickham, bishop of Winchester, of crimes rather powerfully objected than plainly proved against him; whereupon the bishop's temporals were taken from him, and he denied access within twenty miles of the king's court.†

I confess there is a village in the East-riding of Yorkshire, called Skipwith; but I have no assurance of this judge's nativity therein; though ready to remove him thither upon clearer information.

[AMP.] Sir WILLIAM SKIPWITH, junior.—He was inferior to the former in place (whom I behold as a puisne judge); but herein remarkable to all posterity, that he would not comply, neither for the importunity of king Richard the Second, nor the example of his fellow judges,‡ (in the 10th year of that king's reign) to allow that the king by his own power might rescind an Act of Parliament. "Solus inter impios mansit integer Gulielmus Skipwith, miles; clarus ideò apud posteros;" and shined the brighter for living in the midst of a crooked generation,§ bowed with fear and favour into corruption.

I know well, that the collar of SSS (or *Esses*) worn about the necks of judges (and other persons of honour) is wreathed into that form, whence it receiveth its name; chiefly from *Sanctus Simon Simplicius*, an uncorrupted judge in the primitive times. May I move that every fourth link thereof, when worn, may mind them of this Skipwith, so upright in his judgment in a matter of the highest importance.

Having no certainty of his nativity, I place him in this county, where his name at Ormesby hath flourished ever since his time in a very worshipful equipage.

[AMP.] Sir WILLIAM HUSEE, Knight, was born, as I have cause to believe, in this county, where his name and family flourish in a right worshipful equipage. He was bred in the study of our municipal law, and attained to such eminency therein, that by king Edward the Fourth, in the one and twentieth of his reign, he was made lord chief justice of the King's Bench.||

---

* Sir Henry Spelman's Glossary, tit. *Justitiarius*.
† Bishop Godwin, in the Bishops of Winchester.
‡ See Sir Robert Belknap, title LAWYERS, in Leicestershire.
§ Sir Henry Spelman, in Glossary, verbo *Justitiarius*.
|| Spelman's Glossary, p. 417.

King Henry the Seventh (who in point of policy was only directed by himself) in point of law was chiefly ruled by this judge, especially in this question of importance.* It happened that in his first parliament many members thereof were returned, who (being formerly of this king's party) were attainted, and thereby not legal to sit in parliament, being disabled in the highest degree, it being incongruous that they should make laws for others, who themselves were not inlawed. The king, not a little troubled therewith, remitted it as a case in law to the judges. The judges, assembled in the Exchequer Chamber, agreed all with Sir William Husee (their speaker to the king) upon this grave and safe opinion, mixed with law and convenience, " that the knights and burgesses attainted by the course of law should forbear to come into the House, till a law were passed for the reversal of their attainders ;" which was done accordingly. When at the same time it was incidently moved, in their consultation, what should be done for the king himself, who likewise was attainted, the rest unanimously agreed with Sir William Husee, " that the crown takes away all defects and stops in blood; and that, by the assumption thereof, the fountain was cleared from all attainders and corruptions." He died in Trinity term, in the tenth year of king Henry the Seventh.†

Sir EDMUND ANDERSON, Knight, was born a younger brother of a gentle extract at Flixborough in this county, and bred in the Inner Temple. I have been informed that his father left him 1000*l.* for his portion, which this our Sir Edmund multiplied into many, by his great proficiency in the common law, being made in the twenty-fourth of queen Elizabeth chief justice of the Common Pleas.

When secretary Davison was sentenced in the Star Chamber for the business of the queen of Scots, judge Anderson said of him, " that therein he had done *justum non juste* ;" and so, acquitting him of all malice, censured him, with the rest, for his indiscretion.‡

When Henry Cuff was arraigned about the rising of the earl of Essex, and when Sir Edward Coke the queen's solicitor opposed him, and the other answered syllogistically, our Anderson (sitting there as judge of law not logic) checked both pleader and prisoner, " ob stolidos syllogismos," (for their foolish syllogisms§), appointing the former to press the statute of king Edward the Third. His stern countenance well became his place, being a great promoter of the established church discipline, and very severe against all Brownists when he met them in his circuit. He died in the third of king James, leaving great estates to several sons; of whom I behold Sir Francis Anderson

* Lord Verulam, in the Life of king Henry the Seventh, p. 242.
† Spelman's Glossary, ut prius.   ‡ Camden's Elizabeth, anno 1587.
§ Idem, anno 1600.

of Edworth in Bedfordshire the eldest, whose son Sir John, by
a second wife Audrey Butler (niece to the duke of Buckingham,
and afterwards married to the Lord Dunsmore in Warwickshire)
was (according to some conditions in his patent) to succeed his
father-in-law in that honour, if surviving him. This I thought
fit to insert, to vindicate his memory from oblivion, who, being
a hopeful gentleman (my fellow colleague in Sidney College),
was taken away in the prime of his youth.

SOLDIERS.

Sir FREDERIC TILNEY, Knight, had his chief residence at
Boston in this county.* He was a man of mighty stature and
strength, above the proportion of ordinary persons. He attended king Richard the First, anno Domini 1190, to the siege
of Acon in the Holy Land, where his achievements were such,
that he struck terror into the infidels. Returning home in
safety, he lived and died at Terington nigh Tilney in Norfolk,
where the measure of his incredible stature was for many years
preserved. Sixteen knights flourished from him successively in
the male line, till at last their heir general being married to the
duke of Norfolk, put a period to the lustre of that ancient family.†

[S. N.] PEREGRINE BERTY, Lord Willoughby, son of Richard Berty, and Katherine duchess of Suffolk. Reader, I crave
a dispensation, that I may, with thy good leave, trespass on the
premised laws of this book; his name speaking his foreign
nativity, born nigh Hidelberg in the Palatinate. Indeed I am
loath to omit so worthy a person. Our histories fully report
his valiant achievements in France and the Netherlands, and
how at last he was made governor of Berwick. He could not
brook the obsequiousness and assiduity of the Court; and was
wont to say, " That he was none of the *reptilia*, which could
creep on the ground." The camp was his proper element;
being a great soldier, and having a suitable magnanimity.

When one sent him an insulting challenge, whilst he lay sick
of the gout, he returned this answer, " That although he was
lame of his hands and feet, yet he would meet him with a piece
of a rapier in his teeth."

Once he took a gennet, managed for the war, which was intended for a present to the king of Spain ; and was desired by
a trumpeter from the general to restore it, offering this lord
1000*l*. down for him, or 100*l*. per annum during his life at his
own choice. This lord returned, "That if it had been any
commander, he freely would have sent him back ; but, being
but a horse, he loved him as well as the king of Spain himself,
and would keep him." Here I will insert a letter of queen
Elizabeth, written to him with her own hand ; and, reader, deal

* Hacluit, in his first volume of Sea Voyages.
† Weever, in his Funeral Monuments, in Norfolk, p. 817.

in matters of this nature, as when venison is set before thee—eat the one, and read the other; never asking whence either came, though I profess I came honestly by a copy thereof, from the original:

"Good Peregrine, we are not a little glad that by your journey you have received such good fruit of amendment; specially when we consider how great vexation it is to a minde devoted to actions of honour, to be restrained by any indisposition of body, from following those courses, which, to your own reputation and our great satisfactisn, you have formerly performed. And, therefore, as we must now (out of our desire of your well doing) chiefly enjoyne you to an especial care to encrease and continue your health, which must give life to all your best endeavours; so we must next as seriously recommend to you this consideration; that in these times, when there is such appearance that we shall have the triall of our best and noble subjects, you seem not to affect the satisfaction of your own private contentation, beyond the attending on that which nature and duty challengeth from all persons of your quality and profession. For if necessarily (your health of body being recovered) you should *elloigne* yourself by residence there from those imployments, whereof we shall have too good store; you shall not so much amend the state of your body, as happily you shall call in question the reputation of your mind and judgment, even in the opinion of those that love you, and are best acquainted with your indisposition and discretion.

"Interpret this our plainness, we pray you, to our extraordinary estimation of you; for it is not common with us to deal so freely with many; and believe that you shall ever find us both ready and willing in all occasions to yeild you the fruits of that interest, which your endeavours have purchased for you in our opinion and estimation. Nor doubting but when you have with moderation made tryal of the success of these your sundry peregrinations, you will find as great comfort to spend your dayes at home as heretofore you have done; of which we do wish you full measure, howsoever you shall have cause of abode or return. Given under our signet, at our manor of Nonesuch, the seventh of October 1594, in the 37th year of our reign.

"Your most loving Soveraign,

"E. R."

It appears by the premises, that it was written to this lord when he was at the Spa in Lukeland, for the recovery of his health, when a second English invasion of the Spaniard was (I will not say feared, but) expected. Now though this lord was born beyond the seas accidentally (his parents flying persecution in the reign of queen Mary), yet must he justly be reputed this countryman, where his ancestors had flourished so many years, and where he was baron Willoughby in right of his mother.   He died anno Domini 1601; and lies buried under a stately monument at Eresby in this county.

Sir EDWARD HARWOOD was born nigh Bourne, in this county, a valiant soldier and a gracious man.   Such who object that he was extremely wild in his youth, put me in mind of the return which one made to an ill-natured man in a company, who with much bitterness had aggravated the debauched youth of an aged and right godly divine : " You have proved," said he, " with much pains what all knew before, that Paul was a great persecutor before he was converted."

I have read of a bird, which hath a face like, and yet will prey upon, a man; who coming to the water to drink, and finding there by reflection that he had killed one like himself, pineth away by degrees, and never afterwards enjoyeth itself. Such in some sort the condition of Sir Edward.   This accident, that he had killed one in a private quarrel, put a period to his carnal mirth, and was a covering to his eyes all the days of his life.   No possible provocations could afterwards tempt him to a duel : and no wonder if one's conscience loathed that whereof he had surfeited.   He refused all challenges with more honour than others accepted them ; it being well known, that he would set his foot as far in the face of an enemy as any man alive. He was one of the four standing colonels in the Low Countries, and was shot at the siege of Maestricht, anno Domini 1632. Death was so civil to him as to allow him leave to rise up on his knees, and to cry " Lord have mercy upon me."   Thus a long death-prayer after short piety is not so good, as a short prayer after a long pious conversation.

SEAMEN.

JOB HARTOP was (as himself* affirmeth) born at Bourne in this county, and went anno 1568 (early days, I assure you, for the English in those parts) with Sir John Hawkins, his general, to make discoveries in New Spain.   This Job was chief gunner in her majesty's ship called the Jesus of Lubec, being the queen's by no other title but as hired for her money, who in the beginning of her reign, before her navy-royal was erected, had her ships from the Hans-towns.

Long and dangerous was his journey; eight of his men at Cape Verd being killed, and the general himself wounded with poisoned arrows, but was cured by a negro drawing out the poison with a clove of garlic,† enough to make nice noses dispense with the valiant smell for the sanative virtue thereof.

He wrote a treatise of his voyage ; and is the first I met with, who mentioneth that strange tree, which may be termed the *tree of food*, affording a liquor which is both meat and

---

* In his Travels, inserted in Hackluit's Voyages, last Part, p. 487.
† Idem, ibidem.

drink; the *tree of raiment*, yielding needles wherewith, and thread whereof, mantles are made; the *tree of harbour*, tiles to cover houses, being made out of the solid parts thereof; so that it beareth a self-sufficiency for man's maintenance.

Job was his name, and patience was with him; so that he may pass amongst the Confessors of this county; for, being with some other by this general, for want of provisions, left on land, after many miseries they came to Mexico, and he continued a prisoner twenty-three years, viz. two years in Mexico, one year in the Contraction-house in Seville, another in the Inquisition-house in Triana, twelve years in the galleys, four years (with the Cross of St. Andrew on his back) in the Ever-lasting-Prison, and three years a drudge to Hernando de Soria; to so high a sum did the inventory of his sufferings amount.

So much of his patience. Now see "the end which the Lord made with him." Whilst enslaved to the aforesaid Hernando, he was sent to sea in a Flemish, which was afterward taken by an English ship, called the Galeon Dudley; and so was he safely landed at Portsmouth, December the second, 1590; and, I believe, lived not long after.

Sir WILLIAM MOUNSON, Knight, was extracted of an ancient family in this shire; and was from his youth bred in sea-service, wherein he attained to great perfection. Queen Elizabeth, having cleared Ireland of the Spanish forces, and desiring carefully to prevent a relapse, altered the scene of war, from Ireland to Spain, from defending to invading.

Sir Richard Leveson was admiral; our Sir William, vice-admiral; anno 1602.

These, without drawing a sword, killed trading quite on the coasts of Portugal, no vessels daring to go in or out of their harbours.

They had intelligence of a caract ready to land in Sisimbria, which was of 1600 ton, richly laden, out of the East Indies; and resolved to assault it, though it seemed placed in an invincible posture. Of itself it was a giant in comparison to our pigmy ships, and had in her three hundred Spanish gentlemen; the Marquess de Sancta Cruce lay hard by with thirteen ships, and all were secured under the command of a strong and well fortified castle. But nothing is impossible to man's valour and God's blessing thereon. After a fair dispute (which lasted for some hours) with syllogisms of fire and sword, the caract was conquered, the wealth taken therein amounting to the value of ten hundred thousand crowns of Portugal account.* But, though the goods gotten therein might be valued, the good gained thereby was inestimable; for henceforward they beheld

* Camden's Elizabeth, anno 1602.

the English with admiring eyes, and quitted their thoughts of invasion. This worthy knight died about the midst of the reign of king James.

WRITERS.

This county hath afforded many; partly because so large in itself; partly because abounding with so many monasteries (whereof two mitred ones, Crowland and Bardney) the seminaries of many learned men; not to speak of the cathedral of Lincoln and embryo university of Stamford, wherein many had their education. Wherefore, to pass by Fœlix Crowlandensis, Kimbertus Lindesius, and others, all of them not affording so much true history as will fill a hollow quill therewith, we take notice of some principal ones; and begin with,

GILBERT of HOLLAND.—He took his name, not as others from a single town, but a great part of ground, the third part of this tripartite county; which, in my apprehension, argues his diligence in preaching thereabouts. But, quitting his native land, he was invited by the famous St. Bernard to go to and live with him at Clarvaulx in Burgundy, where he became his scholar.

Some will prize a crumb of foreign praise before a loaf of English commendation, as subject to partiality to their own countrymen. Let such hear how abbot Trithemius the German commendeth our Gilbert: " Vir erat in Scripturis Divinis studiosus et egregiè doctus, ingenio subtilis, et clarus eloquio."

The poets feign that Hercules for a time supplied the place of wearied Atlas, in supporting the heavens. So our Gilbert was frequently substitute to St. Bernard; continuing his sermons where the other brake off, from those words "in lectulo meo per noctes," &c. unto the end of the book, being forty-six sermons, in style scarce discernible from St. Bernard's. He flourished anno Domini 1200; and was buried at Cistreaux in France.

ROGER of CROULAND was bred a Benedictine monk therein, and afterwards became abbot of Friskney in this county. He was the seventh man in order, who wrote the Life of Thomas Becket. Some will say his six elder brethren left his pen but a pitiful portion, to whom it was impossible to present the reader with any remarkable novelty in so trite a subject. But know, that the pretended miracles of Becket daily multiplying, the last writer had the most matter in that kind. He divided his book into seven volumes, and was full fifteen years in making it, from the last of king Richard the First, to the fourteenth of king John. But whether this elephantine birth answered that proportion of time in the performance thereof, let others decide. He flourished anno Domini 1214.

ELIAS de TREKINGHAM was born in this county, at a village so called, as by the sequent will appear.

Ingulphus* relateth, that in the year of our Lord 870, in the month of September, Count Algar, with others, bid battle to the Danes in Kesteven, a third of this county, and worsted them, killing three of their kings, whom the Danes buried in a village therein, formerly called Laundon, but after Trekingham. Nor do I know any place to which the same name, on the like accident, can be applied, except it be Alcaser in Africa, where, anno 1578, Sebastian the Portugal and two other Moorish kings were killed in one battle.

I confess no such place as Trekingham appeareth at this day in any catalogue of English Towns; whence I conclude it a parish some years since depopulated, or never but a churchless village. This Elias was a monk of Peterborough,† doctor of divinity in Oxford, a learned man, and great lover of history, writing himself a chronicle from the year of our Lord 626, till 1270, at what time it is probable he deceased.

HUGO KIRKSTED was born at that well known town in this county, being bred a Benedictine-Cistercian-Bernardine. A Cistercian is a reformed Benedictine, a Bernardine is a reformed Cistercian; so that our Hugh may charitably be presumed pure, as twice refined. He consulted one Serlo, an aged man, and one of his own order; and they both clubbing their pains and brains together, made a chronicle of the Cistercians from their first coming into England, anno 1131 (when Walter de Espeke founded their first abbey at Rivaux in Yorkshire). Our Hugh did write, Serlo did indite, being almost an hundred years old, so that his memory was a perfect chronicle of all remarkable passages from the beginning of his order.‡ Our Hugo flourished anno Domini 1220.

WILLIAM LIDLINGTON was born, say some, at that village in Cambridgeshire; at a village so named in this county say others, with whom I concur, because he had his education at Stamford. He was by profession a Carmelite, and became the fifth Provincial of his order in England. Monasteries being multiplied in that age, Gerardus a Frenchman, master-general of the Carmelites, in a Synod at Narbonne, deputed two English Provincials of that order, to the great grievance of our Lidlington, refusing to subscribe to the decisions of that Synod. His stubbornness cost him an excommunication from Pope Clement the Fifth, and four years' penance of banishment from his native country. Mean time our Lidlington, living at Paris, ac-

* Pag. 865.
† Bale, de Scriptoribus Britannicis, Cent. iv. num. 31. Pits, de Scriptoribus Angliæ, pag. 35. anno 1270.
‡ Bale, de Scriptoribus Britannicis, Cent. iii. num. 81.

quired great credit unto himself by his lectures and disputations.* At last he was preferred Provincial of the Carmelites in Palestine (whence from Mount Carmel he fetched their original) ; and he himself best knew whether the depth of his profit answered the height of his honour therein, which I suspect the rather, because returning into England he died and was buried at Stamford, anno Domini 1309.

NICHOLAS STANFORD.—He was born at that well known town, once offering to be a university, and bred a Bernardine therein. The eulogy given him by learned Leland ought not to be measured by the yard, but weighed in the balance : " Admirabar hominem ejus ætatis tam argutè, tam solidò, tamque significanter potuisse scribere ;" (I admired much that a man of his age could write so smartly, so solidly, so significantly.) Understand him not, that one so infirm with age, or decrepit in years, but that one living in so ignorant and superstitious a generation, could write so tersely; flourishing, as may be collected, about the year of our Lord 1310.

JOHN BLOXHAM was born at that town in this county, and bred a Carmelite in Chester. I confess it is a common expression of the countryfolk in this county, when they intend to character a dull, heavy, blundering person, to say of him, " he was born at Bloxham ;" but indeed our John, though there first encradled, had acuteness enough, and some will say activity too much for a friar. He advantageously fixed himself at Chester, a city in England, near Ireland, and not far from Scotland, much conducing to his ease, who was supreme Prefect of his order through those three nations, for two years and a half ;† for afterwards he quitted that place, so great was his employment under king Edward the Second and Third, in several embassies into Scotland and Ireland ; flourishing anno 1334.

JOHN HORNBY was born in this county,‡ bred a Carmelite, D. D. in Cambridge. In his time happened a tough contest betwixt the Dominicans and Carmelites about priority.
Plaintiff, Dominican—John Stock (or Stake rather, so sharp and poignant his pen) left marks in the backs of his adversaries.
Judges—John Donwick the chancellor, and the doctors of the university.
Defendant, Carmelite—John Hornby, who, by his preaching and writing, did vindicate the seniority of his order.
But our Hornby, with his Carmelites, clearly carried away the conquest of precedency, and got it confirmed under the authentic seal of the university.

* Ibid. Cent. iv. n. 79.
† Bale, de Scriptoribus Britannicis, Cent. v. p. 399.
‡ Pits, de Angliæ Scriptoribus, num. 636.

However, the Dominicans desisted not to justle with them for the upper hand, until Henry the Eighth made them friends by thrusting both out of the land. Our Hornby flourished anno Domini 1374; and was buried at his convent in Boston.

BOSTON of BURY, for so he is generally called.* I shall endeavour to restore him first to his true name, then to his native country. Some presume Boston to be his Christian; of Bury, his surname. But seeing Boston is no font name, and godfathers were conscientious in those days (I appeal to all English antiquaries) in imposing, if not Scripture or Saints' names, yet such as were commonly known (the christianizing of surnames to baptized infants being of more modern device), we cannot concur with their judgment herein. And now thanks be to Doctor John Caius, who, in the catalogue of his author cited in the "Defence of the Antiquity of Cambridge," calleth him John Boston of Bury, being born at and taking his surname from Boston in this county, (which was customary for the clergymen in those days), though he lived a monk in Bury. Thus, in point of nativities, Suffolk hath not lost, but Lincolnshire hath recovered, a writer belonging unto it.

He travelled all over England, and exactly perused the library in all monasteries, whereby he was enabled to write a catalogue of ecclesiastical writers, as well foreign as English, extant in his age. Such his accurateness, as not only to tell the initial words in every of their books, but also to point at the place in each library where they are to be had. John Leland oweth as much to this John Boston, as John Bale doth to him, and John Pits to them both. His manuscript was never printed, nor was it my happiness to see it; but I have often heard the late reverend archbishop of Armagh† rejoice in this, that he had, if not the first, the best copy thereof in Europe. Learned Sir James WARE transcribed these verses out of it: which, because they conduce to the clearing of his nativity, I have here inserted, requesting the reader not to measure his prose by his poetry, though he dedicated it to no meaner than Henry the Fourth, king of England:

> "Qui legis hunc Librum, Scriptorum, Rex, miserere,
> Dum scripsit verè, non fecit (ut æstimo) pigrum.
> Si tibi displiceat, veniat tua gratia grandis;
> Quam cunctis pandis, hæc sibi sufficiat.
> Scriptoris nomen Botolphi Villa vocatur;
> Qui condemnatur nisi gratum det Deus omen."

Sure it is, that his writings are esteemed the rarity of rarities by the lovers of antiquities; which I speak in humble advice to the reader, if possessed thereof to keep and value them; if not, not to despise his books, if on any reasonable price they may be procured. This John Boston flourished anno Domini 1410.

* Bale, de Scriptoribus Britannicis, Cent. vii. n. 48: and Pits, in anno 1410.
† Dr. James Usher.—ED.

LAURENCE HOLEBECK was born, saith my author,* " apud Girvios;" that is, amongst the Fenlanders. I confess, such people with their stilts do stride over much ground, the parcels of several shires, Norfolk, Suffolk, Cambridge, Huntingdon, Northampton, Lincolnshire. But I have fixed him right in this county, where Holebeck is not far from Crowland in Holland.

He was bred a monk in the abbey of Ramsey, and was very well skilled in the Hebrew tongue, according to the rate of that age : for the Englismen were so great strangers in that language, that even the priests amongst them, in the reign of king Henry the Eighth, as Erasmus reporteth, " Isti quicquid non intelligunt Hebraicum vocant,"† (counted all things Hebrew which they did not understand); and so they reputed a tablet which he wrote upon Walsingham in great Roman letters, out of the road of common cognizance. Holebeck made a Hebrew Dictionary, which was counted very exact according to those days. I. Pits doth heavily complain of Robert Wakefeild (the first Hebrew professor of Cambridge) that he purloined this Dictionary to his private use; whereon all I will observe is this:

It is resolved in the law, that the taking of another man's sheep is felony, whilst the taking away of a sheep-pasture is but a trespass, the party pretending a right thereunto. Thus I know many men so conscientious, that they will not take twenty lines together from any author (without acknowledging it in the margin), conceiving it to be the fault of a plagiary. Yet the same critics repute it no great guilt to seize a whole manuscript, if they can conveniently make themselves the masters, though not owners thereof ; in which act none can excuse them, though we have too many precedents hereof. This Laurence died anno Domini 1410.

BERTRAM FITZALIN. — Finding him charactered *illustri stemmate oriundus*,‡ I should have suspected him a Sussex man, and allied to the earls of Arundel, had not another author positively informed me he was *patriâ Lincolniensi*, bred B. D. in Oxford, and then lived a Carmelite in the city of Lincoln.§ Here he built a fair library on his and his friend's cost, and furnished it with books, some of his own making, but more purchased. He lived well beloved, and died much lamented, the seventeenth of March 1424.

WRITERS SINCE THE REFORMATION.

EDMUND SHEFFEILD (descended from Robert Sheffeild, Recorder of London, knighted by king Henry the Seventh,‖ 1496,

---

* Bale, de Scriptoribus Britannicis, Cent. vii.
† In his Dialogue. Per Religi. Er.
‡ Bale, de Scriptoribus Britannicis, Cent. vii. num. 64.
§ Pits, de Angliæ Scriptoribus, anno 1424.
‖ Stow's Survey of London, p. 574.

for his good service against the rebels at Blackheath) was born at Butterwick in the Isle of Axholm in this county, and was by king Edward the Sixth created baron thereof. Great his skill in music, who wrote a book of sonnets according to the Italian fashion. He may seem, swan-like, to have sung his own funeral, being soon after slain (or murdered rather) in a skirmish against the rebels in Norwich; first unhorsed and cast into a ditch, and then slaughtered by a butcher, who denied him quarter, 1449. He was direct ancestor to the hopeful earl of Mulgrave.

PETER MORWING was born in this county, and bred fellow of Magdalen College in Oxford.* Here I cannot but smile at the great praise which I. Pits bestoweth upon him: "Vir omni Latini sermonis elegantiâ bellè instructus, et qui scripta quædam, tum versu, tum prosâ, tersè nitidèque composuisse perhibetur."†

It plainly appeareth he mistook him for one of his own persuasion; and would have retracted this character, and beshrewed his own fingers for writing it, had he known him to have been a most cordial Protestant.‡ Nor would he have afforded him the phrase of "claruit sub Philippo et Mariâ," who under their reigns was forced, for his conscience, to fly into Germany, where he supported himself by preaching to the English exiles. I find not what became of him after his return into England in the reign of queen Elizabeth.

ANTHONY GILBY was born in this county, and bred in Christ's College in Cambridge, where he attained to great skill in the three learned languages.§ But what gave him the greatest reputation with Protestants, was, that in the reign of queen Mary he had been an exile at Geneva for his conscience. Returning into England, he became a fierce, fiery, and furious opposer of the church discipline established in England, as in our "Ecclesiastical History" may appear. The certain date of his death is to me unknown.

JOHN FOX was born at Boston in this county, and bred fellow in Magdalen College in Oxford. He fled beyond the seas in the reign of queen Mary, where he set forth the first and least edition of the "Book of Martyrs" in Latin, and afterwards, returning into England, enlarged and twice revised the same in our own language.

The story is sufficiently known of the two servants, whereof the one told his master, "he would do every thing;" the other (which was even Esop himself) said, "he could do nothing;" rendering this reason, "because his former fellow servant would

---

* Bale, de Scriptoribus sui temporis.　　　† De Angliæ Scriptoribus, page 757.
‡ P. Morvinus voluntarium in Germaniâ exilium, turpi in Collegio remansioni, prætulit. Dr. Humfred, in Vitâ Juelli, page 73.　　　§ J. Bale.

leave him nothing to do."* But in good earnest, as to the particular subject of our English martyrs, Mr. Fox "hath done every thing" (leaving posterity nothing to work upon); and to those who say "he hath overdone something," we have returned our answer before.†

He was one of prodigious charity to the poor, seeing nothing could bound his bounty but want of money to give away: but I have largely written of his life and death in my "Church History."

THOMAS SPARKS, D.D. was born at South Sommercot in this county, bred in Oxford, and afterwards became minister of Bleachley in Buckinghamshire: an impropriation which the lord Gray of Wilton (whose dwelling was at Whaddon hard by) restored to the church.‡ He was a solid divine and learned man, as by his works still extant doth appear. At first he was a Nonconformist, and therefore was chosen by that party as one of their champions in the Conference of Hampton Court. Yet was he wholly silent in that disputation, not for any want of ability, but because (as afterwards it did appear) he was convinced in his conscience at that conference of the lawfulness of ceremonies, so that some accounted him king James's convert herein. He afterwards set forth a book of Unity and Uniformity, and died about the year of our Lord 1610.

DOCTOR TIGHE was born at Deeping in this county, bred (as I take it) in the university of Oxford. He afterwards became archdeacon of Middlesex, and minister of All-hallows Barking, London. He was an excellent textuary and profound linguist, the reason why he was employed by king James in translating of the Bible. He died (as I am informed by his nephew,§) about the year of our Lord 1620; leaving to John Tighe his son, of Carby in this county, Esquire, an estate of one thousand pounds a year; and none, I hope, have cause to envy or repine thereat.

FINES MORISON, brother to Sir Richard Morison, lord president of Munster, was born in this county of worshipful extraction, and bred a fellow of Peter-house in Cambridge. He began his travels May the first, 1591, over a great part of Christendom, and no small share of Turkey, even to Jerusalem, and afterwards printed his observations in a large book, which for the truth thereof is in good reputation; for of so great a traveller he had nothing of a traveller in him, as to stretch in his reports. At last he was secretary to Charles Blunt, deputy of Ireland,

---

* In vitâ Æsopi.
† In our Description of Berkshire, under the title of CONFESSORS.
‡ So am I informed by his grandchild and heir.
§ Living at Tenterbury in Kent.

saw and wrote the conflicts with and conquest of Tyrone, a discourse which deserveth credit, because the writer's eye guided his pen, and the privacy of his place acquainted him with many secret passages of importance. He died about the year of our Lord 1614.

BENEFACTORS TO THE PUBLIC.

Having formerly presented the reader with two eminent ones, Bishop Wainfleit, founder of New College, and Bishop Fox, founder of Corpus Christi in Oxford ; he (if but of an ordinary appetite) will be plentifully feasted therewith ; so that we may proceed to those who were

SINCE THE REFORMATION.

WILLIAM RATCLIFFE, Esquire, and four times alderman of the town of Stamford, died anno Domini 1530 : gave all his messuages, lands, and tenements in the town, to the maintenance of a free school therein,* which lands for the present yield thirty pounds per annum, or thereabouts, to a school-master and usher. I am informed that an augmentation was since given to their stipend by William Cecil, lord treasurer ; but it seems that since, some intervening accident hath hindered it from taking the true effect.

JANE CECIL, wife to Richard Cecil, Esquire, and coheir to the worshipful families of Ekington and Wallcot, was born in this county, and lived the main of her life therein.† Job, speaking of parents deceased, " His sons," saith he, " come to honour, and he knoweth it not ;"‡ but God gave this good woman so long a life (abating but little of a hundred years) that she knew the preferment of her son, William Cecil, for many years in her life, lord treasurer of England. I say she knew it, and saw it, and joyed at it, and was thankful to God for it ; for well may we conclude her gratitude to God, from her charity to man. At her own charges, anno 1561, she leaded and paved the Friday Market Cross in Stamford ;§ besides fifty pounds given to the poor, and many other benefactions. Her last will was made anno Domini 1588. But she survived some time after, and lies buried, in the same vault with her son, in St. Martin's in Stamford.

[AMP.] GEORGE TRIGG, Gentleman, was, as I collect, a native of this county ; he gave, anno Domini 1586, four hundred pounds, to be lent out for ever, upon good security, without interest, to poor young tradesmen and artificers in Stamford.||

---

* R. Butcher, in his Survey of Stamford, page 82.
† Camden's Eliz. in anno 15. ‡ Job xiv. 21.
§ Richard Butcher, in his Survey of Stamford, page 33.
|| Idem, pages 33 and 38.

He also bestowed a tenement upon the parson and poor of St. John's in the same town.

RICHARD SUTTON, Esquire, was born at Knaith in this county, bred a soldier in his youth, and was somewhat of pay-master by his place; much money therefore passing through, some did lawfully stick on his fingers, which became the bottom of his future estate. He was afterward a merchant in London, and gained great wealth therein. Such who charge him with pur-blindness in his soul, looking too close on the earth, do them-selves acquit him from oppression; that, though *tenax*, he was not *rapax*; not guilty of covetousness, but parsimony.

Indeed, there was a merchant, his comrade, whose name I will conceal (except the great estate he left doth discover it (with whom he had company in common; but their charges were se-veral to themselves. When his friend in travel called for two faggots, Mr. Sutton called for one; when his friend for half a pint of wine, Mr. Sutton for a gill, underspending him a moiety. At last, Mr. Sutton hearing of his friend's death, and that he left but fifty thousand pounds estate, "I thought," said he, " he would die no rich man, who made such needless expences."

Indeed, Mr. Sutton's estate doubled his; and he bestowed it all on Charter-house, or Sutton's Hospital. This is the master-piece of Protestant English charity; designed in his life; com-pleted after his death; begun, continued, and finished, with buildings and endowments, *sine causâ sociâ*, solely at his charges; wherein Mr. Sutton appears peerless in all Christendom, on an equal standard and valuation of revenue. As for the canker of Popish malice endeavouring to fret this fair flower, we have re-turned plentiful answers to their cavils in our "Ecclesiastical History." Mr. Sutton died anno Domini 1611.

ROBERT JOHNSON was born at Stamford, whereof Maurice his father had been chief magistrate. He was bred in Cam-bridge, and entering into the ministry, he was beneficed at Luf-fenham in Rutland, at what time that little county was at a great loss for the education of the children therein; and Mr. Johnson endeavoured a remedy thereof.

He had a rare faculty in requesting of others into his own de-sire, and with his arguments could surprise a miser into charity. He effectually moved those of the vicinage, to contribute, to the building and endowing of schools, money or money worth; stones, timber, carriage, &c.; not slighting the smallest gift, es-pecially if proportionable to the giver's estate. Hereby finding none, he left as many free schools in Rutland, as there were market towns therein; one at Okeham, another at Uppingham, well faced with buildings, and lined with endowments.

Hitherto he was only a nurse to the charity of others, erect-ing the schools aforesaid, as my author observeth,* who after-

* Camden's Britannia, in Rutland, è stirpe collaticiâ.

wards proved a fruitful parent in his own person, becoming a considerable benefactor to Emanuel and Sidney colleges in Cambridge; and, though never dignified higher than archdeacon of Leicester, he left an estate of one thousand pounds per annum, which descended to his posterity. He died about the year of our Lord 1616.

FRANCES WRAY, daughter to Sir Chichester Wray, lord chief justice, was born at Glentworth in this county; and married first unto Sir George St. Paul of this county, and afterwards to Robert Rich, first earl of Warwick of that surname. She was a pious lady, much devoted to charitable actions, though I am not perfectly instructed in the particulars of her benefactions. Only I am sure Magdalen College in Cambridge hath tasted largely of her liberality; who died in the beginning of the reign of king Charles.

MEMORABLE PERSONS.

JAMES YORKE, a blacksmith of Lincoln, and an excellent workman in his profession, insomuch that if Pegasus himself would wear shoes, this man alone is fit to make them, contriving them so thin and light, as that they would be no burden to him. But he is a servant as well of Apollo as Vulcan, turning his *stiddy* into a *study*, having lately set forth a book of heraldry called "The Union of Honour," containing the arms of the English nobility, and the gentry of Lincolnshire. And although there be some mistake (no hand so steady as always to hit the nail on the head), yet is it of singular use and industriously performed; being set forth anno 1640.

LORD MAYORS.

1. John Stockton, son of Richard Stockton, of Bratoft, Mercer, 1470.
2. Nicholas Aldwin, son of Richard Aldwin, of Spalding, Mercer, 1499.
3. William Rennington, son of Robert Rennington, of Boston, Fishmonger, 1500.
4. William Forman, son of William Forman, of Gainsborough, Haberdasher, 1538.
5. Henry Hoberthorn, son of Christ. Hoberthorn, of Waddingworth, Merchant Taylor, 1546.
6. Henry Amcoates, son of William Amcoates, of Astrap, Fishmonger, 1548.
7. John Langley, son of Robert Langley, of Althrope, Goldsmith, 1576.
8. John Allot, son of Richard Allot, of Limbergh, Fishmonger, 1590.
9. Nicholas Raynton, son of Robert Raynton, of Heighington, Haberdasher, 1632.

THE NAMES OF THE GENTRY OF THIS COUNTY,

RETURNED BY THE COMMISSIONERS IN THE TWELFTH YEAR OF KING HENRY THE SIXTH.

William Bishop of Lincoln, and Lion de Welles, chevalier ;— Thomas Meres, and Patricius Skipwith, (knights of the shire) ; —Commissioners.

Johannis Willoughby, militis.
Roberti Ros, militis.
Humfridi Littelbery, armig.
Philippi Tilney, arm.
Johannis Copuldik, arm.
Richardi Laund, arm.
Willielmi Braunche, arm.
Richardi Pynchebek.
Richardi Welby.
Richardi Benynington.
Willielmi Goding de Boston.
Gilberti Haltoft.
Will. Hughbert de Doning.
Will. Quadring de Tofte.
Johan. Pawlyn de Frampton.
Will. Walcote de Spaldyng.
Thom. Overton de Swynshed.
Hug. Dandison de Wrangle.
Roberti Hughson de Boston.
Rich. Whiteb. de Gosberkerk.
Joh. Docking de Whaploade.
Will. Calowe de Holbetch.
Will. Cawode de Whaploade.
Nich. Gyomer de Sutton de Holand.
Godf. Hilton, militis.
Johannis Busshe, militis.
Nicholai Bowel, militis.
Philippi Dymmok, militis.
Johannis Gra, militis.
Johannis Pygot, arm.
Johannis Boys, arm.
Galfridi Painell, arm.
Maunceri Marmeon, arm.
Willielmi Eton, arm.
Johannis Markham.
Johannis Trenthall, gent.
Thom. Holme, gent.
Joh. Saltby de Gunwardby.
Thomæ Repynghale.
Johannis Hesill de Carleton.

Johannis Leek de Grantham.
Will. Mapulbeck de Granth.
Joh. Chevercourt de Stannf.
Nich. Mason de Blankeney.
Joh. Chapelyn de Sleford.
Thomæ Sleford de Kirkeby.
Joh. Hardyng de Kime.
Joh. Wykes, armigeri, de Kisteven.
Hugonis Midleton, militis.
Rogeri Wentworth, arm.
Roberti Auncell de Grymesby.
Willielmi Bleseby de Bleseby.
Thomæ Fereby de Burton.
Johannis Ufflete de Halton.
Johan. Thoresby de Croxby.
And. Godehand de Whalesby.
Joh. Tomlinson de Wotton.
Roberti Morley, arm.
Johannis Abbot de Hatclif.
Johannis Smith de Elkington.
Abbatis de Neusom.
Johan. Teleby Canonici ejusdem Abbatis.
Johannis Cawode de Oxcomb.
Joh. Langton de Somercotes.
Wil. Marshall de Somercotes.
Roberti Pigot de Parva Grymesby.
Thomæ Spaldyng de Claxby.
Johannis Hamon, parsone de Whalesby.
Joh. Boucher de Tynton.
Richardi Alesby de Hatclif, clerici.
Rogeri Glaston, parsone de Aylesby.
Rob. Lackwode de Whalesby.
Johannis Nundye de Whalesby, chapellani.

SHERIFFS
OF LINCOLNSHIRE.

HENRY II.
Anno

1 Rainerus de Bada.
2 Jordanus de Blossevilla.
3 Walterus de Amundevel, for seven years.
10 Petrus de Gossa.
11 Idem.
12 Willielmus de Insula.
13 Aluredus de Poiltona.
14 Philippus de Kime.
15 Idem.
16 Walterus de Grimesby.
17 Idem.
18 Walt. et Al. de Poilton.
19 Walt. et Al. de Poilton.
20 Idem.
21 Idem.
22 Drogo filius Radulphi.
23 Idem.
24 Will. Basset, for seven years.
31 Nigel. filius Alexandri.
32 Idem.
33 Idem.

RICHARD I.

1 Nigellus filius Alexandri.
2 Gerardus de Camvill. Roger de Stikewald.
3 Gerardus de Camvill.
4 Gerard. et Roger. Stikelralde.
5 Idem.
6 Gerardus et Eustacius de Hedenham.
7 Simond Kimmeo et Petrus de Trihanton.
8 Sim. de Kime, et Petrus de Beckering, et Robertus de Trihanton.
9 Idem.
10 Philip. filius Roberti.

JOHAN. R.

1 Robertus de Tateshall.

Anno

2 Ger. de Cemvill et Hugo filius Ricardi, for six years.
8 Thomas de Muleton.
9 Idem.
10 Idem.
11 Huber. de Burgo et Alex. Ormesby (ut Custos).
12 Huber. Alex. (ut Custos).
13 Hubertus de Burozo et Robertus de Aoziulver.
14 Hub. de Burozo et Rob. Aquilum.
15 Hubertus de Burgo et Robertus Aquilum, Alex. de Puncton.
16 Idem.
17 Johannes Marescallus.

HENRY III.

1 Will. Comes Saresb. Will. filius Warner.
2 Will. Comes Sarisb. et Johan. Bonet, for five years.
7 Steph. de Segne et Radulphus filius Regin.
8 Idem.
9 Hugo Lincolne Episcopus, et Rad. filius Regin.
10 Hugo Episcop. et Rad.
11 Radulph. filius Regin.
12 Idem.
13 Idem.
14 Robertus de Rokefeld.
15 Walt. de Cuerame, et Willielmus de Curum.
16 Walt. et Willielmus.
17 Phil. de Ascellus.
18 Philippus.
19 Philippus.
20 Philippus.
21 Robertus Lupus, for four years.
25 Radulphus Basset, for five years.

298   WORTHIES OF LINCOLNSHIRE.

Anno

30 Willielmus de Derleg.
31 Willi. filius de Curzim, for five years.
36 Gilbertus de Cheile, for four years.
40 Roger. Beler. et Roger. et hæres ejusdem.
41 Williel. de Leverton.
42 Joh. de Cookerington.
43 Will. de Angleby, et Wil. de Notingham.
44 Hamo Hauteyn.
45 Idem.
46 Willielmus de Grey.
47 Idem.
48 Idem.
49 Will. et Rich. de Grey, fil. ejus hæres, et Will. de Notingham Clericus.
50 Will. et Rich. Will. et Ja. Panton.
51 Idem.
52 Jacobus Panton, for four years.
56 Tho. de Bolton.

EDWARD I.

1 Thomas.
2 Thomas.
3 Richardus de Harington.
4 Nicolaus de Rye.
5 Idem.
6 Idem.
7 Adamus de Sancto Laudo.
8 Idem.
9 Idem.
10 Radulphus de Arnehall.
11 Radul. de Arnehall, et Walt. de Stuchesle.
12 Idem.
13 Idem.
14 Robert. de Cadworth, for five years.
19 Johan. Dyne.
20 Idem.
21 Johan. et Radulphus de Trihampton.

Anno

22 Robertus la Venur, for four years.
26 Rad. de Paynell, et Rich. de Draycot.
27 Idem.
28 Ricardus de Howell.
29 Hugo de Bussey.
30 Idem.
31 Tho. fil. Eustarchi.
32 Idem, et Johan. Nevill.
33 Thom. de Burnham, for five years.

EDWARD II.

1 Radulphus Paynell.
2 Idem.
3 Thom. de Burnham.
4 Johan. de Nevill, et Rad. de Rye.
5 Idem.
6 Johannes.
7 Johannes.
8 Tho. de Tittele, et Joh. de Nevill.
9 Idem.
10 Johan. de Nevill, et Robertus Stannton.
11 Robertus de Stannton.
12 Robertus et Simon de Landerthorp.
13 Johan. de Bellâ-fide, for four years.
17 Simon le Chamberlaine.
18 Simon et Reginald. Donington.
19 Idem.

EDWARD III.

1 Tho. de Novo Mercato.
2 Simon Kinardsley.
3 Tho. de Novo Mercato.
4 Tho. de Novo Mercato.
5 Rad. de Santo Laudo, et Tho. de Novo Mercato.
6 Reginal. de Donington, et Rad. de Santo Laudo.
7 Idem.
8 Johan. de Trehampton.

Anno

9 Idem.

10 Rad. de Santo Laudo, et Regin. de Donington.

11 Johannes de Bolingbroke, et Joh. de Trehampton.

12 Gilbertus de Beaved.

13 Idem.

14 Willielmus Disney, et Gilbertus de Leddred.

15 Idem.

16 Willielmus Franuke.

17 Johannes de Hundon.

18 Saierus de Rochford.

19 Idem.

20 Johan. de Trehampton.

21 Idem.

22

Anno

23 Saierus de Rochford, for six years.

29 Tho. Fulvetby, et Sajerus de Rochford, for four years.

33 Edw. de Cormil.

34 Idem.

35 Johan. de Boys.

36 Idem.

37 Will. Haudley, for six years.

43 Thomæ de Fulvetby, for four years.

47 Willielmus Bussy.

41 Johannes Hode.

49 Tho. de Kidale.

50 Rogerus Beler.

51 Radulphus Paynell.

SHERIFFS.

RICH. II.

Anno	Name and Arms.	Place.
1	Tho. de Kydale . . .	Ferriby.
	S. a saltire raguled Arg.	
2	Will. de Spaygne.	
3	Johann. Ponger.	
4	Tho. Thimorby . . .	Irenham.
	Arg. three pallets, and four mullets in bend S.	
5	Will. de Belesby . . .	Belesby.
	Arg. a chevron betwixt three steel gads S.	
6	Johannes Ponger.	
7	Johannes Bussy . . .	Hather.
	Arg. three bars S.	
8	Williel. Spaygne.	
9	Johannes Bussy . . .	*ut prius.*
10	Philip. de Tilney . .	Boston.
	Arg. a chevron betwixt three griffins' heads erased G.	
11	Will. de Belesby . . .	*ut prius.*
12	Anketin Mallore.	
13	Walter. Taylboys.	
	Arg. a cross saltire and chief G.; on the last three escalops of the first.	
14	Johannes Bussy . . .	*ut prius.*
15	Johann. Rochford.	
	Quarterly O. and G. twelve bezants on a border S.	
16	Henr. de Recford.	
17	Joh. Cupuldicke . . .	Harrington.
	Arg. a chevron betwixt three crosses crossed G.	
18	Joh. Skipwith . . .	Ormsby.
	Arg. three bars G. in chief a greyhound cursant S.	

Anno   Name.   Place.

19 Joh. Walch   .   .   .   .   Grimsby.
    G. two bars gemelles a bend Arg.
20 Rogerus Welby.
    S. a fess betwixt three flowers-de-luce Arg.
21 Henricus Bidford, et
    Joh. Litelbury, mil.
    Arg. two lions passant gardant G.

HENRY IV.

1 Jo. Cobeldikes, mil. .   .   *ut prius.*
2 Joh. Rochford, mil. .   .   *ut prius.*
    et Tho. Swynford.
3 Ger. Soithil, mil.   .   .   Redborne.
    G. an eagle displayed Arg.
4 T. Willoughby, mil.   .   Eresby.
    Az. a fret of eight pieces Or.
5
6 Thomas Hanlay.
7 Henr. Redford, mil.
8 Rad. Rochford, mil.   .   *ut prius.*
9 T. Chauworth, mil.
    Az. two chevrons O.
10 Joh. Rochford   .   .   .   *ut prius.*
11 Joh. de Waterton.   .   .   Waterton.
    Barry of six Erm. and G. three crescents S.
12 Rob. Waterton   .   .   .   *ut prius.*

HENRY V.

1 Thomas Clarell.
2 Robertus Hilton.
    Arg. two bars Az. over all a flower-de-luce O.
3 T. Cumberworth, mil.   .   Cumberworth.
4 Nicholas Tournay   .   .   Cainby.
    Arg. a chevron betwixt three bulls passant S. armed Or.
5 Joh. Normanvile.
6 Thom. Chaworth   .   .   *ut prius.*
7 Rich. Haunsard   .   .   .   S. Kelsey.
    G. three mullets Arg.
8 Robertus Roos   .   .   .   Melton.
    G. three water-bougets Arg.
9 Rob. et Tho. Clarel.

HENRY VI.

1 Wal. Talboyes, mil. .   .   *ut prius.*
2 Joh. Haytfield.
3 Robertus Hilliard.
4 Joh. Talboys .   .   .   .   *ut prius.*
5 Will. Cupuldicke   .   .   *ut prius.*
6 Henricus Retford.

Anno	Name.	Place.

7 Hamo Sutton . . . . Willoughton.
  Arg. a quarter S. a crescent G.

8 Will. Rither, mil.

9 T. Cumberworth, mil.

10 Rob. Roos, mil. . . . *ut prius.*

11 Johan. Pigot, arm. . . Doddington.
  S. three pickaxes Arg.

12 Tho. Darcy, arm. . . Norton.
  Az. crusuly three cinquefoils Arg.

13 Johan. Cunstable . . Halsham.
  Quarterly G. and Vaire, a bend O.

14 Robert Roos, mil. . . *ut prius.*

15 Thom. Meres, arm. . . Kirton.
  G. a fess betwixt three water-bougets Erm.

16 Philippus Tilney . . . *ut prius.*

17 H. Willoughby, mil. . *ut prius.*

18 [AMP.] Joh. Nevil.

19 Nichol. Bowet, mil.

20 Rog. Pedwardyn . . . Burton Pedwardyn.

21 Johannes Sothil . . . *ut prius.*

22 Thomas Moigne.
  S. a fess dancetté betwixt six annulets O.

23

24 Johan. Harington.
  Arg. a fret S.

25 Thomas Meres . . . *ut prius.*

26 Nicholaus Bowet.

27 Manc. Marmyon, mil. . Scrivelby.
  Vairy Az. and Arg. a bend G.

28 Brian. Stapleton.
  Arg. a lion rampant S.

29 Will. Rither, mil.

30 Nich. Bowet, mil.

31 Johannes Nevil . . . *ut prius.*

32 Rich. Waterton . . . *ut prius.*

33 Hen. Retford, mil.

34 Joh. Tempest, mil.
  Arg. a bend betwixt six martlets S.

35 Joh. Harington, arm. . *ut prius.*

36 Ric. Waterton, arm. . *ut prius.*

37 W. Skipwith, mil. . . *ut prius.*

38 Joh. Marmyon, arm. . *ut prius.*

EDWARD IV.

1 Joh. Burgh, arm. . . . Gainsborough.
  Az. three flowers-de-luce Erm.

2 Tho. Blound, arm.

3

Anno	Name.	Place.

4 Will. Skipwith, mil.   .   *ut prius.*

5 Brian. Stapleton, mil.   .   *ut prius.*

6 Joh. Wichcote, arm.   .   Harpswell.
    Erm. two boars G.

7 Rob. Cunstable, mil.   .   *ut prius.*

8 Thomas Meres   .   .   .   *ut prius.*

9 Ri. Fitz Williams, mil.   Maple-thorp.
    Lozengée, Arg. and G.

10 Rich. Tempest, mil.   .   *ut prius.*

11 Richard Welby   .   .   .   *ut prius.*

12 L. Thornburgh, arm.

13 Thomas Kyme   .   .   .   Freisney.
    G. a chev. betwixt nine crosses crossed O.

14 Joh. Villers, arm.   .   .   Leicestershire.
    A. on a cross G. five escalops O.

15 Th. Wimbech, arm.

16 Rob. Markham, mil.   .   Sidebroke.
    Az. in chief O. a lion issuant G. and border Arg.

17 Tho. Bolles, arm.   .   .   Haugh.
    Az. three cups Arg. holding as many boars' heads
    erected O.

18 [AMP.] Will. Brown.

19 Tho. Tempest, arm. .   .   *ut prius.*

20 Joh. Bushy, mil. .   .   .   *ut prius.*

21 Rob. Talboys, mil.   .   .   *ut prius.*

22 Will. Tirwhit, arm.   .   .   Kettleby.
    Gules, three puits O.

RICHARD III.

1 Thomas Knight.

2 Rob. Dymock, mil.
    S. two lions passant gardant Arg. crowned O.

3 Thomas Meres   .   .   .   *ut prius.*

HENRY VII.

1 Thom. Pinchbeck.

2 Brian. Standford.

3 Johan. Copuldick   .   .   *ut prius.*

4 Tho. Tempest, mil. .   .   *ut prius.*

5 Oliv. St. John, mil.
    Arg. on a chief G. two mullets O. pierced.

6 H. Willougby, mil. .   .   *ut prius.*

7 Thomas Welby   .   .   .   *ut prius.*

8 Joh. Skipwith   .   .   .   *ut prius.*

9 Johan. Husee .   .   .   .   Sleford.
    O. a plain cross V.

10 W. Shiriolli, mil.

11 George Taylboys   .   .   *ut prius.*

Anno	Name.	Place.
12	Mance. Marmyon . .	*ut prius.*
13	Tho. Knight, arm.	
14	Tho. Dalaland, mil. . .	Ashby.
15	Will. Ascue, arm. . . .	Kelsey.

S. a fess O. betwixt three asses passant Arg. maned of the second.

16	Will. Tirwhit, mil. . .	*ut prius.*
17	H. Willoughby, mil. .	*ut prius.*
18	Rob. Dimmock, mil. .	*ut prius.*
19	Leon. Percy, arm.	

O. a lion rampant Az.

20	Will. Ascu, mil. . .	*ut prius.*
21	Milo. Bushy, mil. .	*ut prius.*
22	Rob. Sutton, arm. .	*ut prius.*
23		
24	Will. Ascugh, mil. . .	*ut prius.*

HENRY VIII.

1	Rob. Dymock, mil. . .	*ut prius.*
2	Thomas Parr, mil. . .	Northam.

Arg. two bars Az. a border engrailed S.

3	Edw. Guldeford, arm. .	KENT.

O. a saltire entre four martlets S.

4	Tho. Cheyne, mil.	
5	Mar. Constable, jun. mil.	*ut prius.*
6	G. Fitzwilliams, arm. .	*ut prius.*
7	Leo. Dymmock, mil. .	*ut prius.*
8	Will. Hansard, mil. . .	*ut prius.*
9	Will. Tirwit, mil. . .	*ut prius.*
10	Th. Burgh, jun. mil. .	*ut prius.*
11	Rob. Tirwhit, mil. . .	*ut prius.*
13	Will. Askue, mil. . .	*ut prius.*
	Franc. Brown, arm.	
14	Andr. Billesby, mil. .	*ut prius.*
15	Rob. Tirwhit, mil. . .	*ut prius.*
16	Thom. Burgh, mil. . .	*ut prius.*
17	Gilb. Taylboys, mil. . .	*ut prius.*
18	Will. Skipwith, arm. .	*ut prius.*
19	Tho. Portington, arm.	
20	G. Fitzwilliams, arm. .	*ut prius.*
21	Andr. Bilesby, mil. . .	*ut prius.*
22	Will. Hussey, mil. . .	*ut prius.*
23	Will. Disney, arm. . .	Nort. Dis.

Arg. on a fess G. three flowers-de-luce O.

24	Joh. Markham, mil. .	*ut prius.*
35	G. Fitzwilliams, mil. .	*ut prius.*
26	Joh. Goodrick, arm.	

Arg. on a fess G. betwixt two lions passant gardant S. a flower-de-luce between two crescents O.

Anno	Name.	Place.
27	Edw. Dymock, arm.	*ut prius.*
28	Will. Tirwhit, mil.	*ut prius.*
29	Joh. Harrington, mil.	*ut prius.*
30	W. Newenham, mil.	
31	Will. Sandon, mil.	

O. a chief Az.

32	Rob. Tirwhit, mil.	*ut prius.*
33	Tho. Dymock, arm.	*ut prius.*
34	Rob. Hussey, mil.	*ut prius.*
35	Will. Sandon, arm.	*ut prius.*
36	Franc. Ascugh, mil.	*ut prius.*
37	Will. Dallison, arm.	Laughton.

G. three crescents O. a canton Erm.

38 Andr. Nowel, arm.

O. fretty G. a canton Erm.

EDW. VI.

1	Edw. Dymock, mil.	*ut prius.*
2	Joh. Copledick, mil.	*ut prius.*
3	Fran. Ayscough, mil.	*ut prius.*
4	Richard. Bolles, arm.	*ut prius.*
5	Rich. Thimolby, mil.	*ut prius.*
6	Will. Skipwith, mil.	*ut prius.*

REX PHIL. et MAR. REGINA.

1	Fran. Ascough, mil.	*ut prius.*
	W. Mounson, arm.	S. Carlton.

O. two chevrons G.

2 et 3	E. Dymock, mil.	*ut prius.*
3 et 4	Nic. Disney, arm.	*ut prius.*
4 et 5	T. Litlebery, arm.	*ut prius.*
5 et 6	W. Thorold, arm.	Blanckney.

S. three goats salient Arg.

ELIZ. REG.

1	Rob. Tirwhit, mil.	*ut prius.*
2	Ric. Thimolby, mil.	*ut prius.*
3	Rich. Welby, arm.	*ut prius.*
4	Adlerdus Welby, arm.	*ut prius.*
5	Will. Skipwith, mil.	*ut prius.*
6	Rich. Berty, arm.	Grimsthorp.

Arg. three battering-rams in pale barry Az. armed and garnished O.

7 Tho. St. Pole, arm. . . Snarford.

Arg. a lion rampant bicaudé G. crowned Or.

8	Rich. Disney, arm.	*ut prius.*
9	Joh. Copledick, arm.	*ut prius.*
10	Johan. Carr, arm.	Sleaford.

G. on a chevron Arg. three mullets Sable.

Anno	Name.	Place.

11 Rich. Bolles, arm. . . *ut prius.*

12 Tho. Quadring, arm.
Erm. a fess engrailed G.

13 Anthon. Tharold . . . *ut prius.*

14 Will. Hunston, arm.
S. four fusils Erm. a border engrailed Arg.

15 Rob. Savill, arm.
Arg. on a bend S. three owls of the first.

16 Andr. Gedney, arm. . Bagg. Enderby.
Arg. two lucies saltireways Az.

17 Will. Metham, arm. . Bullington.
Quarterly Az. and Arg. on the first a flower-de-luce O.

18 G. Hennage, arm. . . Haynton.
O. a Greyhound current S. betwixt three leopards' heads
Az. ; a border G.

19 Joh. Mounson, arm. . *ut prius.*

20 Franc. Manby, arm. . . Elsham.
Arg. a lion rampant S. in an orle of escalops G.

21 Tho. St. Pole, arm. . . *ut prius.*

22 W. Fitzwilliams, arm. . *ut prius.*

23 Rob. Carr, jun. arm. . *ut prius.*

24 Daniel Disney, arm. . . *ut prius.*

25 Edw. Tirwhit, arm. . . *ut prius.*

26 Edw. Dymock, mil. . . *ut prius.*

27 Wil. Hennage, arm. . . *ut prius.*

28 Barth. Armyn, arm. . . Osgodby.
Erm. a saltire engrailed G.; on a chief of the second a lion
passant O.

29 Edw. Ascough, arm. . *ut prius.*

30 Geo. St. Pole, arm. . . *ut prius.*

31 Joh. Markham, arm. . *ut prius.*

32 Joh. Savile, arm. . . . Dodington.
Arg. on a bend S. three owls of the first.

33 Carolus Hussey, arm. . *ut prius.*

34 Nic. Sanderson, arm. . Fillingham.
Paly of six Arg. and Az.; on a bend S. three annulets O.

35 Valent. Brown, arm. . Croft.

36 Will. Wray, arm. . . Glentworth.
Az. on a chief O. three martlets G.

37 Philip. Tirwhit, arm. . *ut prius.*

38 Johan. Meres, arm. . . *ut prius.*

39 Tho. Mounson, mil. . . *ut prius.*

40 W. Hennage, mil. . . *ut prius.*

41 Rob. Tirwhit, arm. . . *ut prius.*

42 Th. Grantham, arm. . Goltho.
Erm. a griffin segreant, his tail nowed G.

43 Rog. Dallison, arm. . . *ut prius.*

Anno	Name.	Place.

44 Will. Pelham, arm. . . Broklesby.
　　Az. three pelicans Arg.
　Will. Armyn, mil . . *ut prius.*

JACOB. REX.

1 Will. Armyn, mil. . . *ut prius.*
2 Edw. Marbury, mil. . Girsby.
　　Arg. on a fess engrailed Az. three garbs O.
3 Rich. Amcots, mil.
　　Arg. a castle betwixt three cups covered Az.
4 Will. Welby, mil. . . *ut prius.*
5 Gerv. Helwish, mil. . . Wortley.
　　O. a fess Az. and bend G.
6 Rich. Ogle, mil. . . . Pinchbeck.
　　Arg. a fess betwixt two crescents jess. and as many flowers-
　　de-luce G.
7 Joh. Reade, mil. . . . Wrangle.
　　G. on a bend Arg. three shovelers S. beaked O.
8 Joh. Hatcher, mil. . . Careby.
9 Rob. Tirwhit, arm. . . Camerin.
　　Arms, *ut prius.*
10 Joh. Langton, mil. . . Langton.
　　Quarterly S. and O. a bend Arg.
11 Nic. Sanderson, mil. . *ut prius.*
12 Ed. Carr, mil. et bar. . *ut prius.*
13 Joh. Thorold, mil. . . *ut prius.*
14 Franc. South, mil. . . Kelstern.
　　Arg. two bars G. in chief a mullet S.
15 Anth. Thorold, arm. . *ut prius.*
16 Edw. Hussey, mil. . . *ut prius.*
17 Joh. Buck, mil. . . . Hanby.
　　Barry, bendy O. and Az. a canton Erm.
18 Tho. Taylor, arm. . . Doddington.
19 Ric. Hickson, arm. . . Ropsley.
20 Geo. Southcot, mil. . . Bliburgh.
21 Tho. Midlecot, mil. . . Boston.
22 Will. Lister, arm. . . Coleby.
　　Erm. on a fess S. three mullets Arg.

CAROLUS I.

1 Jo. Wray, mil. et bar. . *ut prius.*
2 Joh. Bolles, arm. . . . Scampton.
　　Arms, *ut prius,* with a flower-de-luce for difference.
3 Jac. Brampton, arm. . Touse.
4 Geor. Hennage, mil. . *ut prius.*
5 Wil. Armyn, bar. . . *ut prius.*
6 Dan. Deligne, mil. . Harlaxon.
　　O. a bend G.; a chief checky Arg. and Az.
7 Edw. Ascough, mil. . . *ut prius.*

Anno	Name.	Place.
8	W. Thorold, mil.	*ut prius.*
9	Jervas. Scroop, mil.	Cokerington.
	Az. a bend O.	
10	W. Norton, mil. et bar.	
11	Wil. Pelham, mil.	*ut prius.*
12	Edw. Hussey, mil.	*ut prius.*
13	Anthonius Irby, mil.	Boston.

Arg. a fret of eight pieces S.; on a canton G. a chaplet O.

| 14 | Tho. Grantham, arm. | *ut prius.* |
| 15 | Jo. Brownlow, arm. | Belton. |

O. an escutcheon, and orle of martlets Sable.

| 16 | Tho. Trollop, arm. | |

V. three bucks passant Arg. maned and unguled O. a border Arg.

| 20 | Thomas Lister, arm. | *ut prius.* |
| 22 | Joh. Hobson, arm. | |

S. a cinquefoil Arg.; a chief checky O. and Az.

RICHARD II.

19. JOAN WALCH.—Proportion of time and place evidence him the same person, of whom I read, in the eighth year of the reign of this king, anno 1385. "On St. Andrew's day, there was a combat fought in the lists at Westminster, betwixt an English esquire, named John Walch of Grimesby, and one of Navarre, called Mortileto de Vilenos, who had accused him of treason to the king and realm; in which combat the Navarrois was overcome, and afterwards hanged for his false accusation."*

HENRY IV.

2. JOHN ROCHFORD, Miles.—The same, no doubt, with him who was sheriff in the 15th of king Richard the Second. I confess there was a knightly family of this name at Rochford in Essex,† who gave for their arms, Argent, a lion rampant Sable, langued, armed, and crowned Gules; quartered at this day by the Lord Rochford earl of Dover, by the Butlers and Bollons descended from them. But I behold this Lincolnshire knight of another family, and different arms, quartered by the earl of Moulgrave, whence I collect his heir matched into that family.

Consent of time and other circumstances argue him the same with Sir John Rochford, whom Bale maketh to flourish under king Henry the Fourth, commending him for his noble birth, great learning, large travel through France and Italy, and worthy pains in translating Josephus's Antiquities, Polychronicon, and other good authors, into English.‡

RICHARD III.

2. ROBERT DIMOCK, Miles.—This Sir Robert Dimock, at the

---

* Stow's Chronicle.   † Camden's Britannia, in Essex.
‡ De Scriptoribus Britannicis, Cent. vii. n. 41.

coronation of king Henry the Seventh, came on horseback into Westminster Hall, where the king dined; and, casting his gauntlet on the ground, challenged any who durst question the king's right to the crown.

King Henry, being pleased to dissemble himself a stranger to that ceremony, demanded of a stander-by what that knight said? To whom the party returned, " He challengeth any man to fight with him, who dares deny your Highness to be the lawful king of England." " If he will not fight with such a one," said the king, " I will." And so sate down to dinner.

HENRY VII.

9. JOHN HUSSE.—This was undoubtedly the same person whom king Henry the Eighth afterwards created the first and last Baron Husee of Sleford, who engaging himself against the king, with the rebellious Commons, anno 1537, was justly beheaded; and saw that honour begun and ended in his own person.

HENRY VIII.

16. THOMAS BURGE, Mil.—He was honourably descended from the heir general of the Lord Cobham of Sterbury in Surrey,* and was few years after created Baron Burge, or Borough, by king Henry the Eighth. His grandchild Thomas Lord Burge, deputy of Ireland, and knight of the Garter (of whom before†) left no issue male, nor plentiful estate; only four daughters,—Elizabeth, married to Sir George Brook; Frances, to the ancient family of Copinger in Suffolk; Anna, wife to Sir Drue Drury; and Katharine, married to . . . . . . Knivet of Norfolk, mother to Sir John Knivet, knight of the Bath at the last instalment; so that the honour, which could not conveniently be divided, was here determined.

KING CHARLES.

9. JERVASIUS SCROOP, Miles.—He engaged with his majesty in Edge-hill fight, where he received twenty-six wounds, and was left on the ground amongst the dead. Next day his son Adrian obtained leave from the king to find and fetch off his father's corpse; and his hopes pretended no higher than to a decent interment thereof.

Hearty seeking makes happy finding. Indeed, some more commended the affection than the judgment of the young gentleman, conceiving such a search in vain amongst many naked bodies, with wounds disguised from themselves, and where pale death had confounded all complexions together.

However, he having some general hint of the place where his father fell, did light upon his body, which had some heat left

---

* Camden's Britannia, in Surrey.   † In this Shire, title STATESMEN, p. 278.

therein. This heat was, with rubbing, within few minutes improved into motion; that motion, within some hours, into sense; that sense, within a day, into speech; that speech, within certain weeks, into a perfect recovery; living more than ten years after, a monument of God's mercy and his son's affection.

He always after carried his arm in a scarf; and loss of blood made him look very pale, as a messenger come from the grave, to advise the living to prepare for death. The effect of his story I received from his own mouth, in Lincoln College.

THE FAREWELL.

It is vain to wish the same success to every husbandman in this shire, as he had, who some seven score years since, at Harlaxton in this county, found a helmet of gold as he was ploughing in the field.

Besides, in treasure trove, the least share falleth to him who first finds it. But this I not only heartily wish but certainly promise to all such who industriously attend tillage in this county (or elsewhere), that thereby they shall find (though not gold in specie, yet) what is gold worth, and may quickly be commuted into it, great plenty of good grain; the same which Solomon foretold, " He that tilleth his land shall have plenty of bread."*

WORTHIES OF LINCOLNSHIRE WHO HAVE FLOURISHED SINCE THE TIME OF FULLER.

Richard BUSBY, grammarian, master of Westminster School, commonly called the "flogging master;" born at Sutton St. Nicholas, or Lutton, 1606; died 1695.

Susannah CENTLIVRE, ingenious dramatic writer; born at Holbeach about 1667; died 1722.

Sir Charles COTTERELL, translator of Cassandra; born at Wilsford; died 1687.

Thomas COWLEY, benefactor, founder of the free school; born at Donnington; died 1718.

Dr. William DODD, divine and author; born at Bourne, 1729; executed for forgery in 1777.

Thomas EMLYN, persecuted Arian divine and author; born at Stamford 1663; died 1743.

Matthew HORBERY, learned and able divine, author on the "Duration of Future Punishment;" born at Haxey 1707; died 1773.

Cyril JACKSON, dean of Christ Church Oxford; born at Stamford 1742; died 1819.

* Prov xxviii. 19.

Sarah JENNINGS, wife of the first Duke of Marlborough, the Atossa in Pope's Satire on Women; born at Burwell; died 1744.

Charles LAMB, essayist and poet; born 1774: died 1834.

John NEWCOME, dean of Rochester, author of Sermons; born at Grantham; died 1765.

Sir Isaac NEWTON, philosopher, astronomer, mathematician, &c.; born at Wolsthorpe in Colsterworth 1642; died 1727.

Simon PATRICK, bishop of Ely, author of Paraphrases and Commentaries on the Old Testament; born at Gainsborough 1626; died 1707.

Francis PECK, antiquary, historian of his native town; born at Stamford 1692; died 1743.

John RASTRICK, nonconformist divine and author; born at Heckington 1749.

Benjamin RAY, miscellaneous writer; born at Spalding; died 1760.

Robert SMITH, mathematician, author of "Harmonics," 1689; died 1768.

Daniel WATERLAND, divine, writer against Arianism; born at Waseley 1683; died 1740.

John WESLEY, founder of Methodism; born at Epworth 1703; died 1791.

Samuel WESLEY, brother of preceding, poet, author of "Battle of the Sexes;" born at Epworth 1690; died 1739.

Francis WILLIS, physician, eminent in cases of insanity; born at Lincoln; died 1807.

⁎ Of this county there have been numerous local histories brought out at different periods; and in 1834 a regular history of the county made its appearance, compiled by Thos. Allen, in 2 vols 4to, from the various works which had preceded him; amongst which may be enumerated the following:—Histories of Lincoln, 1810, and 1816. Terra Incognita of Lincolnshire, by Miss Hatfield, 1816. Account of the Isle of Axholme, &c. by W. Peck, 1815. Account of Boston, and Hundred of Skirbeck, by P. Thompson, 1820. Sketches of the Town and Soke of Horncastle, &c. by G. Weir, 1820. Collections for a topographical, historical, and descriptive Account of the Hundred of Aveland, by J. Moore, 1809. History of the Town and Soke of Grantham, by E. Turnor, F.R.S. 1806. The History of Crowland Abbey, &c., by B. Holdich, 1816. An Essay on the ancient and present state of Stamford, by F. Howgrave, 1726. Antiquarian Annals of Stamford, by the Rev. F. Peck, 1727. The Survey and Antiquities of the Towns of Stamford, &c. by R. Butcher, 1717. The Antiquities of Stamford and St. Martin's, &c. by W. Harrod, 1785. History of Stamford, by J. Drakard, 1822. History of Gainsburgh, by A. Stark, 1817. Account of Scampton, by Rev. C. Illingworth, 1810. Sketches of New and Old Sleaford, &c. 1825. Account of Tattershall, &c. 1813. Monumental Antiquities of Grimsby, by Rev. G. Oliver, 1825.

MIDDLESEX.

It is in effect but the suburbs at large of London, replenished with the retiring houses of the gentry and citizens thereof, besides many palaces of noblemen, and three [lately] royal mansions. Wherefore much measure cannot be expected of so fine ware; the cause why this county is so small, scarce extending, east and west, to 18 miles in length, and not exceeding north and south 12 in the breadth thereof.

It hath Hertfordshire on the north, Buckinghamshire on the west, Essex parted with Lee on the east, Kent and Surrey (severed by the Thames) on the south. The air generally is most healthful, especially about Highgate, where the expert inhabitants report, " that divers that have been long visited with sickness, not curable by physic, have in short time recovered, by that sweet salutary air."*

NATURAL COMMODITIES.

WHEAT.

The best in England groweth in the Vale lying south of Harrow-the-Hill nigh Hessen (where Providence for the present hath fixed my hahitation) ; so that the king's bread was formerly made of the fine flower thereof.†

Hence it was that queen Elizabeth received no composition-money from the villages thereabouts, but took her wheat in kind for her own pastry and bakehouse.

There is an obscure village hereabouts, called Perivale, which my author ‡ will have more truly termed Purevale (an honour I assure you unknown to the inhabitants thereof) because of the clearness of the corn growing therein, though the purity thereof is much subject to be humbled with the mildew, whereof hereafter.§

* John Norden, Speculum Britanniæ, page 22.
† Camden's Britannia, in Middlesex.
‡ Norden, in his Speculum Britanniæ, page 11.
§ In the Farewell to this county.

TAMARISK.

It hath not more affinity in sound with tamarind, than sympathy in extraction (both originally Arabic), general similitude in leaves, and operation; only tamarind in England is an annual (dying at the approach of winter), whilst tamarisk lasteth many years. It was first brought over by bishop Grindal out of Switzerland (where he was exile under queen Mary), and planted in his garden at Fulham in this county; where the soil, being moist and fenny, well complied with the nature of this plant, which since is removed, and thriveth well in many other places. Yet it groweth not up to be timber, as in Arabia, though often to that substance that cups of great size are made thereof. Dioscorides saith, it is good for the tooth-ache (as what is not, and yet indeed what is good for it?) but it is especially used for mollifying the hardness and opening the stopping of the belly.

MANUFACTURES.

LEATHER.

This, though common to all counties, is entered under the manufactures of Middlesex, because London therein is the staple-place of slaughter; and the hides of beasts there bought are generally tanned about Enfield in this county.

A word of the antiquity and usefulness of this commodity. Adam's first suit was of leaves, his second of leather. Hereof girdles, shoes, and many utensils (not to speak of whole houses of leather, I mean coaches) are made. Yea, I have read how Frederick the second Emperor of Germany, distressed to pay his army, made "monetam coriaceam," (coin of leather), making it current by his proclamation; and afterwards, when his soldiers repaid it into his exchequer, they received so much silver in lieu thereof.

Many good laws are made (and still one wanting to enforce the keeping of them) for the making of this merchantable commodity; and yet still much unsaleable leather is sold in our markets.

The lord treasurer Burleigh (who always consulted artificers in their own art) was indoctrinated by a cobbler in the true tanning of leather. This cobbler, taking a slice of bread, toasted it by degrees at some distance from the fire, turning many times till it became brown and hard on both sides. "This, my lord," saith he, "we good fellows call a tanned toast, done so well that it will last many mornings' draughts; and leather, thus leisurely tanned and turned many times in the fat, will prove serviceable, which otherwise will quickly fleet and rag out. And although that great statesman caused statutes to be made according to his instructions, complaints in this kind daily continue and increase. Surely were all, of that occupation, as honest as Simon the tanner (the entertainer of Simon Peter in Joppa) they would be more conscientious in their calling. Let me add, what experience avoweth true, though it be hard to assign the true cause thereof, that when wheat is dear, leather always is cheap; and when leather is dear, then wheat is cheap.

THE BUILDINGS.

HAMPTON COURT was built by that pompous prelate Cardinal Wolsey: once so magnificent in his expenses, that whosoever considereth either of these three, would admire that he had any thing for the other two left unto him; viz. his house-building; house-keeping; house-furnishing.

He bestowed it on king Henry the Eighth, who, for the greater grace thereof, erected it (princes can confer dignities on houses as well as persons) to be an honour, increasing it with buildings, till it became more like a small city than a house. Now whereas other royal palaces (Holdenby, Oatlands, Richmond, Theobald's) have lately found their fatal period, Hampton Court hath happiness to continue in its former estate.

> *Non equidem invideo: miror magis, undique totis*
> *Usque adeo spoliatur agris.*

> " I envy not its happy lot, but rather thereat wonder;
>   There's such a rout, our land throughout, of palaces by plunder."

Let me add, that Henry the Eighth enforested the grounds hereabouts (the last of that kind in England), though they never attained the full reputation of a forest in common discourse.

OSTERLY HOUSE (now Sir William Waller's) must not be forgotten, built in a park by Sir Thomas Gresham, who here magnificently entertained and lodged queen Elizabeth. Her majesty found fault with the court of this house as too great: affirming, "that it would appear more handsome, if divided with a wall in the middle."

What doth Sir Thomas, but in the night-time sends for workmen to London (money commands all things), who so speedily and silently apply their business, that the next morning discovered that court double, which the night had left single before. It is questionable whether the queen next day was more contented with the conformity to her fancy, or more pleased with the surprise and sudden performance thereof; whilst her courtiers disported themselves with their several expressions, some avowing it was no wonder he could so soon *change* a building, who could build a *Change*; others (reflecting on some known differences in this knight's family) affirmed, " that any house is easier divided than united."

PROVERBS

" A Middlesex clown."]

Some English words, innocent and inoffensive in their primitive notion, are bowed by custom to a disgraceful sense ; as *villain*, originally nothing but a dweller in a village and tiller of the ground thereabouts ; *churle*, in Saxon *coorel*, a strong stout husbandman ;* *clown*, from *colonus*, one that plougheth the ground" (without which neither king nor kingdom can be maintained) ; of which Middlesex hath many of great estates.

But some endeavour to fix the ignominious sense upon them, as if more arrant rustics than those of their condition elsewhere ; partly, because nobility and gentry are respectively observed (according to their degree) by people far distant from London, less regarded by these Middlesexians (frequency breeds familiarity) because abounding thereabouts ; partly, because the multitude of gentry here (contraries are mutual commentaries) discover the *clownishness* of others, and render it more conspicuous. However, to my own knowledge, there are some of the yeomanry in this county as completely civil as any in England.

" He that is a low ebb at Newgate, may soon be afloat at Tyburn."†]

I allow not this satirical proverb, as it makes mirth on men in misery, whom a mere man may pity for suffering, and a good man ought to pity them for deserving it. *Tyburn* some will have so called from *tie* and *burne*, because the poor Lollards—for whom this instrument (of cruelty to them, though of justice to malefactors) was first set up—had their necks tied to the beam, and their lower parts burnt in the fire. Others will have it called from *twa* and *burne*, that is, two rivulets, which, it seems, meet near to the place. But whencesoever it be called, may all endeavour to keep themselves from it ; though one may justly be confident, that more souls have gone to heaven from that place, than from all the churches and churchyards in England.

" When Tottenham Wood is all on fire,
  Then Tottenham Street is nought but mire."

I find this proverb in the " Description of Tottenham,"‡ written by Mr. William Bedwell, one of the most learned translators of the Bible. And seeing so grave a divine stooped to so low a subject, I hope I may be admitted to follow him therein. He thus expoundeth the proverb : "When Tottenham Wood, of many hundred acres, on the top of a high hill in the west end of the parish, hath a foggy mist hanging and hovering over it, in manner of a smoke, then generally foul weather followeth ; so that it serveth the inhabitants instead of a prognostication." I am confident there is as much mire now as formerly in Tottenham Street, but question whether so much wood now as anciently on Tottenham Hill.

" Tottenham is turned French."]

I find this in the same place of the same author, but quoting it out of Mr. Heywood. It seems, about the beginning of the

* See Sir Henry Spelman's Glossary.
† John Heywood, in his 26th Epigram upon Proverbs.   ‡ Cap. iii.

reign of king Henry the Eighth, French mechanics swarmed in England, to the great prejudice of English artizans, which caused the insurrection in London, on ill May-day, anno Domini 1517. Nor was the city only, but country villages for four miles about, filled with French fashions and infections. The proverb is applied to such, who, contemning the custom of their own country, make themselves more ridiculous by affecting foreign humours and habits.

PRINCES.

EDWARD, sole surviving son of king Henry the Eighth and Jane his wife, was born at Hampton Court in this county, anno Domini 1537. He succeeded his father in the kingdom, and was most eminent in his generation; seeing the kings of England fall under a fivefold division:

1. Visibly vicious; given over to dissoluteness and debauchery; as king Edward the Second. 2. " Potiùs extra vitia quàm cum virtutibus;" (rather free from vice than fraught with virtue); as king Henry the Third. 3. "In quibus æquali temperamento magnæ virtutes inerant, nec minora vitia;" (in whom vices and virtues were so equally matched, it was hard to decide which got the mastery); as in king Henry the Eighth. 4. Whose good qualities beat their bad ones quite out of distance of competition; as in king Edward the First. 5. Whose virtues were so resplendent, no faults (human frailties excepted) appeared in them; as in this king Edward.

He died July 5, 1553; and pity it is, that he who deserved the best, should have no monument erected to his memory. Indeed, a brass altar of excellent workmanship, under which he was buried (I will not say sacrificed with an untimely death by the treachery of others) did formerly supply the place of his tomb; which since is abolished, under the notion of superstition.

Guess the goodness of his head and heart, by the following letters written to Barnaby Fitz-Patrick (gentleman of his bedchamber, and brought up with him), copied out from the originals by the reverend archbishop of Armagh, and bestowed upon me. Say not they are but of narrow and personal concernment, seeing they are sprinkled with some passages of the *publique*. Neither object them written by a child, seeing he had more man in him than any of his age. Besides, epistles are the calmest communicating truth to posterity; presenting history unto us in her night-clothes, with a true face of things, though not in so fine a dress as in other kinds of writings.

" EDWARD.

" We have received your letters of the eighth of this present moneth, whereby we understand how you are well entertained, for which we are right glad, and also how you have been once to go on pilgrimage : for which cause we have thought good to advertise you, that hereafter, if any such chance happen, you shall desire leave to goe to Mr. Pickering, or to Paris, for your business ; and, if that will not serve, to declare to some man of estimation, with whom you are best acquainted, that as you are loth to offend the French king, because you have been so favourably used, so with safe conscience you cannot do any such thing, being brought up with me, and bound to obey my laws; also that you had commandment from me to the contrary. Yet, if you be vehemently procured, you may go, as waiting on the king, not as intending to the abuse, nor willingly seeing the ceremonies, and so you look on the Masse. But, in the mean season, regard the Scripture, or some good book, and give no reverence to the Masse at all. Furthermore remember, when you may conveniently be absent from the court, to tarry with Sir William Pickering, to be instructed by him how to use yourself. For women, as far forth as you may, avoid their company. Yet, if the French king command you, you may sometime dance, so measure be your meane; else applye yourself to riding, shooting, tennis, or such honest games, not forgetting sometimes (when you have leisure) your learning, chiefly reading of the Scriptures. This I write, not doubting but you would have done, though I had not written but to spur you on. Your exchange of 1200 crowns you shall receive, either monthly or quarterly, by Bartholomew Campaigne, factor in Paris. He hath warrant to receive it by here, and hath written to his factors to deliver it you there. We have signed your bill for wages of the Chamber, which Fitzwilliams hath ; likewise we have sent a letter into Ireland, to our deputy, that he shall take surrender of your father's lands ; and to make again other letters patent, that those lands shall be to him, you, and your heirs lawfully begotten for ever, adjoyning thereunto two religious houses you spake for. Thus fare you well. From Westminster, the 20th of December, 1551."

"Mr. BARNABY,—I have of late sent you a letter from Bartholomew Campaigne, for your payment, by the French ambassador's pacquet. I doubt not but your good nature shall profitably and wisely receive the king's Majesties letter to you, fatherly of a child, comfortably of your sovereign lord, and most wisely of so young a prince. And so I beseech you that you will think, wheresoever you go, you carry with you a demonstration of the king's majesty, coming *à latere suo*, and bred up in learning and manners with him, with your conversation and modesty ; let me therefore believe the good reports of the king to be true ; and let them perceive what the king is, when one brought up with him *habeat virtutis tam clarum specimen*. This I write boldly, as one that in you willeth our master's honour and credit; and, I pray you, use me as one that loveth you in plain terms. Scribled in hast, from Westminster, the 22d of December, 1551.

"Yours to use and have,

"W. CECILL."

"To the King's Majesty.

"According to my bounden duty, I most humbly thank your Highness for your gracious letters of the 20th of December; lamenting nothing but that I am not able by any meanes, nor cannot deserve any thing of the goodness your Highness hath shewed towards me. And as for the avoiding of the company of the ladies, I will assure your highness, I will not come into their company, unless I do wait upon the French king. As for the letter your Majesty hath granted my father for the assurance of his lands, I thank your Highness; most humbly confessing myself as much bound to you as a subject to his sovereign for the same.

"As for such simple news as is here, I thought good to certify your Majesty. It did happen that a certain saint, standing in a blind corner of the street where my lord admiral lay, was broken in the night-time, when my lord was here; which the Frenchmen did think to have been done by the Englishmen; and the Englishmen did think it to have been done by some Frenchmen, of spite, because the Englishmen lay in that street; and now since that time they have prepared another saint, which they call our Ladie of Silver, because the French king that is dead made her once of clean silver, and afterwards was stoln, like as she hath been divers times both stoln and broken in the same place; which lady was, at this present Sunday, being the 27th of this month, set up with a solemn procession; in the which procession came first in the morning divers priests of divers churches, with crosses and banners, and passed by the place where she should stand; then afterwards, about eleven of the clock, came the legat of Rome, in whose company came first afore him sixty black canons of our Ladies Church. Then came after them one that carried the legate's hat, in such sort as they carry the Great Seal in England: then came the master of Paris next to the cardinall which carried the image that should be set up; then came the legate himself, all in red, and with a white surpless, still blessing, accompanied with the bishop of Caen; and after him came the four presidents of the town, with all the councell of the town: also there went before, and came behind, divers officers of the town with tip-staves. And so they have set her up with great solemnity, and defended her with a double grate, to the intent she should be no more stolen nor broken; and the poor people lie still in the foul streets worshipping her. Further, as I am crediblie informed, the legate that lieth here doth give pardons and bulls daily; and one of the king's treasurers standeth by, and receiveth the money to

the king's use.   Other news I have none.   The meanest and
most obligest of your subjects,

" BERNABY FITZ-PATRICK.

" *December the 28th.*"

" EDWARD.

" We have received your letters of the 28th of December,
whereby we perceive your constancy, both in avoiding all kind
of vices, and also in following all things of activity or otherwise that be honest and meet for a gentleman ; of the which we
are not a little glad, nothing doubting your continuance therein.
We understand also, by certain letters you sent to the earl of
Pembroke and Mr. Vice-chamberlaine, that you have some lack
of muletts, and that you desire to have sent to you some of
ours ; whereupon we have considered, that our muletts, being
old and lame, will do you but little service, and at least less
than good ones bought there.   For which cause, we have willed
Bartholomew Champagne to deliver you 300 crownes by exchange, for the buying of your two muletts, over and besides
your former allowance.   Here we have little news at this present, but only that the challenge you heard of before your going
was very well accomplished. At tilt there came eighteen defendants, at tournay twenty, at barriers they fought eight to
eight, on twelfth-night.   This last Christmas hath been well and
merrily past.   Afterwards there was run a match at tilt, six to
six, which was very well runne.   Also, because of the Lord
Riche's sickness, the bishop of Ely was made chancellor of
England during the parliament.   Of late there hath been such
a tide here as hath overflown all medowes and marshes.   All
the Isle of Dogges, all Plumsted Marsh, all Shippey, Foulness
in Essex, and all the sea coast, was quite drowned.   We hear
that it hath done no lesse harme in Flanders, Holland and
Zealand ; but much more, for townes and cities have been there
drowned.   We are advertised, out of Almaine, that duke Morice
is turned from the emperour ; and he, with the Protestants,
levieth men to deliver the old duke of Sax and the land-grave
out of prison.   The cause of our slowness in writing this letter
hath been lack of messengers ; else we had written before time.
Now shortly we will prove how ye have profited in the French
tongue ; for within a while we will write to you in French.
Thus we make an end, wishing you as much good as our selves.
At Westminster, the 25th of January, 1551."

" EDWARD.

" We have received your letters, dated at Paris the twelfth of
this instant, and also Mr. Pickering's letter, written to our
trusty well beloved cousin the duke of Northumberland, on
your behalf ; whereby we perceive both the great preparation for
the wars, which the French king our brother maketh : and also how

that you are ill furnished of all things meet to go such a journey; so that he thinketh that your costs will not be borne under £300. Whereupon we have given order to Bartholomew Campaigne for to deliver you, in Paris, 800 French crowns, over and besides all moneys sent you heretofore; and besides your diet. Also, whereas you seem to find a lack for the moylettis, there was appointed to you 300 French crowns for the buying of the same, because they could not well be transported. Also order is given for your horses to be carried over to you with diligence, which we trust shall like you well. We have no more to you, but to will you not to live too sumptiously as an ambassador, but so as your proportion of living may serve you. We mean, because we know many will resort to you, and desire to serve you. I told you how many I thought convenient you should keep. After you have ordered your things at Paris, go to the court, and learn to have more intelligence if you can; and after to the wars, to learn somewhat to serve us. News from hence I shall write you when you send us some; in the mean season, none but that (thanks be to God) all is well for the present. Fare you well. From Westminster, the 25th of February, 1551."

"Edward.

"We have received your letters of the second and fifteenth of April; whereby we perceive then you were at Nancy, ready to go together with Mr. Pickering to the French camp. And, to the intent you might be better instructed how to use yourself in these wars, we have thought good to advertise you of our pleasure therein. First, we would wish you, as much as you may conveniently, to be in the French king's presence, or at least in some part of his army where you shall perceive most business to be, and that for two causes: one is, because you may have more experience in the wars, and see things that might stand you in stead another day; the other is, because you might be more profitable in the language; for our embassador, who may not wear harness, cannot well come to those places of danger, nor seem so to serve the French king as you may, whom we sent thither for that purpose. It shall be best for you therefore hereafter, as much as you may, to be with the French king; and so you shall be more acceptable to him, and do yourself much good. We doubt not also but of such things as you see there done, you will not fail to advertise us, as you have well begun in your last letters; for thereby shall we judge of your diligence in learning, and seeing things that be there done. We shall be nothing wearied with often advertising, nor with reciting of particularity of things. And to the intent we would see how you profit in the French, we would be glad to receive some letters from you in the French tongue, and we would write to you again therein. We have a little been troubled with the small pox, which hath letted us to write hitherto; but now we have shaken that quite away. Thus fare you well. At Greenwich, the third of May, anno 1552."

"EDWARD.

"We have received your letters, dated at Rheims the fourth of this instant; by which we understand how the French king doth mean now to set forth a new army to resist the emperor, and that for that cause you think you cannot yet ask leave to return, without suspicion, till this bray do cease. In which thing we like your opinion very well; and the rather, because you may peradventure see more things in this short journey (if so be it that the emperor doth march towards you) than you have seen all the while you have been there. Nevertheless, as soon as his business is once overpast, you, with Mr. Pickering's advice, may take some occasion to ask leave for this winter to come home, because you think there shall few things more be done than have been already, in such manner and form as we have written in our former letters. We pray you also to advertise for how long time you have received your diets. Bartholomew Campaigne hath been paid six weeks agone, till the last of September; and we would be very glad to know whether you have received so much at his factor's hands. More we have not to advertise you; and therefore we commit you to God. From Hampton Court, the 7th of October, anno Domini 1552."

MARTYRS.

Smithfield, near London, being *Bonner's* shambles, and the *bon-fire general* of England, no wonder if some sparks thereof were driven thence into the vicinage, at Barnet, Islington, and Stratford Bow, where more than twenty persons were martyred, as in Mr. Fox doth appear. Nor must we forget Mr. John Denley, burnt at Uxbridge, who began to sing a Psalm at the stake; and Dr. Story, there present, caused a prickly faggot to be hurled in his face, which so hurt him that he bled therewith.* Now the singing nightingale needed no thorn, but only the sleeping one to awake it.† We may believe that this martyr's prick-son indeed made good melody in the ears of the God of Heaven.

PRELATES.

RICHARD NORTHALL was, saith my author, born in this county, adding moreover "Prætoris Londinensis, ejusdem cognominis, ut fertur, filius."‡ But take Prætor either for Major or Sheriff, and no such man appeareth in Stow's exact " Survey of London;" so that one may thence safely conclude the

---

* Fox, Acts and Monuments, p. 1685.　　　† Pliny's Natural History.
‡ Bale, de Scriptoribus Britannicis, Cent. vii. n. 6.

negative, no such person in those places, though probably he might hold some other eminent office in that city.*

By the way, the applying the names of Roman magistrates to our English officers, wherein every one followeth their own fancy in assigning the correspondency, hath caused much uncertainty in matters of this nature. But we willingly believe this Robert of wealthy extraction, though he became a Carmelite, and afterwords chaplain to king Richard the Second, who for his good preaching preferred him bishop of Ossory, for a time chancellor of Ireland,† and at last archbishop of Dublin. He wrote a set of sermons for the whole year, lived much beloved for his learning and virtues, and died, no less lamented, anno Domini 1397, on the 20th day of July.

SINCE THE REFORMATION.

WILLIAM WICKHAM, born at Enfield in this county,‡ bred in King's College, was bishop first of Lincoln, then of Winchester, where he may be termed William Wickham junior, in distinction of his name-sake and predecessor; one equal to any of his order in piety and painfulness (though little of him extant in print); superior to all in patience, dying anno 1596 of the strangury, when he had not made water for fourteen days together.§ This mindeth me of an usual prayer amongst the modern Jews (had they no worse customs their company would be welcome unto us), praising God as well for their vents of ejection, as mouths for the admission of nourishment.

SOLDIERS.

FALCATIUS, or FULKE de BRENT, was a Middlesex-man by his nativity, whose family so flourished therein in former ages (remaining in a meaner condition to this day) that an antiquary‖ will have the rivulet Brent, which denominateth Brentford, so named from them; which is preposterous in my opinion, believing them rather named from the rivulet.

This Fulke was a minion to king John, whose dangers endeared martial men unto him; who, the more to oblige his fidelity, gave him in marriage Margaret the daughter of Warrin Fitz-Gerald his chamberlain, late wife to Baldwin de Rivers, many muttering thereat, and the lady herself (it seems) not well satisfied therewith, as beneath her deserts. Hereupon our author:¶

> *Lex connectit eos, amor et concordia lecti,*
> *Sed lex qualis? amor qualis? concordia qualis?*
> *Lex exlex, amor exosus, concordia discors.*

---

* As Prætor, Quæstor, Censor, Tribunus, &c.
† J. Waræus, de Scriptoribus Hibernicis, page 127.
‡ Dr. Hatcher's Manuscript History of the Fellows of King's College in Cambridge.
§ Godwin, in his Catalogue of the Bishops of Winchester.
‖ Norden, in his Description of Middlesex. ¶ Matthew of Westminster.

> " Now both of them being brought into a bed,
>   By law, and love, and concord joined are :
> What law ? what love ? what concord did them wed ?
>   Law lawless, loathed love, concord which did jar."

This Fulke was highly in favour with king Henry the Third;
who, by the valour of this his general, obtained the great victory at Lincoln.

But afterwards, when the land was settled in peace, Fulke
found himself less respected, *set by*, and not *sett by*, hung up
like the axe, when it hath hew'n all the hard timber, on the
wall unregarded.* He endeavoured therefore to embroil the
nation in a new war, and, like a dishonest chirurgeon, wilfully to
blister the sound flesh into a sore, to gain by the curing thereof.
This not succeeding (all being weary of civil war), he presuming
on the king's lenity, and his own merit, (accounting himself too
high to come under the roof of any law) committed many out-
rages of felonies and murders. He was esteemed too bad to
live, such his present desperateness; yet too good to be put to
death, such his former deserts; and therefore (as an expedient
between both) he was condemned to perpetual banishment.
He went to Rome (none had more need to confess his faults),
where he lived obscurely, died miserably, and was buried
ignobly, anno 1226.†

Sir RALPH SADLIER, son of —— Sadlier, esquire, was born
at Hackney, in this county, where he was heir to a fair inheritance. He first was servant to the lord Cromwell, and by him
advanced into the service of king Henry the Eighth; a prince
judicious in men and meat (and seldom deceived in either), who
made him chief secretary of state. He was much knowing
(and therefore most employed) in the Scotch affairs, much complicated with state intricacies, which he knew well to unfold.
It is seldom seen that the pen and sword, gown and corslet,
meet eminently, as here, in the same person; for, in the battle
of Musselborough, he ordered and brought up our scattered
troops (next degree to a rout), inviting them to fight by his
own example; and so for his valour was made a knight
banneret. Of these two kinds, one by way of encouragement
made before, the other by way of reward after, a field victory,
more safe, and no less honourable in my opinion; Sir Ralph
was of the second sort, and the last which survived in England

---

* " Dr. Fuller, in his ' Mixt Contemplations,' p. 23, of the second numbering
has these words, 'being now *set by*, laid aside as useless, and not *sett by*;' whereby
he makes the different senses of the word to consist in the spelling with one or two
t's. It may rather consist in the difference of pronunciation, *set by* and *sett by*. But
in truth there is nothing in either the pronunciation or the orthography; for these
two contrary senses arise from the same word, and the same pronunciation, and
very naturally. To *set by* is to *set aside :* now a thing may be *set aside* as useless or
disregarded, and it may be *set by* as a thing highly valuable : hence the phrase, *little
or nothing set by*, that is valued and esteemed, and *much set by*."—DR. PEGGE.
† Matthew Paris, in anno 1226.

of that order. Yet he was little in stature, tall not in person but performance, queen Elizabeth made him chancellor of the duchy. During his last embassy in Scotland, his house at Standon in Hertfordshire was built by his steward, in his absence, far greater than himself desired; so that he never joined therein, and died soon after, anno 1587, in the 80th year of his age. However, it hath been often filled with good company; and they feasted with great cheer by the hereditary hospitality therein.

I must not forget, how when this knight attended his master the lord Cromwell at Rome (before the English renounced the Papal power) a pardon was granted (not by his own but a servant's procuring) for the sins of that family, for three immediate generations (expiring in R. Sadlier, esquire, lately dead); which was extant, but lately lost or displaced amongst their records; and though no use was made thereof, much mirth was made therewith.

CAPITAL JUDGES, AND WRITERS ON THE LAW.

Sir THOS. FROWICK, Knight, was born at Elinge, in this county, son to Thomas Frowick, esquire; by his wife, who was daughter and heir to Sir John Sturgeon, knight, (giving for his arms, Azure, three sturgeons Or, under a fret Gules) bred in the study of our municipal law; wherein he attained to such eminency, that he was made lord chief justice of the Common Pleas, on the 30th of September, in the eighteenth year of the reign of king Henry the Seventh.

Four years he sat in his place, accounted the oracle of law in his age, though one of the youngest men that ever enjoyed that office. He is reported to have died *floridâ juventute*, before full forty years old, and lieth buried, with Joane his wife, in the church of Finchley in this county, the circumscription about his monument being defaced; only we understand that his death happened on the seventeenth of October, 1506. He left a large estate to his two daughters; whereof Elah the eldest was married to Sir John Spelman (one of the justices of the King's Bench), grandfather to Sir Henry, that renowned knight.

Sir WILLIAM STAMFORD, Knight, was of Staffordian extraction, Robert his grandfather living at Rowley in that county. But William his father was a merchant in London, and purchased lands at Hadley in Middlesex, where Sir William was born August 22, 1509.

He was bred to the study of our municipal laws, attaining so much eminence therein, that he was preferred one of the judges of the Common Pleas. His most learned book of the Pleas of the Crown hath made him for ever famous amongst

Y 2

men of his own profession.   There is a spirit of retraction of
one to his native country, which made him purchase lands, and
his son settle himself again in Staffordshire.   This worthy
judge died August 28th, and was buried at Hadley in this shire,
in the last year of the reign of queen Mary, 1558.

WRITERS.

JOHN ACTON.—I find no fewer than seventeen Actons in
England, so called, as I conceive, originally from *ake*, in Saxon
an *oak*, wherewith anciently, no doubt, those towns were well
stored.*   But I behold the place nigh London as the paramount Acton amongst them.

Our John was bred doctor of the laws in Oxford, and afterwards became canon of Lincoln, being very able in his own
faculty.   He wrote a learned comment on the Ecclesiastical
Constitutions of Otho and Ottobone† (both cardinals and legates
to the Pope in England), and flourished under king Edward
the First, anno 1290.

RALPH ACTON was bred in the university of Oxford, where
he attained (saith my author‡) *magisterium theologicum ;* and,
as I understand, *magister in theologiâ* is a doctor in divinity, so
doctor in artibus is a master of arts.   This is reported to his
eternal commendation : "Evangelium regni Dei fervore non
modico prædicabat in mediis Romanarum superstitionum tene-
bris ;" and though sometimes his tongue lisped with the *siboleth* of the superstition of that age ; yet generally he uttered
much precious truth in those dangerous days, and flourished
under king Edward the Second, anno 1320.

[AMP.] ROGER TWIFORD.—I find eleven towns so named
in England (probably from the confluence of two fords thereabouts), and two in this county.   He was bred an Augustinian
friar, studied in both universities, and became a doctor of divinity.   In his declining age he applied himself to the reading of
the Scripture and the Fathers, and became a painful and profitable preacher.   I find him not fixed in any one place, who is
charactered, " Concionum propalator per diœcesin Norvicen-
sem," (an itinerant, no errant, preacher through the diocese of
Norwich.§)   He was commonly called goodluck (" and goodluck have he with his honour") because he brought good success
to others (and consequently his own welcome) with him whithersoever he went, which made all places and persons ambitious and
covetous of his presence.   He flourished about the year of our
Lord 1390.

* Bale, de Scriptoribus Britannicis, Cent. iv. num. 66.
† Idem, Cent. v. n. 13.   ‡ Idem, ibidem.
§ Bale, de Scriptoribus Britannicis, Cent. vii. n. 17.

ROBERT HOWNSLOW was born in this county, at Hounslow, a village well known for the road through, and the Heath besides it. He was a friar of the order of the Holy Trinity, which chiefly employed themselves for the redemption of captives.* Indeed locusts generally were the devourers of all food; yet one kind of locusts were themselves wholesome, though coarse food, whereon John Baptist had his common repast. Thus friars, I confess, generally were the pests of the places they lived in; but, to give this order their due, much good did redound from their endeavours; for this Robert being their Provincial for England, Scotland, and Ireland, rich people by him were affectionately exhorted, their alms industriously collected, such collections carefully preserved, till they could be securely transmitted, and thereby the liberty of many Christian captives effectually procured. He wrote also many Synodal sermons, and epistles of consequence to several persons of quality, to stir up their liberality. He flourished, says Pitseus, anno Domini 1430; a most remarkable year by our foresaid author, assigned either for the flourishing or for the funerals of eleven famous writers (yet so as our Robert is *dux gregis*, and leads all the rest) all contemporaries; whereas otherwise, for two or three eminent persons to light on the same year, is a fair proportion through all his book " De Illustribus Angliæ Scriptoribus."

SINCE THE REFORMATION.

WILLIAM GOUGE, born at Stratford-Bow in this county, bred in King's College in Cambridge, where he was not once absent from public service morning and evening the space of nine years together. He read fifteen chapters in the Bible every day; and was afterwards minister of Blackfriars in London.† He never took a journey merely for pleasure in all his life; he preached so long, till it was a greater difficulty for him to go up into the pulpit, than either to make or preach a sermon; and died aged seventy-nine years, leaving the examples of his humility, faith, patience, &c. to the imitation of posterity; being buried in his own church, December 19, 1653.

BENEFACTORS TO THE PUBLIC.

A *nameless* HERMIT‡ (dwelling in the hermitage where now the school is) on his own cost, caused gravel to be digged in the top of Highgate-hill, where now is a fair pond of water: and therewith made a causeway from Highgate to Islington; a two-handed charity, providing water on the hill, where it was wanting, and cleanness in the vale, which before, especially in winter, was passed with much molestation.

* Bale, de Scriptoribus Britannicis, Cent. vii. n. 17; and Pits.
† These Memoirs are extracted out of the sermon preached at his funeral.—F.
‡ Norden, in his Speculum Britanniæ, p. 22.

SINCE THE REFORMATION.

ALICE, daughter of Thomas Wilkes, was a poor maid born in Islington, where her cap was casually shot through with an arrow without any hurt to her head.   She afterwards was thrice married to wealthy husbands (whereof justice Owen the last); and built at Islington, near to the place of her deliverance, a proper alms-house, by her well endowed. This lady expended to charitable uses, here and elsewhere, what amounted to the full sum of two thousand three hundred pounds and upwards; and lieth buried, as I take it, in Islington.*

Sir JULIUS CÆSAR, Knight, was born in this county, his father having a house nigh unto Tottenham.†   His father was a doctor of physic to queen Elizabeth, and descended of the ancient family of the Dalmarii in Italy.   This his son was bred in Oxford; and, after other intermediate preferments, was advanced chancellor of the duchy of Lancaster, and sworn a privy counsellor on Sunday the 6th of July 1607, and afterwards was preferred master of the rolls.‡

A person of prodigious bounty to all of worth or want, so that he might seem to be almoner-general of the nation. The story is well known of a gentleman, who once borrowing his coach (which was as well known to poor people as any hospital in England), was so rendezvoused about with beggars in London, that it cost him all the money in his purse to satisfy their importunity; so that he might have hired twenty coaches on the same terms. Sir Francis Bacon, Lord Verulam, was judicious in his election, when, perceiving his dissolution to approach, he made his last bed in effect in the house of Sir Julius.

He continued more than twenty years master of the rolls; and, though heaved at by some expectants, sate still in his place, well poized therein with his gravity and integrity: " Vir tantarum elemosynarum non movebitur," (a man of so great alms and prayers, made by him and for him, shall not be removed.) Nor was it without a prosperous omen, that his chief house in Hertfordshire was called Benington; that is, " Villa benigna," (the bountiful village), as one author will have it;§ or as another " Villa beneficii," (the town of good turns‖), from the river so named running by it. What shall I speak of his arms, viz. Gules, three roses Argent; on a chief of the first so many roses of the second; embleming the fragrancy of the memory he hath left behind him.¶

* On taking down the old church at Islington, in 1751, the fragments of Lady Owen's monument were removed to the alms-houses which she founded.—ED.
† John Norden, in Description of Middlesex.   ‡ Stow's Annals.
§ Norden, in Hertfordshire.   ‖ Camden's Britannia, in Hertfordshire.
¶ So blazoned by Peacham, in his " Practice of Blazonry," page 186.

His monument in Great St. Helen's, London, being out of the road of ordinary fancies, was thus designed by himself.

The ensuing description is contrived in form of a deed, and imitateth ruffled parchment, in allusion to his office, as master of the Rolls :

> "Omnibus Christi fidelibus ad quos hoc præsens scriptum pervenerit : Sciatis, me Julium Dalmare, alias Cæsarem, Militem, utriusque Doctorem, Elizabethæ Reginæ Supremæ Curiæ Admiralitatis Judicem, et unum è Magistris Libellorum, Jacobo Regi à Privatis Conciliis, Cancellarium Scaccarii, Scriniorum Magistrum, hac præsenti charta mea confirmasse me, annuente Divino Numine, naturæ debitum libenter soliturum, quamprimum Deo placuerit. In cujus rei memoriam manum meam et sigillum apposui. Datum 27 Februarii, 1635."

JULIUS CÆSAR

Here his seal of coat of arms is affixed, and beneath them is written " Irrotulatur Cœlo."

He died the twenty-eighth day of April, anno Domini 1636, in the seventy-ninth of his age.

MEMORABLE PERSONS.

PETER FABEL.—I shall probably offend the gravity of some to insert, and certainly curiosity of others to omit, him. Some make him a friar, others a lay gentleman ; all a conceited person, who, with his merry devices, deceived the devil, who by grace may be resisted, not deceived by wit. If a grave bishop, in his sermon,* speaking of Brute's coming into this land, said it was but a *bruit*, I hope I may say, without offence, that this *Fabel* was but a *fable*, supposed to live in the reign of king Henry the Sixth.

. . . . TRESTRAM was a gardener by his occupation, living at Brentford in this county. This man, anno Domini 1609, fell into a most violent inflammation of the lungs, accompanied with a terrible fever, shortness of breath, stitch of both sides, dry cough, and an unquenchable thirst. Doctor Theo-

---

* At the funeral of king James.

dore Deodate,* being his neighbour (then physician to prince
Henry and the lady Elizabeth) beholding him of a ruddy and
sanguine complexion, adventured to let him blood, though he
was of threescore and sixteen years of age.

Once he let him blood about twenty ounces, by which
evacuation (his blood being extremely putrefied) he felt ease for
three hours; but afterwards all his accidents returned as violent
as before.

Next morning he repeated the bleeding in the same quantity,
whereby the patient only found a momentary ease, his pain
returning as violent as before.

The third day, remembering the rule of Hippocrates, that
blood must be let to the changing of the colour, he adventured
again on as copious a phlebotomy as before; whereby the sick
man found extraordinary ease, who in three days had lost more
than sixty ounces of blood.

This Trestram survived eight years after; and died anno
1619,—a most eminent instance against those who endeavour to prove the decay of the world, because men cannot
spare so much by blood-letting as in former ages.

LORD MAYORS.

1. Henry Frowicke, son of Henry Frowicke, of Tottenham,
    Mercer, 1435.
2. William Marrow, son of Stephen Marrow, of Stebunheath,
    Mercer, 1455.
3. William Hallin, son of Nicholas Hallin, of Fulham, Fish-
    monger, 1459.
4. Humphrey Heyford, son of Roger Heyford, of Stratford Bow,
    Goldsmith, 1470.
5. Christopher Askew, son of John Askew, of Edmonton, Dra-
    per, 1533.
6. John Lyon, son of Thomas Lyon, of Peryfare, Grocer,
    1554.
7. Thomas Curteis, son of John Curteis, of Enfield, Fish-
    monger, 1557.
8. John Jolles, son of Thomas Jolles, of Stratford Bow, Dra-
    per, 1615.

THE NAMES OF THE GENTRY OF THIS COUNTY,

RETURNED BY THE COMMISSIONERS IN THE TWELFTH YEAR OF KING HENRY
THE SIXTH, 1433.

Richard bishop of London, and the Prior of the Hospital of St.
    John's of Jerusalem;—John Ash, and Richard Maidestone,
    (knights for the shire);—Commissioners to take the oaths.
Johannis Harpeden, mil.   Thomæ Chaleton, mil.[a]

* From his own letter, printed in Dr. Hakewill's Apology, p. 242.

Johannis Boys, mil.
Henrici Somer.
Johannis Frampton.
Thomæ Hasele.
Thomæ Frowyk.[b]
Simonis Campe.
Alexandri Anne.
Willielmi Wrothe.[c]
Johannis Chichele.
Roberti Warner.
Johannis Shordyche.[d]
Edmundi Bibbesworth.
Walteri Grene.
Thomæ Holgyll.
Thomæ Malton.
Johannis Drayton.

Willielmi Swanlond.
Willielmi Norton.
Johannis Barnvile.
Richardi Richmond.
Roberti Oliver.
Willielmi Bray.
Roberti Foster.
Henrici Filingsley.
Johannis Bronn.
Roberti Charyngworth.
Richardi Skarburgh.
Richardi Bronn.
Johannis Elryngton.[e]
Willielmi Brokherst.
Johannis Danyell.

What is generally true of the gentry in all counties, that, being *in continuo fluxo,*

" Labitur, et labetur, in omne volubilis ævum,"

is most true in this county, where the stream thereof runneth most rapid, to make more speedy room for succession; so that the gentry in Middlesex seem sojourners, rather than inhabitants therein. Is it not strange, that of the thirty-three fore-named families, not three of them were extant in the shire one hundred and sixty years after, viz. anno Domini 1593, as appeareth by the alphabetical collection set forth by Mr. Norden in that year.* I impute the brevity (as I may term it) of such gentry in this county to the vicinity of London to them, or rather of them to it; and hope that worshipful families now fixed in Middlesex will hereafter have longer continuance.

[a] THOMÆ CHALETON, *Militis.*—I can hardly believe him of the same family, (R being slipped out in the writing thereof) with Thomas Carleton, who died anno Domini 1447, being buried under a much defaced monument in Edmonton church, and whom the inhabitants deliver by tradition to have been a man of great command in this county.

[b] THOMÆ FROWYK.—He was owner of Gunnersbury in the parish of Great Ealing, wherein he lies buried; and was father of famous Judge Frowyk, of whom before.

[c] WILLIELMI WROTH.—Ancestor to Sir Henry Wroth, still living at Durance, whose great grandfather, Sir Thomas Wroth, fled over for his religion into Germany, in the reign of queen Mary; and it is observable that he, who then went away for

* In his Speculum Britanniæ, p. 42.

his conscience, hath alone of all this catalogue his name remaining in this county. As for William Wroth, mentioned in this catalogue, he was son to William Wroth, esquire, who died the 20th of March, the ninth of Henry the Fourth,[*] who was the son of John Wroth, who married Maud sole daughter unto Thomas Durand, by whom the house of Durands was devolved unto him.

JOHN SHORDYCHE.—So called from Shoreditch on the north of Bishopsgate in London, whereof he was owner, as also of the manor of Hackney; I say *Shoreditch*, so named here (in the twelfth of king Henry the Sixth) and some hundred years before, quasi *Shoreditch*, or the *ditch* that was the *sewer* or public drain to the north-east part of the city. Hereby appeareth the vanity of their conceits who will have it so called from Jane Shore (the minion of Edward the Fourth), reported to die here pitifully (as much pitied, though not relieved) in the reign of king Richard the Third.

Reader, be pleased to take notice, that though Mr. Norden, in his survey of this county, passeth over this surname in silence, yet the progeny of this John Shoreditch hath still a considerable estate at Icknam therein.

[e] JOHANNIS ELRYNGTON.—These had a house sometime at Neusdon,[†] in this county, but are since extinct; and the last I find of the name was John Elryngton, filicer of the city of London, and keeper of the records of the Common Pleas; who, dying 1504, is buried with an inscription in Hackney church.

THE SHERIFFS.

Some perchance may expect, that in conformity to other counties, I should here insert the sheriffs of Middlesex, reserving those of London to the description of that city. These proceed on an old vulgar error, that the sheriffs aforesaid have their several jurisdictions divided accordingly; whereas indeed both are jointly and equally sheriffs of London and [sheriff of] Middlesex, having not only concurrent but united power in all places. Nor know I any difference betwixt them, save that he who is first chosen taketh place, and he who liveth the nearest to the Tower hath the Poultry, the other Wood-street-counter, assigned to his service. But more of them in London.

All I will add is this: the gentry in Middlesex have herein a privilege above any county in England, that they are not eligible (except also they be freemen of London) to be sheriffs of this shire, which doth cut off from them the occasion of much expences.

---

[*] Ex bundello Inquisitionum anno 2 Regis Hen. V., num. 4, in Turre London.
[†] Norden, p. 37.

THE BATTLES.

Brentford Fight, Nov. 12*th,* 1642.—It began on the south-west side of the town, near Zion-house : some execution being done by great guns, and a boat on the Thames with many therein sunk, and Captain Quarles (an active citizen on the parliament side) drowned before he could recover the shore.

Soon was the scene of this tragedy removed to the north of the town, near Acton ; and the king's forces fell fiercely on the regiment of Colonel Denzil Hollis, then present in parliament, and put them to the worst.

Here the Welch, under Sir . . . . Salisbury their leader, made true the Greek proverb, ὁ φεύγων πάλιν μαχήσεται, (he that flieth will fight again.) These who shewed swift heels at Edgehill battle, use as stout arms [as any] in this fight; for formerly they were little better than naked ; whereas, since, they had recovered armour to fence their bodies, and resolutions to arm their minds.

Next day, being Sunday, marched out the militia of London ; but both armies may be said to have kept the Sabbath, facing each other without any considerable action. It is incredible how many cart-loads of victuals were carried out from London, enough to have feasted their soldiers for some days, and fed them for some weeks. In the evening the king's forces drew off towards Kingston.

The number of the slain on both sides amounted not to a thousand; and the reputation of the victory on the king's side was more than the effect thereof; for then the royalists did *nose* and *beard* the populous city of London, and did *triumphare* (though not *in*) *sub hostico*. Indeed the accession of citizens to the king answered not rational expectation ; wealth, though loyal, being always fearful, and loath to hazard a certain estate.

This is most sure, that many scores of prisoners taken by the king were by him freely dismissed, without other ransom than a strict oath to serve no more against him. Now, what oath-office is kept in London I know not, nor what Pope therein had power to dispense with so sacred an obligation. But these met with such confessors, who seemingly satisfied them in the violation of this oath, so that some weeks after they appeared on the same side as fierce as before.

THE FAREWELL.

This county is much infested with the mildew. That it is, I know to my cost; but could not purchase the knowledge what it is, much less how it might be prevented at the same price, though having diligently inquired into the name and nature thereof.

Some will have it called *mildew,* quasi *maldew,* or *ill-dew ;* others *meldew,* or *honey-dew,* as being very sweet (oh, how luscious and noxious is flattery!), with the astringency thereof causing an atrophy on consumption in the grain. His etymology was peculiar to himself who would have it termed *mildew*, because it grindeth the grain aforehand, making it to dwindle away almost to nothing.

It falleth (be it mist or dew) when corn is almost ripe for the sickle, and antedateth the harvest (not before it is welcome, but) before it is wished by the husbandman, grain being rather withered than ripened thereby. If, after the fall, a good rain or strong wind cometh, it washeth and wipeth it off, so that no mischief is done; otherwise the hot sun arising sealeth (to use the husbandman's phrase) the mildew upon the straw, and so intercepteth the nourishment betwixt the root and the ear, especially if it falleth not on the *house* (which is but another case, and hath another tunicle under it) but on the stripped straw near to the top of the stalk.

Grain growing under hedges (where the wind hath least power) is most subject thereunto; though wheat of all grain is most, bearded wheat of wheat is least, liable unto it: not that the *haums* thereof are spears to fright the mildew from it; but advantageous gutters, to slide it away the sooner, which sticketh on notted or pollard wheat.

Inland counties, Northamptonshire, Bedfordshire, &c. complain the least, maritime the most, of mildew; which insinuateth the vapours of the sea to be casual thereof. Some hold that, seeing it falls from the skies, earth hath no guard for heaven's blow, save prayer, which in this very case is prescribed by Solomon.* But others conceive, that human may be subordinate to spiritual means; to prevent, not the falling but the hurting of this dew in such a degree, and hopefully expect the remedy from the ingenuity of the next generation.

I am the rather confirmed in my hopes, because a help hath been found out against the smutting of wheat, at least wise in some good proportion; I say the smutting of wheat, which makes it a negro, as mildew makes it a dwarf; viz. by mingling the seed with lime, as your husbandmen will inform you.

And for my *Vale* to this county, I heartily desire, that either God would of his goodness spare the fruits of the earth from so hurtful a casualty, or put it into the minds of men (if it may stand with his will) to find out some defensive, in some part, to abate the malignity thereof.

* Kings viii. 37.

LONDON.

It is the second city in Christendom for greatness, and the first for good government. There is no civilized part of the world but it hath heard thereof, though many with this mistake, that they conceive London to be the country, and England but the city therein.

Some have suspected the declining of the lustre thereof, because of late it vergeth so much westward, increasing in buildings in Covent Garden, &c. But by their favour (to disprove their fear) it will be found to burnish round about, to every point of the compass, with new structures daily added thereunto.

It oweth its greatness, under God's divine providence, to the well-conditioned river of Thames, which doth not (as some tyrant rivers in Europe) abuse its strength in a destructive way, but employeth its greatness in goodness, to be beneficial to commerce, by the reciprocation of the tide therein. Hence it was that when king James, offended with the city, threatened to remove his court to another place, the Lord Mayor (boldly enough) returned, "that he might remove his court at his pleasure, but could not remove the river of Thames."

Erasmus * will have London so called from *Lindus*, a city of Rhodes; averring a great resemblance betwixt the language and customs of the Britons and Grecians. But Mr. Camden (who no doubt knew of it) honoureth not this his etymology with the least mention thereof. As improbable, in my apprehension, is the deduction from Lud's-town,—*town* being a Saxon, no British termination. And that it was so termed from *Lan Dian*, a temple of Diana (standing where now St. Paul's doth), is most likely, in my opinion.

MANUFACTURES.

Natural Commodities are not to be expected to grow in this place, which is only the field of art, and shop-general of England; Cheapside being called the best garden only by metaphor; seeing otherwise nothing but stones are found therein. As for London Manufactures, they are so many, I shall certainly lose myself in this labyrinth, if offering to enter. In leaving, therefore, all intermediate inventions to others, I will only in-

---

* In his adage, *Rhodii Sacrificium.*

sist on the Needle and the Engine, as the least and greatest instruments employed therein.

NEEDLES.

The use hereof is right ancient, though sewing was before needles; for we read that our first parents made themselves aprons by sewing fig-leaves together,* either fastening them with some glutinous matter, or with some sharp thing joining them together.

A pin is a blind needle, a needle a pin with an eye. What nails do in solid, needles do in supple bodies, putting them together; only they remain not there formally, but virtually, in the thread which they leave behind them. It is the woman's pencil; and embroidery [*vestis acu picta*] is the master-piece thereof. I say embroidery, much used in former, neglected in our age, wherein modern gallants (affecting variety of suits) desire that their clothes should be known by them, and not, as our ancestors, they by their clothes, one suit of state serving them for several solemnities.

This industrious instrument, *needle*, quasi *ne idle* (as some will have it), maintaineth many millions. Yea, he who desireth a blessing on the plough and the needle (including that in the card and compass) comprehendeth most employments at home and abroad, by land and by sea.

All I will add is this: that the first fine Spanish needles in England were made in the reign of queen Mary, in Cheapside, by a negro; but such his envy, that he would teach his art to none; so that it died with him. More charitable was Elias Crowse, a German, who, coming over into England about the eighth of queen Elizabeth, first taught us the making of Spanish needles; and since we have taught ourselves the using of them.

THE ENGINE.

This general word, communicable to all machines or instruments, *use*, in this city, hath confined to signify that which is used to quench scare-fires therein. One Mr. Jones, a merchant (living in Austin Friars), fetched the first form thereof from Neuremberg, and obtained a patent of king James, that none should be made without his approbation.

Two were begun but not finished, in his life-time, who died in the great plague, primo Caroli Primi; since which time, William Burroughs, city founder, now living in Lothbury, hath so completed this instrument, that his additions amount to a new invention, having made it more secure from breaking, and easy to be cleansed; so that, with the striking out of a wedge, it will cleanse itself, and be fit to work again in four minutes.

Since, the aforesaid party hath made about three score of these engines for city and country. The cooper, carpenter,

* Gen. iii. 7.

smith, founder, brazier, and turner, contribute their skills to the perfecting of it. Yet may the price thereof be compassed for thirty-five pounds.

It hath gained, because it hath saved, many pounds, and (which is invaluable) many lives of men, in this city.* The best (though not the biggest) was lately in the church of St. James, Clerkenwell, as hath many times been experimented. "A good musician makes a good instrument;" and it was a poor blue-cap (better known by his work than name) who played so well thereon, that (though not, with the left-handed Gibeonites, to hit the mark within a hair's breadth) he could hit within the scantling of a shilling. Since a newer at St. Bridget's church is a better; and no wonder if the younger out-active those who are more ancient. All wished this engine may be brought forth once a quarter, to be scoured, oiled, and trimmed, but not to be used. But if there be an occasion thereof, may it effectually perform that for which it was intended!

THE BUILDINGS.

ST. PAUL'S.

This is the only cathedral in Christendom dedicated solely to that Saint; great the pillars (little legs will bow under so big a body), and small the windows thereof; darkness in those days being conceived to raise devotion; besides, it made artificial lights to appear with the more solemnity. It may be called the Mother Church indeed, having one babe in her body, St. Faith's, and another in her arms, St. Gregory's. Surely such who repair to divine service in St. Faith may there be well minded of their mortality, being living people, surrounded with the antiperistasis of the dead both above and beneath them. For the present, I behold St. Paul's church as one struck with the dead palsy on one side, the east part and quoir thereof being quick and alive, well maintained and repaired, whilst the west part is ruinous and ready to fall down.† Little hopes it will be repaired in its old decays, which is decayed in its new reparations, and, being formerly an ornament, is now an eye-sore to the City; not to say unto the citizens in general, some being offended that it is in so bad, and others that it is in no worse, condition.

The repairing of this church was a worthy monument of the piety and charity of archbishop Laud; not only procuring the bounty of others, but expending his own estate thereon. We despair not but that his majesty's zeal, in commending this work to their care, will in due time meet with the forward bounty of the citizens. It is no sin to wish, that those who

---

* In a very few years after this was written, the great Fire of London destroyed, indiscriminately, both engines and buildings.—ED.

† St. Paul's Cathedral was, soon after, among the dreadful ruins of the city.—ED.

have plundered the cloak and cover of St. Paul's (not left behind *by*, but) violently taken *from* him, might be compelled to make him a new one of their own cost; at leastwise to contribute more than ordinary proportions thereunto.

As for the parochial churches in London, they have all either cast their skins with the snake, or renewed their bills with the eagle, having at the least their fronts beautified, if not their bodies rebuilt; amongst which St. Clement's, Eastcheap, is not to be forgotten, the monument of the bounty of Baldwin Hamey, doctor in physic; so that what is written in a modest challenge to the papist, on the entry into the new-built church of St. Giles-in-the-Fields, may be inscribed on the rest: " Heus, Viator! anne bonis operibus effœtum est hoc seculum?"

THE BRIDGE.

The middle thereof is properly in none, the two ends in two counties, Middlesex and Surrey. Such who only see it beneath, where it is a bridge, cannot suspect it should be a street; and such who behold it above, where it is a street, cannot believe it is a bridge. It was made with great cost, and is maintained with daily charge against the battery and assault of the tide. The sad riddle is generally known to all, which happened here some twenty years since, when a lamentable fire could not be quenched, because there was such store of water, hindering all access thereunto.

THE EXCHANGE.

This was built by Sir Thomas Gresham, Knight, anno Domini 1571, in imitation of that at Antwerp, but so that the copy exceedeth the original. Queen Elizabeth named it the Royal Burse; but it is commonly called the Exchange, or Change, because, by bargains driven there, wares are changed for wares, and wares for money, and money for money. Yet, because much of mutability is imported in the word Change, it may be a fit remembrancer to merchants meeting here, not to build their hopes of perpetuity on what is so subject to vicissitude and alteration. Well may this place be termed the Change, where poor men so soon become rich by good success, and rich men poor by losses and casualties unexpected!

THE TOWER.

This, to waive the fable of Julius Cæsar, was first founded by king William the Conqueror, finished by William Rufus, encompassed with a ditch by William Longcamp bishop of Ely, enlarged by king Henry the Third, fortified by king Edward the Fourth, beautified by king Richard the Third, repaired by king Henry the Eighth; since whose time no considerable addition thereunto. The mortar thereof (to make it, belike, the more tenacious) was, saith my author,* tempered with the blood of beasts; and this Tower was built to secure London in both senses, to awe or defend it, as occasion should require. It is a palace, a prison, a liberty, a town, a castle, and what not? most remarkable for the Armory, Mint, Wardrobe, and [formerly] the unicorn's horn therein.

ARMORY.

I place this before the Mint, because of Solon's speech to Crœsus, that " he that hath the best steel will command all his gold and silver." Here many justly admire at the prodigious greatness of some ancient corslets. If Tully, seeing a little man wearing a long sword, said pleasantly, that he was " alligatus gladio," (tied to his sword,) surely at the sight hereof, he would conclude wearers imprisoned in their arms. This hath put men on many conjectures; some collecting hence the strength and stature of the former ages far above ours; others parallel them with the shields left by Alexander to lie in India, purposely to possess posterity with an untruth, about the proportion of the persons of his soldiers. If I may interpose my conjecture (and if he may speak of John of Gaunt who never fought in his armour), I conceive those arms, so signally great, not made to march in (as too ponderous for any under a giant); but to stand therein in a breach, where they might be serviceable.

Nor can a general diminution of men's strength be justly inferred from the disproportion of arms in our and former ages. I say general diminution, seeing all ages, even in the same country, have produced some of greater, some of lesser dimensions. For, if we compare the common armour used three hundred years since (and yet extant in the Tower) with ours of modern use, no such sensible difference will be found betwixt them as should argue an universal decay. It is confessed that their arrows exceeded ours both in bigness and length. But a learned author† imputeth this rather to their continual practice in shooting from their infancy, than to their strength and stature; so that it is rather disuse than disability in our age, that we cannot shoot the like; and, since the invention of guns, the light use we make of arrows have made them the lighter in the making.

MINT.

Many of these anciently in most cities, and some towns. These afterwards (as so many spangles in one piece of gold) were united in the Tower.

Of late it was much employed to coin the plate of our nation, to make state money; whence one said,

* Fitz-Stephen, in his Description of London.
† Dr. Hakewill, in his Apology, p. 221.

Cæsaris effigies nulla est, sed imaginis expers,
Crux duplex super est dira, gemensque Lyra.

And another,

" May their success like to their coin appear,
Send double crosses for their single cheer."

Sure I am, their coin goeth under a general suspicion of being
as bad as their cause. But I hope hereafter, when the question
is asked of our coiners, " Whose image and superscription is
this ?" it will be returned, " The *Cæsar's* of England."

WARDROBE.

This was not that for the king's wearing apparel, or liveries
of servants, kept elsewhere in a house so called, in the parish
of St. Andrew's Wardrobe ; but for vests or robes of state,
with rich carpets, canopies, and hangings, to be used on great
solemnities. Here lately was a rich piece of arras, presenting
the sea-fight in eighty-eight, and having the living portraitures
of the chiefest commanders wrought in the borders thereof.
On the same token, that a captain, who highly prized his own
service, missing his picture therein, complained of the injury to
his friend, professing of himself that he merited a place there
as well as some therein remembered, seeing he was engaged in
the middle of the fight ; " Be content," quoth his friend, " thou
hast been an old pirate, and art reserved for another *hanging*."*

There were also kept in this place the ancient clothes of
our English kings, which they wore on great festivals ; so that
this wardrobe was, in effect, a library for antiquaries, therein to
read the mode and fashion of garments in all ages. These king
James, in the beginning of his reign, gave to the earl of Dun-
bar ; by whom they were sold, resold, and re-resold at as many
hands almost as Briareus had, some gaining vast estates thereby.

THE UNICORN'S HORN.

Amongst the many precious rarities in the Tower, this (as another in Windsor castle) was, in my memory, shewn to people. It
belongs not to me to inquire what is become of them, but rather
to discuss, 1. Whether there be such a creature as an unicorn ?
2. What kind of animal it is ? 3. What the fashion and colour ?
and 4. What the use and effect of his horn ? For the first,
they produce a weak proof who allege them to be the supporters
of the Scottish arms, and of the arms of some English gentlemen, particularly of the family of Paris in Cambridgeshire ;
seeing most heralds wear the addition of painters, and the fancy
of painters pretends to the privilege of a lawless liberty. But,
besides that it is uncivil to give the lie to a common tradition,
the former existence of such a creature (and surely no species

* Lord Verulam, in his Essays.

is wholly lost) is cleared from several places of Scripture:
" God hath as it were the strength of an unicorn."* "Will
the unicorn be willing to serve thee ?"† " My horn shalt thou
exalt like the horn of an unicorn,"‡ &c. True it is, the word in
the original§ importeth nothing of any horn therein (as doth
the Latin *unicornis*, and the Greek *monoceros*). Yet I am confident it is rightly rendered, because it is so rendered; such was
the learning and piety of the persons employed in that translation.

Proceed we now to the second query, about the kind thereof.
Surely it is distinct from the rhinoceros (carrying a horn, not
on his forehead, but on his nose) because the exaltation of his
horn is not considerable, as not bunching forth much above a
foot in the prominency thereof. He is commonly pictured,
bodied like a buck, with a horn advanced out of his forehead,
some two yards in proportion; and this his picture confuteth
his picture, seeing generally he is held to be no beast of prey,
but which feedeth on the grass; and if so, his mouth cannot
meet with the ground; the interposition of his horn, so fancy-
fully fixed, making so great distance betwixt them.

The plain truth is, I, who first questioned whether there
were any unicorns, am since convinced that there are so many
sorts of them: the Indian ox, the Indian ass, the oryx, &c.
famous for carrying one horn; but which is the prize in this
lottery I cannot decide, seeing none alive in our land have seen
a four-footed beast of that kind; and Julius Scaliger saith truly,
" Ex libris colligere quæ prodiderunt authores longè est pericu-
losissimum ; rerum ipsarum cognitio vera è rebus ipsis est."

Olaus Worme, one no less a curious inquirer into the mysteries
than careful preserver of the rarities of nature, physician at this
day unto the king of Denmark, in a learned work which he
lately set forth, endeavoureth to prove all under a general mistake who fancy a unicorn a fourfooted beast, proving the same
to be a fish in the northern seas, of twenty-two feet in length, a
long horn in his forehead (no more cumbersome in the portage
than ears are to other beasts) ; with which horn he tilteth at his
prey, and, having pierced it through, doth afterward feed upon it.

If it be objected to the contrary, that in Scripture he is
ranked amongst the quadrupeds ; "And the unicorns shall
come down with them, and the bullocks with the bulls ; and
their land shall be soaked with blood, and their dust made fat
with fatness ;"‖ it will be answered, that unicorns there are not
real but metaphorical (rendered appellatively *robusti* in some
translations) ; importing that strong enemies, both by water and
land, shall invade Idumea, to the utter destruction thereof.

Come we now to the fashion and colour of the horn, conceiv-

---

* Num. xxiii. 22.   † Job xxxix. 9.   ‡ Psal. xcii. 10.
§ ראם Reem.   ‖ Isa. xxxiv. 7.

ing it no considerable controversy concerning the length and bigness thereof, quantity not varying the kind in such cases. Some are plain, as that in St. Mark's in Venice; others wreathed about, as that at St. Dyonis near Paris, with anfractuous spires, and cocleary turnings about it, which probably is the effect of age, those wreaths being but the wrinkles of most vivacious unicorns. The same may be said of the colour; white, when newly taken from his head; yellow, like that lately in the Tower, of some hundred years' seniority; but whether or no it will ever turn black, as that of Ælian's and Pliny's description, let others decide.

The last query remains, of the virtue of this horn, which some exalt so high, that it is not only antidotal to several venoms, and substances destructive by their qualities, which we can command ourselves to believe; but also that it resisteth poisons which kill by second qualities, that is, by corrosion of parts; wherein I concur with my learned author, and doubt "such exceed the properties of its nature, and the promises of experiment will not secure the adventure;"* and I believe few mountebanks will be so daring as to poison themselves on the security of such an *alexipharmacon*.

I have done, reader, with this subject, when I have told thee that two of my worthy friends (yea, the friends to mankind by their general generosity), Dr. Baldwin Hamey, and Sir Francis Prugean; the one had the horn itself, (which to my dim eyes at some distance seemed like a taper of wreathed wax), the other hath the socket (as I may term it) of the fish, into which this horn was fixed. I have heard that, upon experiment, a great cure against poison hath been done with some grains thereof; and it is improbable that the vigour of nature should extrude that so specious to sight, which is not also sovereign to service. Since I am informed that the same Dr. Hamey hath parted with the propriety thereof to the college of physicians; and they have solemnly presented this unicorn's horn to his majesty, to supply the place of that in the Tower, which our civil wars have embezzled.

PROVERBS.

" A London jury; hang half, and save half."]

Some affirm this of an Essex, others of a Middlesex jury; and my charity believes it equally *true*, that is, equally *untrue*, of all three. What gave occasion first to this libelling proverb I know not. This I know, reports of this nature, like round bodies down precipices, once moved move themselves, and a mouse may stir what a man cannot stay in this kind. The best

---

* Thomas Browne, doctor of physic, in his "Enquiries into Vulgar Errors," B. iii. cap. 23.

is, though none can hinder a slanderer from speaking, they may hinder them from speaking truth.

This proverb would fain suggest to credulous people, as if Londoners, frequently impannelled on juries, and loaded with multiplicity of matters, aim more at dispatch than justice ; and, to make quick riddance (though no haste to hang true men), acquit half, and condemn half. Thus they divide themselves *in æquilibrio,* betwixt justice and mercy, though it were meet the latter should have the more advantage, and the beam break on the pitiful side. Others extend this proverb also to their arbitrations betwixt party and party ; as if, not minding the merits of the cause, they cleave the thing controverted into equal moieties betwixt plaintiff and defendant.

The falseness of these suggestions will appear to such who, by perusing history, do discover the London jurors most conscientious in proceeding *secundùm allegata et probata,* always inclining to the merciful side in saving life, when they can find any cause or colour for the same ; and amongst many thousands take two most memorable instances.

The first, Sir Nicholas Throgmorton, who, on the 17th of April 1554, was (in the reign of queen Mary) arraigned for high treason in Guildhall, before Sir Thomas White, lord mayor, the earls of Shrewsbury and Derby, Sir Thomas Bromley, lord chief justice, &c. Mr. Edward Griffin, the attorney-general, pressed the prisoner very sorely for his correspondence with the Carews in the west, and his being privy to the rising of Sir Thomas Wyat. Sir Nicholas pleaded many hours for himself, no less stoutly than wisely, yet with due submission to the court, till at last his jury passed upon him ; whose names, *ad perpetuam rei memoriam,* are here inserted : 1. Wheston ; 2. Lucar ; 3. Yoong ; 4. Martin ; 5. Beswik ; 6. Barscarfeld ; 7. Kightleie ; 8. Low ; 9. Painter ; 10. Banks ; 11. Calthrop ; 12. Cater.*

These acquitted the prisoner ; and though much menaced by the court, stood stoutly to their verdict, for which they were all imprisoned, five of them fined† and paid 260*l.* a-piece, the rest lower sums ; and, after their discharge from durance, commanded to attend the council-table at an hour's warning.‡

The other is of a person who was lately arraigned in Guildhall, and whom I list not to name ; partly because he is easily guessed ; partly because he was of so turbulent a spirit, that his name would set all my book at dissension. He, being charged with what concerned his life, was, by an uncorrupted jury, though heavily pressed to the contrary, clearly acquitted ; and one passage (omitted in his printed trial) I must here insert.

Speaking his farewell to the jury, now ready to depart the bar, he requested them to remember a statute in the reign of king Henry the Seventh, as making much in his behalf. "Sir-

---

* Holinshed's Chronicle, p. 1105.   † Idem, p. 1126.
‡ Stow's Chronicle, page 624, who saith they were fined 500*l.* a-piece.

rah," said one judge on the bench to this prisoner, "I know that statute better than you do." To whom he calmly replied, "I believe you, Sir! but I desire that these gentlemen of the jury should understand it but as well as I do." And so it seems they did, for his life was saved thereby.

"A fool will not part with his bauble for the Tower of London."

This Tower anciently was, and in part still is, the magazine of England's wealth. There the silver, the mint of money; and there the brass and iron to defend it, the armory and store-house of ordnance; yet fools so doat on their darling fancies, that they prize them above all this treasure. But, alas! "quod scribimus et legimus, et ridemus, hoc facimus, (we do our-selves what we deride in others.) Every one is addicted to some vanity or other, which he will not part with on any conditions, so weak and wilful we are by nature. He that will not freely and sadly confess that he is much a fool, is all a fool.

"London lick-penny."]

The countryman coming up hither, by his own experience, will easily expound the meaning thereof. The best is, it is also London get-penny, to those who live here, and carefully follow their vocations.

"London Cockneys."

Let us observe, first, the antiquity of this Proverb, then the meaning; lastly, the application thereof to Londoners. It is more than four hundred years old; for, when Hugh Bigot added artificial fortifications to the natural strength of his castle at Bungay in Suffolk, he gave out this rhyme, therein vaunting it for impregnable:

> "Were I in my castle of Bungey,
>   Upon the river of Waveney,
>   I would not care for the king of Cockeney."*

Meaning thereby king Henry the Second, then peaceably pos-sessed of London, whilst some other places did resist him; though afterwards he so humbled this Hugh, that he was fain, with large sums of money and pledges for his loyalty, to redeem this his castle from being razed to the ground.

I meet with a double sense of this word *Cockney*: some tak-ing it for, 1. One *coaks'd* or *cocker'd* (made a wanton or nestle-cock of, delicately bred and brought up), so that when grown men or women they can endure no hardship, nor comport with pains-taking. 2. One utterly ignorant of husbandry or housewifery, such as is practised in the country, so that they may be persuaded any thing about rural commodities; and the original thereof, and the tale of the citizen's son, who knew not the language of a cock, but called it neighing, is commonly known.

Here I take no notice of his fancy who will have it called

* Camden's Britannia, in Suffolk.

Cockney by transposition, " quasi *incoct*," (raw and rude*), as forced and far-fetched.

The name is generally fixed on such who are born within the sound of Bow-bell, and are tender enough, and sufficiently ignorant in country businesses. One merrily persuaded a she-citizen, that, seeing malt did not grow, the good housewives in the country did spin it ; " I knew as much," said the Cockney, " for one may see the threads hang out at the ends thereof." However, be it known unto all people, that as there are delicate and silly folk in the country ; so are there as hardy men and skilful housewives in the city ; no disparagement to any of what place soever.

" An ill word meets another, and it were at the Bridge of London."]

This is a Scottish proverb,† and indeed a Scottish text needs a Scottish comment thereon. However, I thus guess at the meaning thereof : London-bridge is notoriously known for a narrow pass and numerous passengers ; so that, people meeting thereon, a quarrel will quickly be engendered, if one of them hath not the wit or patience to step into a shop if on foot, if on horseback to stay in the void places. Thus words quickly inflame a difference, except one of the parties have the discretion of silence, yielding, or departure.

" Billingsgate language."]

Billings was formerly a gate, though now rather *portus* than *porta*, being the prime landing-place, and market for some sea commodities. Now, although as fashionable people live there as elsewhere in the city, yet much rude folk repair thither ; so that one may term this the Esculine Gate of London, from the dross and dregs of the baser people flocking thither. Here one may hear *linguas jurgatrices :* yea, shrewd words are sometimes improved into smart blows betwixt them. I doubt not but that Rome, Venice, Paris, and all populous cities, have their Billingsgate language in those places where rude people make their rendez-vous.

" Kirbie's castle, and Megse's glory,
    Spinola's pleasure, and Fisher's folly."]

These were four houses about the city, built by citizens, large and sumptuous above their estates, whose memories are likely longer to continue by this rhyme than by their own pompous buildings.

The first of these is so uncastled, the glory of the second so obscured, that very few know (and it were needless to tell them) where these houses were fixed.

As for Spinola (a Genoan, made free-denizen) the master and fellows of a college in Cambridge know too well what he was, by their expensive suit, known to posterity by Magdalen College case. If his own country (I mean the Italian) curse did

---

* Minsew's Dictionary, in the word *Cockney*.
† Proverb by David Ferauson, minister at Dunfermline.

overtake him, and if the plague of building did light upon him, few, I believe, did pity him.

As for the last, it was built by Jasper Fisher, free of the Goldsmiths, one of the six clerks in chancery, and a justice of peace, who, being a man of no great wealth (as indebted to many), built here a beautiful house, with gardens of pleasure, and bowling-alleys about it, called Devonshire House at this day.*

However, it seems this was an ancient vanity, even in the days of king David : "Their inward thought is, that their houses shall continue for ever, and their dwelling-places to all generations. They call their lands after their own names."†

"He will follow him like a St. Anthony's pig."]

St. Anthony is notoriously known for the patron of hogs, having a pig for his page in all pictures, though for what reason unknown, except, because being an hermit, and having a cell or hole digged in the earth, and having his general repast on roots, he and hogs did in some sort intercommon both in their diet and lodging.

There was a fair hospital built to the honour of St. Anthony, in Bennet's Fink in this city; the protectors and proctors whereof claimed a privilege to themselves, to garble the live pigs in the markets of the city; and such as they found starved, or otherwise unwholesome for man's sustenance, they would slit in the ear, tie a bell about their necks, and let them loose about the city.‡

None durst hurt or take them up (having this livery of St. Anthony upon them) ; but many would give them bread, and feed them in their passage, whom they used to follow whining after them. But, if such pigs proved fat, and well liking (as often they did), the officers of St. Anthony's hospital would seize on them for their own use.

The proverb is appliable to such who have servile saleable souls, who, for a small reward, will *lacquey* many miles, pressing their patrons with their unwelcome importunity.

"He was born within the sound of Bow-bell."]

This is perhaps the periphrasis of a Londoner at large, born within the suburbs thereof; the sound of this bell exceeding the extent of the lord mayor's mace. It is called *Bow-bell*, because hanging in the steeple of *Bow-church*; and *Bow-church* because built upon *bows* or arches. John Dun, mercer, gave, in 1472, two tenements to maintain the ringing of this bell nightly at nine o'clock, which sounded to servants a retreat from their work, and a march to their supper and bed ;§ and therefore conceived by some masters to ring too soon, by most apprentices too late. William Copland, the king's merchant, about the year 1520, gave a bigger bell for the same purpose,

---

* Stow's Survey, p. 175.
‡ Stow's Survey of London, p. 190.
† Psalm xlix. 11.
§ Idem, p. 269.

and had the hansel thereof himself, being first rung as a knell at his burial.

> ———————————— " St. Peter's in the poor,
>   Where no tavern, alehouse, or sign at the door."]

Under correction, I conceive it called " in the poor," because the Augustinian friars, professing wilful poverty, for some hundred of years, possessed more than a moiety thereof. But, as one gave for his motto, " Malim dives esse quàm haberi," this parish may say, " Malim pauper vocari quàm esse ;" which ever was (not to say is) one of the richest in London ; which their signless houses do avouch, being a sign of the eminency of their inhabitants, *ubi quisque sui ipsius index*, sufficiently notified and distinguished by themselves.

How ancient the use of signs in this city on private houses, is to me unknown. Sure I am, it was generally used in the reign of king Edward the Fourth ; witness that dear jest of a well-meaning citizen, who lost his life in those dangerous times for saying " he would leave the crown to his son."

I suspect this proverb is lately a little discomposed, and that some public houses for entertainment have stept or crept into this parish.

> " To dine with Duke Humphrey."]

This proverb hath altered the original meaning thereof ; for first it signified *alienâ vivere quadrâ*, to eat by the bounty or feed by the favour of another man ; for Humphrey duke of Gloucester (commonly called the good duke) was so hospitable, that every man of fashion, otherwise unprovided, was welcome to dine with him : it not being so proper for strangers to sup in those days with the greatest housekeepers. The said duke was so bountiful, that his alms-dish of silver was very massy when empty (what then when full?) which alms-dish came afterwards into the possession of the duke of Somerset, who sent it to lord Rivers, to sell the same, to furnish himself for a sea-voyage.[*]

But, after the death of good Duke Humphrey (when many of his former alms-men were at a loss for a meal's meat), this proverb did alter its copy ; to dine with duke Humphrey importing to be dinnerless.

A general mistake fixed this sense ; namely, that Duke Humphrey was buried in the body of St. Paul's church, where many men chew their meat with feet, and walk away the want of a dinner ;[†] whereas indeed that noble person interred in St. Paul's was Sir John Beauchamp, constable of Dover,[‡] warden of the Cinque Ports, knight of the Garter, son to Guy earl of Warwick, and brother to Thomas earl of Warwick ; whilst Duke Humphrey was honourably buried at St. Alban's.

---

[*] Stow's Survey of London, p. 75.
[†] Old St. Paul's church was then a public walk.—ED.
[‡] Stow's Survey of London, p. 368.

" I will use you as bad as a Jew."]

I am sure I have carried the child home, and laid it at the father's house, having traced this proverb by the tract from England in general to London, thence to the Old Jewry, whence it had its first original; that poor nation (especially on Shrove Tuesday) being intolerably abused by the English, whilst they lived in the land.

I could wish, that wheresoever Jews live, they may not find so much courtesy as to confirm them in their false, yet not so much cruelty as to discourage them from the true, religion; till which time I can bemoan their misery, condemn the Christian's cruelty, and admire God's justice in both.

See we it here now fulfilled, which God long since frequently foretold,* and threatened; namely that he would make "the Jews become a proverb," if continuing rebellious against him. I pass not for the flouts of profane Pagans, scoffing at the Jew's religion, "Credat Judæus Apella;"† but to behold them thus *proverbiascere*, for their rebellions against God, minds me of the performance of God's threatening unto them.

" Good manners to except my lord mayor of London."]

This is a corrective for such, whose expressions are of the largest size, and too general in their extent, parallel to the logic maxim, " Primum in unoquoque genere est excipiendum," as too high to come under the roof of comparison. In some cases, it is not civil to fill up all the room in our speeches of ourselves, but to leave an upper place void, as a blank reserved for our betters.

" I have dined as well as my lord mayor of London."]

That this proverb may not cross the former, know, that *as well* is not taken for *as dubiously* or *daintily*, on variety of costly dishes, in which kinds the lord mayor is paramount for magnificence; for (not to speak of his solemn invitations, as when Henry Pickard, lord mayor, 1357, did in one day entertain a mess of kings,‡ Edward king of England, John king of France, David king of Scots, and the king of Cyprus, besides Edward prince of Wales, and many prime noblemen of the land,) his daily dinners are feasts, both for plenty, guests, and attendants. But the proverb hath its modest meaning; " I have dined as well," that is, as comfortably, as contentedly, according to the rule, " satis est quod sufficit," (enough is as good as a feast), and better than a surfeit; and indeed nature is contented with a little, and grace with less.

" As old as Paul's steeple."]

Different are the dates of the age thereof, because it had two births or beginnings; for, if we count it from the time wherein it was originally co-founded by king Ethelbert, with the body of the church, anno 1610, then it is above a thou-

* Deut. xxviii. 37.   1 Kings ix. 7.   Jer. xxix. 9.   † Horace's Satires.
‡ Stow's Survey of London, p. 87.

sand and forty years of age. But, if we reckon it from the year 1087, when burnt with lightning from heaven, and afterwards rebuilt by the bishops of London, it is not above five hundred years old. And though this proverb falls far short of the Latin ones, " Antiquius Arcadibus, antiquius Saturno ;" yet serveth it sufficiently to be returned to such, who pretend those things to be novel, which are known to be stale, old, and almost antiquated.

" He is only fit for Ruffian's-hall."]

A ruffian is the same with a swaggerer, so called because endeavouring to make that side to swag or weigh down, whereon he engageth. The same also with swash-buckler, from swashing, or making a noise on bucklers. West Smithfield (now the horse-market) was formerly called Ruffian's-hall, where such men met casually and otherwise, to try masteries with sword and buckler.* More were frighted than hurt, hurt than killed, therewith, it being accounted unmanly to strike beneath the knee, because in effect it was as one armed against a naked man. But, since that desperate traitor Rowland Yorke first used thrusting with rapiers, swords and bucklers are disused,† and the proverb only appliable to quarrelsome people (not tame, but wild barreters) who delight in brawls and blows.

" A loyal heart may be landed under Traitors' Bridge."]

This is a bridge under which is an entrance into the Tower (over against Pink-gate), formerly fatal to those who landed there, there being a muttering that such never came forth alive, as dying (to say no worse) therein, without any legal trial. The proverb importeth, that passive innocence, overpowered with adversaries, may be accused without cause, and disposed at the pleasure of others ; it being true of all prisoners, what our Saviour said to and of St. Peter, " Another shall carry thee whither thou wouldst not."‡

Queen Elizabeth may be a proof hereof, who, in the reign of queen Mary her sister, first staid, and denied to land at those stairs, where all traitors and offenders customably used to land, till a lord (which my author would not, and I cannot name) told her " she should not choose ;" and so she was forced accordingly.§

" To cast water into the Thames."]

That is, to give to them who had plenty before ; which notwithstanding is the dole general of the world. Yet let not Thames be proud of his full and fair stream, seeing water may be wanting therein, as it was anno 1158, the fourth of William Rufus,‖ when men might walk over dryshod ; and again anno

* Continuer of Stow's Annals, p. 1024.
† Camden's Britannia, in anno 1587.   ‡ John xxi. 18.
§ Fox, Acts and Monuments, p. 2092.
‖ Stow's Chronicle, in anno notato.

1582, a strong wind lying west and by south, which forced out the fresh and kept back the salt-water.*

"He must take him a house in Turn-again Lane."†]

This, in old records, is called Wind-again Lane,‡ and lieth in the parish of St. Sepulchre's, going down to Fleet-dike; which men must turn again the same way they came, for there it is stopped.§ The proverb is applied to those, who, sensible that they embrace destructive courses, must seasonably alter their manners, which they may do without any shame to themselves; it is better to come back through Turn-again (though a narrow and obscure) lane, than to go (on an ill account) straight forwards in a fair street hard by, whence " vestigia nulla retrorsum," as leading westward to execution.

"He may whet his knife on the threshold of the Fleet."]

The Fleet is a place notoriously known for a prison, to which many are committed for their contempts,‖ more for their debts; so called it is from a brook running by, as that (of Tigris in Armenia) from its former fleetness, though now it creepeth slow enough; not so much for age, as the injection of city excrements wherewith it is so obstructed.

The proverb is appliable to those who never owed ought; or else, having run into debt, have crept out of it; so that now they may defy danger and arrests; yea, may *triumphare in hostico*, laugh in the face of the serjeants. Surely the threshold of the Fleet, so used, setteth a good edge on the knife, and a better on the wearer thereof, actuating him with a spirit free from all engagements.

"All goeth down Gutter-lane."]

There is a small lane (inhabited anciently by gold-beaters) leading out of Cheapside, east of Foster-lane, which orthography presents to the reader by the name of *Guthurun*-lane, from him the once owner thereof.¶ But common people (we must speak with 'the *volge*, and think with the wise) call it Guttur-lane, pleading for their mis-pronouncing it, that the narrow form thereof is like the throat or gullet, and such a one would have pleased Apicius the epicure, who wished to himself *tricubitale guttur*.

The proverb is appliable to those who spend all in drunkenness and gluttony, mere belly-gods, whom the philosopher* called γαστριμάργους. I confess the word, both in sound and

---

* Stow's Chronicle, in anno notato.
† J. Heywood, in his Epigrams, num. 69.
‡ Stow's Survey of London, p. 427.
§ The whole neighbourhood has since been so completely metamorphosed, that to a modern resident these allusions would be unintelligible; Fleet Dike, which was formerly navigable as far as Holborn-hill, having been long covered over. Many other allusions of Fuller, from local alterations, are equally obscure.—ED.
‖ It is now the prison of the Court of Chancery.—ED.
¶ Stow's Survey of London, p. 338.   ** Aristotle, Moral, l. 3.

sense, hath some affinity with that of St. Paul's of the Cretians, γαστέρες ἀργαὶ, (idle-bellies;*) save that our *gastrimargi* are far worse, so named from the mere madness and distraction of their appetite.

" As lame as St. Giles Cripple-gate."]

St. Giles was by birth an Athenian, of noble extraction and great estate, but quitted all for a solitary life. He was visited with a lameness (whether natural or casual I know not); but the tradition goes, that he desired not to be healed thereof for his greater mortification : if so, his judgment differed from all the good lame men in the Gospel, importunate for ease from their infirmity. He is accounted the patron of cripples; and whereas churches dedicated to other saints of better footman-ship get the speed of him, and come into the city, generally lame St. Giles laggeth behind in the suburbs, as in London, Cambridge, Salisbury, &c.

Cripplegate was so called before the Conquest,† from cripples begging of passengers therein. And indeed they may prescribe for their custom, ever since the lame man begged an alms of Peter and John at the beautiful gate of the Temple.‡

This proverb may seem guilty of false heraldry, lameness on lameness; and, in common discourse, is spoken rather merrily than mournfully, of such who for some light hurt lag behind, and sometimes is applied to those who out of laziness (none so lame as they that will not go) counterfeit infirmity.

" You are all for the Hoistings, or Hustings."]

It is spoken of those who by pride or passion are mounted or elated to a pitch above the due proportion of their birth, quality, or estate ; such as are all *in altitudinibus,* so that com-mon persons know not how to behave themselves unto them. It cometh from the hustings, the principal and highest court in London (as also in Winchester, Lincoln, York, &c.), so called from the French word *haulser,* to raise or lift up.

The mention of the Hustings, a court so called, mindeth me of another court, called the Court of Hall-mote; and I am resolved to run the hazard of the reader's anger with this my digression, to rectify a mistake in some, and prevent it in others.

"This is derived of hall and mote, as much as to say, the hall court, *i. e. conventus civium in aulam publicam ;* every company in London having a hall, wherein they kept their courts; and this court anciently called hall-mote, or folk-mote."§

With whom *verbatim* concurreth (who would not willingly dissent from him in point of common law) the learned doctor Cowel in his " Interpreter."

But let all take heed that they confound not this court with another more ancient (and more proper for the cognizance of the

* Titus i. 12.   † Stow's Survey of London, p. 32.   ‡ Acts iii. 2.
§ Sir Edward Coke, Institut. part iv. cap. 9.

pen of a divine) ; viz. Haly-mote Court, being a court derived
from *haly*, which is holy, and *mote* a meeting, being an assembly
kept before the lord mayor and sheriffs, for the regulation of
the company of the bakers in London (wherein the staff of
bread, and therein the life of the poor, is so much concerned) ;
formerly kept on the Lord's-day (whence it took its name)
before the feast of St. Thomas. But a court of common council, December the 15th, 1609, altered that court until the
Thursday before St. Thomas's day ; as since, by a later act of
the same council, it is removed unto the Monday before the
said festival. The ancient title of this court ran as followeth :
" Curia sancti motûs tenta in Guilhaldeâ civitatis London,
coram majore et vicecomitibus civitatis London, die Dominico
proximo ante festum sancti Thomæ Apostoli, ad horam sextam
ante meridiem ejusdem diei, secundùm consuetudinem civitatis
London."

Such who are learned in the laws, and are pleased to reflect
on the name of my author and worthy friend* will not in the
least degree suspect the truth hereof.

Before I come to enrol the list of the WORTHIES of this city,
I premise the words Londinas and Londinensis, as some have
curiously stated their senses ; according to whose fancy, 1. *Londinas* signifieth one born in London, wheresoever he doth live.
2. *Londinensis* signifieth one living in London, wheresoever he
was born.

Could this be made a truth, this distinction would be very
serviceable to me in this work ; but it will not hold water ; finding, on due inquiry, that by the best critics both are used pro-
miscuously, for any either born or living in that city, save that
Londinas (answering to the question *cujas*) signifieth persons
alone, whilst Londinensis importeth either persons or things relating to that city ; as Turris Londinensis, Pons Londinensis, &c.

PRINCES.

KATHERINE, third daughter of king Henry the Third and
queen Eleanor, was born at London, anno Domini 1252, November the 25th, being St. Katherine's day, whose name was
therefore given unto her at the font, by Boniface archbishop of
Canterbury, her uncle and godfather.† She died in her very
infancy, on whom we will presume to bestow this epitaph :

> " Wak't from the womb, she on this world did peep,
>   Disliked it, closed her eyes, fell fast asleep."

She lieth interred at Westminster, in the space betwixt the
chapels of king Edward and St. Bennet.

JOAN, eldest daughter and third child of king Edward the

---

* Mr. Richard Smith, still living (1659) ; " quondam seneschallus curiæ sancti-
motus antedictæ."—F.
† Speed's Chronicle, p. 551.

Second and queen Isabel, was born in the Tower of London, about the year 1316.* She was afterwards married to David the Second, king of Scotland, continuing his wife twenty-eight years. This was she (as I conceive†) who was commonly called Joan Make-peace (and we know " Blessed are the peace-makers"); improving her power (though sometimes with small success) to do good offices betwixt the two kingdoms. Coming into England to visit her brother king Edward the Third, she deceased here without issue, anno 1357, and lieth buried in Greyfriars, London.

It will not be amiss, in reference to her name, here to observe, that Joan (which is feminine to John) was a frequent name in the royal family of England, as also amongst foreign princes; and no wonder, seeing we find a worthy woman of that name benefactress to our Saviour himself.‡ However, seeing in later times it hath been counted but a coarse and homely name, and some proverbs of contempt have been cast thereon; it hath since been mollified into Jane (sounding finer, it seems, to an English ear), though this modern name will hardly be found in any English writer three hundred years ago.

KATHERINE, youngest daughter to king Henry the Seventh and Elizabeth his queen, was born in the Tower of London, on the 2nd day of February, anno Domini 1503, deceasing few days after.

It is a sad, and probably too true an, account of an ancient man, which is given in his epitaph,

" Here lies the man was born, and cried,
Lived sixty years, fell sick, and died."§

What was a bad character of his aged unprofitableness, is a good one of this infant lady's innocence, of whom we know nothing, save that she sucked, fell sick, and deceased. Only let me add, she was the last princess born in the Tower; our English kings hereafter removing their residence to Bridewell and White-hall; and using the Tower, not so much as a palace for the state as prison for the strength thereof.

[AMP.] ANNA BOLLEN, daughter of the Lord Thomas Bollen, earl of Wiltshire, was (as some of her honourable relations still surviving do conjecture) born in London, and became second wife to king Henry the Eighth. Indeed he passionately affected her when but a lord's daughter, but did not marry her till she was a princess; created by him marchioness of Pembroke, partly to make her the more proportionable match, and

* Speed's Chronicle, p. 576.
† Others apply it to Joan daughter to king John, wife to Alexander the Second, king of Scotland.—F.   ‡ Luke viii. 3.   § Camden's Remains.

partly to try how she would become a coronet, before she wore a crown.

The Papists much disparage her memory (malice will lie, or must be dumb) making all her wit to consist in boldness, her beauty in a French garb, and her modesty in a cunning coyness ; whereas indeed she was a lady accomplished in body (was it likely king Henry would love what was not lovely ?) and virtuous in mind, and, whilst a favourite of the king's, a favourer of all good men, and great promoter of the Gospel. The inconstancy of her husband's affections is conceived by most moderate men (what else soever was pretended) her chiefest crime, and cause of her death, which happened anno 1536.

[AMP.] KATHERINE HOWARD, daughter to the Lord Edmund Howard, son to Thomas duke of Norfolk, was (though her father had large lands and houses in many places) probably born in London, and at last became fifth wife to king Henry the Eighth. Such as desire to know the names, number, and success of all six, may conceive king Henry thus speaking on his death-bed :

> " Three Kates, two Nans, and one dear Jane, I wedded ;
> One Spanish, one Dutch, and four English wives :
> From two I was divorced, two I beheaded,
> One died in child-bed, and one me survives."

Of this Katherine Howard little is reported ; and yet too much, if all be true, of her incontinency, which cost her her life. The greatest good the land got by this match was a general leave to marry cousin-germans, formerly prohibited by the canon, and hereafter permitted by the common law ; a door of lawful liberty left open by God in Scripture, shut by the Pope for his private profit, opened again by the king, first for his own admittance (this Katherine being cousin-german to Anna Bollen, his former wife), and then for the service of such subjects as would follow him upon the like occasion. This lady was beheaded anno Domini 1540.

SAINTS.

Not to speak of St. Sedd, born in this city, and afterwards bishop thereof, of whom we find nothing reported, save that he was very instrumental to the converting of the Mercians ;* we begin with

WULSINE, who was born in this city of worthy parents, breeding him up in the devotion of that age ;† and became a Benedictine monk ; till at last by his fast friend St. Dunstan, he was preferred, first abbot of Westminster, whence he was after-

---

* Hierom Porter, Lives of the Saints, p. 25.
† Hierom Porter, in his Flowers of the Lives of English Saints, January 8.

wards removed to be bishop of Sherburne in Dorsetshire. A mighty champion he was for a monastical life, and therefore could not be quiet till he had driven all the secular priests out of Sherburne, and substituted monks in their room. I read not of any miracle done by him, either whilst living or when dead, save that, in the juncture of both, he is said with St. Stephen to have seen Heaven opened, &c. He had contracted great intimacy with one Egeline, a virtuous knight, who died on the same day with him, and he enjoined his monks that they should both be buried in one grave. Their joint death happened January the 8th, anno 985.

THOMAS BECKET, son to Gilbert Becket, merchant, and Maud his wife, was born in this city, in the place where now Mercers-chapel is erected. I have, reader, been so prodigal in the large description of his life, in my " Ecclesiastical History," that I have no new observable left to present you with. Only when I consider of the multitude of vows, made by superstitious pilgrims to his shrine (where the stones were hallowed with their bended knees), I much admire at their will-worship, no vows appearing in Scripture but what were made to God alone. And therefore most impudent is the attempt of those papists, tampering to corrupt Holy Writ in favour of such vows, reading in the vulgar Latin, Prov. xx. 25 : " Ruina est homini devotare sanctos, et post vota retractare," (it is a snare to a man who often maketh vows to Saints, and after vows retracteth them) ; instead of, " Ruina est homini devorare sancta, et post vota retractare," (it is a snare to a man who devoureth that which is holy, and after vows to make inquiry.)

This Becket was slain, as is notoriously known, on Innocents-day, in his own church of Canterbury, 1170.

MARTYRS.

WILLIAM SAUTRE, alias *Chatris*, parish priest of the church of St. Osith's, London, was the first Englishman that was put to death by fire, for maintaining the opinions of Wicliffe.

In the primitive times (pardon, reader, no impertinent digression) such the lenity and tenderness of the fathers of the church towards heretics, that, contenting themselves with condemning their blasphemous opinions, they proceeded to no penalty on their persons. Yea, in after ages, when the Christian emperor would have punished the furious Donatists with a pecuniary mulct, the holy men of those times so earnestly interceded, as to procure the remission.* And St. Augustine himself, who was most zealous in his writing against these Donatists,† professeth he had rather be himself slain by them, than by detecting them be any cause they should undergo the

* Augustine, Epistle 68. † Epistle 127, and Retract. lib. ii. cap. 5.

punishment of death; whereas henceforward in England many were brought to the fire by the bishops and others of the clergy, whose opinions were neither so blasphemous, nor deportment so inhuman, as ancient heretics.

I confess, not only simple heresy was charged on this Sautre, but also a relapse thereinto after abjuration; in which case such is the charity of the canon law, that such a person is, "seculari judicio sine ullâ penitus audientiâ relinquendus,"* (not affording any audience to one relapsed, though he should revoke his opinions.) Quite contrary to the charitable judgment of St. Chrysostom, who sticked not to say, Χιλιάκις μετανοήσας εἰσελθε, (if thou fall a thousand times, and repent thee of thy folly, come boldly into the church.†)

There is some difference amongst authors, about the legal proceedings against this Sautre, by what power he was condemned to die:

Walsingham will have him die during the sitting of the parliament, secundo Henrici Quarti, by virtue of the law then made against heretics.‡ Others will have him put to death, not by any statute-law then made, but as convicted in a provincial council of the archbishop of Canterbury.

The latter seemeth most true, because the writ *De Hæretico comburendo* (sent down by the advice of the lords temporal to the mayor of London, to cause his execution) bare date the 26th of February; whereas it was ordered in that parliament that the penal statutes made therein should not take effect till after Whitsuntide.§

But, by what power soever it was done, poor Sautre was burnt in Smithfield, about the 28th of February, 1400. One criticism of cruelty and hypocrisy is most remarkable. The close of the archbishop's sentence of degradation, when Sautre was committed over to the secular court, endeth with this expression, "Beseeching the court aforesaid, that they will receive favourably the said William, unto them thus re-committed.||"

We are much beholding to Baronius, for the better understanding this passage; informing us that it was ever fashionable with their clergy to this day, that when they consign a heretic over to the secular for execution, "they effectually intercede that he may not be punished with death."¶ For it appeareth in Prosper, that four bishops were excommunicated anno 392, for being accusers of Priscilian (the first heretic who was confuted with steel), that age conceiving all tendency to cruelty utterly inconsistent with clerical profession. And hence it was, thinks the aforesaid Baronius, that this custom was taken up, of the clergy's mock-mercy, in their dissembled mediation for

* De Hæret. cap. 9. & tit. eod. cap. 4. in sexto.
† Socrates de Chrysostomo, lib. 6. cap. κά. lat. 19.
‡ Hypodigma Neustria, anno 1401, p. 158.
§ Rot. Parl. 2 Hen. IV. num. 116.
|| Fox, Acts and Monuments, p. 517.   ¶ Tom. iv. anno 386. num. 23.

condemned heretics. I say dissembled: for, if the lay, having them in his power, shall defer the doing of it more than ordinary, it is the constant tenet of the Canonists (relying on a bull of Alexander the Fourth, 1260,) he is to be compell'd unto it by spiritual censures.

We have been the larger upon this Sautre's death, because he was the English Protestant (pardon the *prolepsis*) Proto-martyr. But every son must not look to be an heir; we will be shorter on the rest in this city, contenting ourselves with their bare names, except some extraordinary matter present itself to our observation.

JOHN BADBY was an artificer in Blackfriars in London, con-demned, and burned in Smithfield, about 1401. Henry Prince of Wales (afterwards king Henry the Fifth) happened to be present at his execution, who not only promised him pardon on his recantation, but also a stipend out of the king's treasury, sufficient for his support; all which Badby refused. He was put into an empty tun (a ceremony of cruelty peculiar to him alone), and the fire put therein.

At the first feeling thereof, he cried "Mercy, mercy,"* begging it of the God of heaven; which noble prince Henry mistook for a kind of revocation of his opinions, and presently caused the fire round about him to be quenched, renewing his promises unto him with advantage; which Badby refused the second time, and was martyred.

But, reader, I will engage no deeper in this copious subject, lest I lose myself in the labyrinth thereof. Joseph left off to number the corn in Egypt, "for it was without number;"† the cause alone of my desisting in this subject. Yea, bloody Bonner had murdered many more, had not that hydropical humor which quenched the life of queen Mary extinguished also the fires in Smithfield.

PRELATES.

Here in this city we are at a greater loss, as to this topic, than in any shire in England; for in vain it is for any man to name himself Thomas of London, John of London, &c.; such sur-names not reaching their end, nor attaining their intention, viz., to diversify the person, the laxity of so populous a place leaving them as unspecified as it found them. We therefore have cause to believe, that many clergymen, both bishops and writers, born in this city, did not follow suit with others of their coat, to be named from the place of their nativity, but from their fathers; the reason why we can give so slender an account of them as followeth.

* Fox, Acts and Monuments, p. 522.   † Gen. xli. 49.

2 A 2

SIMON OF GAUNT was born in this city* (his mother being an English woman, his father a Fleming); and, being bred in good literature, became so famous, that by king Edward the First he was preferred bishop of Salisbury, 1298. He gave the first leave to the citizens thereof to fortify that place with a deep ditch, partly remaining, and a strong wall wholly demolished at this day. Now, seeing good laws are the best walls of any foundation, no less was his care for the church than city of Salisbury, making good statutes, whereby it was ordered even unto our age. He died about the year 1315.

JOHN KITE was borne in London, bred in Oxford, sent ambassador into Spain, made a Grecian titulary archbishop (receiving thence as much profit as men shear wool from hogs), and at last the real bishop of Carlisle :† yet is his epitaph, in the church of Stepney, neither good English, Latin, Spanish, or Greek, but a barbarous confusion, as followeth:

> " Under this stone closyd et marmorate
> Lyeth John Kite, Londoner natiffe.
> Encreasing in virtues, rose to hygh estate
> In the fourth Edward's chappel by his yong life
> Sith which the Seuinth Henries service primatife
> Proceeding still in virtuous efficase
> To be in favour with this our king's grase.
> With witt endewyed chosen to be legate,
> Sent into Spain, where he right joyfully
> Combined both princes in pease most amate.
> In Grece archbishop elected worthely
> And last of Carlyel ruling postorally :
> Keeping nobyl houshold with great hospitality.
> On thousand fyve hundred thirty and seuyn
> Inuyterate with carys consumed with age,
> The nineteeth of Jun, reckonyd full euyn
> Passed to Heauyn from worldly pylgramage,
> Of whose soul good peopul of Cherite
> Prey, as ye wold be preyd for, for thus must you lye ;
>   Jesu mercy, Lady help.'

These, if made 300 years ago, had been excusable ; but such midnight verses are abominable, made, as it appears, in the dawning of good learning and pure language. Yet, because some love poetry, either very good or very bad, that if they cannot learn from it, they may laugh at it, they are here inserted.

WILLIAM KNIGHT was born in this city, bred Fellow of New College in Oxford, on the same token that there have been ten of his surname, Fellows of that foundation.‡ He proceeded doctor of law ; and a noble pen § makes him secretary to king Henry the Eighth. Sure it is, he was the first person employed to the Pope, to motion to him the matter of his divorce ; ad-

* J Bale, J. Pits ; and Bishop Godwin, in the Bishops of Salisbury.
† Godwin, in the Bishops of Carlisle.
‡ Register of that College, in anno 1493.
§ Lord Herbert, in the Life of Henry VIII. p. 216.

vertising the king, by his weekly dispatches, how slowly his cause (though spurred with English gold) crept on in the court of Rome. After his return, the king rewarded his industry, fidelity, and ability, with bestowing the bishopric of Bath and Wells upon him.

In Wells (with the assistance of Dean Woolman) he built a stately covered cross in the market-place, for the glory of God and conveniency of poor people, to secure them from the weather; adding this inscription, " Laus Deo, pax vivis, requies defunctis." He died September 29, anno 1547.

NICOLAS HEATH was born, and had his childhood, in the city of London, being noted for one of St. Anthony's pigs therein (so were the scholars of that school commonly called, as those of St. Paul's, Paul's pigeons); * and bred first in Christ's College, then Fellow of Clare Hall in Cambridge.† By king Henry the Eighth (to whom he was almoner) he was preferred bishop, first of Rochester, then of Worcester; deprived by king Edward the Sixth; restored by queen Mary, who advanced him archbishop of York and lord chancellor of England. A moderate man, who would not let the least spark of persecution be kindled in his diocese, if any in his province.

In the conference at Westminster betwixt Papists and Protestants, primo Elizabethæ, he was a kind of moderator, but interposed little. Infected by his fellow-prisoner-Popish-prelates, he could not be persuaded to take the oath of supremacy, for which he was deprived. He led a pious and private life, on his own lands, at Cobham in Surrey, whither queen Elizabeth came often to visit him; and died about the year of our Lord 1566.

SINCE THE REFORMATION.

JOHN YOUNGE, D.D. was born in Cheapside, and bred in Pembroke Hall in Cambridge, whereof he became master; hence he was preferred rector of St. Giles, Cripplegate, and at last bishop of Rochester;‡ a constant preacher, and to whose judgment queen Elizabeth ascribed much in church-matters.

Better bishoprics were often offered to, and as often refused by him; particularly when Norwich was proffered him, by one who affirmed it to be a higher seat, bishop Young pleasantly returned, " Yea, but it is a harder, and not so easy for an old man, since the cushion was taken away from it;" meaning, since Dr. Scambler had *scambled* away the revenues thereof. He died anno Domini 1605; and lieth buried at Bromley church in Kent, where his son most solemnly and sumptuously interred him, though he enjoined all possible privacy, and on his death-bed forbad all funeral expences. But in such cases it may become

* Stow's Survey of London.   † Richard Hall, in the Life of Bishop Fisher.
‡ So am I informed by Sir John Young, his grandchild.—F.

the charity and affection of the survivors, to do what beseems not so well the modesty and discretion of the dying to desire.

WILLIAM COTTON, D.D. was born in this city (though his infancy was much conversant about Finchley in Middlesex), as his nearest relation* hath informed me. He was bred in Queen's College in Cambridge; preferred by queen Elizabeth archdeacon of Lewes, and canon residentiary of St. Paul's. Hence he was advanced and consecrated bishop of Exeter, November the 12th, 1598.

During his sitting there, Mr. Snape, a second Cartwright (not for abilities but activity), came out of Jersey, and plentifully sowed the seeds of nonconformity in his diocese, which the vigilancy of this stout and prudent prelate plucked up by the roots, before they could come to perfection.

In his old age he was apoplectical, which malady deprived him of his speech some days before his death; so that he could only say "Amen, amen," often reiterated. Hereupon some scandalous tongues broached this jeer, "that he lived like a bishop, and died like a clark;" and yet let such men know, that no dying person can use any one word more expressive; whether it be an invocation of his help in whom all the promises are Amen; or whether it be a submission to the Divine Providence in all, by way of approbation of former, or option of future things.

I will only add and translate his epitaph, transcribed from his monument.

A Paulo ad Petrum pia te Regina vocavit :
Cum Petro et Paulo cæli Rex arce locavit.

"Whom th' queen from Paul to Peter did remove :
Him God with Paul and Peter plac'd above."

He lieth buried in the north side of the choir of Exeter ; but his monument is distanced from the place of his interment, in a north-east chapel. His death happened anno Domini 1621.

LANCELOT ANDREWS, D.D. was born in this city, in Tower Street; his father being a seaman of good repute belonging to Trinity-house. He was bred scholar, fellow, and master of Pembroke Hall in Cambridge.

He was an inimitable preacher in his way; and such plagiaries who have stolen his sermons could never steal his preaching, and could make nothing of that whereof he made all things as he desired. Pious and pleasant bishop Felton (his contemporary and colleague) endeavoured in vain in his sermon to assimilate his style; and therefore said merrily of himself, "I had almost marred my own natural trot, by endeavouring to imitate his artificial amble." But I have spoken largely of this peerless prelate in my "Church History. He died anno Domini 1626.

* Edward Cotton, D.D. his son.

THOMAS DOVE, D.D. was born in this city, as a credible person * of his nearest relation hath informed me, bred a *tanquam* (which is a fellow's fellow) in Pembroke Hall in Cambridge. He afterwards became an eminent preacher: and his sermons, substantial in themselves, were advantaged by his comely person and graceful elocution. Queen Elizabeth was highly affected, and anno 1589 preferred him dean of Norwich, advancing him eleven years after to the bishopric of Peterborough.† He departed this life, 1630, in the thirtieth year of his bishopric, on the thirtieth of August, who kept a good house whilst he lived, and yet raised a family to knightly degree.

JOHN HOWSON, D.D. was born in St. Bride's parish in this city;‡ bred a scholar in St. Paul's School; whence going to Oxford, he became a student and canon of Christ-church, and afterwards was consecrated bishop of Oxford, May 9, 1619, being his birth-day in his climacterical, then entering upon the 63rd year of his age.§

His learned book, "In what case a Divorce is lawful," with his Sermons against Sacrilege, and Stating of the Pope's supremacy, in four sermons, enjoined on him by king James (to clear his causeless aspersion of favouring Popery), and never since replied unto by the Romish party, have made him famous to all posterity. He was afterwards removed to the bishopric of Durham, but continued not long therein; for he died, in the 75th year of his age, 6th of February, anno Domini 1631, and was buried in St. Paul's in London.

JOHN DAVENANT, D.D. born in Watling-street, was son to John Davenant, a wealthy citizen, whose father was of Davenant's Lands in Essex. When an infant newly able to go, he fell down a high pair of stairs, and rising up at the bottom smiled, without having any harm; God and his good angels keeping him for further service in the church.

When a child, he would rather own his own frowardness, than another's flattery; and, when soothed up by the servants, "that not John but some other of his brothers did cry," he would rather appear in his own face, than wear their disguise; returning, "that it was none of his brothers, but John only cried."

He was bred first fellow-commoner, then fellow, then Margaret professor, then master of Queen's College in Cambridge. At a public election, he gave his negative voice against a near kinsman, and a most excellent scholar;‖ "Cousin," said he,

---

* Mr. Thursby.   † See more of him in my "Church History."—F.
‡ So am I informed by his own daughter, the widow of famous Master Farnaby, since re-married to Mr. Cole in Suffolk.—F.
§ H. Holland, in his printed additions to Bishop Godwin.
‖ Mr. John Gore (afterwards knighted) of Gilesden in Hertfordshire

" I will satisfy your father, that you have worth, but not want, enough to be one of our society."

Returning from the synod of Dort, he was elected bishop of Sarum, 1621.

After his consecration, being to perform some personal service to king James at Newmarket, he refused to ride on the Lord's-day; and came (though a day later to the Court) no less welcome to the king, not only accepting his excuse, but also commending his seasonable forbearance.

Taking his leave of the college, and of one John Rolfe, an ancient servant thereof, he desired him to pray for him, and when the other modestly returned, that he rather needed his lordship's prayers: " Yea, John," said he, " and I need thine too, being now to enter into a calling wherein I shall meet with many and great temptations." " Præfuit qui profuit," was the motto written in most of his books; the sense whereof he practised in his conversation.

He was humble in himself, and (the consequence thereof) charitable to others. Indeed, once invited by bishop Field, and not well pleased with some roisting company there, he embraced the next opportunity of departure after dinner. And when bishop Field proffered to light him with a candle down stairs, " My lord, my lord," said he, " let us lighten others by our unblameable conversation;" for which speech some since have severely censured him, how justly I interpose not. But let others unrelated unto him write his character, whose pen cannot be suspected of flattery, which he when living did hate, and dead did not need.

We read of the patriarch Israel, that the time drew nigh, that he must die ;* *must*, a necessity of it. Such a decree attended this bishop, happy to die, before his order (for a time) died, April 1641: and with a solemn funeral he was buried in his own cathedral; Dr. Nicholas (now dean of St. Paul's) preaching an excellent sermon at his interment.

MATTHEW WREN, D.D. was born in this city (not far from Cheapside); but descended (as appears by his arms) from the worshipful family of the Wrens in Northumberland. He was bred fellow of Pembroke-hall in Cambridge, where he kept the extraordinary Philosophy Act before king James. I say, kept it, with no less praise to himself, than pleasure to the king; where if men should forget, even dogs would remember, his seasonable distinction, what the king's hounds could perform above others, by virtue of their prerogative.

He afterwards became an excellent preacher; and two of his sermons in the university were most remarkable.

One preached before the judges on this text, " And let judg-

* Gen. xlvii. 29.

ment run down like waters, and righteousness as a mighty stream ;"* at what time the draining of the fens was designed, suspected detrimental to the university.

The other, when newly returned from attending prince Charles into Spain, on the words of the Psalmist, " Abyssus abyssum invocat;" (one depth calleth another.†)

He was afterwards preferred master of Peter-house, dean of Windsor, bishop of Norwich and Ely. Some in the Long Parliament fell so heavily on him, that he was imprisoned in the Tower almost fifteen years, and his cause never heard. Surely, had the imposers been the sufferers hereof, they would have cried it up for a high piece of injustice; but, as St. Paul had the credit to be brought with entreaties out of prison by those who sent him thither,‡ so this prelate hath had the honour, that the same parliamentary power (though not constituted of the same persons) which committed him, caused his enlargement, still living 1661.

STATESMEN.

Sir THOMAS MORE was, anno Domini 1480, born in Milk-street, London (the brightest star that ever shined in that *via lactea*), sole son to Sir John More, knight, one of the justices of the King's Bench.§

Some have reported him of mean parentage, merely from a mistake of a modest word, in an epitaph of his own making, on his monument in Chelsea church; where *nobilis* is taken not in the civil but common law sense, which alloweth none noble under the degree of barons. Thus men cannot be too wary what they inscribe on tombs, which may prove a record (though not in law, in history) to posterity.

He was bred first in the family of archbishop Morton, then in Canterbury college (now taken into Christ-church) in Oxford, where he profited more in two, than many in ten years' continuance.

Thence he removed to an inn of Chancery called New Inn, and from thence to Lincoln's Inn, where he became a double reader. Then did his worth prefer him to be judge in the sheriff of London's Court, whilst a pleader in others. And although he only chose such causes which appeared just to his conscience, and never took fee of widow, orphan, or poor person ; he gained in those days four hundred pounds per annum.

Being made a member of the House of Commons, he opposed king Henry the Seventh, about money for the marriage of his daughter Margaret : whereat the king was much discontented, when a courier told him, " that a beardless boy (beard was

---

* Amos v. 24.   † Psalm xiii. 7.   ‡ Acts xvi. 39.
    § The sum hereof is taken out of his printed Life (rare to be had) written by a nephew of his, more fairly and impartially than any would expect from so near a relation.—F.

never the true standard for brains) had obstructed his desires;" which king, being as certain, but more secret than his son in his revenge, made More the mark of his displeasure; who, to decline his anger, had travelled beyond the seas, had not the king's going into another world stopped his journey.

King Henry the Eighth coming to the crown, and desirous to ingratiate himself by preferring popular and deserving persons, knighted Sir Thomas, and made him chancellor of the duchy of Lancaster, the king's personal patrimony.

Finding him faithful in lesser matters (according to the method of the Gospel), he made him in effect ruler of all, when lord chancellor of England; a place wherein he demeaned himself with great integrity, and with no less expedition.

In testimony of the latter, it is recorded, that, calling for the next cause, it was returned unto him, "There are no more to be heard, all suits in that court depending, and ready for hearing, being finally determined."

Whereon a rhythmer:

> "When *More* some years had chancellor been,
>   No more suits did remain;
> The same shall never more be seen
>   Till *More* be there again."

Falling into the king's displeasure for not complying with him about the queen's divorce, he seasonably resigned his chancellor's place, and retired to his house in Chelsea, chiefly employing himself in writing against those who were reputed heretics. And yet it is observed to his credit (by his great friend Erasmus) that, whilst he was lord chancellor, no Protestant was put to death; and it appears by some passages in his "Utopia," that it was against his mind that any should lose their lives for their consciences.

He rather soiled his fingers than dirtied his hands in the matter of the holy maid of Kent; and well wiped it off again. But his referring (or rather not accepting) the oath of supremacy, stuck by him, for which he was sixteen months imprisoned in the Tower, bearing his afflictions with remarkable patience. He was wont to say, "that his natural temper was so tender, that he could not endure a fillip;" but a supernatural principle (we see) can countermand, yea help natural imperfections.

In his time (as till our memory) Tower prisoners were not dieted on their own, but on the king's charges; the lieutenant of the Tower providing their fare for them. And when the lieutenant said, "that he was sorry that commons were no better," "I like," said Sir Thomas, "your diet very well; and if I dislike it, I pray turn me out of doors."

Not long after, he was beheaded on Tower-hill, 1535. He left not above one hundred pounds a year estate; perfectly hating covetousness, as may appear by his refusing four or five thousand pounds offered him by the clergy.* Among his

Latin books his Utopia beareth the bell, containing the idea of a complete common-wealth in an imaginary island (but pretended to be lately discovered in America); and that so lively counterfeited, that many, at the reading thereof, mistook it for a real truth; insomuch that many great learned men, as Budeus, and Johannes Paludanus, upon a fervent zeal, wished that some excellent divines might be sent thither to preach Christ's Gospel;† yea, there were here amongst us at home sundry good men and learned divines, very desirous to undertake the voyage, to bring the people to the faith of Christ, whose manners they did so well like.

By his only son, Mr. John More, he had five grandchildren; Thomas and Augustin, born in his life time, who proved zealous Romanists: Edward, Thomas, and Bartholomew (born after his death) were firm Protestants; and Thomas, a married minister of the Church of England.

MARGARET MORE.—Excuse me, reader, for placing a lady among men and learned statesmen. The reason is, because of her unfeigned affection to her father, from whom she would not willingly be parted (and for me shall not be) either living or dead.

She was born in Bucklersbury in London at her father's house therein, and attained to that skill in all learning and languages that she became the miracle of her age. Foreigners took such notice hereof, that Erasmus hath dedicated some epistles unto her. No woman that could speak so well did speak so little; whose secrecy was such, that her father entrusted her with his most important affairs.

Such was her skill in the Fathers, that she corrected a depraved place in Cyprian; for whereas it was corruptly written "Nisi vos sinceritatis," she amended it, "Nervos sinceritatis."‡

Yea, she translated Eusebius out of Greek; but it was never printed, because I. Christopherson had done it so exactly before.

She was married to William Roper, of Eltham in Kent, esquire, one of a bountiful heart and plentiful estate. When her father's head was set up on London Bridge, it being suspected it would be cast into the Thames, to make room for divers others (then suffering for denying the king's supremacy), she bought the head, and kept it for a relic (which some called affection, others religion, others superstition in her); for which she was questioned before the council, and for some short time imprisoned, until she had buried it; and how long she herself survived afterwards, is to me unknown.

THOMAS WRIOTHESLEY, Knight of the Garter, was born in Barbican,§ son to William Wriothesley, York herald, and grandchild to John Wriothesley (descended from an heir general of

---

* Mr. More, in the Life of his Grandfather, p. 405.　　† Idem, p. 359.
‡ This is acknowledged by J. Costerus, and Pamelion, on that place.
§ The house of his nativity is called Garter-court.

the ancient family of the Dunstervilles) king of arms. He was
bred in the university of Cambridge; and if any make a doubt
thereof, it is cleared by the passage of Mr. Ascham's letter unto
him,* writing in the behalf of the university when he was lord
chancellor, " Quamobrem Academia cum omni literarum ratione,
ad te unum conversa (cui uni quam universis aliis se chariorem
intelligit) partim tibi ut alumno suo, cum authoritate imperat:
partim, ut patrono summo, demissè et humiliter supplicat, &c."

He afterwards effectually applied his studies in our municipal
law, wherein he attained to great eminency. He was by king
Henry the Eighth created baron of Titchborne at Hampton
Court, January the first, 1543, and in the next year, about the
beginning of May, by the said king made chancellor of England.
But, in the first of king Edward the Sixth, he was removed from
that place (because a conscientiously rigorous Romanist); though,
in some reparation, he was advanced to be earl of Southampton.
He died at his house, called Lincoln's place, in Holborn, 1550,
the 30th of July; and lies buried at St. Andrew's in Holborn.

WILLIAM PAGET, Knight, was born in this city, of honest
parents,† who gave him pious and learned education, whereby
he was enabled to work out his own advancement; privy councillor to four successive princes, which, though of different persuasions, agreed all in this, to make much of an able and trusty
minister of state.

1. King Henry the Eighth made him his secretary, and employed him ambassador to Charles the emperor, and Francis king
of France.

2. King Edward the Sixth made him chancellor of the duchy,
comptroller of his househeld, and created him baron of Beaudesert.

3. Queen Mary made him keeper of her privy seal.

4. Queen Elizabeth dispensed with his attendance at court,
in favour to his great age, and highly respected him.

Indeed, duke Dudley, in the days of king Edward, ignomini-
ously took from him the garter of the order; quarrelling, that by
his extraction he was not qualified for the same. But, if all be
true which is reported of this duke's parentage,‡ he of all men
was most unfit to be active in such an employment. But no
wonder if his pride wrongfully snatched a garter from a subject,
whose ambition endeavoured to deprive two princes of a crown.
This was restored unto him by queen Mary, and that with ceremony and all solemn accents of honour, as to a person "who
by his prudence had merited much of the nation."§ He died
very old, anno 1563; and his corpse (as I remember) is buried
in Lichfield, and not in the vault under the church of Drayton
in Middlesex, where the rest of that family, I cannot say lie (as

* Page 200. † Out of the Herald's Visitation of Staffordshire.
‡ See Edmund Dudley, in our Description of Staffordshire.
§ Camden, Elizabeth, anno 1563.

whose coffins are erected), but are very completely reposed in a peculiar posture, which I meet not with elsewhere; the horror of a vault being much abated with the lightness and sweetness thereof.

THOMAS WENTWORTH was born (his mother coming casually to London) in Chancery Lane, in the parish of St. Dunstan's in the West.* Yet no reason Yorkshire should be deprived of the honour of him whose ancestors long flourished in great esteem at Wentworth Woodhouse in that county.

He was bred in St. John's College in Cambridge, and afterwards became a champion patriot on all occasions. He might seem to have a casting voice in the House of Commons; for where he was pleased to dispose his yea or nay, there went the affirmative or negative. It was not long before the court gained him from the country; and then honours and offices were heaped on him; created baron and viscount Wentworth, earl of Strafford, and lord deputy of Ireland.

When he went over into Ireland, all will confess he laid down to himself this noble foundation; vigorously to endeavour the reduction of the Irish, to perfect obedience to the king, and profit to the exchequer. But many do deny the superstructure (which he built thereon) was done by legal line and plummet.

A parliament was called in England; and many crimes were, by prime persons of England, Scotland, and Ireland, charged upon him. He fenced skilfully for his life; and his grand guard was this, that (though confessing some misdemeanors) all proved against him amounted not to treason.

And indeed *number* cannot create a *new kind;* so that many trespasses cannot make a riot, many riots one treason, no more than many frogs can make one toad. But here the distinction of accumulative and constructive treason was coined, and caused his destruction.

Yet his adversaries politicly brake off the edge of the axe, which cut off his head, by providing his condemnation should not pass into precedent to posterity; so that his death was remarkable, but not exemplary. Happy had it been, if (as it made no precedent on earth, so) no remembrance thereof had been kept in Heaven.

Some hours before his suffering, he fell fast asleep, alleged by his friends as an evidence of the clearness of his conscience; and hardly to be paralleled, save in St. Peter, in a "dead sleep,"† the night before he was to die, condemned by Herod. His death happened in 1641.

He hath an eternal monument in the matchless meditations of king Charles the First; and an everlasting epitaph in that weighty character there given him, "I looked upon my lord of Strafford as a gentleman, whose abilities might make a prince

* Register of St. Dunstan's. † Acts xii. 6.

rather afraid than ashamed, in the greatest affairs of state, &c."*

God alone can revive the dead. All that princes can perform is to honour their memory and posterity; as our gracious sovereign king Charles hath made his worthy son Knight of the Garter.

LYONEL CRANFIELD, son to Randal Cranfield, citizen, and Martha his wife, daughter to the Lady Dennis of Gloucestershire,† (who by her will, which I have perused, bequeathed a fair estate unto her) was born in Basinghall Street, and bred a merchant, much conversant in the custom-house.

He may be said to have been his own tutor, and his own university. King James being highly affected with the clear, brief, strong, yea and profitable sense he spake, preferred him lord treasurer 1621, baron of Cranfield, and earl of Middlesex. Under him it began to be *young flood* in the Exchequer (wherein there was a very *low ebb* when he entered on that office); and he possessed his treasurer's place some four years, till he fell into the duke of Buck's (the best of friends, and worst of foes) displeasure. Some say this lord, who rose chiefly by the duke (whose near kinswoman he married) endeavoured to stand without, yea, in some cases (for the king's profit) against him; which independency and opposition that duke would not endure. Flaws may soon be found, and easily be made breaches, in great officers; who, being active in many, cannot be exact in all matters.

However, this lord, by losing his office, saved himself, departing from his treasurer's place, which in that age was hard to keep; insomuch that one asking, "what was good to preserve life?" was answered, "Get to be lord treasurer of England, for they never do die in their place;" which indeed was true for four successions.

Retiring to his magnificent house at Copt-hall, he there enjoyed himself contentedly; entertained his friends bountifully, neighbours hospitably, poor charitably. He was a proper person, of comely presence, cheerful yet grave countenance, and surely a solid and wise man. And though their soul be the fattest who only suck the sweet milk, they are the healthfullest who (to use the Latin phrase) have tasted of both the breasts of fortune. He died, as I collect, anno 1644; and lieth interred in a stately monument in the abbey at Westminster.

WRITERS ON THE LAW.

FLETA, or FLEET.—We have spoken formerly of the Fleet as a prison; but here it importeth a person disguised under that name, who, it seems, being committed to the Fleet, therein wrote a book of the common laws of England, and other anti-

* Εἴκων Βασιλικὴ, Med. 2. p. 6.
† Register of the Parish of St. Michael, Basinghall.

quities. There is some difference concerning the time when this learned book of Fleta was set forth; but it may be demonstrated done before the fourteenth of the reign of king Edward the Third: for he saith that "it is no murder except it be proved that the party slain was English, and no stranger;"* whereas this was altered in the fourteenth year of the said king,† when the killing of any (though a foreigner, living under the king's protection) out of prepensed malice, was made murder.

He seemeth to have lived about the end of king Edward the Second, and beginning of king Edward the Third.‡ Seeing in that juncture of time two kings in effect were in being, the father in right, the son in might, a small contempt might cause a confinement to that place; and as loyal subjects be within it as without it. Sure it is, that (notwithstanding the confinement of the author) his book hath had a good passage, and is reputed law to posterity.

CHRISTOPHER ST. GERMAN.—Reader, wipe thine eyes, and let mine smart, if thou readest not what richly deserves thine observation; seeing he was a person remarkable for his gentility, piety, chastity, charity, ability, industry, and vivacity.

1. *Gentility;* descended from a right ancient family, born (as I have cause to believe) in London; and bred in the Inner Temple, in the study of our laws. 2. *Piety;* he carried Saint in his nature (as well as in his surname), constantly reading and expounding every night to his family a chapter in the Bible. 3. *Chastity;* living and dying unmarried, without the least spot on his reputation. 4. *Charity;* giving consilia and auxilia to all his people gratis.§ Indeed I read of a company of physicians in Athens, called ἀνάργυροι, because they would take no money of their patients; and our St. German was of their judgment as to his clients. 5. *Ability;* being excellently skilled in civil, canon, and common law; so that it was hard to say wherein he excelled. Add to these his skill in Scripture; witness his book called "The Doctor and Student," where the former vies divinity with the law of the latter. 6. *Industry;* he wrote several works, wherein he plainly appeareth not only a favourer of but champion for the reformation. 7. *Vivacity;* living to be above eighty years old; and, dying anno Domini 1593, was buried at St. Alphage, London, near Cripplegate.

WILLIAM RASTAL was born in this city (sister's son to Sir Thomas More); and was bred in the study of our common law; and whoever readeth this passage in Pits, will thence conclude him one of the two chief justices of England: "Factus est civilium et criminalium causarum alter ex duobus per Ang-

* Lib. i. cap. 30.   † Statutes 14 Edward III. cap. 4.
‡ Cowel's Interp. de verbo *Fleta.*
§ Bale, de Scriptoribus Britannicis, Cent. viii. n. 75.

liam supremis judicibus ;"* whereas in deed he was but one of
the justices of the King's Bench : yet his ability and integrity
did capacitate him for higher preferment, being also a person
of industry.

He wrote the Life, and set forth the Works, of his uncle
More; and made a collection of, and comment on, the Statutes
of England.

Great was his zeal to the Romish religion : flying into Flanders, with the changing of his country (under king Edward the
Sixth), he changed the nature of his studies ; but then wrote
worse books on a better subject, I mean divinity. He undertook bishop Jewel, as much his over-match in divinity, as
Rastal was his in the common law. The Papists are much
pleased with him, for helping their cause (as they conceive) ;
and we are not angry with him, who hath not hurt ours in any
degree.

He died at Louvain, 1565 ; and lieth buried, with his wife, in
the same tomb; and this epitaph may be bestowed on him :

> " Rastallus tumulo cum conjuge dormit in uno,
>   Unius carnis pulvis et unus erit."

Know that Winifred Clement, his wife, was one of the greatest
female scholars, an exact Grecian, and (the crown of all) most
pious according to her persuasion.

SOLDIERS.

No city in Europe hath bred more (if not too many of late) ;
and indeed we had had better tradesmen if worse soldiers. I
dare not adventure into so large a subject, and will instance but
in one (to keep possession for the rest) ; submitting myself to
the reader's censure, whether the parties' merit or my private
relation puts me on his memorial.

Sir THOMAS ROPER, son of Thomas Roper, servant to queen
Elizabeth, was born in Friday-street in London, whose grandfather was a younger son of the house of Heanour in Derbyshire. Indeed Furneaux was the ancient name of that family,
until Richard Furneaux married Isald the daughter of . . . . .
Roper, of Beighton, in the county of Derby, esquire ; and on
that consideration was bound to assume the name of Roper, by
indenture dated the seventh of Henry the Sixth.† This Sir
Thomas, going over into the Low Countries, became page to
Sir John Norrice, and was captain of a foot company at sixteen
years of age. What afterwards his martial performances were,
to avoid all suspicion of flattery (to which my relation may
incline me) I have transcribed the rest out of the original of his
patent.

" Cum Thomas Roper, Eques auratus, è secretioribus concili-

---

* Pits, de Angliæ Scriptoribus, ætat. 16, anno 1565.
† Dugdale, in his Antiquities of Warwickshire illustrated, p. 212.

ariis nostris in regno nostro Hyberniæ, jampridem nobis bellicæ
virtutis splendore clarus innotuerit; utpote qui quamplurimis
rebus per eum in nuperrimo bello hujus regni fortiter gestis,
præclarum nomen et strenui militis et prudentis ducis reporta-
vit : cujus virtus precipuè in recessu in provinciâ nostrâ
Conaciæ propè Le Boyle emicuit, ubi paucissimis admodum
equestribus ingentes equitum turmas per regni meditullia
hostiliter grassantes fortiter aggressus : ita prudentiâ suâ singu-
lari receptui cecinit, ut non modo, et se, et suos, sed etiam
totum exercitum ab ingenti periculo liberavit, hostesque quam-
plurimos ruinæ tradidit :

" Qui etiam, cùm provincia nostra Ultoniæ bello deflagaverat,
ob exploratam animi fortudininem, ab honoratissimo comite
Essexiæ exercitus tunc imperatore, unus ex omnibus designatus
fuit ad duellam cum Makal, uno ex fortissimis Tyronentium
agminum ducibus suscipiendam, nisi prædictus Makal duello
prædicto se exponere remisisset :

" Cumque etiam prædictus Thomas Roper, in nuperrimo bello
apud Brest, in regno Galliæ, se maximis periculis objiciendo, et
sanguinem suum effundendo, fortitudinem suam invectam
demonstravit :

" Qui etiam in expeditione Portugalenci se fortiter ac honori-
ficè gessit, ac etiam apud Bergen in Belgio cùm per Hispanos
obsideretur, invictissimæ fortitudinis juvenem in defensione
ejusdem se præbuit :

" Qui etiam in expugnationis Kinsalensis die prima acie juxta
oppidum propissimè constitutus fuerat, Hispanosque ex eo
oppido sepius eodem die prosilientes, fortissimè felicissiméque,
et ad maximam totius exercitus incolumitatem repulit et profli-
gavit :

" Sciatis igitur quòd nos, intuitu præmissorum, dominum
Thomam Roper, militem, &c."

("Whereas Thomas Roper, knight, one of our privy councillors of our kingdom of Ireland, long since hath been known
unto us, famous with the splendour of his warlike virtue; as
who, by the many achievements valiantly performed by him in
the late war of this kingdom, hath gained the eminent repute
both of a stout soldier and a discreet commander; whose
valour chiefly appeared in his retreat near Le Boyle in our
province of Connaught, where, with very few horse, he undaunt-
edly charged great troops of the horse of the enemy, who, in a
hostile manner, foraged the very bowels of the kingdom, and by
his wisdom made such a singular retreat, that he not only
saved himself and his men, but also delivered the whole army
from great danger, and slew very many of his enemies:

" Who also, when our province of Ulster was all on fire with
war, being one out of many, was, for the tried resolution of his
mind, chosen by the right honourable the earl of Essex, then

general of the army, to undertake a duel with Makal, one of the stoutest captains in the army of Tyrone, had not the said Makal declined to expose himself to the appointed duel:

"And also when the aforesaid Thomas Roper, in the late war in the kingdom of France at Brest, by exposing himself to the greatest perils, and shedding of his own blood, demonstrated his courage to be unconquerable:

"Who also, in the voyage to Portugal, behaved himself valiantly and honourably, as also at Bergen in the Netherlands, when it was besieged by the Spaniards, approved himself a young man of invincible valour in the defence thereof:

"Who also, in the day wherein Kinsale was assaulted, was placed in the first rank, nearest of all unto the town; and, with no less success than valour, to the great safety of the whole army, beat back and put to flight the Spaniards, who in the same day made several sallies out of the town:

"Know, therefore, that we, in intuition of the premises, have appointed the aforesaid Thomas Roper, knight, &c.")

Then followeth his patent, wherein king Charles, in the third of his reign, created him Baron of Bauntree, and Viscount Baltinglasse in Ireland.

I will only add, from exact intelligence, that he was a principal means to break the hearts of Irish rebels; for whereas formerly the English were loaded with their own clothes, so that their slipping into bogs did make them, and the stopping of their breeches did keep them prisoners, therein; he first being then a commander, put himself into Irish trowsers, and was imitated first by all his officers, then soldiers; so that thus habited they made the more effectual execution on their enemies. He died at Roper's Rest, anno Domini 164 . ; and was buried with Anne his wife (daughter to Sir Henry Harrington) in Saint John's church in Dublin.

SEAMEN.

I behold these seamen as the sea itself, and suspect, if I launch far therein, I shall see land no more: besides, I know there be many laws made against forestallers, and would be loath to fall under that penalty, for preventing the pains of some able perosn, a member of the Trinity-house, who may write a just tract thereof.

CIVILIANS.

Sir HENRY MARTIN, Knight, was born in this city, where his father left him forty pounds a year; and he used merrily to say, that if his father had left him fourscore, he would never have been a scholar, but lived on his lands; whereas this being (though a large encouragement, but) a scant maintenance, he plied his book for a better livelihood. He was bred a fellow in

New College in Oxford; and, by the advice of bishop Andrews, addressed himself to the study of the civil law.

By the advice of the said bishop, Master Martin had weekly transmitted unto him, from some proctors at Lambeth, the brief heads of the most important causes which were to be tried in the high commission. Then, with some of his familiar friends in that faculty, they privately pleaded those causes amongst themselves, acting in their chamber what was done in the court. But Mr. Martin, making it his work, exceeded the rest in amplifying and aggravating any fault, moving of anger and indignation against the guilt thereof, or else in extenuating and excusing it, procure pity, obtain pardon, or at least prevail for a lighter punishment. Some years he spent in this personated pleading, to enable himself against he was really called to that profession.

Hence it was that afterwards he became so eminent an advocate in the high commission, that no cause could come amiss to him ; for he was not to make new armour, but only to put it on, and buckle it ; not to invent, but apply arguments to his client. He was at last knighted, and made judge of the prerogative for probate of wills, and also of the admiralty in causes concerning foreign traffic ; so that, as king James said pleasantly, " he was a mighty monarch in his jurisdiction over land and sea, the living and dead." He died, very aged and wealthy, anno Domini 1642.

PHYSICIANS.

[REM.] RICHARDUS ANGLICUS was certainly a man of merit, being eminently so denominated by foreigners (amongst whom he conversed) from his country ; and he who had our nation for his name, cannot have less than London for his lodging in this our CATALOGUE OF WORTHIES. He is said to have studied first in Oxford, then in Paris, where he so profited in the faculty of physic, that he is counted, by Simphorianus Champerius* (a stranger to our nation, and therefore free from flattery), one of the most eminent writers in that profession. Now, because he was the first Englishman whom I find famous in that calling, may the reader be pleased with a receipt of the several names of the books left by him to posterity : 1. " A Tractate of Urins :" 2. " Of the Rules of Urins :" 3. " Of the Signs of Diseases :" 4. " Of Prognostick Signs :" 5. " Of Letting Bloud :" 6. " Of Anatomy according to Galen :" 7. " Of Feavors :" 8. " A Correction of Alchymy :" 9. " A Mirour of Alchymy :" 10. " Of Physick : 11. " Repressive :" 12. " Of the Signs of Feavors†."

Leland reporteth, that, besides these, he wrote other works,

* In tractatu quinto de ejus Artis Scriptoribus.
† Bale, de Scriptoribus Britannicis, Cent. iii. n. 92 ; and Pits, in anno 1230.

which the envy of time hath denied unto us.   He flourished about the year of our Lord 1230.

JOHN PHREAS was born in this city, bred fellow of Baliol college in Oxford, where he contracted familiarity with his colleague and Mæcenas, J. Tiptoft earl of Worcester.*   He afterwards travelled into Italy, and at Ferrara was a constant auditor of Gwarinus, an old man and famous philosopher.

Hitherto our Phreas made use only of his ears; hereafter of his tongue, when of hearer he turned a teacher; and see the stairs whereby he ascended:—1. He read Physic at Ferrara, concerning medicinal herbs: 2. Then at Florence, well esteemed by the duke thereof: 3. Then at Padua (beneath Florence in beauty, above it in learning), an university where he proceeded doctor of physic: 4. Then at Rome, where he was gracious with Pope Paul the Second, dedicating unto him many books translated out of Greek.

The Pope rewarded him with the bishopric of Bath and Wells;† dying before his consecration, poisoned (as is vehemently suspected) by some who maligned his merit:

"Heu mihi quod nullis livor medicabilis herbis!"

Solomon himself, who wrote of all simples, from "the Cedar in Lebanus, to the Hyssop on the wall,"‡ could find no defensative against it; which made him cry out, "But who can stand before envy?"‡   No wonder, therefore, if our Phreas, (though a skilful botanist) found men's malice mortal unto him.   He died at Rome, anno Domini 1465; and Leland's commendation of him may serve for his epitaph, if but "Hic jacet Johannes, Phreas" be prefixed before it; "qui primus Anglorum erat, qui propulsâ barbarie, patriam honesto labore bonis literis restituit."

ANDREW BORDE, doctor of physic, was (I conceive) bred in Oxford, because I find his book, called "The Breviary of Health," examined by that university.   He was physician to king Henry the Eighth, and was esteemed a great scholar in that age.   I am confident his book was the first written of that faculty in English, and dedicated to the college of physicians in London.

Take a taste out of the beginning of his dedicatory epistle: "Egregious doctors and masters of the eximious and arcane science of physic, of your urbanity exasperate not yourselves against me for making this little volume of physic, &c."

Indeed his book contains plain matter under hard words; and was accounted such a jewel in that age (things whilst the first are esteemed the best in all kinds) that it was printed, "cum

* Bale, de Scriptoribus Britannicis, Cent. viii. n. 38.   † Idem, ibidem.
‡ 1 Kings iv. 33.   § Proverbs xxvii. 4.

privilegio ad imprimendum solum," for William Middleton, anno 1548. He died, as I collect, in the reign of queen Mary.

WRITERS.

NOTHELMUS OF LONDON.* Having casually let slip his *fore-lock*, I mean his episcopal capacity (being successively bishop of London and archbishop of Canterbury) under which he ought to be entered, we are fain to lay hold on his *hind part* (that his memory may not escape us), taking notice of him as a writer. In his age shined a constellation of three learned men, Bede, Alcuinus, and our Nothelme, whom the two former, by their letters, invited to write (a performance proper for his pen) the guests of Gregory the Great, and the disciples sent by him, with Austin the monk, for the conversion of Britain. Nothelme, the more effectually to enable himself for this work, went to Rome, obtained leave from Pope Gregory the Second to peruse his records; then sent his completed collections to Bede, to be inserted in his "Church History." Bede, in gratitude, (according to the courteous custom of the learned exchange) dedicated to him his Thirty Questions on the Books of Kings. His death happened anno Domini 739.

WILLIAM FITZ-STEPHEN was descended, saith Leland, of Norman nobility, but born in this city, and bred a monk in Canterbury. He wrote many learned works; and one in Latin, of the description of London, since commendably (because rare to come by) translated and added to the "Survey of London."

Say not that London then was but the suburbs to the London now, for the bigness and populousness thereof; seeing, in Fitz-Stephen's time, it accounted thirteen conventual, and a hundred and six-and-thirty parochial churches, not producing so many at this day; so that it seems, though there be more bodies of men, there be fewer houses of God therein.

As for the populousness thereof in his time, it was able to set forth sixty thousand foot, which I believe it may treble in our time. It could also then raise twenty thousand horsemen, which would pose it at this day to perform. But, as railing Rabshekah made Jerusalem weaker [not able to set two thousand riders on horses], so possibly Fitz-Stephen might make London stronger than it was. I hope one may safely wish this city may be better in holiness, as bigger in houses, than it was when Fitz-Stephen flourished, 1190.

ALBRICIUS OF LONDON.—Leland maketh him a native of this city, and signally learned; though little is extant of his writings, save a work of "the Original of Heathen Gods." Herein

---

* Bale, de Scriptoribus Britannicis, Cent. ii. n. 8.

he sheweth how mankind having, by error and ignorance, left and lost the true God, multiplied deities, that a mock-infinite (viz. what was but indefinite in number) should supply His place who was infinite in nature. Albricius flourished anno Domini 1217.

[REM.] WILLIAM SENGHAM, born of mean but honest parents, being one of a meek nature and quick wit, was brought up in learning, wherein he attained to great perfection. He wrote many books; and one, " de Fide et Legibus," wherein Bale* highly praiseth this passage: "There is no other law for the salvation of men, besides the Gospel of Christ our Lord."

Now although this be but a plain expression of the common truth, yet was it beheld as an oracle in that ignorant age. Thus a beam of noon day, might it be seen at midnight, would shine as the sun itself. Besides, these words were uttered in that age, when impudent friars began to obtrude on the world a fifth-forged Gospel, consisting of superstitious ceremonies, and called Æternum Evangelium, which did much mischief in the church amongst credulous men. This William is supposed by some an Augustinian friar, who flourished anno Domini 1260.

[REM.] LAURENTIUS ANGLICUS was certainly an Englishman, and probably a Londoner; but brought up and living most of his time in Paris, where he was master of the college which had an Englishman for the sign thereof.† Hence I collect it for building little better than our ordinary inns for entertainment, where probably our countrymen had their lodgings for nothing. This Laurence, being a learned and pious person, stoutly opposed that mock Gospel commonly called Evangelium Æternum,‡ with the mendicant friars the champions thereof. He wrote a smart book " contra Pseudo-prædicatores ;" but afterwards, being frightened with the Pope's thunderbolts and the friars' threatenings, he cowardly recanted. But what saith Solomon,§ "A just man falleth seven times ;" [the vulgar Latin addeth *in die*, in one day], and riseth again, as we hope this Laurence did, who flourished anno Domini 1260.

NICHOLAS LYRE‖ was (as Barnabas a Jew Cypriot, and Saul a Jew Cicilian) a Jew Englishman, the first by nation, the second by nativity. He had the Rabbins at his fingers' ends; but conversed so long with, that at last he was converted by, some Franciscans to be a Christian ; and I behold Nicholas [conqueror of his people] as his font name then given him, as predictory of those victories he afterwards got, by his disputings

---

* Bale, de Scriptoribus Britannicis, Cent. iv. n. 17.   † Ibid. Cent. iv. n. 30.
‡ See more hereof in the life of John Driton, in Sussex.—F.
§ Proverbs xxiv. 15.   ‖ Bale, de Scriptoribus Britannicis, Cent. v. n. 12.

and writings, over his own countrymen. Nor doth the church of God more complain of Nicholas, that proselyte of Antioch, the last of the seven deacons, and first founder of the Nicholaitans whom God hated, than it doth commend our Nicholas, who vigorously confuted the Jews; who expect the rising of the sun in the afternoon, waiting for Messias still to come.

I read, how, some fifty years before, Henry the Third founded a house called *Domus Conversorum* (where now the office of the Rolls is kept in Chancery-lane) where converted Jews were accommodated with lodging, and a small salary. But I believe Lyre made no use thereof, contenting himself to live first in Oxford, then in Paris, a Franciscan friar; and wrote " Comments on all the Old and New-Testament;" whereof so different the editions, that I am certainly informed, one is so bad, one can hardly give too little; and one is so good, one can hardly give too much for it. Though sometimes he may be wide of the mark, and this harp be out of tune, yet uncharitable their censure of " Lyra delirat," whilst Luther highly praiseth him, because his wanton wit did not gad after empty allegories, but, with the good housekeeper, stays at home; keeping himself close to the text in his literal interpretations.* Now though there were many Jewish synagogues in England (at York, Cambridge, Northampton, &c.); yet, the Old Jewry in London equalling all the rest in numerousness, Lyre's birth is here assigned with best assurance, though dying in Paris about the year 1340.

BANKINUS of LONDON, not *Bancks* of London (who taught his horse reason, to perform feats above belief,) but one of higher parts, and worse employed. Being an Augustinian friar, he set himself wholly to suppress the poor Wickliffites; and, being ready to dispute against them in a public council, was taken off in his full speed with the following accident, worthy of the reader's observation :

" Sed terræ-motus, justissimâ summi Dei vindictâ, subitò exortus, diruptis passim domorum ædificiis, immanes eorum impetus fregit, ac vires infirmavit ;" (but an earthquake, by the just revenge of the most high God, suddenly arising, by breaking asunder the buildings of the houses, brake their cruel assaults, and weakened their forces.†)

This, if literally true, deserved a *downright* (and not only so *slenting* a) mention. But, hitherto meeting it in no other author, I begin to suspect it meant metaphorically of some consternation of mind, wherewith God's restraining grace charmed the adversaries of the truth. Bankinus flourished under king Richard the Second, anno 1382.

* In his comment on the Second, and again on the Ninth, chapter of Genesis.
† Bale, de Scriptoribus Britannicis, Cent. vi. n. 97.

ROBERT IVORY was, saith Leland, none of the meanest natives of this city; a Carmelite, and president general of his order; D. D. in Cambridge. He wrote several books; and, *prece et precio*, procured many more, wherewith he adorned the library of White-friars in Fleet-street.* He died November the fifth, 1392.

[REM.] JULIANA BARNES was born *ex antiquâ et illustri domo*. Understand it not in the sense wherein the same was said of a certain Pope, born in a ruinous cottage, where the sun did shine through the rotten walls and roof thereof. But indeed she was descended of a respectable family, though I, not able to find the place, am fain to use my marginal mark of greatest uncertainty.

She was the Diana of her age for hunting and hawking; skilful also in fishing, and wrote three books of these exercises, commending the practice thereof to the gentry of England.†

The city of Leyden is scited in the very bottom of the Low Countries; so that the water settled there would be soon subject to putrefaction, were it not by engines forced up, that it might fall, and so by constant motion kept from corruption. Idleness will betray noble men's minds to the same mischief, if some ingenious industry be not used for their employment.

Our Julian also wrote a book of heraldry. Say not the needle is the most proper pen for the woman; and that she ought to meddle with making no coats, save such as Dorcas made for the widows, seeing their sex may be not only pardoned, but praised for such lawful diversions. No gentleman will severely censure the faults in her heraldry; but rather imitate Julius Scaliger, who, passing his verdict on all poets, and coming to do the like on Sulpitia a Roman poetess (living under Domitian), thus courteously concludeth, " Ut tam laudabilis Heroinæ ratio habeatur, non ausim objicere ei judicii severitatem."‡ She flourished, anno Domini 1460, under king Henry the Sixth.

ROBERT FABIAN was born and bred in this city, whereof he became sheriff 1493.§ Treating his guests with good cheer and welcome, he doubled his dishes with pleasant discourse, being an excellent historian, witness two chronicles of his own writing: 1. From Brutus to the death of king Henry the Second; 2. From the first of king Richard, to the death of king Henry the Seventh.

He was also an excellent poet, both in Latin, French, and English.

* Bale, de Scriptoribus Brit., Cent. vi. n. 96.   † Idem, Cent. viii. n. 33.
‡ De Arte Poeticâ, liber Hyper-Criticus, capite sexto.
§ Bale, Cent. viii. n. 62.; et J. Pits, anno 1512.

A modern master wit,* in the contest betwixt the poets of our age for the laurel, maketh Apollo to adjudge it to an alderman of London, "because to have most wealth was a sign of most wit." But, had the scene of this competition been laid seven-score years since, and the same remitted to the umpirage of Apollo, in sober sadness he would have given the laurel to this our alderman.

As for his histories, if the whole strain of them doth λονδινίζειν, it must be indulged to him that followed the genius of his own education. He died at London, 1512; and was buried in the church of All-hallows, where he hath a tedious and barbarous epitaph;† as commonly (reader, I should be glad to have my observation confuted) who hath worse poetry than poets on their monuments? After his death, cardinal Wolsey caused so many copies of this book as he could come by to be burnt, because therein he had opened the coffers of the church too wide, and made too clear discovery of the revenues of the clergy.‡

THOMAS LUPSET was born in this city, and was related to most English and some foreign learned eminencies of his age :§ 1. Bred a child in the house of dean Colet: 2. Under William Lilly in St. Paul's school: 3. Sent to Oxford, where he became Greek professor: 4. Resigns his place to his friend Ludovicus Vives: 5. Travelled into Italy, and at Padua was familiar with cardinal Pole: 6. Was known unto Erasmus, who giveth him this character, " Hujus ingenio nihil gratius, nihil amantius : " 7. Intended divinity diverted by cardinal Wolsey : 8. At Paris was tutor to Thomas Winter, a ward to the cardinal: 9. Returning into England, was known to king Henry the Eighth : 10. Began to grow into his favour, when cut off with a consumption, 1532, in the prime of his life.

He died in London; and lieth buried in the church of Saint Alphage nigh Cripplegate, without a monument.

SINCE THE REFORMATION.

JOHN RASTALL was a citizen and printer of London ; by marriage a-kin to Sir Thomas More;|| and when the said Sir Thomas and bishop Fisher wrote in defence of purgatory, to prove it by Scripture, Rastall undertook to maintain it by reason. Surely he that buys the two former books deserveth to have this last given him, to make him a *saver*. Some will say, the former two endeavoured to prove the fire, and Rastall the smoke of purgatory. But, to pass by his works in divinity, he was a good mathematician ; and made a comedy of Europe, Asia, and

---

* Sir John Suckling.   † Exemplified in Stow's Survey, p. 214.
‡ Bale, ut prius.   § Bale, and Pits.
|| Bale, de Scriptoribus Britannicis, Cent. viii. n. 74.

Africa, which, my author saith,* was very witty, and very large; and I can believe the latter, seeing he had three parts of the world for his subject; and how long would it have been had America been added? He wrote a book against John Frith; but afterwards (convinced with his adversary's arguments) recanted it of his own accord; the cause why we have placed him since the Reformation. He wrote a book of "the Terms of Law," and made an Index to Justice Fitz-Herbert; yea, I behold this John as father to Rastall the famous lawyer, of whom before.† He died and was buried at London 1536.

EDWARD HALL.—We may trace him from his cradle to his coffin, as followeth: 1. He was a citizen of London by his birth.‡ 2. He was bred a scholar at Eton. 3. Thence he removed, and was one of the foundation of King's College.§ 4. Thence he went to Gray's-Inn, and studied the municipal law. 5. He became common-sergeant of London; for the well discharging whereof, he, 6. Was advanced to be one of the judges in the sheriff's court. 7. Wrote an elegant history of the wars of York and Lancaster, from king Henry the Fourth, till the end of king Henry the Eighth.‖ 8. Died, a very aged man, 1547.

He was, as by some passages in his book may appear, in that age well affected to the Reformation. He lieth buried in the church of Saint Sithes¶ (contracted, I think, for Saint Osith's), where I cannot recover any epitaph upon him.

WILLIAM FULKE, D. D. was born in this city; bred first fellow of Saint John's, then master of Pembroke-hall in Cambridge.** His studies were suitable to his years: when young, a good philosopher, (witness his book of Meteors); afterwards his endeavours ascended from the middle region of the air to the highest heavens, when he became a pious and solid divine.

Now the Romanists, seeing they could no longer blind-fold their laity from the Scriptures, resolved to fit them with false spectacles, and set forth the Rhemish translation; which by doctor Fulke was learnedly confuted, though he never attained any great preferment in the church.

Here it is worth our pains to peruse the immediate succession of masters in Pembroke-hall, because unparalleled in any English foundation;—Edmund Grindall, archbishop of Canterbury; Matthew Hutton, archbishop of York; John Whitgift, archbishop of Canterbury; John Young, bishop of Rochester; William Fulke, D.D.; Lancelot Andrews, bishop of Winchester; Samuel Harsnet, archbishop of York; Nicholas Felton, bishop of Ely.

---

* Bale, ut prius.　　　　　　　† In this city, title, " Writers on the Law."
‡ Stow's Survey, p. 92.　　　§ Hatcher's MS. of King's College.
‖ Bale, de Scriptoribus Britannicis, Cent. ix.
¶ Stow's Survey, p. 276.　　** Parker, in his Scheliton Cant.

Here, though all the rest were episcopated, doctor Fulke was but *doctor Fulke* still, though a man of great merit. This proceeded not from any disaffection in him to the hierarchy (as some would fain suggest); but principally from his love of privacy, and place of Margaret professor, wherein he died anno Domini 1589.

EDMOND SPENSER, born in this city,* was brought up in Pembroke-hall in Cambridge, where he became an excellent scholar; but especially most happy in English poetry, as his works do declare; in which the many *Chaucerisms* used (for I will not say affected by him) are thought by the ignorant to be blemishes, known by the learned to be beauties, to his book; which notwithstanding had been more saleable, if more conformed to our modern language.

There passeth a story commonly told and believed, that Spenser presenting his poems to queen Elizabeth, she, highly affected therewith, commanded the lord Cecil, her treasurer, to give him a hundred pounds; and when the treasurer (a good steward of the queen's money) alleged that sum was too much; "Then give him," quoth the queen, "what is reason;" to which the lord consented; but was so busied, belike, about matters of higher concernment, that Spenser received no reward; whereupon he presented this petition in a small piece of paper to the queen in her progress:

> " I was promis'd on a time,
> To have reason for my rhyme;
> From that time unto this season,
> I receiv'd nor rhyme nor reason."

Hereupon the queen gave strict order (not without some check to her treasurer) for the present payment of the hundred pounds she first intended unto him.

He afterwards went over into Ireland, secretary to the lord Gray, lord deputy thereof; and though that his office under his lord was lucrative, yet got he no estate; but, saith my author, " peculiari poetis fato, semper cum paupertate conflictatus est."† So that it fared little better with him than with William Xilander the German (a most excellent linguist, antiquary, philosopher, and mathematician,) who was so poor, that (as Thuanus saith) he was thought, " fami non fame scribere."‡

Returning into England, he was robbed by the rebels of that little he had; and, dying for grief in great want, anno 1598, was honourably buried nigh Chaucer in Westminster, where this distich concludeth his epitaph on his monument:

> *Anglica te vivo vixit plausitque poesis,*
> *Nunc moritura timet te moriente mori.*

> " Whilst thou didst live, liv'd English poetry,
> Which fears, now thou art dead, that she shall die."

---

* Camden's Elizabeth, in anno 1598. † Idem, ibidem.
‡ Obit. Virorum Doctorum, anno 1576.

Nor must we forget, that the expense of his funeral and monument was defrayed at the sole charge of Robert, first of that name, earl of Essex.

JOHN STOW, son of Thomas Stow, who died anno 1559, grandchild to Thomas Stow, who died 1526 (both citizens of London, and buried in Saint Michael's in Cornhill,) was born in this city, bred at learning no higher than a good grammar-scholar; yet he became a painful, faithful, and (the result of both) useful historian.

Here, to prevent mistake by the *homonymy* of names, I request the reader to take special notice of three brace of English writers:

1. *Sir Thomas* (commonly with the addition of *de la*) *More*, who lived under, and wrote the life of, king Edward the Second. —2. *Sir Thomas More*, the witty and learned chancellor of England.

1. *John Leland*, bred in Oxford, the most exquisite grammarian of his age, who flourished anno 1428.—2. *John Leland*, bred in Cambridge, the most eminent antiquary under king Henry the Eighth.

1. *John Stow*, a Benedictine monk of Norwich, anno 1440, who wrote various collections, much cited by Caius in his History of Cambridge.—2. *John Stow*, this Londoner, and historian.

I confess, I have heard him often accused, that (as learned Guicciardini is charged for telling *magnarum rerum minutias*) he reporteth *res in se minutas*, toys and trifles, being such a smell-feast, that he cannot pass by Guildhall, but his pen must taste of the good cheer therein. However, this must be indulged to his education; so hard it is for a citizen to write a history, but that the fur of his gown will be felt therein. Sure I am, our most elegant historians who have wrote since his time (Sir Francis Bacon, Master Camden, &c.) though throwing away the basket, have taken the fruit; though not mentioning his name, making use of his endeavours. Let me add of John Stow, that (however he kept tune) he kept time very well, no author being more accurate in the notation thereof.

Besides his " Chronicle of England," he hath a large " Survey of London;" and I believe no city in Christendom, Rome alone excepted, hath so great a volume extant thereof. Plato was used to say, " That many good laws were made, but still one was wanting; viz. a law to put all those good laws in execution." Thus the citizens of London have erected many fair monuments to perpetuate their memories; but still there wanted a monument to continue the memory of their monuments (subject by time, and otherwise, to be defaced) which at last by John Stow was industriously performed.

He died in the eightieth year of his age, April 5, 1605; and is buried at the upper end of the north isle of the choir of St. Andrew's Undershaft;* his Chronicle since continued by another, whose additions are the lively emblem of the times he writeth of, as far short of Master Stow in goodness, as our age is of the integrity and charity of those which went before it.

GILES FLETCHER was born in this city,† son to Giles Fletcher, doctor in law, and ambassador into Russia; of whom formerly in Kent. From Westminster school he was chosen first scholar, then fellow of Trinity college in Cambridge: one equally beloved of the Muses and the Graces, having a sanctified wit; witness his worthy poem, intituled " Christ's Victory," made by him being but bachelor of arts, discovering the piety of a saint, and divinity of a doctor. He afterward applied himself to school divinity (cross to the grain of his genius as some conceive), and attained to good skill therein. When he preached at St. Mary's, his prayer before his sermon usually consisted of one entire allegory, not driven, but led on, most proper in all particulars. He was at last (by exchange of his living) settled in Suffolk, which hath the best and worst air in England; best about Bury, and worst on the sea-side, where Master Fletcher was beneficed. His clownish and low-parted parishioners (having nothing but their shoes high about them) valued not their pastor according to his worth; which disposed him to melancholy, and hastened his dissolution. I behold the life of this learned poet, like those half-verses in Virgil's Æneid, broken off in the middle, seeing he might have doubled his days according to the ordinary course of nature; whose death happened about the year 162 . . He had another brother, Phineas Fletcher, fellow of King's college in Cambridge, and beneficed also in Norfolk; a most excellent poet, witness his " Purple Island," and several other pieces of great ingenuity.

JOHN DONNE was born in this city, of wealthy parentage, extracted out of Wales; one of an excellent wit, large travel, and choice experience. After many vicissitudes in his youth, his reduced age was honoured with the doctorship of divinity, and deanery of Saint Paul's.

Should I endeavour to deliver his exact character, I (who willingly would not do any wrong) should do a fourfold injury: 1, to his worthy memory, whose merit my pen is unable to express: 2, to myself, in undertaking what I am not sufficient to perform: 3, to the reader, first in raising, then in frustrating his expectation: 4, to my deservedly honoured Master Isaac Walton, by whom his life is so learnedly written.

It is enough for me to observe, he died March 31, anno Domini 1631; and lieth buried in Saint Paul's, under an inge-

---

* In his own Survey of London (continued after his death), p. 152.
† So was I informed bv Mr. John Rainsey, who married his relict.—F.

nious and choice monument, neither so costly as to occasion envy, nor so common as to cause contempt.

ROMISH EXILE WRITERS.

JOHN HEIWOOD was born in London,* and was most familiar with Sir Thomas More, whom he much resembled in quickness of parts, both undervaluing their friend to their jest, and having " ingenium non edentulum, sed mordax." I may safely write of him, what he pleasantly writes of himself; " that he applied mirth more than thrift; made many plays, and did few good works."† He hath printed many English proverbial epigrams; and his " Monumenta Literaria " are said to be " non tam labore condita, quam lepore condita." He was highly in favour with queen Mary; and, after her death, fled for religion beyond the seas.

It is much, that one so fanciful should be so conscientious. He lived, and (for ought I find) died at Mechlin, about the year 1566. Gasper Heiwood, his son, was a great jesuit, and executed here in queen Elizabeth's reign.

MAURICE CHAMNEE, most probably born in this city, was bred a friar in Charter-house, now called Sutton's hospital. He was imprisoned, for refusing the oath of supremacy, with eighteen of his order, all which lost their lives for their obstinacy, whilst our Maurice (like Job's messenger) " only escaped alone " to tell of his fellows' misfortune, and write the history of the execution. Some of Chamnee's party report to his praise, " that martyrdom was only wanting to him, and not he to martyrdom."‡ Others more truly tax him, for warping to the will of king Henry the Eighth, not so much to decline his own death, as to preserve his convent from destruction, who sped in the first, and failed in the latter. However, fearing some after-claps, he fled beyond the seas, passing the rest of his life in the Low Countries, dying anno Domini 1581.

EDMUND CAMPIAN was born in this city, and bred fellow in Saint John's college in Oxford, where he became proctor anno 1568,§ when queen Elizabeth visited that university. Being made deacon by the Protestant church, he afterwards renounced that order, and fled beyond the seas. A man of excellent parts; though he who rode post to tell him so, might come too late to bring him tidings thereof; being such a valuer of himself, that he swelled every drop of his ability into a bubble by his vain ostentation. And indeed few who were reputed scholars, had more of Latin, or less of Greek, than he had.

He was sent over with father Parsons into England, to reduce it to the church of Rome; to this purpose he set forth his " Ten

---

* Pits, de Angliæ Scriptoribus, anno 1556.
† In his Five Hundred of Epigrams, num. 100.
‡ Pits, de Scriptoribus Angliæ, in anno 1581.   § Ibid.

Reasons," so purely for Latin, so plainly and pithily penned, that they were very taking, and fetched over many (neuters before) to his persuasion.

It was not long before he was caught by the setters of the secretary Walsingham, and brought to the Tower, where one of his own religion said, that he was "exquisitissimis cruciatibus tortus," (racked with most exquisite torments.*)

Yet the lieutenant of the Tower truly told him, "that he had rather seen than felt the rack,† being so favourably used therein, that, being taken off, he did presently go to his lodging without help, and used his hands in writing. Besides, (as Campian confessed) he was not examined upon any point of religion, but only upon matters of state.

Some days after he was engaged in four solemn disputations, to make good that bold challenge he had made against all Protestants:—Place, the chapel in the Tower : Auditors, the lieutenant of the Tower; Mr. Bele, clerk of the council; with many Protestants and Papists.

> *Question* 1.—Aug. 31, 1581, (opposers, Alexander Nowell, dean of Paul's, and William Day, dean of Windsor.)
>
> " Whether the Protestants had cut off many goodly and principal parts of Scripture from the body thereof?"—Campian's answer in the affirmative.
>
> *Question* 2.—Sept. 18, (opposers, William Fulk, D. D., and Roger Goad, D. D.)
>
> " Whether the Catholic church be not properly invisible ?"—Campian's answer in the negative.
>
> *Question* 3.—Sept. 23, (opposers, William Fulk, D. D., and Roger Goad, D. D.)
>
> " Whether Christ be in the Sacrament substantially very God and man in his natural body ?" And "Whether, after the consecration, the bread and wine are transubstantiated?"—Campian's answer in the affirmative.
>
> *Question* 4.—Sept. 27, (opposers, John Walker and William Clarke.)
>
> " Whether the Scriptures contain sufficient doctrine for our salvation ?" And " Whether faith only justifieth ?"—Campian's answer in the negative.

An authentic author‡ giveth this impartial account of Campian in his disputation, "ad disputandum productus, expectationem concitatam ægrè sustinuit;" and, in plain truth, no man did ever boast more when he put on his armour, or had cause to boast less when he put it off. Within a few days, the queen was necessitated, for her own security, to make him the subject of

---

* Pits, de Angliæ Scriptoribus, in anno 1581.
† In the Prince's Report of the first day's conference, fol. 1.
‡ Camden, in his Elizabeth, anno 1580.

severity, by whose laws he was executed in the following
December.

BENEFACTORS TO THE PUBLIC.

THOMAS POPE, Knight, was born in this city, as my worthy
friend Doctor Seth Ward, the head, and others of the Society of
Trinity College in Oxford, have informed me.   I behold him as
Fortunæ suæ fabrum, the smith who (by God's blessing) ham-
mered out his own fortune without any patrimonial advantage.
Indeed, he lived in an age which one may call the harvest of
wealth, wherein any that would work might get good wages, at
the dissolution of abbeys.

Herein he was much employed, being, under the lord Cromwell, an instrument of the second magnitude, and lost nothing
by his activity therein.   However, by all the printed books of
that age, he appeareth one of a candid carriage; and in this
respect stands sole and single by himself, that, of the abbey-
lands which he received, he refunded a considerable proportion
for the building and endowing of Trinity College in Oxford.
He died, as I collect, about the beginning of the reign of queen
Elizabeth.

There are in Oxfordshire many descendants from him, continuing in a worshipful estate, on the same token, that king
James came in progress to the house of Sir William Pope,
knight, when his lady was lately delivered of a daughter, which
babe was presented to king James with this paper of verses in
her hand; which because they pleased the king, I hope they
will not displease the reader :

> " See this little mistress here,
>   Did never sit in *Peter's* chair;
> Or a triple crown did wear,
>   And yet she is a *Pope*.
> No benefice she ever sold,
> Nor did dispence with sins for gold,
> She hardly is a sevenight old,
>   And yet she is a *Pope*.
> No King her feet did ever kiss,
> Or had from her worse look then this ;
>   Nor did she ever hope,
>   To saint one with a rope,
>   And yet she is a *Pope*.
>
> A female *Pope*, you'll say ; a second *Joan ?*
> No, sure ; she is *Pope Innocent*, or none."

I behold the earl of Down in Ireland (but living in Oxfordshire) the chief of the family.

THOMAS CURSON, born in Allhallows, Lombard-street, armourer, dwelt without Bishopsgate.   It happened that a stage-
player borrowed a rusty musket, which had lain long leger in
his shop : now, though his part was comical, he therewith acted

an unexpected tragedy, killing one of the standers-by, the gun casually going off on the stage, which he suspected not to be charged.

Oh the difference of divers men in the tenderness of their consciences! Some are scarce touched with a wound, whilst others are wounded with a touch therein. This poor armourer was highly afflicted therewith, though done against his will, yea without his knowledge, in his absence, by another, out of mere chance. Hereupon he resolved to give all his estate to pious uses. No sooner had he gotten a round sum, but presently he posted with it in his apron to the court of aldermen, and was in pain till by their direction he had settled it for the relief of the poor in his own and other parishes; and disposed of some hundreds of pounds accordingly, as I am credibly informed by the then churchwardens* of the said parish. Thus, as he conceived himself casually (though at great distance) to have occasioned the death of one, he was the immediate and direct cause of giving a comfortable living to many. He died anno Domini 16..

EDWARD ALLIN was born in the aforesaid parish, near Devonshire-house, where now is the sign of the Pie. He was bred a stage-player; a calling which many have condemned, more have questioned, some few have excused, and far fewer conscientious people have commended. He was the Roscius of our age, so acting to the life that he made any part (especially a majestic one) to become him. He got a very great estate, and in his old age, following Christ's council (on what forcible motive belongs not to me to inquire), "he made friends of his unrighteous mammon," building therewith a fair college at Dulwich in Kent, for the relief of poor people.

Some, I confess, count it built on a foundered foundation, seeing in a spiritual sense none is good and lawful money save what is honestly and industriously gotten. But perchance such who condemn Master Allin herein, have as bad shillings in the bottom of their own bags, if search were made therein. Sure I am, no hospital is tied with better or stricter laws, that it may not *sagg* from the intention of the founder. The poor of his native parish, Saint Botolph Bishopsgate, have a privilege to be provided for therein before others. Thus he, who out-acted others in his life, out-did himself before his death, which happened anno Domini 1626.

WILLIAM PLAT was born in this city (as his heir hath informed me), son to Sir Hugh Plat, grand-son to Richard Plat, alderman of London. He was a fellow-commoner bred in Saint John's College in Cambridge, and by his will bequeathed thereunto lands to maintain fellows and scholars (fellows at

---

* John Cheston, George Carter.

thirty, scholars at ten pounds per annum) so many as the estate would extend unto.

But this general and doubtful settlement was liable to long and great suits betwixt the college and the heirs of the said William, until, anno 1656, the same were happily composed betwixt the college and John Plat, clerk, (heir to the foresaid William) when a settlement was made by mutual consent, of four scholars at ten, and two fellows at fifty pounds, per annum. Here I mention not thirty pounds yearly given by him to the poor of Hornsey and Highgate, with a lecture founded therein. This William Plat died anno 1637.

ALEXANDER STRANGE, son to a doctor in law, was born in London,* bred in Peter-house in Cambridge, where he commenced bachelor of divinity, and afterwards for forty-six years was vicar of Layston,† and prebendary of Saint Paul's, where his *prebenda-submersa*, the corpse whereof was drowned in the sea, afforded him but a noble a year.

Now, because Layston church stood alone in the fields, and inconveniently for such who were to repair thereunto, he built at Buntingford (a thorough road market, mostly in his parish) a neat and strong chapel, *è stipe collatitiâ*, from the bounty others gave, and he gathered. Wherefore, having laid the foundation, before well furnished for the finishing thereof, he gave for his motto, " Beg hard, or beggard."

None could tax him (with the Scribes and Pharisees) for "binding heavy burthens and grievous to be borne, and laying them on other men's shoulders, whilst he himself would not move them with one of his fingers."‡ First, because the burthens were not heavy, being light in the particulars; though weighty in the total sum. Secondly, he bound them on none, but professed himself bound unto them, if pleased to take them up for a public good. Thirdly, he put his, and that a bountiful, hand unto them, purchasing land out of his own purse to pay for the daily reparation thereof. He also promoted the building of a free school in the said place, to which some sisters, worshipfully born in the same town, wealthily and honourably married, were the foundresses; yet so as it will still be thankful to contributors thereunto for better accommodation.

This Master Strange, being no less prosperous than painful in compounding all differences among his neighbours, being a man of peace, went to eternal peace December 8, in the eightieth year of his age, 1650.

TO THE READER.

" Pauperis est numerare," (they have but few who have but a number). It passeth my power to compute the Benefactors,

---

* So was I informed by his careful executors.—F.
† So read I in his epitaph in the chapel.—F.   ‡ Matthew xxiii. 4.

natives of this city, whose names are entered in fair tables (the counterpart of the original, no doubt, kept in heaven) in their respective parishes; so that in this city it is as easy to find a steeple without a bell hanging in it, as a vestry without such a memorial fixed to it. Thither I refer the reader for his better satisfaction; and proceed to the

LORD MAYORS OF LONDON.

1. John Rainwell, son of Rob. Rainwell, Fishmonger, 1426.
2. Nicholas Wotton, son of Tho. Wotton, Draper, 1430.
3. Robert Large, son of Tho. Large, Mercer, 1439.
4. Stephen Foster, son of Robert Foster, Fishmonger 1454.
5. Ralph Varney, son of Ralph Varney, Mercer, 1465.
6. John Tate, son of John Tate, Mercer, 1473.
7. Bartholom. James, son of Edw. James, Draper, 1479.
8. John Percivall, son of Roger Percivall, Merchant-Taylor, 1498.
9. Richard Haddon, son of W. Haddon, Mercer, 1506.
10. William Brown, son of John Brown, Mercer, 1507.
11. Henry Kebble, son of Geo. Kebble, Grocer, 1510.
12. William Brown, son of John Brown, Mercer, 1513.
13. George Monox, son of [not named] Draper, 1514.
14. Thomas Seymer, son of John Seymer, Mercer, 1526.
15. William Holleis, son of Wm. Holleis, Baker, 1539.
16. George Barn, son of Geo. Barn, Haberdasher, 1552.
17. William Garrett, son of John Garrett, Grocer, 1555.
18. William Chester, son of John Chester, Draper, 1560.
19. Thomas Rowe, son of Rob. Rowe, Merchant-Taylor, 1568.
20. William Allen, son of Wm. Allen, Mercer, 1571.
21. James Hawes, son of Tho. Hawes, Cloth-worker, 1574.
22. Nicholas Woodrofe, son of David Woodrofe, Haberdasher, 1579.
23. John Branche, son of John Branche, Draper, 1580.
24. Thomas Blanke, son of Tho. Blanke, Haberdasher, 1582.
25. George Barne, son of Geo. Barne, Haberdasher, 1586.
26. Martin Calthrop, son of Martin Calthrop, Draper, 1588.
27. John Garrett, son of Wm. Garrett, Haberdasher, 1601.
28. Thomas Low, son of Simon Low, Haberdasher, 1604.
29. Henry Rowe, son of Tho. Rowe, Mercer, 1607.
30. John Swinnerton, son of Tho. Swinnerton, Merchant-Taylor, 1612.
31. Sebastian Harvey, son of James Harvey, Ironmonger, 1618.
32. William Cockain, son of W. Cockain, Skinner, 1619.
33. Martin Lumley, son of James Lumley, Draper, 1623.
34. John Goare, son of Gerrard Goare, Merchant-Taylor, 1624.
35. Robert Ducy, son of Henry Ducy, Merchant-Taylor, 1630.
36. Robert Titchborn, son of ——— Titchborn, Skinner, 1656.

SHERIFFS
OF LONDON AND MIDDLESEX.

Anno   HEN. II.

1 Quatuor Vic.
2 Gervasius, et Johan.
3 Gervasius, et Johan. filius
    Radulphi.
4
5 Remiencus fili. Berigarii,
    et socii ejus.
6
7 Johan. filius Radulphi.
8 Erisaldus Sutarius, et
    Vital. cl'icus.
9 Remiencus filius Boringa-
    rii, et Will. fil. Isab.
    for seven years.
16 Johan. Bievinitte, et
    Bald. cl'icus.
17 Rad. Orificus, et Rad.
    Vinter. Andre. Buck-
    erol, Adlord. Crispus,
    David de Cornhill, et
    Rog. Blundus, for four
    years.
21 Bricknerus de Haverhil, et
    Pet. fil. Walter.
22 Idem.
23 Will. fil. Isab.
24 Waleran. Johan. filius Ni-
    gelli.
25 Will. fil. Isab., et
    Arnulphus Buxell.
26 Will. et Regin. le Viell.
27 Idem.
28 Idem.
29 Will. et fil. Isab. for six
    years.

RICHARD I.

1 Henri. de Cornhill, et
    Rich. fil. Renner.
2 Rich. filius Renner, ut su-
    pra.
3 Will. et Hen. fil. Renner.
4 Nichol. Duke, et
    Pet. Neveley.
5 Rog. Duke, et

Anno

    Rich. fil. Alwin.
6 Will. fil. Isabel, et
    Will. fil. Arnold.
7 Rob. Besont, et
    Joh. de Josue.
8 Gerard. de Anteloch, et
    Rob. Durant.
9 Rog. Blunt, et
    Nichol. Ducket.
10 Constant. filius Arnold. et
    Rob. le Beau.

R. JOHAN.

1 Arnold. filius Arnold. et
    Rich. filius Barthol.
2 Rog. Dorset, et
    Jacob. Bartholomew.
3 Walter. filius Alic. et
    Simon de Aldermanbury.
4 Norman. Blundell, et
    Johan de Eely.
5 Walt. Broune, et
    Will. Chamberlain.
6 Tho. Haverel, et
    Hamon. Brond.
7 Johan. Walgrave, et
    Rich de Winchester.
8 Johan. Holihand, et
    Edm. filius Gerard.
9 Rog. Winchester, et
    Edm. Hard Le.
10 Petrus Duke, et
    Tho. Neal.
11 Petr. le Josue, et
    Will. Blound.
12 Adam Whiteley, et
    Step. le Grasse.
13 Johan. filius Pet. et
    Joh. Garland.
14 Randolp. Eyland, et
    Constan. Josue.
15 Martin, filius Alic. et
    Petr. Bate.
16 Solom. Basinge, et
    Hug. Basinge.

Anno

17 Joh. Travers, et
And. Newland.

HENRY III.

1 Benedict. Seinturer, et
Will. Bluntivers.
2 Tho. Bockerel, et
Rad. Holyland.
3 Johan. Veile, et
Johan. le Spicer.
4 Rich. Wimbledon, et
Johan. Veile.
5 Rich. Renger, et
Johan. Veile.
6 Rich. Renger, et
Tho. Lambart.
7 Idem.
8 Johan. Travars, et
And. Bockerell.
9 Idem.
10 Rog. Duke. et
Martin filius Will.
11 Idem.
12 Steph. Bokerel, et
Hen. Cocham.
13 Idem.
14 Will. Winchester, et
Rob. filius Johan.
15 Rich. Walter. et
Johan. de Woborne.
16 Micha. de S. Helen, et
Walter. de Enfeild.
17 Hen. de Edmonton, et
Gerard. Bat.
18 Sim. fil. Mar. et
Rog. Blunt.
19 Rad. Ashwy, et
Johan. Norman.
20 Gerard. Bat. et
Rich. vel Rob. Hardle.
21 Hen. Cobham, et
Jordan. de Coventry.
22 Johan. Toloson, et
Gervasius.
23 Johan. Codras, et
Joh. Wilhall.
24 Reymond Bongey, et
Rad. Ashwy.

Anno

25 Johan. Gisors, et
Mich. Tony.
26 Tho. Duresme, et
Johan. Voil.
27 Johan. filius Joh. et
Rad. Ashwy.
28 Hugo Blunt, et
Adam. Basing.
29 Rad. Foster, et Nic. Bat.
30 Rob. de Cornhill, et
Adam. de Bewley.
31 Simon. filius Mar. et
Laurent. Frowick.
32 Johan. Voile, et Nic. Bat.
33 Nich. fil. Josue, et
Galf. Winchester.
34 Rich. Hardell, et
Joh. Toloson.
35 Humf. Bat, et
Will. fil. Richardi.
36 Laur. Frowick, et Nic. Bat.
37 Will. Duresme, et
Tho. Wimborne.
38 Johan. Northampton, et
Rich. Picard.
39 Rad. Ashwy, et
Rob. Limon.
40 Steph. Doe, et
Hen. Walmond.
41 Mich. Bocherel, et
Joh. Minor.
42 Rich. Otwell, et
Will. Ashwy.
43 Rob. Cornhill, et
Joh. Adrian.
44 Idem.
45 Adam. Brouning, et
Hen. Coventry.
46 Johan. Northampton, et
Rich. Picard.
47 Johan. Taylor, et
Rich. Walbrook.
48 Rob. de Mount-Piter, et
Osbert de Suffolk.
49 Greg. Rokesley, et
Tho. de Detford.
50 Edward Blunt, et
Petr. Anger.

Anno

51 Jahan. Hind, et
Johan. Walraven.

52 Johan. Adrian, et
Lucas de Baten-Court.

53 Walter. Harvey, et
Will. Duresme.

54 Tho Baseing, et
Rob. Cornhill.

55 Walt. Potter, et
Phil. Taylor.

56 Greg. Rokesley, et
Hen. Walleys.

57 Rich. Paris, et
Johan. de Wodeley.

EDWARD I.

1 Johan. Horne, et
Walt. Potter.

2 Nico. Winchester, et
Hen. Coventry.

3 Lucas de Batencourt, et
Hen. Frowick.

4 Johan. Horne, et
Rad. Blunt.

5 Rob. de Arer, et
Rad. le Fewre.

6 Johan. Adrian, et
Walt. Langley.

7 Rob. Baseing, et
Will. le Meyre.

8 Tho. Fox, et
Rad. Delamore.

9 Will. Farenden, et
Nich. Winchester.

10 Will. le Meyre, et
Rich. Chigwell.

11 Rad. Blunt, et
Ankerin de Betavill.

12 Johan. Goodcheap, et
Martin. Box.

13 Steph. Cornhill, et
Rob. Rokesley.

14 Walt. Blunt, et
Johan. Wade.

15 Tho. Cross, et
Gualt. Hawteyne.

16 W. Hereford, et
Tho. Stanes.

Anno

17 W. Betaine, et
Johan. de Canter.

18 Fulke of St. Edmond, et
Salom. Langford.

19 Tho. Romaine, et
W. de Leyre.

20 Rad. Blunt. et
Hamond. Box.

21 Hen. Bol vel Bolle, et
Elias Russel.

22 Rob. Rokesley, jun. et
Mort. Aubery.

23 Hen. Box, et
Rich. Glocester.

24 Johannis Dunstable, et
Adam. de Halingbury.

25 Tho. de Suffolk, et
Adam de Fulham.

26 Rich. Refham, et
Tho. Sely.

27 Johan. Armenter, et
Hen. Fingrith.

28 Lucas de Havering, et
Rich. Champnes.

29 Rob. Callor, et
Pet. de Bescant.

30 Hugo Pourte, et
Sim. Paris.

31 W. Combmartin, et
Johan. de Burford.

32 Rog. Paris, et
Johan. de Lincolne.

33 Will. Cawson, et
Regin. Thunderley.

34 Galf. et Sim. Billet.

EDWARD II.

1 Nic. Pigot, et Nigel Drury.

2 W. Baseing, et
Jam. Butteler.

3 Rog. le Palmer, et
Jacobus de Saint Edmons.

4 Sim. Cooper, et
Petr. Blackney.

5 Sim. Metwood, et
Rich. Wilford.

6 Johan. Lambin, et
Will. Lutkin.

Anno

7 Rob. Gurden, et
  Hugo Garton.
8 Steph. Abingdon, et
  Hamond Chigwell.
9 Hamond Goodcheap, et
  Willielm. Bodeleigh.
10 Will. Caston, et
  Rad. Balancer.
11 Johan. Prior, et
  Will. Furneux.
12 Johan. Pointell, et
  Joh. Dalling.
13 Sim. de Abington, et
  Johan. Preston.
14 Renauld. at Conduit, et
  Will. Prodham.
15 Rich. Constantine, et
  Rich. de Hackney.
16 Johan. Grantham, et
  Rich. de Ely.
17 Adam. de Sarisbury, et
  Johan. de Oxford.
18 Benet. de Fulham, et
  Johan. Cawson.
19 Gilb. Mordon, et
  Joh. Causton.
20 Rich. Rothing, et
  Rog. Chauntclere.

EDWARD III.

1 Hen. Darcy, et
  Johan. Haughton.
2 Sim. Frances, et
  Hen. Combmartin.
3 Rich. Lazar, et
  Will. Gisors.
4 Rob. of Ely, et
  Tho. Wharwood.
5 Johan. Mocking, et
  And. Auberey.
6 Nico. Pike, et
  Johan. Husband.
7 Johan. Hamond, et
  Will. Hansard.
8 Johan. Kingstone, et
  Walt. Turke.
9 Walt. Mordon, et
  Rich. Upton.
10 Johan. Clarke, et

Anno

Will. Curtes.
11 Walt. Neale, et
  Nic. Crane.
12 Will. de Pomfrett, et
  Hugo Marbler.
13 Will. Thorney, et
  Rog. Frosham.
14 Adam. Lucas, et
  Barth. Morris.
15 Rich. de Barkeinge, et
  Johan. de Rokesley.
16 Johan. Loufkin, et
  Rich. Killingbery.
17 Johan. Steward, et
  Joh. Aylesham.
18 Geffred. Witchingham, et
  Tho. Leg.
19 Edmund. Hemenhall, et
  Johan. de Gloucester.
20 Joh. Croyden, et
  Will. Clopton.
21 Adam. Brapson, et
  Rich. Fas, vel Bas.
22 Hen. Picard, et
  Sim. Dolseby.
23 Adam. de Bury, et
  Rad. de Lynn.
24 Johan. Notte, et
  Will. de Worcester.
25 Johan. Wroth, et
  Gilb. de Stenineshorpe.
26 Johan. Peache, et
  Joh. Stotley.
27 Will. Wold vel Wild, et
  Johan. Little.
28 Will. Nottingham, et
  Rich. Smelt.
29 Wal. vel Tho. Forster, et
  Tho. Brandon.
30 Rich. Nottingham, et
  Tho. Dolsell.
31 Stephen. Candish, et
  Barth. Frostlinge.
32 Johan. Barnes, et
  Johan. Buris.
33 Sim. de Bennington, et
  Johan. de Chichester.
34 Johan. Dennis, et
  Walt. Berny.

Anno

35 Will. Holbech, et
   Jacob. Tame.
36 Johan. de S. Alban. et
   Jacob. Andrew.
37 Rich. de Croyen, et
   Johan. Hiltoft.
38 Johan. de Metford, et
   Simon. de Mordon.
39 Johan. Bukylsworth, et
   Johan. vel Tho. Ireland.
40 Johan. Ward, et
   Tho. de Lee.
41 Johan. Turnegold, et
   Will. Dickman.
42 Rob. Girdeler, et
   Adam Wimondham.

Anno

43 Joh. Piell, et
   Hugo Holdich.
44 Will. Walworth, et
   Rob. Gayton.
45 Adam. Staple, et
   Rob. Hatfeiled.
46 Johan. Philpot, et
   Nich. Brembar.
47 Johan. Aubery, et
   Johan. Fished.
48 Rich. Lyons, et
   Will. Woodhouse.
49 Johan. Hadley, et
   Will. Newport.
50 Johan. Northampton, et
   Rob. Land.

KING JOHN.

5. WALTER BROWN.—This is he who, with Rosia his wife, founded the hospital of Saint Mary without Bishopsgate, commonly called Saint Mary Spittle.

HENRY THE THIRD.

31. SIMON FITZ-MARY.—He founded the hospital of Mary, called Bethlehem* (corruptly Bedlam) without Bishopsgate.

SHERIFFS

OF LONDON AND MIDDLESEX.

RICHARD II.

Anno   Name and Arms.

1 Andr. Pikeman.
  Nich. de Twiford.
    Arg. two bars, and on a canton S. a buckle of the first.
2 Johan. Bosham.
  Tho. Cornwallis.
3 Johan. Helesdon.
  Will. Barret.
4 Walt. Doget.
  Will. Knightcott.
5 Johan. Hende.
    Arg. a chevron Az. three escalop shells of the feild; on a
      chief of the second a lion passant of the first.
  Johan. Rote.
6 Adam. Bam.
    Erm. on a chief indented S. an annulet between two
      trefoils Arg.

---

* Since removed into St. George's-fields, in the county of Surrey.—ED.

Anno Name and Arms.

 Johan. Sely.
7 Johan. More.
  Arg. a fess dancetté G. and S. between three mullets of
  six points pierced of the third.
 Simon. Winchcombe.
8 Nich. Exon.
  G. a cross between twelve croslets fitched O.
 Johan. Fresh.
  Vert, a fess engrailed O.; in chief an annulet S.
9 Johan. Churchman.
 Johan. Organ.
10 Will. Moore.
 Will. Stanndon.
  S. on a chevron between three lions' heads erased Arg.
  seven cloves proper.
11 Hugo. Tastolfe.
 Will. Venour.
  G. on a fess O. five escalops, three and two, S.
12 Tho. Austen.
 Adam. Carleille.
13 Johan. Lovey.
 Johan. Walcott.
  Arg. on a fess S. three escalops O.
14 Tho. Vynant.
 Johan. Francis.
  Erm. on canton S. a harp Arg.
15 Johan. Chadworth.
  Arg. on a bend S. three trefoils of the first.
 Hen. Vauner.
16 Gilb. Muchfeld.
 Tho. Newton.
17 Urogo. Barentin.
  S. three eaglets Arg.; in the midst an annulet O.
 Rich. Whittington.
  G. a fess compony O. and Az.; in the dexter canton an
  annulet.
18 Will. Brampton.
 Tho. Knoll.
  Az. semé of croslets and a cross recercilte O.
19 Will. Shiringham.
 Roger. Ellis.
20 Tho. Wilford.
 Will. Panker.
21 Johan. Woodcoke.
  O. on a bend G. three crosses bottony fitched at foot of
  the first.
 Will. Askham.
  G. a fess O. between three dolphins naiant Arg.
22 Johan. Warner.

Anno   Name and Arms.

    Johan. Wade.

HENRY IV.

1 Will. Walderne.
    Arg. a bend between three griffins' heads erased S.
    Will. Hide.
2 Will. Gnote.
    Johan. Wakely.
3 Rob. Chichley.
    O. a chevron engrailed between three cinquefoils G.
    Rich. Merlaw.
    Quarterly G. and S. an orle of martlets of the second.
4 Tho. Polle.
    Tho. Fawkoner.
    Paly of six Arg. and S.; on a bend Vert three trefoils
      of the first.
5 Tho. Polle.
    Tho. Fawkoner.
    Arms, *ut prius.*
6 Hen. Barton.
    Erm. a saltire S. voided of the field.
    Will. Crowmer.
    Arg. a chevron engrailed between three choughs
      proper.
7 Nich. Wotton.
    Arg. a saltire engrailed S.
    Galf. Brooke.
8 Hen. Halton.
    Hen. Pounfrayt.
9 Will. Norton.
    Tho. Dukes.
10 Johan. Law.
    Will. Chichley.
    Arms, as before.
11 Johan. Penn.
    Tho. Pike.
12 Johan. Raynwell.
    Per pale indented Arg. and S. a chevron G.
    Walt. Cotton.

HENRY V.

1 Johan. Sutton.
    Johan. Michell.
2 Johan. Michell.
    S. a chevron between three escalops O.
    Tho. Aleyn.
3 Will. Cambrigg.
    Az. a cross patonce between four swans Arg.
    Adam. Everard.

Anno   Name and Arms.

4   Johan. Coventre.
> Arg. on a chevron S. between three columbines proper a bezant.

Rob. Widington.

5   Hen. Rede.

Johan. Gedney.
> Arg. on a fess Az. three eaglets displayed O. between as many leopards' heads G.

6   Johan. Parvies.
> O. a fess Vert, over all a saltire G.

Rad. Barton.

7   Johan. Botiller.

Rob. Whitingham.

8   Johan. Welles.
> Lozengy O. and Erm. a lion rampant G.

Johan. Botiller.

9   Will. Weston.

Rich Gosselin.

HENRY VI.

1   Will. Eastfield.
> S. a chevron between three boys' heads Arg. crined O.

Rob. Tatersall.

2   Tho. Wadeford.

Nich. James.

3   Johan. Bithwater.

Sim. Seaman.

4   Will. Milreth.

Johan. Brockle.
> Checkée O. and Vert, a chief Arg.

5   Rob. Arnold.

Johan. Higham.

6   Rob. Otteley.
> Arg. three lions' heads erased within a border engrailed S.

Hen. Frowicke.

7   Johan. Abbot.

Tho. Duffhous.

8   Will. Rus.

Rad. Holland.

9   Rob. Large.
> Arg. a bend Az. between three mullets G.

Walt. Chichley.
> O. a chevron betwixt three cinquefoils G.

10   Steph. Brown.
> Arg. two chevrons S. ; on a canton Erm. an annulet of the second.

Johan. Hatherley.

Anno   Name and Arms.

11 Johan. Padesley.

Arg. three flowers-de-luce Az. charged on the middle with annulets O.

Johan. Oylney.

G. besanty, two flanches S.; on each a lion rampant gardant Arg.

12 Tho. Chalton.

Az. a lion rampant regardant Arg. crowned O.

Johan. Linge.

13 Tho. Brunewell.

Simon Eyre.

G. a porcupine saliant Arg. quilted and chained about the neck O.

14 Rob. Clopton.

G. a fess Erm. between six mascles O.

Tho. Chatworth.

Erm. three pyles S.; on a canton O. a flower-de-luce Az.

15 Will. Gregory.

Per pale O. and Az. two lions rampant indorsed and regardant, counterchanged.

Tho. Marsted.

16 Will. Chapman.

Will. Halys.

17 Hugo. Dike.

Nich. Yoo, sive Goo.

18 Rob. Markhall.

Phil. Malpas.

19 Johan. Sutton.

Will. Wettenhall.

20 Will. Combes.

Rich. Rich.

21 Tho. Beaumond.

Rich. Norden.

22 Johan. Norman.

O. three bars G.; on a chief Arg. as many flower-de-luces S.

Nich. Wyford.

23 Steph. Foster.

S. a chevron engrailed Erm. between three pheons Arg.

Hugo. Wich.

Arg. on a chevron G. five plates between three quatrefoils slipt Vert.

24 Johan. Darby.

Galf. Felding.

Arg. on a fess Az. three lozenges O.

25 Rob. Horne.

Anno   Name and Arms.

Galf. Bullen.
> Arg. a chevron G. between three bulls' heads couped. S. armed O.

26 Will. Abram.
Tho. Scot.
> Arg. a chevron between three gridirons S.

27 Will. Catlowe.
Will. Marrowe.
> Az. a fess engrailed O. between three maidenheads Arg. crined of the second.

28 Tho. Caning.
Will. Hulyn.
> Arg. a chevron Az. within a border engrailed S.

29 Will. Dere.
Johan. Middleton.

30 Math. Philip.
> S. semé of flowers-de-luce O. a lion rampant Ermine, crowned O.

Chri. Marter.

31 Rich. Lee.
> Az. on a fess between two cotises O. three leopards' heads G.

Rich. Allyn.
> Az. a pale engrailed Erm.

32 Johan. Walden.
Tho. Cooke.
> O. a chevron compony G. and Az. between three cinque-foils of the third.

33 Will. Tayllour.
Johan. Felde.

34 Johan. Young.
> Lozengy O. and Arg.; on a bend Az. two ebeckes' heads erased of the first.

Tho. Oldgrave.
> Az. a chevron engrailed Erm. between three owls O.

35 Johan. Styward.
Rad. Varny.
> Az. on a cross Arg. five mullets O.

36 Tho. Reyner.
Will. Edward.
> Arg. a fess between six martlets S.

37 Rad. Jocelin.
> Az. a wreath Arg. and S. adorned with four horse-bells O.

Rich. Nedeham.

38 Johan. Stocker.
Johan. Plommer.

EDW. IV.

1 Johan. Lambard.

Anno   Name and Arms.

    Rich. Fleming.

2 Geor. Ireland.

    Johan. Lock.

3 Will. Hampton.

      G. a fess checky O. and Az. within a border Arg.

    Barth. James.

      Az. on a chevron between three lions passant gardant O. as many escalops S.

4 Rob. Basset.

    Tho. Muschamp.

5 Johan. Tate.

      Per fess O. and G. a pale counterchanged, between three Cornish choughs.

    Johan. Stone.

6 Hen. Wever, mil.

    Will. Constantin.

7 Johan. Brown.

      Az. a chevron between three escalops O. within a border engrailed.

    Johan. Stockton.

      G. a chevron vairy Arg. and S. between three mullets Arg.

8 Hum. Hayford.

      Arg. a chevron S. between three roebucks tripping G.

    Tho. Stalbroock.

9 Will. Heriot.

      Per pale Ermine and Erminois three crescents counterchanged.

    Simon. Smith.

10 Rob. Drope.

      Arg. gutté de poix; on a chief G. a lion passant gardant O.

    Rich. Gardiner.

      Per fess Arg. and S. a pale counterchanged between three griffins' heads erased of the field.

11 Johan. Crosbey.

    Johan. Warde.

12 Johan. Shelley.

    Johan. Aleyn.

13 Tho. Bledlowe.

    Johan. Brown.

14 Will. Stocker.

    Rob. Billesdon.

      Az. a bend cotised O.; in the sinister chief an eagle's head erased of the second.

15 Tho. Hill.

      S. a chevron Erm. between three lions passant guardant.

Anno   Name and Arms.

Edw. Shaw.
> Arg. a chevron between three lozenges Erm. within a border G.

16 Rob. Colwich.

Hugo. Brice.
> Arg. fretty G. a plain cross of the first, within a border Az. verdoy of cinquefoils O.

17 Rich. Rawson.

Will. Horne.

18 Hen. Collet.
> S. on a chevron between three hinds tripping Arg. as many annulets of the first.

Johan. Stocker.

19 Rob. Harding.

Rob. Byfeld.

20 Tho. Ilam.

Johan. Ward.

21 Will. Bacon.

Tho. Daniell.

22 Rob. Tate.
> Arms, as before.

Rich. Chawry.
> Arg. on a chevron S. between three birds Az. as many annulets of the first.

RICHARD III.

1 Johan. Mathew.
> Gyronny of six S. and G., a lion rampant O. within a border Az. charged with crosses patée O.

Will. White.
> S. on a chevron between three ewers Arg. as many martlets G.

2 Tho. Northland.

Mill. Marten.
> O. two bars G. on the first an escutcheon Erm.

3 Rad. Astry.
> Barry wavy Arg. and Az. on a chief G. three bezants.

Tho. Breteyn.

HENRY VII.

1 Johan. Tate.
> Arms, as before.

Johan. Swan.

2 Johan. Percival.
> Per chevron G. and Az. three greyhounds' heads erased Arg.

Hugo. Clopton.
> Paly of four O. and Az. a lion rampant counterchanged.

Anno   Name and Arms.

3 Tho. Frukell.
   Will. Remington.
      Gyronny of eight Erm. and Az. a dolphin naiant O.
4 Rad. Tilney.
      Arg. a chevron between three griffins' heads erased G.
   Will. Isacke.
5 Will. Capell.
      G. a lion rampant betwixt three crosses botony fitchy O.
   Johan. Brooke.
6 Hen. Coote.
   Hugo. Pemberton.
7 Tho. Wood.
   Will. Brone.
      Per pale indented O. and Arg. a chevron between three
         escalop-shells G.
8 Will. Welbeck.
   Will. Purches.
      Arg. a lion rampant Az., whereon a fess S. charged with
         three besants.
9 Rob. Fabian.
   Johan. Winger.
      Arg. on a chevron between three mascles S. as many
         besants.
10 Nich. Alwyn.
      Arg. a fess nubilée Az. between two lions passant S.
   Johan. Warner.
11 Tho. Knesworth.
      Erm. a chevron wavy G. between three greyhounds
         passant.
   Hen. Somer.
12 Johan. Shawe.
      Arms, as before.
   Rich. Haddon.
      O. a man's leg couped at the thigh Az.
13 Barth. Rede.
      Per pale G. and S. a croslet botony fitched at the base
         between four flowers-de-luce O.
   Tho. Windew.
14 Tho. Burdbury.
      S. a chevron Erm. between three round buckles Arg. the
         tongues pendant.
   Steph. Jenings.
      Arg. a chevron G. betwixt three plumets S.
15 Jac. Wilford.
   Rich. Brond.
16 Johan. Hawes.
   Will. Stede.
17 Laur. Aylemer, mil.

Anno   Name and Arms.

    Hen. Hedde.

18 Hen. Kebill.

    Arg. a chevron engrailed G.; on a chief Az. three mullets O.

    Nich. Nynis.

19 Chri. Hawes.

    Tho. Grannger.

20 Rog. Acheley.

    G. on a fess engrailed between three griffins' heads erased O. as many crosses pattée fitched S.

    Will. Brown.

    Arms, as before.

21 Rich. Shore.

    Rog. Grove.

22 Will. Coppinger.

    Bendy of six, Arg. and G. on a fess Vert three plats withim a border of the second.

    Will. Fitz-Will.

23 Will. Botiler.

    Arg. on a fess componé G. and Az. betwixt six croslets of the third three annulets O.

    Johan Kirkby.

24 Tho. Exmewe.

    Arg. a chevron checky G. and Arg. between three escalop shells S.; within a border of the second ennurny of leopards' heads, and entoir of annulets O.

HENRY VIII.

1 George Monox.

    Arg. on a chevron S. between three holly-leaves proper as many besants; on a chief G. a bird between two anchors O.

    Johan. Doget.

2 Johan. Wilborne.

    Johan. Rest.

3 Nich. Shelton.

    Tho. Mirfin.

4 Rob. Fenrother.

    Rob. Aldernes.

5 Johan. Brugges.

    Arg. on a cross S. a leopard's head O.

    Rog. Basford.

    S. three dancing bears O.

6 Jac. Yarford.

    Johan. Mundy.

7 Hen. Warly.

    Rob. Baily.

Anno   Name and Arms.

8 Tho. Seymor.
    S. a fess imbattled with three ogresses betwixt as many
      wings Arg.
  Johan. Thirston.
9 Tho. Baldry.
  Rad. Simonds.
10 Johan. Aleyn.
  Jacob. Spens.
11 Johan. Wilkenson.
  Nich. Pertrich.
    Checké Arg. and S. on a bend G. three escalops O.
12 Johan. Kime.
    G. a chevron betwixt nine cross croslets O.
  Johan. Skevington.
    Arg. three bulls' heads erased S.
13 Johan. Bretton.
  Tho. Pargiton.
14 Johan. Rudston.
  Johan. Champnes.
    Per pale Arg. and S. a lion rampant within a border en-
      grailed counterchanged.
15 Mich. English.
    S. three lions passant Arg.
  Johan. Junis.
16 Rad. Dodmer.
  Will. Roche.
17 Johan. Counton.
  Chri. Askew.
18 Steph. Peacocke.
  Nich. Lambard.
19 Johan. Hardy.
  Will. Howles.
20 Rad. Warren.
  Johan. Long.
21 Mich. Dormer.
    Az. ten billets, four, three, two, and one, O.; in a chief of
      the second a lion issuant S. armed and langued G.
  Walt. Champion.
22 Will. Dauntsey.
  Rich. Cophin.
23 Rich. Gresham.
  Edw. Altam.
24 Rich. Reynolds.
  Johan. Prise.
25 Will. Forman.
  Tho. Kitson, mil.
26 Nich. Lawson.

Anno	Name and Arms.

Will. Denham.
27 Hum. Munmoth.
Johan. Cotes.
28 Rob. Paget.
Will. Bowyer.
29 Johan. Gresham.
Tho. Lewyn.
30 Will. Wilkinson.
Nich. Gibson.
   Az. three storks rising proper.
31 Johan. Fairy.
Tho. Huntlowe.
32 Mart. Bowes.
Will. Louton.
33 Roland. Hill, mil.
Hen. Suckley.
34 Hen. Hoberthorne.
Hen. Amcotts.
   Arg. a castle betwixt three cups covered Az.
35 Rich. Tolus.
Johan. Dobes.
36 Johan. Wilford.
And. Judde.
37 Georg. Barnes.
Rad. Aleyn.
38 Rich. Jerveys.
Tho. Curtys.

EDWARD VI.

1 Rob. Chertesey.
Tho. White.
2 Will. Lock.
Johan. Ayliffe.
3 Johan. Yorke.
Rich. Turke.
4 Agust. Hinde.
Johan. Lyon.
5 Johan. Lambert.
Johan. Cooper.
6 Johan. Maynard.
   Arg. a chevron Az. betwixt three hands G.
Will. Gerrard.

REX. PHIL. ET. MA. REGINA.

1 Tho. Offley.
   Arg. on a cross Az. formée flurt. a lion passant O. be-
   twixt four Cornish choughs proper.
Will. Hewet.

2 David. Woodroffe.
  Will. Chester.
3 Tho. Leigh.
  Johan. Macham.
4 Will. Harpur.
  Johan. White.
5 Rich. Mallary.
  Jaco. Altham.
6 Johan. Hales.
  Rich. Champion.

REG. ELIZAB.

1 Tho. Lodge.
  Rog. Martin.
2 Chri. Diaper.
  Tho. Roo.
3 Alex. Avenon.
  Hum. Baskervill.
      Arg. a chevron G. betwixt three hearts proper.
4 Will. Allen.
  Rich. Chamberlain.
5 Edw. Banckes.
  Rowland. Haward.
6 Edw. Jackman.
  Lion. Ducket.
7 Johan. Rivers.
      Az. two bars dancetté O.; in chief three bezants.
  Jacob. Hawys.
8 Amb. Nicolas.
  Johan. Langley.
9 Thomas Ramsey.
      S. a chevron Erm. betwixt three rams' heads erazed Arg.
  Will. Bond.
10 Johan. Cliffe.
   Jacob. Bacon.
11 Hen. Becher.
   Will. Dane.
12 Fran. Barnham.
   Will. Boxe.
13 Johan. Milles.
   Johan. Braunch.
14 Rich. Pipe.
      Az. crusuly, two pipes O.
   Nich. Woodroffe.
15 Jacob. Harvey.
   Tho. Pullyson.
16 Tho. Blancke.
   Anth. Gamage.

Anno   Name and Arms.

17 Edw. Osborn.
    Wolstans. Dixie.
18 Will. Kimpton.
    Georg. Barne.
19 Nich. Backhouse.
    Fran. Bowyer.
        O. a bend vairy betwixt two cotises G.
20 Georg. Bonde.
    Tho. Starkey.
21 Mart. Calthorpe.
        Checky O. and Az. a fess Erm.
    Johan. Hart.
22 Rod. Woodcock.
    Johan. Allott.
23 Rich. Martin.
    Will. Webbe.
24 Will. Rowe.
        Arg. on a chevron Az. between three trefoils parted per
            pale G. and Vert, as many bezants.
    Cutb. Buckell.
25 Will. Masham.
    Johan. Spencer.
26 Steph. Slany.
    Hen. Willingsley.
27 Anth. Ratliffe.
    Hen. Prannell.
28 Rob. House.
    Will. Elkin.
29 Johan. Catcher.
    Tho. Skynner.
30 Hugo. Offeley.
        Arg. on a cross Az. formée fleury a lion passant O. be-
            tween four Cornish choughs proper.
    Rich. Saltenstall.
31 Rich. Gourney.
    Steph. Soame.
        G. a chevron betwixt three mallets O.
32 Nich. Mouseley.
        S. a chevron betwixt two mallets Arg.
    Rich. Brooke.
33 Will. Rider.
        Az. three crescents O.
    Benedic. Barnham.
34 Johan. Gerrard.
    Rob. Taylor.
35 Pavel. Banning.
    Pet. Haughton.

Anno   Name and Arms.

36 Rob. Lee.
    Tho. Benett.
37 Tho. Lowe.
    Leon. Holliday.
38 Johan. Watts.
    Ricard. Goddard.
39 Hen. Rowe.
    Johan. Moore.
40 Edw. Holmenden.
    Rob. Hampson.
41 Rog. Clarke.
    Hum. Welde.
42 Tho. Cambell.
    Will. Craven.
      Arg. a fess betwixt six cross croslets fitchy G.
43 Hen. Anderson.
      Arg. a chevron betwixt three cross croslets S.
    Will. Glover.

JACOB. REX.

1 Jam. Pemberton.
      Arg. a chevron betwixt three buckets S.
    Johan. Swynnerton.
      Arg. a cross formée flurt S.
2 Will. Rumney.
    Tho. Middleton.
3 Tho. Hayes, mil.
      Erm. three leopards' heads erazed G.
    Oliver. Stile, arm.
4 Clem. Scudamore.
      G. three stirrups leathered and buckled O.
    Johan. Jolles, mil.
5 Will. Walthall.
    Johan. Leman.
      Az. a fess betwixt three dolphins Arg.
6 Galf. Elwis.
    Nich. Stile.
7 Georg. Booles.
      Az.three cups Arg. holding as many boars' heads erected O.
    Rich. Farrington.
8 Rich. Pyott.
    Fran. Jones.
9 Edw. Barkham.
      Arg. three pallets G.; over all a chevron.
    Georg. Smithes.
10 Edw. Rotheram.
    Alex. Prescot.

Anno   Name and Arms.

11 Tho. Bennett.
      Hen. Jay.
12 Pet. Proby.
      Mart. Lumley.
13 Will. Gore. } G. a fess betwixt three croslets fitchy O.
      Johan. Gore. }
14 Allanus Cotton.
      Cut. Harbert.
15 Will. Holeday.
      Rob. Johnson.
16 Rich. Herve.
      Hugo. Hamersley.
17 Rich. Deane.
      Jacob. Cambell.
18 Edrus. Allen.
      Rob. Ducy.
        O. two lions passant G.
19 Geor. Whitmore.
        Vert, fretty O.
      Nich. Ranton.
20 Johan. Hodges.
      Hum. Handford, il.
21 Tho. Moulson.
      Rad. Freeman.
        Az. three lozenges Arg.
22 Roland. Heylinge.
      Rob. Parkhurst.

           CAR. REG.

1 Jahan. Poole.
     Chri. Clitherowe.
2 Edrus. Bromfeild.
     Rich. Fenn.
3 Maur. Abbot, mil.
     Hen. Garway.
       Arg. a pile surmounted by a fess, between four leopards
         heads G.
4 Rowland Backhouse.
     Will. Acton, mil. and bar.
5 Edmund Wright.
     Humph. Smith.
6 Arthur Abdey.
       O. two chevrons betwixt three cinquefoils S.
     Rob. Cambell.
7 Sam. Cranmer.
     Hen. Prat.
       Arg. on a chevron S. between three pellets, each charged
         with a martlet of the field, as many mascles O.
8 Hugo Perry.

Anno   Name and Arms.

    Hen. Andrews.
 9 Gilb. Harrison.
    Rich. Gurney.
       Paly counter-paly of six pieces per fess O. and Az.
10 John Highlord.
       S. a bend flory Arg.
    Joh. Cordell.
11 Tho. Soame.
    Joh. Gaire.
12 Will. Abell.
    Jac. Gerrard.
13 Tho. Atkin.
    Edw. Rudge.
14 Isaac Pennington.
    Joh. Woolaston.
       S. three mullets pierced Arg.
15 Tho. Adams.
       Erm. three cats Az.
    Johan. Warner.
       O. a chevron betwixt three boars' heads erased S.
16 Johan. Towse.
    Abram. Reynardson.
       Arg. two chevrons engrailed and a canton G. whereon a
         a mascle of the field.
17 Georg. Garret, mil.
    Georg. Clarke.
       Arg. on a bend G. between three ogresses as many swans
         proper.
18 Johan. Langham.
       Arg. three bears' heads erased S. muzzled O.
    Tho. Andrews.
       Arg. on a chevron engrailed betwixt three trefoils Vert as
         many mullets O.
19 Johan. Fouke.
       Vert, a flower de-luce Arg.
    Jacob. Bunce.
20 Will. Gibbs.
    Rich Chambers.
21 Johan. Kendrick.
    Tho. Foot.
       Arg. a chevron, and in the dexter-point a trefoil S.
22 Tho. Cullum.
    Simon. Edmunds.

    The reader (whom I presume no less charitable than judi-
cious) will not be offended with the many naked blanks, or
armless spaces, annexed to these sheriffs. He that thinks the
sheriffs of London as cognizable persons (especially so long
since) as those of other counties, may with equal truth maintain

the springs of rivers as easily discernible as their channels. For the sheriffs of counties were men of known and grown estates, equally eminent for the roots whence they sprang, as for the branches springing from them; whereas many sheriffs of London (like those plants which the gardeners term annual, lasting but a year) appear only eminent during their shrievalty, and afterwards no motion or mention of them, especially of such as died before their mayoralty; the true reason why we could attain so few arms with any assurance.

HENRY VI.

18. PHILIPPUS MALPAS.—He gave by his testament £125 to relief of poor prisoners; and every year, for five years, 400 shirts and smocks, 40 pair of sheets, 150 gowns of frieze to the poor. To 500 poor people in London, every one 6s. 8d.; to poor maids' marriages, 100 marks; to highways, 100 marks; 20 marks' the year to a graduate to preach; £20 unto preachers at the Spittle on the three Easter holidays, &c.*

20. RICHARD RICH.—He was a mercer, and founded alms-houses at Hodsden in Hertfordshire,† which no doubt were by him competently endowed; though now the alms-houses are as poor as the alms-folk, the one needing repairing, as much as the other relieving.

EDWARD IV.

17. RICHARD RAWSON.—He gave by testament large legacies to the prisoners, hospitals, and lazar-houses. To other poor, to highways, to the water-conduits, besides to poor maids' marriages, £340; and his executors to build a large house in the churchyard of St. Mary's Spittle, wherein the mayor and his brethren do use to sit, and hear the sermons in Easter holidays.‡

20. THOMAS ILAM.—He newly builded the great conduit in the Cheap, of his own charges, to the great convenience of the city.§

HENRY VII.

HENRY KEBLE.—He gave to highways £200,‖ to poor maids' marriages 100 marks, &c.; to seven alms-men in London 6d. the week for ever. He was, when living, a great benefactor to the building of Aldermary church, and by his testament gave £1000 towards the finishing thereof. How barbarously he was afterwards requited, and his body cast out of the grave, we have formerly largely bemoaned, and with just indignation.¶

---

* Stow's Survey of London, p. 88.   † Idem, p. 89.   ‡ Idem, ibidem.
§ Idem, ibidem.   ‖ Idem, ibidem.
¶ First Book, in the Chapter of CHURCHES, see vol. i. p. 31.

HENRY VIII.

1. GEORGE MONOX.—He re-edified the decayed parish-church of Waltamstow, or Walthamstow, in Essex; he founded there a free-school, and alms-houses for thirteen alms-people; he made also a causeway of timber over the marshes from Walthamstow to Lock-bridge.*

THE FAREWELL.

And now, being to take my farewell of this great city, I cannot forget the verse, which I find, amongst others, in Master Camden's commendation thereof:

Urbs pietate potens, numeroso cive superba.
" Potent in piety, in her people proud."

But see the Romish charity, who confine all piety to Popery. The Index Expurgatorius, printed at Madrid by Lewes Sanchez 1612, commandeth the fore-part of the verse, concerning their piety, to be expunged; letting the latter moiety, of their pride, to remain.

May I in this particular be the humble remembrancer of the city (without the least intrenching on his place who worthily dischargeth that office)† to cross and confute that peevish and partial Index.   Let it be their endeavours to delete out of their hearts all high conceits of their populousness, and effectually to express grace and goodness in their conversations.

Nor let the city of London ever forget " quantillum interfuit inter maximam civitatem et nullam," (how little distance there lately was betwixt the greatest city and none at all), if gates and bars (as it is generally received) be the essential difference of a city.   But God, who can produce light out of darkness, can make the plucking down of the gates, to be the setting up of the city.   Wherefore though the eleventh day of March be generally beheld as the first day of Spring, London may date her Spring from the eleventh day of February 1659, when she effectually felt the vernal heat after a long winter of woe and misery.

I heartily wish this honourable city whatever may conduce to the continuance and increase of the happiness thereof.   Especially that the river of Thames, the life of London (as which easeth, adorneth, enricheth, feedeth, and fortifieth it), may have its channel constantly continued.   The Miller's riddle,

" If I have water I will drink wine;
But if I have no water, I must drink water,"

is appliable to this city: so long as Thames water continues, Londoners may *wine* it; but should it fail, they must drink

---

* Stow's Survey of London, p. 90.
† This is a very ancient and respectable office in the City of London.—ED.

water indeed, and some perchance brackish too, as made of their tears.

I will not pry too nearly and narrowly into the fancy of our poet, speaking of the ruins of old Rome:

> " Ne ought, save Tiber hasting to his fall,
> O world's inconstancy ! remains of all :
> That which is firm doth flit and fall away,
> And that is flitting doth abide and stay. *

And yet, by his leave, greater rivers than Tiber have, in process of time, had their streams, by casualties or neglect, partly drained, wholly dried, or otherwise diverted. My humble request therefore to the officers of the city is, effectually to own their concernment in the river of Thames, in clearing and cleansing it from shoals, sands, and other obstructing encroachments,† that they may leave it as well to posterity, as they found it from their fathers.

WESTMINSTER.

Westminster is the greatest city in England next to London, not only in position, but by the dimensions thereof. For let it be taken (as truly it ought) extensively with the liberty of Lancaster from Temple-bar, and it filleth as much ground (not to say containeth more reasonable souls) than any city in the land. But as a proper man seemeth a dwarf, when placed next to a giant; such the infelicity of Westminster, whose due greatness, devoured by the vicinity of London, is insensible in the eyes of beholders.

It was anciently called Thorney, and afterwards Westminster, for distinction from St. Paul's, called in ancient times Eastminster.‡

THE BUILDINGS.

The Abbey church is beheld as a rare structure, with so small and slender pillars (greatest legs argue not the strongest man) to support so weighty a fabric, built by king Henry the Third, and afterwards much enlarged and beautified by the abbots thereof.

Adjoining to it is the chapel of king Henry the Seventh, which Leland calls " the miracle of the world." Indeed, let the

---

* Bella, in his Ruins of Rome, translated by Spenser.

† The Lord Mayor of London is, by his office, Conservator of the Thames : and a committee of aldermen and other members of the Court of Common Council, are annually appointed to superintend the improvement of the navigation, and to prevent encroachments.—Ed.

‡ Bale, de Scriptoribus Britannicis, Cent. ii. p. 173, in Vità Gilberti Westmonasteriensis.

Italians deride our English, and condemn them for Gothic buildings; this they must admire, and may here take notes of architecture (if their pride would permit them) to perfect theirs accordingly.

In this chapel the founder thereof, with his queen, lieth interred, under a monument of solid brass,* most richly gilded, and artificially carved. Some slight it for the cheapness, because it cost but a thousand pounds in the making thereof.† Such do not consider it as the work of so thrifty a prince, who would make a little money go far; besides that it was just at the turning of the tide (as one may term it) of money, which flowed after the finding out of the West Indies, though ebbing before.

Amongst the civil structures, Westminster-hall is eminent, erected by king William Rufus for the hall to his own court, built with cobwebless beams, conceived of Irish-wood. Sure I am, we then had no command in that island, as first subdued by king Henry the Second. It is one of the greatest rooms in Christendom; and indeed it needeth to be of good capacity, to receive so many plaintiffs and defendants, being at such mutual distance of affection.

Next is White-hall, the palace of our English kings, which one termed a good hypocrite, promising less than it performeth, and more convenient within than comely without; to which the nursery of St. James's was an appendant.

As for the houses of noblemen all along the Strand, I desire to be excused from commending some, lest it should, by cavilling spirits, be implicitly interpreted a dispraise of the rest. Besides, I am ignorant under what name to commend them to posterity; so many houses daily, new-dipt, assume to themselves new names, according to the alteration of their owners. I conclude them therefore *all best*, and *best of all* whilst they continue in the hands of their present possessors.

PROVERBS.

"As sure as Exchequer pay."]

All know, that the Exchequer was formerly the treasury of the kings of England, kept in this city, the pleading part on the one side, and the paying part on the other side of Westminster-hall. This proverb was in the prime thereof in the reign of queen Elizabeth, who maintained her Exchequer to the height, that her Exchequer might maintain her. The pay thereof was sure inwards, nothing being remitted which was due there to the queen: and sure outwards, nothing being detained which was due thence from the queen, full and speedy payment being made thereof. This proverb began to be crost about the end of the reign of king James, when the credit of the Exchequer

---

* Or copper rather.   † Godwin, in his Annals of King Henry VIII. anno 1.

began to decay; and no wonder if the streams issuing thence were shallow, when the fountain to feed them was so low, the revenues of the crown being much abated.

"There is no redemption from Hell."]

There is a place partly under, partly by the Exchequer Court, commonly called Hell; I could wish it had another name, seeing it is ill jesting with edge-tools, especially with such as are sharpened by Scripture. I am informed that formerly this place was appointed a prison for the king's debtors, who never were freed thence, until they had paid their uttermost due demanded of them. If so, it was no Hell, but might be termed purgatory, according to the popish erroneous persuasion. But, since, this proverb is applied to moneys paid into the Exchequer, which thence are irrecoverable upon what plea or pretence whatsoever.

"As long as Megg of Westminster."]

This is applied to persons very tall, especially if they have hop-pole height, wanting breadth proportionable thereunto. That such a giant woman ever was in Westminster, cannot be proved by any good witness (I pass not for a late lying pamphlet); though some, in proof thereof, produce her grave-stone on the south-side of the cloisters, which (I confess) is as long and large and entire marble as ever I beheld. But be it known, that no woman in that age was interred in the cloisters, appropriated to the sepultures of the abbot and his monks. Besides, I have read, in the records of that abbey, of an infectious year, wherein many monks died of the plague, and were all buried in one grave, probably in this place, under this marble monument. If there be any truth in the proverb, it rather relateth to a great gun, lying in the Tower, commonly called Long Megg, and in troublesome times (perchance upon ill May-day in the reign of king Henry the Eighth) brought to Westminster, where for a good time it continued. But this *nut* (perchance) deserves not the cracking.

PRINCES.

EDWARD the First was born in Westminster, being a Prince placed, by the posture of his nativity, betwixt a weak father and a wilful son. Yet he needed no such advantage for foils, to set forth his real worth. He was surnamed Longshanks, his step being another man's stride, and was very high in stature. And though ofttimes such who are built four stories high are observed to have little in their cock-loft, yet was he a most judicious man in all his undertakings; equally wise to plot, as valiant to perform; and (which under Divine Providence was the result of both) happy in success, at sea, at land, at home, abroad, in war, in peace. He was so fortunate with his sword at the beginning of his reign, that he awed all his enemies with his scabbard before the end thereof. In a word, he was a prince of so much merit, that nothing under a Chronicle can make his complete character.

EDWARD, sole son to king Henry the Sixth and Margaret his queen, was born at Westminster, on the 13th day of October 1453.* Now, when his father's party was totally and finally routed in the battle at Tewksbury, this prince, being taken prisoner, presented to king Edward the Fourth, and demanded by him, "On what design he came over into England?" returned this answer, "That he came to recover the Crown, which his ancestors for three descents had no less rightfully than peaceably possessed."

An answer, for the truth, befitting the son of so holy a father as king Henry the Sixth; for the boldness thereof, becoming the son of so haughty a mother as queen Margaret. But presently king Edward dashed him on the mouth with his gauntlet, and his brother Richard Crookback stabbed him to the heart with his dagger. A barbarous murder, without countenance of justice in a legal or valour in a military way. And his blood then shed was punished not long after.

Here I am not ashamed to make this observation; that England had successively three Edwards, all princes of Wales, sole or eldest sons to actual kings; two dying violent, all untimely deaths, in their minority, before they were possessed of the crown; viz. 1. Edward, son to Henry VI., stabbed in the seventeenth year of his age. 2. Edward, son to Edward IV., stifled in the tenth year of his age. 3. Edward, son to Richard III., pined away in the eleventh year of his age.

The murder of the second may justly be conceived the punishment of the murder of the first; and the untimely death of the last (of whom more in Yorkshire†) a judgment for the murder of the two former.

EDWARD, eldest son of Edward the Fourth and Elizabeth his queen, was born in the sanctuary of Westminster, November 4, 1471. His tender years are too soft, for a solid character to be fixed on him. No hurt we find done by him, but too much on him, being murdered in the Tower by the procurement of his uncle protector. Thus was he born in a spiritual, and killed in a temporal, prison. He is commonly called king Edward the Fifth, though his hand was asked but never married to the English crown; and therefore, in all the pictures made of him, a distance interposed forbiddeth the banns betwixt them.

ELIZABETH, eldest daughter of king Edward the Fourth and Elizabeth his queen, was born in Westminster on the eleventh of February 1466.‡ She was afterwards married to king Henry

---

* Speed's Chronicle, p. 684.　　　　† In the title of " PRINCES.
‡ Idem, p. 703.

the Seventh; and so the two houses of York and Lancaster united first hopefully in their bed, and afterwards more happily in their issue. Besides her dutifulness to her husband, and fruitfulness in her children, little can be extracted of her personal character. She died (though not in child-bearing) in child-bed, being safely delivered on Candlemas-day, anno 1503, of the lady Catharine; and, afterwards falling sick, languished until the eleventh of Februrary, and then died, in the thirty-seventh year of her age, on the day of her nativity.* She lieth buried with her husband in the chapel of his erection, and hath an equal share with him in the use and honour of that his most magnificent monument.

[AMP.] CECILY, second daughter to king Edward the Fourth by Elizabeth his queen, bearing the name of Cecily duchess of York, her grandmother and godmother, was born at Westminster. In her childhood mention was made of a marriage betwixt her and James (son to James the Third) prince of Scotland. But that motion died with her father, heaven (wherein marriages are made) reserving that place for Margaret her eldest sister's eldest daughter.

She long led a single life, but little respected of king Henry the Seventh her brother-in-law. That politic king, knowing that, if he had none or no surviving issue by his queen, then the right of the crown rested in this Cecily, sought to suppress her from popularity, or any public appearance. He neither preferred her to any foreign prince, nor disposed of her to any prime peer of England, till at last this lady wedded herself to a Lincolnshire lord, John Baron Wells, whom king Henry advanced Viscount, and no higher. After his death, my author† saith, she was remarried, not mentioning her husband's name;‡ whence I conclude him an obscure person, and this lady rather married than matched, such the distance betwixt their degrees. Probably this Cecily, consulting her comfort more than her credit, did it of design, so to be beneath the jealousy of king Henry the Seventh. She left no children, and the date of her death is uncertain.

CHARLES the Second (son to king Charles the First, of blessed memory, and Mary youngest daughter to Henry the Fourth, king of France) was born at Saint James's, May 29, 1630. Great was the general rejoicing thereat. The university of Oxford congratulated his birth with printed poems; and it was taken ill, though causelessly, by some, that Cambridge did not do the like; for then the wits of the university were sadly distracted into several counties, by reason of the plague therein.

---

* Speed's Chronicle, p. 703.
† Idem, in the end of the reign of king Edward the Fourth.
‡ Some say his name was *Kyme*.

And I remember, Cambridge modestly excused herself in their poem made the year after, at the birth of the lady Mary; and it will not be amiss to insert and translate one tetrastic, made by my worthy friend, Master Booth, of Christ's College, Cambridge.

> *Quod fuit ad nixus academia muta priores,*
> *Ignoscat princeps Carolus, ægra fuit.*
> *Spe veniente novâ si tunc tacuisset amores,*
> *Non tantùm morbo digna, sed illa mori.*

> " Prince Charles, forgive me, that my silent quill,
>   Joy'd not thy birth; alas sore sick was I.
> New hopes now come; had I been silent still,
>   I should deserve both to be sick and die."

His birth was accompanied with two notable accidents in the heavens. The star Venus was visible all day long, as sometime it falls out near her greatest elongation. And two days after there was an eclipse of the sun, about eleven digits, observed by the greatest mathematicians.[*]

And now, reader, give me leave to be silent myself, and present thee with the expressions of a most ingenious gentleman :

" To behold this babe, heaven itself seemed to open one eye more than ordinary.——Such asterisks and celestial signatures affixt to times so remarkable as this, usually are ominous, prophetically hinting and pointing out somewhat future of eminent contingency."[†]

Yea, such have since been the occurrences in the life of this pious prince, that, rightly considered, they will appear (not only eminent above the common standard of actions, but) full of miracle and amazement.

He was, on the first of January 1650, at Scone, crowned king of Scotland; being before invaded by an army under the conduct of Oliver Cromwell. Soon after quitting that kingdom, he marched for England; and on the third of September 1651, nigh Worcester,[‡] was fought, and lost the day, though he (to use my author's expression[§]) " acted beyond the expectation of his friends, and to the great applause of his very enemies." Narrow search was made after his person, yea a thousand pounds (a bait his politic enemies made sure would have been bit at) promised to such who should betray him. Yet God (whose angels were his life-guard) miraculously preserving him out of the hands of his enemies, he safely passed over into France to the queen his mother.

During his continuance beyond the seas, great were the proffers tendered unto him if forsaking the Protestant religion; but, alas! as soon might the impotent waves remove the most

---

[*] Bainbridge and Gassendus.
[†] Hamond L'Estrange, in the reign of king Charles the First, p. 112.
[‡] See " BATTLES " in Worcestershire.
[§] Doctor Heylin, in his Life of King Charles, p. 155.

sturdy rocks, as they once unfix him; such his constancy, whom neither the frowns of his afflictions, nor smiles of secular advantages, could make to warp from his first principles.

At length his piety and patience were rewarded by God, with a happy restitution to his undoubted dominions; and he, after a long and tedious exile, landed at Dover, May 25, 1660, to the great joy of his three kingdoms.

A prince whose virtues I should injure, if endeavouring their contraction within so narrow a scantling. And yet I cannot pass over that wherein he so much resembleth the king of heaven (whose vicegerent he is); I mean his merciful disposition, doing good unto those who spitefully used and persecuted him.

And now it is my hearty prayer, that God, who appeared so wonderfully in his restoration, would continue still gracious to us in his preservation, confounding the plots of his adversaries, that upon him and his posterity the crown may flourish for ever.

MARY, eldest daughter of king Charles the First and queen Mary, was born at Saint James's, November 4, 1631. When her royal father, out of his paternal love, began to cast about for a fitting consort, this peerless princess (though tender in years, rich in piety and wisdom) made it her humble request she might be matched as well in her religion as affection; which happened answerable to her desires; for, not long after, a marriage, treated betwixt her and count William of Nassau, eldest son to Henry prince of Orange, was concluded; and this royal pair wedded accordingly, May 2, 1641. The February following, having at Dover taken her leave of the king her father (the last time she ever saw him on earth) she embarked for, and within few days landed in, Holland.

His majesty's affairs in England daily growing worse and worse, at length the sad news of his horrid murder arrived at her ears: this was seconded with the loss of her husband the prince of Orange, who deceased October 8, 1650. Yet such her signal patience, that she underwent the weight of so many heavy afflictions, sufficient to break the back of a mean Christian, with a courage far surpassing the weakness of her sex. But, amidst these her calamities, God was pleased to remember mercy, blessing her the November ensuing with a hopeful son.

The complexion of the times being altered in England, she came over to congratulate the happiness of her brother's miraculous restitution; when, behold, sickness arrests this royal princess, no bail being found by physic to defer the execution of her death, which happened 1660. On the 31st of December following, she was honourably [though privately] interred at Westminster, in the chapel of king Henry the Seventh; and no eye so dry but willingly afforded a tear to bemoan the loss of so worthy a princess.

JAMES, third son of king Charles and queen Mary, was born October 13, 1633, at St. James's. He was commonly styled duke of York, though not solemnly created until January 27, 1643. At the rendition of Oxford, he was taken prisoner; and some two years after, through the assistance of one colonel Bamfield, made his escape, landing safe in Holland. Hence he went for France; where he so prudently deported himself, that he soon gained the favour and honour of the whole court. Yea, such was this prince's valour and prowess, that, before arrived at the age of one and twenty years, he was made lieutenant general of the forces of the king of France; a thing which sounds highly to the esteem of this duke, being a sufficient argument as well of his policy as magnanimity; seeing a wise head is equally required warily to consult, as a stout heart resolutely to act, for the due performance of that office.

This trust he discharged to the admiration of all, achieving so many noble and heroic exploits, which rendered him renowned throughout the Christian world. Yet such the baseness and ingratitude of the French, that, concluding a peace with Oliver Cromwell, the Usurper of England, they wholly forgot his former services, and consented to the expulsion of this prince and his royal brothers out of that kingdom.

True valour cannot long lie neglected. Soon was he courted by Don John de Austria into Flanders, where, in the action at Dunkirk, he far surpassed his former deeds, often forgetting that he was a prince, to shew himself a true soldier; such his hazarding his person, really worth ten thousand of them, to the great molestation of his true friends.

Since God, out of his infinite love to the English, hath safely returned this duke to his native country; where that he may long live, to be the joy and delight of the whole nation, I shall constantly beg of God in my daily devotions.

ELIZABETH, second daughter of king Charles the First and queen Mary, was born at Saint James's, anno 1635, on the 28th day of December. She proved a lady of parts above her age, the quickness of her mind making recompence for the weakness of her body. For the remainder of her life, I will hold my peace; and listen to my good friend Master John Buroughs,* thus expressing himself in a letter unto me:

"The Princess Elizabeth, with her brother Henry duke of Gloucester, being, by order of Parliament, to be removed to Carisbrook-castle in the Isle of Wight (where his most excellent majesty was lately a prisoner) were accordingly received by Mr. Anthony Mildmay, from the earl and countess of Leicester, at Penshurst in Kent; and began their unwilling journey on Friday, 9th of August, 1650. On the 16th of the same month, they were first lodged in Carisbrook-castle aforesaid.

* Now Clerk of Stationers-hall, then an attendant of the Lady.—F.

"The princess being of a melancholy temper (as affected above her age with the sad condition of her family) fell sick about the beginning of September following, and continued so for three or four days, having only the advice of doctor Bignall, a worthy and able physician of Newport. After very many rare ejaculatory expressions, abundantly demonstrating her unparalleled piety, to the eternal honour of her own memory, and the astonishment of those who waited on her, she took leave of the world on Sunday the eighth of the same September.

"Her body, being embalmed, was carefully disposed of in a coffin of lead, and on the four and twentieth of the said month, was brought (in a borrowed coach) from the Castle to the town of Newport, attended thither with her few late servants. At the end of the town the corpse was met and waited on by the mayor and aldermen thereof in their formalities to the church, where, about the middle of the east part of the chancel in Saint Thomas's chapel, her highness was interred in a small vault purposely made, with an inscription of the date of her death engraved on her coffin."

The hawks of Norway, where a winter's day is hardly an hour of clear light, are the swiftest of wing of any fowl under the firmament, nature teaching them to bestir themselves, to lengthen the shortness of the time with their swiftness. Such the active piety of this lady, improving the little life allotted her, "in running the way of God's commandments."

ANNE, third daughter to king Charles the First and queen Mary, was born at Saint James's, March 17, anno Domini 1637. She was a very pregnant lady above her age, and died in her infancy when not full four years old. Being minded by those about her to call upon God even when the pangs of death were upon her ;[*] "I am not able," saith she, "to say my long prayer (meaning the Lord's-prayer); but I will say my short one, Lighten mine eyes, O Lord, lest I sleep the sleep of death."[†] This done, the little lamb gave up the ghost.

KATHARINE, fourth daughter to king Charles the First and queen Mary, was born at White-hall (the queen-mother then being at Saint James's), and survived not above half an hour after her baptizing ; so that it is charity to mention her whose memory is likely to be lost, so short her continuance in this life, the rather, because her name is not entered, as it ought, into the register of Saint Martin's in the Fields ; as indeed none of the king's children, save Prince Charles, though they were born in that parish. And hereupon a story depends.

I am credibly informed that, at the birth of every child of the king born at White-hall or Saint James's, full five pounds

---

[*] Mistress Conant, a Rocker, to whom she spake it.—F.   [†] Psalm xiii. 3.

were ever faithfully paid to some unfaithful receivers thereof, to record the names of such children in the register of Saint Martin's. But the money being embezzled (we know by some, God knows by whom) no memorial is entered of them. Sad, that bounty should betray any to such baseness, and that which was intended to make them the more solemnly remembered, should occasion that they should be more silently forgotten!

Say not, Let the children of mean persons be written down in registers; kings' children are registers to themselves, or all England is a register to them; for sure I am, this common confidence hath been the cause that we have been so often at a loss about the nativities and other properties of those of royal extraction.

CHARLES STUART, son to the illustrious James Stuart duke of York, by Anne, daughter to the Right Honourable Edward Hide earl of Clarendon and lord chancellor of England and Frances his lady, descended of the ancient family of the Aylesburies, high-sheriffs for many years together of Bedford and Buckinghamshire, in the reign of king Edward the Second and Third,* was born at Worcester-house, 22d day of October 1660, and christened by the Right Reverend Father in God, Gilbert, lord bishop of London, his majesty, and George duke of Albemarle being his godfathers, and Mary the queen-mother his godmother; he was declared duke of Cambridge, a title which, to the great honour of that university, for these four hundred years, hath been only conferred either on foreign princes, or persons of the royal blood. This princely infant died May 5, 1661.

SAINTS.

Saint WULSY, being a man reputed when living (and reported when dead) of great virtue and innocency,† was, by Saint Dunstan, created the first abbot of Westminster, where he lived many years very exemplary for his conversation, until his death, which happened anno Domini 960. Then was his body buried in the same monastery; and the 26th day of September was kept by the citizens of London with great veneration of his miracle-working memory.

MARTYRS.

I meet with none in this city, and in my mean judgment it is most observable that London having two pages (as I may term them) attending it, viz. Westminster and Southwark, both joined to it in buildings, should be so different from it in condition; in London, we have no room to hold martyrs; in the other two, no martyrs to take up any room.

Inquiring the cause thereof, we find these three places (though

---

* See our list of " SHERIFFS," in that county.
† Matthew of Westminster, ad ann. Domini 958.

contiguous, not to say continued) in the reign of queen Mary under three several jurisdictions : London under bloody Bonner, who made havoc of all he could come at ; Southwark, under politic Gardiner, who took wit in his anger, of whom formerly ;* this Westminster under John Fecknam, abbot thereof with power episcopal, a man cruel to none, courteous and charitable to all who needed his help or liberality.

CONFESSORS.

Rain (which country people say goeth by planets) goeth by Providence. " I caused it to rain upon one city, and caused it not to rain upon another."† Persecution observeth the same method, ordered by the same power and pleasure. A shower of blood fell upon London, whilst Westminster, the next city, did escape ; so that I find neither martyr nor confessor therein. Meeting with none before, let us proceed to

PRELATES SINCE THE REFORMATION.

RICHARD NEILE was born in King's Street in this city, and was bred in St. John's College in Cambridge ; he was afterwards vicar of Cheshunt in the county of Hertford, presented thereunto by the honourable family of the Cecils. He was the first and last native of this city who became the dean, and so the supreme magistrate thereof. Through many bishoprics, of Coventry and Lichfield, Durham, and Winchester, he was at last preferred archbishop of York, being also privy councillor to king James and king Charles. He died anno Domini 1641.

JOHN WARNER, D.D. was born in the parish of Saint Clement Danes, within the precincts of this city ; bred in Magdalen College in Oxford ; at last preferred bishop of Rochester.‡

This worthy bishop, perceiving the want of a fixed font in the cathedral church of Canterbury, bestowed one upon it ; whether more curious or costly my author§ could not decide it, being both ways so excellent and exquisite ; a gift the more remarkable, because the first which hath been offered by any private hand to that church of later times.|| But I suspect now this font itself is washed away, in the deluge of our late wars, under the notion of superstition.

God hath given him a great estate, and a liberal heart to make use of it ; keeping good hospitality in the Christmas at Bromley. As he fed many poor, so he freed himself from much trouble ; being absent when the rest of the bishops subscribed their protest in Parliament, whereby he enjoyed liberty in the restraint of others of his order. He was an able and active advocate for episcopacy in the House of Lords, speaking for them as long

---

* See "Martyrs" in ... shire. † Amos iv. 7.
‡ So informed from his own mouth.—ED.
§ W. Somner, in the Antiquity of Canterbury, p. 181. || Idem, ibidem.

as he had any voice left him; and then willing to have made signs in their just defence, if it might have been permitted him.

But it is now high time for me to put out my candle, when day-light shines so bright; I mean to desist from charactering of persons who are so perfectly known to so many alive. I will only add, this eminent prelate hath since seen the happy restitution of his order, enjoying again his former dignity, who now is (and long may be) living, 1661.*

STATESMEN.

Sir FRANCIS BACON, Knight, youngest son to Sir Nicholas Bacon, lord keeper, was born in York House, anno 1560; for, being demanded his age by queen Elizabeth, he returned, "that he was two years younger than her majesty's reign." He was bred in Trinity College in Cambridge, and there first fell into a dislike of Aristotle's Philosophy, as barren and jejune, enabling some to dispute, more to wrangle, few to find out truth, and none, if confining themselves to his principles.

Hence it was that afterwards he traded so largely in experiments; so that, as Socrates is said to be the first who stooped towering speculations into practical morality, Sir Francis was one of the first who reduced notional to real and scientifical philosophy.

He was afterwards bred in Gray's Inn, in the study of our municipal law, attaining to great eminency, but no preferment therein, during the reign of queen Elizabeth; imputable to the envy of a great person, who hindered his rising, for fear to be hindered by him if risen, and eclipsed in his own profession. Thus the strongest wing of merit cannot mount, if a stronger weight of malice doth depress it. Yet was he even then favourite to a favourite, I mean the earl of Essex, and more true to him than the earl was to himself: for, finding him to prefer destructive before displeasing counsel, Sir Francis fairly forsook not his person (whom his pity attended to the grave) but practices; and herein was not the worse friend for being the better subject.

By king James he was made his solicitor, and afterwards his attorney (then privileged, contrary to custom, to sit a member *in Dom. Com.*); and at last lord chancellor of England.† His abilities were a clear confutation of two vulgar errors (libels on learned men): first, that judgment, wit, fancy, and memory, cannot eminently be in conjunction in the same person; whereas our knight was a rich cabinet, filled with all four, besides a golden key to open it, Elocution. Secondly, "That he who is something in all is nothing in any one art;" whereas he was singular *in singulis*, and, being in-at-all, came off with credit.

Such who condemn him for pride, if in his place, with the

---

* He died in 1666.—ED.   † See his life written by Dr. Rawleigh.

fifth part of his parts, had been ten times prouder themselves. He had been a better master if he had been a worse, being too bountiful to his servants, and either too confident of their honesty, or too conniving at their falsehood. The story is told to his advantage, that he had two servants, one in all causes patron to the plaintiff (whom his charity presumed always injured), the other to the defendant (pitying him as compelled to law); but taking bribes of both, with this condition, to restore the money received if the cause went against them. Their lord, ignorant hereof, always did impartial justice; whilst his men (making people pay for what was given them) by compact shared the money betwixt them, which cost their master the loss of his office.

Leading a private life, he much delighted to study in the shade of solitariness; and many useful discoveries in nature were made by him, so that he may be said to have left nothing to his executors, and *all* to his heirs, under which notion the learned of all ages may be beheld. His vast bounty to such who brought him presents from great persons occasioned his want afterwards, who, in rewarding them, so remembered that he had been lord chancellor, that he forgot that he was but the lord Verulam.

A Viscounty that began ended in him dying issueless; it being remarkable, that though we have had two earls (of several families)* of Saint Alban's; yet was there no Lord Verulam, as if it were reserved for that ancient Roman colony to be buried in its own reverend ruins and in this peerless lord's everlasting memory, much admired by English, more by outlandish men; distance diminishing his faults to be invisible to foreign eyes, whilst we behold his affections abated with his failings.

He died, anno Domini 1626, in the house of the Earl of Arundel at Highgate, and was buried in St. Michael's church in St. Alban's, Master Mutis his grateful servant erecting a monument for him. Since I have read that, his grave being occasionally opened, his skull (the relic of civil veneration) was by one King, a doctor of physic, made the object of scorn and contempt; but he, who then derided the dead, is since become the laughing-stock of the living.

WRITERS.

Sulcard of Westminster was an Englishman by birth, bred a Benedictine monk. He was one of an excellent wit, meek disposition, candid behaviour, and in great esteem with king Edward the Confessor.† What progress he made in learning, may easily be collected from what is recorded in an old manuscript; " In Westmonasterio vixerunt simul Abbas Ead-

---

* Lord Burgh of Ireland, and Lord Henry Jermyn.
† Bale, de Scriptoribus Britannicis, Cent. ii. num. 55

winus et Sulchardus Cœnobita; sed Sulchardus doctrinâ major erat." He flourished anno Domini 1070, under king William the Conqueror.

GILBERT of WESTMINSTER, bred first monk, then abbot thereof. He gave himself to the study of human learning, then of divinity, and, through the guidance of Anselme archbishop of Canterbury, attained to great knowledge in the Scriptures. Afterwards he studied in France, visited Rome, in his return from whence he is reported to have had a disputation with a learned Jew, which afterwards he reduced into the form of a dialogue, and, making it public, he dedicated it to Saint Anselme. He died anno 1117, and was buried in Westminster.

MATTHEW of WESTMINSTER was bred a monk therein, and as accomplished a scholar as any of his age. Observable is the grand difference betwixt our English history, as he found it, and as he left it. He found it, like Polyphemus when his eye was bored out, a big and bulky body, but blind. Memorable actions were either presented without any date, which little informed, or too many dates, which more distracted, the reader. Our Matthew reduced such confused sounds to an articulate and intelligible voice, regulating them by a double directory of time, viz. the beginnings and deaths of all the kings of England and archbishops of Canterbury. He wrote one history from the beginning of the world to Christ; a second, from Christ's Nativity to the Norman Conquest; a third, from thence to the beginning of king Edward the Second, augmenting it afterwards with the addition of his life, and king Edward the Third's. He named his book " Flores Historiarum ; " and if sometimes (for it is but seldom) he presenteth a flower less fragrant, or blasted bud, the judicious reader is not tied to take what he tenders, but may select for his own ease a nosegay of the choicest flowers thereof. He died about the year 1368.

SINCE THE REFORMATION.

BENJAMIN JONSON was born in this city. Though I cannot, with all my industrious inquiry, find him in his cradle, I can fetch him from his long coats. When a little child, he lived in Harts-horn-lane near Charing-cross, where his mother married a bricklayer for her second husband.

He was first bred in a private school in Saint Martin's church; then in Westminster school; witness his own epigram;*

> " Camden, most reverend head, to whom I owe
> All that I am in arts, all that I know;

* Epigram 14.

How nothing's that to whom my country owes
The great renown and name wherewith she goes," &c.

He was statutably admitted into Saint John's College in Cambridge (as many years after incorporated an honorary member of Christ Church in Oxford) where he continued but few weeks for want of further maintenance, being fain to return to the trade of his father-in-law. And let them blush not that have, but those who have not, a lawful calling. He helped in the new structure of Lincoln's-Inn, when, having a trowel in his hand, he had a book in his pocket.

Some gentlemen, pitying that his parts should be buried under the rubbish of so mean a calling, did by their bounty manumise him freely to follow his own ingenious inclinations. Indeed his parts were not so ready to run of themselves, as able to answer the spur; so that it may be truly said of him, that he had an elaborate wit wrought out by his own industry. He would sit silent in a learned company, and suck in (besides wine) their several humours into his observation. What was *ore* in others, he was able to refine to himself.

He was paramount in the dramatic part of poetry, and taught the stage an exact conformity to the laws of comedians. His comedies were above the *volge* (which are only tickled with downright obscenity), and took not so well at the first stroke as at the rebound, when beheld the second time; yea, they will endure reading, and that with due commendation, so long as either ingenuity or learning are fashionable in our nation. If his later be not so spriteful and vigorous as his first pieces, all that are old will, and all that desire to be old should, excuse him therein.

He was not very happy in his children, and most happy in those which died first, though none lived to survive him. This he bestowed as part of an epitaph on his eldest son, dying in infancy:

" Rest in soft peace; and, ask'd, say here doth lye,
Ben Jonson his best piece of poetry." *

He died anno Domini 1638; and was buried about the belfry, in the abbey church at Westminster.

MASTERS OF MUSIC.

[S.N.] CHRISTOPHER TYE, doctor of music, flourished in the reign of king Henry the Eighth and king Edward the Sixth, to whom he was one of the gentlemen of their chapel, and probably the organist. Music, which received a grievous wound in England at the dissolution of abbeys, was much beholding to him for her recovery; such his excellent skill and piety, that he kept it up in credit at court and in all cathedrals

* Epigram 45.

during his life. He translated the Acts of the Apostles into verse; and let us take a taste of his poetry:

" In the former treatise to thee
    Dear friend Theophilus ;
I have written the veritie
    Of the Lord Christ Jesus.

Which he to do, and eke to teach,
    Began until the day
In which the Spirit up did him fetch,
    To dwell above for aye.

After that he had the power to do
    Even by the Holy Ghost ;
Commandements then he gave unto
    His chosen least and most.

To whom also himself did shew
    From death thus to revive :
By tokens plain unto his few
    Even forty days alive.

Speaking of God's kingdome with heart,
    Chusing together them ;
Commanding them not to depart
    From that Jerusalem.

But still to wait on the promise
    Of his Father the Lord ;
Of which ye have heard me ere this
    Unto you make record."

Pass we now from this poetry (being music in *words*) to his music (being poetry in *sounds*), who set an excellent composition of music of four parts to the several chapters of his aforementioned poetry, dedicating the same to king Edward the Sixth, a little before the death of that good prince, and printed it anno Domini 1553. He also did compose many excellent services and anthems of four and five parts, which were used in cathedrals many years after his death, the certain date whereof I cannot attain.

JOHN DOULAND was (as I have most cause to believe) born in this city; sure I am he had his longest life and best livelihood therein, being servant in the chapel to queen Elizabeth and king James. He was the rarest musician that his age did behold; having travelled beyond the seas, and compounded English with foreign skill in that faculty, it is questionable whether he excelled in vocal or instrumental music. A cheerful person he was, passing his days in lawful merriment, truly answering the anagram made of him,* " JOHANNES DOULANDUS," (*annos ludendo hausi.*)

Christian the Fourth, king of Denmark, coming over into England, requested him of king James ; who unwillingly willing parted with him. Many years he lived (as I am credibly informed) in the Danish court, in great favour and plenty, generally employed to entertain such English persons of quality as came thither. I cannot confidently avouch his death at Denmark, but believe it more probably than their assertion who report him returned and dying in England about the year 1615.

BENEFACTORS TO THE PUBLIC.

JAMES PALMER, B.D. was born in this city, and bred in Magdalen College in Cambridge. The company of Carpenters in London gave him an exhibition towards his maintenance there,

* By Ralph Sadler, Esq. of Standon in Hertfordshire, who was with him at Copenhagen.—F.

or lent it him rather; for, since, his bounty hath repaid them the principal with plentiful consideration. He was afterwards for many years the constant preacher of Saint Bridget's in Fleet-street, the only church preferment he enjoyed. I perceive thus craft and cruelty may raise a quick and great, but plain frugality (especially if vivacious) will advance a better and surer, estate. Though sequestered in these times, what he had formerly gained in his place he hath since bestowed in building and endowing, over against the new chapel in Westminster, a fair alms-house for twelve poor people. Besides this, many and great have his gifts been to ministers' poor widows. And wonder not, reader, if they be unknown to me, which were unknown to his own left hand.—All this he did in his life-time. Oh, it giveth the best light, when one carrieth his lanthorn before him! The surest way that one's will shall be performed, is to see it performed. Yea, I may say that his poor people in his almshouse are in some sort provided for, not only from head to foot, but also from body to soul, he constantly preaching to them twice a week. He died anno 1659.

MEMORABLE PERSONS.

[S. N.] EDMOND DOUBLEDAY, Esquire, was of a tall and proper person, and lived in this city. Nor had this large case a little jewel, this long body a lazy soul, whose activity and valour was adequate to his strength and greatness, whereof he gave this eminent testimony.

When Sir Thomas Knevet was sent, November 4, 1605, by king James, to search the cellar beneath the Parliament-house, with very few, for the more privacy, to attend him, he took Master Doubleday with him. Here they found Guy Faux, with his dark-lanthorn, in the dead of the night, providing for the death of many the next morning. He was newly come out of the Devil's Closet (so I may fitly term the inward room where the powder lay, and the train was to be laid) into the outward part of the cellar. Faux beginning to bustle, Master Doubleday instantly ordered him at his pleasure, up with his heels, and there with the traitor lay the treason flat along the floor, by God's goodness detected, defeated. Faux vowed (and, though he was a false traitor, herein I do believe him) that, had he been in the inner room, he would have blown up himself and all the company therein. Thus it is pleasant music to hear disarmed malice threaten, when it cannot strike. Master Doubleday lived many years after, deservedly loved and respected; and died about the year of our Lord 1618.

THE FAREWELL.

Seeing the well-being (yea being) of this city consisteth in the king's court and in the courts of justice, I congratulate the happy return of the one, praying for the long continuance of the other; yea, may the lawyers in Westminster-hall never again plead in their armour (as they did in the time of Wyat's rebellion), but in their peaceable gowns and legal formalities. Nor doth this wish only extend to the weal of Westminster, but all England; for no such dearth in a land, as what is caused from a drought of justice therein; for, if "judgment do not run down as waters, and righteousness as a mighty stream,"* injustice, like an ocean, will drown all with its inundation.

WORTHIES OF MIDDLESEX WHO HAVE FLOURISHED SINCE THE TIME OF FULLER.†

Jeremy BENTHAM, political writer; born in London 1747; died 1832.

Charles BOYLE, Earl of Orrery, statesman and scholar, antagonist of Bentley; born at Little Chelsea 1676; died 1731.

Isaac Hawkins BROWNE, Esq., M.P., F.R.S., essayist; born in London 1746; died 1818.

Right Hon. Geo. CANNING, illustrious statesman; born in London 1770; died 1827.

Edward Daniel CLARKE, LL.D., traveller and classical scholar; born 1767; died 1821.

George COLMAN, dramatic writer; born in London 1762; died 1836.

Charles COMBE, M.D., classical scholar, and editor of "Horace;" born in London 1743; died 1807.

Taylor COMBE, antiquary, classical scholar, and author; born 1774; died 1826.

Rev. J. J. CONYBEARE, antiquary and author; born 1779; died 1824.

Rev. Archdeacon COXE, historian, biographer, and traveller; born in London 1747; died 1828.

Daniel DANCER, miser; born near Harrow 1716; died 1794.

Daniel FINCH, third Earl of Nottingham, statesman and scholar; born at Kensington 1689; died 1730.

Henry FOX, Lord Holland, statesman, rival of Pitt Earl of Chatham; born at Chiswick 1705; died 1774.

Charles James FOX, son of the preceding, illustrious statesman and scholar; born 1748; died 1806.

Richard GOUGH, the modern Camden; born 1735; died at Enfield 1809.

Joseph GRIMALDI, clown; born in London 1779; died 1837.

* Amos v. 24.

† Many distinguished individuals, who from their long connexion with the Metropolis might, without any impropriety, be classed under this head, will be found in the respective counties which gave them birth.—ED.

Edmund HALLEY, astronomer and mathematician; born at Haggerston 1656; died 1741.

William HAWES, physician, founder of the Humane Society; born at Islington 1753; died 1808.

Richard HEBER, M.P., classical scholar and celebrated bibliomaniac; born in Westminster 1773; died 1834.

Nathaniel HODGES, physician, historian of the plague; born at Kensington; died 1684.

John Gale JONES, political orator; born in London 1771; died 1838.

John HOWARD, philanthropist, visitor of prisons; born at Hackney 1726; died 1790.

Edmund KEAN, great tragic actor; born in London 1787; died 1832.

Dr. William KING, principal of St. Mary's Hall, Oxford, politician, poet, and scholar; born at Stepney 1663; died 1712.

Edward LOVIBOND, poet, author of " Tears of Old May Day;" born near Hampton; died 1775.

Charles MATTHEWS, comedian; born in London 1770; died 1835.

Richard MEAD, physician and author; born at Stepney 1673; died 1754.

Rev. Dr. MILNER, F.S.A., catholic divine and learned author; born in London 1752; died 1826.

Sir George NARES, judge; born at Stanwell 1716.

James NARES, musician and composer; born at Stanwell 1715; died 1783.

Joseph NOLLEKENS, eminent sculptor; born in London 1737; died 1823.

Richard NORTHALL, archbishop of Dublin; born at Northall; died 1397.

William PAGE, divine, schoolmaster, and translator; born at Harrow; died 1663.

Charles PRATT, first Earl Camden, lord chancellor; born at Kensington 1714; died 1794.

Sir Thomas Stamford RAFFLES, great Oriental scholar; born at sea 1781; died 1826.

Stephen Peter RIGAUD, Savilian professor of Astronomy at Oxford, &c.; born at Richmond 1774; died 1839.

Sir Samuel ROMILLY, M.P., celebrated advocate and statesman; born in 1757; died 1818.

William SHARPE, eminent engraver; born in London 1749; died 1824.

George STEEVENS, commentator on Shakspeare; born at Poplar 1735; died 1809.

Charles Alfred STOTHARD, historical draughtsman and painter; born in London 1787; killed 1821.

Brook TAYLOR, author on Linear Perspective; born at Edmonton 1685; died 1731.

Thomas TAYLOR, the Platonist, metaphysician, and Greek translator; born in London 1758; died 1836.

Mrs. THICKNESSE, accomplished authoress of " The School of Fashion," &c.; born in London 1737; died 1824.

Richard WESTALL, R.A., historical painter; born in London; died 1837.

Robert WOODCOCK, painter of sea-pieces; born at Chelsea 1690.

₊ Of Middlesex, there has been no general historian; and indeed, from the ever fluctuating nature of property and constant change of families, in this populous and wealthy county, it is almost impossible there could have been a regular topographical history.   So early as 1593, however, the " Speculum Britanniæ," (the first Part containing an historical and chorographical Description of Middlesex) was brought out; and in 1663, the " Visitation of Middlesex " was published by Ryley and Dethick. Since that period innumerable histories, local descriptions, and illustrative views of London, Westminster, and places adjoining, have made their appearance.   " Of London, strictly speaking (says Mr. John Nichols) there is no topographical description; and it is almost impossible that there should be. Independent of the numerous chartered companies, almost each of which possesses a considerable share of property in the city, the number of freeholders is very large. Yet there are few or no great families, through whom the descent of property can be regularly traced, as in the surrounding counties; where in every parish the manor or manors have passed, if not from father to son, at least by purchase from one family to another."—The .earliest description of London was written in Latin by Fitz-Stephen, which has been more than once translated into English, and forms the basis of every subsequent history. In its Ecclesiastical history and antiquities, London has been fortunate. In addition to the laudable endeavours of John Stow, to which Dr. Fuller acknowledges frequent obligations, may be added the still more accurate researches of his continuator, Mr. Strype; Howel's " Londinopolis;" the " New View of London," 1708;. Newcourt's Repertorium, 1708; Warburton's London and Middlesex, 1749; the Survey of London by Seymour; besides the Works of Maitland, Entick, Nousthouck, Pennant, Malcolm, &c.

The histories of the city of Westminster have in general been included in the many volumes descriptive of London. But there are several separate publications, particularly on the antiquities of its beautiful and magnificent Abbey Church. Of these, the first printed account is by Camden, in 1600; followed by Taylor in 1684; by Dart in 1722; by Widmore in 1731 and 1743; and by Smith in 1807.

In addition to the preceding, the following list of Works, illustrative of the history of the County and the Metropolis, may be enumerated in alphabetical order:—

Bayley's Tower of London. Brayley's Londinia. Bruce's Account of Savoy Palace.   Charities of London, from Report of Parliamentary Commissioners.   Colnaghi's Views of London and Westminster, by Watts, Angus, and Medland, with Descriptions.   Denham's Account of St. Dunstan's in the West. Ducarel's History of St. Katharine's.   Dugdale's St. Paul's, by Ellis. Ecclesiastical Topography, or History of 100 Churches near London.   Ellis's History of Shoreditch, 1798. Faulkner's History of Fulham, of Kensington, and of Chelsea. Fisher's Plates to illustrate Lysons's Environs. Gwilt's St. Paul's Cathedral. Gwynne's London Improved. Ironside's History of Twickenham, 1797. Kempe's Account of St. Martin-le-Grand. Lysons's Environs of London, 1795; and also an Account of various Parishes in the County of Middlesex, 1800. Middleton's Agriculture of Middlesex, 1807. Nash's Views to illustrate Pennant's London. Nelson's History and Antiquities of Islington. New View of London, 1701. Nichols's Account of Guildhall, the History of Canonbury, and Account of St. Katharine's Hospital, &c. Park's Hampstead. Dr. Wm. Robinson's Histories of Edmonton, of Tottenham, of Stoke Newington, and of Enfield. Smith's History of Marylebone, of Westminster, and Ancient Topography of London. Topham's St. Stephen's Chapel. Wilkinson's Account of St. Martin Outwich. Wilson's Christ's Hospital, &c. &c. —ED.

MONMOUTHSHIRE.

MONMOUTHSHIRE.—I may fitly call this an English-Welsh county;* for, though it lie west of Severn, yea of Wye itself, and though the Welsh be the common language thereof, yet it doth wear a double badge of English relation. First, whereas formerly all Welch counties sent but one knight to the Parliament, this had the privilege of two, conformable to the shires of England. Secondly, it is not subject to the Welch jurisdiction; but such itinerant judges as go Oxford Circuit have this county within the compass of their commission.

MANUFACTURES.

CAPS.

These were the most ancient, general, warm, and profitable coverings of men's heads in this Island. It is worth our pains to observe the tenderness of our kings to preserve the trade of cap-making, and what long and strong struggling our state had to keep up the using thereof, so many thousands of people being maintained thereby in the land,† especially before the invention of Fulling-mills, all caps before that time being wrought, beaten, and thickened by the hands and feet of men, till those mills, as they eased many of their labour, ousted more of their livelihood. Thus ingenious inventions conducing to the compendious making of commodities, though profitable to private persons, may not always be gainful to the public, to which what employs most is most advantageous; as capping anciently set fifteen distinct callings on work, as they are reckoned up in the statute :‡

1. Carders; 2. Spinners; 3. Knitters; 4. Parters of Wool; 5. Forcers; 6. Thickers; 7. Dressers; 8. Walkers; 9. Dyers; 10. Battelers; 11. Shearers; 12. Pressers; 13. Edgers; 14. Liners; 15. Band-makers; and other exercises.

---

* In Dr. Fuller's time, Monmouthshire was considered a Welch county. It is now an English one.—Ed.

† Eight thousand in London, Stat. 13 Elizabeth, cap. 19 ; and probably twice as many in the land beside.

‡ 13 Elizabeth, cap, 19.

No wonder then if so many statutes were enacted in Parliaments, to encourage this handicraft, as by the ensuing catalogue will appear.

1. Anno 22 Edward IV. cap. 5. "That none thicken any cap or bonnet in any fulling-mill, upon pain to forfeit forty shillings."

2. Anno 3 Henry VIII. cap. 15. "That no caps or hats ready wrought should be brought from beyond the seas, upon the forfeiture of forty shillings." Yet because, notwithstanding this statute, some still presumed to import foreign wares, it was enacted,

3. Anno 21 Henry VIII. cap 9. "That such outlandish hats should be sold at such low prices as are specified in the statute;" merely to deter the merchant from importing them, because such their cheapness that they would turn to no account.

4. Anno 7 Edward VI. cap. 8. Fulling-mills beginning now to take footing in England, the statute made 22 Edward IV. was revived, to stand and remain in full force, strength, and effect.

5. Anno 8 Elizabeth, cap. 11. Fulling-mills still finding many to favour them, the pains and profit of cap-making was equally divided betwixt the mills and the cap-makers; it being enacted, "That no cap should be thickened or fulled in any mill, until the same had first been well scoured and closed upon the bank, and half footed at least upon the foot-stock."

6. Lastly, to keep up the usage of caps, it was enacted, the 13 Eliz. cap. 19, "That they should be worn by all persons (some of worship and quality excepted) on sabbath and holidays, on the pain of forfeiting ten groats for omission thereof.

But it seems nothing but hats would fit the heads (or humour rather) of the English, as fancied by them fitter to fence their fair faces from the injury of wind and weather; so that, in the 39th of queen Elizabeth, this statute was repealed. Yea, the cap, accounted by the Romans an emblem of liberty, is esteemed by the English (except falconers and hunters) a badge of servitude, though very useful in themselves, and the ensign of constancy, because not discomposed, but retaining their fashion, in what form soever they be crowded.

The best caps were formerly made at Monmouth, where the Cappers' chapel doth still remain, being better carved and gilded than any other part of the church. But, on the occasion of a great plague happening in this town, the trade was some years since removed hence to Beaudly in Worcestershire, yet so that they are called Monmouth caps unto this day. Thus this town retains, though not the profit, the credit of capping; and seeing the child still keeps the mother's name, there is some hope in due time she may return unto her.

All I will add is this: if at this day the phrase of "wearing a Monmouth cap" be taken in a bad acception, I hope the inha-

bitants of that town will endeavour to disprove the occasion thereof.

PRINCES.

HENRY of MONMOUTH,* so called from that well-known town wherein he was born. He was son to king Henry the Fourth (by Mary, one of the daughters and heirs of Humfrey de Bohun earl of Hereford, and) whom he succeeded on the throne (being the fifth of that name); and began his reign March 20, anno 1413.

He cannot be excused from extravagancies in his youth, seeing the king his father expelled him his council (substituting his younger brother the duke of Clarence president in his stead) for the same. Yet, as those bodies prove most healthful, which break out in their youth, so was his soul the sounder for venting itself in its younger days; for no sooner was his father dead, but he reclaimed himself, and became a glory to his country, and a constant terror to his enemies. Yea, he banished all his idle companions from court, allowing them a competency for their subsistence.

When the lord chief justice (who had secured him when prince for striking him for the commitment of some of his lewd companions) begged his pardon for the same, he not only forgave him, but rewarded his justice, for distributing it without fear or partiality.

In his reign a supplication was preferred, that the temporal lands given to pious uses, but abusively spent, might have been seized to the king. This was wisely awarded by Chichley archbishop of Canterbury, by putting the king on the design of recovering France. Yea, this king, by his valour, reduced Charles the Sixth king of France to such a condition, that he in a manner resigned his kingdom into his hand.

And here the Frenchmen found him as good (or rather worse) as his promise, which he made to the dauphin (who sent him a barrel of Paris tennis-balls), sending such English balls, that they proved to their great loss.

He died at Bois St. Vincent in France, the last day of August, anno 1422; and was brought over with great solemnity, and interred in Westminster Abbey.

SAINTS.

Saint AMPHIBALUS, a citizen of Carleon. See the Saints in HEREFORDSHIRE.

Saint AARON was a wealthy citizen of Carleon in this county, who, for the testimony of the Christian faith, was martyred under the tyrant emperor Dioclesian. By the way, we may ob-

---

* In the original edition, the name of Henry of Monmouth was here inadvertently omitted by Dr. Fuller, and inserted under RADNORSHIRE; but it is now given in its proper place.—ED.

serve the names of the three first British martyrs as to their language :

1. Alban, of Latin original : 2. Amphibalus, of Greek original : 3. Aaron, of Hebrew original.

It seems that the Christian Britons at the font quitted their native names as barbarous, and imposed on their children those of the learned languages. This Aaron was martyred, anno Domini 303.

Saint JULIUS.—It is pity to part so fast friends, both being citizens of Carleon. Yea, " they were lovely in their lives, and in their deaths they were not divided," both suffering martyrdom together; and therefore, like Philip and Jacob, one day is assigned to their memories in the Calendar.

Nor must I forget how Carleon, the place of their abode, though now a small town, was once a great city, stretching so far on both sides of the river, that Saint Julian's (a house of late of Sir William Herbert's) was sometime within the city, though now about a mile south-west thereof, being a church dedicated anciently to the memory of this Saint Julius.*

CARDINALS.

GEFFERY of MONMOUTH is by some† very firmly avouched to have been created a Cardinal; but by what Pope, and with what title, uncertain ; but my worthy author justly suspecteth the truth hereof; alleging that popes in that age advanced few foreigners at so great a distance to that title, except their merits to the see of Rome (which appears not to this Jeffery) were very great.‡ Let me add, that it is improbable so much honour should be done unto him whilst living, who was so solemnly disgraced after his death; whose books (extant in his life) were afterwards by the court of Rome publicly prohibited. See him, therefore, in this shire, under the title of WRITERS.

JOHN of MONMOUTH, so called from the place of his nativity, D. D. and canon of Lincoln, was chosen, anno 1296, bishop of Llandaff, the manner whereof was remarkable ; for, when Robert Kilwarby complained to Pope Celestine, how that cathedral had been for seven years without a bishop (caused either by the troublesomness of those times, or the *exility* of revenue thereof,) his Holiness remitted his election wholly to the discretion of this archbishop, to confer that vacant see on whomsoever he pleased. The archbishop, knowing all eyes intent on his integrity herein, resolved on a Welchman by his birth (as most proper for and acceptable in the place), and on one of merit for the function.

Both qualifications met in this John of Monmouth, as British

---

* Camden's Britannia, in Monmouthshire.　　† Cicaonius.
‡ Bishop Godwin, in the Catalogue of the Bishops of St. Asaph.

by his birth and alliance, and charactered to be " doctus et pius
theologus.* One of his successors in that bishopric acknowledgeth that he was "multimodis sedi suæ benefactor;" and
more particularly, that he procured the rectory of Newland, in
the Forest of Dean, to be appropriated thereunto.† But one
bishop [Anthony Kitchin by name] more *unlanded Llandaff* in
one, than all his predecessors endowed it in *four hundred* years.
This John dying April 8, 1323, was buried in Saint Mary's
chapel, whose epitaph in French is hardly legible at this day on
his marble monument.

WALTER CANTILUPE was son to William [the elder] lord
Cantilupe, whose prime residence was at Abergavenny in this
county. One of high birth, higher preferment (made, by king
Henry the Third, bishop of Worcester), and highest spirit. In
his time the Pope's legate came into England, and complained
of many clergymen keeping their livings against the canons, intending either to force such irregular incumbents into avoidance
(so to make room for the Pope's favourites) or else to compound for their continuance at his arbitrary price. But our
Walter would not yield to such extortion. Indeed he was one
of a keen nature; and his two-edged spirit did cut on both
sides, against—

The Pope.—Telling Rusland, his legate, coming hither 1255,
that he would prefer to be hanged on the gallows, rather than
ever consent to such expilation of the church.‡

The King.—Siding with the barons, he encouraged them in
their civil wars, promising heaven for their reward, though
this doctrine cost him an excommunication from the Pope.

Lying on his death-bed, he was touched with true remorse
for his disloyalty, and, upon his desire, obtained absolution.§
He died February the fifth, 1267, whom I behold as uncle unto
Thomas Cantilupe, the sainted bishop of Hereford.

SOLDIERS.

RICHARD de CLARE was born (as from all concentred pro-
babilities may be conjectured) at Strigule castle in this county,
and had the title of earl of Strigule and Pembroke. He was
otherwise surnamed Strong-bow, from drawing so strong a bow,
and had *brachia projectissima*, saith my author;|| though I can
hardly believe that *reacher*, which another writeth of him, that
" with the palms of his hands he could touch his knees, though
he stood upright."¶ More appliable to him is the expression

* Harpsfield, Histor. Eccl. Ang. p. 490.
† Godwin, in his Catalogue of Bishops in Llandaff.
‡ Antiq. Brit. anno prædicto. § Godwin, in the Bishops of Worcester.
|| Camden's Britannia, in this County.
¶ Mills, in his Catalogue of Honour, p. 1082.

of Tully, "Nihil egit levi brachio,"* being a person of effectual performance.

It happened that Mac Murugh lord of Leinster, in the year of our Lord 1167, being expelled his territory for several tyrannies, by the lords of Meath and Connaught, repaired to our king Henry the Second, and invited him to invade Ireland. But that politic king, fearing, if failing in success, to forfeit the reputation of his discretion, would not engage in the design; but permitted such subjects of his who had a mind "militare propriis stipendiis," to adventure themselves therein.

Amongst these Richard Strongbow was the principal, going over into Ireland with twelve hundred men, too great for an earl's train, yet too little for a general's army, to make a national invasion; yet so great his success, that in a short time he possessed himself of the ports of Leinster and Munster, with large lands belonging thereunto; insomuch that king Henry grew jealous of his greatness, remanded him home, and commanded him to surrender his acquests into his hands; which done, he received them again by re-grant from the king, save that Henry reserved the city of Dublin for himself.

This Strongbow is he who is commonly called "Domitor Hiberniæ," "the Tamer of Ireland;" though the natives thereof then, and many hundred years after, paid rather verbal submission, than real obedience, to our English kings. Yea, some of their great lords had both the power and title of kings in their respective territories; witness the preface in the commission whereby king Henry the Second made William Fitz Adelme his lieutenant of Ireland; "Archiepiscopis, Episcopis, Regibus, Comitibus, Baronibus, et omnibus fidelibus suis in Hibernià, salutem;" where kings are postposed to bishops, which speaketh them *royolets* by their own ambition, and by no solemn inauguration. This Earl Richard died at Dublin 1177; and lieth buried in Trinity Church therein.

Sir ROGER WILLIAMS, born of an ancient family at Penross in this county, was first a soldier of fortune under Duke D'Alva, and afterwards successively served queen Elizabeth; having no fault, save somewhat over-free and forward to fight.

When a Spanish captain challenged Sir John Norris to fight a single combat (which was beneath him to accept, because a general,) this Roger undertook the Don. And after they had fought some time (both armies beholding them) without any hurt, they pledged each other a deep draught of wine, and so friendly departed.†

Another time, at midnight, he assaulted the camp of the prince of Parma, nigh Venloe, slew some of the enemy,

---

* Epist. ad Atticum, lib. iv.   † Camden's Elizabeth, in anno 1581.

and pierced to the tent of the general, as highly blamed by some for rashness, as commended by others for his valour. He bravely defended Slufe, whilst any hope of help.*

WILLIAM HERBERT, earl of Pembroke, with Sir Richard Herbert his brother, were both undoubtedly born in this county; but whether or no at Ragland castle, is uncertain. Both valiant men, and as fast friends to king Edward the Fourth, as professed foes to Richard Nevil earl of Warwick. They gave the last and clearest evidence hereof in the battle of Banbury, where we find it reported, that these two leading the army of the Welch, with their pole-axes, twice made way through the battle of the northern-men (which sided with king Henry the Sixth) without any mortal wound.

There passeth a tradition in the noble family of the Herberts of Cherbury, that this Sir Richard their ancestor slew that day one hundred and forty men with his own hands ; which, if done in charging, some censure as an act of impossibility; if after a rout in an execution, as a deed of cruelty. But others defend both truth and courage therein, as done in passing and repassing through the army. Indeed guns were, and were not, in fashion in that age, used sometimes in sieges, but never in field service ; and next the gun, the pole-axe was the mortal weapon, especially in such a dead hand as this knight had, with which, " Quot icti, tot occisi." He is reported also to be of a giant's stature, the peg being extant in Montgomery castle, whereon he used to hang his hat at dinner, which no man of an ordinary height can reach with his hand at this day.

However, both these brave brethren, circumvented with the subtlety of their foes (odds at any time may be bet on the side of treachery against valour) were brought to Banbury, beheaded, and buried, the earl at Tintern, and Sir Richard at Abergavenny, in this county.

WRITERS.

JEFFREY of MONMOUTH was born in, and named from, Monmouth. He was also called ap Arthur, from his father (as I suppose) ; though others say, because he wrote so much of king Arthur † but, by the same proportion, Homer may be termed Achillides, and Virgil the son of Æneas. Yea, this Jeffrey, by an ancienter title, might be surnamed ap Bruit, whose story he asserteth. He translated and compiled the various British authors into one volume.

I am not so much moved at William Newbrough calling this his book *ridicula figmenta*, as that Giraldus Cambrensis, his countryman, and (as I may say) *con-sub-temporary*, should term it *fabulosam historian.* Indeed he hath many things from the British bards, which, though improbable, are not *ipso facto*

* Camden's Elizabeth, in anno 1586.
† Bale, de Scriptoribus Britannicis, Cent. ii. num. 86.

untrue.   We know Herodotus, nicknamed by some *Pater Fa-bularum,* is by others acknowledged to be *Pater Historiarum.*

The truth is, that both Novelants and Antiquaries must be content with many falsehoods; the one taking reports at the first rebound, before come to; the other raking them out of the dust, when past their perfection.

Others object, that he is too hyperbolical in praising his own country; a catching disease, seeing Livy mounts Italy to the skies, and all other authors respectively.   And why should that be mortal in our Monmouth, what is but venial in others? And if he be guilty in mistiming of actions, he is not the only historian without company in that particular.

However, on the occasion of the premises, his book is prohibited by His Holiness, whilst the lying legend is permitted to be read without control.   Thus Rome loves "questuosa, non inutilia figmenta," (falshoods whereby she may gain.)   Some conceive it to be his greatest fault, that he so praiseth the ancient church in Britain, making it independent from the see of Rome, before Austin the monk came hither.   One maketh him a cardinal, which is improbable; whilst it is more certain that he was bishop of St. Asaph, and flourished anno 1152.

THOMAS of MONMOUTH was probably born, certainly bred and brought up, in the chief town of this county.*   Nor doth it move me to the contrary, because Pits calls him an Englishman, Monmouth in that age being a frontier garrison, peopled with English inhabitants.

It happened at this time many Jews lived in Norwich, where their habitation was called Abraham's-hall, though therein not practising the piety of that worthy patriarch.†   He, out of conformity to God's command, sacrificed his one and only son; they, contrary to His will in his word, crucified the child of another, William by name.   His sepulchre‡ was afterwards famed for many miracles, whereof this Thomas wrote an history and dedicated it to William de Turbes, bishop of Norwich, though he lived above six score miles from the place of those strange performances; but probably the farther the better; "major è longinquo reverentia;" and miracles are safest reported, and soonest believed, at some competent distance. He flourished anno 1160, under king Henry the Second.

BENEFACTORS TO THE PUBLIC.

[AMP.] HENRY PLANTAGENET, first duke of Lancaster, was born in Monmouth castle, the chief seat of his barony. He is commonly surnamed *de torto collo,*§ or the wry-neck, and by others the good duke of Lancaster,‖ by which name we en-

---

* Bale, de Scriptoribus Britannicis, Cent. ii. num. 94.   † Idem, ibidem.
‡ The Shrine of this reputed Saint was in Lincoln Cathedral.—ED.
§ Speed's Chronicle, in the foundation of Bene't College.
‖ Mills,   Catalogue of Honour, in the Dukes of Lancaster.

title him, it being fitter to call men from what was to be praised, than what to be pitied in them; not from their natural defects, but moral perfections. His bounty commends him to our mention in this place, being head of the guild of Corpus-Christi in Cambridge, and the first founder of a college so called in that university. Indeed the land was but little he conferred thereon, but great the countenance of so eminent a person in procuring and settling their mortmain. He died in the year of our Lord 1361; and was buried in the collegiate church at Leicester, which he founded. Blanch, his only daughter which had issue, was married to John of Gaunt, duke of Lancaster.

SINCE THE REFORMATION.

WILLIAM JOHNES was a native of the town of Monmouth; a person whose estate was very considerable in several respects; viz. in—

1. His *emptiness;* being forced out of Monmouth, for not being able to pay ten groats: as the late recorder of that corporation* hath informed me. How had he been *undone,* if he had *not* been undone!

2. His *filling;* flying to London, he became first a porter, and then (his brains being better than his back) a factor; and going over to Hamburgh, by his industry and ingenuity made such a vent for Welch cottons, that what he found *drugs* at home, he left *dainties* beyond the sea.

3. His *re-funding,* founding a fair school-house in the place of his nativity, allowing fifty pounds yearly for the master, thirty for the usher, with one hundred marks salary to a lecturer; besides a stately alms-house for twenty poor folk, each of them having two rooms and a garden, with half a crown a week, besides other conveniences.

All which his benefactions, and many more,† he by will submitted to the oversight of the honourable company of Haberdashers in London, who at this day right worthily discharge their trust herein. He died anno Domini 16 . .

MEMORABLE PERSONS.

WILLIAM EVANS was born in this county, and may justly be accounted the giant of our age for his stature, being full two yards and a half in height: he was porter to king Charles the First, succeeding Walter Persons in his place, and exceeding him two inches in height, but far beneath him in an equal proportion of body; for he was not only what the Latins call *compernis,* knocking his knees together, and going out squalling with his feet, but also halted a little; yet made he a shift to dance in an antimask at court, where he drew little Jeffrey

---

* Henry Milbourne, Esq.
† Reckoned up in Stow's Survey of London, p. 103.

the dwarf out of his pocket, first to the wonder, then to the laughter, of the beholders. He died anno Domini 163. .

SHERIFFS.

This was made a shire by act of parliament in the 27th year of king Henry the Eighth, but it seems not solemnly settled till five years after.

HEN. VIII.

Anno	Name and Arms.	Place.
32	Car. Herbert, arm.	

Per pale, Az. and G. three lions rampant Arg.

33	Walt. Herbert, arm.	. *ut prius.*
34	Walt. ap Robert, arm.	
35	Hen. Lewis, arm.	
36	Re. ap Howel, arm.	

G. a lion rampant guardant Arg.

37	Joh. Hen. Lewis, arm.	
38	Anth. Welsh, arm.	

Az. six mullets, three, two, one, O.

EDW. VI.

1	Th. ap Morgan, arm. .	Lanterra².

O. a griffin segreant S.

2	Car. Herbert, mil. . .	*ut prius.*
3	Will. Morgan, mil. . .	*ut prius.*
4	Will. Herbert, arm. .	*ut prius.*
5	Walt. Herbert, arm. .	*ut prius.*
6	Will. Herbert, arm. .	*ut prius.*

MAR. REG.

1	Anth. Welsh, arm. . .	*ut prius.*
2	Walt. ap Robert.	
3	Will. Joh. Thomas.	
4	Roul. Morgan, arm. .	*ut prius.*
5	Hen. Lewis, arm.	
6	Tho. Morgan, mil. . .	*ut prius.*

ELIZ. REG.

1	Tho. Herbert, arm. . .	*ut prius.*
2	Geo. James, arm.	
3	Rog. Williams.	
4	Will. Herbert . . .	Colebrook.
5	Will. Herbert. . . .	J. Julian.
6	Will. Morgan, arm. . .	Tredegar.

Arms, *ut prius.*

7	Joh. Henry Kemis.

Vert, on a chevron O. three pheons S.

Anno   Name and Arms.

8   Wil. Joh. ap Roger   .   *ut prius.*
9   Will. Morgan, arm.
10   Christ. Welsh, arm.   .   *ut prius.*
11   Row. Morgan, arm. .   .   *ut prius.*
12   Will. Herbert   .   .   *ut prius.*
13   Tho. Herbert .   .   .   *ut prius,*
14   Will. Morgan, arm. .   .   *ut prius.*
15   Milo Morgan .   .   .   *ut prius.*
16   Row. Kemis, arm.   .   .   *ut prius,*
17   Christ. Welsh, arm.   .   *ut prius.*
18   Rich. Morgan .   .   .   *ut prius.*
19   Wil. Joh. ap Roger.
      Per pale, Az. and G. three lions rampant Arg.
20   Will. Lewes, arm.
21   Will. Herbert, mil.   .   .   *ut prius.*
22   Tho. Morgan, arm. .   .   *ut prius.*
23   Edw. Morgan, arm.   .   *ut prius.*
24   Edw. Morgan, arm. .   .   *ut prius.*
25   Mat. Herbert, arm. .   .   *ut prius.*
26   Will. Lewes, arm.   .   .   *ut prius,*
27   Rich. Morgan, arm. .   .   *ut prius.*
28   Jo. Jones, arm.
      S. a stag standing at gaze Arg. attired and unguled O.
29   Hen. Morgan   .   .   *ut prius.*
30   Hen. Herbert, arm. .   .   *ut prius.*
31   Nich. Herbert, arm.   .   *ut prius.*
32   Edw. Lewis, arm.   .   .   *ut prius.*
33   Wal. Vaughan, arm.
34   Row. Morgan, arm. .   .   *ut prius.*
35   Walt. Jones, arm.   .   .   *ut prius.*
36   Math. Herbert, arm.   .   *ut prius.*
37   Mat. Prichard, arm.
      S. a lion rampant Arg.
38   Andr. Morgan, arm.   .   *ut prius.*
39   Hen. Herbert, arm. .   .   *ut prius.*
      Will. Morgan, arm. .   .   *ut prius.*
40   Hen. Billingsley.
41   Rich. Kemis, arm.   .   .   *ut prius.*
42   Edw. Kemis, arm.   .   .   *ut prius.*
43   Edw. Morgan, arm. .   .   *ut prius.*
44   Hen. Morgan, arm. .   .   *ut prius.*
45   Joh. Gainsford, arm.

JACOB.

1   Joh. Gainsford, arm.
2   Row. Williams, arm.
3   Valen. Prichard, arm.
4   Will. Price, arm.

Anno   Name and Arms.

5 Walt. Mountague.
    Arg. three fusils in fess G. a border S.
6 Car. Jones, arm. . . . *ut prius.*
7 Hen. Lewis, arm.
8 Will. Ramlyns, arm.
9 Will. Morgan, mil. . . *ut prius.*
10 Rog. Batherne, arm.
11 Egid. Morgan, arm . . *ut prius.*
12 Will. Jones, arm. . . *ut prius.*
13 Tho. Vanne, arm.
14 Tho. Morgan, arm. . . *ut prius.*
15 Geo. Milbourn, arm.
    G. a chevron betwixt three escalops Arg.
16 Will. Hughes, arm.
17 Tho. Cocks, arm.
18 Walt. Aldey, arm.
19 Rob. Jones, arm. . . *ut prius.*
20 Will. Walter, arm.
21 David Lewis, arm.
22 Ed. Morgan. arm. . . *ut prius.*

CARO. I.

1 Car. Somerset, arm.
2 Car. Williams, mil.
3 Will. Keymis, arm. . . *ut prius.*
4 Will. Thomas, arm.
5 Joh. Walter, arm.
6 Will. Baker, arm.
7 Nich. Keymeis, arm. . *ut prius.*
8 Nich. Arnold, arm.
9 Lodo. Vanne, arm.
10 Geo. Milborne, arm. . *ut prius.*
11 Hen. Probert, arm.
12 Tho. Morgan, arm. . . *ut prius.*
13 Will. Herbert, arm. . . *ut prius.*
14 Nich. Moor, arm.

THE FAREWELL.

I understand that, in January 1607, part of this county which they call The Moor, sustained a great loss, by the breaking-in of the Severn sea, caused by a violent south-west wind, continuing for three days together:* I heartily desire the inhabitants thereof may for the future be secured from all such dangerous inundations (water being a good servant, but bad master) by His providence, who bindeth the sea in a girdle of sands, and saith to the waves thereof, Thus far shall ye go, and no further.†

---

* Camden's Britannia, in this County.   † Job xxxviii. 2.

WORTHIES OF MONMOUTHSHIRE WHO HAVE FLOURISHED
SINCE THE TIME OF FULLER,

Rev. Dr. John EVANS, Baptist divine; author of Sketch of all Denominations of the Christian World, &c.; born at Usk 1767; died 1827.

Charles GODWIN, antiquary, friend of Hutchins the historian of Dorset; born at Chepstow 1698.

William HOPKINS, divine, born at Monmouth 1706.

Edmund JONES, historian of his native village; born at Aberystwith.

Thomas LLYWELLYN, Baptist, editor of editions of the Welsh Bible; died 1796.

Sir Charles Hanbury WILLIAMS, M.P. poet, and diplomatist; born at Pontypool 1709; died 1759.

** This county has not been without its historians since the time of Fuller. In 1796, Mr. David Williams produced the History of Monmouthshire; and in 1801, the Rev. Wm. Coxe brought out his Historical Tour. Mr. Cha. Heath has also published an historical and descriptive Account of the Town of Monmouth (1804), besides descriptions of Raglan Castle, Tintern Abbey, Chepstow, &c. In 1831, the Rev. T. D. Fosbroke also produced an account of Raglan Castle.—ED.

NORFOLK.

NORFOLK hath the German Ocean on the north and east thereof; Suffolk, severed by the river Waveny, on the south side; Cambridgeshire, parted by the river Ouse, and a small part of Lincolnshire, on the west. It extendeth full fifty miles from east to west; but from north to south stretcheth not above thirty miles.

All England may be carved out of Norfolk, represented therein, not only to the kind but degree thereof. Here are fens and heaths, and light and deep, and sand and clay-ground, and meadows and pasture, and arable and woody, and (generally) woodless land; so grateful is this shire with the variety thereof. Thus, as in many men, though perchance this or that part may justly be cavilled at, yet all put together complete a proper person: so Norfolk, collectively taken, hath a sufficient result of pleasure and profit; that being supplied in one part which is defective in another.

This county hath the most churches of any in England (six hundred and sixty); and, though the poorest livings, yet (by some occult quality of their good husbandry, and God's blessing thereon) the richest clergymen. Nor can there be given a greater demonstration of the wealth and populousness of this county, than that in the late act for an assessment upon England, at the rate of sixty thousand pounds by the month, for three months, Norfolk, with the city of Norwich, is rated at three thousand two hundred sixty-six pounds, thirteen shillings, and fourpence, the highest proportion of any shire in England. And, though Norfolk hath little cause to please and less to pride itself in so dear purchased pre-eminence, yet it cannot but account it a credit to see itself not undervalued.

NATURAL COMMODITIES.

It shareth plentifully in all English commodities, and aboundeth with the best and most.

RABBITS.

These are an army of natural pioneers, whence men have learned " cuniculos agere," the art of undermining. They thrive best on barren ground, and grow fattest in the hardest frosts. Their flesh is fine and wholesome. If Scottish men tax our language as improper, and smile at our wing of a rabbit, let us laugh at their shoulder of a capon.

Their skins were formerly much used, when furs were in fashion; till of late our citizens, of Romans are turned Grecians, have laid down their grave gowns, and taken up their light cloaks; men generally disliking all habits, though emblems of honour, if also badges of age.

Their rich or silver-hair-skins, formerly so dear, are now levelled in prices with other colours; yea, are lower than black in estimation, because their wool is most used in making of hats, commonly (for the more credit) called half-beavers, though many of them hardly amount to the proportion of semi-demi-castors.

HERRINGS.

Great store and very good of these are caught nigh Yarmouth, where once every year, on the feast of Saint Michael, is a fair held for the sale of fish; and such the plenty of herrings there constantly vended, that incredible the sum which is raised thereby. Indeed, the fishing for herrings is a most gainful trade; fish, though contemptible in itself, considerable in its company, swimming in shoals, that what the whale hath in bigness the herring hath in number. (It may well mind such who excel in strength and valour, not to boast or be proud thereof, seeing the greatest courage may be soon pressed to death under unequal number.) Yea, red-herrings, in England mostly eaten for sauce to quicken the appetite, serve in Holland and elsewhere for food to satisfy hunger.

I will conclude the natural commodities of this county, with this memorable passage, which I have read in a modern author.*

" The lord F. W. assured me of a gentleman in Norfolk, that made above £10,000. sterling of a piece of ground not forty yards square; and yet there was neither mineral nor metal in it. He after told me, it was only a sort of fine clay, for the making a choice sort of earthenware; which some that knew it, seeing him dig up, discovered the value of it, and, sending it into Holland, received so much money for it."

My belief tireth in coming up to the top of this story, suspecting the addition of a cipher. But, if it were so, how much would it have enriched us, if those mock-China dishes had been made in England!

MANUFACTURES.

WORSTEDS.

These first took their name from Worstead†, a village in this

---

county. Originally it is nothing but woollen-thread spun very fine, and for the more strength twisted together. But oh! it surpasseth my skill to name the several stuffs (being worsted disguised with weaving and colouring) made thereof.

It argueth the usefulness and public profit of this commodity (which first found a general repute in England toward the end of the reign of king Henry the Sixth) that there are no fewer than fourteen statutes now in force in the well-ordering thereof to merchantable proof; and appointing which of them may, which may not, be transported. Not to speak of four wardens of worsted weavers to be chosen yearly within the city of Norwich, and other four out of the county of *Northfolk,* with their solemn oath, office, and authority.*

As for worsted stockings, they were first made in England, anno 1564, by William Rider,† an ingenious apprentice living against Saint Magnus church, at the foot of London bridge. This William chancing to see a pair of knit worsted stockings in the lodging of an Italian merchant, who had brought them from Mantua, borrowed them; and, making the like by that pattern, presented them to William earl of Pembroke, who first wore them in England.

PROVERBS.

"Norfolk dumplings."]

This cannot be verified of any dwarfish or diminutive stature of people in this county, being as tall of their bodies, and as tall of their arms too, I assure you, as any in England. But it relates to the fare they commonly feed on, so generally called. I wish, much good may it do them, and that their bodies thereby may be enabled for all natural, civil, and spiritual performances.

"Norfolk wiles."]

Such the skill of the common people hereof in our common law, wherein they are so versed, "ut si nihil sit litium, lites tamen ex juris apicibus serere callent.‡ If I must go to law, I wish them rather of my counsel than my adversary's; for whereas "pedibus ambulando" is accounted but a vexatious suit in other counties, here (where men are said to study law as following the plough-tail) some would persuade us, that they will enter an action for their neighbour's horse but looking over their hedge. Now, although we listen to this but as a jeer, yet give me leave to observe two parts in wiles; *wittiness,* which all must commend; *wickedness,* which all must condemn.

Sure I am, that in Scripture§ a *wile* always "malè audit," is taken in an evil sense, as wherein the simplicity of the dove is stung to death by the subtilty of the serpent. But no more

---

* Stat. 7 Edward IV. c. 3.   † Stow's Chronicles, p. 869.
‡ Camden's Britannia, in this County.
§ Numbers xxv. 18. Ephesians vi. 11. Joshua ix. 4.

hereof, lest Norfolk men commence a suit against me, though I verily believe many therein are of as peaceable dispositions as any in other places.

"A Yarmouth Capon."]

That is, a red-herring. No news for creatures to be thus disguised under other names; seeing critics by a Libyan bear, "sub pelle Libystidis ursæ," understand a lion, no bears being found in the land of Libya. And I believe few capons (save what have more fins than feathers) are bred in Yarmouth. But, to countenance this expression, I understand that the Italian friar (when disposed to eat flesh on Fridays) calls a capon "piscem è corte," (a fish out of the coop.)

"He is arrested by the Bailie of Marshland."]

The air of Marshland in this county is none of the wholesomest, being surrounded with the sea and fens on all sides. Hence it is that strangers coming hither are clapt on the back with an ague, which sometimes lasts them longer than a stuff suit. The best is, when such prisoners have paid the bailiff's fees and garnish, and with time and patience have weathered out the brunt of that disease, they become habited to the air of the country, and arrive in health at a very great age.

PRINCES.

I meet with no prince since the Conquest taking his first breath in this county; probably, because so remote from the principal place of royal residence.

PRELATES.

Gilbert Berkeley was born in this county;* but descended from the ancient barons of that name, as appeareth by his arms. He was consecrated bishop of Bath and Wells in the first of queen Elizabeth, and sate therein twenty-two years. He died of a lethargy, being eighty years of age, 1581; and is buried on the north-side of the communion-table of his own cathedral.

John Aylmer, brother to Sir Robert Aylmer, knight, was born, at Aylmer-hall, in the parish of Tilseley, in this county as his nearest surviving relations have informed me, from whom I have received the following information.

When he was but a child, going toward school, Henry Gray, duke of Suffolk, having some discourse with, took so much liking unto him, that, after he had been bred some years in the university of Cambridge, he made him his chaplain, and committed his daughter the lady Jane Gray to his tuition.

In the reign of queen Mary he fled over beyond sea, and was little less than miraculously saved from the searchers of the ship

* Godwin, in his Catalogue of the Bishops of Norwich.

by the ingenuity of a merchant, who put him into a great wine-but, which had a partition in the middle; so that master Aylmer sate in the hind part, whilst the searchers drank of the wine which they saw drawn out of the head or other end thereof.

Returning into England, he was made archdeacon of Lincoln, and at last bishop of London. He was happy in a meet yoke-fellow, having a gracious matron to his wife, by whom he had many children, and one son, to which archbishop Whitgift was godfather, and named him Tob-el; that is, The Lord is good, in memorial of a great deliverance bestowed on this child's mother; for, when she was cast out of her coach in London (by a mastiff casually seizing upon the horses), she received no harm at all, though very near to the time of her travail.

Bishop Aylmer was well learned in the languages, a ready disputant, and deep divine. He was eighteen years bishop of London; and, dying anno 1594, in the 73d year of his age, had this for part of his epitaph, which bishop Vaughan (sometime his chaplain, afterwards his successor) made upon him:

> *Ter senos annos præsul, semel exul, et idem*
> *Bis pugil in causâ religionis erat.*

> " Eighteen years bishop, and once banished hence,
> And twice a champion in the truth's defence."

I understand it thus: once a champion in suffering, when an exile for religion, and again in doing, when chosen one of the disputants at Westminster against the popish bishops *primo Elizabethæ;* except any expound it thus: once champion of the doctrine against papists, and afterwards against the discipline of the non-conformists, none more stoutly opposing, or more foully belibelled, of them.

God blessed him with a great estate, the main whereof he left unto Samuel Aylmer, his eldest son (high sheriff of Suffolk in the reign of king Charles). And amongst his youngest sons (all well provided for) Doctor Aylmer, rector of Haddam in Hertfordshire, was one of the most learned and reverend divines in his generation.

JOHN TOWERS was born in this county, bred fellow of Queen's College in Cambridge, and became chaplain to William earl of Northampton, who bestowed on him the benefice of Castle-Ashby in Northamptonshire. He was preferred dean, and at last bishop, of Peterborough.

He was a good actor when he was young, and a great sufferer when he was old; dying (about the year 1650) rich only in children and patience. Nothing but sin is a shame in itself; and poverty as poverty (especially since our Saviour hath sanctified it by suffering it) is no disgrace.

CAPITAL JUDGES, AND WRITERS ON THE LAW.

RALPH DE HENGHAM, so named from a fair market town in this county, was made lord chief justice of the King's Bench in Michaelmas Term in the second year of king Edward the First, when the king was newly returned from the Holy Land.* He sat sixteen years in that place (saving that one Winborne was, for a year or two, interposed†) : and, at the general purging and garbling of the judges, which happened in the 18th year of the aforesaid king : when all the judges (except two, John de Metingham and Elias de Bekingham) were cast out by the Parliament for their corruption, fined, banished, and imprisoned‡ ; then this Ralph was amerced in seven thousand marks, for bribery, and ejected out of his place.

Some will say, Let him wither in silence : why do you mention him amongst the Worthies of our nation ? I answer, Penitence is the second part of innocence ; and we find this Ralph, after his fine paid, made chief justice of the Common Pleas,§ " sub resipiscendi fiduciâ," (under the confidence generally conceived of his amendment.")‖ He died the next, being the 19th year of the reign of king Edward the First ;¶ he lies buried in the church of Saint Paul, where he hath, or had, this epitaph :

> " Per versus patet hos Anglorum quod jacet hic flos
> Legum, qui tuta dictavit vera statuta.
> Ex Hengham dictus Radulphus vir benedictus."

One must charitably believe that he played a good after-game of integrity ; and, if enjoying longer life, he would have given a clearer testimony thereof.

WILLIAM PASTON, Esq. son of Clement Paston, Esq. and Beatrix his wife (sister and heir to Geoffrey Sommerton, Esq.) was born at Paston, in this county. He was learned in the laws of this realm, and first was serjeant to king Henry the Sixth, and was after by him preferred second judge of the Common Pleas. I confess, having confined our catalogue to Capital Judges or Writers on the Law, he falls not under our method in the strictness thereof. But I appeal to the reader himself, whether he would not have been highly offended with me, had I in silence passed over a person so deserving his observation.

He was highly in favour with king Henry the Sixth, who allowed him, besides the ordinary salary assigned to other judges, one hundred and ten marks (reader, behold the standard of money in that age, and admire), with two gowns, to be taken

---

* Sir Henry Spelman, in the Glossary, page 416.
† Viz. anno Regis 10 et 13.   ‡ Tho. Walsingham, anno 1290.
§ 6 Sept. 1 Edward II. inter Pat. pars 1. memb. 21.
‖ This was in 29 Edw. I. 1301. He was again apointed o that office in 1308 by patent, dated 6th Sept. 1 Edw. II.—ED.
¶ He died in 1309, the second year of king Edward II.

yearly out of the Exchequer, as by the ensuing letters patent will appear:

"Henricus, Dei gratiâ, Rex Anglie et Francie, et Dominus Hibernie, Omnibus ad quos presentes litere pervenerint, Salutem : Sciatis quod de gratiâ nostrâ speciali, et ut dilectus et fidelis noster Willielmus Paston, unus justiciariorum nostrorum de Communi Banco statum suum decentius manutenere, et expensas, quas ipsum in officio predicto facere oportebit, sustinere valeat ; concessimus ei centum et decem marcas percipiendas singulis annis ad scaccarium nostrum, ad terminos Pasche et Sancti Michaelis per equales portiones ; et duas robas per annum percipiendas, unam videlicet cum *pellurâ* ad festum Natalis Domini, et aliam cum *limrâ* ad festum Pentecostes, ultra feodum consuetum, quamdiu ipsum stare contigerit in officio supradicto. In cujus rei testimonium, has literas nostras fieri fecimus patentes. Teste meipso, apud Westminst. xvº. die Octobris, anno nostri octavo."

What *pellura* is I understand *fur;* but what *limra* is (if rightly written) I would willingly learn from another, though some are confident it is taffeta.

I wonder the less at these noble favours conferred on the said William Paston, judge ; for I find him in grace with the two former kings, being made serjeant by king Henry the Fourth, and of his council for the duchy of Lancaster ; and in the reign of king Henry the Fifth, he was in such esteem with Sir John Fastolfe, knight, that he appointed him one of his feoffees, whom he enabled, by a writing under his hand, to recover debts from the executors of king Henry the Fifth.

This William Paston married Agnes, daughter and heir of Sir Edmund Berrey, by which marriage the Pastons * rightly quarter at this day the several coats of Hetherset, Wachesham, Craven, Gerbredge, Hemgrave, and Kerdeston : and received both advancement in blood and accession of estate. This said William Paston died at London, August 14, 1444 ; and lies buried in Norwich ; so that his corps, by a peculiar exception, do straggle from the sepulture of their ancestors, who from Wolstan de Paston (who three years after the Conquest came into England to William earl of Glandwill,†) were all interred at Paston. He left rich revenues to John Paston, esquire, his eldest son, who married Margaret daughter and heir of John Mautby ; and no mean estate to William his second surviving son, who married Anne daughter to Edmund duke of Somerset.

---

* Of this family was Robert Paston, created Baron Paston and Viscount Yarmouth, in 1673, and Earl of Yarmouth in 1679 ; titles which, in 1682, descended to his son William ; at whose death, in December 1732, without surviving issue, they became extinct.—Ed.

† Out of the book of William Botyner, fol. 20. sometime herald to Sir John Fastolfe, written in the reign of king Henry VI. and containing all the ancient gentry of this county.—F.

Sir EDWARD COKE, Knight, son of Robert Coke, esquire, and of Winefred Knightly his wife, was born at Mileham, in this county; bred, when ten years of age, at Norwich school, and thence removed to Trinity College in Cambridge. After four years' continuance there, he was admitted into Clifford's Inn, London, and the year following entered a student of the municipal law in the Inner Temple. Such his proficiency therein, that at the end of six years (exceeding early in that strict age) he was called to the bar, and soon after for three years chosen reader in Lyon's Inn. Here his learned lectures so spread forth his fame, that crowds of clients sued to him for his counsel, and his own suit was the sooner granted, when tendering his affections, in order to marriage, unto Briget daughter and coheir of John Paston, esquire.

She was afterwards his incomparable wife; whose portion, moderately estimated, *viis et modis*, amounted unto thirty thousand pounds, her virtues not falling under valuation; and she enriched her husband with ten children.

Then began preferment to press upon him; the city of Norwich choosing him recorder, the county of Norfolk their knight to parliament, the queen her speaker therein, as also successively her solicitor and attorney. King James honoured him with knighthood, and made him chief justice, first of the Common Pleas, then of the King's Bench. Thus, beginning on a good bottom left him by his father, marrying a wife of extraordinary wealth, having at the first great and gainful practice, afterwards many and profitable offices, being provident to choose good pennyworths in purchases, leading a thrifty life, living to a great age, during flourishing and peaceable times (born as much after the persecution under queen Mary, as dying before our civil wars), no wonder if he advanced a fair estate, so that all his sons might seem elder brethren, by the large possessions left unto them.

Some falsely character him a back-friend to the church and clergy, being a grand benefactor to the church of Norwich, who gratefully, under their public seal, honoured him with the ensuing testimony:

" Edwardus Coke, Armiger, sæpius et in multis difficillimis negotiis ecclesiæ nostræ auxiliatus est, et nuper eandem contra Templorum Helluones, qui dominia, maneria, et hæreditamenta nostra devorare sub titulo obscuro (*Concelatum* dicunt) sponte suâ nobis insciis, et sine mercede ullâ, legitimè tutatus est; atque eandem suam nostri defensionem, in perpetuam tantæ rei memoriam, quam posterorum (si opus fuerit), magnâ cum industriâ et scriptis redegit, et nostræ ecclesiæ donavit."

As for the many benefices in his own patronage, he freely gave them to worthy men; being wont to say, in his law-language, that he would have church-livings pass by livery and seisin, not bargain and sale.

Five sorts of people he used to fore-design to misery and poverty; chemists, monopolizers, councillors, promoters, and rhyming poets. For three things he would give God solemn thanks; that he never gave his body to physic, nor his heart to cruelty, nor his hand to corruption. In three things he did much applaud his own success; in his fair fortune with his wife, in his happy study of the laws, and in his free coming by all his offices, *nec prece, nec pretio ;* neither begging nor bribing for preferment.

His parts were admirable : he had a deep judgment, faithful memory, active fancy ; and the jewel of his mind was put into a fair case, a beautiful body, with a comely countenance; a case which he did wipe and keep clean, delighting in good clothes, well worn; and being wont to say, " that the outward neatness of our bodies might be a monitor of purity to our souls."

In his pleadings, discourse, and judgments, he declined all circumlocutions, usually saying, " The matter lies in a little room." In all places, callings, and jurisdictions, he commended modesty and sobriety within their boundaries, saying, " If a river swells beyond its banks, it loseth its own channel."

If any adverse party crossed him, he would patiently reply, " If another punisheth me, I will not punish myself." In the highest term of business, he made vacation to himself at his table ; and would never be persuaded privately to retract what he had publicly adjudged, professing, he was a judge in a court and not in a chamber. He was wont to say, " No wise man would do that in prosperity, whereof he should repent in adversity." He gave for his motto, " Prudens qui patiens;" and his practice was accordingly, especially after he fell into the disfavour of king James.

The cause hereof the reader may find in our English chronicles, whilst we behold how he employed himself when retired to a private life, when he did *frui suo infortunio,* and improved his loss to his advantage. He triumphed in his own innocency, that he had done nothing illegally, calling to mind the motto which he gave in his rings when made serjeant, " Lex est tutissima cassis," (the law is the safest helmet.)

And now he had leisure to peruse what formerly he had written, even thirty books, with his own hand ; most pleasing himself with a manual, which he called his " Vade mecum," from whence, at one view, he took a prospect of his life passed, having noted therein most remarkables. His most learned and laborious works on the laws will last to be admired by the judicious posterity whilst Fame hath a trumpet left her, and any breath to blow therein His judgment lately passed for an oracle in law; and if, since, the credit thereof hath causelessly been questioned, the wonder is not great. If the prophet himself, living in an incredulous age, found cause to complain,

" Who hath believed our report ?"* it need not seem strange, that our licentious times have afforded some to shake the authenticalness of the " reports " of any earthly judge.

He constantly had prayers said in his own house, and charitably relieved the poor with his constant alms. The foundation of Sutton's hospital (when indeed but a foundation) had been ruined before it was raised, and crushed by some courtiers in the hatching thereof, had not his great care preserved the same. The free-school at Thetford was supported in its being by his assistance; and he founded a school, on his own cost, at Godwick in this county.

It must not be forgotten, that Dr. Whitgift (afterwards archbishop of Canterbury) was his tutor, who sent unto his pupil, when the queen's attorney, a fair New Testament, with this message : " He had now studied common law enough, let him hereafter study the law of God."

Let me add to this, that when he was under a cloud at court, and ousted of his judge's place, the lands belonging to the church of Norwich, which formerly he had so industriously recovered and settled thereon, were again called into question, being begged by a peer, who shall pass nameless. Sir Edward desired him to desist, telling him, that otherwise he would put on his gown and cap, and come into Westminster-hall once again, and plead there in any court in justification of what he had done. He died at Stoke Poges in Buckinghamshire, on Wednesday the 3d of September, being the 83rd year of his age, whose last words were, " Thy kingdom come, Thy will be done."

Sir THOMAS RICHARDSON, Knight, was born at Mulbarton in this county, his father being minister thereof. He was bred in the study of our municipal law, and became the king's serjeant therein. Afterwards, on the 28th of November 1626, he was sworn chief justice of the Common Pleas, that place having been void ten months before.

But coming now to our own times, it is safest for me to break off. Virgil, I remember, put a period to his Eclogue with

——— *Et Hylax in limine latrat.*

——— ——— " We'll versify no more,
For do but hark, Hylax doth bark at th' entrance of the door."

Seeing many will be ready to carp, it is safest for me to be silent, whilst his brass monument on the south side of Westminster Abbey thus entertaineth the reader :

" Deo O. M.
Thomæ Richardsoni, Iceni, Equitis Aurati,
Humanum Depositum.
Ille Juris Municip. omnes gradus exantlavit;

* Isaiah liii. 1.

Conventus tertii ordinis ann. Jacobi Regis 21 et 22
Prolocutor extitit;
Fori Civilis (Communium Placitorum vocant)
Supremum Magistratum quinquennium gessit;
Ad summum tandem Primarii per Angliam Judicis Tribunal
A Rege Carolonevectus;
Expiravit anno ætatis 66, Salutis MDCXXXIIII.
Tho. Richardson fil. unicus, Eques Aur. Baro Scotiæ designatus,
Patri incomparabili posuit."

This judge married, for his second lady, Elizabeth Beaumont, the sister (as I take it) of Mary countess of Buckingham, and the relict of Sir John Ashburnham, knight. She was by king Charles created baroness of Craumount in Scotland, and (though issueless by the judge) the honour descended to his grandchild.

SOLDIERS.

ROBERT VENILE, Knight; one, I confess, whose name I never heard of, till meeting with this memorable note in a modern historian :*

"And here must not be forgotten, Robert Venile, knight, a Norfolk man; who when the Scots and English were ready to give battle, a certain stout champion of great stature, commonly called Tournboll, coming out of the Scots army, and challenging any English man to meet him in a single combate; this Robert Venile accepteth the challenge, and marching towards the champion, and meeting by the way a certain black mastife dog, which waited on the champion, he suddenly, with his sword, cut him off at the loyns, and afterwards did more to the champion himself, cutting his head from off his shoulders."

This put me with blushing enough (that one so eminent in himself should be altogether to me obscure) upon the inquiry after this valiant knight; but all my industry could not retrieve him in any author, so that he seems to me akin to those spirits who appear but once, and finally vanish away.

Sir OLIVER HINGHAM was born, richly landed, and buried in Hingham, an eminent market-town in this county. A right valiant man, whom king Edward the Third left governor of Aquitaine in France; an honourable but difficult place, being to make good a great country with a few men, against a fierce and numerous enemy. Yet he gave a good account of his trust. When the French lay before Bordeaux, the citizens thereof, to abuse the enemy's hopes, set open their gates, displaying the *golden lilies*, the French arms, on their towers, as if they were theirs. The French were no sooner securely entered, but brave Oliver, captain of this city, and warden of the whole country

* Sir Richard Baker's Chronicle, 3 Edward III. p. 181.

for king Edward, gave them such an entertainment, that they drank not so much claret-wine in the city, as they left blood behind them.* This happened in the thirteenth year of the reign of king Edward the Third.

This Sir Oliver lived many years after, and was made knight of the Garter; and lies buried at Hingham, under a fair tomb of freestone curiously wrought, with his resemblance in his coat-armour (having a crowned owl out of an ivy-bush for his crest†), lying upon a rock, beholding sun, moon, and stars (because a great traveller), all lively set forth in metal, with four and twenty mourners about his monument.

JOHN FASTOLFE, Knight, was a native of this county, as I have just cause to believe, though some have made him a Frenchman, merely because he was baron of Sineginle in France, on which account they may rob England of many other Worthies. He was a ward (and that the last) to John duke of Bedford, a sufficient evidence, to such who understand time and place, to prove him of English extraction. To avouch him by many arguments valiant, is to maintain that the sun is bright, though since the stage hath been over-bold with his memory, making him a thrasonical puff, and emblem of mock valour.

True it is, Sir John Oldcastle did first bear the brunt of the one, being made the make-sport in all plays for a coward. It is easily known out of what purse this black penny came; the Papists railing on him for a heretic, and therefore he must also be a coward, though indeed he was a man of arms, every inch of him, and as valiant as any in his age.

Now as I am glad that Sir John Oldcastle is put out, so I am sorry that Sir John Fastolfe is put in, to relieve his memory in this base service, to be the anvil for every dull wit to strike upon. Nor is our comedian excusable, by some alteration of his name, writing him Sir John Falstaff (and making him the property of pleasure for king Henry the Fifth, to abuse), seeing the vicinity of sounds entrench on the memory of that worthy knight, and few do heed the inconsiderable difference in spelling of their name. He was made knight of the Garter by king Henry the Sixth; and died about the second year of his reign.

Sir CLEMENT PASTON, Knight, fourth son to Sir William Paston, son to Sir John Paston, a famous soldier, and favourite to king Edward the Fourth (sent by him with the lord Scales to conduct the lady Margaret, the sister of the king, to her husband Charles duke of Burgundy), son to William Paston the judge, was born at Paston in this county. When a youth he was at the burning of Conquest in France; and afterwards by

---

* Holinshed and Stow.   † Weever's Funeral Monuments, p. 817.

king Henry the Eighth was made captain of one of his ships of war; and in a sea-fight took a French galley, and therein the admiral of France prisoner, called the Baron of Blancard, whom he brought into England, and kept at Castor nigh Yarmouth, till he had paid 7000 crowns for his ransom, besides the spoil of the galley, wherein he had a cup and two snakes of gold, which were the admiral's, and which Sir Clement used during his life on festivals, and at his death bequeathed them to his family for a monument. He received divers wounds, and was left for dead at Musselborough field in Scotland. When Sir Thomas Wyat, in the reign of queen Mary, was worsted at Ludgate, and desired, for the more civil usage, to render himself to a gentleman, he submitted himself (saith our historian) to Sir Clement Paston. He served at Newhaven, having command of some ships of queen Elizabeth; and was pensioner to two kings and two queens successively. So rare was his happiness, that he spent his old age honourably, quietly, and in good house-keeping in this county, where, at Oxnead, he built a goodly house for hospitality; and an hospital hard by, for six poor serving men, retainers to his name and family, allowing them convenient maintenance. He died anno Domini 1599; and lieth buried in a fair tomb in the church at Oxnead.

SEAMEN.

No county in England doth carry a *top* and *gallant* more high in maritime performances than Norfolk. Witness the proportion of Yarmouth alone in the ensuing catalogue of ships, used by king Edward the Third against Calais :—

The South-fleet ships 493; the mariners thereof 9630. The North-fleet ships 217; the mariners thereof 4521. Ships of London 25; mariners of London 662. Ships of Yarmouth 43; mariners of Yarmouth 1950, or 1075.

Know, reader, I cannot, with all my diligence and interest, recover the original of this catalogue, as extant, not in the Tower (where by my friend's favour I could do something), but in the king's great wardrobe in London, out of which it is cited by our author.* But our times (I fear) have brushed it away with the rest of the wardrobe. However, give me leave to make some annotations thereon :

1. These ships, as by their great number appeareth, were small vessels; yet as good as any in that age of England, and better (witness their victories) than any in France.

2. The proportion may seem strange, that Yarmouth should afford well nigh twice as many ships and mariners as London itself.

3. Except it was that the king spared London at this time, as the sure reserve for his navy on all occasions.

---

* Hackluit, in his English Voyages, Vol. I. p. 118, &c.

4. Or except there be a mistake in the numbers (figures in writing, as well as figures in rhetoric, may, with a small dash, have their *meiosis* made an *hyperbole*). And the various lections in the mariners of Yarmouth doth something shake (though not shatter) the credit of the account.

5. The numbers may be very true, Yarmouth in that age being so populous a place that (though but one parish) a lamentable plague in one year did sweep thence 7000 men to the grave.*

Thus, though the church (and that very large) could never hold their living, the churchyard could contain the dead ; seeing persons alive will not be pressed in their pews so close, as corpse may be crowded together in their graves. But let us proceed to the particular seamen of this county ; and let none be offended if a friar be put in the front before all the rest : viz.

NICHOLAS of LYNN,† born in that town ; bred in Oxford, and is generally accounted a Franciscan friar. But my author, being a Carmelite himself, makes him one of his own order.‡ And all acknowledge him an excellent musician, mathematician, and astrologer.

It is reported of him, how in the year 1330, being the thirtieth year of the reign of the king Edward the Third, he sailed, with others, to the most northern islands in the world. Then leaving his company, and taking his astrolabe, he, by the help of art-magic (so mathematicians are nick-named by the ignorant), went as far as the pole itself, where he discovered four indraughts of the ocean, from the four opposite quarters of the world, from which many did conceive, as well the flowing of the sea, as blasts of the winds, to have their original. Were these things true, and had they been known to the ancients, as it would have spared philosophers much pains in disputing the moon the cause of the motion of the tide in the sea, so had it spoiled Virgil's fancy in making the country of Æolia the only magazine of the winds.§

Sure I am, Gerardus Mercator hath so graced the fancy of this friar, that he made his description of the countries about the arctic pole conformable to this his imaginary discovery, preferring to fill that his map with a fiction, than otherwise to leave it altogether empty. But the other parts of his book have more solid and substantial truths, or else weak were the shoulders of his atlas to support the world therewith.

But to return to friar Nicholas. One tells us he wrote a book of his discoveries, and intituled it " Inventio Fortunata."||
Sure it is, he was highly honoured by our learned Chaucer ; wit-

---

* Camden's Britannnia, in Norfolk.
† Bale, de Scriptoribus Britannicis, Cent. vi. num. 25.   ‡ Idem, ibidem.
§ In the second of his Æneid. || Dr. John Dee.

ness his testimony of him, styling Freere N. Linne "a reverend clerk." But all his learning could not fence him from death, which happened about the year 1360 : and he was buried in Lynn, the town of his nativity.

PETER READ.—What he was, his ensuing epitaph on his monument, in the south aisle in St. Peter's church in Norwich, will fully acquaint you :

"Here under lieth the corps of Peter Read, Esquire, who hath worthily served not only his prince and country, but also the emperor Charles the Fifth, both at his conquest of Barbary, and his siege at Tunis, as also in other places. Who had given him by the said emperour, for his valiant deeds, the order of Barbary. Who died the 29th day of December, in the year of our Lord God, 1566."

We place him among Seamen, because finding first his mention in Hakluit's Voyages,* and salt water is the proper element of the pen of that author.

Secondly, because his service was performed at Tunis, a porttown in a sea expedition. Now, although we confess it follows not that he was born in or about Norwich, because buried therein (vast ofttimes the distance betwixt the cradles and coffins of far-travellers) ; yet let none dislike his placing here, but such who can disprove it, and depose the negative, that elsewhere he had his nativity.

It is observable that this Sir Peter, knighted by the emperor, as appears in his epitaph (let me add anno 1538), is only styled, not less modestly than truly, Esquire upon his monument. I confess, some maintain that though higher honours (Baron, Count, &c.) are only local, to be owned by the person receiving them in that place where they are given him; yet that knighthood given by a sovereign prince is universal, and passeth current through all Christendom. But others, their equals, as stiffly deny it; and one who is their superior, (I mean queen Elizabeth) who, in the case of Count Arundle, would not admit of any foreign honour conferred on any of her subjects, avowing that her sheep should only be known by her own mark.†

WRITERS.

JOHN BACONTHORPE was born in a village so called in this county ;‡ bred a Carmelite in the convent of Blackney, and afterwards studied first in Oxford, then in Paris; one remarkable on many accounts :

First, for the dwarfishness of his stature,

"Scalpellum calami atramentum chartâ libellus,"

His pen-knife, pen, ink-horn, one sheet of paper, and any of his books, would amount to his full height. As for all the books

---

* Vol. I. p. 99.   † See it discussed at large in Camden's Elizabeth.
‡ Bale, de Scriptoribus Britannicis, Cent. v. num. 1.

of his own making, put together, their burden were more than his body could bear.

Secondly, for his *high* spirit in his *low* body. Indeed his soul had but a small diocese to visit, and therefore might the better attend the effectual informing thereof. I have heard it delivered by a learned doctor in physic (at the Anatomy lecture in London), who a little before had been present at the embowelling and embalming of duke Hamilton and the lord Capel, that the heart of the former was the largest, the latter the least, he had ever beheld; inferring hence, that contracted spirits act with the greatest vigorousness.

Thirdly, for his high title, wherewith he was generally termed the resolute doctor. Two sorts of people he equally disliked, sceptics who are of none; and unconstant people who are [successively] of all opinions; and whilst others turned about like the wheel, he was as fixed as the axletree in his own judgment. Yet this his resoluteness was not attended with censuring of such who were of another opinion, where equal probability on either side allowed a latitude to dissent.

He groped after more light than he saw, saw more than he durst speak of, spake of more than he was thanked for by those of his superstitious order ; amongst whom, (saith Bale) neither before, nor after, arose the like for learning and religion. Most agree in the time of his death, anno 1346, though dissenting in the place of his burial; assigning Blackney, Norwich, London, the several places of his interment.

JOHN COLTON, born at Terrington in this county, was chaplain to William Bateman, bishop of Norwich, and first master (by the appointment of the founder) of Gonvil-hall in Cambridge.* Leland allows him a man *plus quam mediocriter doctus et bonus ;* for which good qualities king Henry the Fourth advanced him archbishop of Armagh and primate of Ireland.† He was employed to the court of Rome in the heavy schism between pope Urban the Sixth and Clement the Seventh, which occasioned his writing of his learned treatise, "De Causâ Schismatis;" and because, knowing the cause conduceth little to the cure without applying the remedy, he wrote another book " De Remediis ejusdem." It seemeth he resigned his arch-bishopric somewhat before his death, which happened in the year of our Lord, 1404.‡

ALAN of LYNN was born in that famous mart-town in this county,§ and brought up in the university of Cambridge, where he proceeded doctor of divinity, and afterwards became a Carmelite in the town of his nativity. Great his diligence in read-

---

* Parker, in his Skeletos Cantabrigiensis.
† So saith Pits, but mistaken ; for it was king Richard the Second, p. 382.
‡ J. Warens, de Scriptoribus Hibernicis, p. 129.
§ Bale, de Scriptoribus Britannicis, Cent. vii. num. 54.

ing many and voluminous authors; and no less his desire that others with him should reap the fruit of his industry, to which end he made indexes of the many writers he perused.

An index is a necessary *implement*, and no *impediment*, of a book, except in the same sense wherein the carriages of an army are termed *impedimenta*. Without this, a large author is but a labyrinth without a clue to direct the reader therein. I confess there is a lazy kind of learning, which is only *indical*; when scholars (like adders which only bite the horse heels) nibble but at the tables, which are *calces librorum*, neglecting the body of the book. But, though the idle deserve no crutches (let not a staff be used *by* them, but *on* them;) pity it is the weary should be denied the benefit thereof, and industrious scholars prohibited the accommodation of an index, most used by those who most pretend to contemn it.

To return to our Alan; his Herculean labour in this kind doth plainly appear to me, who find it such a toil and trouble to make but an index of the indexes he had made of the authors following.

1. Ægidius. 2. Alcuinus. 3. Ambrosius. 4. Anselmus. 5. Aquinas. 6. Augustinus. 7. Baconthorpe. 8. Basil. 9. Bede. 10. Belethus Bles. 11. Bernard. 12. Berthorius. 13. Cassianus. 14. Cassiodorus. 15. Chrysostome. 16. Cyril. 17. Damascen. 18. Gerard. Laodic. 19. Gilbert. 20. Gorham. 21. Gregory. 22. Haymo. 23. Hierome. 24. Hilary. 25. Hugo. 26. Josephus. 27. Neckam. 28. Origen. 29. Pamph. Eusebius. 30. Phil. Ribot. 31. Raban. 32. Remigius. 33. Richard.

All these J. Bale,* professeth himself to have seen in the Carmelites' library at Norwich, acknowledging many more which he saw not.

Now, although it be a just and general complaint, that indexes for the most part are heteroclites,—I mean, either redundant in what is needless, or defective in what is needful; yet the collections of this Alan were allowed very complete. He flourished anno 1420; and was buried at Lynn, in the convent of Carmelites.

WILLIAM WELLS was born (saith Pits†) at Wells, the cathedral see in Somersetshire, wherein no doubt he is mistaken: for (be it reported to any indifferent judgment, that) seeing this William had his constant converse in this county (living and dying an Augustinian in his convent at Lynn), and seeing there is a Wells no mean market-town in this shire, with more probability he may be made to owe his nativity and name to Norfolk. He was for twenty years Provincial of his order in England, doctor of divinity in Cambridge, an industrious man and good writer; abate only the *siboleth* of barbarism,

---

* De Scriptoribus Britannicis, p. 553.   † De Angliæ Scriptoribus, p. 609.

the fault of the age he lived in. He died and was buried at Lynn, 1421.

JOHN THORPE was born in a village so called in this county; bred a Carmelite at Norwich, and doctor at Cambridge. Logic was his master-piece; and this Dædalus wrote a book intituled " The Labyrinth of Sophisms;" and another, called " The Rule of Consequences;" for which he got the title of *Doctor Ingeniosus*.* This minds me of a prognosticating distich on the physiognomies of two children:

" Hic erit ingenuus, non ingeniosus; at ille
    Ingeniosus erit; non erit ingenuus."

The latter of these characters agreeth with our Thorpe, who had a pound of wit for a dram of good nature; being of a cruel disposition, and a violent persecutor of William White and other godly Wichliffites. He died anno Domini 1440; and lieth buried at Norwich.

His name causeth me to remember his namesake of modern times, lately deceased, even Mr. John Thorpe, B. D. and fellow of Queen's College in Cambridge, my ever honoured tutor; not so much beneath him in logic, as above him in the skill of divinity and in holy conversation.

[AMP.] JOHN SKELTON is placed in this county, on a double probability. First, because an ancient family of his name is eminently known long fixed therein. Secondly, because he was beneficed at Dis, a market-town in Norfolk. He usually styled himself (and that *nemine contradicente* for ought I find) " The king's orator and poet laureat." We need go no further for a testimony of his learning than to Erasmus, styling him, in his letter to king Henry the Eighth, " Britannicarum literarum lumen et decus."

Indeed he had scholarship enough and wit too much; seeing one saith truly of him, " Ejus sermo salsus in mordacem, risus in opprobrium, jocus in amaritudinem."† Yet was his satirical wit unhappy to light on three " Noli me tangere's;" viz. the rod of a schoolmaster, the cowls of friars, and the cap of a cardinal. The first gave him a lash, the second deprived him of his livelihood, the third almost ousted him of his life.

WILLIAM LILLY was the schoolmaster whom he fell foul with, though gaining nothing thereby, as may appear by his return. And this I will do for William Lilly (though often beaten for his sake), endeavour to translate his answer;

Quid me, Sceltone, fronte sic apertâ
Carpis, vipereo potens veneno ?
Quid versus trutinâ meos iniquâ

* Bale, de Scriptoribus Britannicis, Cent. vii. num. 100.
† Pits, de Angliæ Scriptoribus, in anno 1529.

Libras ? dicere vera num licebit ?
Doctrinæ tibi dum parare famam,
Et doctus fieri studes poeta,
Doctrinam nec habes, nec es poeta.

" With face so bold, and teeth so sharp
    Of viper's venom, why dost carp ?
    Why are my verses by thee weigh'd
    In a false scale ?—May truth be said ?
    Whilst thou, to get the more esteem,
    A learned poet fain wouldst seem :
    Skelton, thou art, let all men know it,
    Neither learned, nor a poet."

The Dominican friars were the next he contested with, whose
viciousness lay pat enough for his hand ; but such foul lubbers
fell heavy on all which found fault with them.   These instigated
Nix bishop of Norwich to call him to account for keeping a
concubine, which cost him (as it seems) a suspension from his
benefice.

But cardinal Wolsey (*impar congressus* betwixt a poor poet
and so potent a prelate) being inveighed against by his pen, and
charged with too much truth, so persecuted him, that he
was forced to take sanctuary at Westminster, where abbot Islip
used him with much respect.   In this restraint he died, June
21, 1529 ; and is buried in Saint Margaret's chapel with this
epitaph :

" J. Sceltonus Vates Pierius hic situs est."

The word *vates* being poet or prophet, minds me of this
dying Skelton's prediction, foretelling the ruin of cardinal
Wolsey.   Surely one unskilled in prophecies, if well versed in
Solomon's Proverbs, might have prognosticated as much, that,
" Pride goeth before a fall."*

We must not forget, how, being charged by some on his
death-bed, for begetting many children on the aforesaid concubine, he protested, " that in his conscience he kept her in the
notion of a wife, though such his cowardliness, that he would
rather confess adultery (then accounted but a *venial*) than own
marriage, esteemed a *capital* crime in that age."

SINCE THE REFORMATION.

JOHN BARRET was born of an honest family at Lynn in this
county ;† bred a Carmelite of Whitefriars in Cambridge, when
learning ran low, and degrees high, in that university ; for many
usurped scarlets, qualified only with ignorance and impudence
(properties seldom parted) : so that a scholar could scarcely be
seen for doctors, till the university, sensible of the mischief
thereby, appointed doctor Cranmer (afterwards archbishop of
Canterbury) to be the *poser-general* of all candidates in divinity ;
amongst whom he stopped Barret for insufficiency.

* Proverbs xvi. 18.
† J. Bale, in his book intituled " Scriptores nostri temporis."

Back goes Barret to Lynn; turns over a new, yea many new leaves, plying his book to purpose, whose former ignorance proceeded from want of pains, not parts; and in short time became a tolerable, a good, an excellent, and admirable scholar; and, commencing doctor with due applause, lived many years a painful preacher in Norwich, always making honourable mention of doctor Cranmer as the means of his happiness.* Indeed he had been ever, if not once, a dunce, who, if not debarred, had never deserved his degree. Bale saith, that, in the reign of queen Mary, he returned to his vomit, and became a great papist. But his praises are better to be believed than his invectives; and seeing wood, not growing crooked, but warping with weight, may be straightened again, we charitably believe that, though complying in times of persecution, he returned to the truth in the reign of queen Elizabeth, in the beginning whereof he died.

EDMOND GOURNEY, born in this county, was bred in Queen's and Bene't College, in Cambridge, where he commenced bachelor of divinity, and afterwards was beneficed in this shire. An excellent scholar, who could be humorous, and would be serious, as he was himself disposed; his humours were never profane towards God, or injurious towards his neighbours; which premised, none have cause to be displeased, if in his fancies he pleased himself.

Coming to me in Cambridge when I was studying, he demanded of me the subject whereon I studied. I told him, " I was collecting the witnesses of the truth of the Protestant religion through all ages, even in the depth of Popery, conceiving it feasible though difficult to evidence them."

" It is a needless pains," said he, " for I know that I am descended from Adam, though I cannot prove my pedigree from him." And yet, reader, be pleased to take notice, he was born of as good a family as any in Norfolk. His book against Transubstantiation, and another on the Second Commandment, are learnedly and judiciously written. He died in the beginning of our civil wars.

BENEFACTORS OF THE PUBLIC.

GODFREY BOLLEN, Knight, son of Jeffrey Bollen, was born at Salle in this county.† Being but a second brother, he was sent into the city to acquire wealth, " ad ædificandum domum antiquam:" unto whose achievements fell in both the blood and inheritance of his eldest brother, for want of issue male;‡ by which accumulation he attained great wealth, and anno Domini 1457 was Lord Mayor of London. By his testament, made in the next year, he gave liberally to the prisoners, hospitals, and

* Fox, Acts and Monuments, in the Life of Archbishop Cranmer.
† Stow's Survey, p. 567.   ‡ Fragmenta Regalia.

lazar-houses.* Besides, he gave one thousand pounds † (the greatest sum I meet with in that age to pious uses) to poor householders in London; and two hundred pounds to those in Norfolk. But it was the height of his and our happiness that he was great-grandfather, by the mother's side, to queen Elizabeth.

JAMES HOBART was born in this county, though I dare not say at Halleshall, which he left to his posterity. He was attorney-general, and of the privy council, to king Henry the Seventh; by him dubbed knight, at such time as he created Henry his son prince of Wales. This worthy patriot (besides his many benefactions to his parish church in London) built a fair bridge over the river Waveny,‡ betwixt this county and Suffolk, and a firm causeway thereby, with many other works of charity, so that the three houses of his issue, planted in this county, with fair possessions, may be presumed to prosper the better for the piety of this their ancestor.

ANDREW PERNE was born at Bilny; bred in Peter-house, whereof he was fellow and master, as also proctor and vice-chancellor of Cambridge and dean of Ely.§ Very bountiful he was to his college, wherein he founded a fellowship and scholarships; besides many rare manuscripts he acquired to their library.‖ But his memory ought most to be honoured (saving God's living temples, is better than building dead colleges) on this account, because, in the days of queen Mary, he was the screen to keep off the fire of persecution from the faces and whole bodies of many a poor Protestant; so that by his means no Gremial of the university was martyred therein.

I know he is much taxed for altering his religion four times in twelve years (from the last of king Henry the Eighth to the first of queen Elizabeth); a Papist, a Protestant, a Papist, a Protestant; but still Andrew Perne. However, be it known, that though he was a bending willow, he was no smarting willow, guilty of compliance not cruelty, yea preserving many who otherwise had been persecuted.

He was of a very facetious nature, excellent at *blunt-sharp* jests, and perchance sometimes too tart in true ones. One instance of many; this dean chanced to call a clergyman *fool* (who indeed was little better); who returned, " that he would complain thereof to the lord bishop of Ely."—" Do," saith the dean, " when you please; and my lord bishop will *confirm* you."

Yet was doctor Perne himself at last heart-broken with a jest (as I have been most credibly informed from excellent hands,)

* Viz. the donation of Sir Simon Eyre.   † Stow's Survey, p. 89.
‡ Camden's Britannia, in Norfolk.
§ Parker, in his Sceletos Cantab. in MS.
‖ Some have questioned whether the MSS. were of his gift.—F.

on this occasion. He was at court with his pupil archbishop Whitgift in a rainy afternoon, when the queen was (I dare not say wilfully, but) really resolved to ride abroad, contrary to the mind of her ladies, who were on horseback (coaches as yet being not common) to attend her. Now one Clod the queen's jester was employed by the courtiers to laugh the queen out of so inconvenient a journey. "Heaven," saith he, "Madam, dissuades you, it is cold and wet; and earth dissuades you, it is moist and dirty. Heaven dissuades you, this heavenly-minded man archbishop Whitgift; and earth dissuades you, your fool Clod, such a lump of clay as myself. And if neither will prevail with you, here is one that is neither heaven nor earth, but hangs betwixt both, Doctor Perne, and he also dissuades you." Hereat the queen and the courtiers laughed heartily; whilst the Doctor looked sadly, and, going over with his grace to Lambeth, soon saw the last of his life.

SINCE THE REFORMATION.

Sir Thomas Gresham was born in this county; bred a mercer and merchant in the city of London, where God so blessed his endeavours, that he became the wealthiest citizen in England of his age, and the founder of two stately fabrics,—the Old Exchange,* a kind of college for merchants; and Gresham College, a kind of Exchange for scholars.

I have learned from goldsmiths, that vessels made of silver and gilt are constantly burnished; seldom or never those few which are made of massive gold, whose real intrinsic worth disdaineth to borrow any foil from art. Let lesser donations be amplified with rhetorical praises. Nothing need be said of this worthy knight's gifts but his *gifts;* and take them truly copied from the original of his will, as followeth:

" First, concerning the building in London called the Royal Exchange, with all shops, cellars, vaults, tenements thereunto belonging; I will and dispose one moiety to the mayor, commonalty, and citizens of London, upon confidence that they perform the payments, and other intents hereafter limited.

" The other moiety of the said buildings, to the wardens and commonalty of the mystery of Mercers, of the city of London, upon trust that they perform the payments, and other intents hereafter mentioned.

" I will and dispose, that they the said mayor and commonalty do give and distribute, for the sustentation, maintenance, and finding four persons, from time to time to be chosen, nominated, and appointed by the said mayor, &c. to read the lectures of divinity, astronomy, music, and geometry, within mine own dwelling house in the parish of Saint Helen's. I give and dispose, out of this moiety, two hundred pounds, to be payed to the four readers sufficiently learned, fifty pounds to each yearly.

* Burnt down in Jan. 1839.—Ed.

" I likewise give the said mayor, &c. fifty-three pounds, six shillings and eight-pence, to be yearly distributed in manner following:

" Unto eight alms-folks, whom the said mayor, &c. shall appoint to inhabit my eight alms-houses, in the parish of Saint Peter's Poor, the sum of six pounds thirteen shillings four pence, to each of them, to be paid at four usual terms, &c.

" I likewise dispose out of this moiety fifty pounds yearly, to be distributed by the said mayor, &c. to the prisoners in Newgate, Ludgate, the King's-bench, the Marshalsea, the Counter in Wood Street, ten pounds to each prison, to be paid among the poor thereof.

" The other moiety of the said building disposed to the Mercers, I will and dispose out of it, to be by them paid, one hundred and fifty pounds to the finding, &c. three persons, to be by the wardens, &c. chosen, nominated, and appointed, to read the lectures of law, physic, and rhetoric.

" That the said Mercers shall, out of their moiety, yearly expend one hundred pounds, at four several dinners, for the whole company of the said corporation, in the Mercer's hall in London, on every quarter day.

" That they shall distribute to the several hospitals of Christ's Church, Saint Bartholomew's, the Spittle at Bedlam, the hospital for the poor in Southwark, and the Poultry Counter, fifty pounds yearly, in money or other provisions; ten pounds to each.

" My mansion house, with the gardens, stables, &c. I give to the mayor and commonalty of London, and also to the wardens and commonalty of the mystery of Mercers, to have and to hold in common; upon trust and confidence that they observe, perform, and keep my will, and true meaning hereafter expressed.

" My will, intent, and meaning is, that the said mayor, and commonalty, and their successors, and that the said wardens and commonalty of the Mercers, shall permit and suffer seven persons, by them from time to time to be elected and appointed as aforesaid, meet and sufficiently learned to read the said seven lectures, to have the occupation of all my said mansion house, gardens, &c.; for them and every of them there to inhabit, study, and daily to read the said several lectures. And my will is, that none shall be chosen to read any of the said lectures so long as he shall be married; neither shall receive any fee or stipend appointed for the reading of the said lectures.

" Moreover, I will and dispose that the said mayor and commonalty, and Mercers, shall enjoy the said Royal Exchange, &c. for ever, severally by such moieties as is before expressed; provided they do, in the term of fifty years, provide and obtain sufficient and lawful dispensations and licenses, warrant and authority, upon trust and confidence, and to the intent that they shall severally and for ever maintain and perform the payment, charges, and all other intents and meanings thereof before limited and expressed, according to the intent and true meaning of these presents.

"And that I do require and charge the said corporations and chief governors thereof, with circumspect diligence, and without long delay, to procure and see to be done and obtained such licences, as they will answer for the same before Almighty God: for if they, or any of them, should neglect to obtain such licences, no prince nor counsel in any degree will deny or defeat the same; and if conveniently by my will or other conveyance, I might assure it, I would not leave it to be done after my death; then the same shall revert to my heirs, whereas I do mean the same to the Commonweal; and then their default thereof shall be to the reproach and condemnation of the said corporation before God, &c."

This worthy knight completed his second change, I mean of a mortal life for a blessed eternity, on the 21st of November 1579; and lieth buried in the parish church of Saint Helen's.

Sir WILLIAM PASTON, Knight, son and heir to Erasmus Paston, of Paston, esquire, is justly recounted a public benefactor. True it is, the family whence he was extracted were always forward in deeds of charity, according to the devotion of the days they lived in. Witness their bountiful donations to the abbeys of St. Bennet, in the Holme and Bromholme in this county. After the Reformation, they had not (with too many) less heat, because more light; but continued the stream, though they changed the channel, of charity. This Sir William erected a very fair school, with thirty pounds per annum for the maintenance thereof, at Northwalsam, in this county; a deed, no doubt, acceptable to the God of heaven.

Solomon saith, "Teach a child in the trade of his youth." But, alas! it is above the reach of poor parents to teach the children, lacking learning to do it themselves, and livelihood to hire others; save where such good persons as this worthy knight have made provision for them. This Sir William married Frances the daughter of Sir Tho. Clear of Stokesby; and was great grand-father to Sir William Paston, the bountiful promoter of all my weak endeavours.

HENRY HOWARD, youngest son of Henry Howard, earl of Surrey, and brother to Thomas Howard, last duke of Norfolk, was born at Shotesham in this county.* He was bred a serious student for many years in King's College, in Cambridge, then in Trinity-hall, going the ordinary path and pace to the degree of mastership, without any honorary advantage.† Here he be-

---

* The Continuer of Stow's Annals, p. 1012.
† Cowel's Epistle Dedicatory to his Institutions.

came a great and general scholar; witness his large and learned work, entitled, "A Dispensative against the Poison of supposed Prophecies," and dedicated to Sir Francis Walsingham. His fortune, left him by his father, was not great; and he lived privately all the reign of queen Elizabeth, till king James advanced him in honour and wealth.

Here, for variety sake, and the better to methodize our matter, we will make use of a distinction, common in the custom-house about bills of lading, *Inwards* and *Outwards*, observing what greatness were *imported* on him, what gratitude was *exported* and performed by him.

Inwards.—1. King James created him Baron of Marnhill, in Dorsetshire. 2. Earl of Northampton. 3. Lord Privy Seal. 4. Lord Warden of the Cinque Ports. 5. Knight of the Garter. 6. Cambridge chose him her chancellor.

Outward.—1. He founded and endowed an hospital, for twelve poor women and a governor, at Rising in this county. 2. Another for twelve poor men and a governor, at Clun in Shropshire. 3. Another at Greenwich in Kent, for a governor and twenty poor men, of whom eight are to be chosen out of Shotesham, the place of his nativity.

He died the 15th of June, 1614; and was buried in the ancient chapel of the castle of Dover.

MEMORABLE PERSONS.

—— SHARNBORN, born at, and Lord of, Sharnborn, a considerable manor in this county. This manor William the Conqueror, out of the plenitude of his power, conferred on one Warren, a Norman soldier.

But Sharnborn was not so tame as silently to sit down, and suffer a stranger peaceably to possess his inheritance, which his English ancestors for many years had enjoyed; but fairly traversed his title (I will not say in Westminster-hall, as of later erection in the reign of king Rufus, but) in that public place where pleas were held in that age.

Surely none but a Norfolk-man durst go to law with the Conqueror, and question the validity of his donations. Yea, brave Sharnborn got the better of the suit; and the king's grant was adjudged void. This is pertinently pressed by many, to prove that king William (though in name) was in very deed no conqueror, but came in by composition to keep the laws of England.

Now, as I am heartily sorrowful that Sharnborn, possessed ever since (almost 600 years) by that name and family, should in our age be sold and aliened from it (whose heir males are just now extinct); so am I cordially glad that it is bought by a worthy person, Francis Ash, esquire; which, with some limitation, hath freely settled it (being of good yearly value) on Emanuel College: and may they as long enjoy it as the former owners, if, before that term, the day of judgment put not a period to all earthly possessions!

LORD MAYORS.

1. Godfry Bullen, son of Geffrey Bullen, of Salle, probably Mercer, 1457.
2. Bartholomew Rede, son of Robert Rede, of Cromer, Goldsmith, 1502.
3. Richard Gresham, son of John Gresham, of Holt, Mercer, 1537.
4. John Gresham, son of John Gresham, of Holt, Mercer, 1547.
5. Thomas Cambell, son of Robert Cambell, of Fullsam, Ironmonger, 1609.
6. John Leman, son of John Leman, of Gillingham, fishmonger, 1616.
7. Edward Barkham, son of Edward Barkham, of Southacre, Draper, 1621.

THE NAMES OF THE GENTRY OF THIS COUNTY,

RETURNED BY THE COMMISSIONERS IN THE TWELFTH YEAR OF KING HENRY THE SIXTH, 1433.

William bishop of Norwich, and John de Morley, chevalier;— Robert Clifton, mil. and John Roys (knights for the shire);— Commissioners to take the oaths.

Abbatis de Langle.	Tho. Kerderston.
Abbatis de Creek.	Hen. Inglose, mil.
Abbatis de Wendelyng.	Tho. Tudenham, mil.
Abbatis de Derham.	Rog. Harsick, mil.
Prioris Sancte Fidis.	Hen. Richford, mil.
Prioris de Walsyngham.	Johan. Curson, mil.
Prioris de Tetford.	Henry Grey.
Prioris de Linne.	Willielmi Calthorp.
Prioris de Yernemouth.	Johan. Fitz-Rauf de Moris.
Prioris de Ingham.	Thomæ Willoughby.
Prioris de Cokysforde.	Oliveri Groos.
Prioris de Westar.	Thomæ Chaumbir.
Prioris de Penteneye.	Edmundi Winter.
Prioris de Castelacre.	Nich. Apilyerde.
Prioris de Bromhill.	Will. Apilyerde.
Prioris de Childham.	Nicholai Castel.
Prioris de Wyrmingheye.	Edmundi Stapulton.
Prioris de Bokynham.	Thomæ Pigot.
Prioris de Bromholm.	Henrici Walpole.
Prioris de Hyking.	Thomæ Trusbute.
Prioris de Petreston.	Willielmi Byllingford.
Prioris de Flycham.	Willielmi Daubeney.
Prioris de Bæston.	Thomæ Astele.
Johan. Clyfton, mil.	Radulphi Lampet.
Briani Stapulton, mil.	Johannis Woodehouse.

Johan. Berney de Redham.
Joh. Berney de Wythingham.
Georgii Holkham.
Willielmi Yelverton.
Edmundi Wychyngham.
Johan. Heydon.
Will. Grey de Merston.
Willielmi Raimis.
Thomæ Dengayne.
Johannis Clepisby.
Johannis Strange.
Richardi Gogh.
Christopheri Strange.
Henrici Catte.
Johannis Bakon.
Henrici Nottyngham.
Henrici Sharyngton.
Roberti Martham.
Willielmi Bellingford.
Walteri Aslak.
Thomæ Lovell.
Thomæ Shuldham.
Simonis Fincham.
Will. Walton.
Thomæ Derham.
Roberti Godard.
Thomæ Kervile.
Hen. Stormer.
Johan. Hamond.
Georg. Hethe.
Johan. Fox de Castelacre.
Nich. Bokkyng.
Nich. Stonwell.
Will. Spynk.
Thomæ Chelton.
Johan. Bekkeswell.
Johan. Rysele.
Roberti Popyngeay.
Johan. Wentworth.
Walt. Eton.
Will. Thurleton.
Will. Tweyth.
Edmundi Sekford.
Johan. Michell.
Thomæ Boys.
Johan. Dory.
Johan. Bacheler.
Thomæ Selors.
Thomæ Brigge.

Thomæ Gurney.
Will. Brampton.
Johan. Clare.
Johan. Austyn.
Johan. Bolle.
Roberti Brom.
Johan. Knight.
Galfridi Grey.
Johan. Bullok.
Johan. Brustbon.
Simonis Godknap.
Robert. Padyrys.
Robert. Blogge.
Rich. Chirche.
Ade Mundforth.
Johan. Gigges.
Will. Dyton.
Galfridi Craneweys.
Edmundi Massingham.
Osberti Mundford.
Tho. Fyssher.
Johan. Seche.
Will. Thakker.
Will. Barbour.
Johan. Crane.
Johan. Holdernese.
Leonardi Claxton.
Tho. Fannyngham.
Tho. Botylsham.
Johan. Thursby.
Johan. Wesingham.
Rich. Frank.
Nich. Frank.
Johan. Wythe.
Johan. Parlementer.
Will. Wythe.
Rad. Brecham.
Roberti Walsyngham.
Will. Kirton.
Johan. Stannton.
Johan. Miryoll.
Johan. Syff.
Tho. Spicer.
Tho. Salysbury.
Johan. Waryn.
Johan. Warner.
Rich. Lychour.
Johan Bury.
Johan. Brekerope.

Edmundi Goldyng.
Johan. Tylney.
Andr. Swanton.
Will. Kellowe.
Johan. Abbot.
Johan. Frewill.
Will. Stapulton.
Johan. Wayte.
Johan. Gybbon.
Rober. Brandon.
Nich. Wythe.
Johan. Nicolasson.
Johan. Andrewe.
Alexan. Draper.
Tho. Midleton.
Johan. Thorn.
Will. Sylk.
Simon. Body.
Nich. Benpre.
Edmund. Bonet.
Tho. Feltwell.
Rad. Midylton.
Rich. Baker.
Johan. Howard.
Johan. Eye.
Rich. Deye.
Rich. Billingforth.
Johan. Tremche.
Will. Bullman.
Will. Candelere.
Will. Stokker.
Johan. Bosse.
Johan. Sturmy.
Will. Fyrsk.
Johan. Parker.
Sen. Hetersite.
Rog. Scot.
Johan. Joye.
Hen. Warner.
Tho. Manning.
Rich. Cans.
Tho. Norwold.
Johan. Bredeman.
Georg. Palgrave.
Johan. Rede.
Will. Ede.
Tho. Gyle.
Tho. Candeler.
Tho. Stywarp.

Johan. Walpell.
Tho. Canon.
Johan. Mortoft.
Rich. Vewtre.
Johan. Alcok.
Will. James.
Johan. Tylls.
Rog. Brook.
Johan. Bee.
Will. Tanerham.
Rich. Baret.
Johan. Loumour.
Tho. Walisch.
Galf. Brewster.
Will. Newegate.
Johan. Man.
Pet. Hokkeham.
Will. Seyne.
Johan. Monk.
Johan. Lewes.
Johan. Seforth.
Tho. Colles.
Johan. Chapman.
Edmundi Clerk.
Tho. Bertram.
Rob. Norwich.
Johan. Sweyn.
Johan. Puttok.
Tho. Trunch.
Johan. Wynse.
Johan. Byrston.
Tho. Stipoard.
Rich. Cordy.
Johan. Webbe.
Rich. Wode.
Johan. Spark.
Johan. Atte Mere.
Johan. Ely.
Johan. Dany.
Edmundi Wode.
Tho. Richeforth.
Johan. Dawes.
Alani Twkke.
Simon Cook.
Nich. Parke.
Johan. Legge.
Rich. Henke.
Rob. Ling.
Tho. Mounsewes.

Tho. Yekesworth.
Johan. Trench.
Johan. Elyngham.
Johan. Bettys.
Johan. Porter.
Johan. Bemys.
Johan. Molitis.
Edw. Wylnby.
Will Moletis.
Tho. Holley.
Nich. Holley.
Robert. Holley.
Simon. Dykone.
Johan. Westhaw.
Edmund. Parker.
Galf. Fox.
Johan. Draper.
Johan. Homerston.
Hen. Aphagh.
Will. Atte Hagh.
Hugo. Bedenham.
Will. Prentys.
Johan. Watterden.
Tho. Burgh.
Johan. Doggyng.
Geor. Wyton.
Will. Sparkam.
Johan. Baily.
Hen. Thursby.
Johan. Mersch.
Galf. Cobbe.
Denys Wellys.
Tho. Moket.
Edmundi Cole.
Will. Cole.
Johan. Scorowr.
Johan. Reppes.
Walt. Wedurby.
Johan. Brechinham.
Will. Payn.
Alex. Payn.
Johan. Brygg.
Johan. Crosse.
Steph. Silvestre.
Bob. Teyser.
Tho. Bowde.
Johan. Swayn, jun.
Johan. Grenede Folsham.
Rob. Kervyle.

Simon. Tyller.
Johan. Arnald.
Rich. Carleton.
Edmundi Michell.
Johan. Wodesende.
Will. Stubbe.
Johan. Lawyes.
Hen. Lesingham.
Johan. Jucewode.
Nich. Rake.
Will. Fox.
Johan. Green.
Will. Dallyng.
Nich. Waterman.
Will. Norwhich.
Johan. Tasburgh.
Johan. Brampton.
Robert. Brese.
Edmundi Ade.
Tho. Pye.
Rich. Rede.
Johan. Gerard.
Johan. Dam.
Johan. Bernard.
Johan. Lynford.
Tho. Stodhagh.
Rich. Ballord.
Tho. Walsham.
Johan. Spany.
Johan. Penny.
Johan. Hastynges.
Rich. Stotevyle.
Tho. Arnald.
Robert. Elys.
Will. Granour.
Rich. Elys.
Johan. Berhyng.
Rog. Hoddes.
Will. Baily.
Johan. Crancle.
Nich. Baxter.
Robert. Dooke.
Nich. Pykeryng.
Robert. Kent.
Tho. Unphry.
Walt. Heylot.
Tho. Rycheman.
Johan. Howard.
Johan. Levoth.

Johan. Ansell.
Robert. Fyllisson.
Rog. Calleston.
Tho. Halle.
Robert. Martham.
Galf. Walle.
Johan. Panne.
Johan. Cobald.
Johan. Phelipp.
Johan. Merschgate.
Robert. Cupper.
Tho. Eyre.
Johan. Cobbe.
Rich. Flykke.
Robert. Heyloth.
Johan. Mannyng.
Simon. Falsham.
Robert. Hendy.
Lauren. Oky.
Radulph. Bronnyng.
Johan. Pepyr.
Tho. Martyn.
Johan. Roche.
Johan. Span.
Oliv. Kevet.
Johan. Deynes.
Johan. Holler.

Johan. Fuller.
Johan. Puttok.
Edmund. Rysyng.
Robert. Atte Lee.
Johan. Broune de Weveton.
Johan. Meleman.
Tho. Brydge.
Thom. Roose.
Galf. Bolayn.
Will. Blonnevyse.
Edmund. Yonghousbond.
Edmund. Godewyn.
Tho. Twytwell.
Rich. Holdyche.
Johan. Holtman.
Robert. Randes.
Tho. Glaveyn.
Robert. Wyrmegey.
Tho. Person.
Robert. Wylly.
Johan. Maynard.
Johan. de Pulham.
Willielm. Arnald de Crommer.
Robert. Russell.
Johan. Wodewane.
Ade Williamson, et
Robert. Cravell.

SHERIFFS

OF NORFOLK AND SUFFOLK.

HENRY II.

Anno

1 Rich. Basset, et
  Alberi. de Veer.
2 Will. de Nova Villa, et
  Will. de Jeaxmeto.
3 Will. de Caisuei, sive
  Caisuer.
4
5 Will.
6
7
8
9 Will. de Chaisu.
10 Oggerus Dapifer, for six
  years.
16 Barth. Glanvill, et

Anno

Vinar. Capellanus, et
Will. Bardull, for six years.
22 Vinar. Cappellanus, for
  eleven years.
33 Vin. pro dimid. ann. et
  Will. fil. Hervei dimid.

RICHARD I.

1 Will. fil. Hervei.
2 Idem.
3 Rob. fil. Rog. et
  Pet. de Edichfeld.
4 Rob. fil. Rog. et
  Sam. de Salia.
5 Idem.
6 Idem.

7 Osber. de Longo Campo.
8 Idem.
9 Idem.
10 Rob. fil. Rog. et
   Rich. de Gosfeld.

JOH. REG.

1 Rod. fil. Rog. et
   Rich. de Gosfeld.
2 Idem.
3 Pet. de Mealton.
4 Idem.
5 Idem.
6 Alex. de Dunham, et
   Alex. Banister.
7 Idem.
8 Johan. de Cornheard, for
   four years.
12 Walt. de Huntingfeld, et
   Will. Esturmi.
13 Idem.
14 Rob. fil. Rog. et
   Will. fil. Rosicke.
15 Will. sive Walt. de Huntingfeld, Will. Escurmi.
16 Johan. fil. Rob. et
   Rob. de Kent.
17 Johan. fil. Rob. fil. Rogeri.

HENRY III.

1
2 Hubert. de Burge.
3 Idem.
4 Idem.
5 Hu. et Rich. de Frefing-
   feld.
6 Hubert. et Rich. Ducket.
7 Idem.
8 Hub. et Tho. Ingolde-
   thorpe.
9 Idem.
10 Hugo Rufus.
11 Idem.
12 Herb. de Alencum, for
   five years.
17 Rob. de Brivas.
18 Idem.

19 Tho. de Heningham.
20 Idem.
21 Tho. Ingoldesthorpe.
22 Idem.
23 Rob. de Broyons.
24 Johan. de Ulecott.
25 Idem.
26 Hen. de Heketon, et
   Hamo Passeleve.
27 Idem.
28 Hamo Passeleve, for six
   years.
34 Rob. de Savage, for six
   years.
40 Will. de Swyneford.
41 Idem.
42 Idem.
43 Hamo Hanteyn.
44 Hamo et Hen. de Stanho.
45 Idem.
46 Phil. Marnium, et
   Will. de Hekam.
47 Nich. Espigornel, for five
   years.
52 Rob. de Norton.
53 Idem.
54 Idem.
55 Will. Giffard.
56 Idem.

EDWARD I.

1 Will. Giffard.
2 Idem.
3 Rob. fil. Johannis.
4 Wal. de Shelfhaugre.
5 Idem.
6 Walt. Granimt.
7 Johan. Brito, et
   Will. de Bedham.
8 Idem.
9 Idem.
10 Will. de Doinge.
11 Idem.
12 Will. de Rochinger, for
   six years.
18 Rich. de Belhus.
19 Will. de Nedham.

Anno

20 Idem.
21 Idem.
22 Will. de Gerbe.
23 Idem.
24 Idem.
25 Will. de Rideston.
26 Idem.
27 Will. de Sutton.
28 Idem.
29 Will. de Ailton.
30 Rob. Hereward, for five years.
35 Egid. de Mumpinzon.

EDWARD II.

1 Tho. de Sancto Omero.
2 Hen. de Seagrave.
3 Rob. Baygnard.
4 Idem.
5 Idem.
6 Rob. et Alex. de Claveringe.
7 Rich. de Claveringe.
8 Rich. de Refham.
9 Ric. et Alex. de Claveringe.
10 Johan. de Fitten, et Will. de Rungeton.
11 Johan. Howard.
12 Johan. Seafoule.
13 Johan. Howard, et Edw. Hemingne.
14 Idem.
15 Idem.
16
17 Egid. de Wachesham.
18 Idem.
19 Idem.

EDWARD III.

1 Tho. de Lindringham, et Rob. de Walkefare.
2 Johan. de Londham.
3 Idem.
4 Idem.
5 Rog. de Kirdeston.
6 Rog. de Bourne, et

Anno.

Rog. de Kirdeston.
7 Rog. de Bourne, et Edw. de Baconsthorpe.
8 Johan. de Cailly.
9 Idem.
10 Rob. de Causton.
11 Idem.
12 Johan. de Harsike.
13 Rob. Causton, et Joh. Harsike.
14 Rob.
15 Tho. Belisforde.
16 Edw. de Creting.
17 Idem.
18 Idem.
19 Johan. Haward.
20 Will. de Midleton.
21 Idem.
22 Idem.
23 Johan. de Colby.
24 Idem.
25 Will. de Midleton.
26 Idem.
27 Edw. de Creting.
28 Idem.
29 Tho. de Mareux.
30 Guido Seynclere.
31 Idem.
32 Idem.
33 Johan. de Battlesden.
34 Idem.
35 Tho. de Sancto Omero, for four years.
39 Rog. Gyney.
40 Will de Clere.
41 Tho. Morieux.
42 Idem.
43 Rog. Holdich.
44 Idem.
45 Edw. de Thopre.
46 Rob. Bacon.
47 Johan. Holbroke.
48 Johan. Mantby.
49 Will. de Kirdeston.
50 Oliver de Calthrope.
51 Johan. de Browes.

HENRY II.

16. BARTH. GLANVILL, et VINAR. CAPELLANUS.—It may seem strange that this *Vinar. Capellanus*, that is *Vinar. the Chaplain*, should be sheriff so many years together. One would have sought for a person of his profession rather in the pulpit than in the shire-hall. But in that age men in orders did not only engross places of judicature, but also such as had military and martial relation, whereof the sheriffs' place in some sort may seem to partake. Sure I am, that under the reign of king Charles, one prick'd sheriff of Rutland escaped by pleading that he was a deacon. But now all this is said, this *Vinar. the chaplain* may still be a layman, seeing in England " Multi clerici sunt laici," (many clerks by name are no clerks by profession.) Chaplain may be his surname, and the same with *de Capella* or *Capell*—a right ancient name, I assure you.

SHERIFFS OF NORFOLK AND SUFFOLK.

RICH. II.

Anno	Name and Arms.	Place.
1	Johan. Harsikes.	
	Or, a chief indented S.	
2	Steph. de Hales.	
3	Joh. de Mantby.	
4	Will Winter.	
	Checky, Or and S. a fess Arg.	
5	Will de Kirdeston.	
6	Joh. de Volveston.	
7	Joh. Tudenham.	
8	Andr. Cavendish . . .	Cavendish.
	S. three bucks' heads cabossed Arg. attired Or.	
9	Rad. Bigot, mil.	
	Parti per pale, O. and Vert, a lion ramp. G.	
10	Galf. Michell.	
11	Tho. Corsonn.	
	Ermin. a bend componé Arg. and S.	
12	Idem	*ut prius.*
13	Hugo Fastolfe.	
	Quarterly O. and Az. ; on a bend G. three escalops Arg.	
14	Rob. Carbonell.	
15	Johan. Knivett . . .	Buckenham.
	Arg. a bend within a border engrailed S.	
16	Will. Winter	*ut prius.*
17	Will. Argente, mil.	
	G. three cups covered Arg.	
18	Gilb. Debenham.	
	S. a bend betwixt two crescents O.	

Anno	Name.	Place.

19 Tho. Corsonn . . . . *ut prius.*
20 Idem . . . . . . *ut prius.*
21 Will Rees.
    Arg. three spears' heads G. ; chief O.
22 Idem . . . . . . *ut prius.*

HENRY IV.

1 Joh. Gournay.
    Paleways of six pieces O. and Az.
2 Joh. Heningham.
    Quarterly, O. and G. a border S. charged with escalop
      shells Arg.
    Edw. Oldhall.
3 Joh. Inglesthorpe.
    G. a cross engrailed Arg.
4 Rob. Ramsey.
    G. three rams' heads cabossed Arg.
5 Idem . . . . *ut prius.*
6 Nic. Winchingham.
7 Rob. Berney, mil. . . Parkhall R.
    Per pale G. and Erm. a cross engrailed Erm.
8 Will Rees . . . . . *ut prius.*
9 Rad. Ramsey . . . . *ut prius.*
10 Oliver Groose.
    Quarterly Arg. and Az. on a bend S. three martlets O.
11 Rob. Berney, mil. . . *ut prius.*
12 Tho. Lovell.
    Arg. a chev. Az. betwixt three squirrels seiant G.

HENRY V.

1 Edw. Oldhall.
2 Joh. Heaveningham. . *ut prius.*
3 Joh. Spencer.
    Quarterly, Arg. and G. a bend S. in the second and third
      a fret O.
4 And. Botiller.
    G. a fess componée Arg. and S. betwixt six crosses patée
      fitché Arg.
5 Edw. Winter . . . . *ut prius.*
6 Oliv. Groos . . . . *ut prius.*
7 Joh. Fitz Rauf.
    G. a fess vairy.
8
9 Idem.

HENRY VI.

1 Rob. Clifton, mil.
    S. semée of cinquefoils and a lion ramp. Arg. within a

Anno   Name.   Place.

   border of the first, charged with verdoy of trefoils of the second.

2 Joh. Shardlow.
   Ar. a chevron G. betwixt three croslets Az.
3 Bri. Stapilton.
   Az. a lion ramp. queué fourché O.
4 Oliver Groose . . . . *ut prius.*
5 Johan. Tirrey.
6 Gib. Debenham . . . *ut prius.*
7 Hen. Drury, ar. . . . Halsted, S.
   Arg. on a chief Vert the letter Tau betwixt two mullets pierced O.
8 Hen. Dray, ar.
   Az. a fess betwixt two chevrons O.
9 Joh. Shardlow, m. . . *ut prius.*
10 Joh. Ropley.
11 Tho. Thudenham, mil.
12 Hen. Grey, arm. . . . *ut prius.*
13 Joh. Fitz-Rauf . . . *ut prius.*
14 Tho. Chambre.
15 Johan. Hopton.
   Erm. on two bars S. six mullets O.
16 Joh. Heaveningham . *ut prius.*
17 Tho. Brewes.
   Az. semée of croslets and a lion rampant O.
18 Milo. Stapilton . . . *ut prius.*
19 Rog. Chamberlain.
20 Will. Calthrope.
   Checky O. and Az. a fess Erm.
21 Tho. Brewes . . . . *ut prius.*
22 Joh. Fitz-Rauf . . . *ut prius.*
23 Joh. Hopton, arm. . . *ut prius.*
24 Will. Tirrell.
   Arg. two chev. Az. within a border engrailed G.
25 Tho. Daniel.
26 Phil. Wentworth.
   S. a chev. betwixt three leopards' heads O.
27 Egid. St. Loe, arm.
28 Johan. Gray . . . . *ut prius.*
29 Johan. Germin . . . Rushbroke, Suf.
   S. a crescent betwixt two mullets Arg.
30 Johan. Clopton.
   S. a bend Arg. betwixt two cotises dancetté O.
31 Tho. Sharnebrone.
32 Joh. Denston.
33 Joh. Wingfeld . . . Letheringham.
   Arg. on a bend G. cotised S. three wings of the first.
34 Joh. Clapton, arm. . . *ut prius.*

Anno	Name.	Place.

35 Rich. Bothe, arm.
  Arg. three boars' heads erased S. tusked O.
36 Egid. St. Loe, arm.
37 Will. Calthorpe . . . *ut prius.*
38 Phil. Wentworth . . *ut prius.*

EDWARD IV.

1 Tho. Hayward, mil.
2 Tho. Mountgomery.
  G. a chev. betwixt three flower-de-luces O.
3 Idem . . . . . . *ut prius.*
4 Will. Calthrope, arm. . *ut prius.*
5 Alex. Cressener.
6 Will. Hopton, arm. . . *ut prius.*
7 Tho. Mountgomery . . *ut prius.*
8 Joh. Twyer.
9 Rog. Ree, arm.
10 Joh. Heveningham . . *ut prius.*
11 Will. Knivett, at. . . *ut prius.*
12 Joh. Wingfeld, mil. . *ut prius.*
13 Rog. Ree, mil.
14 Rob. Radliffe.
15 Joh. Hasting, arm.
  Or. a maunch G.
16 Will. Calthorp, mil. . *ut prius.*
17 Tho. Howard, mil.
  G. a bend betwixt six croslets fitchée Arg.
18 Rob. Radliffe, arm.
19 Will. Hopton, arm. . . *ut prius.*
20 Will. Knivett, mil. . . *ut prius.*
21 Alex. Cressener.
22 Hen. Wenthworth . . *ut prius.*

RICHARD III.

1 Joh. Wingfeild, arm. . *ut prius.*
2 Rad. Willoughby.
  Rich. Pole.
  Per pale O. and S. a saltire engrailed counterchanged.
3 Johan. Paston.
  Arg. six flower-de-luces Az. a chief indented O.

HENRY VII.

1 Johan. Paston . . . *ut prius.*
2 Edm. Bedingfeld.
  Erm. an eagle displayed G.
3 Rad. Shelton, mil.
  Az. a cross O.
4 Rob. Lovell . . . . *ut prius.*

Anno   Name.   Place.

5 Simon. Wiseman.
    S. a chevron Erm. betwixt three cronells of a tilt-spear
        Arg.
6 Phil. Lewes, arm.
7 Rob. Brandon, mil.
    Barry of ten Arg. and G.; over all a lion rampant O.
        crowned per pale Arg. of the second.
8 Joh. Wingfeld, mil. . . *ut prius.*
9 Will. Carewe, mil.
10 Rob. Southwell.
11 Rog. Le Strange, arm. .   Hunstanton.
    G. two lions passant Arg.
12 Rob. Curson, mil. . . *ut prius.*
13 Edw. Arundell, mil.
14 Phil. Calthrope, mil. . *ut prius.*
15 Will. Bolein, mil.
    Arg. a chevron betwixt three bulls' heads S. armed O.
16 Hum. Catesby, arm.
17 Rob. Clere, mil.
    Arg. on a fess Az. three eagles O.
18 Edw. Jeney, mil.
19 Idem.
20 Johan. Shelton . . . *ut prius.*
21 Idem . . . . . . *ut prius.*
22 Phil. Bothe, mil. . . *ut prius.*
23 Rob. Brandon, mil. . . *ut prius.*
24 Idem . . . . . . *ut prius.*

                HENRY VIII.

1 Ric. Wentworth   . . *ut prius.*
2 Joh. Hevingham   . . *ut prius.*
3 Rog. Townesend   . . Raynham.
    Az. a chevron Erm. betwixt three escalops Arg.
4 Lio. Talmarsh, arm.   .   Helmingham.
    Arg. a fret S.
5 Tho Gibbon, arm.
    O. a lion rampant S. debrused with a bend G. charged
        with three escalops Arg.
6 Joh. Heydon, mil.
    Quarterly Arg. and G. a cross engrailed counterchanged.
7 Ant. Wingfeld, mil. . . *ut prius.*
8 Ric. Wentworth, mil. . *ut prius.*
9 Will. Paston, arm. . . *ut prius.*
10 Rog. Townsend, arm. . *ut prius.*
11 Joh. Heydon, mil. . . *ut prius.*
12 Hum. Wingfeld, arm. . *ut prius.*
13 Th. Bedingfeld, mil. . *ut prius.*
14 Joh. Shelton, mil. . . *ut prius.*

Anno	Name.		Place.
15	Joh. Heveningham	. .	*ut prius.*
16	Joh. Heydon, mil.	. .	*ut prius.*
17	Rog. Townsend	. . .	*ut prius.*
18	Fran. Lovell, arm.	. .	*ut prius.*
19	Phil. Filvey, mil.		
20	Will. Paston, mil.	. .	*ut prius.*
21	Edw. Bedingfeld	. .	*ut prius.*
22	Tho. Jermyn, arm.	. .	*ut prius.*
23	Hen. Fermour, mil.		
24	Tho. le Strange, mil.	.	*ut prius.*
25	Tho. Lush, or Rush.		
26	Rich. Southwell.		
27	Walt. Hubard, mil.	. .	Blickling.

S. an étoile with eight points betwixt two flanches Erm.

28	Will. Drury, mil.	. .	*ut prius.*
29	Edm. Windham	. . .	Cowtherk.

Az. a chev. betwixt three lions' heads erased O.

30	Fran. Lovell, mil.	. .	*ut prius.*
31	Edw. Knivett, mil.	. .	*ut prius.*
32	Will. Fermoure, mil.		
33	Tho. Jermyn, mil.	. .	*ut prius.*
34	Johan. Jermyn, mil.	.	*ut prius.*
35	Fran. Lovell, mil.	. .	*ut prius.*
36	Will. Drury, mil.	. .	*ut prius.*
37	Edw. Windham, mil.	.	*ut prius.*
38	Hen. Hubbard, arm.	.	*ut prius.*

EDWARD VI.

1	Joh. Robsart, mil.		

Vert, a lion rampant O. vulned in the shoulder.

2	Nich. le Strange	. . .	*ut prius.*
3	Edm. Windham, mil.	. .	*ut prius.*
4	Will. Walgrave.		

Parti per pale Arg. and G.

5	Joh. Robsat, mil.	. .	*ut prius.*
6	Tho. Cornwallis	. . .	Brome, S.

S. guttée Arg. on a fess of the second three Cornish choughs of the first.

PHILIP. ET MARI.

1	Tho. Woodhouse	. .	Kimberley, Norf.

S. a chevron betwixt three cinquefoils Erm.

1,2	Joh. Shelton, mil.	. .	*ut prius.*
2,3	Joh. Sulyard, arm.	. . .	SUFFOLK.

Arg. a chevron G. betwixt three pheons S.

3,4	Chri. Heydon, mil.	. .	*ut prius.*

Anno   Name.   Place.

4,5 Hen. Doly, mil.

      G. three bucks' heads cabossed Arg.

5,6 Amb. Jermyn, arm.   .   *ut prius.*

ELIZAB. REG.

 1 Joh. Apleyard, arm.   .   SUFFOLK.

      Az. a chevron O. betwixt three owls Arg.

 2 Rob. Wingfeld, arm.   .   *ut prius.*

 3 Tho. Tindall, mil.

 4 Will. Buts, mil.

 5 Tho. Woodhouse   .   .   *ut prius.*

 6 Owin Hopton, mil. .   .   *ut prius.*

 7 Will. Paston, mil.   .   .   *ut prius.*

 8 Lion. Talling, arm.

 9 Edw. Clere, arm.   .   .   *ut prius.*

10 Will. Walgrave .   .   .   *ut prius.*

11 Chri. Heydon, mil. .   .   *ut prius.*

12 Edw. Witipole.

13 Rad. Shelton, arm. .   .   *ut prius.*

14 Amb. Jermyn, mil. .   .   *ut prius.*

15 Hen. Doly, arm. .   .   .   *ut prius.*

16 Tho. Felton, arm.   .   .   Playford.

      G. two lions passant Erm. crowned O.

HENRY VII.

14. PHILIP CALTHROPE, Miles.—He was a very grave gentleman (and lived to a great age); yet withal of a very merry and pleasant conceit, whereof take this instance:

He sent as much cloth of fine French tawny as would make him a gown, to a tailor in Norwich. It happened, one John Drakes, a shoe-maker, coming into the shop, liked it so well, that he went and bought of the same as much for himself, enjoining the tailor to make it of the same fashion. The knight, being informed hereof, commanded the tailor to cut his gown as full of holes as his shears could make, which purged J. Drakes of his proud humour, that he would never be of the gentleman's fashion again.

HENRY VIII.

29. EDMUND WINDHAM.—He was a gentleman of a fair estate in this county, great birth and alliance (whose grandmother was daughter to John Howard duke of Norfolk); but, it seems, somewhat, given to his passion. This caused him (in the 33rd of this king's reign) to strike Master Clere, a gentleman of his own county, in the king's tennis-court. For this he was arraigned, in the great hall at Greenwich, before Master Gage, comptroller of the king's household, and other justices; and

one quest of gentlemen, another of yeomen passed upon him, to inquire of the same stripe; by whom he was found guilty, and had judgment to lose his right hand. Then was he brought in to solemn execution by Sir William Pickering, knight martial; and, confessing his fault, desired that the king, of mercy, would be pleased to take his left hand, and spare his right; for therewith (said he) I may hereafter be able to do his grace service." The king, informed hereof by his justices, granted his full pardon, neither to lose hand, land, nor goods; but restored him to his liberty. (See more of him in the third of king Edward the Sixth.)

EDWARD VI.

3. EDMUND WINDHAM, Mil.—Of him before in the twenty-ninth of king Henry the Eighth. He now made good his former promise to the son, which he made to his father, of using his right hand in the service of his sovereign; for in this year Ket's rebellion began in this county, which this sheriff endeavoured with all his power and policy to suppress, till at last it proved a task beyond his strength to perform.

QUEEN MARY.

1. THOMAS WOODHOUSE, Mil.—Though he be the first of his surname whom we meet in our catalogue, I find many of his family anciently employed in state affairs. In a manuscript collection (extant in the library of Sir Thomas Cotton) of persons summoned to parliament by king Edward the Third, I read,

1. "Rex dilecto Clerico suo Roberto de Woodhouse, archidiacono de Richmund, thesaurario, salutem: Negotia nos et statum regni contingentia, &c. vobis mandamus, firmiter injungentes, quòd, omnibus aliis prætermissis, &c."

2. John Woodhouse, Esq. was servant, and one of the executors, to king Henry the Fifth.[*]

3. Sir William Woodhouse (near related to our sheriff) was vice-admiral of our English fleet at Musselburgh-field.[†]

4. Philip Woodhouse, Esq. was very active at the taking of Cadiz; and knighted there, for his good service, by the earl of Essex.[‡]

And ever since there hath been a military inclination in this family, which hath manifested itself on several occasions.

* Stow's Chronicle, p. 362.
† Sir John Hayward, in the Life of Edward VI. p. 15.
‡ Camden's Elizabeth, anno 1596.

SHERIFFS OF NORFOLK ALONE.

ELIZ. REG.

Anno   Name and Arms.   Place.

17 Tho. Townsend, arm. . Rainham.
      Az. a chev. Erm. betwixt three escalops Arg.
18 Drugo Drury, arm.
      Arg. on a chief Vert, the latter Tau betwixt two mullets
        pierced O.
19 Hen. Weston, mil.
20 Baing. Gaudy, arm.
      Vert. a tortoise passant Arg.
21 Tho. Knivett, mil.
      Arg. a bend within a border engrailed S.
22 Edw. Clere, mil.
      Arg. on a fess Az. three eaglets O.
23 Arth. Heveningham.
      Quarterly O. and G. a border S. charged with esca-
        lop-shells Arg.
24 Will. Paston, mil.
      Arg. six flower-de-luces Az. a chief indented O.
25 Will. Heydon, mil.
      Quarterly, Arg. and G. a cross engrailed counter-
        changed.
26 Hen. Woodhouse . . Kimberley.
      S. a chev. betwixt three cinquefoils Erm.
27 Tho. Hogan. arm.
      Arg. a chev. engrailed vairy.
      Hen. Hogan, arm. . . ut prius.
      O. and G. betwixt three hurts, each charged with three
        lions' legs erased Arg.
28 Nath. Bacon, arm. . . SUFFOLK.
      G. on a chief Arg. three mullets S.
29 Clem. Paston, arm. . . ut prius.
30 Joh. Peiton, mil.
      S. a cross engrailed O.
31 Rob. Southwell.
32 Hen. Dolney, arm.
33 Milo. Corbett, arm. . . Sprouston.
      O. a raven proper.
34 Hen. Gaudy, arm. . . ut prius.
35 Basing. Gaudy, mil. . . ut prius.
36 Phil. Woodhouse . . ut prius.
37 Tho. Clere, arm. . . ut prius.
38 Hum. Guibon, arm.
      O. a lion rampant S. debrused with a bend G. charged
        with three escalops Arg.
39 Nich. Bacon, mil. . . ut prius.

Anno	Name.	Place.

40 Clem. Spelman, mil.
    S. platée proper, two flaunches Arg.

41 Nath. Bacon, arm. . . *ut prius.*

42 Ric. Jenkinson, arm.
    O. two bars gemelles G. betwixt three boars' heads and necks erased S.

43 Basen. Gaudy, mil. . . *ut prius.*

44 Arth. Hemingham . . *ut prius.*

45 Edm. Doyley, et 1 Jac.
    G. three bucks' heads cabossed Arg.

JAC. REG.

1 Edm. Doyley, arm. . . *ut prius.*

2 Hen. Spelman, mil. . . *ut prius.*

3 Rad. Hare, mil.
    G. two bars and a chief indented O.

4 Le 'Stran. Mordant.
    Arg. a chev. betwixt three étoiles S.

5 Hen. Gawdy, mil. . . *ut prius.*

6 Hamo Le 'Strange . . Hunstanton.
    G. two lions passant Arg.

7 Tho. Barney, mil. . . Parkhall R.
    Per pale G. and Erm. a cross engrailed Erm.

8 Chri. Gawdy, mil. . . *ut prius.*

9 Tho. Corbet, arm. . . *ut prius.*

10 Tho. Lewer, mil.

11 Jac. Calthrope, mil.
    Checky O. and Az. a fess Erm.

12 Joh. Heveningham . . *ut prius.*

13 Ric. Jenkinson, arm. . *ut prius.*

14 Aug. Palgrave, mil.
    Az. a lion passant Arg.

15 Anth. Drury, mil. . . *ut prius.*

16 Tho. Holland, mil.
    Az. semée of flower-de-luces; a lion ramp. guardant Arg.

17 Hen. Beddingfeld.
    Erm. an eagle displayed G.

18 Tho. Heirne, mil.

19 Will. Yelverton, bar.
    Arg. three lioncels rampant G.; a chief of the second.

20 Rich. Berney, bar. . . *ut prius.*

21 Le 'Stran. Mordant . *ut prius.*

22 Tho. Woodhouse . . *ut prius.*

CAR. REG.

1 Tho. Holle, arm.
    O. on a chevron S. three unicorns' heads erased Arg.

Anno	Name.	Place.

2 Car. Le Groose, mil.
   Quarterly, Arg. and Az. on a bend S. three mullets O.
3 Fran. Gawdy, arm. . . *ut prius.*
4 Rob. Gawdy, mil. . . *ut prius.*
5 Rog. Townsend, bar. . *ut prius.*
6 Fran. Mapes, arm.
7 Tho. Pettus, arm. . . Recheath.
   G. a fess Arg. betwixt three annulets O.
8 Jo. Hobart, mil. et bar. Blickling.
   S. an étoile with eight points betwixt two flanches Erm.
9 Will. Heveningham . . *ut prius.*
10 Joh. Wentworth . . . *ut prius.*
11 Edr. Barkham, mil.
   Arg. three pallets G.; over all a chevron.
12 Will. Paston, arm. . . *ut prius.*
13 Edr. Asteley, arm.
14 August. Holt, arm. . . *ut prius.*
15
16
17 Thomas Guibon, mil. . *ut prius.*
18 Joh. Coke, arm.
   Parti per pale G. and Az. three eagles displayed Arg.
19
20 Valen. Pell, mil.
21
22 Tho. Barney, arm. . . *ut prius.*

QUEEN ELIZABETH.

18. Drugo Drury, Arm.—This Sir Dru, being afterwards
knighted, was joined in commission with Sir Amias Paulet, to
keep Mary queen of Scots; and discharged his dangerous trust
therein. It moveth me not, that I find both these knights
branded for Puritans ;* being confident that nick-name, in relation to them both, was first pronounced through a Popish
mouth, causelessly offended at their religion.

KING CHARLES.

5. Roger Townsend, Baronet.—He was a religious gentleman, expending his soul in piety and charity; a lover of
God, his service, and servants. A grave divine saith most
truly, "that encroachments on the church are like breaches of
the seas, a thousand to one if they ever return."† But this
worthy knight may be said to have turned the tide, restoring
impropriations to the church, to some hundreds in yearly valuation. He married Mary, daughter and co-heir of Horatio Lord

* Camden's Elizabeth, anno 1584.
† Mr. Bolton, in his Funeral Notes on Judge Nichols.

Vere of Tilbury; by whom he had Sir Horace, who for his worth was deservedly created a baron at the coronation of king Charles the Second.

THE FAREWELL.

And now being to take my leave of this county, I wish the inhabitants thereof may make good use of their so many churches, and cross that pestilent proverb, " The nigher to the church, the farther from God;" substituting another (which will be a happy change) in the room thereof, viz. "The more the churches, the more sincere the devotion."

NORWICH.

NORWICH is (as you please) either a city in an orchard, or an orchard in a city, so equally are houses and trees blended in it; so that the pleasure of the country and populousness of the city meet here together. Yet, in this mixture, the inhabitants participate nothing of the rusticalness of the one, but altogether of the urbanity and civility of the other.

NATURAL COMMODITIES.

FLOWERS.

The Dutch brought hither with them, not only their profitable crafts, but pleasureable curiosities. They were the first who advanced the use and reputation of flowers in this city. A flower is the best-complexioned grass (as a pearl is the best-coloured clay); and daily it weareth God's livery, for " He clotheth the grass in the field."* Solomon himself is outbraved therewith, as whose gallantry only was adopted, and on theirs innate, and in them. In the morning (when it groweth up) it is a lecture of Divine Providence. In the evening (when it is cut down withered) it is a lecture of human mortality.

Single flowers are observed much sweeter than the double ones (poor may be more fragrant in God's nostrils than the rich); and let florists assign the cause thereof, whether because the sun doth not so much dry the intricacies of such flowers which are duplicated.

Great the art in meliorating of flowers; and the rose of roses, [rosa mundi] had its first being in this city. As Jacob used an ingenious invention to make Laban's cattle speckled or ringstreaked,† so, much the skill in making tulips feathered and variegated with stripes of divers colours.

* Matthew vi. 30.   † Genesis xxx. 39.

In my judgment those flowers carry it clearly, which acquit themselves to a double sense, sight and smell; for though in some things it may be true, *optimè quæ minimè olent*, yet in flowers (besides a negation of an ill) the position of a good scent is justly required.

MANUFACTURES.

STUFFS.

" It is an ill wind which bloweth no man good." Even storms bring wrecks to the admiral. The cruelty of Duke d'Alva, as it blew the Dutch out of their own, brought them into this city, and with them their manufactures, which the English quickly learned from them, until Norwich became the staple of such commodities for the whole land. For the nimble woof, its artificial dancing in several postures about the standing warp produceth infinite varieties in this kind.

Expect not I should reckon up their several names, because daily increasing, and many of them are *binominous*, as which, when they began to tire in sale, are quickened with a new name. In my childhood there was one called *stand-far-off* (the emblem of hypocrisy), which seemed pretty at competent distance, but discovered its coarseness when nearer to the eye: also *perpetuano*, so called from the lasting thereof, (though but a counterfeit of the clothes of the Israelites, which endured in the Wilderness forty years*), *satinisco*, *bombicino*, *Italiano*, &c. Comineus saith, that a favourite must have a handsome name which his prince may easily call on all occasions; so a pretty pleasing name, complying with the buyer's fancy, much befriendeth a stuff in the sale thereof.

By these means Norwich hath beaten Sudbury out of distance in the race of trading. Indeed in the starting (the south having the better of the north; and *bury*, or city, being before *wich*, or *vicus*, a village) Sudbury had the advantage; but now Norwich is come first to their mark.

THE BUILDINGS.

The cathedral therein is large and spacious, though the roof in the cloisters be most commended. When, some twenty years since, I was there, the top of the steeple was blown down; and an officer of the church told me, "that the wind had done them much wrong; but they meant not to put it up;" whether the wrong or the steeple, he did not declare.

Amongst private houses, the duke of Norfolk's palace is the greatest I ever saw in a city out of London. Here a covered bowling-alley (the first, I believe, of that kind in England) on the same token that when Thomas last duke of Norfolk was taxed for aspiring (by marriage of the queen) to the crown of

---

* Deuteronomy xxix. 5.

Scotland, he protested to queen Elizabeth, " that, when he was in his bowling-alley at Norwich, he accounted himself as a king in Scotland."*

As for the bishop's palace, it was formerly a very fair structure, but lately *unleaded,* and new covered with *tile* by the purchasers thereof; whereon a wag, not unwittily,

> " Thus palaces are altered ; we saw
> John *Leyden,* now Wat *Tyler,* next Jack *Straw.*"

Indeed there be many thatched houses in the city; so that Luther (if summoned by the emperor to appear in this place) would have altered his expression, and said, instead of " *tiles* of the house," that, " if every *straw* on the roof of the houses were a devil, notwithstanding he would make his appearance." However, such thatch is so artificially done (even sometimes on their chancels) that it is no eye-sore at all to the city.

PHYSICIANS.

JOHN GOSLIN, born in this city,† was first fellow, and afterwards master of Caius College in Cambridge, proctor of the university, and twice vice-chancellor thereof: a general scholar, eloquent Latinist, a rare physician, in which faculty he was regius professor. A strict man in keeping, and magistrate in pressing, the statutes of college and university, and a severe punisher of the infringers thereof. And here, courteous reader, let me insert this pleasant passage (seeing Cato himself may sometimes smile) without offence.

I remember, when this doctor was last vice-chancellor, it was highly penal for any scholar to appear in boots, as having more of the gallant than civil student therein. Now a scholar undertook, for a small wager, much beneath the penalty, to address himself *ocreated* unto the vice-chancellor, which was beheld by others as a desperate adventure. Carrying his state in his urinal, he craved his advice for an hereditary numbness in his legs (and something of truth therein), which made him, in his habit, to trespass on the university's statutes, to keep them warm. The vice-chancellor, pitying instead of punishing him, prescribed him his best receipts ; and so, by this *fraus honesta,* he effected his desires.

This doctor was a worthy benefactor to Catharine hall (to which he had no relation, save what his bounty created), bestowing thereon the fair Bull Inn, of considerable value. If he who giveth a night's lodging to a servant of God shall not lose his reward, certainly he that bestoweth *inn and all* upon the sons of the prophets shall find full compensation ; the rather, because that hall, pent formerly for lack of ground, and complaining with the sons of prophets, " The place where we dwell, is too strait for us,"‡ may now say with Isaac, " The Lord hath

* Camden's Elizabeth, anno 1569.   † Parker, Sceletos Cantabrigiæ, MS.
‡ 2 Kings vi. 1.

made room for us;"* by this convenient addition.   He died in his vice-chancellorship, anno 1625.

JOHN CAIUS, born in this city, son to Robert Caius, was bred fellow in Gonvil Hall in Cambridge. Hence he travelled into Italy, where he studied much, and wrote several learned treatises ; returned home, became physician to queen Mary, and improved Gonvil Hall into a college. He bestowed good land *on,* erected fair buildings *in,* bequeathed thrifty statutes *to,* produced a proper coat of arms *for,* and imposed a new name *on,* this foundation, Gonvil and Caius College. He wrote an excellent book of the Antiquity of Cambridge. When king James passed through this college, the master thereof presented him a Caius " De Antiquitate Cantabridgiæ," fairly bound ; to whom the king said, " What shall I do with this book ?" give me rather Caius " De Canibus," a work of the same author, very highly praised, but very hardly procured. Few men might have had a longer, none ever had a shorter epitaph,—" FUI CAIUS."

WRITERS SINCE THE REFORMATION.

ROBERT WATSON, born in this city, was excellently well skilled in the laws, and (saith Bale) " à Dispensatione sive Administratione domesticâ," (English it as you please) to Archbishop Cranmer. Being imprisoned for his religion, he often disputed during his restraint with several Papists, concerning transubstantiation ;† and at length, having gained his enlargement, wrote a treatise in elegant Latin (dedicating the same to such who with him suffered banishment for their religion), wherein he relateth the accidents of his life.   I cannot attain to any certainty in the date of his death.

BENEFACTORS TO THE PUBLIC.

WILLIAM BAITMAN was born in this city,‡ bred in Cambridge, and afterwards became first archeacon, and then by king Edward the Third made bishop of this his native see.   One of a high spirit, to maintain the prophet and privileges of his place ; and I charitably presume him watchful over his sheep (souls subjected to his charge), because he was so careful of his deer ; for the stealing whereof he enjoined penance § to Robert Lord Morley, and made him perform them, in the cathedral of Norwich, notwithstanding the king's threatening letters to the contrary.

This prelate, in his travels beyond the seas, perceiving that our English common law was *outlawed* in those parts, and apprehending the absolute necessity that the English should have skill in the canon and civil laws (for the managing of foreign

---

* Genesis xxvi. 22.   † Bale, de Scriptoribus Britannicis, Cent. ix. num. 81.
‡ Godwin's Catalogue of the Bishops of Norwich.   § Idem, ibidem.

negociations) erected a college in Cambridge, called Trinity Hall,
for the study thereof. As he was father to Trinity, he was foster-
father to Gonvil Hall, in the same university, removing it to a
more convenient place, building, and settling the revenues
thereof, according to the will of the founder. King Edward the
Third, resolving to follow his title to the crown of France, sent
this bishop to the Pope, to acquaint him with his intentions, in
which embassage he died, at Avignon, 1354.

SINCE THE REFORMATION.

THOMAS LEGG was born in this city;* bred first fellow in
Trinity, then Jesus College in Cambridge, until he was chosen
by doctor Caius (then surviving) the nineteenth† master of
Gonvil Hall, and the second of Gonvil and Caius College. He
was doctor of the law and Arches, one of the masters of the
Chancery, twice vice-chancellor of the university, and thirty-
four years master of his college therein. There needeth no
other testimony for to avouch his great learning, than the character given him by J. Lipsius, in his (hitherto unprinted)
Epistle, " In Antiquitatis studio tam egregiè versatus es, ut id
de teipso potes quod de se *Apollo* Ennî : 'A me omnes Canta-
brigienses consilium expetunt in literis incerti, quos ego, meâ
ope, ex incertis certos, compotesque consilii dimitto.' "

This doctor, though himself a serious man, used to recreate himself with delightful studies, observing gravity in his very pleasures. He composed a tragedy of the destruction of Jerusalem;
and having at last refined it to the purity of the public standard,
some plagiary filched it from him, just as it was to be acted.
He formerly had made a tragedy of the life of king Richard the
Third, presented with great applause (queen Elizabeth, I suppose, being a beholder thereof) in Saint John's College Hall.
On the same token that John Palmer (afterwards dean of Peterborough) who acted king Richard therein, had his head so possessed with a prince-like humour, that ever after he did what then
he acted, in his prodigal expences ; so that (the cost of a sovereign ill befitting the purse of a subject) he died poor in prison, notwithstanding his great preferment.

Great the bounty of doctor Legg unto his college, bequeathing
600 pounds for the building of the east part thereof; besides
several lesser liberalities. Yea, be it remembered, that after Thomas
Bacon, fifteenth master of the college, had been a malefactor
thereunto, leaving it much indebted, the four succeeding masters (ill examples avoided do good) doctor Caius, Legg, Branth-
waite, Gosling, (all natives of Norwich) were signal benefactors ;
though masters of, but stewards for, the house ; making it, for
the main, their heir at their decease. Doctor Legg died July
12, 1607, in the 72nd year of his age.

* Ex Annalibus Coll. Gonv. et Caii.
† In Sceletos Cantabrigiæ, he is accounted but the 17th.

THE FAREWELL.

I heartily wish that this city may long flourish in its full lustre. In tendency whereunto, may the thatch of all their houses, by Divine Providence, be effectually secured from the merciless element of fire (as which knoweth not to be a king, but must be tyrant), whose furious raging is seldom bounded, unless by the want of fuel to feed on! Yea, may their straw in due time advance into tile, that thereby their houses may for the future be better fenced for another element; I mean the injury of wind and rain.

WORTHIES OF NORFOLK WHO HAVE FLOURISHED SINCE THE TIME OF FULLER.

Thomas ALLEN, author and nonconformist divine; born at Norwich 1608; died 1673.

Joseph AMES, historian and typographical antiquary; born at Yarmouth 1688-9; died 1759.

William BELOE, divine, critic, and translator of Herodotus; born at Norwich 1758; died 1817.

Robert BRADY, historian and learned physician; born at Denver; died 1700.

Edward BROWNE, physician to Charles II. president of the College, Norwich; born at Norwich 1642; died 1708.

Sir William BROWNE, popular physician and author; born near Lynn 1692; died 1774.

Sir Charles BURNEY, learned Grecian, and critic; born at Lynn 1757; died 1817.

William CAPON, antiquarian draughtsman and scene-painter; born at Norwich 1757; died 1827.

Thomas CHESTERTON, physician and nonconformist divine; born at Downham 1715; died 1770.

Samuel CLARKE, divine and philosopher; born at Norwich 1675; died 1729.

John Henry COLLS, poet and dramatist; born at Letheringset 1764; died 1823.

John COSIN, bishop of Durham, learned author and benefactor; born at Norwich 1595; died 1672.

William D'OYLEY, divine and philanthropist; born at Bergh-Apton 1745; died 1814.

Anthony ELLYS, bishop of St. David's, author; born at Yarmouth 1690; died 1761.

Sir John FENN, antiquary, publisher of " Paston Letters;" born at Norwich 1739; died 1794.

Lady FENN, wife of Sir John, authoress of works for the

instruction of youth under the name of Mrs. Lovechild; born at East Dereham; died 1814.

Robert FORBY, divine, author of the "Vocabulary of East Anglia;" born at Stoke; died 1825.

Sir Andrew FOUNTAINE, antiquarian collector and numismatist, friend of Pope and Swift; born at Narford 1675; died 1753.

John FRANSHAM, "the Norwich polytheist," author; born at Norwich 1730; died 1810.

Thomas GIRDLESTONE, physician and translator of Anacreon; born at Holt 1758; died 1820.

Timothy GOODWIN, archbishop of Cashel; born at Norwich 1696; died 1729.

Luke HANSARD, printer of the House of Commons; born at Norwich 1752; died 1828.

Thomas HARMER, dissenter, orientalist, and biblical critic; born at Norwich 1715; died 1788.

Henry HEADLEY, poet, critic, and editor of Ancient Poetry; born at Irstead 1766; died 1788.

Thomas HERRING, archbishop of York and Canterbury; born at Walsoken 1691; died 1757.

James HOOKE, musical composer; born at Norwich 1746; died 1813.

Thomas HOWES, divine and author; born at Mourningthorpe 1729; died 1814.

William HURN, divine and poet; born at Hockham; died 1829.

Dr. Benjamin IBBOT, ingenious and learned writer and divine; born at Beachamwell 1680; died 1725.

John IVES, antiquary and author; born at Yarmouth 1750; died 1776.

Edward JERNINGHAM, poet; born 1727; died 1812.

Sir Benjamin KEENE, statesman, ambassador to Spain; born at Lynn Regis 1697; died 1757.

Edmund KEENE, brother of the above, bishop of Ely, "the builder of palaces;" born at Lynn Regis 1714; died 1781.

Henry KETT, scholar and divine; born at Norwich 1761; died 1826.

Edward KING, Pres. A.S., author of "Munimenta Antiqua;" born at Norwich 1734; died 1807.

John Glen KING, author of "Rites of the Greek Church;" born 1732; died 1787.

John LENG, bishop of Norwich, editor of Aristophanes; born 1665; died 1727.

Sir Roger L'ESTRANGE, political and miscellaneous writer; born at Hunstanton hall 1616; died 1704.

Roger LONG, mathematician, astronomer, and divine; born at Croxton Park, near Thetford, 1680; died 1770.

Thomas MARTIN, " honest Tom Martin," antiquary and historian of his native town; born at Thetford 1696; died 1771.

Horatio NELSON, Viscount, hero of the Nile and Trafalgar; born at Burnham Thorpe 1758; died 1805.

Sir William NELSON, Clarencieux king-at-arms, antiquary; born at Aslacton 1592; died 1661.

Thomas PAINE, deist and republican, author of " Rights of Man," &c.; born at Thetford 1737; died 1809.

John PEARSON, bishop of Chester, expositor of the Creed; born at Creak or Snoring 1612-13; died 1686.

Richard PEARSON, brother of the bishop, traveller and Grecian scholar; born at Creak; died 1670.

Richard PORSON, critic and Greek scholar; born at East Ruston 1759; died 1808.

William RAWLEIGH, editor of Bacon's works; born at Norwich about 1588; died 1667.

James SAYERS, satirical poet and caricaturist; born at Yarmouth; died 1823.

Frank SAYERS, physician, poet, and metaphysician; died 1817.

Thomas SHADWELL, poet-laureat, dramatist, and historiographer; born at Stanton-hall or Weeting, about 1640; died 1692.

Sir Cloudesley SHOVEL, admiral; born at Cockley Cley or Cockthorpe 1650; drowned 1708.

Sir James Edward SMITH, founder and president of the Linnæan Society; born at Norwich 1759; died 1828.

Benjamin STILLINGFLEET, naturalist and poet; born at Wood Norton 1700; died 1771.

Henry SWINDEN, historian of his native town; born at Yarmouth; died 1772.

George first Marquis TOWNSHEND, general and statesman; born 1723-4; died 1807.

Horatio WALPOLE, Lord Walpole of Woolterton, statesman, brother to Sir Robert; born at Houghton 1678; died 1757.

Sir Robert WALPOLE, first Earl of Orford, statesman; born at Houghton 1676; died 1745.

Lord Chief Justice WALSINGHAM, of the Common Pleas; born at Merton 1719; died 1781.

Henry WHARTON, divine, author of " Anglia Sacra;" born at Worstead 1664; died 1694-5.

Thomas Dunham WHITAKER, divine, antiquary, and historian; born at Rainham 1759; died 1821.

William WILKINS, architect, author of an essay on Norwich Castle; born at Norwich about 1747.

Robert WOODHOUSE, mathematician, author of the " Principles of Analytical Calculation," &c.; born at Norwich; died 1827.

" *₊* Since the time of Dr. Fuller the county of Norfolk has been successful in its topographical historians. In 1698, Sir H. Spelman published his " Icena sive Norfolciæ descriptio topographica ;" and in 1789 appeared a History of the County of Norfolk, by the Rev. F. Blomefield, and the Rev. C. Parkin ; which was re-published in 11 vols. 8vo. in 1805. Other Works have been subsequently produced by Matchett, and by Cotman. In 1816, Mr. Britton brought out a History of the See and Cathedral of Norwich ; some partial notices having been published by Sir T. Browne so early as 1712. Several Histories of Yarmouth have also been produced by various authors, viz. by H. Swinden (1772) ; by the Rev. C. Parkin (1776) : by the Rev. R. Turner, and by J. Preston (1819) ; and by J. H. Druery (1826). Histories of King's Lynn, by B. Mackerell (1788), and by W. Richards (1812), and Histories of Thetford, Holkham, &c., have also made their appearance.—Ed.

NORTHAMPTONSHIRE.

NORTHAMPTONSHIRE, being a long narrow inland county, is stretched from north-east to south-west, and bordereth on more counties than any other in England, being nine in number; viz. —on the east, 1. Cambridgeshire; 2. Huntingdonshire;—on the west, 3. Warwickshire;—on the north, 4. Lincolnshire; 5. Rutland; 6. Leicestershire;—on the south, 7. Bedford-shire; 8. Buckinghamshire; 9. Oxfordshire.

It is as fruitful and populous as any in England, inso-much that sixteen several towns with their churches have at one view been discovered therein by my eyes, which I confess none of the best; and God grant that those who are sharper-sighted may hereafter never see fewer !*

Sure I am there is as little waste ground in this, as in any county in England (no mosses, mears, fells, heaths (whiter-ing, but a beauty-spot), which elsewhere fill so many shires with much emptiness); Northamptonshire being an apple, with-out core to be cut out, or rind to be pared away.

Northamptonshire challengeth that all the rivers running through or by it are its natives, as bred in it (which argueth the elevation and height of the ground thereof), which I believe no other county in England can say. Besides, it lend-eth two considerable rivers, Avon to Warwick, and Cherwell to Oxfordshire.

The language of the common people is generally the best of any shire in England. A proof whereof, when a boy, I received from a hand-labouring man herein, which since hath convinced my judgment: "We speak, I believe," said he, "as good Eng-lish as any shire in England, because, though in the sing-ing psalms, some words are used to make the metre unknown to us, yet the last translation of the Bible, which no doubt was done by those learned men in the best English, agreeth per-fectly with the common speech of our country."

Know, reader, that doctor Bowle, my worthy friend, and most skilful botonographist, hath taken notice of a heath in this county nigh to Stamford, whereof he giveth this commen-

---

* Other men have discovered two and thirty.—F.

dation, "as fine a place for variety of rare plants as ever I beheld;"* who, I am sure, hath seen, in this king, as much, both here and beyond the seas, as any of his age and profession.

NATURAL COMMODITIES.

Now though this shire shares as largely as any in those profits which are general to England, grass, corn, cattle, &c.; yet it is most eminent for

SALT-PETRE.

In Latin *Sal petræ*, rather so called because " exudat è petris," (it usually sweats out of rocks), than because it is wrought up at the last to a rocky or a stony consistency. Some conceive it utterly unknown to the ancients, which learned Hoffman will not allow, only it was disguised unto them, under the name of *Sal nitrum*, though our modern use was unknown to them, that *Pulvis nitrosus*, or gunpowder, might be made thereof. It is ἐυφλώγιστος, what will easily take fire, the best test of the goodness thereof.

But why is salt-petre (common to all counties) insisted on in Northamptonshire? Because, most thereof is found in dovehouses, and most dove-houses in this great corn county. Yet are not those emblems of innocency guilty in any degree of those destructions, which are made by that which is made thereof. All that I will add of salt-petre is this: I have read in a learned writer† that " Salt-petre-men, when they have extracted salt-petre out of a floor of earth one year, within three or four years after they find more generated there, and do work it over again."

PIGEONS.

These of all fowls live most sociably in a commonwealth together, seeing their government is not, as bees, monarchical. They are generally reported without gall; understand it, their gall is not sequestered into a distinct vessel, as in other creatures. Otherwise we find the effects thereof in their animosities among themselves (whose bills can peck as well as kiss) as also (if their crops be not clearly drawn) in the bitterness of their flesh. They are most swift in flight, and the steerage of their tails conduceth much to their steady mounting upright. An envious man, having caught his neighbour's pigeons in a net, feeding on his stack, plucked off their tails, and let them go; which, though they could fly forward home, yet were soon after found dead in the dove-cote, famished for want of food, as unable to fly up perpendicularly, and so out at the louver.

Pigeons, against their wills, keep one Lent for seven weeks in

* Phytologia Britannica, p. 82. † Dr. Jorden, of Mineral Baths, c. 11.

the year, betwixt the going out of the old, and growing up of the new, grain. Probably, our English would be found as docible and ingenious as the Turkish pigeons, which carry letters from Aleppo to Babylon, if trained up accordingly. But such practices, by these *wing-posts*, would spoil many a *foot-post* living honestly by that painful vocation.

I find a grievous indictment drawn up against the poor pigeons for felony, as the grand plunderers of grain in this land. My author, computing six and twenty thousand dove-houses in England and Wales,* and allowing five hundred pair in each house, four bushels yearly for each pair, hath mounted the annual waste they make to an incredible sum. And, if the moiety of his proportions hold true, doves may be accounted the causers of death, and justly answer their etymology in Hebrew, *Jonah*, which is deduced from a root, signifying to spoil or to destroy. The advocates for pigeons plead, that they pick up such loose corn which otherwise would be lost, and uselessly trodden into the earth ; that probably Divine Providence, which feedeth the fowls, by some natural instinct directeth them to such grain which would be barren and fruitless; that their dung, incredibly fruitful for the manuring of ground, abundantly recompenseth the spoil done by them.

However, if pigeons be guilty of so great stealth, they satisfy the law for the same, being generally killed for man's meat; and a *corrected pigeon* (let blood under both wings) is both pleasant and wholesome nourishment.

THE MANUFACTURES.

This county can boast of none worth naming, whereof this the reason; sufficient the fruitfulness thereof in corn, grass (and what not, necessary for nature ?) for its plentiful subsistance. The elder brother who hath the inheritance of his own to maintain him, need not be bound an apprentice, let the younger turn tradesman, and enlarge his narrow portion by his industry. It is enough for Northamptonshire to sell their wool, whilst that other countries make cloth thereof. I speak not this (though it be my native country) to praise Northamptonshire men for not *using*, but that Northamptonshire men may praise God for not *needing*, manufactures. However, the town of Northampton may be said to stand chiefly on other men's legs ; where (if not the best) the most and cheapest boots and stockings are bought in England.†

I am credibly informed by a good friend, that the manufacture of clothing hath, by prudent and able persons, been endeavoured effectually (understand me, in design, not success) in this county; and yet (though fine their wool) their cloth ran

---

* Samuel Hartlib, of Husbandry, his Legacy, p. 227.

† The county of Northampton is still famous for its manufactory of boots and shoes.—ED.

so coarse, it could not be sold without loss. Thus God hath innated every country with a peculiar genius; and when art crosseth nature, neither succeed; but both exceed where both concur.

BUILDINGS.

As Saint Peter hath the primacy of all the other Apostles, so the cathedral dedicated unto him in this county challengeth the precedency of all in England, for a majestic western front of *columel* work. But, alas! this hath lately felt the misfortune of other fabrics in this kind. Yea, as in a gangrene one member is cut off to preserve the rest; so I understand the cloisters of this cathedral were lately plucked down, to repair the body thereof; and am heartily glad God in his mercy hath restored the only remedy (I mean its lands) for the cure thereof.

As for civil structures, Holdenby-house lately carried away the credit, built by Sir Christopher Hatton, and accounted by him the last monument of his youth. If Florence be said to be a city so fine that it ought not to be shown but on holidays, Holdenby was a house which should not have been shown but on Christmas-day. But, alas! Holdenby-house is taken away, being the emblem of human happiness, both in the beauty and brittleness, short flourishing, and soon fading thereof. Thus one demolishing hammer can undo more in a day than ten edifying axes can advance in a month.

Next is Burleigh-house nigh Stamford, built by William Lord Cecil. Who so seriously compareth the [late] state of Holdenby and Burleigh, will dispute with himself, whether the offices of the lord chancellor or treasurer of England be of greater revenues; seeing Holdenby may be said to show the seal, and Burleigh the purse, in their respective magnificence, proportionable to the power and plenty of the two great officers that built them.

Withorpe must not be forgot (the least of noble houses, and best of lodges), seeming but a dim reflection of Burleigh, whence it is but a mile distant. It was built by Thomas Cecil earl of Exeter, "to retire to," as he pleasantly said, "out of the dust, whilst his great house of Burleigh was a sweeping."

Castle Ashby, the noble mansion of the earl of Northampton, succeeds, most beautiful before a casual fire deformed part thereof. But, seeing fire is so furious a plunderer, that it giveth whatsoever it taketh not away, the condition of this house is not so much to be condoled, as congratulated.

Besides these, there be many others, no county in England yielding more noblemen; no noblemen in England having fairer habitations. And although the freestone, whereof they be built, keepeth not so long the white innocence, as brick doth the blushing modesty thereof; yet, when the fresh lustre is abated, the full state thereof doth still remain.

THE WONDERS.

There is within the demesnes of Boughton (the barony of the right honourable Edward Lord Montague) a spring which is conceived to turn wood into stone.   The truth is this, the coldness of the water incrustateth wood (or what else falleth into it) on every side with a stony matter, yet so that it doth not transubstantiate wood into stone; for the wood remaineth entire within, until at last wholly consumed, which giveth occasion to the former erroneous relation.   The like is reported of a well in Candia, with the same mistake, that "quicquid incidit lapidescit."   But I have seen, in Sidney College in Cambridge, a skull brought thence, which was candied over with stone, within and without, yet so as the bone remained entire in the middle, as by a casual breach thereof did appear.   This skull was sent for by king Charles; and whilst I lived in the house, by him safely again returned to the college, being a prince as desirous in such cases to preserve others' propriety, as to satisfy his own curiosity.

MEDICINAL WATERS.

WELLINGBOROUGH-WELL.

Some may conceive it called Wellingborough, from a sovereign well therein anciently known, afterwards obstructed with obscurity, and re-discovered in our days.   But Master Camden doth *marr* their *mart*, avouching the ancient name thereof Wedlingburough.   However, thirty years since, a water herein grew very famous, insomuch that queen Mary lay many weeks thereat.   What benefit her majesty received by the spring here, I know not.   This I know, that the spring received benefit from her majesty; and the town got credit and profit thereby.   But it seems all waters of this kind have (though far from the sea) their ebbing and flowing; I mean in esteem.   It was then full tide with Wellingborough-well, which ever since hath abated, and now I believe is at low water in its reputation.

PROVERBS.

" The mayor of Northampton opens oysters with his dagger."]

This town being eighty miles from the sea, sea-fish may be presumed stale therein.   Yet have I heard that oysters (put up with care, and carried in the cool) were weekly brought, fresh and good, to Althorp, the house of the lord Spencer, at equal distance.   Sweeter, no doubt, than those oysters commonly carried over the Alps, well nigh 300 miles, from Venice to Vienna, and there reputed (far-fetched and dear-bought) dainties to great persons, though sometimes very valiant their savour.   Nor is this a wonder, seeing Pliny tells us, that our English oysters did " Romanis culinis servire," (serve the kitchens of Rome); pickled as some suppose, though others believe them preserved by an ingenions contrivance (epicures bear their brains in their bowels); and some conceive them carried in their shells. But, seeing one of their own emperors gave for his motto, "Bonus odor hostis, melior civis occisi;" (good is the smell of an enemy, but better the smell of a citizen of Rome killed); I say unto such a Roman nose, stinking may be better than sweet oysters; and to their palates we'll leave them.

"He that must eat a buttered fagot, let him go to Northampton."]

Because it is the dearest town in England for fuel, where no coals can come by water, and little wood doth grow on land. Camden saith of this county in general, that it is "silvis, nisi in ulteriori et citeriori parte, minùs lætus." And if so when he wrote, fifty years since, surely it is less woody in our age.

What *reformation* of late hath been made in men's judgments and manner, I know not; sure I am, that *deformation* hath been great in trees and timber: who verily believe that the clearing of many dark places, where formerly plenty of wood, is all the new light this age produced.

Pity it is no better provision is made for the preservation of woods, whose want will be soonest for our fire, but will be saddest for our water, when our naval walls shall be decayed. Say not that want of wood will put posterity on witty inventions for that supply, seeing he is neither a pious nor prudent parent, who spends his patrimony on design that the industry and ingenuity of his son may be quickened thereby.

PRINCES.

ELIZABETH, daughter of Sir Richard WOODEVILL, by the Lady Jaquet his wife (formerly the relict of John duke of Bedford) was born at Grafton Honour in this county; in proof whereof, many strong presumptions may be produced.* Sure I am, if this Grafton saw her not first a child, it beheld her first a queen, when married to king Edward the Fourth.

This Elizabeth was widow to Sir John Grey, who lost his life for the house of Lancaster; and petitioned king Edward to take off the sequestration from her jointure.

Beauty is a good solicitress of an equal suit, especially where youth is to be the judge thereof. The king fell much enamoured of her feature; whilst the lady put herself into a chaste posture, and kept a discreet distance, neither forward to accept, nor froward to decline, his favour.

She confessed herself too worthless to be his wife, yet pleaded too worthy to be his wanton; till at last the king was content to take her upon her own terms, though a widow, and his subject. She got more greatness than joy, height than happiness,

* The Woodvils had formerly, for four generations, lived at Grafton, as appears by the Lieger-book of Pipwell Abbey.

by her marriage; her husband keeping company with others for his pleasure, her for posterity. Nor was it long before the tempest of his lust drave him to another *Shore,* which had a greater share in his affections.

This lady lived to see the death of her husband, murder of her two sons, restraint of herself and rest of her children. And though her condition was altered and bettered by the marriage of her eldest daughter to king Henry the Seventh, yet that cunning king (who always weighed his love in the balance of policy) was not over-dutiful to her, nor over-loving to her daughter. She died anno Domini 14. . .

But her memory is most remarkable to posterity for finishing Queen's College in Cambridge (wherein I had my first breeding; and for it, and all therein, shall ever have an unfeigned affection); begun by queen Margaret (wife to king Henry the Sixth) an implacable enemy to her husband, so that the two houses of Lancaster and York had their first amity in that foundation; a a comfortable presage, that in process of time they should be publicly and effectually united.

RICHARD PLANTAGENET, son to Richard Plantagenet duke of York, was born at Fotheringhay castle in this county. He was somewhat rumpled in his mother's womb (which caused his crooked back): otherwise handsome enough for a soldier. Ajax and Ulysses, valour and eloquence, met in his person, having as well a tongue to flatter, as an arm to fight.

He compassed the crown by cruelty, and the killing of his nephews, the two sons of king Edward the Fourth. When king, he made good laws, which never procured him the people's love, as who beheld vice for his native colour, and virtue for his painted complexion, on design to make himself popular.

He lost the crown and his life in the battle of Bosworth; where it may be verified of him, what Livy saith of Hannibal when beaten by Scipio, that "in that fight he performed all the offices of a wise general and valiant soldier; only fortune did not befriend him."

If any except that king Richard in this battle was too prodigal of his own person, engaging it too far for a general; his condition did excuse him herein, with whom it was all one, to die as to survive success. His memory hath since met with a modern pen,* who hath not only purged, but praised, it to the height; † and pity it is, that so able an advocate had not a more meriting person to his client. He was slain anno Domini 1435.

KATHARINE PARR, daughter to Sir Thomas Parr, and last wife to king Henry the Eighth, may probably be presumed a

---

* George Buck, Esquire.

† King Richard has since found another able advocate in the Hon. Horace Walpole, afterwards earl of Orford.—ED.

native of this shire. However, to prevent cavils, we resign her over to Westmoreland, where (God willing) we shall meet with her character.

SAINTS.

WERBURGH was daughter to Wolpher prince of Mercia, who had his chief palace of residence* at Wedon in the Street in this county, which place her father bestowed on her for her portion. She was bred a nun, under Saint Audery her aunt, and abbess at Ely, until such time that she was able, of herself, to go alone without leading, in a monastical life. Returning to Wedon, she turned that place, which had been her father's palace, into a monastery.

Besides Wedon, she had the inspection of two other monasteries, Trekingham in Lincolnshire, and Hamburge, noted by my author† near Ely in Cambridgeshire, though no such place appear in any modern maps or catalogue. She parted herself, whilst living, successively betwixt these three places; but on her death-bed, commanded her body to be buried at Hamburge, when, contrary to her will, it was carried to the monastery of Trekingham, and the gates thereof fast locked, and carefully watched, to keep so great a treasure.

Reader, if the day be as long with thee when thou readest, as it was with me when I wrote, the ensuing story, time may the better be afforded for the perusal thereof. My author‡ proceeds:

"But see a wonder." [It were well if we could see; whereas now, by his leave, we do but hear it.] "They which were appointed to watch the same fell into a deep sleep, so as the people of Hamburge§ coming in the night for the body, the gates, both of the monastery and church, were opened themselves without men's hands; and, taking it away without any resistance, they interred it at Hamburge, as before her death she requested.

Wonder not they were so ambitious for her body; for, as Werburgh was her name, which by a great antiquary‖ is interpreted the keeper or conserver of a burgh or town, so all presumed she would prove a tutelary patroness to the place which possessed her body: seeing some have reported, that she hath miraculously driven away all geese from Wedon, that they shall destroy no grain thereabout.¶ If this be true, then, as a certain Jupiter amongst the heathens was called Jupiter Ἀπόμυιος, Jupiter the flie-flapper,** who drave away those offensive insects, let this saint hereafter be termed Werburga Ἀποχήνιος, the chaser

---

* Camden's Britannia, in this county.
† The English Martyrology, in the third day of February.　　　‡ Idem, ibidem.
§ Mr. Nichols says that this is an error in the original from which Dr. Fuller cites the passage. According to Nasmith's Tanner, the place intended was probably Romburc or Rumburgh, a small Benedictine cell in Suffolk.—ED.
‖ R. Verstegan, p. 212.
¶ "Cujus miracula in fugandis hinc anseribus, scriptores creduli decantarunt." Camden's Britannia, in Northamptonshire.　　　** Apud Pausaniam, in Eliacis.

away of noisome geese, which spoil grain, grass, and water, where they come. She died anno Domini 675. Her body was afterwards taken up, and translated to Chester, where Hugh Lupus, somewhat after the Conquest, built the fair monastery of Saint Werburgh's to her memory, converted into a cathedral by king Henry the Eighth.

MARTYRS.

This county affordeth no Marian martyrs, thanks be to a good and gracious God; a meek and moderate man, David Pool, bishop of Peterborough; whom I here mention the more willingly, not knowing where to fix his nativity. However, " Unus Homo nobis."

One martyr we had; not chargeable on the bishop, but his bloody archdeacon's account; John Curd, of Syrsam, a shoemaker, burnt in Northampton.*

As for Augustine Dudley, parson of Castor, though some of his family credibly informed me that he was martyred, yet, on inquiry, his sufferings amounted not to loss of life; and therefore the less wonder that they escaped the drag-net of Master Fox's diligence.

CARDINALS.

HENRY CHICHLEY was born at Higham Ferrers, in this county; and, by the author of " Antiquitates Britannicæ " is avouched, made cardinal by the title of Saint Eusebius. But because this appeareth not in his epitaph on his tomb (wherein an exact inventory of all his dignities) the truth thereof is justly suspected; and I reserve his character, to be ranked amongst the " Benefactors to the Public."

PRELATES.

RICHARD ADAM of NORTHAMPTON.—We compound them for several reasons: First, because natives of the same town. Secondly, both going over into Ireland, there became bishops of the same see. Thirdly, because the history of them is, *singly*, so slender it cannot subsist alone; though, *twisted* together, it is possible that their memories may support one the other; for we have nothing more of them than the dates of their consecrations and deaths. The former, consecrated bishop of Fernose, October the 13th, 1282, died anno 1304.† The latter, consecrated 1322, died October the 29th, 1346, having first seen his cathedral church burnt and destroyed by the rebels.‡

WILLIAM le ZOUCH, son to .... lord Zouch, was born at Haringworth in this county; as a branch of that honourable

* Fox, Acts and Monuments, anno 1557.
† Sir James Ware, de Præsulibus Lagentiæ, page 58.
‡ Idem, p. 59.

family,* still alive, and critical in their pedigrees, hath credibly informed me. From dean he became archbishop of York, 1342.

King Edward the Third, going over to France, committed the north to the care of this prelate. Soon after, David king of Scots, with a great army, invaded it; he promised himself Cæsar's success, to come and conquer, see and subdue; the rather because he believed that, the flower of the English chivalry being gone into France, only priests and peasants were left behind. Our archbishop, with such forces as he could suddenly provide, bid him battle at Durham, on Saint Luke's eve; whereon the Scotch king found such a *fast*, he had little list to *feast* the day following, being routed and taken prisoner. Hence a poet of that age,

"Est pater invictus, sicco de stipite dictus :"

Zouch in French signifying the dry stump of a stick. However, his honourable family flourished as a green tree for many years, till withered in our memory, when Edward the last lord Zouch died, without issue male, in the beginning of king Charles.

To return to our prelate; he began a beautiful chapel on the south side of his cathedral, intending to be interred therein; but dying before the finishing thereof, was buried before the altar of Saint Edmund, 1352.

ROBERT BRAYBROOKE was born at a village in this county, well known for the carcass of a castle therein. He was consecrated bishop of London, January 5, 1381; and afterwards, for six months, was chancellor of England. He died 1404, being buried under a marble-stone in the chapel of Saint Mary; which is all we can recover of this prelate; and if it be enough to satisfy the reader's hunger, he need not leave anything for manners in the dish.

LIONELL WYDEVILL, or WOODVILL, was born at Grafton (since called Grafton-Honor) in this county; bred in the university of Oxford, whereof for a time he was chancellor; then made bishop of Sarisbury, 1482. As he was at first preferred, so his memory is still supported from sinking in silence, rather by the buttresses of his great relations, than the foundation of his own deserts: for he was son to Jaquet duchess of Bedford, and Richard Wydevill earl of Rivers; brother to Elizabeth queen of England; brother-in-law to king Edward the Fourth; uncle to king Edward the fifth; and father (say some) to Stephen Gardener, bishop of Winchester. Heart-broken with grief, with the tragedies he beheld in his own family, caused by the cruelty of king Richard the Third, he died about the year of our Lord, 1484.

* Dr. Richard Zouch, Professor of law in Oxford.

SINCE THE REFORMATION.

JAMES MONTAGUE, son to Sir Edward Montague, knight, was born at Boughton, in this county; bred in Christ's college in Cambridge. He was afterwards master, or rather nursing-father, to Sidney College; for he found it in bonds to pay twenty marks per annum to Trinity College, for the ground whereon it is built; and left it free, assigning it a rent for the discharge thereof. When the King's Ditch in Cambridge, made to *defend* it by its *strength*, did in his time *offend* it with its *stench*, he expended a hundred marks to bring running water into it, to the great conveniency of the university. He was afterwards bishop, first of Bath and Wells, then of Winchester, being highly in favour with king James, who did ken a man of merit as well as any prince in Christendom. He translated the works of king James into Latin, and improved his greatness to good offices therewith. He died anno Domini 1618; and lieth buried within his fair monument, within his fairer monument—I mean a goodly tomb in the church of Bath, which oweth its well-being and beauty to his munificence.

FRANCIS GODWIN, son to Thomas Godwin, bishop of Bath and Wells, was born at Haningham in this county;* bred in Christ's church in Oxford; doctor of divinity, and sub-dean of Exeter. He was born in the fourth year of the reign of queen Elizabeth, anno 1561; and in the fortieth year of his age, 1601, by her majesty made bishop of Llandaff; a bishopric better proportioned to his modesty than merits, as which was much impaired by his predecessor; so that one did truly say, " A bad *Kitching* did for ever spoil the *good meat* of the bishops of Llandaff."† He was a good man, grave divine, skilful mathematician, pure Latinist, and incomparable historian. The church of Llandaff was much beholding to him; yea, the whole church of England; yea, the whole church militant; yea, many now in the church triumphant had had their memories utterly lost on earth, if not preserved by his painful endeavours in his " Catalogue of English Bishops." I am sorry to see that some have made so *bad* use of his *good* labours, who have lighted their candles from his torch, thereby merely to discover the faults of our bishops, that their personal failings may be an argument against the prelatical function. He was translated, by king James, to the bishopric at Hereford, and died, very aged, in the reign of king Charles, anno Domini 1633.

JOHN OWEN was born at Burton Latimers, in this county; his father being the worthy and grave minister thereof. He was bred a fellow in Jesus college in Cambridge, where he com-

---

* Witness himself in his Catalogue of Llandaff.
† Anthony Kitchin, who marred this See with selling and letting long leases.—F.

menced doctor of divinity; and was chaplain to king Charles, whilst he was a prince. A modest man, who would not own the worth he had in himself; and therefore others are the more engaged to give him his due esteem.

In the vacancy of the bishopric of Saint Asaph, king Charles, being much troubled with two competitors, advanced doctor Owen, (not thinking thereof) as an expedient to end the contest. Indeed his majesty was mistaken in his *birth*, accounting him a Welchman; but not in his *worth*, seeing he deserved a far better preferment. Besides he was, though not *ortus*, *oriundus è Wallia*, and by his father (being a Welchman) he was related to all the best families in North Wales. He out-lived his vote in Parliament. and survived to see all contempt cast on his order, which he bare with much moderation, and died anno Domini 1651.

ROBERT SKINNER, D.D., was born at Pisford in this county, where his father was minister, bred fellow of Trinity college, in Oxford, afterwards an eminent preacher in London, and dean of . . . . . . Hence he was preferred bishop of Bristol, and afterwards of Oxford; and is still, and long may he be, living.*

STATESMEN.

Sir CHRISTOPHER HATTON was born (I collect at Holdenby) in this county, of a family rather ancient than wealthy, yet of no mean estate. He rather took a *bait* than made a *meal* at the inns of court, whilst he studied the laws therein. He came afterwards to court in a mask, where the queen first took notice of him, loving him well for his handsome dancing, better for his proper person, and best of all for his great abilities. His parts were far above his learning, which mutually so assisted each other, that no manifest want did appear; and the queen at last preferred him lord chancellor of England.

The gown-men, grudging hereat, conceived his advancement their injury, that one not thoroughly bred in the laws should be preferred to the place. How could he cure diseases unacquainted with their causes; who might easily mistake the justice of the Common-law for rigour, not knowing the true reason thereof? Hereupon it was, that some sullen serjeants at the first refused to plead before him, until, partly by his power, but more by his prudence, he had convinced them of their errors, and his abilities. Indeed he had one Sir Richard Swale, doctor of the civil laws (and that law, some say, is very sufficient to dictate equity) his servant-friend, whose advice he followed in all matters of moment.

A scandal is raised, that he was popishly affected; and I cannot blame the Romanists, if desirous to countenance their

* He had been rector of Launton in Oxfordshire; bishop of Bristol 1636; translated to Oxford 1640; and to Worcester 1663. He died in 1671.—ED.

cause with so sonsiderable a person. Yet most true it is, that
his zeal for the dicipline of the Church of England gave the first
being and life to this report.

One saith, that he was "a mere vegetable of the court,* that
sprung up at night, and sunk again at his noon;" though indeed
he was of longer continuance. Yet it brake his heart, that the
queen (who seldom gave boons, and never forgave due debts)
rigorously demanded the present payment of some arrears,
which Sir Christopher did not hope to have remitted, but did
only desire to be forborne: failing herein in his expectation,
it went to his heart, and cast him into a mortal disease.
The queen afterwards did endeavour what she could to recover
him, bringing, as some say, cordial broths unto him with her
own hands ; but all would not do. Thus no pulleys can draw
up a heart once cast down, though a queen herself should set
her hand thereunto. He died anno Domini 1591; and is
buried, under a stately monument, in the choir of Saint Paul's.

Sir WILLIAM FITZ-WILLIAMS, born at Milton in this
county, married the sister of Sir Henry Sidney, lord deputy of
Ireland. Yea, he himself was five times lord deputy of that
kingdom;† a sufficient evidence of his honesty and ability,
seeing queen Elizabeth never trusted twice, where she was once
deceived in a minister of state. She so preserved him in the
power of his place, that, sending over Walter earl of Essex (a
person higher in honour) to be governor of Ulster, it was ordered
that the earl should take his commission from the lord deputy.‡

An intelligent pen§ alloweth him serviceable towards the
reduction of that kingdom, in two eminent particulars. First,
in raising a composition in Munster, then in settling the possessions of the lords and tenants in Monaghan, one of the last acts
of state (tendering to the reformation of the civil government)
performed in the reign of queen Elizabeth. His vigilancy was
most conspicuous in the eighty-eighth, when the routed Armada,
in its return, did *look*, dared not to *land*, in Ireland, except
against their wills driven by tempest, when they found the
shore worse than the sea unto them. I confess, some impute the Irish rebellion‖ which afterwards broke out to this
deputy's severity, in imprisoning suspected persons for concealing Spanish goods, though this only gave the Irish a mantle for
their intended wickedness. He died anno Domini 15 . .

Sir ISAAC WAKE was born in this county, whose father,
Arthur Wake, clerk, was parson of Billing, master of the hos-

* Fragmenta Regalia, in his Character.
† " Guil. Fitz-Williams, jam *quintum* Hiberniæ Pro-rex."—Camden's Elizabeth,
anno 1587.
‡ Idem, anno 1573.
§ Sir John Davis, in his " Dicoveries of Ireland," p. 257.
‖ Camden, anno 1588.

pital of Saint John's in Northampton, and canon of Christ's Church, and son to John Wake of Saucy Forrest, esquire, of a most ancient and honourable family.* He was bred fellow of Merton College in Oxford, proctor and orator of that university. He was afterwards secretary to Sir Dudley Carleton, secretary of state ; and from his, was advanced into the king's service, and employed ambassador to Venice, where he neglected his own commodity, to attend his majesty's employment ; the reason that he died rich only to his own conscience. Coming from Venice, he was appointed lieger for France, and designed secretary of state, had not death prevented him at Paris. He was accomplished with all qualifications requisite for public employment ; learning, languages, experience, abilities, and what not.

King Charles, hearing of his death, commanded his corpse to be decently brought from Paris into England, allowing the expences for his funeral, and enjoining his nearest relations to attend the performance thereof. These accordingly met his body at Boulogne in France, and saw it solemnly conveyed into England, where it was interred in the chapel of the castle of Dover, anno Domini 16 . .

CAPITAL JUDGES, AND WRITERS ON THE LAW.

[AMP.] MARTIN de PATESHULL.—Let him remain here, till any show me a town called Pateshulle, in any other county of England ; which village in this shire gave the name, and afforded the habitation, to that ancient family.† Though a clergyman, he was, in the first of king Henry the Third, made justice of the Lower Bench, or Common Pleas,‡ wherein he continued for twelve years and upwards, as appeareth by the date of his death, out of an excellent author :§ " Eodem anno obiit Martinus de Pateshulle, decanus S. Pauli London. 18 Cal. Decem. vir miræ prudentiæ, et legum regni peritissimus."

He was the fourth dean of Saint Paul's, as reckoned up in Bishop Godwin's Catalogue. In that age we see, clergymen were not only trusted with the spirit (I mean the equity) but also with the letter of the law, being judges in those courts wherein were the most strict proceedings.

Sir THOMAS de BILLING was born in this county (where two villages, his namesakes, near Northampton) ; and had his habitation, in great state, at Ashwell in this shire. He was made chief justice of the King's Bench in the sixth,‖ and so continued till the one and twentieth of Edward the Fourth, whose lands (and those very large) have since, by the Lovells,

---

* So am I informed from Mr. George Wake, late fellow of Magdalen College in Oxford, and his near kinsman.—F.
† Camden's Britannia, in Northamptonshire.
‡ Sir Henry Spelman's Glossary, verbo *Justitiarius.*
§ Florilegus in anno 1226, being the 14th of Henry III.
‖ Sir Henry Spelman, ut prius.

descended to the Shirlies.* Nothing else have I to observe of him, save that he married, for his second wife, Mary, the daughter and heir of Robert Nesenham, of Conington in Huntingdonshire, the relict of William Cotton (whose issue possess her inheritance at this day), and she lieth entombed in Westminster.†

Sir WILLIAM CATESBYE was born in this county, where his family long flourished at Ashby Saint Leger. He was first advanced by William Lord Hastings, by whose countenance he came to the notice, then favour, of Richard the Third, though ill requiting it, when betraying him who caused his preferment. Take his character (transcribing in this kind, is safer than indicting) from an author‡ above exception. "This Catesby was a man well learned in the laws of this land; and surely great pity it was that he had not more truth, or less wit."

If any object, that being neither lord chief justice, chief baron, nor any writer on the law, he falleth not under my pen, by the charter of method prefixed to this catalogue, know, that, though formerly *none*, he was eminently *all* officers, in every court of judicature, all the judges shaking at his displeasure. Witness the libel which Collingborn made, and which cost him his life for the same:

> " The *Rat*,§ and the *Cat*,‖ and *Lovel* the *Dog*,
> Do govern all England under the *Hog*."¶

The time of his death is uncertain; but, because we find him not molested in the reign of king Henry the Seventh (which, had he survived, surely had happened) it is probable he died before his patron and preferrer, king Richard the Third.

Sir RICHAD EMPSON.—It is pity to part them, seeing Empson may be called the Catesbye to king Henry the Seventh, as Catesbye the Empson to king Richard the Third; both countrymen, eminent for *having*, odious for *abusing*, their skill in law; active for the prince, injurious to the people. This Sir Richard was chancellor of the duchy of Lancaster; and from a sieve-maker's son (at Towcester in this county, where he was born) came to *sift* the estates of the most wealthy men in England.

For king Henry the Seventh, vexed that he had refused Columbus's proffer (whereby the West Indies, being found out fortunately, fell to Ferdinand king of Spain), resolved to discover Indies in England; and, to this purpose, made Empson promoter general, to press the penal statutes all over the land.

---

* Camden's Britannia, in Northamptonshire.
† Stow's Survey of London, p. 519.
‡ Sir Thomas More, printing the Continuation of John Harding's Chronicle, fol. 56.   § Ratcliffe.   ‖ Catesbye.
¶ King Richard the Third, who gave a boar for his crest.

Empowered hereby, this prowling knight did grind the faces of rich and poor, bringing the *grist* thereof to the king, and keeping the *toll* thereof to himself, whereby he advanced a vast estate, which now, with his name, is reduced to nothing. He united the two houses of York and Lancaster in the king's coffers, taking no notice of parties or persons for their former good service, but making all equally obnoxious to fines and forfeitures. But, in the beginning of the reign of king Henry the Eighth, he was arraigned, condemned, and beheaded, August the 17th, 1510. Say not that princes, if sacrificing their ministers to popular fury, will want persons faithfully to serve them, seeing such exemplary justice will rather fright officers from false-deserving them; for, in fine, no real profit can redound to the sovereign, which resulteth from the ruin of his subjects.

I must not forget how there was an old man in Warwickshire, accounted very judicious in judicial astrology, of whom Sir Richard Empson (then in his prime) did scoffingly demand, "When the sun would change?" To whom the old man replied, "Even when such a wicked lawyer as you go to heaven."* But we leave him to stand and fall to his own Master, and proceed.

EDWARD MONTAGUE, son of Thomas Montague, born at Brigstock in this county, was bred in the Inner Temple, in the study of the laws, until his ability and integrity advanced him lord chief justice of the King's Bench, in the thirtieth of Henry the Eighth. He gave for his motto, "Equitas Justitiæ Norma." And although equity seemeth rather to *resent* of the Chancery than the King's Bench, yet the best justice will be worm-wood without a mixture thereof. In his times, though the golden showers of abbey-lands rained amongst great men, it was long before he would open his lap (scrupling the acceptation of such gifts); and at last received but little in proportion to others of that age.

In the thirty-seventh of king Henry the Eighth, he was made chief justice of the common pleas; a descent in honour, but ascent in profit; it being given to old age, rather to be thrifty than ambitious.

In drawing up the will of king Edward the Sixth, and settling the crown on the lady Jane, for a time, he swam against the tide and torrent of Duke Dudley,† till at last he was carried away with the stream, as in our "Church History" is largely related.

Ousted of his judge's office in the first of queen Mary, he returned into Northamptonshire; and what contentment he could not find in Westminster-hall, his hospital-hall at Boughton af-

* Camden's Remains.
† John Dudley, the powerful and ambitious duke of Northumberland, afterwards beheaded by queen Mary.—ED.

forded unto him.   He died anno 1556 ; and lieth buried in the parish church of Weekly.

Sir AUGUSTIN NICOLLS, son to Thomas Nicolls, sergeant at law, was born at Eckton in this county.   Now though, according to the rigour of our fundamental premises, he cometh not within our cognizance under this title, yet his merit will justify us in presenting his character.

He was bred in the study of the common law, wherein he attained to such knowledge, that queen Elizabeth made him a (king James his own) sergeant ; whence he was freely preferred one of the judges of the Common Pleas ; I say freely, king James commonly calling him " the judge that would give no money."   Not to speak of his moral qualifications and subordinate abilities ; he was renowned for his special judiciary endowments ; patience to hear both parties all they could say, a happy memory, a singular sagacity to search into the material circumstances ; exemplary integrity, even to the rejection of gratuities after judgment giving.

His forbearing to travel on the Lord's day wrought a reformation on some of his own order.   He loved plain and profitable preaching ; being wont to say, " I know not what you call puritanical sermons ; but they come nearest to my conscience."

The speech of Cæsar is commonly known, " Oportet imperatorem stantem mori ;" which Bishop Jewell altered, and applied to himself, " Decet Episcopum concionantem mori ; " of this man it may be said, " Judex mortuus est jura dans," dying in his calling, as he went the northern circuit ; and hath a fair monument in Kendall-church in Westmorland.

Sir ROBERT DALLINGTON, Knight, was born at Geddington in this county ; bred a Bible clerk (as I justly collect) in Bene't College ; and after became a schoolmaster in Norfolk.   Here having gained some money, he travelled over all France and Italy, being exact in his observations ; and was, after his return, secretary to Francis earl of Rutland.   He had an excellent wit and judgment, witness his most accurate aphorisms on Tacitus. At last he was knighted, and preferred master of the Charterhouse, where the schoolmaster,* at his first entering, welcomed him with a speech in Latin verse, spoken by a schoolboy ; but sure he was more than a boy who indited it.   It is hard to say, whether Sir Robert was more pleased or displeased with the last distic therein :

> *Partem oneris vestri minimam ne despice, curam*
> *Nec Pueros iterùm tædiat esse tuam.*

> " Do not the least part of your trust disdain,
>   Nor grudge of boys to take the care again."

* Dr. Gray.

He lived to be a very aged man, past seventy-six, and died anno Domini 1637.

JOHN FLETCHER, son of Richard Fletcher, D. D. was (as by proportion of time is collectible) born in this county, before his father was bishop of Bristol or London, and whilst as yet he was dean of Peterborough. He had an excellent wit, which, the back friends to stage-plays will say, was neither idle nor well employed; for he and Francis Beaumont, esquire, like Castor and Pollux (most happy when in conjunction) raised the English to equal the Athenian and Roman theatre; Beaumont bringing the ballast of judgment, Fletcher the sail of phantasy; both compounding a poet to admiration.

Meeting once in a tavern, to contrive the rude draught of a tragedy, Fletcher undertook to kill the king therein; whose words being overheard by a listener (though his loyalty not to be blamed herein), he was accused of high treason; till, the mistake soon appearing, that the plot was only against a dramatic and scenical king, all wound off in merriment.

Nor could it be laid to Fletcher's charge, what Ajax doth to Ulysses:*

———*Nihil hic Diomede remoto.*

" When Diomede was gone,
  He could do nought alone."

For, surviving his partner, he wrote good comedies himself, though inferior to the former; and no wonder, if a single thread was not so strong as a twisted one. He died (as I am informed) in London, of the plague, in the first of king Charles, 1625.

Sir HENRY MONTAGUE, knight, third son to Sir Edward Montague, knight, grand-child to Sir Edward Montague, knight, lord chief justice of the King's Bench, was born at Boughton in this county. One skilful in mysterious arts, beholding him when a schoolboy, foretold that, by the pregnancy of his parts, he would raise himself above the rest of his family; which came to pass accordingly. He was bred first in Christ's College at Cambridge; then in the Middle Temple, where he attained to great learning in the laws, and passed through many preferments, viz. 1. Serjeant at law; 2. Knighted by king James, July 22, 1602; 3. Recorder of London; 4. Lord Chief Justice of the King's Bench, November 18, 1616; 5. Lord Treasurer of England, December 16, 1620; 6. Baron of Kimbolton; 7. Viscount Mandeville; 8. President of the Council, September 29, 1621; 9. Earl of Manchester; 10. Lord Privy Seal.

He wisely perceiving that courtiers were but as counters in the hands of princes, raised and depressed in valuation at pleasure, was contented rather to be set for a smaller sum, than to be

* Ovid, Metam. lib. 13.

quite put up into the box. Thus, in point of place and preferment, being pleased to be what the king would have him (according to his motto, " Movendo non mutando me,") he became
almost what he would be himself, finally advanced to an office of
great honour. When lord privy seal, he brought the Court of
Requests into such repute, that what formerly was called the
alms-basket of the chancery, had in his time well nigh as much
meat in, and guests about it (I mean suits and clients) as the
chancery itself. His Meditations on Life and Death, written in
the time of his health, may be presumed to have left good impressions on his own soul, preparatory for his dissolution, which
happened 1642.

WRITERS.

JOHN of NORTHAMPTON, in Latin *Johannes Avonius*, was
born in the town of Northampton, "in ipso insulæ umbilico,"
(saith Bale[*]); and is not mistaken in his proportion. This
mindeth me of a village in this county, sufficiently known, commonly called Navesby, whose orthography critics will have
Navelsby, as in the middle of England. This John became a
Carmelite in his native town, and so addicted himself to the study
of mathematics, that he became one of the most eminent in that
age for practical experiments. He was author of a work which
he called "The Philosopher's Ring." This was not, like "the
philosopher's stone," a thing merely imaginary, nor yet was it
a work of the "Cyclopedy of Arts" (as the sound may seem to
import); but it was, in plain truth, a perpetual almanac. I
say almanac, which word though many make of Arabic extraction, a great antiquary [†] will have it derived from the the Dutch,
Al-mon-aght; that is to say, *Al-mon-heed*, the regard or observation of all moons. However, this work of John was beheld as a
master-piece of that age, and since commented upon by other
writers. He flourished anno Domini 1340.

ROBERT HOLCOT was born in a village of this county so
named, bred in the university of Oxford, and afterwards became
a Dominican in Northampton.[‡]   A deep scholar, and yet commended to be prudent *in rebus agendis,*[§] and accounted one of
the greatest schoolmen in that age. Nor was he only a candle,
or domestic light, confined within the walls of his own country ;
but his learning was a public luminary to all Christendom, as
appears by the praise which Trithemius[||] bestoweth upon him.
" Vir in Divinis Scripturis eruditissimus, et secularium literarum non ignarus ; ingenio præstans, et clarus eloquio, declamator

* Cent. v. num. 75.   † Verstegan, of Decayed Intelligence, p. 58.
‡ Camden's Britannia, in Northamptonshire.
§ Bale, de Scriptoribus Britannicis, cent. vi. num. 8.
|| De Scriptoribus Eccles. fol. 136.

quoque sermonum egregius. Scripsit multa præclara opuscula, quibus nomen suum posteris notificavit."

He died at Northampton of the plague, anno 1349, before he had finished his lectures on the Seventh of Ecclesiastes. I say of the plague, which at that time so raged in England, that our chroniclers* affirm, scarce a tenth person of all sorts was left alive; insomuch that, the churches and churchyards in London not sufficing for their interments, a new churchyard was consecrated in West Smithfield, wherein fifty thousand were buried, who at the time died of the pestilence.†

Robert Dodford was born in a village so called in this county (where the Wirlyes, gentlemen of good account, have long had their habitation); so named, as I take it, from a *ford* over the river Avon, and *dods*, water weeds (commonly called by children cats' tails) growing thereabouts. He was bred a Benedictine monk in the abbey of Ramsey; and applied himself to the study of the Hebrew tongue, wherewith the library (of which he was keeper) in that convent did much abound.‡ He wrote Postils on the Proverbs, and other sermons, which the envy of time hath intercepted from us. He is said to have flourished about the year 1370, by Bale; though Pits (on what account I know not) maketh him more ancient by an hundred years.

Peter Pateshull was, no doubt, born in that village, not far from Northampton; bred an Augustinian in Oxford. However, falling afterwards into some dislike of his order, he procured from Walter Dysse (legate to pope Urban the Sixth) a dispensation to relinquish it; and was made the Pope's honorary chaplain. Afterwards, by often reading the works of Wickliffe (but especially his book of "Real Universals,"§) he became of his judgment; and after the death of Wickliffe, preached and promoted his doctrine; he wrote an exposition of the Prophecy of Hildegards (a stinging comment on a nettling text); and so taxed the pride and laziness of all friars, that his book was burnt by command from the Pope; and the writer thereof had been burnt also, had he not seasonably secured himself by his flight beyond the seas.

This mindeth me of a passage of a friar, who burned a book of Peter Ramus, after the death of the author thereof; and then and there used this distich, in some imitation of Ovid:

> *Parve, nec invideo (sine me) liber ibis in ignem,*
> *Hei mihi quod domino non licet ire tuo.*

" Small book, thy fate I envy not,
Without me feel the flame ;

* Stow's Ann. page 245. † Idem, ibidem.
‡ Bale, de Scriptoribus Britannicis, Cent. iv. num. 41.
§ Idem, Cent. vii. numb. 2.

> Oh had it been thy master's lot,
> He might have felt the same."

But our Pateshull was out of reach in Bohemia, betwixt which and England, a great intercourse in that age, since king Richard had married a sister of Wincelaus king of Bohemia. We behold him as an advancer of Wicklivisme in that county, for which John Huss and Hierome of Prague were afterwards condemned. He flourished in the year of our Lord 1390.

SINCE THE REFORMATION.

ROBERT CROWLEY was born in this county ;* bred master of arts in Magdalen College in Oxford. It happened that one Miles Hogheard, whom Pits† maketh a learned writer, and entituleth him, " Virum doctum, pium, et in fide Catholicâ mirè zelosum," (though in master Fox it appeareth, by his own confession, that he was but an hosier in London,) wrote railing books against the poor Protestants. Our Crowley took him to task, and confuted him in several treatises. Under queen Mary, he fled over to Frankfort ; and returning under queen Elizabeth, was made vicar of Saint Giles without Cripplegate, London, where he lieth buried under a fair plated stone in the chancel. He died on the 18th of June, 1588.‡

EUSEBIUS PAGET was born at Cranford in this county, as Master Ephraim Paget, his aged son, late minister of St. Edmond the King, Lombard Street, hath informed me. He was admitted, at twelve years of age, into Oxford, where, when a boy, he brake his right arm with carrying the pax,§ though surely some casualty beside so light a weight concurred thereunto. He was commonly called the golden *sophister*, and yet he proved no *leaden* graduate. Many years he was a painful minister in London ; and was author of that excellent book called "The History of the Bible," and catechism of "The Forty short Questions," which hath done as much good to unbook-learned people, as any of that kind. The certain date of his death I cannot attain.

JOHN PRESTON, D.D. was born at Heyford in this county ; bred in Queen's College in Cambridge, whose life (interwoven much with church and state matters) is so well written by his pupil, Master Thomas Ball, that all additions thereunto may seem "carrying of coals to Newcastle." However, seeing he who carrieth charcoal (a different kind from the native coal of that place) may meet with a chapman there, on the same confidence a word or two of this doctor.

Before he commenced Master of Arts, he was so far from eminency, as but a little above contempt. Thus the most generous wines are the most muddy before they are fine. Soon after, his

---

* Bale de Scriptoribus Britannicis, Cent ix. num. 80.
† De Angliæ Scriptoribus, 1556.　　　‡ Stow's Survey of London, page 313.
§ As his said son related to me.—F.

skill in philosophy rendered him to the general respect of the university.

He was the greatest pupil-monger in England in man's memory, having sixteen fellow commoners (most heirs to fair estates) admitted in one year in Queen's College, and provided convenient accommodations for them. As William the popular earl of Nassau was said to have won a subject from the king of Spain, to his own party, every time he put off his hat; so was it commonly said in the college, that every time when Master Preston plucked off his hat to doctor Davenant the college-master, he gained a chamber or study for one of his pupils; amongst whom one Chambers, a Londoner (who died very young), was very eminent for his learning.

Being chosen master of Emanuel College, he removed thither with most of his pupils; and I remember when it was much admired where all these should find lodgings in that college, which was so full already, "Oh!" said one, "Master Preston will carry *Chambers* along with him."

The party called Puritan then being most active in Parliament, and doctor Preston most powerful with them, the duke rather used than loved him, to work that party to his compliance. Some thought the doctor was unwilling to do it; and no wonder he *effected* not, what he *affected* not. Others thought he was unable, that party being so diffusive, and then, in their designs (as since in their practices) divided. However, whilst any hope, none but doctor Preston with the duke, set by and extolled, and afterwards, set by and neglected, when found useless to the intended purpose. In a word, my worthy friend fitly calls him the court-comet, blazing for a time, and fading soon afterwards.

He was a perfect politician, and used (lapwing-like) to flutter most on that place which was furthest from his eggs; exact at the concealing of his intentions, with that simulation, which some make to lie in the marches of things lawful and unlawful. He had perfect command of his passion; with the Caspian Sea never ebbing nor flowing; and would not alter his composed pace for all the whipping which satirical wits bestowed upon him. He never had wife, or cure of souls; and, leaving a plentiful, no invidious estate, died anno Domini 1628, July 20. Pass we now from one who was all judgment and gravity, to another (place and time making the connexion) who was all wit and festivity, viz.

THOMAS RANDOLPH, born at Houghton in this county, was first bred in Westminster School, then fellow in Trinity College at Cambridge. The Muses may seem not only to have smiled, but to have been tickled at his nativity, such the festivity of his poems of all sorts. But my declining age, being superannuated to meddle with such ludicrous matters, consigneth the censure and commendation of his poems (as also of his countryman Peter Haulsted, born at Oundle in this county) to younger pens, for whom it is most proper. Master Randolph died anno Domini 1671.

NICHOLAS ESTWICK, B.D. was born at Harrowden (the barony of the Lord Vaux) in this county. A solid Protestant: to counterpoise Kellison, a violent Papist, and native of the same village. He was bred fellow of Christ's College in Cambridge, being there beheld as a pious and judicious divine, always cheerful without the least levity, and grave without any moroseness. He was afterwards presented by the Lord Montague parson of of Warton, where he lived a painful preacher 40 years, less than a deacon in his humility, and more than an archbishop in his own contentment. Hence he was [unwillingly-willing] preferred by the earl of Rutland to Bottesford in Leicestershire, where he had hardly inned one harvest, before, like a ripe sheaf, he was brought into the barn of the grave. Thus, though young trees are meliorated with transplanting, yet old ones seldom live, and never flourish after their removal. Let his works witness the rest of his worth, some of whose books are published, others prepared for the press; and I wish them a happy nativity, for the public good. Coming to take his farewell of his friends, he preached on the forenoon of the Lord's-day, sickened on the afternoon; and was buried with his wife in the same grave, in Warton chancel, the week following, 1657.

ROMISH EXILE WRITERS.

MATTHEW KELLISON was born in this county, at Harrowden,* his father being a servant and tenant of the Lord Vaux, in whose family his infancy did suck in the Romish persuasions. He afterwards went beyond the seas, and was very much in motion. 1. He first fixed himself at the college of Rheims in France: 2. Thence removed to the English college at Rome, where he studied in philosophy and divinity: 3. Returned to Rheims, where he took the degree of Doctor: 4. Removed to Douay, where for many years he read school-divinity: 5. Re-returned to Rheims, where he became King's Professor, and rector of the university.

So much for the travails of his feet; now for the labours of his hands (the pains of his pen) those of his own opinion can give the best account of them. He wrote a book to king James, which his majesty never saw; and another against Sutliff, with many more; and was living 1611.

BENEFACTORS TO THE PUBLIC.

HENRY CHICHELY, son of Thomas and Agnes Chichely, was born at Higham Ferrers, in this county; bred in Oxford, and designed by Wickham himself (yet surviving) to be one of the

---

* Pits, p. 811.

fellows of New College. He afterwards became chaplain to R. Metford bishop of Sarum, who made him archdeacon, which he exchanged for the chancellor's place of that cathedral. This bishop, at his death, made him his chief executor, and bequeathed him a fair gilt cup for a legacy. By king Henry the Fourth he was sent to the Council of Risa, 1409, and by the Pope's own hands was consecrated bishop of St. David's at Vienna, and thence was advanced archbishop of Canterbury by king Henry the Fifth.

During his reign, in the Parliament at Leicester, a shrewd thrust was made at all abbeys, not with a rebated point, but with sharps indeed, which this archbishop, as a skilful fencer, fairly put by, though others will say he guarded that blow with a silver buckler; the clergy paying to the king vast sums of money to maintain his wars in France, and so made a foreign diversion for such active spirits, which otherwise, in all probability, would have antedated the dissolution of monasteries.

Under king Henry the Sixth he sat sure in his see, though often affronted by the rich cardinal Beaufort of Winchester, whom he discreetly thanked for many injuries. A cardinal's cap was proffered to and declined by him; some putting the refusal on the account of his humility, others of his pride (loth to be junior to the aforesaid cardinal); others of his policy, unwilling to be more engaged to the court of Rome. Indeed he was thorough-paced in all spiritual popery which concerned religion (which made him so cruel against the Wicklivites); but in secular Popery (as I may term it, touching the interest of princes) he did not so much as rack, and was a zealous assertor of the English liberties against Romish usurpation.

Great his zeal to promote learning, as appears by three colleges erected and endowed at his expence and procurement: 1. One, with an hospital for the poor, at Higham Ferrers, the place of his nativity. 2. Saint Bernard's in Oxford, afterwards altered and bettered by Sir Thomas White into Saint John's College. 3. All-Souls in Oxford, the fruitful nursery of so many learned men.

He continued in his archbishopric (longer than any of his predecessors for 500 years) full twenty-nine years; and died April 12, 1443.

WILLIAM LAXTON, son to John Laxton, of Oundle in this county, was bred a grocer in London, where he so prospered by his painful endeavours, that he was chosen lord mayor, anno Domini 1544. He founded a fair school and alms-house at Oundle in this county, with convenient maintenance, well maintained at this day by the worshipful company of grocers; and hath been, to my knowledge, the nursery of many scholars most eminent in the university.

These Latin verses are inscribed in the front of the building:

Oundellæ natus, Londini parta labore,
Laxtonus posuit senibus puerisque levamen.

" At Oundle born, what he did get
    In London with great pain,
Laxton to young and old hath set
    A comfort to remain."

He died anno Domini 1556, the 29th of July; and lieth buried, under a fair tomb, in the chancel of Saint Antony's, London.

SINCE THE REFORMATION.

NICHOLAS LATHAM was born at Brigstock,* in this county, and afterwards became minister of All-Saints' church in Barnwells. This man had no considerable estate left him from his father, nor eminent addition of wealth from his friends, nor enjoyed any dignity in the church of England, nor ever held more than one moderate benefice. And yet, by God's blessing on his vivacious frugality, he got so great an estate, that he told a friend he could have left his son, had he had one, land to the value of five hundred pounds by the year. But, though he had no issue, yet, making the poor his heirs, he left the far greatest part of his estate to pious uses; founded several small schools with salaries in country villages; and founded a most beautiful almshouse at Oundle in this county; and I could wish that all houses of the like nature were but continued and ordered so well as this is, according to the will of the founder. He died anno Domini 1620; and lieth buried in the chancel of his own parish, having lived seventy-two years.

EDWARD MONTAGUE, Baron of Boughton, and eldest son to Sir Edward Montague, knight, was born in this county; a pious, peaceable, and hospitable patriot. It was not the least part of his outward happiness, that, having no male issue by his first wife, and marrying when past fifty years of age, he lived to see his son enriched with hopeful children. I behold him, as bountiful Barsillia,† superannuated for courtly pleasures, and therefore preferring to live honourably in his own country, wherein he was generally beloved, so that popularity may be said to have affected him, who never affected it : for, in evidence of the vanity thereof, he used to say, " do the common sort of people nineteen courtesies together; and yet you may lose their love, if you do but go over the stile before them." He was a bountiful benefactor to Sidney College, and builded and endowed an alms-house at Weekly in this county.

" To have no bands in their death,"‡ is an outward favour many wicked have, many godly men want; amongst whom, this

* So saith the inscription on his monument.   † 2 Samuel xix. 35.
‡ Psalm lxxiii. 4.

good lord, who died in restraint in the Savoy, on the account of his loyalty to his sovereign. Let none grudge him the enjoying of his judgment, a purchase he so dearly bought, and truly paid for, whose death happened in the year of our Lord 164 . .

MEMORABLE PERSONS.

There is a memorial entered on the wall of the cathedral of Peterborough, for one who, being sexton thereof, interred two queens therein [Katharine Dowager, and Mary of Scotland,] more than fifty years intervening betwixt their several sepultures. This vivacious sexton also buried two generations, or the people in that place twice over. Thus having built many houses (so I find graves frequently called *domus æternales)* for others, some (as it was fitting) performed this last office unto him. Thus though sextons often meet with bad savours arising from corpse too much (or rather too little) corrupted, yet is the instance of his long life alleged by such who maintain that the smelling to perfect mould made of men's consumed bodies is a preservative of life.

LORD MAYORS.

1. John Rest, son of Will. Rest, of Peterborough, Grocer, 1516.
2. Will. Laxton, son of John Laxton, of Yongdell, Grocer, 1544.
3. Ralph Freeman, son of Will. Freeman, of Northampton, Clothworker, 1633.

Reader, this is one of the twelve counties whose gentry were not returned into the Tower, in the reign of king Henry the Sixth.

SHERIFFS.

HENRY II.

Anno
1 Rich. Basset, et Albrus de Vere.
2 Simon fil. Petri.
3 Idem.
4
5 Idem.
6
7 Idem.
8 Hugo Gubion.
9 Idem.
10 Simon fil. Petri, et Hugo Gubion.
11 Simon, for five years.
16 Rob. fil. Gawini, for five years.

Anno
21 Hugo de Gundevill.
22 Idem.
23 Idem.
24 Tho. fil. Bernardi, for six years.
30 Tho. et Rad. Morin.
31 Galfr. fil. Petri.
32 Idem.
33 Idem.

RICHARD I.

1 Gal. fil. Petri.
2 Rich. Engaigne.
3 Idem.
4 Gal. fil. Petri, et Rob. fil. Radulph.

Anno

5 Idem.

6 Gal. et Simon de Patis-
hull.

7 Simon de Patishull, for
four years.

JOH. REG.

1 Simon. Patishull, for five
years.

6 Rob. de Sancei, et
Hen. filius Petri.

7 Idem.

8 Pet. de Stores, et
Gilb. Groc.

9 Wal. de Preston, et
Joh. de Ulcot, ut Custos.

10 Walt. de Preston, ut Custos.

11 Rob. de Braybrook, ut
Custos.

12 Rob. ut Custos.

13 Rob. et Hen. fil. ejus.

14 H. Braybrook, ut Custos.

15 Rob. et Hen. ut Custos.

16 Hen. de Braybrook, ut
Custos.

17 Idem.

HEN. III.

1 Falc. de Breantre, et Rad.
de Bray, for eight years.

9 Rad. de Trublevil, et Rad.
Washingbury, for four
years.

13 Steph. de Segne, et Will.
de Marawast, for six
years.

19 Hen. de Rada, for five
years.

25 Will. de Coleworth.

26 Idem.

27 Alan. de Maidwell, for six
years.

33 Simon de Thorp.

34 Idem.

35 Rob. Basset.

36 Idem.

37 Will. de Insula.

Anno

38 Hugo de Manneby.

39 Idem.

40 Will. de Insula.

41 Hugo de Manneby.

42 Idem.

43 Eustacius de Watford.

44 Simon de Patishull.

45 Idem.

46 Idem.

47 Alanus de Tash.

48 Alanus de Insh.

49 Idem.

50 Idem.

51 Warin. de Basingburn, et
Joh. de Oxenden Cl'ic.

52 Joh. de Moyne, et
Nich. de Maunden.

53 Idem.

54 Idem.

55 Will. de Boyvill.

EDWARD I.

1 Will. de Bowvill.

2 Gilb. de Kirkby, for five
years.

7 Tho. de Arden.

8 Rob. de Band.

9 Rob. de Band in Charta
quidem Asp. H. for nine
years.

18 Joh. Druell, for twelve
years.

30 Rob. de Veer.

31 Joh. de Ashton, for five
years.

EDWARD II.

1

2 Almaric. de Nodardus, et
Simon de Greenhull.

3 Joh. de Willoughby.

4 Idem.

5 Idem.

6 Gal. de Bradden.

7 Tho. Wale.

8 Eustac. de Barnby.

9 Joh. de Ashton.

10 Joh. de Hoby.

Anno		Anno	
11	Joh. de Honby.	15	Idem.
12	Joh. et Egid. de Cugelio.	16	Tho. de Babenham.
13	Joh. de Honby, Egid. de Cugelio, et Joh. de Wittebur, Egid. de Cugegio, et Joh. de Wittlebur.	17	Tho. de Buckton.
		18	Rob. Pandeley.
		19	Idem.
		20	Idem.
14	Hum. de Basingburne, et Joh. Sto. Mauro.	21	Walt. Parles.
		22	Idem.
15	Hum. Basingburne.	23	Rich. Blundel.
16		24	Idem.
17	Joh. de Sto. Mauro, et Joh. Daundelin.	25	Pet. Mallore.
		26	Walt. Parles.
18	Joh. et Joh.	27	Idem.
19	Joh. Daudelin.	28	Idem.
		29	Joh. de Kaynes, for four years.

EDWARD III.

Anno		Anno	
1	Will. de Sto. Mauro, et Simon de Lanshall.	33	Andre. Landwath.
2	Will. de Sto. Mauro.	34	Walt. Parles.
3	Tho. Wake.	35	Rich. Wydevill, for eight years.
4	Idem.	43	Tho. de Preston.
5	Tho. de Buckton.	44	Idem.
6	Idem.	45	Ricn. Wydenell.
7	Will. Lovell, for four years.	46	Rob. Hotot.
		47	Simon Ward.
11	Tho. Wake.	48	Joh. Karnell.
12	Idem.	49	Tho. de Preston.
13	Tho. Wake de Blisworth.	50	Rob. Poteleyn.
14	Idem.	51	Joh Karnell.

SHERIFFS OF NORTHAMPTONSHIRE.

RICHARD II.

Anno	Name and Arms.	Place.
1	Tho. de Preston . . .	Preston.
2	Joh. Lions.	
3	Joh. Paveley.	
	Erm. on a fess Az. three crosses patée O.	
4	Joh. Widevill . . .	Grafton.
	Arg. a fess and canton G.	
5	Johan. Lions.	
6	Ro. Atte Chaumbre.	
	Arg. three chevrons S.	
7	Nich. Litlinges.	
8	Rog. Chaumbre . . .	*ut prius.*
9	Joh. Widevill . . .	*ut prius.*
10	Joh. Paveley . . .	*ut prius.*
11	Ro. de la Chaumbre .	*ut prius.*
12	Rad. Parles.	

Anno   Name.   Place.

13 Joh. Paveley, mil. . . *ut prius.*
14 Joh. Widevill . . . *ut prius.*
15 Joh. Tindall . . . Deane.
     Arg. a fess indented, and three crescents in chief G.
16 Joh. Mallore . . . Winewick.
     O. three lions passant guardant S.
17 Johan. Mulsho.
     Erm. on a bend S. three goats' heads erased Arg. armed O.
18 Idem . . . . . *ut prius.*
19 Idem . . . . . *ut prius.*
20 Joh. Warwick.
     Checky G. and Az. a chevron Erm.
21 Joh. Mulsho . . . *ut prius.*
22 Idem . . . . . *ut prius.*

HENRY IV.

1 Joh. Warwike . . . *ut prius.*
2 Joh. Cope . . . . Canons Ashby.
     Arg. on a chevron Az. betwixt three roses G. slipped and leaved three flower-de-luces O.
     Joh. Chetwood . . . Warkworth.
     Quarterly, Arg. and G. four crosses patée counterchanged.
3 Egid. Malorye.
4 Warin. Lucyen.
5 Idem.
6 Rich. Wedenhall.
7 Tho. Widevill . . . *ut prius.*
8 Rad. Grene . . . . Greens Norton.
     Az. three bucks trippant O.
9 Rad. Parles.
10 Tho. Mulsho . . . *ut prius.*
11 Tho. Widevill . . . *ut prius.*
12 Mat. Swetenham.

HENRY V.

1 Tho. Wake . . . . Blisworth.
     O. two bars and three torteaux in chief G.
2 Rad. Grene . . . *ut prius.*
3 Tho. Widevill . . . *ut prius.*
4 Tho. Grene, mil. . . *ut prius.*
5 Joh. Manutell.
6 Tho. Wake . . . *ut prius.*
7 Tho. Pilkinton.
     Arg. a cross patonce voided G.
8 Tho. Wodevill . . . *ut prius.*
9 Idem.   . . . *ut prius.*

HENRY VI.

Anno	Name.	Place.
1	Tho. Wodevill . . .	*ut prius.*
2	Tho. Holland	Brackley.

Az. semy de flower-de-luces a lion rampant guardant Arg.

3 Johan. Wakerley.
4 Joh. Catesby . . . . Catesby.

Az. two lions passant S. couronné O.

5 Tho. Chaumbre . . . *ut prius.*
6 Johan. Kivett.
7 Tho. Widevill . . . Grafton.
8 Georg. Longvill . . . Little Billing.

G. a fess indented betwixt six cross croslets Arg.

9 Will. Branuspatch.
10 Joh. Colpeper.

Arg. a bend engrailed G.

11 Tho. Chaumbre . . . *ut prius.*
12 Tho. Wodevill . . . *ut prius.*
13 Tho. Wake . . . . *ut prius.*
14 Joh. Holland, mil. . . *ut prius.*
15 Will. Vaux . . . . . Harrowden.

Checky Arg. and G. on a chevron Az. three roses O.

16 Rich. Widevill . . . *ut prius.*
17 Tho. Chaumbre . . . *ut prius.*
18 Eustat. Burnby.

Arg. two bars a lion passant gardant in chief G.

19 Tho. Holland . . . . *ut prius.*
20 Tho. Green, mil. . . *ut prius.*
21 Will. Catesby . . . . *ut prius.*
22 Joh. Marbury.
23 Hen. Green . . . . Drayton.

Arg. a cross engrailed G.

24 Walt. Mauntell.
25 Tho. Wake . . . . *ut prius.*
26 Joh. Holland, mil. . . *ut prius.*
27 Eustat. Burnby . . . *ut prius.*
28 Will. Vaux . . . . *ut prius.*
29 Tho. Wake . . . . *ut prius.*
30 Will. Catesby, arm. . . Ashby St. Legers.

Arms, *ut prius.*

31 Nich. Griffin, arm. . . Dingly.

S. a griffin segreant Arg.

32 Will. Vaux . . . . *ut prius.*
33 Tho Green, mil. . . . *ut prius.*
34 Will. Catesby, mil. . . *ut prius.*
35 Nich. Griffin, mil. . . *ut prius.*
36 Tho. Green, arm. . . *ut prius.*
37 Rob. Olney . . . . Catesby.

Anno   Name.   Place.

38 Will. Mauntell, arm.

EDWARD IV.

1 Will. Fairfax, arm.
    Arg. three bars gemelles G.; over all a lion rampant S.
2 Tho. Walker. arm.
3 Idem.
4 Walt. Mountell.
5 Hen. Green, arm. . . Draiton.
    Arms, *ut prius.*
6 Hen. Hudleston.
    G. fretty Arg.
7 Rad. Hastings.
    Arg. a maunch S.
8 Rog. Salisbury, arm.
    G. a lion rampant Arg. crowned betwixt three crescents O.
9 Guido Walston.
10 Will. Newenham.
11 Rad. Hastings . . . *ut prius.*
12 John Hulcot.
13 Hen. Hudleston . . . *ut prius.*
14 Rich. Griffin, arm. . . *ut prius.*
15 Ric. Knightly, arm. . Fawsley.
    Quarterly Erm. and O. three pales G.
16 *Nullus Titulus in hoc Rotulo.*
17 Rog. Salsbury . . . *ut prius.*
18 Will. Chaumbre . . . *ut prius.*
19 Will Catesby, mil. . . *ut prius.*
20 Will. Newenham.
21 Rob. Pemberton, arm. . Rushden.
    Arg. a chevron betwixt three buckets S. handled and
      hooped O.
22 Tho. Lovell . . . . Astwell.
    Barry nebuly of six O. and G.

RICHARD III.

1 Wittelbury.
2 Rog. Wake, arm. . . . *ut prius.*
3 Rich. Burton, arm.
    Az. a fess between three talbots' heads erased O.

HENRY VII.

1 Hen. Veer, ar. . . . Addington.
    Quarterly G. and O. in the first a mullet Arg.
2 Rich. Knightly . . . *ut prius.*
3 Guido Wolston.
4 David Phillipps.

Anno	Name.	Place.

5 Tho. Haliswood.

Arg. on a chevron G. three lozenges Erm. betwixt three owlets S.; on a chief Az. three nut-trees O.

6 Tho. Lovel, arm.. . . *ut prius.*

7 Guid. Walston, mil.

8 Rob. Witlebury.

9 Joh. Danvers, arm.

G. a chevron Arg. betwixt three mullets of six points O.

10 Joh. Dyve, arm. . . . Haddon.

Parti per pale Arg. and G. a fess Az.

11 Nick. Vaux, mil. . . . *ut prius.*

12 Will. Hertwell.

13 Will. Salisbury, arm. . *ut prius.*

14 Hum. Catesby, arm.. . *ut prius.*

15 Rich. Burton, ar. . . *ut prius.*

16 Fulc. Wodehull, a.

17 Nich. Vaux, mil. . . . *ut prius.*

18 Tho. Andrews, arm. . Harlston.

G. a saltire O. surmounted with another Vert.

19 Joh. Dyve, arm. . , *ut prius.*

20 Rich. Griffin, mil. . . *ut prius.*

21 Tho. Lovell, arm. . . *ut prius.*

22 Joh. Tresham, arm. . . Rushton.

Parti per saltire S. and O. six trefoils of the second.

23 Tho. Cheyne, mil.

Checky O. and Az. a fess G. fretty Erm.

24 Joh. Mulshow, arm. . . *ut prius.*

HENRY VIII.

1 Tho. Parre, mil. . . Green's-Norton.

Arg. two bars Az. a border engrailed S.

2 Ric. Knightley, mil. . *ut prius.*

3 Joh. Spew, arm.

4 Rad. Lane, arm. . . . Horton.

Parti per pale Arg. and G. three saltires Arg.

5 Joh. Catesby, arm. . . *ut prius.*

6 Rob. Mathew, arm. . . Braden.

7 Nich. Wodehull.

8 Nich. Vaux, mil. . . *ut prius.*

9 Will. Parre, mil. . . . *ut prius.*

10 Will. Gascoigne.

Arg. on a pale S. a luce's head erased O.

11 Tho. Lucy, mil.

G. crusuly O. three lucies hauriant Arg.

12 Joh. Mulshow, arm. . *ut prius.*

13 Will. Parre, mil. . . Horton.

14 Joh. Clark, mil.

15 Will. Fitz-Will. sen.   .   Milton.
    Lozengy Arg. and G.
16 Tho. Tresham, arm .   .   *ut prius.*
17 Walt. Mauntel, mil.
18 Hum. Stafford, mil.
    O. a chevron G. and a quarter Erm.
19 Nich. Odell, arm.
20 Will. Fitz.-Will. mil.   .   *ut prius.*
21 Joh. Clarke, mil.   .   .   Stamford.
    Az. fretty Arg.
22 Rich. Cave, arm.
    Az. a fess Erm. betwixt six sea-mews' heads erazed Arg.
23 Will. Spencer, mil.   .   .   Althorp.
    David Sissill, arm.   .   .   Stamford.
    Barry of ten Arg. and Az. on six eschutcheons S. as many
      lions rampant of the first.
24 David Cecill, arm.   .   .   *ut prius.*
25 Will. Parr, mil.   .   .   .   *ut prius.*
26 Tho. Griffin, mil.   .   .   *ut prius.*
27 Joh. Clarke, mil.   .   .   *ut prius.*
28 Will. Newenham.
29 Will. Parr, mil.   .   .   .   *ut prius.*
30 Anth. Catesby, arm.   .   *ut prius.*
31 Tho. Tresham, mil.   .   .   *ut prius.*
32 Will. Newenham.
33 Rob. Kikeman, mil.
34 Rich. Catesby, mil.   .   .   *ut prius.*
35 Tho. Brudenell, arm.   .   Dean.
    Arg. a chevron G. betwixt three caps Az. turned up Er-
      mine.
36 Tho. Griffin, mil.   .   .   *ut prius.*
37 Joh. Cope, arm.
38 Tho. Cave, arm.   .   .   .   *ut prius.*

EDW. VI.

1 Hum. Stafford, mil.   .   .   *ut prius.*
2 Tho. Tresham, mil.   .   .   *ut prius.*
3 Rich. Catesby, mil.   .   .   *ut prius.*
4 Tho. Andrews, arm.   .   .   *ut prius.*
5 Joh. Spencer, arm.   .   .   *ut prius.*
6 Tho. Lovell, arm.   .   .   *ut prius.*

PHIL. et MAR.

1 Tho. Cave, mil.   .   .   .   *ut prius.*
1,2 Val. Knightley, mil.   .   *ut prius.*
2,3 Tho. Tresham, mil.   .   .   *ut prius.*
3,4 Tho. Andrews, mil.   .   .   *ut prius.*
4,5 Joh. Fermor, mil.
    Arg. a fess S. betwixt three leopards' heads erased G.

Anno   Name,   Place.

5,6 Joh. Spencer, mil;   .   .   *ut prius.*

ELIZ. REG.

1 Edw. Montague, arm. .   Boughton.
   Arg. three fusils in fess G. a border S.
2 Tho. Lovell, arm.   .   .   Astwell.
   Barry nebulé of six O. and G.
3 Tho. Spencer, arm.   .   .   Althorp.
   Arg. a fess Ermin. betwixt sea-mews' heads erased Arg.
4 Tho. Catesby, arm.   .   .   Ashby St. Legers.
   Arg. two lions passant S. couronné O.
5 Rob. Lane, mil.   .   .   .   Horton.
   Parti per pale Az. and G. three saltires Arg.
6 Edm. Brudenel, arm.   .   Dean.
   Arg. a chevron G. betwixt three caps Az. turned up Erm.
7 Hum. Stafford, mil. .   .   Blatherwick.
   O. a chevron G. and a quarter Erm.
8 Edw. Elmes, arm.   .   .   Lilford.
   Erm. two bars S. each charged with five elm-leaves trans-
      posed O.
9 Ric. Knightley, mil.   .   Fawsley.
   Quarterly Erm. and O. three pales G.
10 Tho. Andrews, arm.   .   Cherwello'
   G. a cross O. surmounted of another Vert.
11 Will. Sanders, arm.
   Parti per pale S. and Arg. three elephants' heads coun-
      terchanged.
12 Ed. Mountague, mil.   .   *ut prius.*
13 Joh. Spencer, mil.   .   .   *ut prius.*
14 Tho. Lovel, arm.   .   .   *ut prius.*
15 Tho. Tresham, arm. .   .   Rushton.
   Parti per saltire S. and O. six trefoils of the second.
16 Edm. Onley, arm.
17 Rog. Cave, arm.   .   .   .   Stanford.
   Az. fretty Arg.
18 Tho. Brooke, arm.   .   .   Great Oakley.
   O. on a fess Az. three escalops of the first.
19 Edm. Brudnell, mil.   .   *ut prius.*
20 Tho. Cecil, mil.   .   .   .   Burghley.
   Barry of ten Arg. and Az. on six escutcheons S. as many
      lions rampant of the first.
21 Will. Chauncy, arm.   .   Edgecot.
   O. three chevronels engrailed G.
22 Rich. Knightly, mil.   .   *ut prius.*
23 Joh. Isham, arm.   .   .   Longport.
   G. a fess and three piles in chief wavy, in point Arg.
24 Edw. Griffin, arm.   .   .   Dingley.
   S. a griffin surgeant Arg.

Anno	Name.	Place.

25 Joh. Spencer, mil. . . *ut prius.*
26 Euseb. Isham, arm. . . *ut prius.*
27 Barth. Tate, arm.
28 Tho. Andrews, arm. . . *ut prius.*
29 Edw. Saunders, arm. . *ut prius.*
30 Ed. Mountague, mil. . *ut prius.*
31 Geor. Farmer, mil. . . Easton.
    Arg. a fess S. betwixt three leopards' heads erased G.
32 Joh. Spencer, mil. , . *ut prius.*
33 Edw. Watson, arm. . . Rockingham.
    Arg. on a chevron engrailed Az. betwixt three martlets S.
        as many crescents O.
34 Anth. Mildmay, arm. . Apethorp.
    Arg. three lions rampant Az.
35 Thob. Chauncy, arm. . *ut prius.*
36 Joh. Read, arm.
    G. on a bend Arg. three shovellers S. beaked O.
37 Edw. Mountague . . *ut prius.*
38 Tho. Molsho, arm. . . Thingdon.
    Erm. on a bend S. three goats' heads erased Arg. armed
        O.
39 Rich. Chetwood, arm.
40 Eras. Draydon, arm. . Canons Ashby.
    Az. a lion rampant; in chief a globe betwixt two stars O.
41 Will. Browne, arm.
42 Ed. Montague, arm. . *ut prius.*
43 Rob. Spencer, mil.
    Quarterly, Arg. and G. the second and third charged with
        a fret O.; over all on a bend S. three escalops of the
        first.
44 Geo. Sherley, arm. . . Astwell.
    Paly of six O. and Az. a canton Erm.
45 Wil. Tate, arm. et 1 Jac.

JAC. REG.

1 Will. Tate, arm.
2 Art. Throgkmorton.
    G. on a chevron Arg. three bars gemellée S.
3 Joh. Freeman, arm. . . Great Billing.
4 Will. Samuell, mil.
5 Wil. Fitz-Will. mil. . . Milton.
    Lozengée Arg. and G.
6 Tho. Elmes, arm. . . Greens-Norton.
    Arms, *ut prius.*
7 Will. Saunders . . . *ut prius.*
8 Tho. Tresham, mil. . . Newton.
    Arms, *ut prius.*
9 Joh. Isham, mil. . . . *ut prius.*

Anno	Name.		Place.
10	Euse. Andrews, mil.	.	*ut prius.*
11	Joh. Wiseman, arm.		

  S. a chevron betwixt three cronells (or spear burs) Arg.

12	Will. Willmer, arm.	.	Sywell.
13	God. Chibnall, arm.	.	Orlebere.
14	Tho. Brooke, mil.	. .	*ut prius.*
15	Hat. Farmer, mil.	. .	*ut prius.*
16	Sim. Norwich, mil.	. .	Branton.
17	Eras. Dryden, bar.	. .	*ut prius.*
18	Lodi. Pemberton, mil.	.	Rushton.

  Arg. a chevron betwixt three buckets S. handled and
   hooped O.

19	Joh. Hanbury, mil.	. .	Kelmarsh.
20	Mose. Troyoll, arm.		
21	Edw. Shugburgh, arm.	.	Nazeby.

  S. a chevron betwixt three mullets Arg.

22	Wil. Chauncy, mil.	. .	*ut prius.*

CAR. REG.

1	Ric. Knightley, arm.	.	*ut prius.*
2	Joh. Davers, mil.		

  G. a chevron inter three mullets O.

3	Joh. Worley, arm.	. .	Dodford.
4	Hen. Robinson, mil.	.	Cransley.
5	Tho. Elmes, arm.	. .	*ut prius.*
6	Fran. Nicholls, arm.	.	Faxton.
7	Joh. Hewett, bar.	. .	Hemington.

  S. a chevron counter-battillé betwixt three owls Arg.

8	Lo. Watson, mil. et bar.	*ut prius.*
9	Rich. Samwell, mil.	
10	Joh. Driden, bar.	. .	*ut prius.*
11	Caro. Cokaine, arm.	. .	Rushton.

  Arg. three cocks G.

12	Rob. Banaster, mil.	

  Arg. a cross patée S.

13	Joh. Handbury, mil.	.	*ut prius.*
14	Phil. Hollman, arm.		
15	Chri. Yelverton, mil.	.	Easton.

  Arg. three lioncels rampant G. a chief of the second.

16	Anth. Haslewood.	
17	Will. Wilmer, mil.	
18		
19	Edr. Farmer, arm.	. .	*ut prius.*
20	Idem.	
21		
22	Will. Ward, arm.	

  Az. a cross patée O.

16. RICHARD WIDEVILL, alias WODEVILL. — He was a
vigorous knight, and married Jaquet duchess of Bedford, of
most ancient extraction in this county, which (as it appears in
the Ledger-book of Sopewell abbey) had flourished four generations before him at Grafton Honor in this county. Malicious,
therefore, the cavil of Richard duke of York (which the stage
poet hath got by the end), affirming " that they were made
noble, who were not worth a *noble ;*" when this knight was, by
his son-in-law king Edward the Fourth, created earl of Rivers;
and although his issue male failed in the next generation, yet
am I confident, that besides the apparent royal line, an
ordinary herald may, with little pains, derive all the ancient
nobility of England from his six daughters, most honourably
married.

23. HENRY GREEN.—He was a wealthy man (but of a
different family from those of Greens-Norton, as appears by
his arms), who first built the fair house of Drayton in this
county. He had one sole daughter and heir, Constance, married to John Stafford earl of Wiltshire, to whom she bare
Edward Stafford, earl of Wiltshire, who died without issue; so
that her large inheritance devolved unto the family of the Veers;
of whom anon.*

1. HENRY VEER, Arm.—He was son to Richard Veer,
esquire, of Addington, by Isabel his wife, sister, and, at last,
sole heir to Henry Green, of Drayton, esquire, of whom formerly.† This Henry was afterwards knighted; and, dying
without issue-male, Elizabeth his daughter and co-heir was
married to John first lord Mordant, to whom she brought
Drayton-house in this county, and other fair lands, as the partage of her portion.

11. NICHOLAS VAUX, Mil.—He was a jolly gentleman, both
for camp and court, a great reveller, good as well in a march as
a mask; being governor of Guines in Picardy, whom king
Henry the Eighth, for his loyalty and valour, created baron of
Harowden in this county, ancestor to Edward Lord Vaux, now
living [1659.]

This Sir Nicholas, when young, was the greatest gallant of
the English court; no knight, at the marriage of prince Arthur,
appearing in so costly an equipage; when he wore a gown of
purple velvet, dight with pieces of gold, so thick and massive,
that it was valued (besides the silk and furs) at a thousand

* In the first of King Henry VII. p. 182.   † In the 23d of Henry VI.

pounds;* and the next day wore a collar of SS. which weighed (as goldsmiths reported) eight hundred pounds of nobles.

Some will wonder, that Empsom and Dudley (the royal promoters then in prime) did not catch him by the collar, or pick a hole in his gown, upon the breach of some rusty penal sumptuary statute; the rather, because lately the earl of Oxford was heavily fined for supernumerous attendance. But know, that king Henry could better bear with gallantry than greatness in his subjects, especially when such expence cost himself nothing, and conduced much to the solemnity of his son's nuptials. Besides, such plate, as wrought, employed artizans; as massive, retained its intrinsical value, with little loss, either of the owners or commonwealth.

HENRY VIII.

1. THOMAS PAR, Mil.—His former residence was at Kendal castle in Westmoreland, whence he removed into this county, having married Maud, one of the daughters and co-heirs of Sir Thomas Green, of Greens-Norton.* He was father to queen Katharine Par (which rendereth a probability of her nativity in this county), and to William marquis of Northampton; of whom hereafter.

15. WILLIAM FITZ-WILLIAMS, sen. Mil.—This must be the person of whom I read this memorable passage in Stow's Survey of London :‡

"Sir William Fitz-Williams the elder, being a merchant-tailor, and servant sometime to cardinal Wolsey, was chosen alderman of Bread-street-ward in London, anno 1506. Going afterward to dwell at Milton in Northamptonshire, in the fall of the cardinal, his former master, he gave him kind entertainment there, at his house in the country. For which deed, being called before the king, and demanded how he durst entertain so great an enemy to the state, his answer was, 'that he had not contemptuously or wilfully done it; but only because he had been his master, and (partly) the means of his greatest fortunes.' The king was so well pleased with his answer, that saying himself had few such servants, he immediately knighted him, and afterwards made him a privy councillor."

But we have formerly spoken of the benefactions of this worthy knight, in the county of Essex, whereof he was sheriff in the sixth of king Henry the Eighth.

13. WILLIAM PAR, Mil.—I have cause to be confident, that this was he who, being uncle and lord chamberlain to queen Katharine Par, was afterwards, by king Henry the Eighth, created baron Par of Horton. Left two daughters only, married into

---

* Stow's Chronicle, page 483.
† Mills, in Catalogue of Honour, p. 1026.　　　‡ Page 89.

the families of Tressame and Lane.   The reader is requested to distinguish him from his namesake nephew, sheriff in the 25th of this king's reign ; of whom hereafter.

21. JOHN CLARKE, Mil.—I find there was one Sir John Clarke, knight, who, in the fifth of Henry the Eighth, at the siege of Terrowane, took prisoner Lewis de Orleans, duke of Longevile, and marquis of Rotueline.   This Sir John bare, for his paternal coat, Argent, on a bend Gules three swans proper between as many pellets.

But afterwards, in memory of his service aforesaid, by special command from the king, his coat armour was rewarded with a canton sinister Azure, and thereupon a demi-ram mounting Argent, armed Or, between two flowers-de-luce in chief of the last ; over all a baton dexter-ways Argent, as being the arms of the duke his prisoner, and by martial law belonging to him·*

He lieth buried in the next county, viz. in the church of Tame in Oxfordshire, where his coat and cause thereof is expressed on his monument.   If this be not the same with Sir John Clarke our sheriff, I am utterly at a loss, and desire some other's courteous direction.

All I will add is this : If any demand why this knight did only give a parcel and not the entire arms of the duke his prisoner, a learned antiquary† returns this satisfactory answer : that he who taketh a Christian captive is to give but part of his arms (to mind him of charitable moderation in using his success) ; intimating withal, that one taking a Pagan prisoner may justify the bearing of his whole coat by the laws of armoury.

I must not conceal that I have read, in a most excellent manuscript, viz. the " View of Staffordshire," made by Sampson Erderswicke, esquire, that one William Stamford, in that county, had good land given him therein, for taking the duke of Longevile prisoner, August the 16th, in the fifth of king Henry the Eighth.   History will not allow two dukes of Longevile captives ; and yet I have a belief for them both, that Sir John Clarke and William Stamford were *causæ sociæ* of his captivity ; and the king remunerated them both, the former with an addition of honour, the latter with an accession of estate.

23. WILLIAM SPENCER, Miles ; and DAVID SISSILL, Arm.

24. DAVID CECILL, Arm.—Sir William Spencer dying [it seems] in his shrievalty, David Sissill supplied the remainder of that, and was sheriff the next year.   This David had three times been alderman ‡ of Stamford § (part whereof, called Saint Mar-

---

* Gwillim's Display of Heraldry, page 2, edition 1.
† Camden, in Remains.
‡ The head officer of Stamford was then so styled ; see before in Lincolnshire.
§ R. Butcher, in Survey of Stamford, p. 43.

tin's, is in this county), viz. 1504, 1515, and 1526 ; and now twice sheriff of the county, which proves him a person both of birth, brains, and estate ; seeing, in that age, in this county so plentiful of capable persons, none were advanced to that office, except esquires at least of much merit. The different spelling of his name is easily answered, the one being according to his extraction, of the Sitsilts of Alterynnis in Herefordshire ; the other according to the vulgar pronunciation. All I will add is this, that his grandchild William Cecil (afterwards baron of Burghley, and lord treasurer of England), being born anno 1521, was just ten years of age in the shrievalty of this David his grandfather.*

25. WILLIAM PAR, Mil.—He was son to Sir Thomas Par, of whom before. Ten years after, viz. in the 35th year of his reign, king Henry the Eighth (having newly married his sister queen Katharine Par), made him Lord Par of Kendall, and earl of Essex, in right of Anne Bourcher his wife.

King Edward the Sixth created him marquis of Northampton. Under queen Mary, he was condemned for siding with queen Jane ; but pardoned his life, and restored to his lands, as by queen Elizabeth to his honour. Much was he given to music and poetry ; and wanted not personal valour, not unskilful, though unsuccessful, in military conduct, as in the employment against Ket. He died anno Domini 1571, without issue.

QUEEN MARY.

2, 3. THOMAS TRESSAM, Mil.—He was a person of great command in this county, and was zealous (against the court faction) in proclaiming and promoting queen Mary to the crown. She therefore, in gratitude, made him the first and last lord prior of the re-erected order of St. John of Jerusalem. Dying without issue, and being buried in Rushton church, his large lands descended to his kinsman and heir Thomas Tressam; of whom hereafter.

QUEEN ELIZABETH.

6. EDMUND BRUDENELL, Arm.—This is that worthy person, of whom (afterwards knighted) Master Camden entereth this honourable memorial :† " E quibus Edmundus Brudenel, Eques auratus, non ita pridem defunctus, venerándæ antiquitatis summis fuit cultor et admirator." He may seem to have entailed his learned and liberal inclinations and abilities, on his (though not son) heir, Thomas Lord Brudenell of Stoughton, than whom none of our nobility more able in the English antiquities.

15. THOMAS TRESSAM, Arm.—The queen knighted him, in

---

* Camden's Elizabeth, in anno 1598.   † Britannia, in Northamptonshire.

the 18th year of her reign, at Kenilworth. Hard to say whether greater his delight or skill in buildings, though more forward in beginning than fortunate in finishing his fabrics ; amongst which the market house at Rothwell, adorned with the arms of the gentry of the county, was highly commendable. Having many daughters, and being a great housekeeper, he matched most of them into honourable, the rest of them into worshipful and wealthy, families. He was zealous in the Romish persuasion (though as yet not convicted), which afterwards cost him a long confinement in Wisbeach castle.

20. Thomas Cecill, Mil.—He was eldest son to Sir William Cecill, then baron of Burghley, who would not have him by favour excused from serving his country. He afterwards was earl of Exeter ; and married Dorothy, one of the coheirs of the Lord Latimer. These jointly bestowed one hundred and eight pounds per annum on Clare-hall in Cambridge.

28. Thomas Andrews, Arm.—He attended the execution of the queen of Scots at Fotheringhay castle, demeaning himself with much gravity, to his great commendation.*

34. Anthony Mildmay, Esq.—He was son to Sir Walter, privy-councillor, and founder of Emanuel College. This Anthony was by queen Elizabeth knighted, and sent over into France on an embassy ; upon the same token he was at Geneva the same time (reader, I have it from uncontrollable intelligence) when Theodore Beza, their minister, was convented before their Consistory, and publicly checked for preaching too eloquently ; he pleaded, " that what they called eloquence in him, was not affected but natural ; and promised to endeavour more plainness for the future." Sir Anthony, by grace co-heir to Sir Henry Sherington, had one daughter, Mary, married to Sir Francis Fane, afterwards earl of Westmoreland.

43. Robert Spencer, Mil.—He was the fifth knight of his family in an immediate succession,† well allied and extracted, being a branch descended from the Spencers earls of Gloucester and Winchester.‡ By king James, in the first of his reign, he was created baron Spencer of Wormeleiton in the county of Warwick. He was a good patriot, of a quick and clear spirit, as by one passage may appear.

Speaking in parliament of the valour of their English ancestors, in defending the liberties of the nation ; " Your ancestors," said the earl of Arundel, " were keeping of sheep (that lord and his predecessors being known for the greatest sheep-masters in England) when those liberties were defended."—" If they were

* Camden's Elizabeth, anno 1587.
† Camden's Britannia, in Northamptonshire.
‡ Guillim's Display of Heraldry, p. 274, first edition.

in keeping of sheep," returned the other, " yours were then in plotting of treason." Whose animosities for the present cost both of them a confinement; yet so that afterwards the Upper House ordered reparations to this lord Spencer, as first (and causelessly) provoked.*

This lord was also he who, in the first of king James, was sent (with Sir William Dethick, principal King of Arms) to Frederick duke of Wirtemburg, elected into the order of the Garter; to present and invest him with the robes and ornaments thereof, which were accordingly, with great solemnity, performed in the cathedral of Stutgard.†

KING JAMES.

2. ARTHUR THROGKMORTON, Mil.—He was son to that eminent knight, Sir Nicholas Throgkmorton (of whom in Warwickshire); and his sister was married to Sir Walter Raleigh. This Sir Arthur was a most ingenious gentleman; and, dying without issue-male, his large estate was parted amongst his four daughters, married to the lord Dacres, the lord Wotton, Sir Peter Temple of Stow, baronet, and Sir Edward Partridge.

3. JOHN FREEMAN, Arm.—He died without issue; and was a most bountiful benefactor to Clare-hall in Cambridge; giving two thousand pounds to the founding of fellowships and scholarships therein.

12. WILLIAM WILLMER, Arm.—He was the first pensioner, as doctor James Montague the first master, and Sir John Brewerton first scholar, of the house in Sidney College; being all three of them (but in several proportions) benefactors to that foundation.

22. WILLIAM CHAUNCY, Mil.—These have been very (but I know not how) ancient in this county, but far ancienter in Yorkshire; for I meet with this inscription on a monument at Sabridgeworth in Hertfordshire:

"Hic jacent Johannes Chancy, Ar., filius et heres Johannis Chancy, Ar., filii et heredis Willielmi Chancy, Mil. quondam Baronis de Shorpenbek in com. Ebor., et Anna uxor ejus, una filiarum Johannis Leventhorp, Ar., qui quidem Johannes obiit VII Maii MCCCCLXXIX. et Anna, II Decemb. MCCCCLXXVII. quorum animabus . . . ."

It appeareth to me, by a well-proved pedigree, that Henry Chancy, Esq. of Yardlebury in Hertfordshire is the direct descendant from the aforesaid John Chancy, whose epitaph we have inserted.

* Wilson, in the Life of King James. † Stow's Chronicle, p. 128.

KING CHARLES.

7. JOHN HEWET, Bart.—He had not one foot of land nor house (hiring Hemington of the lord Montague) in the whole county, though several statutes* have provided that the sheriff should have sufficient land in the same shire to answer the king and his people. The best is, this baronet had a very fair estate elsewhere. And, as our English proverb saith, "What is lost in the hundred will be found in the shire;" so what was lost in the shire would be found in the land. However, this was generally beheld as an injury; that, because he had offended a great courtier, the shrievalty was by power imposed upon him.

THE FAREWELL.

The worst I wish this my native county is, that Nine (a river which some will have so termed from *nine* tributary rivulets) were Ten; I mean, made navigable from Petersburgh to Northampton; a design which hath always met with many backfriends, as private profit is (though a secret) a sworn enemy to the general good.

Sure I am, the Hollanders (the best copy of thrift in Christendom) teach their little ditches to bear boats. Not that their waters are more docible in this kind than ours; but they are the more ingenious and industrious schoolmaster of the lesson of public advantage, making every place in their province to have access unto every place therein by such cheap transportation.

WORTHIES OF NORTHAMPTONSHIRE WHO HAVE FLOURISHED SINCE THE TIME OF FULLER,

Dr. Stephen ADDINGTON, learned dissenting divine and author; born at Northampton 1729; died 1796.

Sir William ADDINGTON, a magistrate and author; born at Litchborough 1749.

Vincent ALSOP, author and nonconformist divine; born at Wilby; died 1703.

Caleb ASHWORTH, dissenting divine, tutor, and author; born 1709; died 1774.

Matthew BARKER, author and nonconformist divine; born at Cransley; died 1698.

Ralph BATHURST, divine, physician, and Latin poet; born at Hawthorpe 1620; died 1704.

* 9 Edward II. Lincolnshire; 4 Edward III. c. 9; 5 Edward III. c. 4.

Edward BERNARD, mathematician, astronomer, Orientalist, and critic; born at Paulers Pury 1638; died 1697.

Sir John BLENCOWE, M.P., justice of the King's Bench; born at Marston St. Lawrence 1642; died 1726.

William BLENCOWE, third son of the judge, decipherer to the Government; born at Marston St. Lawrence 1682-3; died 1712.

William BURKITT, commentator on the New Testament; born at Hitcham 1650; died 1703.

Alban BUTLER, learned catholic divine and historian of the Saints; born at Apletree 1710; died 1773.

William CAREY, LL.D. Oriental scholar; born at Paulers-Pury 1761; died 1834.

Esther CHAPONE, poet and moralist; born at Twywell 1727; died 1801.

Samuel CLARKE, divine and Orientalist; born at Brackley 1624; died 1669.

Thomas COGAN, physician and author on ethical philosophy and theology; born at Rowell 1736; died 1818.

Elisha COLES, author of " Practical Discourses of God's Sovereignty;" died 1688.

Elisha COLES, nephew of the preceding, lexicographer; born 1640; died 1684.

Philip DODDRIDGE, D.D. learned dissenting divine and commentator; born at Northampton 1702; died 1751.

John DRYDEN, dramatic, political, and satirical poet and translator; born at Aldwinkle All Saints 1631; died 1700.

John FREIND, physician, politician, and elegant writer; born at Croughton 1675; died 1728.

Robert FREIND, brother of John, scholar, celebrated for Latin epitaphs; born at Croughton 1667; died 1751.

Francis GASTRELL, bishop of Chester, author of " Christian Institutes;" born at Slapton 1662; died 1725.

Dr. John GILL, baptist, Orientalist, commentator on the Bible; born at Kettering 1697; died 1771.

Simon GUNTON, historian of the cathedral, Peterborough; died 1676.

James HERVEY, author of " Meditations," pious divine; born at Hardingstone 1713-14; died 1758.

Sir John HILL, physician, voluminous writer, butt of the wits; born at Peterborough 1716; died 1775.

Selina Countess of HUNTINGDON, charitable founder of sixty-four chapels, some colleges and seminaries; born at Astwell 1707; died 1791.

George JEFFREYS, poet and miscellaneous writer; born at Weldon 1678; died 1755.

William JONES, divine, institutor of the " British Critic;" born at Lowick 1726; died 1800.

William LAW, nonjuring divine, author of " Serious Call;" born at King's Cliffe 1686; died 1761.

Sir Creswell LEVINZ, justice of Common Pleas, and author; born at Evenley 1627; died 1700-1.

Owen MANNING, divine, and historian of Surrey; born at Orlingbury 1721; died 1801.

Charles MONTAGUE, first earl of Halifax, K.G. " Mæcenas," statesman and poet; born at Horton 1661; died 1715.

John NEWTON, astronomer and mathematician; born at Oundle 1622; died 1678.

Richard NEWTON, divine, founder of Hertford College, Oxford; born at Yardley Hastings 1675; died 1753.

William PALEY, divine, philosopher, and theologian; born at Peterborough 1743; died 1805.

Samuel PARKER, bishop of London, historian of his own times; born at Northampton 1640; died 1687.

John PARKHURST, divine, lexicographer, and critic; born at Catesby 1728; died 1797.

Thomas PAYNE, " honest Tom Payne," bookseller and bibliopolist; born at Brackley 1717; died 1799.

Philip THICKNESSE, lively writer, and eccentric character; born at Farthinghoe 1719; died 1792.

Leonard WELSTED, poet, satirized by Pope; born at Abington 1689; died 1747.

Daniel WHITBY, learned divine, author of " Commentaries," &c. ; born at Rushden 1638; died 1726.

John WILKINS, bishop of Chester, philosopher; born at Fawsley 1614; died 1672.

Thomas WOOLSTON, divine, and author of some works of a deistical tendency; born at Northampton 1669; died 1732-3.

⁎ The county of Northampton has been fortunate in its topographers. Norden appears amongst the earliest of its historians. He laid the foundation for the History of the County by John Bridges, which was edited by the Rev. P. Whalley, in 2 vols. fol. 1791. In 1822, a very superior edition, in folio, was undertaken by Mr. Geo. Baker, which occupied many years' attention, and certainly reflects great credit on the enterprising spirit and indefatigable research of the author. Other local histories and descriptions have also made their appearance; as the Rev. S. Gunton's History of Peterborough (1686); the Rev. J. Mastin's History of Naseby (1792); Guide to Burleigh (1815); Rev. H. K. Bonney's Historic Notices of Fotheringhay (1821); Cole's History of Weston Favell (1827), &c.—ED.

NORTHUMBERLAND.

NORTHUMBERLAND hath the bishopric of Durham (separated by the river Derwent running into Tyne) on the south ; Cumberland on the south-west; the German Ocean on the east; and Scotland on the north and west ; parted with the river Tweed, Cheviot hills, and elsewhere (whilst our hostility with the Scots) *mutuo metu,* with mutual fear, now turned into mutual faith, both nations knowing their own, and neither willing to invade, the bounds of others.

It is somewhat of a pyramidal form, whose basis, objected to the south, extendeth above forty, whilst the shaft thereof, narrowing northward, ascendeth to full fifty miles. Nature hath not been over indulgent to this county in the fruitfulness thereof ; yet it is daily improved, since (to use the prophet's expression) they have beat their swords into plough-shares, and spears into pruning-hooks ;* and surely such plough-shares make the best furrows, and such comfortable pruning-hooks cut with the best edge.

It must not be forgotten, how, before the uniting of England with Scotland, there lay much waste ground in the northern part of this county, formerly disavowed, (at leastwise not owned by any) only to avoid the charges of the common defence.† But afterward, so great, sudden, and good the alteration, that, the borders becoming safe and peaceable, many gentlemen inhabiting thereabouts, finding the ancient waste ground to become very fruitful, in the fourth of king James put in their claims, and began to contend in law about their bounds, challenging their hereditary right therein.

THE BUILDINGS.

One cannot rationally expect fair fabrics here, where the vicinity of the Scots made them to build not for state but strength. Here it was the rule with ancient architects, " what was firm, that was fair ;" so that it may be said of the houses of the gentry herein, " Quot mansiones, tot munitiones," as either

---

* Isaiah ii. 4.   † Stow's Chronicle, p. 819.

being all castles or castle-like, able to resist (though no solemn siege) a tumultary incursion.

Before we come to the WORTHIES of this county, be it premised, that Northumberland is generally taken in a double acception; first, as a county, (whose bounds we have fore-assigned); and secondly, as a kingdom, extending from Humber to Edinburgh-Frith, and so taking in the southern part of Scotland. Here then we have an opportunity to cry quits with Demster the Scottish historian, and to repair ourselves of him for challenging so many Englishmen to be Scots; should we bring all them in for Northumberlanders which were born betwixt Berwick and Edinburgh, whose nativities we may, in the rigour of right, justify to be English, if born therein whilst the tract of ground was subjected to the Saxon heptarchy. But, because we will have an unquestionable title to what we claim to be ours, we are content to confine ourselves to Northumberland in the county capacity thereof.

PROVERBS.

" To carry coals to Newcastle."]

That is to do what was done before; or to busy one's self in a needless employment. Parallel to the Latin, " Aquam mari infundere," " Sidera cœlo addere," " Noctuas Athenas," (to carry owls to Athens), which place was plentifully furnished before with fowl of that feather.

" From Berwick to Dover, three hundred miles over."]

That is, from one end of the land to the other. Semnable the Scripture expression, " From Dan to Beersheba." Such the the Latin proverbs, " A carceribus ad metam;" " A capite ad calcem;" when one chargeth through an employment, from the beginning to the end thereof.

" To take Hector's cloak."]

That is to deceive a friend who confideth on his faithfulness; and hereon a story doth depend. When Thomas Percy, earl of Northumberland, anno 1569, was routed in the rebellion which he had raised against queen Elizabeth, he hid himself in the house of one Hector Armstrong, of Harlow, in this county, having confidence he would be true to him, who, notwithstanding, for money betrayed him to the Regent of Scotland. It was observed that Hector, being before a rich man, fell poor of a sudden, and so hated generally, that he never durst go abroad, insomuch that the proverb " To take Hector's cloak,"* is continued to this day among them, when they would express a man that betrayeth his friend who trusted him.

" We will not lose a Scot."]

That is, " we will lose nothing, how inconsiderable soever,

---

* Bishop Carleton, in thankful remembrance.

which we can save or recover." Parallel to the Scripture expression, "We will not leave an hoof behind us."* The proverb began in the English borders, when during the enmity betwixt the two nations, they had little esteem of, and less affection for, a Scotchman; and is now happily superseded, since the union of England and Scotland into Great Britain.

" A Scottish mist may wet an Englishman to the skin."]

That is, " Small mischiefs in the beginning, if not seasonably prevented, may prove very dangerous." This limitary proverb hath its original in these parts, where mists may be said to have their fountain north, but fall south of Tweed, arising in Scotland, and driven by the winds into England, where they often prove a sweeping and soaking rain. Sure I am, our late civil war began there, which since hath wet many an Englishman in his own heart's blood; and whether at last the Scotch have escaped dry, that is best known to themselves.

" A Scottishman and a Newcastle grind-stone, travel all the world over."]

The Scots (gentry especially), when young, leave their native land (hard their hap if losers by their exchange), and travel into foreign parts, most for maintenance, many for accomplishment. Now no ship sets safe to sea without a carpenter, no carpenter is able without his tools, no tools useful without a grind-stone, no grindstone so good as those of Newcastle. Some indeed are fetched from Spain, but of so soft a grit that they are not fit for many purposes. Hence it is that these grindstones, though mostly in motion, may be said fixed to ships as most necessary thereunto.

" If they come, they come not;"
        And,
" If they come not, they come."]

We must fetch an Œdipus from this county, to expound this riddling proverb, customary in the wars betwixt the crowns of England and Scotland. For the cattle of people living hereabout, turned into the common pasture, did, by instinct and custom, return home at night, except violently intercepted by the freebooters and borderers, who, living between two kingdoms, owned no king, whilst " Vivitur ex rapto," (catch who catch may). Hence many in these parts, who had an herd of kine in the morning, had not a cow-tail at night, and alternately proved rich and poor by the trade aforesaid. If therefore these borderers came, their cattle came not; if they came not, their cattle surely returned. Now although a sprig of these borderers hath lately been revived (disguised under the new name of mosstroopers); yet the union of the two kingdoms hath, for the main, knocked this proverb out of joint, never (I hope) to be wholly set again.

* Exod. x. 26.

SCOTTISH PROVERBS CURRENT IN THIS COUNTY.

" Lang or ye cut Falkland-wood with a penknife."*]

It is spoken of such who embrace unproportionable and improbable means to effect the ends propounded to themselves, to as much purpose as to lave the sea with a cockle shell. Falkland was one of the king of Scotland's royal palaces in Fife, having a bonny wood (whereof great want in the south of this land, where one can hardly find a stick to beat a dog) about it; so that an axe is proper, and no penknife (fit only to fell a forest of feathers with the timber of quills therein) for such employment.

" He is an Aberdeen's man,† taking his word again."]

It seems the men of that town, a fair haven in the county of Mar, have formerly been taxed for breach of promise. I hope if true (if ever of either) only of the old Aberdeen, now much decayed, and famous only for salmon-fishing. If of the new, then I believe it of the townsmen, not scholars living in the university, founded by bishop Elphinstone. However, we have formerly observed,‡ what is to be believed in such satirical proverbs.

" He was born in August."]

At the first hearing thereof, I took it for a fortunate person, that month beginning the return of profit for the pains of the year past. I know amongst the Latins some months were counted more unhappy than others, witness the by-word "Mense Maio nubunt malè." But, since, I perceive a man may miss his mark, as well by *over* as *under* shooting it, and one may be too serious in interpreting such common speeches: for I am informed by a Scottish man, that it is only the periphrasis of a liquorish person, and such said to be born in August, whose tongues will be the tasters of every thing they can come by, though not belonging to them.

" A Yule feast may be quat at Pasche."]

That is, Christmas cheer may be digested, and the party hungry again, at Easter. No happiness is so lasting, but in short time we must forego and may forget it. The northern parts call Christmas *Yule* (hence the *yule-block, yule-oaks, yule-songs*, &c.), though much difference about the cause thereof. Some, more enemies to the ceremony than the cheer of Christmas, to render that festival the more offensive, make the word of Paganish extraction, deriving it from Iulus the son of Æneas; an etymology fetched far from England, and farther from truth.

But, to omit many forced and feigned deductions, that worthy doctor§ hits the mark, bringing it from the Latin *jubilo* (a word

---

* Scottish Proverbs, by David Fergusson, minister at Dunfermline, Litera L.
† Scottish Proverbs, ut supra, lit. H.
‡ Proverbs in Gloucestershire, " You are a man of Duresly."
§ Dr. Henry Hammond.

as ancient as Varro), signifying the rural shouting for joy, so that it is a name general for festivals, as Lammas Yule, &c. though Christmas be so called without any addition, as the feast κατ᾽ ἐξοχὴν, above all others. It is more than probable that the Latins borrowed their *jubilo* from the Hebrew יובל, the long sound of the trumpet, whence their Jubilee got the name. And seeing Christ's birth was a freeing us from the slavery of sin, I see not how Yule can be cavilled at in that signification.

SAINTS.

Saint EBBA was born in Northumberland, being daughter to Edilfrid the king thereof. When her father was taken prisoner, she got hold of a boat in Humber; and, passing along the raging ocean, she safely landed at a place in Merch in Scotland, which is called the promontory of Saint Ebb unto this day.

Becoming prioress of Coldingham in that country, to preserve her own and fellow-nuns' chastity from the pagan Danes, she cut off her own nose, and persuaded the rest to do the like; that their beauty might be no bait, whilst their deformity did secure their virginity. Sure I am, that since, more have lost their noses in prosecution of their wantonness, than in preservation of their chastity. As for the Danes, being offended that these nuns would not be the objects of their lusts, they made them the subjects of their fury, burning them and their monastery together.

But such the reputed holiness of Saint Ebb, that many churches, commonly called Saint Tabbs,* are in North-England dedicated unto her, and her memory is continued in the name of Ebb-Chester, a little village in the bishopric of Durham. She flourished about the year 630.

PRELATES SINCE THE REFORMATION.

GEORGE CARLETON was born in this county (nigh the borders of Scotland) at Norham, his father being the keeper of the important castle therein; bred in Merton college in Oxford. Hear what our English antiquary† saith of him, "Whom I have loved in regard of his singular knowledge in divinity, which he professeth; and in other more delightful literature, and am loved again of him, &c." He was one of the four divines sent by king James to the Synod of Dort, each of them there observed in their respective eminencies: "In Carletono prælucebat Episcopalis gravitas, in Davenantio subactum judicium; in Wardo multa lectio; in Hallo expedita concionatio." Doctor Carleton was then bishop of Llandaff, and afterwards of Chichester. His good affections appear in his treatise, entituled, "A thankful remembrance of God's mercy;" solid judgment, in his "Confutation of Judicial Astrology;" and clear invention,

---

* Camden's Britannia, p. 745.
† Camden's Britannia in Northumberland, p. 816.

in other juvenile exercises. Indeed, when young, he was grave in his manners; so when old he was youthful in his parts, even unto his death, which happened in the first of king Charles.

VALENTINE CARY was born at Berwick (which, though north of Tweed, is reduced to this county) extracted from the Carys, barons of Hunsdon.* He was first scholar of Saint John's-college in Cambridge, then fellow of Christ's College, afterwards of St. John's again, and at last master of Christ's College; so that I meet not with any his peer herein, thus bounded and re-bounded betwixt two foundations. But the best is, they both had one and the same foundress, Margaret countess of Richmond. He was vice-chancellor of Cambridge, anno 1612; dean of Saint Paul's; and at last bishop of Exeter; a complete gentleman and excellent scholar. He once unexpectedly owned my nearest relation in the high commission court, when in some distress; for which courtesy, I, as heir to him who received the favour, here publicly pay this my due thanks unto his memory.

Though some contest happened betwixt him and the city of Exeter; yet, I am credibly informed, when that city was visited with the sickness, he was bountiful above expectation, in relieving the poor thereof. He died anno Domini 1626; and lies buried under a plain stone in the church of Saint Paul's, London,† though he hath another monument of memorial in the church of Exeter.

RICHARD HOLEWORTH, D. D. was born at Newcastle in this county; preferred fellow of Saint John's College in Cambridge, rector of Saint Peter's in the poor of London, archdeacon of Huntingdon, and at last master of Emanuel College.

During his continuance in London, he did "dominari in concionibus;" and although it be truly observed, that the people in London honour their pastors (as John Baptist) πρὸς ὥραν, for an hour (or short time), yet this doctor had his hour measured him by a large glass, continuing in public esteem till the beginning of these civil wars: when the times turned, and he, standing still, was left to the censure of factious innovators.

Most candid his disposition; and, if he had the infirmity of ingenious persons, to be choleric, he prevented others checking it in him, by checking it first in himself.

He suffered long imprisonment in Ely-house and the Tower, for a sermon he made when vice-chancellor of Cambridge; and at last, restored to his liberty, waited on his majesty in the Isle of Wight. He is here entered amongst the bishops, because proffered Bristol, but refused it; and such who know least of his mind, are most bold to conjecture the cause of it. He slight-

---

* Parker, in his Sceletos Cantab. MS.   † Survey of London, p. 776.

ed not the smallness thereof; because, such his manners, loyalty, and conscience, that he would have thanked his sovereign for an injury, much more for a smaller courtesy. Wherefore such only shoot by the aim of their own fancies, who report him to have said, "he would not wear a Bristol stone."

Sure I am that England had, if any more able, none more zealous to assert episcopacy; and let that suffice us, that he esteemed the acceptance thereof, in that juncture of time, unsafe and unseasonable for himself. He afterwards took the deanery of Worcester; though he received no profit, the place received honour from him, being the last who was entitled (and indeed it was no more) with that dignity.

Pity it is so learned a person left no monuments (save a sermon) to posterity; for I behold that posthume work as none of his, named by the transcriber, "The Valley of Vision," a scripture expression,* but here misplaced. *Valley* it is indeed, not for the fruitfulness but lowness thereof (especially if compared to the high parts of the pretended author), but little vision therein. This I conceived myself in credit and conscience concerned to observe, because I was surprised to *preface* to the book; and will take the blame, rather than clear myself, when my innocency is complicated with the accusing of others.

Dying about the year 1650, he was buried in his own parish church, in Saint Peter's, Broad Street: his ancient friend Doctor Jefferies of Pembroke-hall taking for his text, "My days are like a shadow that decline;"† Thomas Rich and Richard Abdi, esquires, his executors and worthy friends, ordering his funeral with great solemnities and lamentation.

SOLDIERS.

To speak of this county in general, it breedeth most hardy men. He who deduced the Merches (so truly called from *mercke* a limitary bound) from frequent *marching* and warlike expeditions therein, missed the word, but hit the matter. These borderers have been embroiled in several battles against the Scotch; witness the battle of Chevy-Chase, whereof Sir Philip Sidney ‡ is pleased to make this mention. "Certainly I must confess my own barbarousness, I never heard the old song of Percy and Douglas, that I found not my heart moved more than with a trumpet, and yet it is sung but by some blind crowder, with no rougher voice than rude style; which being so evil apparelled in the dust and cobweb of that uncivil age, what would it work trimmed in the gorgeous eloquence of Pindar?"

True it is, the story is not true in the letter and latitude thereof; no earl of Northumberland being ever killed in Chevy-Chase, as by the perusal of the ensuing catalogue will appear.

* Isaiah xxii. 1.5.   † Psalm cii. 11.
‡ In his "Defence of Poesie."

1. Henry Percy, the first earl, lost his life in a battle against king Henry the Fourth, anno Domini 1408.

2. Henry Percy his grandchild, the second earl, was slain on the side of king Henry the Sixth, against king Edward the Fourth, anno 1455.

3. Henry his son, taking part with king Henry the Sixth, was slain at Touton-field, in the first of king Edward the Fourth.

4. Henry his son, promoting a tax for the king, was killed, in a tumultuous rout at Cockledge, eighteen miles from York, in the fourth of king Henry the Seventh.

5. Henry his son, died a natural death, in the eighteenth of king Henry the Eighth.

6. Henry his son, died peaceably at Hackney near London, the nine and twentieth of king Henry the Eighth, in whose reign the scene is laid for the aforesaid tragedy in Chevy-Chase.

This I thought fit to have said, partly, to undeceive people, lest long possession might create a title in their belief to the prejudice of truth ; partly, that the noble family of the Percys (what need a good head of hair wear a perriwig ?), for birth and valour equal to any subjects in Christendom, should not be beholding to an untruth to commend their martial achievement. Yet, though there be more fancy in the varnish, there is much faith in the groundwork of this relation, presenting a four-fold truth to posterity. First, that on light causes heavy quarrels have happened betwixt the Scotch and English in the borders. Secondly, that the Percys,* with other families in this county (mentioned in this ballad) were most remarkable therein. Thirdly, that generally the English got the better in these broils. Lastly, that, for the most part, they were victories without triumphs, wherein the conqueror might sigh for his conquest, so dear the price thereof.

PHYSICIANS.

WILLIAM TURNER was born at Morpeth in this county ;† bred in the university of Cambridge, where he became an excellent Latinist, Grecian, orator, and poet. He was very zealous in the Protestant religion, writing many books in the defence thereof, and much molested for the same by bishop Gardiner and others. He was kept long in durance ; and, escaping at last by God's providence, fled over beyond sea. At Ferrara in Italy he commenced doctor of physic, there gaining his degree with general applause. He wrote a great " Herbal," and a book of physic for the English gentry, as also several treatises of plants, fishes, stones, metals, &c.‡ He went afterwards into

---

* A third part of the county, from which the duke of Northumberland takes his title, belongs to him. Alnwick Castle, where he lives, is a vast and magnificent edifice.—Ed.

† Bale, de Scriptoribus Britannicis, Cent. viii. num. 95.   ‡ Idem.

Germany, where he lived in great credit and practice; and, as I conjecture, died there in the reign of queen Mary. Reader, I conceive him worthy of thy special notice, because he was both a confessor and physician; qualifications which meet not every day in the same person.

THOMAS GIBSON.—It is pity to part him from the former, because symbolising in many particulars of concernment: 1. Both born in this county, and in the same town of Morpeth:* 2. Flourishing at the self-same time: 3. Physicians by profession; and it is said of this Thomas, that he did "ægritudinum sanationes incredibiles," (incredible cures of diseases:)† 4. Writing of the same subject, of the nature of herbs; 5. Professed enemies to Popery.

This Thomas wrote many other books; and one entitled, "The Treasons of the Prelates since the Conquest;" which work, had it come to the hand of a modern author,‡ happily it might have much helped him in that subject. He was alive in the last of queen Mary; and Bale sendeth forth a hearty prayer for the continuance of his health and happiness.

WRITERS.

RALPH FRESBOURNE was born in this county,§ bred a soldier, scholar, traveller (being a man of great estate), and at last turned a friar. He attended Richard earl of Cornwall, and king of the Romans, into the Holy-Land. Here he became acquainted with the friars living on Mount Carmel, which were then much molested with the inroads of Pagans. Our Ralph, pitying their condition, and much taken with their sanctity and (as some say) miracles, brought them over with him into England, and built them a house at Holme, nigh Alnwick, in Northumberland, "in loco Carmelo Syriæ non dissimili," saith my author,‖ in a place not unlike to Carmel in Syria. Thus pence are like shillings; and as Carmel had a hill, with the river Kishon running under it, a forest beside it,¶ and the midland-sea some three miles from it; so this had the river Alne, a park adjoining, and the German-sea at the same distance.

But Northumberland was but a cold Carmel for these friars;** who soon got themselves warmer nests, in Kent, Essex, London, and where not? multiplying more in England than in any other country, as Mantuan†† observeth, and hath not ill expressed:

---

* Bale, de Scriptoribus Britannicis, Cent. viii. num. 54.　　† Idem, ibidem.
‡ Master William Spring.
§ Bale, de Scriptoribus Britannicis, Cent. iv. num. 1.; and Pits, in anno 1274.
‖ Bale, ut prius.　　　　¶ Isaiah xxxvii. 24.
** The Lord Vessey was so great a benefactor to this convent, that by some he is reputed the founder thereof.
†† Fastorum, lib. viii.

> *Cur apud Anglorum populos ita creverit, audi :*
> *Anglicus in Syrias veniens exercitus olim,*
> *Achonem Tyrii positam prope litora ponti,*
> *Quæ prius occurrit, subitis oppresserat armis.*

> " Hear, why that they so much in England thriv'd :
> When th' English erst in Palestine arriv'd,
> The city Acon on the shore of Tyre,
> As next at hand, with arms did soon acquire."

And after some verses interposed :

> *Ista duces tanta intuiti miracula, secum*
> *In patriam duxere viros, quibus arma negabant*
> *In laribus sedem Assyriis : et templa domosque*
> *Construxere novas.   Paucis ita floruit annis*
> *Relligio, quasi virga solo depacta feraci,*
> *Et veluti palmes robur translata recepit.*

> " The captains, seeing so great wonders wrought,
> These friars with them into England brought :
> What war denied at home, they here anew
> Churches and houses built.   In years but few,
> Increasing twig-like set by happy band,
> Or tree transplanted to a fruitful land."

This Ralph wrote books of pious Exhortations and Epistles ; and, after he had been fourteen years provincial of his own order, died and was buried at Holme aforesaid, anno Domini 1274.

JOHANNES SCOTUS.—We have formerly asserted the very *Society* of this *Scotus's* nativity to belong to England, and have answered the objections to the contrary.   He was born at Dunston, a village in the parish of Emildon in this county,* as appeareth by a writing in a book of his in Merton College, wherein he was bred.   He was a Franciscan by order ; and of such nimble and solid parts, that he got the title of *Doctor Subtilis.*

Hitherto all schoolmen were (like the world before the building of Babel) " of one language, and of one speech ; "† agreeing together in their opinions, which hereafter were divided into two regiments, or armies rather, of Thomists and Scotists, under their several generals opposing one another.   Scotus was a great stickler against the Thomists for that " sinful opinion, that the Virgin Mary was conceived without sin ; " which if so, how came she to rejoice in God her Saviour ?‡   He read the sentences thrice over in his solemn lectures, once at Oxford, again at Paris, and last at Cologne, where he died, or was killed rather, because, falling into a strong fit of an apoplexy, he was interred whilst yet alive, as afterwards did appear.§   Small amends were made for his hasty burial, with a handsome monument erected over him, at the cost of his order (otherwise, whether as Scot, scholar, or Franciscan, he had little wealth of his own) in the choir before the High Altar.   On his monument

---

* Camden's Britannia, in Northumberland.   † Genesis xi. 1.
‡ Luke i. 47.   § Camden's Britannia, in Northumberland.

are inscribed the names of fifteen Franciscans, viz. three popes, and two cardinals on the top, and ten doctors (whereof six English) on the sides thereof;* all his contemporaries, as I conceive. He died anno Domini 1308.

BENEFACTORS TO THE PUBLIC.

STEPHEN BROWN, grocer, son of John Brown, was born at Newcastle upon Tyne in this county, afterwards knighted, and made lord mayor of London, 1438;† in which year happened a great and general famine, caused much by unseasonable weather, but more by some (huckstering husbandmen) who properly may be termed knaves in *grain*, insomuch that wheat was sold for three shillings a bushel (intolerable according to the standard of those times), and poor people were forced to make bread of fern roots. But this Sir Stephen Brown sent certain shipsto Dantzic, whose seasonable return with rye suddenly sunk grain to reasonable rates, whereby many a languishing life was preserved. He is beheld one of the first merchants, who, in want of corn, shewed the Londoners the way to the barn-door—I mean, into Spruseland, prompted by charity (not covetousness) to this his adventure. It may be said that, since his death, he hath often relieved the city on the like occasion, because, as Symmachus‡ well observeth, " Author est bonorum sequentium, qui bonum relinquit exemplum."

ROBERT WOODLARKE was born, saith my author,§ at Wakerly in this county. True it is, in my late " Church History," I have challenged him for Northamptonshire; 1. because there is no Wakerly‖ in Northumberland; 2. because there is a Wakerly in Northamptonshire. But, on second thoughts, I resign him clear to his county, loath to higgle for a letter or two (misprinted perchance) in the name of a town. This Woodlarke was the last of the first original fellows, and third provost of King's College in Cambridge. He bought three tenements in Miln-street, and (by a mortmain procured from king Edward the Fourth) erected of them a small college, by the name of Saint Katharine's Hall.

" As is the man, so is his strength." Great matters cannot be expected from so private a person, who never attained to any prelatical preferment, who was bountiful to his foundation to the utmost of his ability. Herein he stands alone, without any to accompany him, being the first and last who was master of one college, and at the same time founder of another. This his *Zoar* hath since met with many worthy benefactors, who have advanced it to be considerable both in buildings and reve-

* Pits, de illustribus Angliæ Scriptoribus, p. 393.
† Stow's Survey of London, p. 564.   ‡ Lib. nono, Ep. 70.
§ John Scot, in his Tables of Cambridge.
‖ Consult Speed's Alphabetical Tables, and Villare Anglicanum.

nues. The date of his death I cannot with any certainty affix.

MEMORABLE PERSONS.

MACHELL VIVAN is a Scottish-man by his birth; but, because beneficed in this county so many years, shall (by the reader's leave) pass for an Englishman, so far as to be here inserted; the rather, because he will minister to the present and future ages just matter of admiration, as, by the perusing of the ensuing letter from my credible friend, well known in London (where his surviving father was not long since the prime magistrate thereof) will appear:

" There is an acquaintance of mine, and a friend of yours, who certified me of your desire of being satisfied of the truth of that relation I made, concerning the old minister in the north. It fortuned, in my journey to Scotland, I lay at Alnwick in Northumberland one Sunday by the way; and understanding from the host of the house where I lodged, that this minister lived within three miles of that place, I took my horse after dinner, and rid thither, to hear him preach, for my own satisfaction. I found him in the desk, where he read unto us some part of the common prayer, some of holy David's Psalms, and two chapters, one out of the Old the other out of the New Testament, without the use of spectacles. The Bible, out of which he read the chapters, was a very small printed Bible. He went afterwards into his pulpit, where he prayed and preached to us about an hour and a half. His text was, " Seek you the kingdom of God, and all things shall be added unto you." In my poor judgment, he made an excellent good sermon, and went cleverly through, without the help of any notes. After sermon, I went with him to his house, where I proposed these several following questions to him. Whether it was true, the book reported of him concerning his hair? whether or no he had a new set of teeth come? whether or no his eye-sight ever failed him? and whether in any measure he found his strength renewed unto him? He answered me distinctly to all these; and told me, he understood the news-book reported his hair to become a dark brown again; but that is false: he took his cap off, and shewed me it. It is come again like a child's, but rather flaxen than either brown or gray. For his teeth, he hath three come within these two years, not yet to their perfection; while he bred them he was very ill. Forty years since he could not read the biggest print without spectacles, and now (he blesseth God) there is no print so small, no written hand so small, but he can read it without them. For his strength, he thinks himself as strong now as he hath been these twenty years. Not long since he walked to Alnwick to dinner and back again, six north-country miles. He is now an hundred and ten years of age, and, ever since last May, a hearty body, very cheerful, but stoops very much. He had five children after he was eighty years of age, four of them lusty lasses now living with him, the other died lately; his wife yet hardly fifty years of age. He writes himself *Machell Vivan.* He is a Scottish-man, born near Aberdeen. I forget the town's name where he is now pastor; he hath been there fifty years.

"Your assured loving friend, THOMAS ATKIN."

"Windsor, 28 September, 1657."

A most strange accident! for waiving the poetical fiction of Æson's Re-juvenescency in Medea's bath, it will hardly be paired. To begin with Scripture, Caleb (or *all-heart*) his professing himself as able for any action at eighty, as forty years before,* speaketh no renovation, but continuation of his strength. And whereas David saith, that "his youth was renewed as an Eagle's,"† he is to be understood in a metaphorical, yea spiritual sense, of the vigorousness and sprightliness of grace in his heart, seeing otherwise his great debilitation doth appear at seventy years,‡ scarce a moiety of this man's age. As for the many miracles, wrought by our Saviour, though extending to the cleansing of lepers, curing diseases, casting out devils, yea reviving the dead, yet they never countermanded nature in this kind, by recruiting the strength of an aged person. As for human history, I meet not with any to mate him in all particulars. The nearest that treadeth on his heels, is the countess of Desmond, married in the reign of king Edward the Fourth, and yet alive anno 1589, and many years since, when she was well known to Sir Walter Raleigh, and to all the nobles and gentlemen in Munster; but chiefly to the earls (for there was a succession of them worn out by her vivacity) of Desmond, from whose expectation she detained her jointure. The lord Bacon casteth up her age to be a hundred and forty at least, adding withal, "Ter per vices dentisse," (that she recovered her teeth, after her casting them three several times.)

All I will add is this, had this happened in foreign parts, addicted to Popery, near the shrine of some Saint, superstition, with her sickle, might have reaped a great harvest thereby.

———— ANDERSON, a townsman and merchant of Newcastle, talking with a friend on Newcastle bridge, and fingering his ring, before he was aware let it fall into the river, and was much troubled with the loss thereof, until the same was found in a fish caught in the river, and restored unto him.§ The same is reported by Herodotus, in his third book, of Polycrates, a petty king, and the minion of fortune, and may be an instance of the recurrency of remarkable accidents, according to Solomon's observation, "There is no new thing under the sun."‖

---

* Joshua xiv. 11.   † Psalm ciii. 5.   ‡ 1 Kings i. 1.
§ "Vox Piscis," printed anno 1626, p. 13.   ‖ Eccles. i. 9.

NAMES OF THE GENTRY OF THIS COUNTY,

RETURNED BY THE COMMISSIONERS IN THE TWELFTH YEAR OF KING HENRY THE SIXTH, 1433.

Thomas bishop of Durham, and Ralph earl of Westmoreland;—
Thomas Lilborn, and John Carington, (knights for the shire);
—Commissioners to take the oaths.

Rob. Umfravile, mil.
Rad. Gray, mil.
Rob. Ogle, senior, mil.
Rob. Ogle, jun. mil.
Johan. Bertram, mil.
Will. Elmeden, mil.
Johan. Midleton, mil.
Will. Svynbarn, mil.
Johan. Maners, mil.
Math. Whitfeld, mil.
Will. Carnaby.
Johan. Fenwyk.
Johan. Midelton.
Tho. Ilderton.
Rob. Raymes.
Tho. Haggerston.
Rob. Maners.
Laur. Acton.
Tho. Gray de Norton.
Tho. Blekensop.
Row. Thirwall.

Ric. Fetherstanhalgh.
Gilb. Rotherford.
Will. Muschaunce.
Gilb. Eryngton.
Will. Clenell.
Johan. Heron de Netherton.
Tho. Reed de Redesdale.
Roger Ushere.
Tho. Midleton.
Joh. Ellerington.
Joh. Park.
Rich. Lilburne.
Tho. Elwick.
Joh. Eryngton.
Nic. Heron de Meldon.
Joh. Trewyk.
Joh. Chestre.
Lion. Chestre.
Joh. Horsley de Horsley.
Jaco. Buk de Morpath.

OBSERVATIONS.

The fable is sufficiently known of the contest betwixt the wind and the sun, which first should force the traveller to put off his clothes. The wind made him wrap them the closer about him; whilst the heat of the sun soon made him to part with them.

This is moralized in our English gentry. Such who live southward near London (which, for the lustre thereof, I may fitly call the sun of our nation), in the warmth of wealth, and plenty of pleasures, quickly strip and disrobe themselves of their estates and inheritance; whilst the gentry living in this county, in the confines of Scotland, in the wind of war (daily alarmed with their blustering enemies), buckle their estates (as their armour) the closer unto them; and since have no less thriftily defended their patrimony in peace, than formerly they valiantly maintained it in war.

The commissioners of this county did not over-weary themselves in working, when they returned these persons; presenting no under-wood, yea, no standels, but only timber oaks, men of great wealth and worship in this shire, as appears by the thinness of their number, but one and twenty.

SHERIFFS
OF NORTHUMBERLAND.

Anno   HENRY II.

1 Odardus.
2 Will. de Vesci Milo.
3 Idem.
4
5 Idem.
6
7 Will. de Vesci Milo, for nine years.
16 Rog. Statevill, for fifteen years.
31 Rog. de Glanvill, for three years.

RICHARD. I.

1 Rog. de Glanvill.
2 Will. de Stutevill, et Regin. Basset.
3 *Null. Tit. Com. in hoc Rotulo.*
4
5
6 Hug. Bardoph. for four years.
10 Idem, et Ob. fil. Will.

JOH. REG.

1 Hugo Bardolfe.
2 Will. Stutevill, et Joh. Laleman.
3 Rob. filius Rog. et Rad. de Furnell, for three years.
6
7
8 Rob. filius Rog. et Rob. de Kent.
9 Rob. filius Rog. et Ang. de Corvo.
10 Rob. filius Rog. et Tho. Haltem.
11 Rob. filius Rog. et Will. de Blunvill.

Anno

12 Idem.
13 Idem.
14
15 Idem.
16 Almericus Archid. Dunelm, et Phil. Ulecott.
17 Phil. de Ulecot, et Will. de Stratton.

HENRY III.

1 Phil. de Ulcot, for four years.
5 Rob. de Wittester alias Wirceser.
6 Idem.
7 Will. Briewere, jun. et Rog. Langford.
8 Will. Briever, jun. ut Custos, et Tho. de Tetleburn.
9 Joh. filius Rob. et Will. Coniers, for three years.
12 Joh. filius Rob.
13 Bri. fil. Alani, et Hug. de Magneby, for three years.
16 Bri. fil. Alani, et Joh. de Mersley, for four years.
20 Rich.
21 Hu. de Bolebet, et Alan. de Kirkby, for seven years.
28 Hug. de Bolebet, et Rob. de Camho, for three years.
31 Will. Heyrun, for eleven years.
42 Joh. de Plesset.
43 Idem.
44 Tho. filius Mich.
45 Idem.

Anno

46 Adam de Gesenor, et
   Hug. de Hereford, cl'icus.
47 Adam de Cresenor, et
   Joh. Lidegreynes, for five
   years.
52 Wischardus de Charny.
53 Idem.
54 Rich. de Charny, for three
   years.

EDWARD I.

1 Rob. de Hampton, for
   three years.
4 Joh. de Lichegreynes, for
   three years.
7 Walt. de Cannblion.
8 Idem.
9 Tho. de Dyneleston, for
   eight years.
17 Rich. Knoul, for five years.
22 Hu. Gobium, for three
   years.
25 Joh. de Kirkby.
26 Rob. de Balliclo.
27 Idem.
28 Rog. Mynot.
29 Idem.
30 Joh. de Camblion.
31 Lucas Talboys.
32 Idem.
33 Joh. de Creppinge, et
   Joh. de Sheffeld, for three
   years.

EDWARD II.

1 Rob. de Fandon.
2 Guid. Charroum.
3 Johan. de Cannton.
4 Idem.
5 Will. de Felton, et
   Joh. de Cannton, for three
   years.

Anno

EDWARD III.

1 Joh. de Insula, et
   Joh. de Fenwick.
2 Joh. de Littlebourne, for
   five years.
7
8 Rog. Mauduit.
9 Hob. Dardins, for three
   years.
12 Williel. Felton, for six
   years.
18 Rob. Bertram, et
   Rob. de Fenwicke.
19 Idem,
20 Rob. Reyms.
21 Idem.
22 Johan. Clifford.
23 Idem.
24
25 Joh. Coupeland, for three
   years.
28
29
30
31 Alan. de Strocker.
32 Idem.
33 Hen. de Strocker.
34 Idem.
35 Johan. Heronn.
36 Rog. de Widrington.
37 Rich. de Horsele.
38 Hen. de Strocher, for five
   years.
43 Rich. de Horsele, for three
   years.
46 Rob. Umfravil.
47 Tho. Surtis.
48 Johan. Fenwicke.
49 Barthram. Monboucher.
50 Tho. de Ilderton.
51 Rob. Umfravil.

EDWARD III.

25. JOHN COUPELAND.—This was he, who five years ago
(viz. in the 20th of this king's reign) took David Bruce king of
Scotland prisoner, in the battle at Nevil's-cross. Buchanan, an

author not always to be credited in the concernments of his own nation (seldom allowing victory to the English valour, but either to their treachery or unequal numbers), reporteth, how Coupeland, having disarmed his royal prisoner, " duos* pugno dentes excussit," which I will not English, as confident never done by Englishman, our Chronicles taking no notice of such a cruelty; but that he treated him with strictness beseeming a prisoner, and respect becoming a prince, until he had surrendered him to king Edward, who rewarded him with knighthood; and lest his honour, without means to support it, should seem burdensome to him and contemptible to others, he gave him five hundred pounds per annum, to be paid four hundred out of the customs of London, the other out of those of Berwick, until such time as lands of the same value were settled on him and his heirs for ever.

SHERIFFS OF NORTHUMBERLAND.

RICH. II.

Anno	Name and Arms.	Place.
1	Bert. Monboucher.	
2	Tho. Surties.	
3	Bert. Monboucher.	
4	Idem.	
5	Adam de Atholl.	
	G. on a chevron O. three étoiles S.	
6	Rob. de Clifford.	
	Checky O. and Az. a fess G.	
7	Johan. Heronn.	
8	Hen. de Percy, co. Northumb.	Alnwick.
	O. a lion rampant Az.	
9	Idem	*ut prius.*
10	Idem	*ut prius.*
11	Idem	*ut prius.*
12	Rad. de Eure.	
	Quarterly, O. and G. on a bend S. three escalops Arg.	
13	Idem	*ut prius.*
14	Joh. de Filton, mil.	
15	Hen. de Percy, com. Northumberland	*ut prius.*
16	Idem	*ut prius.*
17		
18		
19		
20	Hen. de Percy . . .	*ut prius.*
21	Idem	*ut prius.*

---

* Rerum Scoticarum, lib. ix. fol. 89, p. 2.

Anno   Name.   Place.

22 Joh. de Fenwick.   .   .   Fenwick.
     Per pale G. and Arg. six martlets counterchanged.

HEN. IV.

1 Hen. de Percy, fil.
     com. Northumberland } *ut prius.*
2 Ger. Heron, mil. et
   Rob. Umfravill.
     Arg. a fess betwixt six cinquefoils G.
3 Joh. Milford, mil.
4 Joh. Clavering, mil.
     Quarterly O. and G. a bend S.
5
6 Rob. Umfravill, mil.   .   *ut prius.*
7 Rob. Lisle, mil.
     O. a fess betwixt two chevrons S.
8 Rob. Herbotell.
9 Tho. Grey.
     G. a lion ramp. within a border engrailed Arg.
10 Rob. Tempest.
     Arg. a bend betwixt six martlets S.
11 Joh. Widrington.
     Quarterly, Arg. and G. a bend S.
12 Joh. Bertram.
     O. an orle Az.

HENR. V.

1 Joh. Maveres.
     O. two bars Az. a chief G.
2 Edw. Hastings, mil.
     Arg. a maunch S.
3 Rob. Lisle   .   .   .   .   *ut prius.*
4 Joh. Bertram   .   .   .   *ut prius.*
5 Rob. Ogle.
     Arg. a fess betwixt three crescents G.
6 Edw. Hastings   .   .   *ut prius.*
7 Will. Elmeden.
8 Tho. Surtis.
9 Idem.

HENR. VI.

1 Joh. Bertram, mil. .   .   *ut prius.*
2 Joh. Midleton.
3 Joh. Bertram, mil.   .   .   *ut prius.*
4 Joh. Widerington   .   .   *ut prius.*
5 Will. Lambton.
6 Hen. Fenwick, arm.   .   *ut prius.*
7 Will. Carnaby, arm.

Anno	Name.	Place.
8	Joh. Woderington . .	*ut prius.*
9	Joh. Bertram . . .	*ut prius.*
10	Rog. Woderington . .	*ut prius.*
11	Joh. Midleton.	
12	Math. Whitfeld.	

Arg. a bend betwixt two cotizes engrailed S.

13	Joh. Bertram, mil. . .	*ut prius.*
14	Rog. Woderington . .	*ut prius.*
15	Will. Eure, mil. . . .	*ut prius.*
16	Rob. Ogle, mil. . . .	*ut prius.*
17	Joh. Bertram	*ut prius.*
18	Rob. Herbotell, mil.	
19	Joh. Heron	Gawby.
20	Idem.	
21	Rog. Woderington. . .	*ut prius.*
22	Joh. Heron.	
23	Rob. Claxston.	
24	Will. Haringe.	
25	Tho. Wellden.	
26	Bertr. Herbotell.	
27	Tho. Nevill, mil.	

G. a saltire Arg.

28	Ro. de Woderington .	*ut prius.*
29	Rog. Thornton.	
30	Joh. Heronford.	
31	Rob. Mitford.	
32	Joh. Burcester.	
33	Rob. Mavers, arm. . .	*ut prius.*
34	Rad. Grey, mil. . . .	Chillingham.

G. a lion rampant within a border engrailed Arg.

35	Joh. Heron, mil.	
36	Rog. Thornton.	
37	Will. Bertram . . .	*ut prius.*
38	Rad. Grey, mil. . . .	*ut prius.*

EDW. IV.

1	Joh. Midleton, mil.	
2	George Lumley, mil.	
3	Idem.	
4	Rob. Maures, mil. . .	*ut prius.*
5	Ger. Woderington . .	*ut prius.*
6	Will. Bowes, mil.	

Erm. three bows bent G.

7	Joh. Nevill, mil. . .	*ut prius.*
8	Geor. Lumley, mil.	
9	Idem.	
10	Idem.	
11	Idem.	

Anno	Name and Arms.	Place.
12	Joh. Woderington	*ut prius.*
13	Idem	*ut prius.*
14	Idem	*ut prius.*
15	Hen. com. North.	*ut prius.*
16	Idem	*ut prius.*
17	Idem	*ut prius.*
18	Idem	*ut prius.*
19	Idem	*ut prius.*
20	Idem	*ut prius.*
21	Idem	*ut prius.*
22		

RICHARD III.

1	Hen. com. North.	*ut prius.*
2	Rad. Herbotle, mil. subvic.	
3	Hen. com. North.	*ut prius.*
4	Rob. Maneret, mil.	

HENR. VII.

1	Hen. com. North.	*ut prius.*
2	Idem	*ut prius.*
3	Idem	*ut prius.*
4	*Nullus Tit. Com. in hoc*	
5	*Rotulo.*	
6		
7		
8		
9	Rog. Fenwick, arm.	*ut prius.*
10		
11		
12	Rob. Grey	Horton.
	Arms, *ut prius.*	
13	Geor. Taylboys, mil.	

Arg. a cross S. and chief G. on the last, three escalops of the first.

14		
15		
16		
17	Edw. Radcliff, mil.	

Arg. a bend engrailed S.

18		
19	Rad. Eure, mil.	*ut prius.*
20		
21	Tho. Ilderton, mil.	
22		
23	Nich. Ridley, arm.	
24		

HENRY VIII.

Anno	Name.	Place.
1	Nich. Ridley, arm.	
2	Idem.	
3	Idem.	
4		
5		
6		
7	Rad. Fenwick, arm. . .	*ut prius.*
8		
9		
10	Chri. Thirkill, arm.	
11	Geor. Skelton, arm.	
12	Chri. Dacre, mil.	
	G. three escalops Arg.	
13	Will. Elleker, arm.	
	Arg. a fess betwixt three water-bougets G.	
14		
15		
16	Will. Elleker, mil. . .	*ut prius.*
17	Will. Heron, mil.	
18	Will. Eure, mil. . . .	*ut prius.*
19	Cut. Ratcliffe, arm. . .	*ut prius.*
20		
21		
22	*(Recorda manca.)*	
23		
24		
25		
26		
27		
28		
29		
30		
31		
32	Joh. Woderington . .	*ut prius.*
33	Leon. Cornaby, mil.	
34	Joh. de Lavale, mil.	
	Erm. two bars Vert.	
35	Tho. Hilton, mil.	
	Arg. two bars Az. over all a flower-de-luce O.	
36	Joh. Collingwood.	
37	Tho. Hilton, mil. . .	*ut prius.*
38	Joh. Horsley, arm.	

EDWARD VI.

1	Joh. de Lavele, mil. .	*ut prius.*
2	Tho. Hilton, mil. . .	*ut prius.*

Anno	Name.	Place.

3 Joh. Foster, mil.
> Arg. a chevron Vert betwixt three hunters' horns S.

4 Joh. Gray, mil. . . . *ut prius.*

5 Rob. Collingwood.

6 Joh. Witherington . . *ut prius.*

PHIL. et MAR.

1 Joh. de Lavele, mil. . *ut prius.*

1, 2

2, 3

3, 4

4, 5

5, 6 Geo. Ratcliffe, mil. . *ut prius.*

ELIZ. REG.

1 Joh. Witherington . . *ut prius.*

2 Alb. Fetherston. . . Fetherstonhaugh.
> G. a chevron betwixt three feathers Arg.

3 Rob. Lawson, arm.

4 Hen. Percy, mil. . . *ut prius.*

5 Rad. Grey, mil. . . . *ut prius.*

6 Tho. Foster, arm. . . *ut prius.*

7 Joh. de Lavele, arm. . *ut prius.*

8 Georg. Heron, arm.

9 Cut. Carnaby, arm.

10 Cut. Collingwood.

11 Rob. Raydes, arm.

12 Nich. Ridley, arm.

13 Joh. de Lavele, mil. . *ut prius.*
> Geor. Heron, mil.

14 Tho. Foster, arm. . . *ut prius.*

15 Cut. Caneyby, arm.

16 Tho. Grey, mil. . . . *ut prius.*

17 Rob. de Lavele, mil. . *ut prius.*

18 Rob. Midleton, arm.

19 Fran. Russel, mil.
> Arg. a lion rampant G.; on a chief S. three escalops of the first.

20 Will. Fenwicke, arm. . *ut prius.*

21 Hen. Witherington . . *ut prius.*

22 Cut. Colingwood.

23 Joh. Heron, arm.

24 Rad. Grey, arm. . . . *ut prius.*

25 Rob. de Lavele, arm. . *ut prius.*

26 Jam. Ogle, arm. . . . *ut prius.*

27 Rich. Radley, arm.

28 Rob. Clauding, arm.

Anno	Name.	Place.

29 Hen. Anderson, arm.
30 Idem.
31 Will. Fenwick, arm. . . *ut prius.*
32 Ale. Fetherston, arm. . . *ut prius.*
33 Rad. Grey, arm. . . . *ut prius.*
34 Rob. de Lavele, arm. . . *ut prius.*
35 Rad. Grey, arm. . . . *ut prius.*
36 Tho. Bradford, arm.
37 Idem.
38 Geor. Muschampe.
     O. three bars G.
39 Edw. Grey, arm. . . *ut prius.*
40 Idem . . . . . . *ut prius.*
41 Tho. Midleton, arm.
42 Geo. Muschamp, arm. . *ut prius.*
43 Edw. Talbot, arm.
     Arg. three lions rampant Purpure.
44 Nich. Foster, arm.
     Arg. a chevron Vert betwixt three hunters' horns S.
45 Will. Selby, jun. arm.
     et 1 Jacob.

JACO. REX.

1 Will. Selby, jun. arm.
2 Rad. de Lavale, arm. . *ut prius.*
3 Hen. Witherington . . *ut prius.*
4 Will. Selby, mil.
5 Geor. Selby, mil.
6 Rad de Lavale, mil. . *ut prius.*
7 Edw. Talbot, arm. . . *ut prius.*
8 Joh. de Lavale, arm. . *ut prius.*
9 Rad. Grey, mil. . . . *ut prius.*
10 Claud. Foster, arm. . . *ut prius.*
11 Rad. Seldy, mil.
12 Joh. Clavering, mil.
     Quarterly, O. and G. a bend S.
13 Hen. Anderson, mil.
14 Will. Selby, mil.
15 Rob. Brandlinge.
16 Tho. Midleton, arm.
17 Joh. Fenwicke, mil. . . *ut prius.*
18 Mat. Foster, arm. . . *ut prius.*
19 Rad. de Lavale, mil. . *ut prius.*
20 Will. Muschampe . . *ut prius.*
21 Joh. Clavering, mil. . . *ut prius.*
22 Joh. de Lavale, mil.
     Erm. two bars Vert.

CAR REG.

Anno	Name.	Place.
1	Cutb. Heron, arm.	
2	Fran. Bradling, arm.	
3		
4	Tho. Swinborn, mil. et duobus Tumid.	
5		
6	Rob. Bradling, arm.	
7	Nic. Towneley, arm.	
8	Nich. Tempest, mil.	*ut prius.*
9	Tho. Midleton, arm.	
10		
11	Will. Carniby, mil.	
12	Will. Witherington. Quarterly, Arg. and G. a bend S.	
13	Rob. Bewick, arm.	
14		
15		
16		
17		
18		
19	*Ingratum bello debemus inane.*	
20		
21		
22		

The reader is sensible of more blanks and interruptions in these sheriffs, than in any other catalogue; whereof this reason may be assigned; because the sheriffs of Northumberland never accounted to the king's majesty in his Exchequer (from which accounts the most perfect list is made) until the third year of king Edward the Sixth. Yea, they assumed such liberty to themselves, as to seize the issues and profits of their Bailiwick, and convert them to their own use, with all other debts, fines, and amercements, within the said county, and all emoluments accruing from alienations, intrusions, wards, marriages, reliefs, and the like.

This, though it tended much unto the detriment and loss of the crown, was for many years connived at, chiefly to encourage the sheriffs in their dangerous office, who, in effect, lay constant *perdues* against the neighbouring Scots. But after that their care was much lessened, by settling the lord-wardens of the Marches, it was enacted, in the third of king Edward the Sixth, that the sheriffs of Northumberland should be accountable for their office, as others, in the Exchequer.*

* Anno 2 and 3 Edward VI. cap. 34.

QUEEN ELIZABETH.

19. Francis Russell, Mil.—He was son to Francis, and father to Edward earl of Bedford. He married Julian, daughter (whom Mills* calls Elionar, and makes her co-heir) to Sir John Foster aforesaid, which occasioned his residence in these parts. It happened on a truce-day, June 27, 1585, that the English meant to treat, whilst the Scots meant to fight, being three thousand to three hundred. Now, though it was agreed betwixt them (to use the words of the limitary-laws) that they should not hurt each other with word, deed, or look, they fell on the English; in which tumult this worthy knight lost his life. And, because seldom single funerals happen in great families, his father died the same week in the south of England.

THE FAREWELL.

Being now to take our leave of Northumberland, I remember what I have read of Sir Robert Umfrevile, a native of this county —how he was commonly called Robin Mend-market, so much he improved trading hereabouts, in the reign of king Henry the Fourth.† It will not be amiss to wish this county more Mend-markets, that the general complaint of the decay of traffic may be removed. I confess, the knight bettered the markets, by selling therein the plentiful plunder which he had taken from the Scots; but I desire it done by some ingenious and not injurious design, that none may have just cause to complain.

WORTHIES OF NORTHUMBERLAND WHO HAVE FLOURISHED SINCE THE TIME OF FULLER.

Mark Akenside, physician, author of "The Pleasures of Imagination," and other poems; born at Newcastle 1721; died 1770.

Anthony Askew, Greek scholar, collector, Newcastle; born 1722; died 1774.

John Bewick, engraver on wood; born at Ovingham 1760; died 1795.

John Brand, divine, antiquary, historian of his native town; born at Newcastle 1743; died 1806.

Dr. John Brown, divine, poet, and painter; born at Rothbury 1715; died 1766.

William Bulmer, correct and beautiful typographer; born at Newcastle 1757; died 1830.

* In Catalogue of Honour, p. 440.   † Stow's Chronicle, p. 338.

William BURDON, political and miscellaneous writer; born at Newcastle 1764; died 1818.

Sir Robert CHAMBERS, chief justice in the East Indies; born at Newcastle 1737; died 1803.

Lionel CHARLTON, mathematician, author of the History of Whitby; born at Upper Stobbilee in Bellingham 1720; died 1785.

Cuthbert COLLINGWOOD, admiral lord, victor at Trafalgar; born at Newcastle 1749; died 1810.

Thomas COLLINGWOOD, physician, medical author, and dramatist; born at Bates Cross, near Berwick, 1751; died 1822.

Authony COOK, mathematician; born at Woolley; died there 1824.

George COUGHRAN, mathematician, compiler of the Ladies Diary, "a prodigy of genius;" born at Wreighill 1752; died 1774.

Sir Ralph DELAVAL, admiral at the battle of La Hogue; born at North Dissington; died 1707.

Elizabeth ELSTOB, Saxonist; born at Newcastle 1683; died 1756.

William ELSTOB, brother of Elizabeth, divine, Saxonist; born at Newcastle 1673; died 1714.

Sir Charles GREY, first earl Grey, warrior, father of the present earl, Howick; born 1729; died 1807.

Richard GREY, D.D. divine, learned and ingenious author; born at Newcastle 1694; died 1771.

William HEWSON, anatomist and author; born at Hexham 1739; died 1774.

Dr. Charles HUTTON, self-taught mathematician, voluminous author; born at Newcastle 1737; died 1823.

John MITFORD, author and song-writer; born at Mitford Castle; died 1831.

Sir Chaloner OGLE, admiral; born at Kirkley 1680; died 1750.

George PICKERING, poet; born at Simonburn 1758.

James PRINGLE, mathematician and linguist; born at North Shields; died 1824, aged 71.

Joseph RICHARDSON, lawyer and poet; born at Hexham 1774; died 1803.

William RICHARDSON, antiquary, benefactor, and poet; born at Little Harle 1759; died 1824.

John ROTHERAM, pious divine and author; born at Haydon Bridge 1725; died 1789.

John RUSHWORTH, lawyer, republican M.P., editor of "Historical Collections," &c.; born in 1607; died 1690.

Right Hon. John SCOTT, earl of Eldon, and lord chancellor of England; born at Newcastle 1751; died 1838.

Thomas SPENCE, politician, author of a plan to remove pauperism; born at Newcastle; died 1814.

William STEVENSON, author on commerce and agriculture; born at Berwick 1772; died 1829.

Percival STOCKDALE, soldier, poet, and divine; born at Branxton 1736; died 1811.

John TWEDDELL, traveller, scholar, and poet; born at Threepwood 1769; died 1799.

George WALKER, author of "Doctrine of the Sphere;" born at Newcastle; died 1734.

John WALLIS, historian of the County; born at Whitley in Kirkhaugh 1714; died 1793.

₊ The principal historian of this important and interesting county is the Rev. J. Hodgson, the leading Editor of the twelfth volume of the Beauties of England and Wales. He published the History of Northumberland in a succession of Parts between the years 1827 and 1832; and has certainly executed his laborious task with considerable ability. Independently of his own researches, his materials have been chiefly drawn from Wallis's Natural History and Antiquities of Northumberland (1769), and Hutchinson's and Mackenzie's Historical Views of the County, the former published in 1778, and the latter in 1825. Since the appearance of Mr. Hodgson's Work, Sykes's Local Records, or Historical Register of remarkable Events, have been published, in 2 vols. 8vo. 1833. Of local histories, the principal are the Chorographia, or a Survey of Newcastle-upon-Tyne (brought out so early as 1649, by Wm. Grey), and the History and Antiquities of Newcastle, by J. Brand, in 2 vols. 4to. 1789.—ED.

NOTTINGHAMSHIRE.

NOTTINGHAMSHIRE hath Yorkshire on the north, Licolnshire on the east, Leicestershire on the south, and Derbyshire on the west. Nor can I call to mind any county besides this, bounded with four, and but four Shires, (and those towards the four cardinal points) without any parcels of other shires interposed. The pleasantness thereof may be collected from the plenty of noblemen, many having their baronies, and more their residence, therein. It is divided into two parts, the Sand and the Clay, which so supply the defects one of another, that what either half doth afford, the whole county doth enjoy.

NATURAL COMMODITIES.

GLYCYRIZE, OR LIQUORICE.

England affordeth hereof the best in the world for some uses; this county the first and best in England. Great the use thereof in physic, it being found very pectoral and sovereign for several diseases. A stick hereof is commonly the spoon prescribed to patients, to use in any lingences or loaches. If (as Æneas's men were forced to eat their own trenchers) these chance to eat their spoons, their danger is none at all. But liquorice, formerly dear and scarce, is now cheap and common, because growing in all counties. Thus plenty will make the most precious thing a drug; as silver was nothing respected in Jerusalem in the days of Solomon.

WONDERS.

We must not forget how two *ayres* of *lannards* were lately found in Sherwood forest. These hawks are the natives of Saxony; and, it seems, being old and past flying at the game, were let or did set themselves loose; where meeting with *lanerets,* enlarged on the same terms, they did breed together, and proved as excellent in their kind, when managed, as any which were brought out of Germany.

PROVERBS.

" Many talk of Robin Hood, who never shot in his bow."]
That is, many discourse (or prate rather) of matters wherein they have no skill or experience. This proverb is now

extended all over England, though originally of Nottinghamshire extraction, where Robin Hood did principally reside, in Sherwood forest. He was an *arch*-robber, and withal an excellent *archer*; though surely the poet gives a twang to the loose of his arrow, making him shoot one a cloth yard long, at full forty score mark, for compass never higher than the breast, and within less than a foot of the mark.* But herein our author hath verified one proverb, talking at large of Robin Hood, in whose bow he never shot.

One may justly wonder that this archer did not at last hit the mark; I mean, come to the gallows for his many robberies. But see more hereof in the memorable persons of this county.

"To sell Robin Hood's penny-worths."]

It is spoken of things sold under half their value; or, if you will, half sold, half given. Robin Hood came lightly by his ware, and lightly parted therewith; so that he could afford the length of his bow for a yard of velvet. Whithersoever he came he carried a fair along with him, chapmen crowding to buy his stolen commodities. But, seeing the receiver is as bad as the thief, and such buyers are as bad as receivers, the cheap penny-worths of plundered goods may in fine prove dear enough to their consciences.

"As wise as a man of Gotham."]

It passeth publicly for the periphrasis of a fool; and a hundred fopperies are feigned and fathered on the town-folk of Gotham, a village in this county. Here two things may be observed:

1. Men in all ages have made themselves merry without singling out some place, and fixing the staple of stupidity and stolidity therein. Thus the Phrygians were accounted the fools of all Asia, and the anvils of other men's wits to work upon: "Serò sapiunt Phryges, Phryx nisi ictus non sapit." In Grecia take a single city, and then Abdera in Thracia carried it away for dull-heads,

———"Abderitanæ pectora plebis habes."†

But, for a whole country, commend us to the Bœotians for block-heads; and *Bœoticum ingenium* is notoriously known. In Germany *auris Batava* is taken by the poet ‡ for a dull ear, which hath no skill in witty conceits.

2. These places, thus generally slighted and scoffed at, afforded some as witty and wise persons as the world produced. Thus Plutarch himself (saith Erasmus §) was a Bœotian, and Erasmus a Batavian or Hollander; and therefore (his own copyhold being touched in the proverb) he expoundeth *auris Batava* "a grave and severe ear."

But to return to Gotham; it doth breed as wise people as any which causelessly laugh at their simplicity. Sure I am, Mr.

---

* Drayton's Polyolbion, Song xxvi. p. 122. † Martial, l. 10.
‡ Martial, l. 6. § Adag. Bœoticum ingenium.

William de Gotham, fifth master of Michael House in Cambridge, anno 1336, and twice chancellor of the university, was as grave a governor as that age did afford. And Gotham is a goodly large lordship, where the ancient and right well respected family of St. Andrew have flourished some hundreds of years, till of late the name is extinct in, and lands divided betwixt female co-heirs, matched unto very worshipful persons.

> " The little smith of Nottingham,
> Who doth the work that no man can."*]

England hath afforded many rare workmen in this kind; whereof he may seem an apprentice to Vulcan, and inferior only to his master (in making the invisible net) who made a lock and key, with a chain of ten links, which a flea could draw. But what this little smith and great workman was, and when he lived, I know not; and have cause to suspect that this of Nottingham is a periphrasis of *Nemo*, Οὖτις, or a person who never was. And the proverb, by way of sarcasm, is applied to such who, being conceited of their own skill, pretend to the achieving of impossibilities.

MARTYRS.

I meet with none within this county, either before or in the Marian days; imputing the latter to the mild temper of Nicholas Heath, archbishop of York, and diocesan thereof. Yet find we a martyr, though not *in* this yet *of* this county, as a native thereof, here following:

THOMAS CRANMER was born at Arse-lackton † (Speed calls it *Aslackton*) in this county; and, being bred in Jesus' College in Cambridge, became archbishop of Canterbury; and at last (after some intermediate failings) valiantly suffered for the truth at Oxford, anno Domini 1556, March 22.

" *Two* hungry meals," saith our English proverb, " make the *third* a glutton." This may also be inverted, " *Two* glutton meals require the *third* an hungry one;" fasting being then necessary, lest Nature be surcharged. If the reader hath formerly perused Mr. Fox's " Acts and Monuments," and my " Ecclesiastical History," Cranmer's story is so largely related in those two books, there is danger of his surfeit if I should not now be short and sparing therein: only one memorable passage omitted by Mr. Fox (and that is a wonder) I must here insert out of an excellent author: ‡

" After his whole body was reduced into ashes, his heart was found entire and untouched." Which is justly alledged as an argument of his cordial integrity to the truth, though fear too much and too often prevailed on his outward actions: so that what the Holy Spirit recordeth of king Asa was true of him,

---

* Butters of Bees, p. 17.   † Fox, Acts and Monuments, p. 1859.
‡ Bishop Godwin, in his Catalogue of the Archbishops of Canterbury, p. 206,

" Nevertheless the heart of Asa was perfect all his days;"[*] though, good man, he was guilty of many and great imperfections.

The like to this of Cranmer is reported of Zuinglius, " Quòd, cadavere flammis ab hostibus tradito, cor exuri non potuerit;" his foes making this a sign of the obduration and hardness of his heart, his friends of the sincerity thereof. And thus saith my moderate and learned author,[†] " Adeò turbatis odio aut amore animis, ut fit in religionis dissensionibus, pro se quisque omnia superstitiosè interpretatur;" (their minds being so disturbed with hatred or love, as it comes to pass in dissensions of religion, every one interprets all things superstitiously for his own advantage.) The best is, our religion, wherein it differs from Romish errors, hath better demonstration for the truth thereof, than those *topical* and *osier* accidents, liable to be bent on either side, according to men's fancies and affections.

PRELATES SINCE THE REFORMATION.

WILLIAM CHAPPELL was born at Lexington in this county, and bred a fellow in Christ's College in Cambridge, where he was remarkable for the strictness of his conversation. No one tutor in our memory bred more and better pupils, so exact his care in their education. He was a most subtle disputant, equally excellent with the sword and the shield, to reply or answer. He was chosen provost of Trinity College in Dublin, and afterwards bishop of Cork and Ross. Frighted with the rebellion in Ireland, he came over into England, where he rather exchanged than eased his condition, such the wofulness of our civil wars. He died anno 1649, and parted his estate almost equally betwixt his own kindred and distressed ministers; his charity not impairing his duty, and his duty not prejudicing his charity.

CAPITAL JUDGES.

Sir JOHN MARKHAM, descended of an ancient family, was born at Markham in this county, and brought up in the municipal law, till, being knighted by Edward the Fourth, he was made lord chief justice of the King's Bench, in the place of Sir John Fortescue. These I may call the two chief justices of the chief justices, for their signal integrity: for, though the one of them favoured the house of Lancaster, the other of York, in the titles to the crown, both of them favoured the house of Justice in matters betwixt party and party.

It happened that Sir Thomas Cooke,[‡] late lord mayor of London, one of vast wealth, was cast before-hand at the court (where the lord Rivers and the rest of the queen's kindred had

[*] 2 Chronicles xv. 17.   [†] Thuanus, Obit. Doctorum Virorum, anno 1531.
[‡] Fabian, p. 497, and Holinshed, p. 670, and Stow in the 12th of Edward the Fourth.

pre-devoured his estate), aud was only, for formality's sake, to be condemned in Guildhall, by extraordinary commissioners in Oyer and Terminer, whereof Sir John Markham was not the meanest. The fact for which he was arraigned, was for lending money to Margaret the wife of king Henry the Sixth. This he denied; and the single testimony of one Haukins, tortured on the rack, was produced against him.

Judge Markham directed the jury (as it was his place, and no partiality in point of law to do) to find it only misprision of treason; whereby Sir Thomas saved his lands, though heavily fined, and life, though long imprisoned. The king was highly displeased at him, and vowed he should never sit on the bench any more. And here I hope it will not trespass on the grave character of this judge, to insert a modern and pleasant passage, being privy myself to the truth thereof.

A lady would traverse a suit of law, against the will of her husband; who was contented to buy his quiet by giving her her will therein, though otherwise persuaded in his judgment the cause would go against her.

This lady, dwelling in the shire-town, invited the judge to dinner, and (though thrifty enough of herself) treated him with sumptuous entertainment. Dinner being done, and the cause being called, the judge clearly gave it against her. And when in passion she vowed never to invite any judge again, " Nay, wife," said he, " vow never to invite a just judge any more."

Well, king Edward was so vexed, that Sir John Markham was ousted of his chief-justiceship, and lived privately, but plentifully, the remainder of his life, having fair lands by Margaret his wife (daughter and co-heir of Sir Simon Leke, of Cotham in this county), besides the estate acquired by his practice and paternal inheritance.

SEAMEN.

EDWARD FENTON (brother to Sir Jeffrey Fenton, of whom hereafter*) was born in this county; whose nature inclined him wholly to sea-service; and, disdaining to go in a trodden path, he was ambitious to discover unknown passages. His achievements in this nature are related at large in Mr. Hackluit, and excellently contracted in an epitaph on his monument in Deptford church in Kent, erected by the right honourable Roger earl of Cork, who married his brother's daughter :

" Memoriæ perenni Edwardi Fenton, Reginæ Elizabethæ olim pro corpore Armigeri, Jano O-Neal, ac post eum Comite Desmoniæ, in Hiberniâ turbantibus, fortissimi Taxiarchi, qui, post lustratum, improbo ausu, Septentrionalis Plagæ Apochryphum mare, et excussas variis peregrinationibus inertis Naturæ latebras, anno 1588, in celebri contra Hispanos Naumachiâ, meruit Navis Prætoriæ Navarchus. Obiit anno Domini 1603 ;"

being some days after the death of queen Elizabeth.—Observe, by

* Title of WRITERS.

the way, how God set up a generation of military men, both by sea and land, which began and expired with the reign of queen Elizabeth, like a suit of clothes made for her, and worn out with her; for Providence, designing a peaceable prince to succeed her (in whose time martial men would be rendered useless) so ordered the matter, that they all almost attended their mistress, before or after, within some short distance, unto her grave.

WRITERS.

WILLIAM MANSFIELD (named no doubt *from* and born *at* that noted market-town in this county) was bred a Dominican; and, for his skill in Logics, Ethics, Physics, and Metaphysics, in his age highly applauded. And because some prize a dram of foreign before a dram of home-bred praise, know that Leander Bononiensis* (though mistaking his name *Massettus*) giving him the appellation of *inclytus Theologiæ Professor*. He defended Thomas Aquinas against Henricus Gandavensis (though both of them were dead long before), and got great credit thereby. Bale (who is not usually so civil in his expressions) saith that he did strew branches of palms before Christ's ass,† which, if so, was (I assure you) no bad employment. He flourished anno Domini 1320.

WILLIAM NOTTINGHAM was first prebendary, then chapter, of York; bred an Augustinian, and fourteen years the Provincial of his order: resigning which place, he went on some great employment to Rome; and, returning thence by Genoa, fell sick and recovered of the plague, being therein a monument of divine mercy, to prove that disease, though in itself mortal not always *mortiferum*.

Amongst the many books he wrote, his " Concordance on the Evangelists " was most remarkable, which I behold as a leading piece in that kind, though since it hath met with many to follow it; a worthy work, to shew the harmony betwixt those four writers, though it hath met with many to decry the design, being accounted by

Some impossible. As if there were contradictions herein past reconciling: whose opinion cannot be reconciled with piety; seeing the Four Gospels are indited by one and the same spirit of unity and verity, of truth and concord; whilst, in two sentences really contrary, one must be false of necessity.

Others unnecessary. As if it were nothing but the reconciling of those who never fell out; whereas, indeed, there are many seeming oppositions therein, to raise the reputation thereof. " Intellecta ab omnibus sunt, neglecta à plurimis;" and some necessary difficulty becomes Scripture, to quicken our prayers, pains, and patience to understand it.

* In quarto libro suorum Prædicatorum.
† Bale de Scriptoribus Britannicis, cent. v. num. 2.

Bale giveth him this lukewarm (call it hot, because coming from his mouth) commendation, " Non omninò impius in voluminibus quæ composuit."* He died, and was buried in Leicester, anno Domini 1336.

ROBERT WORSOP was born (saith Bale †) in the county, mistaken for the diocese of York, seeing Worsop is notoriously known to be in Nottinghamshire. He was bred an Augustinian in the convent of Tick-hill, not far from Doncaster, where he wrote many books, the one called " The Entrance of Sentences." Bale saith, that at last he was made a bishop, not naming his diocese ; and no such prelate appearing in our English catalogue, it rendereth it suspicious, that either he was some Suffragan, or some titulary bishop of Greece. He died, and was buried at Tick-hill, about the year 1360.

SINCE THE REFORMATION.

Sir JEFFREY FENTON, Knight, born in this county, was for twenty-seven years privy councillor in Ireland to queen Elizabeth and king James.‡ He translated the history of Francis Guicciardini out of Italian into English, and dedicated it to queen Elizabeth. He deceased at Dublin, October 19, 1608 ; and lieth buried in St Patrick's Church, under the same tomb with his father-in-law Dr. Robert Weston, sometime chancellor of Ireland.

JOHN PLOUGH was born in this county,§ a pious and learned minister of the word ; who, for his conscience, fled over into Basle in the reign of queen Mary.

It happened that a book came over into the hands of the English exiles, written against the marriage of ministers, by one Miles Hoggard, a silly hosier in London, but highly opinioned of his learning. It was debated amongst the English, whether this book should be passed over with neglect, or answered. And here the reader is requested to pardon this digression, as proper enough for my profession. Solomon hath two proverbs,‖ the one immediately succeeding, yet seemingly crossing, the other : " Answer not a fool according to his folly, lest thou also be like unto him : "—" Answer a fool according to his folly, lest he be wise in his own conceit."

Some ¶ will have the first precept given to magistrates (who are not to make their authority cheap by engaging against fools), and the latter to belong to all Christians. Others distinguish, that an answer according to his folly may be twofold ; by way of complying with it, which may not, and confuting it, which

---

* Bale, de Script. Brit. cent. v. num. 44.   † Ibid. cent. v. num. 76.
‡ J, Waræus, de Scriptoribus Hiberniæ, p. 137.
§ Bale, in his book termed " Scriptores nostri temporis," p. 111.
‖ Prov. xxvi. 4, 5.   ¶ Mr. Cartwright upon the place.

ought to be done. Most make a difference between the railing fool and the reasoning fool; the former to be ordered, as Hezekiah did Rabshakeh, "Answer him not a word."[*] But, if he be a reasoning fool, who will offer to argue conceited of himself, take him off his speed with a short and seasonable return.

Such a fool this Hoggard was adjudged, whom John Plough undertook to answer, and cut his comb so close, that the other appeared no more. He died in the beginning of the reign of queen Elizabeth.

WILLIAM BRIGHTMAN was born in Nottingham (where some of his brethren were lately alive); bred fellow of Queen's College, in Cambridge, and afterwards beneficed at Hannes in Bedfordshire. No lover of conformity, yet no hater of conformists, being charitable to such who in judgment dissented from him. His memory is most remarkable for his "Comment on the Revelation," by some Protestants approved, praised, admired; by others slighted, contemned, condemned.

Pro —1. His very name, *Brightman*, imports something of illumination and clearness therein. 2. He makes many hard places to be plain, and mysteries to be his histories, by his comment. 3. He foretold many things forty years ago, which we see performed in our days.

Con.— 1. Names are casual; and even *Lucian* himself, as bad as he was, had as much of light and lustre in his name. 2. He makes many plain places hard, and histories to be mysteries by his mis-interpretation; expounding the Seven Asian churches, then literally extant, to be Germany, France, England, &c. 3. Shooting so many arrows, no wonder some few if rather by hap than aim, hit the mark.

Sure I am that time and Mr. Brightman will expound the hardest places in the Revelation; but what credit is to be given to the latter alone I will not engage.

Such who dislike Mr. Brightman's writing, could not but commend his angelical living, who had so much of heaven in his heart. Walking through the vineyard of this world, he plucked and eat a few grapes, but put up none in his vessel, using wealth as if he used it not.

His clay-cottage did crack and fall down in the same minute, so sudden was his death: but he who died daily could on no day be said to die suddenly, being always prepared for his dissolution, which happened anno Domini 16 . .

MEMORABLE PERSONS.

ROBERT HOOD was (if not by birth) by his chiefest abode this country-man. Camden calls him *prædonem mitissimum*,[†] the gentlest thief that ever was: and know, reader, he is entered

---

[*] 2 Kings viii. 36.

[†] His words are taken out of John Major. See his Britannia, in North Riding in Yorkshire.—F.

into our catalogue, not for his thievery, but for his gentleness. Take the character of his (though not good) less bad behaviour from the pen of our poet.*

> " From wealthy abbots' chests, and churls' abundant store,
>   What oftentimes he took, he shar'd amongst the poor:
> No lordly bishop came in lusty Robin's way,
> To him before he went, but for his pass must pay:
> The widow in distress he graciously reliev'd,
>   And remedied the wrongs of many a virgin griev'd."

But who made him a judge? or gave him a commission to take where it might best be spared, and give where it was most wanted? His principal residence was in Sherwood Forest in this county, though he had another haunt (he is no fox that hath but one hole) near the sea in the North Riding in Yorkshire, where Robin Hood's Bay still retaineth his name. Not that he was any pirate, but a land thief, who retreated to those unsuspected parts for his security.

One may wonder how he escaped the hand of justice, dying in his bed for ought is found to the contrary; but it was because he was rather a merry than a mischievous thief (complimenting passengers out of their purses); never murdering any but *deer*, and this popular robber feasted the vicinage with his venison. He played his pranks, in the reign of king Richard the First, about the year of our Lord 1100.

THOMAS MAGNUS.—He was an exposed child, left by his mother in the parish of Newark. What the poet † saith of the father of Cadmus (commanding his son to find his lost sister Europa, or else never to return) that he was,

> *Facto pius et sceleratus eodem,*
> " Expressing in one act a mind,
>   Which was both cruel and was kind,"

may be applied to the mother of this and all such foundlings. Now it happened that some Yorkshire clothiers coming in the dark (very early or late) did light on this child, and resolved to pay both for his nursing and education, the charge whereof would not be great, equally divided betwixt them, according to the proverb:

> *Multorum manibus grande levatur onus.*
> " An heavy work is light to do,
>   When many hands are put thereto."

First then they took order he should be baptized in Newark, by the name of Thomas (probably the best person in their company); and because all of them had interest alike in him, for his sirname they assigned him *Amang-us*, which is *amongst us*, in the Northern pronunciation.

They were very careful in his breeding. I confess Aristotle urgeth it as an argument against the breeding of children in

---

* Drayton's Polyolbion, Song xxvi. p. 127.   † Ovid, Metamorphoses.

common, that the care of all will effectually be the care of none, and so the children be neglected. Not so here, where this Thomas, though he had a commonwealth of foster-fathers, was very well brought up in learning, and became an excellent scholar and statesman, being employed in many foreign embassies. Then took he on him the name of Dr. Magnus* (and was famous thereby both at home and beyond the seas); on which account he might claim kindred with Pompeius Magnus, Carolus Magnus, and Albertus Magnus, and whom not, who was great for arts, arms, or otherwise? It soundeth much in his commendation, that he forgot not his gratitude to the town of his nativity, where he erected a fair school, with other benefactions. He flourished (as I take it) under king Henry the Eighth.

LORD MAYORS.

I cannot, on my best inquiry, recover any native of this county who ever attained to this place of magistracy; but am informed, that now the feet of one do tread near unto the threshold of that door of honour; and doubt not but, when he hath first entered and opened the way, there will be others soon found to follow him.

THE NAMES OF THE GENTRY OF THIS COUNTY,

RETURNED BY THE COMMISSIONERS IN THE TWELFTH YEAR OF KING HENRY THE SIXTH.

John archbishop of York, and Humfrey earl of Stafford;—Richard Stanhope, one of the knights for the shire;—Commissioners to take the oaths.

Thomas Cheworth, chev.
Johan. Zouche, chev.
Will. Plumton, chev.
Hug. Welughby, chev.
Roberti Strelley, chev.
Hen. Perponnt, chev.
Robert Markam, chev.
Gerv. Clyfton, chev.
Will. Meryng, chev.
Hug. Annesley, chev.
Joh. Cokfeld, armig.
Radulphi Makerell.
Thome Nevyll.
Roberti Brewce.
Thome Stanton.
Rad. Leek.
Richardi Sutton.
Thome Stanhope.

Jacobi Stanhope.
Thome Curson.
Willielmi Byrton.
Henrici Perponnt.
Hugonis Hercy.
Johannis Wastnes.
Johannis Gaitford.
Gorgii Clay.
Johannis Husse.
Johannis Hiklinge.
Joh. Barbour de Leek.
Thome Stannton de Sutton.
Roberti Doyle.
Rogeri Perponnt.
Thome Hercy.
Richardi Bevercotes.
Roberti Moresby.
Roberti Morewode.

* Camden's Remains, p. 146.

Johannis Clifton.
Roberti Dunham.
Johannis Serlby.
Willielmi Wilbram.
Thome Geneley.
Thome Schefeld.
Thome Anne.
Johannis Rolley.
Johannis atte Vikars.
Willielmi Boson.
Edm. Nornamuyle.
Richardi Gatford.
Johannis Becard.
Willielmi Remston.
Richardi Strelly.
Thome Meryng.
Willielmi Lassels.
Johannis Powerr.
Willielmi Powerr.
Joh. Leek de Halom.
Thome Okere.
Philippi Barley.
Thome Warberton.
Johannis Alferton.
Willi. Alferton, fil. ejus.
Richardi Ranchestere de Wirssope.
Johannis White de Colyngam.
Johannis Glouseter de Carcoston.
Richardi Walfeld de Newerk.
Roberti Kelom de Newerk.
Willielmi Skrymshire de Muskham.
Roberti Garnon de Muskham.
Johannis Kelom de Kelom.
Rob. Darley de Thorp.
Thome Columboll de Thorp.
Riginaldi Shawe de Estwayte.
Gervasii Bampton de Beston.
Johannis Mathewe de Sterroppe.
Willielmi Crecy de Markham.
Petri Creci de Markham.
Roberti Forsett de Grynley.
Will. Lord de Retford.

Roberti Wytham de Orston.
Radulfi Stuffin de Mansfeld Wodhous.
Johannis Brannspath de Ragnell.
Johannis Brannspath, fil. ejus, de Ragnell.
Tho. Brannspath de Ragnell.
Rad. Barre de Ragnell.
Johannis Crostes de Ragnell.
Johannis Melton de Normanton.
Willielmi Clerk de Gedlynge.
Radulphi Wilbram de Westmerkham.
Galfridi Botelere de Welhagh.
Rob. Norton de Kirton.
Johannis Milnere de Allerton.
Will. Haley de Sutton.
Johan. Morehagh de Mansfeld.
Joh. Arnall de Arnall.
Johan. Spondon de Newerk.
Johan. Dennett de Newerk.
Hugonis Garnon de Muskham.
Johan. Crumwell de Charleton.
Rob. Crumwell, fil. ejus de eadem.
Willielmi Daynell de Egmanton.
Edm. Berkyn de Allerton.
Henrici Payser de Clypston.
Simonis Caldewell de Laxton.
Roberti Bliton de Cannton.
Rob. Waryn de Wanton.
Willielmi Drapour de Welhagh.
Johannis Carleton de Blithe.
Tho. Bagley de Blithe.
Walt. Carleton de Carleton.
Will. Hogekyngson de Misterton.
Joh. Darnall de Misterton.
Williel. Lyndrike de Stockwith.
Willielmi Browet de Walkryngham.
Richardi Caxton de Tuxford.
Johan. Parlethorpe de Laxton.
Tho. Grengorge de Allerton.

SHERIFFS.

This county had the same sheriffs with Derbyshire until the tenth year of queen Elizabeth, wherein they were divided, and since which time these were the particular sheriffs of this shire.

ELIZ. REG.

Anno   Name and Arms.   Place.

10 Tho. Cowper, arm.
   Az. a tortoise erected O.
11 Joh. Biron, arm.
12 Joh. Nevil, arm.   .   .   .   Grove.
   G. a saltire Erm.
13 Rob. Markham, arm.
   Az. in a chief O. a lion issuant G. and border Arg.
14 Gerv. Clifton, mil.   .   .   Clifton.
   S. semé de cinquefoils, a lion rampant Arg.
15 Will. Hollis, mil.   .   .   Houghton.
   Erm. two piles S.
16 Th. Stanhope, mil.   .   .   Shelford.
   Quarterly Erm. and G.
17 Hen. Perpoynt, arm.   .   Holme.
   Arg. a lion rampant S. in an orb of cinquefoils G.
18 Geo. Chaworth, arm.   .   Wiverton.
   Az. two chevrons O.
19 Tho. Markham, arm.   .   *ut prius.*
20 Joh. Biron, arm.
21 Fra. Willoughby, mil.
   O. on two bars G. three water-bougets Arg.
22 Geo. Nevil, arm.   .   .   .   *ut prius.*
23 Will Sutton, arm.   .   .   Arundel.
   Arg. a quarter S. a crescent G.
24 Fran. Molineux, arm.   .   Teversham.
   Az. a cross moline quarter pierced O.
25 Rob. Markham, arm.   .   *ut prius.*
26 Brian Lasles, arm.
   Arg. three chaplets G.
27 Joh. Sydenham, arm.   .   SOMERSETSHIRE.
   S. three rams Arg.
28 Geo. Chaworth, mil.   .   *ut prius.*
29 Tho. Stanhope, mil.   .   .   *ut prius.*
30 Fra. Willoughby, mil.   .   *ut prius.*
31 Joh. Biron, mil.
32 Th. Thornhough, arm.
33 Joh. Hollis, arm.   .   .   *ut prius.*
34 John Basset, arm.
   O. three piles G. a canton Erm.
35 Fra. Willoughby, arm.   .   *ut prius.*
36 Will. Sutton, arm.   .   .   *ut prius.*

Anno   Name.   Place.

37 Rich. Whalley, arm.
38 Joh. Biron, mil.
39 Joh. Thorold, ar.
    S. three goats salient Gules.
40 Hen. Chaworth, arm. . *ut prius.*
41 Brian Lassels, arm. . . *ut prius.*
42 Edw. North, arm.
    Az. a lion passant O. betwixt three flowers-de-luce Arg.
43 Hen. Perpoint, arm. . *ut prius.*
44 Rog. Ascough, mil.
    S. a fess O. between three asses passant Arg.

JACOB.

1 Will. Reyner, mil.
2 Gab. Armstrong, arm.
    G. three right hands couped and armed barways proper.
3 Will. Sutton, mil. . . *ut prius.*
4 Will. Cowper, arm. . . *ut prius.*
5 Jo. Thornhough, ar.
6 Hen. Sacheverell, ar.
    Arg. on a saltire five water-bougets of the first.
7 Joh Molineux, arm. . . *ut prius.*
8 Ger. Clifton, mil. . . *ut prius.*
9 Joh. Molineux, mil. . *ut prius.*
10 Joh Biron, mil.
11 Geo. Perkins, mil.
12 Ro. Williamson, arm. . East-Markham.
    O. a chevron G. betwixt three trefoils S.
13 Rob. Perpoynt, arm. . . *ut prius.*
14 Geo. Lassels, mil. . . *ut prius.*
15 Jo. Thornhough, mil.
16 Tho. Barton, arm.
17 Will. Reason, arm.
18 Tho. Hutchinson, mil.
19 Joh. White, mil.
20 Joh. Digby, arm.
    Az. a flower-de-luce Arg.
21 Math. Palmes, arm.
    G. three flowers-de-luce Arg; a chief Vary.
22 Edw. Goldinge.
    G. a chevron O. betwixt three besan
    Galfr. Markham, ar. . *ut prius.*

CAROL. I.

1 Tim. Pusey, arm.
2 Fra. Williamson, arm. . *ut prius.*
3 Tho. Hewet, mil.
    S. a chevron counter-battillée betwixt three owls Arg.

4 Jer. Teresy, arm.
5 Ith. Perkins, arm.
6 Rob. Sutton, arm. . . *ut prius.*
7 Tho. White, arm.
8 Tho. Bolles, arm.
    Az. three cups Arg. holding as many boars' heads erected O.
9 John Melish, arm.
    Az. two swans Arg. betwixt as many flanches Erm.
10 Joh. Biron, mil.
11 Har. Wasteneys, bar. . Hendon.
    S. a lion rampant Arg. collared G.
12 Geo. Lassels, mil. . . *ut prius.*
13 Fra. Thornhaugh, mil.
14 Joh. Chaworth, arm. . *ut prius.*
15 Tho. Williamson, arm. . *ut prius.*
16 Gilb. et Edw. Nevil, arm. *ut prius.*

QUEEN ELIZABETH.

15. WILLIAM HOLLIS, Mil.—This was that steady and constant house-keeper, who, for his hospitality and other eminent virtues, was commonly called "The good Sir William;" a most honourable title, seeing of God's two grand epithets, *Optimus*, *Maximus*, the former is embraced by too few, the latter affected by too many. This Sir William was son to Sir William Hollis, Lord Mayor of the city of London, father to John Hollis Lord Houghton of Houghton, created earl of Clare in the 22nd of king Charles the First; and grand father to the right honourable John the present earl of Clare [1650].

KING JAMES.

13. ROBERT PERPOINT, Armig.—He was afterwards created Baron Perpoint and Viscount Newark; and afterwards, in the fourth of king Charles the First, earl of Kingston-upon-Hull; one descended of right ancient and noble extraction, whose ancestors, coming over with the Conqueror, first fixed at Hurst-Perpoint in Sussex, thence removed into this county. I find this remarkable passage recorded of Henry de Perpoint, who flourished in those parts in the beginning of king Edward the First.

" *Memorandum*, quòd Henricus de Perponnt, die Lunæ in crastino Octab. Sancti Michaelis, venit in Cancellariâ apud Lincolniam, et publicè dixit quòd sigillum suum amisit, et protestabatur quòd si aliquod instrumentum cum sigillo illo post tempus illud inveniretur consignatum, illud nullius esse valoris vel momenti."*

(" *Memorandum*, that Henry de Perponnt, on Monday the day

---

* Claus. 8 Edwardi I. membrana tertia, in dorso, in Turr. London.

after the Octaves of St. Michael, came into the chancery at Lincoln, and said publicly that he had lost his seal; and protested, that, if any instrument were found sealed with that seal after that time, the same should be of no value or effect.")

He appeareth a person of prime quality, that great prejudice might arise by the false use of his true seal, if found by a dishonest person, so that so solemn a protest was conceived necessary for the prevention thereof.

Robert Perpoint, a descendant from this Henry, was, by king Edward the Third, summoned as a baron to Parliament,* but died (as I am informed) before he sate therein, which hindered the honour of peerage from descending to his posterity.

But this Robert Perpoint was *Robert the younger*, in distinction from his name-sake-ancestor, who lived in great dignity under king Edward the Third, as by the following record will appear:

"Rex Priori S. Johannis Jerusalem in Angliâ, salutem. Cùm dilectus et fidelis noster Robertus de Petroponte, qui fidei nostræ et Edwardi primogeniti nostri hactenus constanter adhæsit, in conflictu habito apud Lewes, captus esset ab inimicis nostris, et detentus in prisonâ Hugonis le Despenser, donec per septingentas marcas finem fecisset cum eodem pro redemptione suâ; unde Walerandus de Munceaus se præfato Hugoni pro prædicto Roberto obligavit per quandam chartam de feoffamento, et scripta obligatoria inter ipsos confecta, quæ vobis liberata fuerant custodienda, ut dicitur: Nos, ipsorum Roberti et Walerandi indempnitati prospicere, et eidem Roberto gratiam facere volentes specialem, vobis mandamus, firmiter injungentes, quòd cartas et scripta prædicta eidem Roberto et Walerando, vel eorum alteri, sine moræ dispendio deliberari faciatis; et nos inde versùs vos servabimus indempnes. In cujus, &c. Teste Rege, apud Westmonasterium, 15 die Octobris."†

("The king to the prior of St. John of Jerusalem in England, greeting. Whereas our beloved and faithful Robert Perpoint, who hitherto hath constantly adhered to our trust, and of our first-born Edward, was taken by our enemies in a skirmish at Lewes, and kept in the prison of Hugh le Despenser, until by seven hundred marks he had made an end with him for his ransoming; whereupon Walerand of Munceaus bound himself to the forenamed Hugh for the foresaid Robert, by a certain charter of feoffment, and obligatory writings made betwixt them, which, as is said, were delivered to you to be kept: We, willing to provide for the safety of the said Robert and Walerand, and to do a special favour to the same Robert, do command you, firmly enjoining, that ye cause the foresaid char-

* Camden's Britannia, in Nottinghamshire.
† Claus. 49 Hen. III. in dorso memb. 6.

ters and writings, without any delay, to be delivered to the same Robert and Walerand, or to one of them; and we shall thenceforth save you harmless. Witness the king, at Westminster, the 15th day of October.")

Whoso seriously considereth how much the *mark*, and how little the *silver*, of our land was in that age, will conclude seven hundred marks a ransom more proportionable for a prince than private person. The best was, that was not paid in effect, which by command from the king was restored again.

THE FAREWELL.

There is in this county a small market town called Blythe, which my author* will have so named *à jucunditate*, from the mirth and good fellowship of the inhabitants therein. If so, I desire that both the name and the thing may be extended all over the shire, as being confident that an ounce of mirth, with the same degree of grace, will serve God more, and more acceptably, than a pound of sorrow.

WORTHIES OF NOTTINGHAMSHIRE WHO HAVE FLOURISHED SINCE THE TIME OF FULLER.

Samuel AYSCOUGH, divine, antiquary, index and catalogue compiler; born at Nottingham 1745; died 1804.

John BLAY, founder of charity school; born at East Leake; died 1731.

John BLOW, musician, excelled in church music, born at North Collingham 1648; died 1708.

William BRIGHTMAN, commentator on the Apocalypse; born at Nottingham; died 1607.

Major John CARTWRIGHT, political reformer, and author; born at Marnham 1740; died 1824.

John Gilbert COOPER, magistrate, biographer of Socrates, essayist, and poet; born 1723; died 1769.

Erasmus DARWIN, physician and poet; born at Elston 1731; died 1802.

Robert DODSLEY, bookseller, poet, and dramatist; born at Anston near Mansfield 1703; died 1764.

Caleb FLEMING, Socinian minister, and author; born at Nottingham 1698; died 1779.

John, celebrated Marquis of GRANBY, warrior; born 1720-21; died 1770.

Richard fourth Viscount and first Earl HOWE, naval commander; born 1726; died 1799.

---

* John Norden, in his Description of Hertfordshire, voce *Benington*.

Dr. Howell, divine, chancellor of Lincoln, author of a History of the World; born at Beckingham; died 1683.

Samuel Jebb, physician, learned editor; born at Nottingham; died 1772.

Andrew Kippis, dissenting divine, biographer; born at Nottingham 1725; died 1795.

Robert Millhouse, self-educated poet; born at Nottingham 1788; died 1839.

Lady Mary Wortley Montague, classical translator, poetess, &c. born at Thoresby 1690; died 1762.

Major Hayman Rooke, traveller, historian of Sherwood Forest, antiquary; died 1806.

Thomas Secker, learned archbishop of Canterbury; born at Sibthorpe 1693; died 1768.

Charles Manners Sutton, archbishop of Canterbury; died 1829.

Dr. Robert Thoroton, physician, historian of this county; born at Screveton, 17th century.

Gilbert Wakefield, classical scholar and critic; born at Nottingham 1756; died 1801.

William Warburton, Bishop of Gloucester, author of "Divine Legation," born at Newark 1698; died 1779.

Sir John Borlase Warren, admiral and author; born at Stapleford 1754; died 1822.

Henry Kirke White, poet, amiable and pious; born at Nottingham 1785; died 1806.

Robert White, astronomer; born at Bingham 1722; died 1773.

Thomas White, bishop of Peterborough in 1685, deprived for refusing the oaths to William and Mary in 1690; died 1698.

Barnard Wilson, divine and author; born at Newark 1689.

Samuel Wright, divine, author of "Happy hour, all hours excelling;" born at Retford 1683.

*** In 1797, Mr. J. Throsby brought out a republication, with considerable additions, of Thoroton's History of Nottinghamshire; and in 1813, the twelfth volume of the Beauties of England and Wales, containing historical and descriptive notices of the county, added materially to the elucidation of its topography.—Of local histories there have been published, Dr. Deering's Historical Account of Nottingham (1751); Harrod's History of Mansfield (1801); and Dickinson's Histories of Newark, and of Southwell (1819).—Ed.

Nuttall and Hodgson, Printers, Gough Square, London.